A GUIDE TO
FEDERAL
AGENCY

RULEMAKING

FIFTH EDITION

Section of Administrative Law
and Regulatory Practice and
Government and Public
Sector Lawyers Division

JEFFREY S. LUBBERS

ABA
SECTION OF
ADMINISTRATIVE LAW
AND REGULATORY
PRACTICE

Printed in the United States of America.

16 15 14   5 4

Lubbers, Jeffrey S.
    A guide to federal agency rulemaking / by Jeffrey S. Lubbers. — 5th ed.
    p. cm.
    Rev. ed. of: A guide to federal agency rulemaking / by Jeffrey S. Lubbers. — 4th ed. (2006).
A publication of the American Bar Association's Section of Administrative Law
ISBN 978-1-61438-579-0

    1. Administrative procedure—United States. 2. Delegated legislation—United States. II. Title.
KF5411.L83 1998
348.73'025—dc21   98-15306
Copy

Dedication

This volume is dedicated to Kenneth Culp Davis and Walter Gellhorn, drafters of the APA, definers of the field of Administrative Law, and teachers to us all.

And to the re-establishment of the Administrative Conference of the United States, from which this book sprang, and which can now continue to build on its notable legacy of administrative law reform.

Table of Contents

About the Author

Jeffrey S. Lubbers is a professor of Practice in Administrative Law at American University's Washington College of Law, where he has also served as a Fellow of Law and Government. He has also taught at the University of Miami School of Law, Georgetown University Law Center, and Washington and Lee University School of Law; the University of Ottawa; and Ritsumeikan University Law School in Kyoto, Japan. He has degrees from Cornell University and the University of Chicago Law School and is a member of the bars of the state of Maryland and the District of Columbia.

Prior to joining the Washington College of Law, he served in various positions with the Administrative Conference of the United States (ACUS), the U.S. government's advisory agency on procedural improvements in federal programs—prior to the agency's shutdown by the 104th Congress in 1995. From 1982 to 1995 he was ACUS's Research Director—a position in the Senior Executive Service. In this position, he developed ideas for new studies, hired outside consultants (mostly law professors) to conduct the studies, reviewed reports, supervised staff attorneys, and assisted ACUS committees in developing recommendations from the studies on a wide variety of administrative law subjects. He worked with congressional committees and agencies to seek implementation of ACUS recommendations and served as Team Leader for Vice President Gore's National Performance Review team on Improving Regulatory Systems in 1993. He was a contributing author for ACUS of the first edition of *A Guide to Federal Agency Rulemaking* and revived the publication for the ABA with the third edition in 1998. With the welcome re-establishment of ACUS in 2010, he was appointed a Special Counsel to the "new ACUS."

Professor Lubbers has published numerous articles on the administrative process and has participated frequently in training programs for government officials in the United States and overseas, with over a dozen trips to China for that purpose. In addition, he has won several prestigious honors for his work in administrative law, including the Presidential Rank of Meritorious Executive and special awards from both the American Bar Association and Federal Bar Association. He is a Fellow of the ABA's Section of Administrative Law and Regulatory Practice and, beginning in 1998, has served as editor of the first 12 editions of the Section's annual volume, *Developments in Administrative Law and Regulatory Practice*.

Preface

When the Administrative Conference of the United States (ACUS) was forced to close its doors in 1995[1] (as it turned out, for 15 years), the American Bar Association's (ABA's) Section of Administrative Law and Regulatory Practice and Government and Public Sector Lawyers Division jointly determined to continue updating and publishing *A Guide to Federal Agency Rulemaking*. The hope was that the loss of ACUS would not mean the end of one of ACUS's most popular and valuable resource guides. As a former officer of ACUS who assisted in the preparation of the first two editions of the *Guide*, I was asked to prepare the third edition in 1998, and then the fourth edition in 2006. This fifth edition continues the tradition, and brings the *Guide* up to date with respect to recent cases and changes introduced during the second term of the Bush II Administration and the first three years of the Obama Administration.

The Foreword to the 1991 edition by then-ACUS Chair Marshall Breger well stated the purpose of the *Guide*,[2] and many of its observations are as valid today as they were then:

> The Administrative Procedure Act established a simple procedure for informal, as opposed to "formal,"[3] rulemaking. Agencies are required to publish a notice of proposed rulemaking that includes "either the terms or substance of the proposed rule or a description of the subjects and issues involved,"[4] and interested persons are to be given an "opportunity to participate in the rulemaking through submission of written data, views, or arguments."[5] The APA afforded agencies great latitude in deciding whether or not to employ additional procedures beyond bare notice and comment.
>
> In the decade or two after the Administrative Procedure Act was enacted, licensing and rulemaking proceedings, formal adjudications, as well as formal rulemaking dominated the administrative law landscape. These processes, however, proved to be too cumbersome for implementing the

---

1. For a description of the events that led to the demise, *see* Toni M. Fine, *A Legislative Analysis of the Demise of the Administrative Conference of the United States*, 30 ARIZ. ST. L.J. 19 (1998). *See also* Gary J. Edles, *Lessons from the Administrative Conference of the United States*, 2 EUR. PUB. L. 571, 599–605 (1996), *reprinted in revised form as The Continuing Need for an Administrative Conference*, 50 ADMIN. L. REV. 101 (1998).
2. ADMINISTRATIVE CONFERENCE OF THE U.S., A GUIDE TO FEDERAL AGENCY RULEMAKING (2d. ed.) (ACUS 1991) at ix–x.
3. Where "formal rulemaking" is required, the trial-type procedures of 5 U.S.C. §§ 556–557 must be followed.
4. 5 U.S.C. § 553(b).
5. *Id.* § 553(c).

flood of new legislation passed in the late 1960s and early 1970s by which
the government sought to remedy newly perceived health, safety, and environmental problems. In a short time, informal rulemaking supplanted the
APA's formal processes as the preferred means of formulating major governmental policies. Indeed, a leading commentator proclaimed such notice
and comment procedures to be "one of the greatest inventions of modern
government."[6]

The increasing use of informal rulemaking to resolve complex, high-
stakes issues led by the mid- and late-1970s to new statutes and court decisions that placed additional procedural hurdles before agencies seeking to
promulgate rules. In addition, the late 1970s and 1980s saw an increased
Presidential involvement in the development of regulatory policies. These
developments are seen by one observer as having "taken the bloom off the
rulemaking rose."[7]

Rulemaking's effectiveness for establishing standards and norms has
been called into question,[8] and some have perceived an increase in agency
use of "non-rule rulemaking," i.e., the setting of standards through memoranda or guidelines intended to have the functional effect of rules.[9] Despite
criticism, however, informal rulemaking continues to be central to the maintenance of the administrative state, and according to the Office of Management and Budget, over 5,000 final rule documents were published in the
Federal Register in 1989.

Given the extensive use of rulemaking in federal agencies, it is important that agency rulemakers have available as clear guidance as possible. As
procedures governing the rulemaking process have proliferated since the
Administrative Procedure Act was enacted, the potential procedural pitfalls
have multiplied. And while some agencies are immersed in the rulemaking
process, other agencies only infrequently extend their toes into it.

---

6. 1 KENNETH CULP DAVIS, ADMINISTRATIVE LAW TREATISE 6.15 (Supp. 1970). *See* Paul Verkuil, *Present at the Creation: Regulatory Reform Before 1946*, 36 ADMIN. L. REV. 511, 520 (1986) (inter-viewing Kenneth Culp Davis and Walter Gellhorn).

7. Antonin Scalia, *Back to Basics: Making Law Without Making Rules*, REGULATION, July/Aug. 1981, at 25, 26.

8. *See* Richard J. Pierce, Jr., *Unruly Judicial Review of Rulemaking*, 5 NAT. RESOURCE & ENV'T 23 (1990) ("In 1990, this ingenious device for policymaking [rulemaking] is in danger of being relegated to a chapter in a legal history book."); JERRY L. MASHAW & DAVID L. HARFST, THE STRUGGLE FOR AUTO SAFETY (1990).

9. *See* Robert A. Anthony, Project on "Non-Rule Rulemaking" (Preliminary Outline to the Ad-ministrative Conference, Dec. 1990), *reprinted as Interpretive Rules, Policy Statements, Guid-ances, Manuals, and the Like—Should Federal Agencies Use Them to Bind the Public?*, 41 DUKE L.J. 1311 (1992).

This Guide to Federal Agency Rulemaking has been prepared to fulfill the Administrative Conference's function of encouraging the exchange of information among agencies.

This fifth edition retains the basic organization of the previous four. Like its predecessors, this edition of the *Guide* has four parts. Part I is an overview of federal agency rulemaking and describes the major institutional "players" and historical development of rulemaking. Part II describes the statutory structure of rulemaking, including the relevant sections of the Administrative Procedure Act (APA) and other statutes that have an impact on present-day rulemaking. Part III contains a step-by-step description of the informal rulemaking process, from the preliminary considerations to the final rule. Part IV discusses judicial review of rulemaking. Appendices include some key rulemaking documents.

While the transitions from the Clinton Administration to the Bush Administration and then to the Obama Administration did not result in a major shift in the rulemaking process—both Presidents Bush and Obama retained the Clinton Executive Order pertaining to White House review of rules—there were some important new initiatives by the Office of Management and Budget. Since 2006, the Supreme Court has issued some significant decisions concerning rulemaking petitions (*Massachusetts v. EPA*) and the "logical outgrowth test" concerning adequate notice in rulemaking (the *Long Island Care at Home* case). It continued the development of the law concerning judicial review of legal interpretations made in rulemaking (so-called *Chevron, Skidmore,* and *Auer* deference) and also of agency fact finding and policy choice under the arbitrary and capricious test (*Fox TV Stations v. FCC*).

Moreover, the rise of "e-rulemaking" has continued to be dramatic since 2006, with the large majority of public comments now being filed electronically—with many ramifications that were absent in the era of "paper" rulemaking. And there have been numerous new significant lower court decisions as well. This edition also continues to emphasize court decisions concerning rulemaking procedure and the judicial review of rules, although, as before, the *Guide* is not intended to be a complete catalog of relevant cases, nor should it be considered the definitive word on their significance. Rather, it should be used as a starting point for discussion or further research on administrative law issues pertaining to agency rulemaking.

I wish to again recognize those who helped out with earlier editions, such as Dan Cohen, Neil Eisner, Fred and Andrew Emery, Ron Levin, Randy May, and David Vladeck. I would also again like to thank those who worked on previous editions, including all my colleagues at ACUS, but especially Michael Bowers, Nancy Miller, and Professor Benjamin Mintz of Catholic University's Columbus School of Law. Over the years, of course, the *Guide* had the benefit of support from ACUS Chairs Loren Smith and Marshall Breger, who wrote Forewords for previous editions; the late Ernest Gellhorn, the longtime chair of ACUS's Committee on Rulemaking; and the many people in various federal agencies and elsewhere who made suggestions on earlier editions and helped make them a success.

For this edition I also received able research and editing assistance from my two research assistants, Emily Baver and Aaron M. Moore, class of 2012, Washington College of Law, American University, and senior editors of the *Administrative Law Review*.

Any errors, of course, are my own.

Jeffrey S. Lubbers
Professor of Practice in Administrative Law
Washington College of Law, American University
Editor, Fifth Edition
March 2012
JSL26@AOL.com

Note about the Administrative Conference
of the United States (1968-1995, 2010-)

The Administrative Conference of the United States (ACUS) is an independent federal agency in the executive branch, established in 1968 as an advisory agency in administrative law and procedure. ACUS has broad authority to conduct studies and make recommendations for improving the efficiency, adequacy, and fairness of the procedures that agencies use to carry out administrative programs and to collect data and publish reports useful for evaluating and improving administrative procedures.

ACUS is composed of the Chairman, the Council, and the Assembly. The Chairman is appointed by the President and serves as the chief executive of the Conference. The Council is composed of the Chairman and 10 members who serve as a "board of directors." The Assembly comprises approximately 100 members, consisting of representatives of federal agencies, boards, and commissions, and private citizens, including lawyers, law professors, and others knowledgeable about administrative law and practice. The Assembly ordinarily meets twice a year in plenary session to consider the adoptions of formal ACUS recommendations. All members serve on standing committees that develop proposed recommendations in their subject matter areas (for example, adjudication, rulemaking, judicial review, and so on). Other agencies and nongovernmental entities are represented by liaison representatives who may participate in committee activities but may not vote in plenary sessions.

The Office of the Chairman contains a small permanent staff of lawyers and support personnel whose responsibility is to administer the day-to-day operations of the agency, organize a research program, serve the membership and committees of the ACUS, and pursue the implementation of adopted recommendations. As part of this responsibility, the Office of the Chairman produced numerous publications and reports, such as the first two editions of *A Guide to Federal Agency Rulemaking*.

The activities of the Administrative Conference were suspended in October 1995 because of the decision of the Appropriations Committees of the 104th Congress to terminate funding for its operations (see the Symposium devoted to ACUS, in 30 *Arizona State Law Review* 19–162 (1998)). However, in both 2004 and 2008, Congress enacted legislation reauthorizing ACUS (Pub. L. No. 108-401, sec. 2(a), Oct. 30, 2004, 118 Stat. 2255; and Pub. L. No. 110-290, sec. 2, July 30, 2008, 122 Stat. 2914). No funding was provided for the first reauthorization, but appropriations were made in 2009, and with the confirmation of Chairman Paul Verkuil in 2010, ACUS resumed its operations. See www.acus.gov.

ACUS recommendations and research reports that formed the foundation for these recommendations, typically prepared by law professor consultants, were published from 1968 to 1995 by the Government Printing Office in annual volumes (*ACUS Reports and Recommendations*) and can now be found on HeinOnline. These volumes are typically cited herein as 19__ ACUS ____. Many of these reports were also subsequently published in law reviews in slightly different form. For the reader's convenience, the more accessible law review citation is usually provided.

ACUS recommendations are, upon adoption, published in the *Federal Register* and, until 1993, were codified in 1 C.F.R. Part 305. The 1993 CFR compilation is also now conveniently available online on the ABA's Administrative Procedure Database [http://www.law.fsu/edu/library/admin/acus/acustoc.html]. In this *Guide*, the *Federal Register* citation is provided where possible. A final listing of ACUS recommendations and statements from 1968 to 1995, with publication citations, was published in 60 Fed. Reg. 56,312 (Nov. 8, 1995). Subsequent ACUS recommendations, beginning in 2010, are available at www.acus.gov.

List of Acronyms Used in the Text

ABA	American Bar Association
ACUS	Administrative Conference of the United States
AFDC	Aid to Families with Dependent Children
ANPRM	Advance Notice of Proposed Rulemaking
APA	Administrative Procedure Act
CAB	Civil Aeronautics Board
CBI	Confidential Business Information
CBO	Congressional Budget Office
CEQ	Council on Environmental Quality
CFPB	Consumer Financial Protection Bureau
CFR	Code of Federal Regulations
CFTC	Commodity Futures Trading Commission
CIA	Central Intelligence Agency
COWPS	Council on Wage and Price Stability
CPSC	Consumer Product Safety Commission
CRA	Congressional Review Act
CRS	Congressional Research Service
DEA	Drug Enforcement Administration
DHS	Department of Homeland Security
DOD	Department of Defense
DOE	Department of Energy
DOI	Department of the Interior
DOL	Department of Labor
DOT	Department of Transportation
DVA	Department of Veterans Affairs
E.O.	Executive Order
EA	Environmental Assessment
EEOC	Equal Employment Opportunity Commission
EIS	Environmental Impact Statement
EPA	Environmental Protection Agency
F.R.A.P.	Federal Rules of Appellate Procedure
FAA	Federal Aviation Administration
FACA	Federal Advisory Committee Act
FAR	Federal Acquisition Regulation
FCC	Federal Communications Commission
FDA	Food and Drug Administration
FDMS	Federal Docket Management System
FEC	Federal Election Commission
FEMA	Federal Emergency Management Agency
FERC	Federal Energy Regulatory Commission

FOIA	Freedom of Information Act
FRFA	Final Regulatory Flexibility Analysis
FTC	Federal Trade Commission
FWS	Fish & Wildlife Service
FWS	Fish and Wildlife Service
GAO	Government Accountability Office (formerly General Accounting Office)
GSA	General Services Administration
GSA	General Services Administration
HHS	Department of Health and Human Services
HUD	Department of Housing and Urban Development
ICC	Interstate Commerce Commission
ICC	Interstate Commerce Commission
IIS	Inflation Impact Statement
INS	Immigration and Naturalization Service
IQA	Information Quality Act
IRFA	Initial Regulatory Flexibility Analysis
MSAPA	Model State Administrative Procedure Act
MSHA	Mine Safety and Health Administration
NARA	National Archives and Records Administration
NASA	National Aeronautics and Space Administration
NEPA	National Environmental Policy Act
NHTSA	National Highway Traffic Safety Administration
NIST	National Institutes of Standards and Technology
NLRB	National Labor Relations Board
NPRM	Notice of Proposed Rulemaking
NPS	National Park Service
NRA	Negotiated Rulemaking Act
NRC	Nuclear Regulatory Commission
NSF	National Science Foundation
OBRA	Omnibus Budget Reconciliation Act
OFR	Office of the Federal Register
OIRA	Office of Information and Regulatory Affairs
OMB	Office of Management and Budget
OPM	Office of Personnel Management
OSHA	Occupational Safety and Health Administration
PRA	Paperwork Reduction Act
PTO	Patent and Trademark Office
RFA	Regulatory Flexibility Act
SBA	Small Business Administration
SBREFA	Small Business Regulatory Enforcement Fairness Act of 1996

SEC	Securities and Exchange Commission
SORNA	Sex Offender Registration and Notification Act
UMRA	Unfunded Mandates Reform Act
USCIS	United States Citizens and Immigration Services
USDA	U.S. Department of Agriculture

PART I

OVERVIEW OF FEDERAL AGENCY RULEMAKING

The extent to which the administrative law of the national government is to be found in executive regulations is not ordinarily appreciated.

Frank J. Goodnow,
THE PRINCIPLES OF ADMINISTRATIVE LAW
IN THE UNITED STATES 87 (1905)

The procedure of administrative rule making is one of the greatest inventions of modern government.

Kenneth Culp Davis,
ADMINISTRATIVE LAW TREATISE § 6.15, at 283 (Supp. 1970)

Over the past few decades, Congress, the courts, and the executive branch have layered so many significant procedural requirements on notice and comment rulemaking that most academics and policymakers agree that the process has become ossified and inefficient.

Stephen M. Johnson,
58 ADMIN. L. REV. 37, 61 (2006)

PART I

Overview of Federal Agency Rulemaking

Passage of the Administrative Procedure Act (APA) in 1946[1] established the basic framework of administrative law governing agency action, including rulemaking. While the provisions of the APA continue to be central to the rulemaking process, a number of developments have, to some extent, undermined the original unifying effect of the APA. Beginning around 1970, Congress enacted a variety of specific regulatory statutes that mandated rulemaking procedures to supplement or supersede the APA's provisions.[2] In addition, agencies have had to significantly modify their rulemaking procedures in response to court-mandated refinements and the increasing complexity and controversial nature of many rulemakings.[3] Succeeding Presidents, beginning with Nixon, have, by executive order, imposed procedural requirements on rulemaking by executive branch agencies that went beyond procedures required by the APA.[4]

---

1. Pub. L. No. 404, 60 Stat. 237, ch. 324, §§ 1–12 (1946). Codified by Pub. L. No. 89-554 (1966) in 5 U.S.C. §§ 551-559, 701–706, 1305, 3105, 3344, 5372, 7521. *See The Administrative Procedure Act: A Fortieth Anniversary Symposium*, 72 VA. L. REV. 215 (1986) (discussing history and contemporary impact of APA on Act's 40th anniversary). This *Guide* refers to the sections in Title 5.

2. *See, e.g.*, Federal Trade Commission Improvement Act, 15 U.S.C. §§ 41–46, 50, 57a–58; Consumer Product Safety Act, 15 U.S.C. §§ 2051–2058, 2060–2061, 2063–2084; Occupational Safety and Health Act, 29 U.S.C. §§ 651–678; Mine Safety and Health Act, 30 U.S.C. §§ 801–804, 811–825, 841–846, 861–878, 901–931. These statutes are often referred to as "hybrid" rulemaking statutes, because they combine elements of both "formal" and "informal" rulemaking. Stephen F. Williams, *"Hybrid Rulemaking" Under the Administrative Procedure Act: A Legal and Empirical Analysis*, 42 U. CHI. L. REV. 401 (1975) (discussing creation of hybrid rulemaking). *See also infra* Part I, subsec. (C) and Part III, ch. 4(c) for a discussion of hybrid rulemaking.

3. *See, e.g.*, Vt. Yankee Nuclear Power Corp. v. Natural Res. Def. Council, 435 U.S. 519, 524 (1978) (reaffirming the principle that "[a]gencies are free to grant additional procedural rights in rulemaking in the exercise of their discretion . . . ."). For then-Professor Scalia's analysis of the case, *see* Antonin Scalia, *Vermont Yankee: The APA, the D.C. Circuit, and the Supreme Court*, 1978 SUP. CT. REV. 345 (1978). For an illuminating history of rulemaking's "collision" "with vigorous judicial review" in the D.C. Circuit, *see* Reuel Schiller, *Rulemaking's Promise: Administrative Law and Legal Culture in the 1960s and 1970s*, 53 ADMIN. L. REV. 1139, 1141 (2001). *See also* Ronald J. Krotoszynski, Jr., *"History Belongs to the Winners": The Bazelon-Leventhal Debate and the Continuing Relevance of the Process/Substance Dichotomy in Judicial Review of Agency Action*, 58 ADMIN. L. REV. 995 (2006).

4. The most important of these is President Clinton's Executive Order 12,866, 3 C.F.R. 644 (1993 compilation), *reprinted in* 5 U.S.C. § 601 and Appendix B to this *Guide*. Its stated purpose is "to enhance planning and coordination with respect to both new and existing regulations; to

3

Additional "regulatory reform" initiatives enacted by Congress have also prescribed procedural requirements for rulemaking. The combination of these add-ons to the rulemaking process has led numerous commentators to fret over the "ossification" of rulemaking.[5]

One of this *Guide*'s major purposes is to provide agency rulemakers, participants, and others interested in agency rulemaking an integrated view of the procedural requirements as they relate to each stage of the rulemaking process. Before embarking on a stage-by-stage discussion, however, the major events in the development of the federal rulemaking process will be summarized.

A. Rulemaking under the Administrative Procedure Act

The APA was the product of a struggle between interests that supported the programs of the New Deal agencies and those that were afraid or suspicious of the power given those agencies.[6] One of the APA's major accomplishments was the establishment of minimal procedural requirements for many types of agency proceedings. However, the APA did not require—as earlier bills would have—that all administra-

---

reaffirm the primacy of Federal agencies in the regulatory decisionmaking process; to restore the integrity and legitimacy of regulatory review and oversight; and to make the process more accessible and open to the public." *Id.* Its importance is unabated in 2011. President Obama's own Executive Order 13,563, "Improving Regulation and Regulatory Review," (Jan. 18, 2011), 76 Fed. Reg. 3821 (Jan. 21, 2011) (reprinted in Appendix C), reaffirmed the role of Executive Order 12,866. He had earlier revoked President Bush's modifications of the Clinton Order. *See* Exec. Order 13,497, "Revocation of Certain Executive Orders Concerning Regulatory Planning and Review" (Jan. 30, 2009), 74 Fed. Reg. 6113 (Feb. 4, 2009) (revoking Exec. Order 13,258 (Feb. 26, 2002) and Exec. Order 13,422 (Jan. 18, 2007)). These and other executive orders governing agency rulemaking are discussed *infra* subsec. (D) and Part III, ch. 2(A), (H).

5. For an overview of the literature on ossification, *see* Lynn E. Blais & Wendy E. Wagner, *Use and Abuse of Information Emerging Science, Adaptive Regulation, and the Problem of Rulemaking Ruts*, 86 Tex. L. Rev. 1701, 1704–11 (2008). For the classic articles *see, e.g.*, Thomas O. McGarity, *Some Thoughts on "Deossifying" the Rulemaking Process*, 41 Duke L.J. 1385 (1992); Richard J. Pierce, Jr., *Seven Ways to Deossify Agency Rulemaking*, 47 Admin. L. Rev. 59 (1995). *But see* Stephen M. Johnson, *Ossification's Demise: An Empirical Analysis of EPA Rulemaking from 2001-2005*, 38 Envtl. L. 767, 767 (2008) (finding that "it did not take EPA much longer to finalize rules subject to the most stringent procedural requirements imposed by the Executive Branch and Congress than it took to finalize rules not subject to those procedures").

6. *See* George B. Shepherd, *The Administrative Procedure Act Emerges From New Deal Politics*, 90 Nw. U. L. Rev. 1557 (1996); Jeffrey S. Lubbers, *APA Adjudication: Is the Quest for Uniformity Faltering?* 10 Admin. L. J. Am. U. 65 (1996); Paul R. Verkuil, *The Emerging Concept of Administrative Procedure*, 78 Colum. L. Rev. 258, 268–74 (1978). *See also* Dennis R. Ernst, *Dicey's Disciple on the D.C. Circuit: Judge Harold Stephens and Administrative Law Reform, 1933-1949*, 90 Geo. L.J. 787 (2002) (detailing pre-APA history).

tive action follow a single, rigid procedural model.[7] Instead, the APA recognized and adopted various agency procedures that are commonly characterized as "formal adjudication," "formal rulemaking," "informal adjudication," and "informal rulemaking."

The emphasis in this *Guide* is on "informal" rather than "formal" rulemaking. Formal rulemaking is triggered only where a statute other than the APA requires a rule to "be made on the record after opportunity for an agency hearing."[8] Although formal rulemaking procedures are discussed in Part II, Chapter 1(B), they will not be analyzed in detail in this *Guide*, as they are seldom used except in some rate-making, agriculture marketing order, and food-additive proceedings.

Section 553 of Title 5, United States Code, is the APA's general rulemaking section; rulemaking governed by it is commonly called "informal," "APA," or "notice-and-comment" rulemaking.[9] The notice-and-comment label derives from the fact that section 553 requires (1) publication of a notice of proposed rulemaking, (2) opportunity for public participation in the rulemaking by submission of written comments, and (3) publication of a final rule and accompanying statement of basis and purpose not less than 30 days before the rule's effective date. It is important to stress that these requirements are the procedural floor below which an agency may not go in prescribing procedures for a particular rulemaking. The APA's drafters contemplated that "[m]atters of great import, or those where the public submission of facts will be either useful to the agency or a protection to the public, should naturally be accorded more elaborate public procedures."[10]

As discussed below,[11] however, even the procedural floor set in section 553 does

---

7. The need for procedural variety and flexibility was shown by the pathbreaking empirical research conducted by the Attorney General's Committee on Administrative Procedure in existence from 1939 to 1941 and chaired by Dean Acheson. *See generally* Attorney General's Committee on Administrative Procedure, Final Report on Administrative Procedure in Government Agencies, S. Doc. No. 77-8 (1941).

8. 5 U.S.C. § 553(c).

9. Professor Herz has noted the increasing tendency of courts and commentators to blur the distinction between formal and informal rulemaking. He described the more frequent use of the oxymoronic phrase "formal notice-and-comment" and ascribed it to the facts that (1) traditional formal rulemaking has "virtually disappeared," (2) agencies increasingly rely on policy statements, where the procedure is even less formal, and (3) the Supreme Court's jurisprudence on the *Chevron* case (discussed in Part IV) has introduced different notions of "formality." Michael Herz, *Rulemaking Chapter, in* Developments in Administrative Law and Regulatory Practice 2002-2003, at 144 (Jeffrey S. Lubbers ed., 2004). Even the Supreme Court has mislabeled informal rulemaking as formal in recent years. *See, e.g.*, Wyeth v. Levine, 555 U.S. 555, 129 S. Ct. 1187, 1203 (2009); Nat'l Cable & Telecomms. Ass'n v. Brand X Internet Servs., 545 U.S. 967, 1004 (2005); Wash. State Dept. of Social and Health Servs. v. Guardianship Estate of Keffeler, 537 U.S. 371, 385 (2003). According to a Westlaw Search of "allfeds," the term "formal rulemaking" appeared in federal cases about twice as often from 2001 to 2011 as it did in the previous decade, although there are very few formal rulemaking statutes on the books.

10. Report on the Administrative Procedure Act, S. Rep. No. 79-752, at 15 (1945).

11. *See infra* Part II, ch. 1(D).

not apply to all rulemaking. Certain types of rules are exempted from some of these requirements, and entire classes of rules are totally exempted from APA notice-and-comment requirements. These exemptions reflect the APA drafters' cautious approach to imposing procedural requirements on a myriad of agency functions, as well as their willingness, in some situations, to permit agencies a measure of discretion in fashioning procedures appropriate to the particular rulemaking involved.

Congress's original willingness to leave to agency discretion rulemaking procedures exceeding the bare minimum required by section 553 has eroded significantly in the subsequent 65 years. Federal courts, Congress, and Presidents have taken steps to require that agencies follow more rigorous procedures. While the Clinton Administration did take some steps to streamline presidential review of rules[12] and the Supreme Court put the brakes on judicial supplementation of procedures in *Vermont Yankee Nuclear Power Corp. v. Natural Resources Defense Council (Vermont Yankee)*,[13] Congress has continued to require new procedural and substantive requirements, as has the Office of Management and Budget (OMB) under Presidents Bush II and Obama. These developments are discussed below in greater detail.

B. Agency Rulemaking and the Courts

Under the APA, persons aggrieved or adversely affected by agency actions, including agency promulgation of rules, have the right to seek judicial review of those actions.[14] Limited exceptions are provided—specifically, where another statute precludes judicial review or the action is committed to agency discretion.[15] Most statutes establishing regulatory programs provide for court review of agency rules.[16] Unless the enabling statute contains a controlling judicial review provision,[17] reviewing courts generally follow section 706 of the APA in determining the scope of judicial review. Because the standards are stated in general terms, and the application of particular standards of review to specific types of proceedings is not defined clearly by the APA, the judicial review provisions have been the subject of much court interpretation. A

---

12. *See infra* subsec. D.
13. *Supra* note 3.
14. 5 U.S.C. §§ 701–706. *See generally infra* Part IV (discussing judicial review of agency actions).
15. 5 U.S.C. § 701(a). The scope of these exceptions has been the subject of court decisions, particularly in the contexts of suits to compel agency action. *See* discussion *infra* Part IV, chs. 2, 3.
16. *See infra* Part IV, ch. 1.
17. Thus, for example, the Occupational Safety and Health Act statute provides that the agency's determination shall be upheld if "supported by substantial evidence in the record considered as a whole." 29 U.S.C. § 655(f). The meaning of the "substantial evidence" test as applied to "informal" or "hybrid" rulemaking has been explicated in a number of court of appeals decisions. *See infra* Part IV, ch. 2.

number of landmark Supreme Court decisions have been important in explicating the relationship between the courts and administrative agencies in the rulemaking area.

The first of these major decisions, *Citizens to Preserve Overton Park, Inc. v. Volpe* (*Overton Park*),[18] involved judicial review of the Secretary of Transportation's decision to authorize a road through a park. The Supreme Court first reaffirmed the presumptive reviewability of agency decisions by narrowly construing exceptions to the right to judicial review contained in section 701(a) of the APA.[19] The Court then applied the "arbitrary and capricious" test of section 706(2)(A), concluding that it "must consider whether the [Secretary's] decision was based on a consideration of the relevant factors and whether there has been a clear error of judgment."[20] The Supreme Court defined the reviewing court's obligation in the following language: "Although this inquiry into the facts is to be searching and careful, the ultimate standard of review is a narrow one. The court is not empowered to substitute its judgment for that of the agency."[21] Finally, the Court, refusing to accept as a basis for the agency decision "post hoc" rationalizations contained in agency affidavits offered for purposes of litigation, stated that to perform its review responsibilities, it must have before it "an administrative record that allows the full, prompt review of the Secretary's action."[22]

Overton Park had a lasting impact on court review of rulemaking even though the proceeding in that case was not rulemaking.[23] The courts continue to apply the presumption of reviewability of agency action,[24] and the Supreme Court's emphasis on the importance of the record to the review process has been extremely influential in the development of rulemaking procedures. The "searching and careful" standard of review described in the *Overton Park* decision, often called "hard look" review, has subsequently been applied by the courts to both substantive and procedural issues.[25]

The application of hard look review to procedural issues in rulemaking resulted in a series of decisions by the courts of appeals, principally the D.C. Circuit, which mandated procedures in agency rulemaking that went beyond the minimum requirements of section 553.[26]

Most of the early hybrid rulemaking judicial decisions involved rulemaking under statutes calling either for a decision after a hearing (but not on the record) or for

---

18. 401 U.S. 402 (1971).
19. *Id.* at 410 (relying on *Abbott Labs. v. Gardner*, 387 U.S. 136 (1967), and holding that there must be "clear and convincing evidence" of legislative intent to restrict judicial review).
20. *Id.* at 416.
21. *Id.*
22. *Id.* at 419. The Secretary of Transportation's determination was set aside and remanded to the district court for "plenary review." *Id.* at 419–20.
23. The action, which involved approval of building a specific road, would more appropriately be characterized as "informal adjudication."
24. *Cf.* Heckler v. Chaney, 470 U.S. 821 (1985), and related cases *infra* Part IV, ch. 3 (discussing the issue of reviewability of agency inaction).
25. *See infra* Part IV, ch. 2(A).
26. *See* Schiller, *supra* note 3.

"substantial evidence" review.[27] Although the courts refused to apply formal rulemaking procedures to these proceedings, they did remand final rules to the agencies for additional development of issues through cross-examination of witnesses or other unspecified procedural devices.[28]

In *Vermont Yankee*,[29] the Supreme Court substantially halted the development of judge-made "common law" of rulemaking procedure. In criticizing the D.C. Circuit's experimentation with hybrid procedure, the Court stated that

> . . . generally speaking [§ 553 of the APA] established the maximum procedural requirements which Congress was willing to have the courts impose upon agencies in conducting rulemaking procedures. Agencies are free to grant additional procedural rights in the exercise of their discretion, but reviewing courts are generally not free to impose them if the agencies have not chosen to grant them.[30]

Although *Vermont Yankee* precludes the invalidation of rules solely because an agency failed to use specific procedures not required by section 553, the decision did not overrule or overturn all the law of informal rulemaking that had been developed by the lower courts.[31] And it did not affect continuing strict court review of agency adherence to the procedural requirements in the APA or in agency regulations.[32]

The late 1970s began a rather sustained period of federal deregulation.[33] Deregu-

---

27. Review of informal rulemaking under the APA is under an "arbitrary or capricious" standard. 5 U.S.C. § 706(1). *See infra* Part IV, ch. 2, for discussion of these standards of review.

28. *See, e.g.*, Portland Cement Ass'n v. Ruckelshaus, 486 F.2d 375 (D.C. Cir. 1973), *cert. denied*, 417 U.S. 921 (1974) (remanding rule on stationary source standards under Clean Air Act for failure to make available test results and procedures used in creating standards, as well as failure to respond to manufacturers' comments); Int'l Harvester v. Ruckelshaus, 478 F.2d 615 (D.C. Cir. 1973) (remanding rule on emissions standards for light-duty vehicles for failure to properly consider availability of technology needed to meet standards). *See also* Symposium, *The Contribution of the D.C. Circuit to Administrative Law*, 40 ADMIN. L. REV. 507 (1988), and the articles cited in note 3, *supra*, for a discussion of these and related cases.

29. 435 U.S. 519 (1978).

30. *Id.* at 524 (footnote omitted).

31. *See* Scalia, *supra* note 3, at 395 ("In sum, it would seem that *Vermont Yankee*'s demand for fealty to the APA must be taken with a grain of salt."). *See also* Jack M. Beermann & Gary Lawson, *Reprocessing* Vermont Yankee, 75 GEO. WASH. L. REV. 856, 860 (2007) ("The decision can be read in at least three different ways: broadly to require strict fidelity to the text of the APA in all respects, narrowly to forbid only the very specific practices rejected in the case, or naturally (so we claim) to forbid imposition of any administrative procedures not firmly grounded in some source of positive statutory, regulatory, or constitutional law.").

32. *See infra* Part IV, ch. 2(A)(5) (discussing judicial review of agency procedures in issuing rules).

33. There is extensive literature on the subject of deregulation and its impact on agency rulemaking. *See, e.g.*, ROBERT E. LITAN & WILLIAM D. NORDHAUS, REFORMING FEDERAL REGULATION (1983); STEPHEN BREYER, REGULATION AND ITS REFORM (1982); Robert L. Rabin, *Federal Regulation in Historical Perspective*, 38 STAN. L. REV. 1189, 1315–26 (1986); Thomas O. McGarity, *Regulatory Reform in*

lation was effected by legislation,[34] through administrative actions—including amendment and repeal of rules—and in some cases through administrative inaction and delay.[35] In 1983, the Supreme Court, in *Motor Vehicle Manufacturers Ass'n v. State Farm Mutual Automobile Insurance Co. (State Farm)*,[36] reversed a major deregulatory action by the Reagan Administration. The Court vacated the National Highway Traffic Safety Administration's rescission of a previously issued rule requiring passive restraints (air bags and passive safety belts) in new automobiles. The Supreme Court first rejected the manufacturers' argument that rescission of a rule should be treated on review as a refusal to promulgate standards, to which a very deferential standard of court review had traditionally been applied.[37] Concluding that "the forces of change do not always or necessarily point in the direction of deregulation," the Court decided that the regulatory direction in which the agency chooses to move "does not alter the standard of judicial review established by law."[38]

Applying the "arbitrary and capricious" standard of review in *State Farm*, the Supreme Court asserted that the "agency must examine the relevant data and articulate a satisfactory explanation of its action, including a 'rational connection between the facts found and the choice made.'"[39] As the Court stated:

> Normally, an agency rule would be arbitrary and capricious if the agency has relied on factors which Congress has not intended it to consider, entirely failed to consider an important aspect of the problem, offered an explanation for its decision that runs counter to the evidence before the agency, or is so implausible that it could not be ascribed to a difference of view or the product of agency expertise.[40]

By insisting on taking a "hard look" at agency deregulatory decisions and requiring rigorous justification for such actions, the Supreme Court limited the sweep of its earlier decision in *Vermont Yankee*. In *State Farm*, the Supreme Court expressly distinguished the imposition of any "additional procedural requirements upon an agency"

---

the *Reagan Era*, 45 MD. L. REV. 253 (1986); Merrick B. Garland, *Deregulation and Judicial Review*, 98 HARV. L. REV. 505 (1985); Marianne K. Smythe, *Judicial Review of Rule Rescissions*, 84 COLUM. L. REV. 1928 (1984).

34. *See* Motor Carrier Act of 1980, Pub. L. No. 96-296, 94 Stat. 793 (codified in scattered sections of 49 U.S.C.); Airline Deregulation Act of 1978, Pub. L. No. 95-504, 92 Stat. 1705 (codified in scattered sections of 49 U.S.C.).

35. The Occupational Safety and Health Administration's delay in issuing a field sanitation standard, which spanned several presidential administrations, is an example. *See* Farmworker Justice Fund v. Brock, 811 F.2d 613 (D.C. Cir. 1987) (decision ordering OSHA to issue standard and ultimately vacated after OSHA issued standard), *vacated as moot*, 817 F.2d 890 (1987).

36. 463 U.S. 29 (1983).

37. *Id.* at 41.

38. *Id.* at 42.

39. *Id.* at 43 (quoting Burlington Truck Lines, Inc. v. United States, 371 U.S. 156, 168 (1962)).

40. *Id.*

but, rather, required the agency to consider in its decisional process an available "technological alternative"—the use of air bags only—"within the ambit of the existing Standard."[41]

In a decision handed down a year after *State Farm*, the Supreme Court, in *Chevron U.S.A. Inc. v. Natural Resources Defense Council (Chevron)*,[42] upheld an Environmental Protection Agency (EPA) rule under the Clean Air Act[43] allowing states to treat all pollution-emitting devices within the same industrial grouping as though they were encased in a single "bubble." Having determined that Congress did not have a "specific intention" concerning the interpretive issue before the Court, the Supreme Court decided that the only question on review was whether the administrative agency's view was a "reasonable one." For a unanimous Court, Justice Stevens stated:

> Judges are not experts in the field, and are not part of either political branch of the Government. Courts must, in some cases, reconcile competing political interests, but not on the basis of the judges' personal policy preferences. In contrast, an agency to which Congress has delegated policy-making responsibilities may, within the limits of that delegation, properly rely upon the incumbent administration's views of wise policy to inform its judgments. While agencies are not directly accountable to the people, the Chief Executive is, and it is entirely appropriate for this political branch of the Government to make such policy choices—resolving the competing interests which Congress itself either inadvertently did not resolve, or intentionally left to be resolved by the agency charged with the administration of the statute in light of everyday realities.
>
> When a challenge to an agency construction of a statutory provision, fairly conceptualized, really centers on the wisdom of the agency's policy, rather than whether it is a reasonable choice within a gap left open by Congress, the challenge must fail. In such a case, federal judges—who have no constituency—have a duty to respect legitimate policy choices made by those who do.[44]

In adopting this highly deferential approach to agency legal interpretations in rulemaking, the Supreme Court in *Chevron* did not attempt to explain its somewhat different approach to factual review in the *State Farm* decision.[45] Nevertheless, *Chevron* spawned a huge volume of cases and articles interpreting both its methodology and application to cases beyond the notice-and-comment rulemaking involved in the *Chevron* case itself.

---

41. *Id.* at 50, 51. On remand, the Department of Transportation issued a new rule relating to passive restraints, 49 Fed. Reg. 28,962 (1984), which was upheld by the D.C. Circuit in *State Farm Mutual Automobile Insurance Co. v. Dole*, 802 F.2d 474 (D.C. Cir. 1986), *cert. denied*, 480 U.S. 951 (1987).
42. 467 U.S. 837 (1984).
43. 42 U.S.C. § 7502(b)(6).
44. 467 U.S. at 865–66.
45. *See* Part IV, ch. 2(A), for a discussion of these cases.

Although its relevance to agency rulemaking is somewhat limited, another Supreme Court decision of special significance to agencies in a period of deregulation is *Heckler v. Chaney*.[46] In that case, various petitioners challenged a decision of the Food and Drug Administration (FDA) not to investigate, under the Federal Food, Drug, and Cosmetic Act, the use by a state of lethal drugs to execute criminals. The Court upheld the FDA decision not to pursue the matter. In an opinion for the majority, Justice Rehnquist stated that the presumption of reviewability of administrative agency action articulated in cases such as *Overton Park* did not apply to suits to force agency action. The Court concluded that decisions by agencies not to enforce or prosecute, whether by civil or criminal process, are "generally committed to an agency's absolute discretion." This "general unsuitability" for judicial review, the Court said, results largely from the fact that decisions not to enforce "often involve[] a complicated balancing of a number of factors which are particularly within [the agency's] expertise."[47]

Although the Supreme Court expressly stated that it was not deciding the reviewability of agency decisions declining to initiate rulemaking proceedings,[48] the decision was cited by the government in challenges to agency decisions not to initiate, or failures to complete, rulemaking. However, the Supreme Court firmly buried that concern in *Massachusetts v. EPA*,[49] which reviewed EPA's denial of a rulemaking petition asking the agency to regulate greenhouse gas emissions from new motor vehicles. In so doing the Court distinguished *Heckler* and said, "There are key differences between a denial of a petition for rulemaking and an agency's decision not to initiate an enforcement action."[50] It reaffirmed that its review was a "narrow" one under the arbitrary and capricious standard,[51] but found that the agency had "offered no reasoned explanation" for its denial.[52]

On the other hand, *Heckler v. Chaney* does clearly affect the reviewability of agency rule *enforcement* (or lack thereof).[53]

---

46. 470 U.S. 821 (1985).
47. *Id.* at 831. These balancing factors include determining whether violations actually occurred, whether the agency's resources should be spent on the particular case, and how the case fits the agency's overall policies. *Id.* at 831. The other reasons for "unsuitability" mentioned by the Court are: (1) in refusing to enforce, the agency is not exercising its "coercive" power, and (2) refusals to enforce are analogous to decisions by a prosecutor not to indict, which have long been considered as the "special province" of the Executive Branch. *Id.* at 831–35.
48. *Id.* at 825 n.2.
49. 549 U.S. 497 (2007).
50. *Id.* at 527. The four dissenting justices did not disagree that EPA's action was reviewable.
51. *Id.* at 527–28.
52. *Id.* at 534.
53. *See infra* Part IV, ch. 3, for a discussion of these cases.

C. Agency Rulemaking and the Congress

Congress has a pervasive influence on agency rulemaking activities.[54] In the first place, Congress decides whether to grant the fundamental authority to an administrative agency to engage in policy making through rulemaking. The enabling regulatory statute typically will, at least in general terms, define the scope of agency authority[55] and describe any specific rulemaking procedures the agency must follow in addition to, or in lieu of, the minimum requirements of 5 U.S.C. § 553.[56] In "hybrid" rulemaking statutes, Congress mandates additional rulemaking procedures normally reserved for adjudication, such as requirements for informal public hearings,[57] cross-examination of witnesses,[58] more extensive statements of justification for proposed and final rules,[59] or the application of the "substantial evidence" test to court review of agency rules.[60] The inclusion of these additional procedures in some regulatory statutes, most of which occurred in the 1970s, reflects in part the influence of pre-*Vermont Yankee* court decisions and the congressional view that the APA procedures, standing alone, did not necessarily ensure adequate public participation or accuracy in agency rulemaking decisions or provide an adequate basis for judicial review.

Congress has also sought to control and expedite agency rulemaking by preventing it through appropriations riders[61] or, contrariwise, imposing statutory deadlines

---

54. *See* Jessica Korn, The Power of Separation: American Constitutionalism and the Myth of the Legislative Veto (1996) (presenting a comprehensive analysis of the many ways Congress exercises effective control over agency policymaking).

55. For example, in *Bowen v. Georgetown Univ. Hosp.*, 488 U.S. 204 (1988), discussed *infra* Part III, ch. 7, the Supreme Court held that the Medicare Act, 42 U.S.C. § 1395x(v)(1)(A), did not authorize the promulgation of retroactive cost-limit rules. The Court stated, "It is axiomatic that an administrative agency's power to promulgate legislative regulations is limited to the authority delegated by Congress." 488 U.S. at 208.

56. *But see* section 559 of the APA, which states that a "[s]ubsequent statute may not be held to supersede or modify [the APA] . . . except to the extent that it does so expressly." 5 U.S.C. § 559. *Discussed in* Coal. for Parity, Inc. v. Sebelius, 709 F. Supp. 2d 10, 18 (D.D.C. 2010).

57. For example, under the Occupational Safety and Health Act, the agency is required to hold a public hearing if an interested person files written objections to a proposed rule and requests a public hearing "on such objections." 29 U.S.C. § 655(b)(3). *See* 29 C.F.R. § 1911.11(d) (implementing 29 U.S.C. § 655(b)(3)).

58. *See, e.g.*, Federal Trade Commission Act, 15 U.S.C. § 57a(c)(2)(B).

59. *See, e.g.*, Consumer Product Safety Act, 15 U.S.C. § 2058(f)(3).

60. *See, e.g.*, FTC Act, 15 U.S.C. § 57a(e)(3); Occupational Safety and Health Act, 29 U.S.C. § 655(f). The "substantial evidence" test as applied to informal or "hybrid" rulemaking has been widely discussed in court decisions. *See also* discussion *infra* Part IV, ch. 2(A)(6).

61. *See, e.g.*, Pub. L. No. 105-78 § 104, 111 Stat. 1467, 1477 (1997) (one of a series of riders prohibiting OSHA from using any appropriations "to promulgate or issue any proposed or final standard regarding ergonomic protection"). For a comprehensive survey of such riders, *see* Curtis W. Copeland, Cong. Research Serv., RL 34354, Congressional Influence on Rulemaking and Regulation Through Appropriations Restriction (Aug. 5, 2008), *available at* http://www.fas.org/sgp/crs/misc/RL34354.pdf. It found nearly two dozen provisions that were designed to prohibit or limit the development, implementation, or enforcement of agency regulations in the Consolidated Appropriations Act for 2008. *Id.* at CRS-8.

for completing rulemaking actions. Congress has been particularly concerned about agency delay and inaction in the public health and environment areas. Thus, for example, the Asbestos Hazard Emergency Response Act of 1986[62] required EPA to publish an advance notice of proposed rulemaking within 60 days of enactment, a proposed rule within 180 days, and final rules within 360 days for seven specific areas relating to asbestos-containing materials in school buildings.[63]

Many other agency statutes have included deadlines for agency rulemaking action.[64] Typically, these statutory deadlines can be enforced only by court suits;[65] however, in some cases, Congress has added so-called "hammers"[66] or other penalties if an agency fails to take timely action. An example of a statutory hammer is the provision in the 1984 amendments to the Resource Conservation and Recovery Act providing EPA with a specified period of time in which to issue regulations. If at the end of that time it had not acted, the hammer would fall—that is, a congressionally specified regulatory result would go into effect.[67] The Nutrition Labeling and Education Act of 1990[68] contained a similar hammer specifying that the agency's *proposed* rule would go into effect if the final rule was not issued within the statutory time limit.[69] New bioterrorism legislation gave the Department of Health & Human Services/FDA 18 months to issue proposed and final rules for registration of food imports, and

---

62. Pub. L. No. 99-519, 100 Stat. 2970 (codified at 15 U.S.C. §§ 2641-56). This Act amended the Toxic Substances Control Act.

63. 15 U.S.C. § 2643(a).

64. For example, the Federal Aviation Administration (FAA) Administrator is directed by statute to "issue a final regulation, or take other final action, not later than 16 months after the last day of the public comment period for the regulations or, in the case of an advanced notice of proposed rulemaking, if issued, not later than 24 months after the date of publication in the Federal Register of notice of the proposed rulemaking." 49 U.S.C. § 106(f)(3)(A). *But see* U.S. GEN ACCOUNTING OFFICE, AVIATION RULEMAKING: FURTHER REFORM IS NEEDED TO ADDRESS LONG-STANDING PROBLEMS 50-62 (GAO-01-821) (July 2001) (finding that the reforms did not improve rulemaking times). It was estimated that Congress imposed about 600 deadlines in various environmental statutes between 1970 and 1983 and added 60 more in the Hazardous and Solid Waste Amendments of 1984. Alden F. Abbott, *The Case Against Federal Statutory and Judicial Deadlines: A Cost-Benefit Appraisal*, 39 ADMIN. L. REV. 171, 173 (1987). *See also* Alden F. Abbott, *Case Studies in the Costs of Federal Statutory and Judicial Deadlines*, 39 ADMIN. L. REV. 467 (1987) (exploring wasted resource costs, agency resource misallocation costs, and regulatory inefficiency costs in context of 11 case studies of deadlines).

65. The issues of court enforcement of statutory deadlines and, more generally, of suits to compel agency action are discussed *infra* Part IV, ch. 3.

66. *See* Sidney A. Shapiro, *Congress' New Direction in Administrative Law*, 13 ADMIN. L. NEWS 8 (Spring 1988).

67. 42 U.S.C. § 6924(d)(1–2).

68. Pub. L. No. 101-535, 104 Stat. 2353 (codified as amended in scattered sections of 21 U.S.C.).

69. *See* M. Elizabeth Magill, *Congressional Control over Agency Rulemaking: The Nutrition Labeling and Education Act's Hammer Provisions*, 50 FOOD & DRUG L.J. 149, 165–70 (1995) (describing FDA's failure to meet strict congressional deadlines for issuance of final nutrition labeling regulations).

included a hammer provision stipulating, in effect, that if the rules were not finalized by the deadline, importers could register as they pleased.[70] And one memorable rider to an appropriations act withheld a portion of the budget of several agency offices until particular final rules were issued.[71]

The Administrative Conference questioned the value of statutory rulemaking dead-lines,[72] as have a number of commentators.[73] Congress continues to impose these deadlines, however, and they often are an important factor in court litigation to force agencies to initiate or complete rulemaking activity.[74]

Congress also seeks to monitor agency rulemaking after its completion. Prior to 1983, Congress had incorporated "legislative veto" provisions into many statutes authorizing agency rules.[75] Such statutes typically provided for review of final agency rules by one or both houses of Congress. In 1983, however, the Supreme Court held in *Immigration and Naturalization Service v. Chadha*[76] that a statutory provision au-thorizing a one-house veto of the suspension of a deportation order by the Attorney General violated the separation of powers doctrine and was therefore unconstitu-tional.[77] Subsequently, the Supreme Court applied *Chadha* to two-house vetoes and to vetoes of rules issued by administrative agencies.[78] Although the legislative veto in

---

70. Public Health Security and Bioterrorism Preparedness and Response Act of 2002, Pub. L. No 107-188, § 305(e), 116 Stat. 594, 669 (June 12, 2002). Interim-final rules were issued October 10, 2003, 68 Fed. Reg. 58,893.

71. *See* Department of Transportation and Related Agencies Appropriations Act, 1988, Pub. L. No 100-202, Title 1, 101 Stat. 1329-358/359 (Dec. 22, 1987) (providing that 5% of appropriated funds be withheld from the Office of the Secretary and Office of General Counsel until several enumerated final rules are issued), *cited in* Neil R. Eisner, *Agency Delay in Informal Rulemaking*, 3 Admin. L.J. 7, 33 n.162 (1989). *See also* Department of Transportation and Related Agencies Appropriations Act, 1990, Pub. L. No 102-388, 106 Stat. 1525 (Oct. 6, 1992) (providing that no funds can be used for pay raises for FAA employees responsible for preparing an environ-mental impact statement until it is prepared).

72. Administrative Conference of the United States [hereinafter ACUS] Recommendation 78-3, *Time Limits on Agency Actions*, 43 Fed. Reg. 27,509 (1978). All ACUS Recommendations are *available at* http://www.acus.gov/library/recommendations.

73. See articles cited *supra* note 64.

74. See cases discussed *infra* Part IV, ch. 3.

75. An inventory of these statutes through 1983 appears as an appendix to the dissenting opinion of Justice White in *INS v. Chadha*, 462 U.S. 919, 1003–13 (1983). The appendix lists 56 statutes with provisions authorizing post-promulgation congressional review. *Id.*

76. 462 U.S. 919 (1983).

77. The *Chadha* decision was the subject of extensive discussion. *See, e.g.*, E. Donald Elliot, INS v. Chadha: *The Administrative Constitution, the Constitution, and the Legislative Veto*, 1983 Sup. Ct. Rev. 125 (1983).

78. United States Senate v. FTC, 463 U.S. 1216 (1983) (holding unconstitutional FTC Improve-ments Act provision authorizing two-house vetoes of FTC rules), *aff'g* Consumers Union v. FTC, 691 F.2d 575 (D.C. Cir. 1982); Process Gas Consumers Group v. Consumers Energy Council of Am., 463 U.S. 1216 (1983) (mem.), *aff'g* Consumer Energy Council of America v. FERC, 673 F.2d 425 (D.C. Cir. 1982) (holding one-house legislative veto in Natural Gas Policy Act of 1978 unconstitutional).

its classic sense is no longer an option for congressional control of rulemaking,[79] in 1995 a congressional review-of-rules procedure was enacted. The law delays the effective date of major rules for at least 60 days and provides expedited procedures for congressional consideration of resolutions of disapproval.[80] The overall scheme avoids *Chadha* problems because it requires bicameral passage of joint resolutions and presentation to the President for signature or veto. However, it is fraught with complexities,[81] and only one rule has been "disapproved," and thus voided, under this process[82]—an ergonomics rule promulgated by the Occupational Safety and Health Administration (OSHA) at the end of the Clinton Administration.[83]

Even beyond this new congressional review process, however, Congress retains other means for overseeing agency rulemaking activity. Statutory requirements limiting agency rulemaking discretion, discussed above, continue to be an important method of congressional control, as are appropriations riders.[84] Another method is the exercise of congressional oversight authority, by either formal or informal means.[85] Congressional committees frequently hold oversight hearings on rulemaking issues and, in some cases, file reports expressing strong views on agency performance on particular matters.[86]

---

79. *See* William F. Leahy, *The Fate of the Legislative Veto After Chadha*, 53 GEO. WASH. L. REV. 168 (1984). The impact of *Chadha* on existing legislative veto provisions remains an issue. Congress has amended several statutes to delete unconstitutional legislative vetoes. However, many statutes containing pre-*Chadha* legislative vetoes remain unchanged. The Supreme Court addressed the severability of such provisions in *Alaska Airlines v. Brock*, 480 U.S. 678 (1987). *See also* New Haven v. United States, 809 F.2d 900 (D.C. Cir. 1987) (holding the legislative veto provision nonseverable).

80. The Small Business Regulatory Enforcement Fairness Act of 1996, Pub. L. No. 104-121, Title II, subtitle E, 110 Stat. 856 (codified at 5 U.S.C. §§ 801–808). *See infra* Part II, ch. 3(J), for a detailed discussion of this Act.

81. *See infra* Part III, ch. 7(A)(6)(b); Daniel Cohen & Peter L. Strauss, *Congressional Review of Agency Regulations*, 49 ADMIN. L. REV. 95 (1997).

82. *See* MORTON ROSENBERG, CONG. RESEARCH SERV., RL 30116, CONGRESSIONAL REVIEW OF AGENCY RULEMAKING: AN UPDATE AND ASSESSMENT OF THE CONGRESSIONAL REVIEW ACT AFTER A DECADE (May 8, 2008), *available at* http://www.fas.org/sgp/crs/misc/RL30116.pdf.

83. Pub. L. No. 107-5 (Mar. 20, 2001), invalidating OSHA's ergonomics program standard issued on Nov. 14, 2000 (65 Fed. Reg. 68,262).

84. *See supra* note 61.

85. There is extensive literature on congressional oversight activity. *See, e.g.,* FREDERICK M. KAISER, ET AL., CONG. RESEARCH OFFICE, RL 30240, CONGRESSIONAL OVERSIGHT MANUAL (June 10, 2011), *available at* http://www.fas.org/sgp/crs/misc/RL30240.pdf.

86. *See, e.g.,* House Comm. on Energy and Commerce; Subcommittee on Oversight and Investigations, Report on *EPA's Asbestos Regulations: A Case Study on OMB Interference in Agency Rulemaking*, 99th Cong., 1st Sess. (Oct. 1985) (criticizing EPA's decision not to regulate asbestos under the Toxic Substances Control Act). EPA reversed its position and initiated a rulemaking. 51 Fed. Reg. 3738 (Jan. 29, 1986).

Informal contacts between agency rulemakers and members of Congress and congressional staff in connection with rulemaking are also frequent.[87] In *Sierra Club v. Costle*,[88] the D.C. Circuit held that it was "entirely proper for congressional representatives vigorously to represent the interests of their constituents before administrative agencies engaged in informal, general policy rulemaking, so long as the individual Congressmen do not frustrate the intent of Congress as a whole as expressed in statute, nor undermine applicable rules of procedure."[89]

Congress also controls agency rulemaking procedure by enacting generic procedural statutes, such as the National Environmental Policy Act,[90] the Paperwork Reduction Act,[91] and the Regulatory Flexibility Act.[92] These statutes, which are designed to improve the quality of agency decisionmaking and further policy goals set forth in the statutes, have had a significant impact on the rulemaking process.[93]

D. Agency Rulemaking and the President

Perhaps the most significant administrative law development during the last few decades has been the increased presidential involvement in federal agency rulemaking.[94] This presidential review, exercised by the Office of Management and Budget's (OMB's) Office of Information and Regulatory Affairs (OIRA), has been the result of numerous executive orders[95] as well as the enactment of the Paperwork Reduction Act.[96] According to testimony of the OIRA Administrator in 2004:

---

87. *See* JEFFREY M. BERRY, FEEDING HUNGRY PEOPLE: RULEMAKING IN THE FOOD STAMP PROGRAM (1984).
88. 657 F.2d 298 (D.C. Cir. 1981).
89. *Id.* at 409. *See* discussion *infra* Part III, ch. 6.
90. 42 U.S.C. §§ 4321–4370d.
91. 44 U.S.C. §§ 3501–3520.
92. 5 U.S.C. §§ 601–612.
93. See *infra* Part II, ch. 3, and Part III, ch. 2, for discussion on these and other generic statutes.
94. See also the companion book published by the ABA Section on Administrative Law and Regulatory Practice, A GUIDE TO JUDICIAL AND POLITICAL REVIEW OF FEDERAL AGENCIES, 211–50, 275–82 (John F. Duffy & Michael Herz eds., ABA 2005). An update of this book is pending.
95. Exec. Order 12,291, 3 C.F.R. 127 (1981 compilation); Exec. Order 12,498, 3 C.F.R. 323 (1985 compilation) (providing guidance on regulatory planning process); Exec. Order 12,606, 3 C.F.R. 241 (1987 compilation); Exec. Order 12,612, 3 C.F.R. 252 (1987 compilation); Exec. Order 12,630, 3 C.F.R. 554 (1988 compilation); Exec. Order 12,866, 3 C.F.R 644 (1993 compilation), Exec. Order, 13,563, "Improving Regulation and Regulatory Review," (Jan. 18, 2011), 76 Fed. Reg. 3821 (Jan. 21, 2011). Some of these Executive Orders are reprinted in 5 U.S.C. § 601 note. Exec. Orders 12,866 and 13,563 are reprinted in the Appendix to this *Guide*. *See generally* Jim Tozzi, *OIRA's Formative Years: The Historical Record of Centralized Regulatory Review Preceding OIRA's Founding*, 63 ADMIN. L. REV. (SPECIAL ED.) 37 (2011) (chronicling the evolution of regulatory review).
96. Pub. L. No. 96-511, 94 Stat. 2812 (1980) (as amended) (codified at 44 U.S.C. §§ 3501–3520). The Paperwork Reduction Act superseded the Federal Reports Act of 1942, Pub. L. No. 77-831, 56 Stat. 1078.

Since OMB began to keep records in 1981, there have been 109,710 final rules published in the Federal Register by federal agencies. Of these published rules, 20,029 were formally reviewed by OMB prior to publication. Of the OMB-reviewed rules, 1,073 were considered "major" or "economically significant" rules, primarily because they were estimated to have an economic impact greater than $100 million in any one year.[97]

More recently, OMB reported that "[b]etween fiscal years 2001 and 2010, Federal agencies published over 38,000 final rules in the *Federal Register*. OMB reviewed 3,325 of these final rules under Executive Order 12866. Of these OMB-reviewed rules, 540 are considered major rules."[98] Note that the percentage of rules reviewed by OMB dropped from 18.3% in the earlier period to less than 8.8% in the most recent one. Moreover, the number of total rules and major rules per year, as reported by OMB, also has dropped significantly in the more recent period.

1. The Development of Presidential Review

Presidential oversight of regulation is not a recent innovation. It has been in effect, in one form or another, since 1971,[99] and it accompanied a major expansion in the scope and complexity of federal regulation that occurred in the 1960s and 1970s when Congress enacted a number of important social and environmental regulatory statutes.[100]

In June 1971, President Nixon established a "Quality of Life Review" program, under which all "significant" draft proposed and final rules were submitted to OMB, which circulated them to other agencies for comment.[101] Agencies were required to

---

97. *Regulatory Reform, Hearing before the House Subcommittee on Energy Policy, Natural Resources and Regulatory Affairs*, 108th Cong. (Nov. 17, 2004) (statement of John D. Graham, Administrator of OIRA), *available at* http://www.whitehouse.gov/omb/legislative/testimony/graham/111704_graham_reg_reform.html.

98. *See* Office of Mgmt. & Budget, Office of Information and Regulatory Affairs, Draft 2011 Report to Congress on The Benefits and Costs Of Federal Regulations and Unfunded Mandates on State, Local, and Tribal Entities 11–12 (2011), *available at* http://www.whitehouse.gov/sites/default/files/omb/legislative/reports/Draft_2011_CBA_Report_AllSections.pdf.

99. *See* Tozzi, note 95. The entire symposium issue contained in 63 Admin. L. Rev. (Special Ed.) (2011) devoted to "OIRA's Thirtieth Anniversary Conference" contains a wealth of information about this topic.

100. *See* Robert. L. Rabin, *Federal Regulation in Historical Perspective*, 38 Stan. L. Rev. 1189 (1986) (providing an excellent history of government regulation).

101. See the papers archived by Jim Tozzi, the career official in charge of Quality of Life Review in the Nixon Administration, for the Center for Regulatory Effectiveness at http://www.thecre.com/ombpapers/centralrev.html. These include "Quality of Life Review #1": Memorandum to Heads of Department and Agencies from George P. Schultz, Director, OMB, Agency Regulations, Standards and Guidelines Pertaining to Environmental Quality, Consumer Protection, Occupational and Public Health and Safety (Oct. 5, 1971).

submit a summary of their proposals, a description of the alternatives that had been considered, and a cost comparison of alternatives. In practice, this program applied to rules pertaining to environmental quality, consumer protection, and occupational health and safety.

In 1974, President Ford issued an executive order requiring executive branch agencies to prepare an "inflation impact statement" (IIS) for each "major" federal action.[102] The order empowered the director of OMB to administer the program, with authority to delegate functions to other agencies, including the Council on Wage and Price Stability (COWPS).[103] Under the IIS program, agencies were required to prepare an IIS for "major" rules[104] prior to publication of the notice of proposed rulemaking (NPRM) and then to forward a summary of the IIS to COWPS upon publication of the NPRM.[105] COWPS would review the IIS and, in its discretion, offer informal criticism of the proposal or participate in the public proceedings on the rule.[106]

President Carter continued presidential review of agency rules by means of Executive Order (E.O.) 12,044, issued in 1978.[107] Under the Order, executive agencies were required to (1) publish semiannual agendas describing and giving the legal bases for any "significant" regulations under development by the agency; (2) establish procedures to identify "significant" rules, to evaluate their need and to have the agency head assure that the "least burdensome of the acceptable alternatives" was proposed; and (3) prepare a "regulatory analysis" that examined the cost-effectiveness of alternative regulatory approaches for "major rules."

President Carter also established a Regulatory Analysis Review Group to review the regulatory analyses prepared for a limited number of proposed major rules and to submit comments on the proposed rules during the public comment period.[108] He created another rulemaking review body, the Regulatory Council, which was charged with coordinating agency rulemaking to avoid duplication of effort or conflicting

102. Exec. Order 11,821, 3 C.F.R. 203 (1971-1975 compilation). When the Executive Order was later extended, the "inflation impact statement" (IIS) was replaced by an "economic impact statement" to better reflect the required analysis, which could be characterized as a loose cost-benefit analysis. *See* OMB Circular No. A-107, § 4(d) (Jan. 28, 1975), *cited in* Charles W. Vernon, III, Note, *The Inflation Impact Statement Program: An Assessment of the First Two Years*, 26 Am. U. L. Rev. 1138, 1141 n.28 (1977).
103. *See* Vernon, *supra* note 102, at 1140.
104. Originally, agencies were left to develop their own criteria for determining what was a "major" proposal, subject to OMB approval; eventually, COWPS adopted a list of suggested criteria that essentially defined a "major" proposal as one entailing a cost of $100 million or more in one year or $150 million or more in two years. *See* Note, *Regulation Analyses and Judicial Review of Informal Rulemaking*, 91 Yale L.J. 739, 746 n.51 (1982).
105. Vernon, *supra* note 102, at 1142.
106. *Id.*
107. 3 C.F.R. 152 (1978 compilation). Jim Tozzi credits the Carter Administration for making "some remarkable contributions to centralized regulatory review." Tozzi, *supra* note 95, at 52.
108. 43 Fed. Reg. 12,668 (1978).

policy in regulation of any area.[109] These efforts to coordinate agency rulemaking were unsuccessfully challenged in several lawsuits.[110]

President Reagan acted quickly after taking office to increase control over executive branch rulemaking. On February 17, 1981, he issued an executive order on federal regulations designed "to reduce the burdens of existing and future regulations, increase agency accountability for regulatory actions, provide for Presidential oversight of the regulatory process, minimize duplication and conflict of regulations, and insure well-reasoned regulations."[111] The new E.O. 12,291 replaced E.O. 12,044, which President Reagan said had "proven ineffective."[112]

E.O. 12,291 contained both substantive requirements and procedural steps to be followed in the development and promulgation of new rules.[113] The Office of Information and Regulatory Affairs (OIRA) in the OMB was given responsibility for implementing E.O. 12,291. OMB's rulemaking review function had been supplemented by the powers it was given in the Paperwork Reduction Act of 1980,[114] by which Congress statutorily established OIRA to, among other things, review and approve or disapprove agency "information collection requests."

The Office of Legal Counsel in the U.S. Department of Justice issued an opinion supporting the validity of E.O. 12,291.[115] The opinion stated that the President's authority to issue the order was based on his constitutional power to "take care that the laws be faithfully executed."[116] While concluding that any inquiry into congressional intent in enacting specific rulemaking statutes "will usually support the legality of Presidential supervision of rulemaking by Executive Branch agencies,"[117] the opinion

---

109. Memorandum from President Carter to executive departments and agencies, titled "Strengthening Regulatory Management" (Oct. 13, 1978). The Regulatory Council included the heads of all executive branch agencies and the heads of any independent agencies that chose to participate on a voluntary basis.

110. *See* Michael S. Baram, *Cost-Benefit Analysis: An Inadequate Basis for Health, Safety, and Environmental Regulatory Decisionmaking*, 8 ECOLOGY L.Q. 473, 512–14 (1980) (discussing controversy over use of cost-benefit analysis); Paul R. Verkuil, *Jawboning Administrative Agencies: Ex Parte Contacts by the White House*, 80 COLUM. L. REV. 943, 944–47 (1980).

111. Exec. Order 12,291, 3 C.F.R. 127 (1981 compilation).

112. Office of the Vice President, Fact Sheet Accompanying Executive Order on Regulatory Management 2 (1981).

113. *See infra* Part III, ch. 2(A) for a discussion of the order's requirements.

114. 44 U.S.C. §§ 3501-3520. It is important to note that OMB's power under the Paperwork Reduction Act extends to independent regulatory agencies in the executive branch. OMB has issued regulations setting forth procedures for clearance of informational requirements contained in agency rules, as well as procedures for collection requests not contained in rules. 5 C.F.R. pt. 1320. *See infra* Part II, ch. 3(d) and Part III, ch. 2(B), for a discussion of the Paperwork Reduction Act.

115. *See* Memorandum from Larry L. Simms, Acting Assistant Attorney General, Office of Legal Counsel, U.S. Department of Justice, Proposed Executive Order titled "Federal Regulation," 5 U.S. Op. Off. Legal Counsel 59 (Feb. 13, 1981), 1981 WL 30877 (O.L.C.). Also *available at* http://www.thecre.com/pdf/DJMemoReaganEO12291PDF.pdf.

116. *Id.* at 60.

117. *Id.* at 61.

stated that presidential supervision of agency rulemaking "is more readily justified when it does not purport wholly to displace, but only to guide and limit, discretion which Congress had allocated to a particular subordinate official."[118]

Despite criticism of this new form of presidential review, President Reagan began his second term by expanding the program through E.O. 12,498, which established a "regulatory planning process" with the purpose of helping to "ensure that each major step in the process of rule development is consistent with Administration policy."[119]

According to OMB, a problem with regulatory review under E.O. 12,291 was that such review "often came late in the regulatory process, after huge investments of agency time and resources, and often after agency staff commitments to constituents had made it extremely difficult to consider any legally acceptable, but previously ignored, regulatory alternative."[120] This resulted, OMB said, in the "bureaucracy often present[ing] agency heads with *faits accompli.*"[121]

E.O. 12,498's regulatory planning process was designed to avoid this problem.[122] Under this procedure, the head of each agency was required to determine at the beginning of the regulatory process whether a proposed regulatory venture was "consistent with the goals of the Administration."[123] At the beginning of the year, agency heads were to develop a plan for managing the agency's most significant regulatory actions. OMB then reviewed the plan for consistency with the administration's program and published the coordinated agency plans in a government-wide document.[124] This document, entitled *Regulatory Program of the United States Government*, governed more than 20 major rulemaking agencies and was published each year during the second Reagan term and the Bush I Administration to inform Congress and the public of the government's regulatory plans.[125]

President Reagan, in 1987 and 1988, issued three additional executive orders, dealing with federalism,[126] interference with property rights,[127] and the family.[128] OMB

---

118. *Id.*
119. OFFICE OF MGMT. & BUDGET, REGULATORY PROGRAM OF THE UNITED STATES GOVERNMENT xiv (1987-1988).
120. *Id.* at xliii.
121. *Id.*
122. President's Memorandum for the Heads of Executive Departments and Agencies, 21 WEEKLY COMP. PRES. DOC. 13 (1985).
123. *Id.*
124. Exec. Order 12,498, §§ 2, 3, 3 C.F.R. 323, 324 (1985 compilation).
125. *See, e.g.,* OFFICE OF MGMT. & BUDGET, REGULATORY PROGRAM OF THE UNITED STATES GOVERNMENT (1990-1991).
126. Exec. Order 12,612, 3 C.F.R. 252 (1987 compilation) (ensuring that executive departments are guided by "principles of federalism").
127. Exec. Order 12,630, 3 C.F.R. 554 (1988 compilation) (relating to "Governmental Actions and Interference with Constitutionally Protected Property Rights").
128. Exec. Order 12,606, 3 C.F.R. 241 (1987 compilation) (intending to "ensure that the autonomy and rights of the family are considered" in formulation of government policy). This order was repealed by Exec. Order 13,045, 62 Fed. Reg. 36,965 (1997). *See infra* Part III ch. 2(H).

was given a role in ensuring coordination of regulatory policy in these areas.[129] President George H.W. Bush basically continued the program of presidential review of agency rulemaking established by President Reagan, although due to congressional opposition to OIRA actions, President Bush's nominee to head OIRA was not confirmed.[130] To counter this weakening of OIRA's authority, President Bush created the Council on Competitiveness, headed by Vice President Quayle, and gave it authority to intervene in major agency rulemakings.[131] Several of the Council's interventions provoked intense criticisms leading up to the 1992 elections.[132]

2. *Executive Order 12,866*

One of President Clinton's first actions was an attempt to reestablish some bipartisan consensus on rulemaking review. His nominee for OIRA administrator was the first subcabinet nominee to be appointed.[133] Following the example of the Reagan Administration, the Clintonites then set out to redraft the extant executive order and produced E.O. 12,866 on September 30, 1993.[134] This Order carried over many of the principles of E.O. 12,291 (and E.O. 12,498), which it superseded,[135] but it also made some significant modifications that simplified the process, made it more selective, and introduced more transparency into the OMB/agency consultations. In drafting this Order, the Clinton Administration followed many of the suggestions of the Administrative Conference in its Recommendation 88-9, "Presidential Review of Agency Rulemaking."[136] Executive Order 12,866 remained operative throughout the Bush II

---

129. *See infra* Part III, ch. 2(H) for further discussion of these executive orders.
130. *See* Delissa Ridgway et al., *The Council on Competitiveness and Regulatory Review: A "Kinder, Gentler" Approach to Regulation?* 6 ADMIN. L.J. AM. U. 691, 698 & n.196 (1993) (comments by Jim Tozzi).
131. The Council was created by a press release from the Vice President's office. *See* Caroline DeWitt, Comment, *The Council on Competitiveness: Undermining the Administrative Procedure Act with Regulatory Review,* 6 ADMIN. L.J. AM. U. 759, 760 n.3 (1993).
132. *See* Ridgway, *supra* note 130. *See also* David B. Rivkin, Jr., *The Unitary Executive and Presidential Control of Executive Branch Rulemaking,* 7 ADMIN. L.J. AM. U. 309 (1993); Thomas O. Sargentich, *The Supreme Court's Administrative Law Jurisprudence,* 7 ADMIN. L.J. AM. U. 273 (1993); Cass R. Sunstein, *The Myth of the Unitary Executive,* 7 ADMIN. L.J. AM. U. 299 (1993).
133. *See* William A. Niskanen, *Clinton Regulation Will Be "Rational": Interview with Sally Katzen, the New OIRA Administrator,* 16 REGULATION, Summer 1993, at 36, *available at* http://www.cato.org/pubs/regulation/regv16n3/v16n3-4.pdf.
134. Exec. Order 12,866, 3 C.F.R 644 (1993 compilation). *See* Appendix B.
135. Somewhat surprisingly, the Order did not, however, supersede the other Reagan Executive Orders requiring various other impact statements in the rulemaking process—most of which remain in effect. *See supra* notes 126–28.
136. ACUS Recommendation 88-9, 54 Fed. Reg. 5207 (1989). The Conference recommended public disclosure of proposed and final agency rules and final agency agendas submitted to OMB, official written policy guidance from OMB, communications from OMB containing factual information relating to the substance of the rulemaking, and "conduit" communications (that

Administration[137] and has been reaffirmed by President Obama,[138] so it continues to be the centerpiece of the White House's involvement in rulemaking.

The Order begins with a lengthy "Statement of Regulatory Philosophy and Principles," which is quite similar to E.O. 12,291 except that it takes pains to specify that measurement of costs and benefits should include both quantifiable and qualitative measures. As with previous orders, E.O. 12,866 retains the traditional (since 1978) level of $100 million annual effect on the economy for those major rules (now referred to as "economically significant" rules) that must be accompanied by cost-benefit assessments when forwarded to OIRA as proposed and final rules. It also provides the standard disclaimer that the Order is not intended to create any enforceable rights in court.[139]

E.O. 12,866 also retains the OIRA review process for other rules, although it requires that only "significant regulatory actions" be subject to review. This includes those $100 million rules plus others that have material adverse effects on "the economy, a sector of the economy, productivity, competition, jobs, the environment, public health or safety, or State, local, or tribal governments or communities." It also includes rules that may materially alter the budgetary impact of benefit programs or the rights of recipients that raise "novel legal or policy issues," or are inconsistent or interfere with actions taken by another agency. The process established for identifying such "significant regulatory actions" relies on agency identification of them in the first instance, vetted by OIRA. Rules that are not so identified may be issued without OIRA review. This selectivity streamlined the review process considerably[140] and made

---

is, communications containing the views, positions, or information from persons outside the government). The recommendation also suggests procedures to be followed by OMB reviewing officials to discourage such "conduit" communications. Finally, the recommendation states that presidential review "should be completed in a timely fashion" by both the reviewing office and the agencies, "with due regard for statutory and other relevant deadlines," but a specific time limit on review was not recommended. The American Bar Association subsequently adopted a resolution urging OMB to complete review within 60 days. A.B.A. Resolution (Feb. 12-13, 1990). The ABA also endorsed Recommendation 88-9 in its entirety. Report 302, Reports with Recommendations, 1990 ABA Annual Meeting, Chicago, IL (Aug. 7-8, 1990).

137. President Bush amended the Order to remove the Vice President from the process. Executive Order 13,258 (Feb. 26, 2002), 67 Fed. Reg. 9385 (Feb. 28, 2002). He also made some more significant amendments in Exec. Order 13,422 (Jan. 18, 2007), 72 Fed. Reg. 2763 (Jan. 23, 2007), but President Obama rescinded all of the changes and reinstated the original Clinton Order. *See supra* note 4. Appendix B contains the unamended text of E.O. 12,866.

138. He did so in Executive Order 13,563, "Improving Regulation and Regulatory Review" (Jan. 18, 2011), 76 Fed. Reg. 3821 (Jan. 21, 2011). Previously his OMB had requested comments on how to improve the OIRA review process. *See* 74 Fed. Reg. 88,19 (Feb. 26, 2009). The public comments are *available at* http://www.reginfo.gov/public/jsp/EO/fedRegReview/publicComments.jsp.

139. Exec. Order 12,866, § 10.

140. The number of rules reviewed dropped considerably under E.O. 12,866 as compared to E.O. 12,291. For a handy "counter" of OIRA's review activity for any given period, *see* http://www.reginfo.gov/public/do/eoCountsSearchInit?action=init. Based on the counter and treating inauguration day as the boundary for presidential administrations, the Reagan/Bush I

it possible to include, for the first time, a firm deadline (of 90 days, with one 30-day extension allowed) for completion of OIRA review. In the event of an unresolved dispute between OIRA and the agency, the issue is bucked to the President, through the Vice-President.

The review process set forth in the Order is intended to be quite transparent. It provides that after the agency has concluded its rulemaking, it should make available to the public all submissions to OIRA and identify all changes made in the rule, noting those made at the behest of OIRA.[141] In addition, OIRA, for its part, must regularize the way it receives any outside communications concerning an agency rule that is subject to review. Only the administrator or his or her designee may receive such communications. OIRA must forward any such communications to the agency within 10 days, invite agency officials to any meetings held with outsiders, and maintain a public log of all such contacts. At the end of the proceeding, OIRA must also make available all documents exchanged with the agency.[142]

In place of the Reagan E.O. 12,498 on regulatory planning, E.O. 12,866 establishes its own yearly planning mechanism. It continues the semiannual publication of the *Unified Agenda of Federal Regulatory and Deregulatory Actions*, which lists all proposed, pending, and completed regulatory and deregulatory actions.[143] And it requires that the October *Agenda* contain each agency's annual regulatory plans, which have been approved by the OMB Director and the other regulatory advisors designated under the Order. These plans must be forwarded to OIRA by June 1 of each

---

Administration reviewed about 1,016 proposed rules and 1,316 final rules per year under E.O. 12,291. Under the Clinton Administration (which operated under the earlier order during much of its first year), the yearly averages dropped to 311 proposed and 363 final rules. Under Bush II the numbers dropped even more to about 246 proposed and 316 final rules. In the first three years of the Obama Administration (thorough January 20, 2012, the numbers stayed about the same, 261 and 314 respectively. (Figures for final rules for the last three Administrations also included interim-final rules.) The overall time for all reviews (including some notices and pre-rule matters) were 24 days (Reagan/Bush), 44 (Clinton), 55 (Bush II), and 50 (Obama). The number of "economically significant rule" reviews (lumping proposed and final rule reviews) were 82, 92, 94, and 124 respectively.

141. *See* U.S. Gov't Accountability Office, Improvements Needed to Monitoring and Evaluation of Rules Development as Well as to the Transparency of OMB Regulatory Reviews (Highlights page) GAO-09-205 (Apr. 20, 2009) ("Agencies used various methods to document OIRA's reviews, which generally met disclosure requirements, but the transparency of this documentation could be improved. In particular, some prior issues persist, such as uneven attribution of changes made during the OIRA review period and differing interpretations regarding which changes are 'substantive' and thus require documentation.").

142. It should be noted, however, that the Order does not require oral communications between OIRA and the agency to be disclosed, nor does it address the participation of non-OMB White House entities in rulewriting; thus, the possibility of another "Quayle Council" is not foreclosed.

143. Since Fall 2007, only the Agenda information required by the Regulatory Flexibility Act (5 U.S.C. §§ 602, 610) is published in the *Federal Register*. The complete *Unified Agenda* is published online at www.reginfo.gov.

year. The plans are also to include agency determinations on which existing rules are
to be reviewed and reconsidered during the ensuing year. These actions do not represent any sharp break from the practices of previous administrations; however, the
Clinton Order was a departure in one regard—for the first time the *independent regulatory agencies* were specifically directed to comply with the planning and agenda
provisions (though *not* with the rule-review process).[144]

Executive Order 12,866 was generally well received by most observers of the regulatory scene, and in the nearly two decades since its issuance, OIRA has worked out a
stable and workable relationship with the agencies in administering it.[145] The once rather
contentious legal and policy debate over the pros and cons of presidential review itself[146] has gradually evolved into a fairly broad agreement that it is not only legal, but
that if properly administered, it is essential to effective executive branch management.[147]

---

144. The Administrative Conference concluded that presidential review "can improve the coordination of agency actions and resolve conflicts among agency rules and assist in the implementation of national priorities" and that it should apply generally to federal rulemaking.
ACUS Recommendation 88-9, *supra* note 136, ¶ 1. Thus, the Conference concluded that "[a]s
a matter of principle, presidential review of rulemaking should apply to independent regulatory agencies to the same extent it applies to rulemaking of executive branch departments and
other agencies." *Id.*, ¶ 2. The National Academy of Public Administration also recommended
that, "[a]s a matter of policy, Congress should consider extending presidential review to
independent regulatory agencies on an agency-by-agency basis." NATIONAL ACADEMY OF PUBLIC
ADMINISTRATION, PRESIDENTIAL MANAGEMENT OF RULEMAKING IN REGULATORY AGENCIES 23 (1987). *See
also* Harold H. Bruff, *Presidential Management of Agency Rulemaking*, 57 GEO. WASH. L. REV.
533, 590–93 (1989); Thomas O. McGarity, *Presidential Control of Regulatory Agency
Decisionmaking*, 36 AM. U. L. REV. 443, 454–62 (1987); Peter L. Strauss & Cass R. Sunstein,
The Role of the President and OMB in Informal Rulemaking, 38 ADMIN. L. REV. 181, 202–05
(1986).
145. Considering its influence, OIRA is still a remarkably small agency, with only 50 full-time
equivalent employees. *See* http://www.reginfo.gov/public/jsp/Utilities/faq.jsp (last visited,
March 17, 2012).
146. *See* Christopher C. DeMuth & Douglas H. Ginsburg, *White House Review of Agency
Rulemaking*, 99 HARV. L. REV. 1075 (1986) (debating the legality of OMB review). *See also*
Alan B. Morrison, *OMB Interference with Agency Rulemaking: The Wrong Way to Write a
Regulation*, 99 HARV. L. REV. 1059 (1986); Strauss & Sunstein, *supra* note 144, at 189; Bruff,
supra note 144; Erik D. Olson, *The Quiet Shift of Power: Office of Management & Budget
Supervision of Environmental Protection Agency Rulemaking Under Executive Order 12,291*,
4 VA. J. NAT. RESOURCES 1, 75–77 (1984); Morton Rosenberg, *Beyond the Limits of Executive
Power: Presidential Control of Agency Rulemaking Under Executive Order 12,291*, 80 MICH.
L. REV. 193 (1981).
147. For example, the legislative hearings on S. 981, "The Regulatory Improvement Act of 1997,"
105th Cong., 1st Sess., which would have, among other things, codified the provisions of E.O.
12,866, were notable because that portion of the bill drew little criticism. On the other hand, the
director of the Public Citizen Litigation Group contended that no empirical evidence exists
supporting the premise that the cost of OIRA review is offset by the benefits, Memorandum to
author from David Vladeck (Oct. 7, 1997). Academic writings now are generally accepting of
OMB review. See, for example, the now especially notable comprehensive analysis in Elena

Some critics, however, maintain that even if presidential oversight may be justified on a theoretical basis, the current program has been implemented almost exclusively to achieve deregulatory goals, in contravention of enabling statutes.[148]

This is not to say, however, that the debate over the need for further regulatory reform was quenched by the issuance of E.O. 12,866. On the contrary, the President's National Performance Review (also known as "Reinventing Government"), initiated in 1993, recommended additional actions to streamline rulemaking,[149] only to be over-

---

Kagan, *Presidential Administration*, 114 HARV. L. REV. 2245, 2384 (2001) (concluding that the development of enhanced presidential control of regulatory administration "within broad but certain limits, both satisfies legal requirements and promotes the values of administrative accountability and effectiveness"). *See also* Curtis Copeland, *The Role of the Office of Information and Regulatory Affairs in Federal Rulemaking*, 33 FORDHAM URB. L.J. 1257 (2006); James F. Blumstein, *Regulatory Review by the Executive Office of the President: An Overview and Policy Analysis of Current Issues*, 51 DUKE L.J. 851, 899 (2001) (finding OIRA review to be "an important and constructive feature of the executive branch"); and the empirical review in Steven Croley, *White House Review of Agency Rulemaking: An Empirical Investigation* 70 U. CHI. L. REV. 821 (2003). *But see* Robin Kundis Craig, *The Bush Administration's Use and Abuse of Rulemaking. Part I: The Rise of OIRA*, 28 ADMIN. & REG. L. NEWS 8 (Summer 2003) (finding OIRA to be an "unreviewable reviewer") and Scott Farrow, *Improving Regulatory Performance: Does Executive Office Oversight Matter?* (July 26, 2000), *available at* http://regulation2point0.org/wp-content/plugins/download-monitor/download.php?id=77 (indicating that although Executive Office review has led to rejection of some regulations that would have been economically inefficient, such review appears to have no efficiency-improving impact on the difference between proposed and final regulations or on the cost effectiveness of regulations that are implemented). For other trenchant critiques *see* Nicholas Bagley & Richard L. Revesz, *Centralized Oversight of the Regulatory State*, 106 COLUM. L. REV. 1260, 1305–10 (2006); RICHARD L. REVESZ & MICHAEL A. LIVERMORE, RETAKING RATIONALITY: HOW COST-BENEFIT ANALYSIS CAN BETTER PROTECT THE ENVIRONMENT AND OUR HEALTH (Oxford, 2008), and the book review, Daniel A. Farber, *Rethinking the Role of Cost-Benefit Analysis*, 76 U. CHI. L. REV. 1355, 1356–57 (2009) ("Revesz and Livermore make a compelling case that CBA has been warped by an antiregulatory ideological agenda and has hampered implementation of valuable environmental policies. Indeed, . . . their critique does not go far enough. CBA has also been used as a means of evading clear statutory mandates.").

148. *See* McGarity, *supra* note 144, at 454–62. There is some empirical evidence that OIRA review is a "one-way ratchet" supporting weaker regulation; *see* Lisa Schultz Bressman & Michael P. Vandenbergh, *Inside the Administrative State: A Critical Look at the Practice of Presidential Control*, 105 MICH. L. REV. 47, 95 (2006); *but see* the response by a former OIRA Administrator, Sally Katzen, *A Reality Check on an Empirical Study: Comments on "Inside the Administrative State,"* 105 MICH. L. REV. 1497 (2007), and the rejoinder, Lisa Schultz Bressman & Michael P. Vandenbergh, *Legitimacy, Selectivity, and the Disunitary Executive: A Reply to Sally Katzen*, 105 MICH. L. REV. 1511 (2007). *See also* Steve Balla, et al., *Outside Communications and OIRA Review*, 63 ADMIN. L. REV. (SPECIAL ED.) 148, 166 (2011) (concluding "surprisingly that . . . delays and changes in agency regulations were not specifically liked with the participation of business firms and other regulated entities"). For more debate on the wisdom of the current system, see the public comments referenced in note 147.

149. *See* OFFICE OF THE VICE PRESIDENT, CREATING A GOVERNMENT THAT WORKS BETTER AND COSTS LESS, NATIONAL PERFORMANCE REVIEW, IMPROVING REGULATORY SYSTEMS (1993), *available at* http://govinfo.library.unt.edu/npr/library/reports/reg.html.

whelmed by the seismic election of 1994, which produced a Republican-controlled 104th Congress and a resulting frenzy of proposed changes to the APA as a whole and to the rulemaking provisions in particular.[150] The most far-reaching "regulatory reform" bills did not pass—in part because of strong opposition from the Clinton Administration, although elements were enacted with bipartisan support in the Unfunded Mandates Reform Act of 1995[151] and the Small Business Regulatory Enforcement Fairness Act of 1996 (SBREFA).[152] Moreover, President Clinton and his National Performance Review announced aggressive new initiatives to cut obsolete regulations; use more consensus-based techniques, such as negotiated rulemaking; and enhance public participation through more grassroots meetings and partnerships.[153]

President Clinton also issued a presidential directive on plain language[154] and a number of other executive orders that remain in effect, concerning: environmental justice in minority populations and low-income populations (E.O. 12,898),[155] civil justice reform (E.O. 12,988),[156] protection of children from environmental risks (E.O. 13,045),[157] federalism (E.O. 13,132),[158] and consultation with Indian Tribal Governments (E.O. 13,175).[159] These are discussed in Part III, Chapter 2(G).

3. Developments in the Bush II Administration

When President George W. Bush took office on January 20, 2001, one of his first actions was to have his Chief of Staff issue a memorandum directing agencies to delay for 60 days all rules issued that had not yet gone into effect and to refrain from sending any additional rules (other than emergency rules) to the *Federal Register* until they were reviewed by an agency head appointed by President Bush.[160]

---

150. *See, e.g.*, Ronald M. Levin, *Administrative Procedure Legislation in 1946 and 1996: Should We Be Jubilant at This Jubilee?*, 10 ADMIN. L.J. AM. U. 55, (1996); Jerry L. Mashaw, *Reinventing Government and Regulatory Reform: Studies in the Neglect and Abuse of Administrative Law*, 57 U. PITT. L. REV. 405 (1996).
151. *See* discussion *infra* Part II, ch. 3(G).
152. *See* discussion *infra* Part II, ch. 3(C) & (J).
153. *See* OFFICE OF MGMT. & BUDGET, OFFICE OF INFORMATION AND REGULATORY AFFAIRS, MORE BENEFITS, FEWER BURDENS—CREATING A REGULATORY SYSTEM THAT WORKS FOR THE AMERICAN PEOPLE, A REPORT TO THE PRESIDENT ON THE THIRD ANNIVERSARY OF EXECUTIVE ORDER 12,866 (1996).
154. White House Memorandum For the Heads of Executive Departments and Agencies, Plain Language in Government Writing (June 1, 1998), *available at* http://govinfo.library.unt.edu/npr/library/direct/memos/memoeng.html.
155. Issued February 11, 1994, published 59 Fed. Reg. 7629 (Feb. 16, 1994).
156. Issued February 5, 1996, published 61 Fed. Reg. 4729 (Feb. 7, 1996).
157. Issued April 21, 1997, published 62 Fed. Reg. 19,885 (Apr. 23, 1997).
158. Issued August 4, 1999, published 64 Fed. Reg. 43,255 (Aug. 10, 1999).
159. Issued November 6, 2000, published 64 Fed. Reg. 67,249 (Nov. 9, 2000).
160. Memorandum for the Heads and Acting Heads of Executive Departments and Agencies from Andrew Card, Jr., Assistant to the President and Chief of Staff (Jan. 20, 2001), 66 Fed. Reg. 7702 (Jan. 24, 2001). For more discussion of the ramifications of the "Card Memorandum," see Part II, ch. 1(D)(4)(f).

The Bush II Administration ultimately determined to maintain E.O. 12,866 as the basis for its review, although the role of the Vice President, prominent in the Clinton Administration, was formally eliminated by an amendment to the Executive Order.[161] In his second term President Bush issued a more significant set of amendments to E.O. 12,866 that (1) required agencies to provide more specific justification for regulation, (2) required agencies to submit "significant guidance documents" to OIRA for review, (3) gave additional authority to the agency's Regulatory Policy Officer, who also was required to be a presidential appointee, (4) required that the agency's Regulatory Plan contain the agency's best estimate of the combined aggregate costs and benefits of all its regulations planned for that calendar year, and (5) urged agencies to "consider whether to utilize formal rulemaking procedures for the resolution of complex determinations."[162] As noted above, at the beginning of his Administration, President Obama revoked these two Orders amending Executive Order 12,866.[163]

OIRA did issue a memorandum in September 2001, putting its own stamp on the E.O. 12,866 process.[164] The memorandum describes the "general principles and procedures that will be applied by OMB in the implementation of E.O. 12866 and related statutory and executive authority."

Significantly, during the Bush Administration, OIRA also announced several new initiatives in its review process. First, it made extensive use of its website to publish its guidelines and other information pertaining to its review process and specific rule reviews. This continues today.[165] Second, it began the practice of issuing public "return letters" that send rules back to the agency for reconsideration, "review letters" that comment on aspects of a particular rule review, and "prompt letters," which are sent on OMB's initiative and contain suggestions for new or stronger regulations. While these letters are still posted on the reginfo.gov website, the Obama Administration has made little use of this practice.[166]

More importantly, during the Bush Administration, OMB also issued four far-reaching documents affecting the regulatory process that remain in effect today. In

---

161. *See* Executive Order 13,258, *supra* note 137.

162. Exec. Order 13,422, "Further Amendment to Executive Order 12866 on Regulatory Planning and Review," (Jan. 18, 2007), 72 Fed. Reg. 2763 (Jan. 23, 2007). *See* Curtis W. Copeland, Cong. Research Serv., RL 33862, Changes to the OMB Regulatory Review Process by Executive Order 13,422 (Feb. 5, 2007), *available at* http://www.fas.org/sgp/crs/misc/RL33862.pdf. For a commentary on these changes, *see Symposium, Reflections on Executive Order 13,422,* 25 YALE J. ON REG. 77 (2008).

163. *See supra* note 4.

164. Memorandum for the President's Management Council from John D. Graham, OIRA Administrator, on Presidential Review of Agency Rulemaking by OIRA (Sept, 20, 2001), *available at* http://www.whitehouse.gov/omb/inforeg_oira_review_process/.

165. *Regulatory Matters*, Office of Mgmt. & Budget, http://www.whitehouse.gov/omb/inforeg_regmatters/.

166. *See* http://www.reginfo.gov/public/jsp/EO/letters.jsp (indicating no prompt or return letters and one review letter in the Obama Administration).

2003 it issued a revised OMB Circular A-4,[167] which provides guidance on the development of regulatory analyses and on the regulatory accounting statements for each major final rule required under the Regulatory Right-to-Know Act. In 2004, it issued the Final Information Quality Bulletin for Peer Review,[168] in 2007 the Final Bulletin for Agency Good Guidance Practices,[169] and in the same year it and the Office of Science and Technology Policy issued a Policy Memorandum on "Updated Principles for Risk Analysis."[170] These are discussed more fully in Part III, Chapter 2. Finally, President Bush issued two executive orders concerning regulations that remain in effect today: (1) analysis of adverse effects on energy supply, distribution, or use (E.O. 13,211)[171] and (2) proper consideration of small entities in agency rulemaking (E.O. 13,272).[172] These are discussed in Part III, Chapter 2(H).

4. Developments in the Obama Administration

On Inauguration Day, President Obama's Chief of Staff issued a memorandum, similar to that issued on the first day of the Bush II Administration, directing agencies to withdraw all proposed or final regulations that have not been published in the *Federal Register*, consider delaying for 60 days (with a public comment period) all published rules that had not yet gone into effect, and to refrain from sending any additional rules (other than emergency rules, or rules subject to legislative or judicial deadlines) to the *Federal Register* until they were reviewed by an agency head appointed by President Obama.[173]

Shortly thereafter, the President revoked the Bush Amendments to Executive Order 12,866[174] and directed the Director of OMB, in consultation with regulatory agencies, to produce a set of recommendations for a new executive order on federal regulatory review within 100 days,[175] followed by an unusual request for public

---

167. *See* http://www.whitehouse.gov/omb/circulars_a004_a-4/.
168. *See* http://www.whitehouse.gov/sites/default/files/omb/memoranda/fy2005/m05-03.pdf.
169. *See* http://www.whitehouse.gov/sites/default/files/omb/memoranda/fy2007/m07-07.pdf.
170. *See* http://www.whitehouse.gov/sites/default/files/omb/memoranda/fy2007/m07-24.pdf.
171. Issued May 18, 2001, published 66 Fed. Reg. 28,355 (May 22, 2001).
172. Issued August 13, 2002, published 67 Fed. Reg. 53,461 (Aug. 16, 2002).
173. Memorandum for the Heads of Executive Departments and Agencies from Rahm Emanuel, Assistant to the President and Chief of Staff (Jan. 20, 2009), 74 Fed. Reg. 4435 (Jan. 26, 2009). *See also* the supplemental memo from OMB Director Peter Orszag, http://www.whitehouse.gov/sites/default/files/omb/assets/agencyinformation_memoranda_2009_pdf/m09-08.pdf. For more discussion of the ramifications of the Emanuel Memorandum, see Part II, ch. 1(D)(4)(f).
174. *See supra* note 137. However, a subsequent March 4, 2009, memo from OMB Director Peter Orszag clarified that notwithstanding the rescission of the Bush Amendments, OMB still expected to review significant guidance documents, *see* http://www.whitehouse.gov/sites/default/files/omb/assets/memoranda_fy2009/m09-13.pdf.
175. Memorandum of January 30, 2009, Regulatory Review, 74 Fed. Reg. 5977 (Feb. 3, 2009).

comments on the same subject.[176] Almost 200 public comments were received.[177]

After about a year of internal consideration, the White House finally settled on its approach to OMB review—basically to reaffirm Executive Order 12,866. It did so on January 18, 2011, with Executive Order 13,563, "Improving Regulation and Regulatory Review."[178] In Section 1(b), the Order stated: "This order is supplemental to and reaffirms the principles, structures, and definitions governing contemporary regulatory review that were established in Executive Order 12866 . . . ."

It did contain a few new mandates and points of emphasis. Most notably, agencies were urged (as appropriate and within legal constraints) to (1) consider "values that are difficult or impossible to quantify, including equity, human dignity, fairness, and distributive impacts"; (2) "afford the public a meaningful opportunity to comment through the Internet on any proposed regulation, with a comment period that should generally be at least 60 days"; (3) "provide, for both proposed and final rules, timely online access to the rulemaking docket on regulations.gov, including relevant scientific and technical findings, in an open format that can be easily searched and downloaded"; (4) for proposed rules, provide "an opportunity for public comment on all pertinent parts of the rulemaking docket, including relevant scientific and technical findings"; (5) seek public input from affected persons "[b]efore issuing a notice of proposed rulemaking"; (6) "identify and consider regulatory approaches that reduce burdens and maintain flexibility and freedom of choice"; (7) "promote retrospective analysis of rules that may be outmoded, ineffective, insufficient, or excessively burdensome, and to modify, streamline, expand, or repeal them in accordance with what has been learned"; and (8) "[w]ithin 120 days of the date of this order, . . . develop and submit to [OIRA] a preliminary plan" for periodically reviewing "its existing significant regulations to determine whether any such regulations should be modified, streamlined, expanded, or repealed so as to make the agency's regulatory program more effective or less burdensome in achieving the regulatory objectives."[179]

The one action mandate in the new Executive Order was for agencies to develop plans for retrospective review of their existing regulations. On May 26, 2011, the OIRA Administrator announced the results of this effort.[180] On July 11, President

---

176. Federal Regulatory Review, 74 Fed. Reg. 8819 (Feb. 26, 2009). The original 19-day comment period was extended by two weeks in a subsequent notice, Federal Regulatory Review, 74 Fed. Reg. 11,383 (Mar. 17, 2009).

177. *See* http://www.reginfo.gov/public/jsp/EO/fedRegReview/publicComments.jsp.

178. 76 Fed. Reg. 3821 (Jan. 21, 2011).

179. Exec. Order 13,563 is reprinted in Appendix C. The OIRA Administrator followed up with a memo elaborating on these requirements. Memorandum for the Heads of Executive Departments and Agencies, and of Independent Regulatory Agencies, from Cass R. Sunstein, M-11-10, (Feb. 2, 2011), *available at* http://www.whitehouse.gov/sites/default/files/omb/memoranda/2011/m11-10.pdf. For a report on the Obama Administration's approach to regulatory review, *see* Helen G. Boutrous, *Regulatory Review in the Obama Administration: Cost–Benefit Analysis for Everyone*, 62 ADMIN. L. REV. 243 (2010).

180. *See* Cass Sunstein, speech to American Enterprise Institute, http://www.whitehouse.gov/sites/default/files/omb/inforeg/speeches/oira-administrator-lookback-at-federal-regulation-05262011.pdf.

Obama issued a follow-up Executive Order extending the terms of E.O. 13,563 to independent regulatory agencies.[181] As the Guide went to press, he issued E.O. 13,609, "Promoting International Regulatory Cooperation."[182]

Other significant OIRA initiatives that relate to rulemaking, including memoranda on electronic rulemaking, scientific integrity, federalism, the Paperwork Reduction Act, and the Privacy Act, will be discussed at the relevant part of this Guide.

5. *Judicial Reaction to Presidential Review*

The D.C. Circuit's opinion in *Sierra Club v. Costle*,[183] a case concerning presidential involvement in EPA rulemaking during the Carter Administration, is often quoted as being supportive of the policy underlying presidential review. The opinion, authored by Judge Patricia Wald, states:

> The court recognizes the basic need of the President and his White House staff to monitor the consistency of executive agency regulations with Administration policy. He and his White House advisers surely must be briefed fully and frequently about rules in the making, and their contributions to policymaking considered. The executive power under our Constitution, after all, is not shared—it rests exclusively with the President. The idea of a "plural executive," or a President with a council of state, was considered and rejected by the Constitutional Convention. Instead the Founders chose to risk the potential for tyranny inherent in placing power in one person, in order to gain the advantages of accountability fixed on a single source. To ensure the President's control and supervision over the Executive Branch, the Constitution—and its judicial gloss—vests him with the powers of appointment and removal, the power to demand written opinions from executive officers, and the right to invoke executive privilege to protect consultative privacy. In the particular case of EPA, Presidential authority is clear since it has never been considered an "independent agency," but always part of the Executive Branch.
>
> The authority of the President to control and supervise executive policymaking is derived from the Constitution; the desirability of such control is demonstrable from the practical realities of administrative rulemaking. Regulations such as those involved here demand a careful weighing of cost, environmental, and energy considerations. They also have broad implications for national economic policy. Our form of government simply could not function effectively or rationally if key executive policymakers were isolated from each other and from the

---

181. Exec. Order No. 13,579, "Regulation and Independent Regulatory Agencies" (July 11, 2011), 76 Fed. Reg. 41,587 (July 14, 2011). Later the OMB issued guidance on that Order, Memorandum from Cass Sunstein to Heads of Independent Regulatory Agencies (July 22, 2011), *available at* http://www.whitehouse.gov/sites/default/files/omb/memoranda/2011/m11-28.pdf.
182. Issued May 1, 2012, 77 Fed. Reg. 26,413 (May 4, 2012). See Part II, ch. 7(a)(3).
183. 657 F.2d 298 (D.C. Cir. 1981). *See infra* Part III, ch. 6 for discussion of *Sierra Club.*

Chief Executive. Single-mission agencies do not always have the answers to complex regulatory problems. An overworked administrator exposed on a 24-hour basis to a dedicated but zealous staff needs to know the arguments and ideas of policymakers in other agencies as well as in the White House.[184]

Sierra Club involved the propriety of nonpublic executive communications in an EPA rulemaking and did not directly address the constitutionality of presidential review. No court has squarely addressed the constitutionality of the presidential review program.[185]

E. Overviews of Rulemaking—Other Views

1. *The Administrative Conference's Comprehensive Review of the "State" of Rulemaking*

In 1993, the Administrative Conference of the U.S. (ACUS) undertook a comprehensive review of the state of rulemaking in the 1990s. The premise for the review was stated in the opening sentences of the eventual recommendation:

> Informed observers generally agree that the rulemaking process has become both increasingly less effective and more time-consuming. The Administrative Procedure Act does not reflect many of the current realities of rulemaking . . . . [T]he APA's simple "informal rulemaking procedures" (set forth in 5 USC § 553) have been overlain with an increasing number of constraints: outside constraints imposed by Congress, the President, and the courts, and internal constraints arising from increasingly complex agency management of the rulemaking process.[186]

---

184. 657 F.2d at 405–06 (footnotes omitted).
185. The constitutional issue was raised in *Public Citizen Health Research Group v. Tyson*, 796 F.2d 1479 (D.C. Cir. 1986), where the petitioning public interest group asserted the invalidity of a portion of OSHA's ethylene oxide standard, in part on the ground that an important provision in the draft standard had been deleted by OSHA at OMB's direction, thus violating separation-of-powers principles. The challenge by petitioner Public Citizen was supported in an *amicus* brief filed by the chairs of several committees of the House of Representatives. The D.C. Circuit, however, reversed OSHA's decision on other grounds without deciding the separation-of-powers issue. *Id.* at 1507. *See also* Nat'l Grain & Feed Ass'n v. OSHA, 866 F.2d 717 (5th Cir. 1989) (rejecting argument that judicial review was obstructed by "alleged off-the-record coercion of OSHA," stating that "agency's final rule must stand or fall on the basis of the record before the agency, not on the basis of some 'secret record' of OMB's"; but remanding rule on other grounds); Envtl. Def. Fund v. Thomas, 627 F. Supp. 566, 570 (D.D.C. 1986) (concluding that OMB, "by insisting on certain substantive changes," significantly delayed publication of proposed rules, thus causing EPA to miss a statutory deadline for promulgating regulations, and declaring that OMB did not have authority under Executive Order 12,291 to delay promulgation of EPA regulations beyond date of statutory deadline or to set new deadline for final rule).
186. ACUS Recommendation 93-4, *Improving the Environment for Agency Rulemaking*, 59 Fed. Reg. 4670 (Feb. 1, 1994) (footnote omitted), *available at* http://www.law.fsu.edu/library/admin/acus/305934.html.

Given that premise, the recommendation sets out a "coordinated framework of proposals aimed at promoting efficient and effective rulemaking." The recommendation addresses the impacts of presidential oversight and congressional structuring of rulemaking and the timing and scope of judicial review. It also suggests some amendments to the APA and agency management initiatives.

This recommendation represents the best thinking of the administrative law experts in the ACUS membership in 1993 on what should be done to remedy the perceived problems with rulemaking. Many of these recommendations seemingly run counter to the continued accretion of procedures and analytical requirements on the rulemaking process. Thus, from the perspective of Recommendation 93-4, the situation has gotten worse instead of better.[187] With its welcome return in 2010, it has resumed its study of the developments in the rulemaking process.[188] I hope that the continued publication of the *Guide* by the American Bar Association can complement this work.

2. The "Blackletter Statement" of the ABA Section of Administrative Law and Regulatory Practice

In November 2001, the ABA Section of Administrative Law and Regulatory Practice, one of the co-sponsors of this *Guide*, completed a multi-year effort to produce *A Blackletter Statement of Federal Administrative Law*.[189] In January 2012 the Section approved an updated version of the rulemaking section,[190] which is reprinted after this Part. This *Guide* is intended to serve as the background report for that portion of the *Blackletter*.

3. Other Overviews of Rulemaking

I would be remiss not to mention some other excellent sources of information about the federal rulemaking process. Jim O'Reilly's regulatory manual[191] and Neil Kerwin and Scott Furlong's authoritative volume written from a public administration point of view[192] are worthy complements to this *Guide*. Shorter helpful treatments can

---

187. *See* Jody Freeman, *Collaborative Governance in the Administrative State*, 45 UCLA L. Rev. 1, 9 (1997) ("Indeed, one could argue that the increasing analytic requirements imposed on agencies and the reinvigoration of aggressive judicial review in recent appellate cases makes the ossification . . . even worse." (footnote omitted)).

188. *See* www.acus.gov for elaboration on ACUS's ongoing research program.

189. *Published at* 54 Admin. L. Rev. 1–83 (2002).

190. 54 Admin. L. Rev. at 30–36, as revised by action of the Council of the Section at its mid-winter meeting in January, 2012, attached to e-mail to author from Section Chair Michael Herz (Feb. 13, 2012).

191. James T. O'Reilly, Administrative Rulemaking: Structuring, Opposing, and Defending Federal Agency Regulations (2d ed.) (Thomson/West 2011).

192. Cornelius M. Kerwin & Scott R. Furlong, Rulemaking: How Government Agencies Write Law and Make Policy (4th ed. CQ Press 2011).

be found in Mark Seidenfeld's detailed "table of requirements" for federal rulemaking,[193] ICF International's "Reg-Map,[194] Curtis Copeland's updated overview for the Congressional Research Service,[195] Anne Joseph O'Connell's empirical review of rulemaking activity from the Reagan Administration through the Bush II Administration,[196] Neil Eisner's ongoing compendium of rulemaking requirements applicable to the U.S. Department of Transportation,[197] and a special issue devoted to "Rulemaking 101" in the Coast Guard's *Proceedings* Journal.[198] Detailed agency guidance on the Federal Trade Commission's demanding hybrid rulemaking process is provided by the Federal Trade Commission's staff manual.[199] The IRS provides its Chief Counsel's handbook on regulation projects.[200] And, using EPA rulemaking as its arena, Washington lawyer Richard Stoll's recent readable book provides some insightful practical advice to all lawyers representing clients in the regulatory process.[201] Finally, the ABA Administrative Law Section's 12 volumes of *Developments in Administrative Law and Regulatory Practice* beginning in 1998-1999 have been very helpful in updating this *Guide*,[202] and the Section's guide to judicial and political review of federal agencies[203] was especially helpful in preparing Part IV.

---

193. Mark Seidenfeld, *A Table of Requirements for Federal Administrative Rulemaking*, 27 Fla. St. L. Rev. 533 (2000).

194. *See* http://www.icfi.com/insights/products-and-tools/reg-map.

195. Curtis W. Copeland, Cong. Research Serv., RL 32240, The Federal Rulemaking Process: An Overview (Feb. 22, 2011), *available at* http://opencrs.com/document/RL32240/2011-02-22/download/1005/.

196. Anne Joseph O'Connell, *Political Cycles of Rulemaking: An Empirical Portrait of the Modern Administrative State*, 94 Va. L. Rev. 889 (2008).

197. Neil Eisner, *U.S. Department of Transportation: Rulemaking Requirements* (April 2011), *available at* http://regs.dot.gov/rulemakingrequirements.htm. *See also* DOT's excellent description of the rulemaking process at http://regs.dot.gov/informalruleprocess.htm.

198. Volume 66, no.4 (Spring 2010), *available at* http://www.uscg.mil/proceedings/spring2010.

199. *See* FTC, Administrative Staff Manual: Operating Manual, Rulemaking ch. 7, *available at* http://www.ftc.gov/foia/ch07rulemaking.pdf.

200. IRS Chief Counsel Regulation Handbook, § 32.1.2, "Procedural Requirements for Regulation Projects," (April 2009), *available at* http://www.irs.gov/irm/part32/irm_32-001-002.html.

201. Richard D. Stoll, Effective EPA Advocacy—Advancing and Protecting Your Client's Interests in the Decision-Making Practice (Oxford Univ. Press 2010).

202. The chapters on rulemaking have been written by Mark Seidenfeld (1998-99), Daniel Cohen & Harold Walther (1999-2000), Marshall Breger (2000-01), Michael Herz (2001-02 & 2002-03), and Richard Stoll & Katherine Lazarski (2003-04 & 2004-05); Katherine Lazarski and Paul Noe (2005-06 & 2006-07); and William S. Jordan III (2007-08 to 2011). All volumes were edited by the author of this *Guide*.

203. *See* A Guide to Judicial and Political Review of Federal Agencies, *supra* note 94.

Excerpts from "A Blackletter Statement of Federal Administrative Law"*

****

PART TWO
INFORMAL RULEMAKING

The following summarizes the procedural requirements that must precede the legally effective promulgation, amendment, or repeal of a rule by a federal agency, as imposed by the Administrative Procedure Act (APA), other procedural statutes, and judicial decisions. Certain additional requirements imposed by Executive Order (primarily E.O. 12,866) are also included. Such requirements are not judicially enforceable, may be and often are waived by the relevant executive office, and are particularly subject to change. Economic impact analysis has been required for the last several presidencies in one form or another, and there is no indication that this requirement will be rescinded any time soon.

I. APPLICABILITY

A. Definition of a Rule

A "rule" is an agency statement designed to implement, interpret, or prescribe law or policy or describing the organization, procedure, or practice requirements of an agency. Although the definition of "rule" in the APA refers to "an agency statement of general or particular applicability," "rule" is usually understood to refer to a pronouncement that is intended to address a class of situations, rather than a named individual. Certain particularized actions, such as rate-setting or the approval of a corporate reorganization, are explicitly included within the statutory definition. A rule may be prospective, retroactive, or both, but an agency normally may not issue a retroactive rule that is intended to have the force of law unless it has express authorization from Congress.

B. Distinction Between Informal and Formal Rulemaking

The procedures described here apply to "informal" (also known as "notice-and-comment") rulemaking. "Formal rulemaking" requires additional trial-type procedures, not described here but essentially the same as those described for initial licensing in the discussion of adjudication. Unless a statute expressly provides for rulemaking "on the record after opportunity for a hearing," or Congress otherwise unequivocally requires formal rulemaking, the requirements for informal rulemaking apply. Agencies engaged in informal rulemaking may provide additional procedures beyond those established by the APA, other applicable statutes, and the agency's own rules, but courts may not require them to do so.

---

* Prepared by the Section of Administrative Law and Regulatory Practice of the American Bar Association, 54 Admin. L. Rev. 1, 30–36 (2002), revised in January 2012, *see supra* note 190.

C. Exemptions

The following types of rules are exempt from all the procedural requirements: rules relating to public property, loans, grants, benefits, and contracts; rules relating to agency management and personnel; and rules that involve a military or foreign affairs function of the United States. However, specific statutes may override these exemptions and agencies may voluntarily forswear them.

The following types of rules are subject to publication and petition requirements, but are exempt from the other procedural requirements set out below: rules regarding agency organization, procedure, and practice; staff manuals; interpretive rules; and general statements of policy. Courts are regularly called upon to police agency invocation of these exemptions. Especially with respect to interpretive rules and policy statements (often lumped together as "guidance") agencies must make sure they do not treat them as binding or seek to add new requirements without seeking public comment.

An agency may also dispense with notice and comment, and/or may make a rule effective immediately, when it finds it has good cause to do so and explains its finding and reasons at the time of publication. Under time pressure, agencies, after such a finding, sometimes adopt "interim final rules" that are both immediately effective and published with an invitation to comment and propose revisions; a subsequent agency revision will treat such a rule as if it were, also, a notice of proposed rulemaking.

Failure to publish a given rule, either in the Federal Register or as described by 5 U.S.C. § 552(a)(2), denies to the agency any possibility of relying on it to the disadvantage of a private party, unless that party has had actual notice of the agency's position.

II. INITIATING RULEMAKING

A. Means to Initiate Rulemaking

An agency may commence a rulemaking on its own initiative, pursuant to statutory mandate, or in response to an outside petition or to suggestions from other governmental actors. Any interested person has the right to petition for the issuance, amendment, or repeal of any rule. The denial of a petition is judicially reviewable and should be at least summarily explained.

B. Developing a Proposed Rule

In developing a proposed rule, an agency may be required to evaluate and prepare appropriate written analyses of (a) overall economic costs and benefits and (b) the extent of new paperwork and information collection requirements. The agency may also be required to analyze more particularized issues, including impacts on (c) the environment, (d) small businesses, (e) state, local, and tribal governments and on the private sector, (f) families, (g) private property rights, (h) the civil justice system, (i) children's health and safety, (j) energy supply, distribution and use, and (k) federalism. Some of the foregoing requirements are limited to economically significant rules, and some are limited to rulemaking by executive agencies. Requirements (a) through (e) are imposed by statute; requirements (f) through (k) were imposed exclusively by a series of executive orders. Requirement (a), although now also required by the Unfunded Mandates Reform Act, was first developed by executive orders—currently, E.O. 12,866. In practice the administration of E.O. 12,866 appears to dominate executive branch implementation of all these requirements. Under that executive order, prior to issuing a Notice of Proposed Rulemaking, an executive agency proposing an economically significant rule must provide the Office of Information and Regulatory Affairs (OIRA), in the Office of Management and Budget (OMB), with an assessment of the proposal's costs and benefits. This analysis may, and typically does, incorporate the analyses required by other statutes and executive orders.

Prior to issuing a Notice of Proposed Rulemaking, an agency may issue and take comments on an Advanced Notice of Proposed Rulemaking and/or establish a negotiated rulemaking committee to negotiate and develop a proposed rule. Under the Negotiated Rulemaking Act, agencies are encouraged to explore the development of consensus proposals for rulemaking with balanced, representative committees under the guidance of a convenor specially appointed for that purpose. Such proposals, if generated, serve as proposed rules under the normal procedure.

Under the Paperwork Reduction Act, all agencies must obtain OIRA clearance of proposed informational collection requirements, including those put in place by rulemaking.

C.   Semi-Annual Agenda

The Regulatory Flexibility Act requires all rulemaking agencies to semi-annually prepare and publish in the Federal Register a regulatory agenda listing all planned regulatory actions that are likely to have a significant economic impact on a substantial number of small entities. Under E.O. 12,866 all rulemaking agencies must prepare an agenda of all regulations under development or consideration. This agenda must include a Regulatory Plan identifying and justifying the most important "significant regulatory actions" the agency expects to issue in proposed or final form in the upcoming fiscal year and must be submitted to OIRA by June 1 each year. This plan is consolidated with the regulatory agenda for publication purposes.

III. NOTICE OF PROPOSED RULEMAKING AND OPPORTUNITY FOR COMMENT

A. Requirements for a Notice of Proposed Rulemaking

An agency must publish in the Federal Register notice of its intent to promulgate, amend, or repeal a rule. Publication in the Federal Register is not necessary if all persons who will be subject to the rule, if adopted, are named and have actual notice.

The Notice of Proposed Rulemaking must include (1) a statement of the time, place, and nature of any public proceedings for consideration of the proposed rule (2) a reference to the agency's statutory authority for the rule and (3) the proposed text of the rule, unless a description of the proposal or the subjects and issues involved will suffice to allow meaningful and informed public consideration and comment. Caselaw has required the agency also to make available in time for comment thereon significant data and studies it knows to be relevant to the proposed rule, including any draft analyses previously made available as under II above.

B. Public Comment on Proposed Rule

After publication of a Notice of Proposed Rulemaking, a reasonable time must be allowed for written comments from the public. Executive Orders have provided that such a comment period should normally be 60 days for significant rules. An agency may, but, unless specifically required to do so by a relevant statute, need not, provide interested persons the opportunity to present oral comments or cross-examine witnesses.

IV. THE RULEMAKING RECORD AND DECISIONMAKING PROCESS

A. Record Requirements

The agency must maintain, and allow and facilitate public examination of, a rulemaking file (often now called a "docket") consisting of (1) all notices pertaining to the rulemaking, (2) copies or an index of written factual material, studies, and reports relied on or seriously consulted by agency personnel in formulating the proposed or final rule, (3) all written comments received by the agency, and (4) any other material specifically required by statute, executive order, or agency rule to be made public in connection with the rulemaking.

The notice-and-comment process and docketing practices have been transformed by the advent of electronic communications. The government's central rulemaking portal, *www.regulations.com*, allows the public to comment on any pending rulemaking, and it also serves as the home for current and past rulemaking dockets. When comments are sent directly to the agency, the agency is supposed to post them to the central portal as soon as feasible.

The obligation to disclose written factual material, studies, and reports relied on or seriously consulted by agency personnel is limited to unprivileged materials. Thus, neither a summary nor a record of predecisional internal agency policy discussions, or like contacts with government officials outside the agency or private consultants, or confidential business information, will ordinarily need to be included in the rulemaking file. Particular agency statutes or rules, however, may forbid or limit such outside communications or require that they be logged and made available to the public. The Executive Orders requiring economic impact analysis provoked concern about this issue, and E.O. 12,866 also includes such requirements.

B. Decisional Process

Again, subject to the obligation to disclose factual material, studies, and reports relied on or seriously consulted, decisionmakers within an agency may freely consult with other agency personnel, government officials outside the agency, and affected persons. Particular statutes or agency regulations may impose logging requirements or other restrictions. A decisionmaker will be disqualified for prejudgment only where the person's mind is unalterably closed.

Under E.O. 12,866 (and the other impact analysis requirements imposed by statute and/or executive order), a final analysis must be prepared in advance of the final rule; that analysis is generally a part of the rulemaking record. An executive agency may not publish a significant final rule until OIRA has completed, waived, or exceeded the time limit for its review of the rule under E.O. 12,866.
A rulemaking must be completed within a reasonable time, or within the time frame, if any, set by the relevant statute. If it is not, the agency does not necessarily forfeit its ability to issue the rule, but interested persons may seek court action to compel completion of the rulemaking.

V. THE FINAL RULE

A. Publication of Final Rule and the Basis and Purpose of the Rule

The agency must publish the operative text of the final rule. The agency must also provide a preamble that adequately explains the justifications, purposes, and legal authority for the rule and indicates compliance with regulatory analysis requirements imposed by statute. The scope of this explanation depends on the importance and impact of the rule. The Administrative Procedure Act calls for only a "concise general statement of . . . basis and purpose." However, courts have required that, especially for rules likely to have significant economic or other impacts the statement (a) must demonstrate that the agency seriously considered significant alternatives to its final rule, important public comments, and relevant information and scientific data and (b) must explain the agency's rejection of any of the foregoing.

After a rule subject to OIRA review has been published, E.O. 12,866 provides that the agency and OIRA disclose specified information pertaining to the review. If the final rule is not a "logical outgrowth" of the proposed rule, a second round of notice and comment is required.

B. Effective Date

A substantive rule of general applicability is unenforceable unless published in the Federal Register, and cannot ordinarily become effective less than 30 days after its publication (unless it grants an exception or relieves a restriction).

No economically significant rule can take effect (a) until 60 calendar days after the agency has submitted a copy of the rule and a concise general statement about it to both Houses of Congress and the Comptroller General and has submitted additional supporting material to the Comptroller General and made such material available to both Houses of Congress, or (b) if a joint resolution disapproving the rule is enacted. Rules relating to agency management or personnel or agency organization, procedure, or practice are exempt from this 60-day requirement.

PART II

THE STATUTORY FRAMEWORK FOR RULEMAKING

This part of the *Guide* presents a general review of the procedural requirements imposed on agencies by the Administrative Procedure Act (APA) and by other generic procedural statutes. Chapter 1 describes the APA requirements for informal rulemaking under 5 U.S.C. § 553 and for those rare instances of formal rulemaking pursuant to the procedures in 5 U.S.C. §§ 556 and 557. Chapter 2 compares the use of agency adjudication with rulemaking for policymaking. Chapter 3 discusses other government-wide procedural statutes that may affect agency rulemaking.

Part III looks at the specific steps in the dominant form of agency rulemaking—informal, or notice-and-comment, rulemaking. Part IV examines judicial review of rulemaking.

Chapter 1

The Administrative Procedure Act's Rulemaking Provisions

This chapter begins by discussing what a rule is under the APA. It then will briefly discuss formal rulemaking, followed by a summary of the informal rulemaking provisions of the APA and a discussion of the exemptions from the APA rulemaking requirements. The last section will cover publication requirements of section 552 of the APA.

A. "Rules" and "Rulemaking" Under the APA

In ordinary usage, a rule is a "prescribed guide for conduct or action."[1] However, an agency rulemaking official trying to decide what procedure to follow in a rulemaking must know the legal definition of rule. For this, the first place to look is the APA, which defines *rule* as follows:

> [T]he whole or part of an agency statement of general or particular applicability and future effect designed to implement, interpret, or prescribe law or policy or describing the organization, procedure, or practice requirements of an agency and includes the approval or prescription for the future of rates, wages, corporate or financial structures or reorganizations thereof, prices, facilities, appliances, services or allowances therefore or of valuations, costs, or accounting, or practices bearing on any of the foregoing.[2]

Rulemaking is defined in the APA as the "agency process for formulating, amending, or repealing a rule."[3]

Standing alone, the APA's definition of rule may not be too helpful. For example, an agency order directing Company X to cease and desist from engaging in a certain unlawful practice would fall within the literal terms of this definition. Yet, it is reasonably clear under the APA that a proceeding leading to the issuance of a cease-and-desist order ordinarily is adjudication and not rulemaking.[4]

---

1. MERRIAM-WEBSTER'S COLLEGIATE DICTIONARY 1023 (10th ed. 2002).
2. 5 U.S.C. § 551(4). The portion of the definition after the word "rates" rarely comes into play.
3. *Id.* § 551(5).
4. *See* ATTORNEY GENERAL'S MANUAL ON THE ADMINISTRATIVE PROCEDURE ACT 15 (1947), *reprinted in* WILLIAM F. FUNK, JEFFREY S. LUBBERS & CHARLES POU, JR., FEDERAL ADMINISTRATIVE SOURCEBOOK 39, 52 (4th ed. 2008).

The definition of *adjudication* sheds little additional light, for it is defined as the agency process for formulating an *order*,[5] which in turn is defined as "a final disposition, whether affirmative, negative, injunctive, or declaratory in form, of an agency in a matter other than rule making but including licensing."[6] Thus, the APA's definitional structure is largely circular, because the definition of adjudication is residual.

To understand the thrust of the APA's distinction between rulemaking and adjudication, one must turn to the discussion in the *Attorney General's Manual on the APA*:

> [T]he entire Act is based upon a dichotomy between rule making and adjudication. Examination of the legislative history of the definitions and of the differences in the required procedures for rule making and for adjudication discloses highly practical concepts of rule making and adjudication. Rule making is agency action which regulates the future conduct of either groups of persons or a single person; it is essentially legislative in nature, not only because it operates in the future but also because it is primarily concerned with policy considerations. The object of the rule making proceeding is the implementation or prescription of law or policy for the future, rather than the evaluation of a respondent's past conduct. Typically, the issues relate not to the evidentiary facts, as to which the veracity and demeanor of witnesses would often be important, but rather to the policy-making conclusions to be drawn from the facts . . . . Conversely, adjudication is concerned with the determination of past and present rights and liabilities. Normally, there is involved a decision as to whether past conduct was unlawful, so that the proceeding is characterized by an accusatory flavor and may result in disciplinary action. Or, it may involve the determination of a person's right to benefits under existing law so that the issues relate to whether he is within the established category of persons entitled to such benefits. In such proceedings, the issues of fact are often sharply controverted.[7]

Given the breadth of the definitions of *rulemaking* and *adjudication* in the APA, it is not surprising that some confusion exists with respect to the proper classification of

---

5. 5 U.S.C. § 551(7).
6. *Id.* § 551(6). Note that all ratemaking (of future effect) is "rulemaking" under this provision.
7. Attorney General's Manual, *supra* note 4, at 14–15 (citations omitted). *See* Bowen v. Georgetown Univ. Hosp., 488 U.S. 204, 216 (1988) (Scalia, J., concurring) (comparing rulemaking and adjudication). *See also infra* chapter 2. For an opinion addressing the issue in terms similar to the Attorney General's Manual, see *Yesler Terrace Cmty. Council v. Cisneros*, 37 F.3d 442 (9th Cir. 1994). In *Yesler Terrace*, the court held that a determination by the Department of Housing and Urban Development that the state of Washington's state-court eviction procedures satisfied HUD's due process requirements constituted rulemaking. 37 F.3d at 448–49. *But see* United States v. Roberts, 2001 WL 1602123 at *7 (S.D.N.Y. 2001) (holding that a DEA determination, made in a criminal case, that drug possessed by defendants was an "analogue" to a controlled substance was an investigation and not rulemaking).

certain agency proceedings. Determining whether an agency action is a "rule" is often vexing and has been the subject of much litigation.[8]

One such case is *Department of Labor v. Kast Metals Corp.*,[9] where the issue was whether the Occupational Safety and Health Administration (OSHA) administrative plan for determining workplace inspection priorities was a rule. The government, relying on the distinction between an "investigation" and "rulemaking," claimed that the inspection plan was "investigative" rather than "prescriptive" because the plan itself "does not require any action on the part of those regulated."[10] In rejecting this argument, the D.C. Circuit stated that the characterization of agency action is a function not of formal definitions, but of the "intrinsic nature of the action in terms of the way the agency does business."[11] The court concluded that the procedure by which the determination to investigate was made was separate from the investigation itself, and the basis for this determination must be classified as a rule under the APA.[12]

Four subsequent cases illustrate that agency acts or policies can be considered as rules even if not issued as such. In *DIA Navigation Co., Ltd. v. Pomeroy*,[13] the court held that an INS policy, applied in a binding fashion via a form given to carriers and based on an internal legal opinion, requiring carriers to pay for the detention of stowaways was a rule that was required to be promulgated through notice-and-comment rulemaking due to its binding effect on the carriers. Similarly, the Fifth Circuit in two cases found determinations by the Department of the Interior (DOI) to be rules. In

---

8. For example, the Fifth Circuit has ruled that an agency action that otherwise would have been an adjudication was transformed into rulemaking because the result was a departure from prior policy, and the agency's "new policy was the basis for the adjudication rather than the facts of the particular adjudication causing [the agency] to modify or re-interpret its rule." Shell Offshore, Inc. v. Babbitt, 238 F.3d 622 (5th Cir. 2001). *See also* Nat'l Ass'n of Home Builders v. U.S. Army Corps of Eng'rs, 417 F.3d 1272, 1284 (D.C. Cir. 2005) (finding Corps' issuance of nationwide dredge-and-fill permits (NWPs) was rulemaking and not adjudication because "each NWP . . . is a legal prescription of general and prospective applicability which the Corps has issued to implement the permitting authority the Congress entrusted to it in section 404 of the [Clean Water Act]."

9. 744 F.2d 1145 (5th Cir. 1984).

10. *Id.* at 1149–50. This distinction was articulated in *United States v. W. H. Hodges & Co., Inc.*, 533 F.2d 276, 278 (5th Cir. 1976) (per curiam).

11. *Kast Metals*, 744 F.2d at 1150 (distinguishing *Appeal of FTC Line of Business Report Litigation*, where the court held that FTC informational report orders constituted not a rule but an investigative act, 595 F.2d 685, 695 & n.48 (D.C. Cir. 1978)).

12. *Id.* The court further held that even if classified as "investigative activity," the language of the OSH Act, read together with the APA, "strongly suggests" that the plan should be classified as a rule. *Id.* at 1151. The court separately concluded that the rule was exempt from notice-and-comment requirements as a "procedural" rule. *Id.* at 1156. Another case found that a settlement agreement and consent decree between the U.S. government and a private company concerning the restoration of the Everglades did not constitute rulemaking. *See* Miccosukee Tribe of Indians of Fla. v. United States, 6 F. Supp. 2d 1346, 1349–50 (S.D. Fla. 1998).

13. 34 F.3d 1255 (3d Cir. 1994).

Phillips Petroleum Co. v. Johnson,[14] an Interior Department royalty-valuation proce-dure, established in an unpublished internal agency paper but applied in a mandatory fashion by the Department, was held to be a rule that required notice-and-comment procedures. In *Shell Offshore Inc. v. Babbitt*, the court struck down a DOI determina-tion denying an offshore leasing rate, ruling it was not an "adjudication" exempt from the rulemaking requirements of the APA; instead, the "new interpretation" of a regu-lation governing acceptance of FERC tariffs was a "new substantive rule" subject to notice and comment.[15] And, in *Military Order of Purple Heart of USA v. Secretary of Veterans Affairs*,[16] petitioners challenged a new Department of Veterans Affairs (DVA) directive requiring that claims awarding $250,000 or more be redetermined after an internal review without notice to the claimants. The DVA argued this was simply a matter of "internal housekeeping," but the court held that the new procedure met the APA definition of a rule and should have followed notice-and-comment procedures.[17]

On the other hand, in *Industrial Safety Equipment Association, Inc. v. EPA*,[18] the D.C. Circuit held that a "guide" issued by the Environmental Protection Agency (EPA) and the National Institute for Occupational Safety and Health recommending the use of only two types of respirators as ideal models for protection against asbestos expo-sure, but not as a mandatory regimen, was not a "rule" under the APA.[19] Finding that Congress did not intend that the APA definition of *rule* be "construed so broadly" that every agency action would be subject to judicial review, the court emphasized the "advisory character" of the guide. Thus, the court concluded, the guide "does not change any law or official policy presently in effect," nor narrow the basis of EPA legal certification of respirators, and therefore did not constitute a rule.[20] In addition, in the context of whether an agency letter was reviewable agency action, the D.C. Circuit has frequently held that letters were not consequential enough to rise to the level of being a rule. In *Independent Equipment Dealers Ass'n v. EPA*, the court said:

14. 22 F.3d 616 (5th Cir. 1994), *modified on other grounds on reh'g*, 1994 WL 484506 (5th Cir. 1994). *See also* Bernard Schwartz, *A Decade of Administrative Law*, 32 TULSA L. REV. 493, 543 (1997), for commentary on these cases.
15. 238 F.3d 622, 629–30 (5th Cir. 2001).
16. 580 F.3d 1293 (D.C. Cir. 2009).
17. *Id.* at 1294 (one panel member dissented on the ground that the rule was exempt from notice and comment as a procedural rule).
18. 837 F.2d 1115 (D.C. Cir. 1988).
19. The particular issue before the court was whether the guide constituted "agency action" subject to review under APA sections 702 and 704. *Id.* at 1117. Because section 551(13) of the APA defines "agency action" as including "the whole or a part of an agency rule," the court confronted the question of whether the guide was a "rule" under the APA. *Id.* at 1120.
20. *Id.* at 1119–21. *Cf.* San Diego Air Sports Ctr., Inc. v. FAA, 887 F.2d 966 (9th Cir. 1989) (holding an FAA letter prohibiting sport parachuting center from "*all* parachuting by any party . . . from the time [FAA] issued" it was a "rule" for review purposes); Thomas v. New York, 802 F.2d 1443 (D.C. Cir. 1986) (holding letter issued by EPA Administrator was rule under APA).

Although the EPA Letter is certainly a statement of "general or particular applicability"—what isn't?—and is arguably of "future effect" insofar as it may inform the future conduct of IEDA's members, the EPA Letter certainly does not "implement, interpret, or prescribe law or policy." By *restating* EPA's established interpretation of the certificate of conformity regulation, the EPA Letter tread no new ground. It left the world just as it found it, and thus cannot be fairly described as implementing, interpreting, or prescribing law or policy.[21]

In discussing the differences between rulemaking and adjudication, the D.C. Circuit agreed with a Federal Communications Commission (FCC) determination that an "Implementation Order" was not rulemaking because the petitioner consistently asked the Commission for a "temporary waiver" and the APA defines *rulemaking* as an "agency process for formulating, amending, or repealing a rule."[22] The court cited two other determinative factors. First, the Implementation Order only applied to previously issued licenses and the APA defines rules as "agency statement[s] of . . . future effect."[23] And second, the Commission's proceeding resembled an adjudicatory proceeding because the agency engaged in "extensive discussion" of standing, which the court observed does not apply to notice-and-comment rulemaking.[24]

In an interesting decision, the D.C. Circuit ruled in a split decision that an EPA industry-wide settlement agreement was not a rule and therefore EPA did not have to subject the agreement to notice and comment.[25] The court ruled that it was merely an exercise of the agency's prosecutorial discretion, whereas the dissenting judge claimed the agency "has attempted to secure the benefits of legislative rulemaking without the burdens of its statutory duties."[26]

Nor was notice and comment required when an agency decided not to promulgate a rule (and withdrew a statement of intent to do so made in an earlier related final rule preamble). The D.C. Circuit observed that "an agency does not enact a new rule when a transition rule expires or when the agency decides not to modify a rule, states that

---

21. 372 F.3d 420, 428 (D.C. Cir. 2004) (emphasis in original), *citing* Indus. Safety Equip. Ass'n v. EPA, 837 F.2d at 1120–21. In *Funeral Consumers Alliance, Inc. v. FTC*, 481 F.3d 860 (D.C. Cir. 2007), the court found that it lacked jurisdiction under the FTC statute's direct review provisions because an agency letter clarifying an aspect of an existing "Funeral Rule" was neither a "rule" nor a "substantive amendment" to a rule. It held that the letter neither "repudiated" nor "supplemented" the rule; instead, it had "merely interpreted the rule." *Id.* at 863, 866. *See also* Gen. Motors Corp. v. EPA, 363 F.3d 442 (D.C. Cir. 2004) (finding letters from an enforcement official at EPA regarding "nascent enforcement actions based on a regulatory interpretation that automobile manufacturing paint purge solvents are 'solid waste'" under the Resource Conservation and Recovery Act to not be reviewable agency action).
22. Goodman v. FCC, 182 F.3d 987, 993–94 (D.C. Cir. 1999) (quoting 5 U.S.C. § 551(5)).
23. *Id.* at 994 (quoting 5 U.S.C. § 551(4)).
24. *Id.* (citations omitted).
25. Ass'n of Irritated Residents v. EPA, 494 F.3d 1027 (D.C. Cir. 2007).
26. *Id.* at 1037 (Rogers, J. dissenting).

additional study is needed, or concludes that no new transition rule is needed."[27] It went on to explain that "*[n]ot* modifying a rule is not the same as 'formulating, amending, or repealing a rule,' the APA definition of 'rule making.'"[28]

Other cases reviewing agency activities with some general applicability have held them not to be rules because they lack sufficient "effect" or do not really "implement, interpret or prescribe law or policy."[29]

With respect to the APA's definition of "rule," the inclusion of agency statements of "particular applicability" probably creates the most difficulty because most people think of rules as addressing general situations and adjudication as addressing particular situations. Although it is true that the great majority of rules have some general application and adjudication is nearly always particularized in its immediate application, the drafters of the APA wished certain actions of a particular nature, such as the setting of future rates or the approval of corporate reorganizations, to be carried out under the relatively flexible procedures governing rulemaking. Consequently, the words "or particular" were included in the definition.[30]

Courts have upheld the classification of agency action as a "rule" even though it only applied to the activities of a single entity,[31] and probably no great change would occur if the words "or particular" were deleted from the definition of rule in section 551 of the APA.[32] It is noteworthy that the definition of "regulation or rule" in Execu-

---

27. Nat'l Mining Ass'n v. Mine Safety & Health Admin., 599 F.3d 662, 670 (D.C. Cir. 2010), *quoting* ICORE, Inc. v. FCC, 985 F.2d 1075, 1082 (D.C. Cir. 1993).

28. 599 F.3d 671, *quoting ICORE*, 985 F.2d at 1082.

29. *See, e.g.*, Reich v. Youghiogheny and Ohio Coal Co., 66 F.3d 111 (6th Cir. 1995) ("Where the rate of interest and the procedures relative to the assessment of the interest were prescribed by law, the DOL's demand for interest could not be considered to be administrative rulemaking."); Nat'l Ornament & Elec. Light Christmas Ass'n v. Consumer Prod. Safety Comm'n, 526 F.2d 1368 (2d Cir. 1975) (holding an agency initiative to have "consumer deputies" visit stores to look for dangerous lights was not rulemaking). *But see* Batterton v. Marshall, 648 F.2d 694 (D.C. Cir. 1980) (holding that a statistical methodology was a statement designed to implement law). *See also* Lincoln v. Vigil, 508 U.S. 182 (1993) (holding a question whether Indian Health Service decision to terminate an entire program was a "rule" need not be reached because it would fit within exemptions from notice and comment).

30. *See* 1 KENNETH CULP DAVIS & RICHARD J. PIERCE, JR., ADMINISTRATIVE LAW TREATISE § 6:1 (3d ed. 1994); Thomas D. Morgan, *Toward a Revised Strategy for Ratemaking*, 1978 U. ILL. L.F. 21, 50 & n.143 (1978) (discussing inclusion of "or particular" in definition).

31. *See, e.g.*, Hercules Inc. v. EPA, 598 F.2d 91, 118–19 (D.C. Cir. 1978) (not requiring either formal rulemaking or adjudicatory procedures in EPA promulgation of effluent limitations even though its requirements directly applied to only a single company); Anaconda Co. v. Ruckelshaus, 482 F.2d 1301, 1306–07 (10th Cir. 1973) (not requiring an adjudicatory hearing in an EPA rulemaking setting emission standards for sulfur oxide, even though the rule applied to only a single entity at the time of issuance).

32. For a thorough discussion of this issue, *see* Ronald Levin, *The Case for (Finally) Fixing the APA's Definition of "Rule,"* 56 ADMIN. L. REV. 1077 (2004) (arguing for a removal of the "or particular" language from § 551(4)). The American Bar Association has long recommended revising the definition to delete the words "or particular." *See The 12 ABA Recommendations*

tive Order 12,866 does not include those words.[33] It should also be noted that several other statutes affecting rulemaking have less inclusive definitions of rule.[34]

The APA definition of "rulemaking" also requires that a rule be "of future effect." This has helped lead to the blackletter law principle that without specific congressional authorization, agencies may not issue retroactive rules.[35]

In addition to classifying agency action as either rulemaking or adjudication, agencies must determine what type of rule they are developing, because different procedural requirements apply to different types of rules. The task of classification is complicated by the great variety of agency actions. Professors Davis and Pierce have observed:

> Agencies issue rules, sub-rules, and sub-sub-rules, seemingly ad infinitum. What agencies denominate "rules" or "regulations" are usually readily recognizable as such, but other statements or announcements that are somewhat in the nature of rules are troublesome and are causes of confusion. Like courts, agencies make "rules" by generalizing in adjudicatory opinions; like courts, they legislate in the process of deciding individual cases. Furthermore, agencies' informal adjudication may be quite voluminous and may be largely recorded, and the products may be rulings, interpretations, staff letters, press releases, official speeches, and many other kinds of announcements. Some agencies have nothing but respectable vertebrates; others have inferior animals and crawling creatures that no one can classify as fish, fowl, or insect.

---

for Improved Procedures for Federal Agencies, 24 ADMIN. L. REV. 389, 389–91 (1972). The Administrative Conference endorsed the ABA proposal with the understanding that "[a] matter may be considered of 'general applicability' even though it is directly applicable to a class which consists of only one or a few persons if the class is open in the sense that in the future the number of members of the class may be increased." ACUS Statement 2, *On ABA Resolution No. 1 Proposing to Amend the Definition of "Rule" in the Administrative Procedure Act.* 38 Fed. Reg. 16,841 (June 27, 1973), *as amended*, 39 Fed. Reg. 23,045 (1974).

33. Exec. Order 12,866, 58 Fed. Reg. 51,735 (Oct. 4, 1993), *reprinted in* Appendix B.
34. The "Congressional Review of Rules" provision of the Small Business Regulatory Enforcement Fairness Act exempts from its coverage "any rule of particular applicability," 5 U.S.C. § 804(3). See discussion of this law at Chapter 3(J) of this Part. The Regulatory Flexibility Act also contains a similar provision, 5 U.S.C. § 601(2), and the Unfunded Mandates Reform Act definition tracks that of the Regulatory Flexibility Act. *See* 2 U.S.C. § 658(10).
35. *See* Bowen v. Georgetown Univ. Hosp., 488 U.S. 204 (1988), discussed *infra*, Part III, ch. 7(A)(6)(c). The APA's definition was relied upon by Justice Scalia in his concurrence. 488 U.S. at 216. *But see* William V. Luneburg, *Retroactivity and Administrative Rulemaking*, 1991 DUKE L.J. 106, 139–41 (arguing that agencies sometimes have a legitimate need to adopt retroactive rules); Ronald Levin, *supra* note 32, at 1083–88 (pointing out that interpretive rules routinely are applied to past events, criticizing Justice Scalia's reasoning, and suggesting removal of the language "of future effect" from the APA definition).

Yet the problem of classification must be taken seriously, because often the required procedure, as well as the degree of authoritative weight, depends on it.[36]

The classification might also determine the applicable requirements for seeking judicial review.[37]

B. *Formal* Rulemaking under the APA

Section 553 is the APA's informal rulemaking section, and it sets forth the notice-and-comment requirements that apply to most "legislative"[38] rulemaking. However, subsection 553(c) states: "When rules are required by statute to be made on the record after opportunity for an agency hearing, sections 556 and 557 of this title apply instead of [subsection (c)]." That sentence establishes the distinction between informal, notice-and-comment rulemaking under section 553 and formal, "on-the-record" rulemaking under sections 556 and 557.

Sections 556 and 557 include requirements that the agency support its rule with substantial evidence in an exclusive rulemaking record,[39] that there be an oral hearing presided over by agency members or an administrative law judge,[40] that the parties be permitted to conduct such cross-examination "as may be required for a full and true disclosure of the facts,"[41] that there be no ex parte communication with the decisionmaker,[42] and that parties be allowed to submit proposed findings and conclusions and present exceptions to the initial or recommended decisions of subordinate agency employees or to tentative agency decisions.[43] Thus, formal rulemaking is a trial-type procedure, even though not all of the APAs for formal adjudication apply to such rulemaking.[44]

---

36. DAVIS & PIERCE, ADMINISTRATIVE LAW TREATISE, *supra* note 30, at § 7:4. For an argument that some agency "administrative agreements," such as memoranda of understanding, should be considered rules under the APA, *see* John M. Scheib, *Administrative Agreements: Should They Be in the Shadows of the Administrative Procedure Act?*, 55 ADMIN. L. REV. 477 (2003).
37. *See, e.g.*, Goodman v. FCC, 182 F.3d 987, 992–94 (finding that an FCC order addressing waiver of certain license requirements was properly characterized as a "non-rulemaking" order for the purpose of determining the time of public notice and, therefore, holding the petition for judicial review was not filed in a timely manner).
38. *See infra* note 128 and accompanying text.
39. 5 U.S.C. § 556(d)–(e).
40. *Id.* § 556(b).
41. *Id.* § 556(d).
42. *Id.* § 557(d). This subsection was added by the Government in the Sunshine Act, Pub. L. No. 94-409, § 4(a), 90 Stat. 1241 (1976). *See infra* Part III, ch. 6, for a discussion of "ex parte," or off-the-record, contacts in the informal rulemaking context.
43. 5 U.S.C. § 557(c).
44. For example, 5 U.S.C. § 556(d) provides that in rulemaking "an agency may, when a party will not be prejudiced thereby, adopt procedures for the submission of all or part of the evidence in written form." Also, the separation-of-functions requirements for adjudication in 5 U.S.C. § 554(d) do not apply to formal rulemaking.

The Supreme Court put a damper on the use of formal rulemaking in *United States v. Florida East Coast Railway*,[45] a proceeding to establish future rates. The Court held that section 1(14)(a) of the Interstate Commerce Act did not mandate use of formal rulemaking procedures to establish incentive per diem charges applicable to railroad use of freight cars because that statute only required a decision "after hearing," rather than the precise phrase "on the record after opportunity for an agency hearing" used in section 553(c).[46] After *Florida East Coast Railway*, one would expect the magic words "on the record" to appear in any statute requiring use of formal rulemaking procedures.[47]

Formal rulemaking always has been the exception rather than the norm,[48] and it is used infrequently today.[49] Surprisingly, however, President Bush included in his short-lived amendments to Executive Order 12,866 a provision that would have inserted encouragement for agencies to "consider whether to utilize formal rulemaking procedures under 5 U.S.C. 556 and 557 for the resolution of complex determinations."[50] Recently there has been a related boomlet by business interests to support greater use of formal rulemaking.[51]

---

45. 410 U.S. 224 (1973).

46. *Id.* at 241.

47. *See* Commodity Exch., Inc. v. CFTC, 543 F. Supp. 1340, 1345–48 (S.D.N.Y. 1982) (providing example of conscious legislative decision not to include the words "on the record" in statute), *aff'd*, 703 F.2d 682 (2d Cir. 1983). On occasion, the question of whether to provide formal or informal rulemaking is debated in Congress during the legislative development of a regulatory statute. *See* Indus. Union Dep't v. Hodgson, 499 F.2d 467, 472–75 (D.C. Cir. 1974).

48. *See* Robert W. Hamilton, *Procedures for the Adoption of Rules of General Applicability: The Need for Procedural Innovation in Administrative Rulemaking*, 60 CAL. L. REV. 1276, 1278–80 (1972). For additional discussion, *see* "Oral Hearings in APA Rulemaking," *infra* Part III, ch. 4(C).

49. One example is the Marine Mammal Protection Act's requirement that regulations by the Secretary of Commerce with respect to the taking and importing of marine mammals must be made on the record after opportunity for an agency hearing. *See* 16 U.S.C. § 1373(d). For a description of a formal rulemaking begun under this section, see http://www.nwr.noaa.gov/ Marine-Mammals/Whales-Dolphins-Porpoise/Gray-Whales/upload/application.pdf at 18. It is also used by the USDA for issuing milk marketing orders under 7 U.S.C. § 608c. *See* White Eagle Co-op Ass'n v. Conner, 553 F.3d 467 (7th Cir. 2009) (rejecting procedural challenges to the formal rulemaking).

50. *See* Exec. Order 13,422 § 5 (Jan. 18, 2007), 72 Fed. Reg. 2763, 2764 (Jan. 23, 2007). The Bush amendments were revoked by President Obama in Exec. Order 13,497, 74 Fed. Reg. 6113 (Feb. 4, 2009).

51. *See, e.g.*, "The Views of the Administration on Regulatory Reform: An Update," Testimony of William L. Kovacs, U.S. Chamber of Commerce, before the House Comm. on Energy & Commerce, Subcomm. on Oversight & Investigations, at 13 (June 3, 2011) ("The Chamber believes formal rulemaking is appropriate for the small category of 'super rules' with significant economic impact and societal impact."), *available at* http://democrats.energycommerce.house.gov/ sites/default/files/image_uploads/Testimony_OI_06.03.11_Kovacs.pdf.

C. *Informal* Rulemaking under Section 553 of the APA

Unless the agency's statute otherwise specifies,[52] agency rulemaking is governed by section 553 of the APA. And unless the rule falls within one of the exemptions in section 553, rulemaking under that section must comply with the following minimum procedural requirements:

1. [A] notice of proposed rulemaking must be published in the *Federal Register* that includes a statement of the time, place, and nature of the public rulemaking proceedings; a reference to the legal authority under which the rule is proposed; and either the terms or a description of the subjects and issues to be addressed by the proposed rule;[53]
2. interested persons must be given an opportunity to submit written data, views, or arguments on the proposal, "with or without opportunity for oral presentation";[54]
3. a "concise general statement" of the "basis and purpose" must accompany the final rule;[55] and
4. subject to certain exceptions, publication of the final rule must take place "not less than 30 days before its effective date."[56]

Because the opportunity for oral presentation is left to agency discretion (item two above), section 553 procedure is accurately referred to as notice-and-comment rulemaking. The meaning and operational impact of these procedural requirements will be discussed in detail in later chapters of the *Guide*.[57] The following discussion deals with the numerous exemptions in section 553, under which certain kinds of rules are either totally or partially exempted from its requirements.

D. Rules Exempt from Section 553's Requirements

Two broad categories of rules—those dealing with military or foreign affairs functions and those relating to agency management or personnel or to public property, loans, grants, benefits, or contracts—are exempted from *all* of the requirements of

---

52. Occasionally Congress will exempt particular rulemakings from notice and comment, *see* section 1601(c) of the 2008 Farm Bill, 7 U.S.C.A. §§ 8781(C)(1), 8781(2)(c), mandating rulemaking within 90 days and exempting the rules from notice and comment as well as from the Paperwork Reduction Act. In other statutes, of course, Congress may require procedures in addition to those in section 553.
53. 5 U.S.C. § 553(b). *See infra* Part III, ch. 3.
54. 5 U.S.C. § 553(c). *See infra* Part III, ch. 4.
55. 5 U.S.C. § 553(c). *See infra* Part III, ch. 7.
56. 5 U.S.C. § 553(d). *See infra* Part III, ch. 7. For certain "major" rules, the effective date is postponed at least an additional 60 days by the congressional-review-of-rules legislation. *See infra* Part II, ch. 3(J).
57. *See generally infra* Part III.

section 553.[58] Broad exemptions from the notice-and-comment process also exist for other types of rules, such as interpretive rules, policy statements, and procedural rules, and more limited exemptions apply to still other rules, such as rules that relieve restrictions. In carving out these exemptions, the drafters of the APA sought to balance the need for public input with competing societal interests favoring the efficient and expeditious conduct of certain government affairs.[59]

Because these exemptions are exceptions to the APA's general policy of providing an opportunity for public participation in rulemaking, which are designed to foster the fair and informed exercise of agency authority, they have traditionally been "narrowly construed and only reluctantly countenanced."[60]

The fact that a particular rule falls within one of the exemptions from the public procedures under section 553 does not mean that the exemption is mandatory, nor is it intended to discourage agencies from using public participation procedures. To the contrary, when Congress enacted the APA, it encouraged agencies to use notice and comment in some exempted cases, and many agencies follow notice-and-comment procedure as a matter of course in making certain kinds of exempted rules. Indeed, some agencies have published rules formally waiving section 553 exemptions, and courts have relied on agency waivers to enforce statutory procedures that otherwise would not apply.[61] Whether agencies will continue to be so willing to waive the various exemptions as the rulemaking process becomes more cumbersome is open to question.[62]

1. Rules Exempt from All of Section 553

a. Proprietary matters: public property, loans, grants, and contracts—Section 553(a)(2) of the APA provides an unqualified exclusion from every requirement of

---

58. 5 U.S.C. § 553(a).

59. Thus, in *American Hospital Ass'n v. Bowen*, 834 F.2d 1037, 1045 (D.C. Cir. 1987), the D.C. Circuit stated that "[t]he reading of the § 553 exemptions that seems most consonant with Congress' purposes in adopting the APA is to construe them as an attempt to preserve agency flexibility in dealing with limited situations where substantive rights are not at stake." *See also* Dep't of Labor v. Kast Metals Corp., 744 F.2d 1145, 1153 (5th Cir. 1984) (noting "tension" between agency efficiency and public input).

60. Am. Fed'n of Gov't Emps., AFL-CIO v. Block, 655 F.2d 1153, 1156 (D.C. Cir. 1981) (quoting New Jersey Dep't of Envtl. Prot. v. EPA, 626 F.2d 1038 (D.C. Cir. 1980); Arthur Earl Bonfield, *Military and Foreign Affairs Function Rulemaking Under the APA*, 71 MICH. L. REV. 221, 237 (1972) [hereinafter Bonfield, *Military and Foreign Affairs Function Rulemaking*].

61. *See, e.g.*, Rodway v. USDA, 514 F.2d 809 (D.C. Cir. 1975).

62. *See infra* note 71 and accompanying text (discussing agency attempts to withdraw waivers). *See also Oversight Hearing on the Congressional Review Act Before the House Subcomm. on Commercial and Administrative Law of the Comm. on the Judiciary* (testimony of Sally Katzen, OIRA Administrator) (noting that the congressional review process may create "perverse incentive" to avoid voluntary use of notice and comment because such use will render rules subject to congressional review).

section 553 for all rules relating to "public property, loans, grants, benefits or contracts." It should be emphasized, however, that although the scope of these "proprietary" exemptions is quite broad, they apply only where an agency action "clearly and directly" involves one of the exempted matters.[63]

These exemptions, which obviously include many important governmental functions, have been strongly criticized. In 1969, the Administrative Conference recommended that the APA be amended to eliminate this exemption, and apart from legislative action, it urged agencies administering exempt programs to voluntarily use notice-and-comment procedure, without awaiting legislative action.[64] The recommendation, emphasizing that the rules covered by the exemption "bear heavily upon non-governmental interests,"[65] stated that the exemption was "unwise" and its elimination will "make for fair, informed exercise of rulemaking authority."[66]

In 1988, Congress followed the Administrative Conference's recommendation when it created the Department of Veterans Affairs (DVA) and required the Department to use notice-and-comment procedures for virtually all of its regulations.[67] Many other departments and agencies with sizable programs in these areas responded to the Conference's recommendation by issuing rules or policy statements voluntarily waiving or limiting exemptions.[68] The effect of such waivers is to subject the agency to the requirements of

---

63. *See* Arthur Earl Bonfield, *Public Participation in Federal Rulemaking Relating to Public Property, Loans, Grants, Benefits or Contracts*, 118 U. Pa. L. Rev. 540, 556 (1970) [hereinafter Bonfield, *Public Participation in Federal Rulemaking*]. *But see* Clipper Cruise Line, Inc. v. United States, 855 F. Supp. 1 (D.D.C. 1994) (holding Interior Department rule governing permitting process for cruise ships entering national park is exempt from notice and comment because it is a matter relating to public property).
64. ACUS Recommendation 69-8, *Elimination of Certain Exemptions from the APA Rulemaking Requirements*, 38 Fed. Reg. 19,782 (July 23, 1973). Other organizations, such as the Advisory Commission on Intergovernmental Relations and the American Bar Association, also recommended eliminating this exemption.
65. *Id.* Federal grant, loan, and procurement programs affect the lives of millions of persons and the character of the federal system as a whole. The extent of this impact today is of a far greater magnitude than it was when the APA, with its exemptions, was enacted in 1946.
66. *Id.*
67. Veterans Judicial Review Act, Pub. L. No. 100-687, §101(a), 102 Stat. 4105, 4106 (1988) (codified at 38 U.S.C. § 223).
68. *See, e.g.*, Dep't of Transp. Regulatory Policies and Procedures, 44 Fed. Reg. 11,034 (Feb. 26, 1979); *see also* Dep't of Housing and Urban Development, Rulemaking: Policy and Procedures, 44 Fed. Reg. 1606 (Jan. 5, 1979) (codified at 24 C.F.R. § 10.1); Dep't of Labor, Rulemaking, 46 Fed. Reg. 35 (Jan. 2, 1981) (codified at 29 C.F.R. § 2.7); Dep't of Health and Human Services, 36 Fed. Reg. 2532 (Feb. 5, 1971); Dep't of Agric., 36 Fed. Reg. 13,804 (1971); Dep't of the Interior, 36 Fed. Reg. 8336 (May 5, 1971); Small Business Admin., 36 Fed. Reg. 16,716 (Aug. 25, 1971). The Department of Defense removed its waiver from its regulations, 32 C.F.R. § 296.3 (2006), *see* 71 Fed. Reg. 12,280 (Mar. 10, 2006), and included it in Administrative Instruction 102, Enclosure 3 at 11–12 (Nov. 6, 2006), *available at* http://www.dtic.mil/whs/directives/corres/pdf/a102p.pdf.

section 553 as if it were promulgating nonexempt rules.[69] Note that agencies that waive the exemptions retain the power to omit notice and comment whenever those procedures are "impracticable, unnecessary, or contrary to the public interest."[70] It also should be mentioned that several agencies have reconsidered their waivers.[71]

Finally, agencies engaged in rulemaking exempted from the APA's procedural requirements by the proprietary exemption may be required by other laws or directives to use some public participation procedures. For example, the Social Security Act provides that regulations prescribing standards for benefits eligibility are subject to Section 553 rulemaking procedures.[72] Congress also required federal procurement regulations to be issued after notice and comment.[73] Moreover, Executive Order 12,866 does not exempt these kinds of rules from its coverage.[74]

---

69. Courts have enforced these waivers in numerous instances. *See, e.g., Yesler Terrace, supra* note 7, at 442; Batterton v. Marshall, 648 F.2d 694, 700 (D.C. Cir. 1980); *Rodway, supra* note 61, at 809. *See also* Gerald H. Yamada, *Rulemaking Requirements Relating to Federal Financial Assistance Programs*, 39 Fed. Cir. B.J. 89, 91–93 (1980).

70. 5 U.S.C. § 553(b)(3)(B). This "good cause" exemption is applicable to all rules and is discussed *supra*, subsec. (D)(4).

71. *See, e.g.*, Housing and Urban Development, Rulemaking Policies and Procedures—Expediting Rulemaking and Policy Implementation, 57 Fed. Reg. 47,166 (Oct. 14, 1992) (proposing withdrawal of its waiver). After receiving 77 comments, mostly opposing the change, HUD modified its proposal somewhat and requested a second round of comments in 1996. 61 Fed. Reg. 42,722 (Aug. 16, 1996). The proposal was withdrawn on January 27, 1998. *See* Rulemaking Policies and Procedures—Expediting Rulemaking and Policy Implementation, Entry 1285, Unified Agenda (April 1998), *available at* http://ciir.cs.umass.edu/ua; *cf.* Pub. L. 104-204, § 215, 110 Stat. 2874, 2904 (requiring HUD to maintain existing rulemaking procedures). *See also* Dep't of Veterans Affairs, Rulemaking Procedures; Public Participation, 62 Fed. Reg. 9969 (Mar. 5, 1997) (removing the broad waiver in 38 C.F.R. § 1.12 on grounds that subsequent statute had partially required notice and comment for DVA rules within exemption and that waiver was too broad and confusing). HHS also proposed to limit its voluntary waiver, *see* 47 Fed. Reg. 26,860 (June 22, 1982), but after receiving numerous negative comments did not act on the proposal.

72. 42 U.S.C. § 421(k)(2).

73. *See, e.g.*, Small Business and Federal Procurement Competition Enhancement Act of 1984, Pub. L. No. 98-577, § 302, 98 Stat. 3066, 3076 (codified in the Office of Federal Procurement Policy Act, at 41 U.S.C. § 418b) (requiring any "procurement policy, regulation, procedure, or form (including amendments or modifications thereto) relating to the expenditure of appropriated funds that has (1) a significant effect beyond the internal operating procedures of the agency issuing the procurement policy, regulation, procedure or form, or (2) a significant cost or administrative impact on contractors or offerors" to be issued after a public comment period of (normally) 60 days). The public comment provision in this Act also applies to rules that otherwise might fit within other exemptions of the APA—such as procedural rules and non-legislative rules. For a case enforcing this provision, *see* Munitions Carriers Conference, Inc. v. United States, 932 F. Supp. 334 (D.D.C. 1996), *rev'd on other grounds*, 147 F.3d 1027 (D.C. Cir. 1998). There, the court held that a military agency's procurement requirement may have fit squarely within the APA's "contracts" exemption from notice-and-comment rulemaking, but was nevertheless covered by 41 U.S.C. § 418b. Such rules must also be included in the Unified Agenda of Federal Regulatory and Deregulatory Actions pursuant to 41 U.S.C. § 421(g).

74. Exec. Order 12,866, § 3(d), 58 Fed. Reg. 51,735 (Sept. 30, 1993).

b. Agency management or personnel—Matters "relating to agency management or personnel" are likewise exempted from all requirements of section 553 of the APA.[75] *Management* has been defined as "the conducting or supervising of something (as a business); . . . the executive function of planning, organizing, coordinating, directing, controlling, and supervising any industrial or business project or activity with responsibility for results."[76] *Personnel* matters generally would include hiring and promotion standards, training, vacation, travel, and leave of absence.[77]

This exemption should not be read as intra-agency only. The *Attorney General's Manual on the APA* construes the exemption to cover many of the managerial functions now performed by the Office of Management and Budget (OMB), as well as interdepartmental committees established by the president for handling internal management problems.[78]

The effect of the personnel exemptions has been reduced significantly by other statutes, such as the Civil Service Reform Act of 1978, which requires the Office of Personnel Management to follow notice-and-comment procedures in formulating government-wide personnel regulations.[79] Those regulations must be published for comment except where "temporary in nature and . . . necessary to be implemented expeditiously as a result of an emergency."[80]

c. Military or foreign affairs—Section 553(a)(1) makes the APA's rulemaking procedures inapplicable "to the extent that there is involved . . . a military or foreign affairs function of the United States." As with proprietary rules, rulemaking involving military or foreign affairs functions is wholly exempted from section 553 requirements.[81] Such

---

75. 5 U.S.C. § 553 (a)(2).
76. WEBSTER'S NEW INTERNATIONAL DICTIONARY 1372 (3d ed. 1986).
77. For cases finding agency rules to be within the scope of the exemption, *see* Favreau v. United States, 317 F.3d 1346, 1359 (Fed. Cir. 2002) (memoranda concerning when the U.S. could recoup prepaid bonuses from military personnel); Hamlet v. United States, 63 F.3d 1097, 1105 (Fed. Cir. 1995) (agency personnel handbook); Stewart v. Smith, 673 F.2d 485, 487 (D.C. Cir. 1982) (Bureau of Prisons' policy of not hiring persons over age of 34). For a case to the contrary, *see* Tunik v. Merit Systems Protection Board, 407 F.3d 1326, 1342–44 (Fed. Cir. 2005) (interpretation of APA's provision concerning removal of ALJs).
78. ATTORNEY GENERAL'S MANUAL, *supra* note 4, at 18, 27.
79. 5 U.S.C. § 1105.
80. *Id.* § 1103(b)(3). *See* Nat'l Fed'n of Fed. Emps. v. Devine, 671 F.2d 607, 610 (D.C. Cir. 1982) (approving health insurance open season postponement). In *Joseph v. U.S. Civil Service Comm'n,* 554 F.2d 1140, 1153 n.23 (D.C. Cir. 1977), the court of appeals required notice and comment for rules concerning exemptions from the Hatch Act because of their widespread public impact.
81. *See* Bonfield, *Military and Foreign Affairs Function Rulemaking, supra* note 60, at 230–31. For a more recent critique of this exemption in the context of the Defense Department rulemakings for military commissions, see Eugene Fidell, *Military Commissions & Administrative Law,* 6 GREEN BAG 379 (2003).

rules are also largely exempt from the coverage of E.O. 12,866.[82]

Several circuits have concluded that "[f]or the [foreign affairs part of the] exemption to apply, the public rulemaking provisions should provoke definitely undesirable international consequences."[83] In a recent example, the Second Circuit applied this test in holding that an Attorney General notice designating the countries whose nationals were subject to a special registration process (that itself had been subject to notice and comment after 9/11) was within the foreign affairs exemption.[84] The exemptions are not limited to activities of the State and Defense Departments, but, like the proprietary exemptions, they are "not to be loosely interpreted."[85] A 1972 report to the Administrative Conference concluded that only rulemaking "directly and intimately" involving these kinds of functions should be exempted.[86]

In this connection, the Ninth Circuit, while agreeing that the exemption could apply to "predominately civilian agencies such as DOE when they are performing a 'military function,'" held that a DOE personnel regulation that provided in part for permanent disqualification from duty of any employee who had ever used hallucinogens, including civilian contractor guards at nuclear facilities, was not within the exemption because the guards were not "performing a military function."[87]

The Administrative Conference recommended that Congress replace the categorical exemption for military or foreign affairs functions with a narrower exemption.[88] First, the Conference's recommendation would make clear that section 553 rulemaking procedures do not apply to matters required by executive order to be kept secret in the interest of national defense or foreign policy.[89] Second, the Conference recommended that repeal of the present exemption "be accompanied by statutory clarification of the agencies' power to prescribe by rule specified categories of rulemaking exempt [by section 553's "good cause" exemption], provided that the appropriate finding and a brief statement of reasons are set forth with respect to each category."[90]

---

82. The exemption covers such rules "other than procurement regulations and regulations involving the import or export of non-defense articles and services." Exec. Order 12,866, § 3(d), 58 Fed. Reg. 51,735 (Sept. 30, 1993).

83. Yassini v. Crosland, 618 F.2d 1356, 1360 n.4 (9th Cir. 1980), *accord,* Zhang v. Slattery, 55 F.3d 732, 744 (2d Cir. 1995).

84. Rajah v. Mukasey, 544 F.3d 427, 436–38 (2d Cir. 2008).

85. *Administrative Procedure Act: Legislative History, S. Doc. No. 248 79-258* (1946) [hereinafter *Legislative History of the APA*], at 9.

86. Bonfield, *Military and Foreign Affairs Function Rulemaking, supra* note 60, at 236–38, 252–53. Professor Bonfield discusses the scope of the exemptions, including agency views. *Id.* at 240–70.

87. Indep. Guard Ass'n of Nev., Local No. 1 v. O'Leary, 57 F.3d 766, 769 (9th Cir. 1995), *amended on other grounds,* 69 F.3d 1038 (9th Cir. 1995).

88. ACUS Recommendation 73-5, *Elimination of the "Military or Foreign Affairs Function" Exemption from APA Rulemaking Requirements,* 39 Fed. Reg. 4847 (Feb. 7, 1974).

89. *Id.* Thus, the exemption would track the language of exemption (b)(1) in the Freedom of Information Act, 5 U.S.C. § 552.

90. ACUS Recommendation 73-5, *supra* note 88.

In response to this recommendation, the Department of Defense has maintained a policy favoring notice and comment in the development of regulations having a substantial and direct impact on the public, and more specifically, that publication is not required if the document "[p]ertains to a military or foreign affairs function of the United States determined to require a security classification in the interests of national defense or foreign policy under the criteria of an E.O. or statute (e.g., foreign military sales)."[91]

Other cases have upheld the government's invocation of the exemption in the context of rules implementing international agreements,[92] rules imposing import quotas,[93] and rules relating to taxation of foreign missions.[94]

2. *Rules of Agency Organization, Procedure, or Practice*

"Rules of agency organization, procedure, or practice" are exempted from the notice-and-comment requirements of section 553.[95] These rules are not, however, exempted from the APA's publication or petition provisions.[96] This exemption has

---

91. Administrative Instruction 102, Enclosure 3 at 12 (Nov. 6, 2006), *available at* http://www.dtic.mil/whs/directives/corres/pdf/a102p.pdf. *See* note 68, *supra*. The Department of Navy's regulation is still codified at 32 C.F.R. § 701.66, but with an outdated cross-reference to DOD's former regulation.

92. Int'l Bhd. of Teamsters v. Peña, 17 F.3d 1478, 1486 (D.C. Cir. 1994) ("The rule at issue here, at least in the aspect challenged by the union, did no more than implement an agreement between the United States and Mexico."). *See also* WBEN, Inc. v. United States, 396 F.2d 601, 616 (2d Cir. 1968) (holding use of exemption valid where the rule implemented a United States-Canada agreement).

93. Am. Ass'n of Exporters & Importers v. United States, 751 F.2d 1239 (Fed. Cir. 1985). The court held that the President may issue regulations to carry out international trade agreements without notice and comment, saying that the purpose of the exemption "was to allow more cautious and sensitive consideration of those matters which 'so affect relations with other Governments that, for example, public rule-making provisions would provoke definitely undesirable international consequences.'" *Id.* at 1249 (quoting H. REP. No. 69-1980, at 23 (1946)).

94. City of New York v. Permanent Mission of India to United Nations, 618 F.3d 172 (2d Cir. 2010) (State Department's promulgation of a notice, pursuant to the Foreign Missions Act, making property tax exemptions for mission and consular staff residences owned by the governments of India and Mongolia in New York City effective retroactively involved a foreign affairs function of the United States.).

95. 5 U.S.C. § 553(b)(A). The reference to "this subsection" in the clause qualifying the § 553(b) exemptions is misleading because the exemptions also extend to § 553(c)'s comment opportunity. *See* ATTORNEY GENERAL'S MANUAL, *supra* note 4, at 30. Note that Exec. Order 12,866 exempts from its coverage rules pertaining to agency "organization" but not those that "describe the procedure or practice requirements of an agency." Exec. Order 12,866 § 3(d), 58 Fed. Reg. 51,735 (Sept. 30, 1993).

96. The drafters of the APA specifically wanted publication of agency rules of practice and procedure so that the public would be aware of them. *See* Batterton v. Marshall, 648 F.2d 694, 707 n.68 (D.C. Cir. 1980). *See also* 5 U.S.C. § 552(a)(1) (providing requirements for publication of procedural rules), discussed *infra* Part III, ch. 7(C).

generally covered matters such as agency rules of practice governing the conduct of its proceedings and rules delegating authority or duties within an agency.

The exemption has generally been based on the distinction between "procedural" and "substantive" rules—a slippery distinction that is hard to apply.[97] For a while, the so-called substantial impact test had some currency. This test exempted from notice-and-comment requirements agency actions that did not themselves alter the rights or interests of parties, unless the agency action "trenches on substantial private rights and interests."[98] The substantial impact test has, however, lost much of its impact in the courts of appeals. Thus, for example, in *American Hospital Ass'n v. Bowen*,[99] the D.C. Circuit observed in 1987 that "[o]ver time our circuit in applying the § 553 exemption for procedural rules has gradually shifted the focus from asking whether a given procedure has a 'substantial impact' on parties to inquiring more broadly whether the agency action also encodes a substantive value judgment or puts a stamp of approval or disapproval on a given type of behavior."[100] According to the court, this "gradual move away from looking solely into the substantiality of the impact reflects a candid recognition that even unambiguously procedural measures affect parties to some degree."[101] After analyzing the case law on the procedural exemption,[102] the court ruled that the Department of Health & Human Services' (HHS) manual governing the procedures for medical peer review inspections in the Medicare program, which was designed to "establish a frequency and focus of PRO [peer review organization] review, urging its enforcement agents to concentrate their limited resources on particular areas where HHS evi-

---

97. Nat'l Motor Freight Traffic Ass'n, Inc. v. United States 268 F. Supp. 90, 96 (D.D.C. 1967) ("The characterizations 'substance' and 'procedural'—no more here than elsewhere in the law—do not guide inexorably to the right result, nor do they really advance the inquiry very far."), *aff'd*, 393 U.S. 18 (1968). However, see the offhand mention of this exemption in dicta by the Supreme Court in *Edelman v. Lynchburg College*, 535 U.S. 106, 114 n.7 (2002) (stating in a footnote that the EEOC was not required to use notice-and-comment procedures in adopting regulations concerning time limits for filing, amending, and verifying charges of discrimination even though Title VII of the Civil Rights Act requires the procedural regulations to "be in conformity with the standards and limitations" of the APA, because of the APA's exemption for "rules of agency organization, procedure, or practice").

98. *Batterton*, 648 F.2d at 708 ("The critical question is whether the agency action jeopardizes the rights and interest of parties.").

99. *See supra* note 59.

100. American Hosp. Ass'n v. Bowen, 834 F.2d 1037, 1047 (D.C. Cir. 1987) (citation omitted).

101. *Id.*

102. Among others, the court discussed the *Kast Metals* case, discussed *supra* text accompanying notes 9–12, where the Fifth Circuit held that the Department of Labor's program for selecting employers for workplace safety inspection was a procedural rule. 834 F.2d at 1147–48. The *Kast* court did so notwithstanding a particularly colorful expression of its view that courts are "not bound by an administrative agency's classification of its own action": "A paisley ribbon will not make up for damaged goods; the substance, not the label, is determinative." 744 F.2d at 1149.

dently believes PRO attention will prove most fruitful,"[103] was a procedural rule and therefore not covered by notice-and-comment requirements.[104]

In 1990, the D.C. Circuit overturned the Federal Aviation Administration's rules of practice for adjudicatory hearings in an administrative civil penalty program. In *Air Transport Ass'n v. DOT*,[105] the court held that the rules were not exempt from notice-and-comment requirements as procedural rules under section 553(b)(3)(A). The court, emphasizing the "housekeeping nature" of the exemption, stated that the distinction created by the exemption was not between substance and procedure, but between the "rights or interests of regulated parties" and "agencies' 'internal operations.'"[106] The court found that the rules "substantially affect . . . defendants' 'right to avail [themselves] of an administrative adjudication'" and that therefore notice and comment were required.[107]

With this decision, the D.C. Circuit appeared to suggest that an agency's decision to limit adjudicatory procedures in the interests of efficiency was in effect a substantive rule and was therefore subject to notice and comment.[108]

However, three years later, the D.C. Circuit revisited *Air Transport* with its decision in *JEM Broadcasting Co. v. FCC*.[109] This case involved a challenge of an FCC

---

103. 834 F.2d at 1050.
104. *Id.* at 1051. The court also ruled that another HHS manual and a program directive containing directions to peer review organizations were likewise procedural. *Id.* at 1051–52. *But see* Reeder v. FCC, 865 F.2d 1298 (D.C. Cir. 1989) (using the "encoding" test to find that FCC amendments to application procedures required notice and comment). On the other hand, the Ninth Circuit in *Southern California Edison Co. v. FERC*, 770 F.2d 779 (9th Cir. 1985) expressly rejected "the notion that procedural rules with a substantial impact are subject to the notice-and-comment requirements," upholding FERC rules pertaining to the procedural aspects of its approval of rates submitted by the Bonneville Power Administration. *Id.* at 783 (citing Rivera v. Becerra, 714 F.2d 887, 890–91 (9th Cir. 1983)). *Cf.* Am. Transfer & Storage Co. v. ICC, 719 F.2d 1283, 1285 (5th Cir. 1983).
105. 900 F.2d 369 (D.C. Cir. 1990), *remanded*, 498 U.S. 1077 (1991), *vacated as moot*, 933 F.2d 1043 (D.C. Cir. 1991).
106. *Id.* at 378 (citations omitted).
107. *Id.* (quoting *Nat'l Motor Freight Traffic Ass'n*, 268 F. Supp. at 96). The dissent argued that the substance/procedure dichotomy remains meaningful despite its difficulty of application and that the rules of practice did not "encode a substantive value judgment or put a stamp of approval or disapproval on a given type of behavior" and in no way affected primary behavior—in this case safety efforts of airlines. *Id.* at 383 (Silberman, J., dissenting) (quoting *American Hospital Ass'n*, 834 F.2d at 1047). *Cf.* S. Cal. Edison Co. v. FERC, 770 F.2d 779 (9th Cir. 1985) (holding similar rules governing procedural aspects of FERC rate approvals exempt from notice and comment); *see also* Chao v. Rothermel, 327 F.3d 223, 227 (3d Cir. 2003) (finding mine safety inspection guidelines to be within the procedural rule exemption because they "set forth procedures for the MSHA inspectors to follow in determining whether there is compliance with already existing mandatory health standards").
108. *See* Jeffrey S. Lubbers & Nancy G. Miller, *The APA Procedural Rule Exemption: Looking for a Way to Clear the Air*, 6 ADMIN. L.J. AM. U. 482 (1992), for a critique of the *Air Transport* case and the jurisprudence up to that point.
109. 22 F.3d 320 (D.C. Cir. 1994).

policy that required rejection of defective applications for FM radio licenses without an opportunity for correction. The FCC had denied JEM's application because it contained a typographical error that affected the coordinates of its planned broadcasting tower, causing inconsistencies in the application. The D.C. Circuit dismissed JEM's petition for review in part on the ground that the FCC's rulemaking was procedural rather than substantive, and thus not subject to the APA's notice-and-comment requirements. In so doing, the D.C. Circuit disavowed its earlier *Air Transport Association* ruling and held that procedural rules that do not change substantive standards are not subject to notice and comment.

In 2000, the D.C. Circuit held that a U.S. Department of Agriculture (USDA) rule eliminating expedited "face-to-face" meetings to approve commercial food labels was within the procedural exemption because the rule was clearly procedural in nature ("procedural on its face"), even though the elimination might have had a "substantial impact" on commercial food processors.[110] The court cited *JEM Broadcasting* in saying:

> This Court has stressed that the "critical feature" of a rule that satisfies the so-called "procedural exception 'is that it covers agency actions that do not themselves alter the rights or interests of parties, although it may alter the manner in which the parties present themselves or their viewpoints to the agency."[111]

It then concluded that:

> The agency's abolition of face-to-face [meetings] did not alter the substantive criteria by which it would approve or deny proposed labels; it simply changed the procedures it would follow in applying those substantive standards.[112]

Importantly, the court made clear that "an otherwise-procedural rule does not become a substantive one, for notice-and-comment purposes, simply because it imposes a burden on regulated parties."[113]

Two years later, the D.C. Circuit returned to the *American Hospital Ass'n* test in *Public Citizen v. Department of State*,[114] where it held that the Department's policy of processing Freedom of Information Act (FOIA) applications did not require notice and comment. The Department had issued an unpublished guidance document that provided that it would only search for documents generated prior to the date of the FOIA request, thus omitting any documents that may have been generated during the search. The court held that it fell within the APA exemption for procedural rules,

---

110. James V. Hurson Assoc. v. Glickman, 229 F.3d 277, 281 (D.C. Cir. 2000).
111. *Id.* at 280. It also cited *National Whistleblower Center v. Nuclear Regulatory Commission*, 208 F.3d 256, 262 (D.C. Cir. 2000). *Id.* at 280–82.
112. *Id.* at 281.
113. *Id.*
114. 276 F.3d 634 (D.C. Cir. 2002).

because the Department's policy applied to *all* FOIA requests equally and therefore did not encode a substantive value judgment—only a desire for the efficient processing of FOIA requests. This result seems somewhat dubious since it did affect requesters' substantive rights under the Freedom of Information Act.[115] In a recent case in which the Department of Homeland Security defended its policy requiring full-body scanners announced without public comment as a procedural rule, a Circuit panel eschewed this test and held that "the change substantively affects the public to a degree sufficient to implicate the policy interests animating notice-and-comment rulemaking."[116]

In a more recent district court case that went the other way,[117] the Department of Labor issued a declaration requiring its administrative law judges to use only initials in the captions of workers' compensation decisions adjudicated under the longshore and black lung laws. Plaintiffs who sought to obtain information from DOL regarding compensation adjudications and thus had an interest in knowing the names of claimants argued that the declaration constituted a substantive rule requiring notice-and-comment procedures. DOL asserted that the rule was merely procedural because it governed simple formatting of adjudicatory decisions, favoring the use of initials to protect claimants' privacy. The district court disagreed with DOL's argument based on the "substantive value judgment" approach to distinguishing between procedural and substantive rules. Here, the declaration "encodes a substantive value judgment" because the DOL declaration expressed the judgment that in all relevant adjudications, the privacy interests of the claimants trumped any public interest in obtaining information about the adjudications. As such, the declaration violated the notice-and-comment requirements of the APA. Obviously, the courts' tests in this area have not been very easy to apply, and agencies are running a risk when they attempt to avoid notice and comment.[118] Perhaps that is why, in 1992, ACUS urged agencies to use

---

115. As Professor Herz points out:

> The court treated the issue as straightforward. However, it is not so clear that this was a procedural rule; it directly affected what records had to be provided in response to a FOIA request. It was thus as "substantive" as a regulation going to the scope of any of the FOIA exemptions, or a rule about whether old records have to be retrieved from an off-site location; in this sense, it was indistinguishable from rules that are undeniably substantive and require notice and comment. This case illustrates the difficulty of defining the scope of the exception, notwithstanding its apparent simplicity.

Michael Herz, *Rulemaking Chapter*, DEVELOPMENTS IN ADMINISTRATIVE LAW AND REGULATORY PRACTICE 2001–2002, at 153 (Jeffrey S. Lubbers ed., 2003). The court, however, struck down the policy as arbitrary and capricious.
116. Elec. Privacy Info. Ctr. v. U.S. Dep't of Homeland Sec., 653 F.3d 1, 6 (D.C. Cir. 2011).
117. Nat'l Ass'n of Waterfront Emps. v. Solis, 665 F. Supp. 2d 10 (D.D.C. 2009).
118. *See* Chamber of Commerce v. U.S. Dep't of Labor, 174 F.3d 206, 211 (D.C. Cir. 1999) (quoting Batterton v. Marshall, 648 F.2d 694, 707 (D.C. Cir. 1980)) ("This distinction is often difficult to apply, as even a purely procedural rule can affect the substantive outcome of an agency proceeding. . . . Because of this difficulty, we apply § 553(b)(3)(A) with an eye toward balancing the

notice-and-comment procedures voluntarily for rules apparently falling within this exemption "except in situations in which the costs of such procedures will outweigh the benefits of having public input and information on the scope and impact of the rules, and of the enhanced public assistance of the rules that would derive from public comment."[119]

3. *Interpretive Rules and Policy Statements (also known as "Non-Legislative Rules")*

"Interpretive rules" and "general statements of policy" are also made exempt from notice-and-comment requirements by section 553(b)(A); moreover, under section 553(d)(2), they can be made effective immediately upon publication in the *Federal Register.*[120] They are, however, not exempt from section 553's petition provision or, generally, from section 552's requirements for publication or public availability,[121] nor are they exempted from the law requiring the submission of rules for congressional review.[122]

The function of the interpretive rule exemption is "to allow agencies to explain ambiguous terms in legislative enactments without having to undertake cumbersome proceedings."[123] The general policy statement exemption is designed "to allow agencies to announce their 'tentative intentions for the future' . . . without binding themselves."[124] There is general agreement that the public interest is served by prompt dissemination of the guidance contained in agency interpretations and policy state-

---

need for public participation in agency decisionmaking with the agency's competing interest in retain[ing] latitude in organizing [its] internal operations."). An easier case was presented by a challenge to an agency delegation of internal appellate authority to a particular office. This was deemed to be well within the procedural exemption. United States v. Gonzales & Gonzales Bonds and Ins. Agency, Inc., 728 F. Supp. 2d 1077 (N.D. Cal. 2010).

119. ACUS Recommendation 92-1, ¶ 2, *The Procedural and Practice Rule Exemption from the APA Notice-and-Comment Rulemaking Requirements*, 57 Fed. Reg. 30,102 (July 8, 1992). ACUS also offered the following test of its own: "A rule is within the terms of the exemption when it both (a) relates solely to agency methods of internal operations or of interacting with regulated parties, and (b) does not (i) significantly affect conduct, activity, or a substantive interest that is the subject of agency jurisdiction, or (ii) affect the standards for eligibility for a government program." *Id.* ¶ 3.

120. This *Guide* uses the term "interpretive" rule instead of the APA's more cumbersome "interpretative" rule.

121. 5 U.S.C. §§ 553(e), 552(a)(1)(D), 552(a)(2)(B). Note also that section 3(d) of Exec. Order 12,866 defines "regulation" to include agency statements "of general applicability and future effect, which the agency intends to have the force and effect of law, that is designed to implement, interpret, or prescribe law or policy or to describe the procedure or practice requirements of an agency . . . ." 58 Fed. Reg. 51,735 (Sept. 30, 1993).

122. *See infra* Part II, ch. 3(J).

123. *Am. Hosp. Ass'n, supra* note 59, at 1045.

124. *Id.* at 1046 (quoting Pac. Gas & Elec. Co. v. FPC, 506 F.2d 33, 38 (D.C. Cir. 1974)).

ments. Moreover, such statements often are indispensable to agency administration because they guide the staff in its day-to-day tasks and structure the exercise of agency discretion.[125] The exemptions for these agency pronouncements reflect the APA drafters' concern that public participation procedures would delay the issuance of interpretive rules or policy statements and could even discourage agencies from issuing them altogether.[126]

The distinctions between such "sub-regulatory"[127] "policy statements" and "interpretive rules," on the one hand, and "substantive" or "legislative" rules[128] requiring notice and comment, on the other, are articulated in the *Attorney General's Manual on the APA*, as follows:

- *Substantive rules*—rules, other than organizational or procedural . . . issued by an agency pursuant to statutory authority and which implement the statute. . . . Such rules have the force and effect of law.
- *Interpretative rules*—rules or statements issued by an agency to advise the public of the agency's construction of the statutes and rules which it administers.
- *General statements of policy*—statements issued by an agency to advise the public prospectively of the manner in which the agency proposes to exercise a discretionary power.[129]

The courts' difficulty in applying these distinctions in particular cases shows, however, that the theoretical distinctions between legislative rules and non-legislative rules (interpretive rules and policy statements) tend to break down and become confused in practice. In 1975, the Second Circuit, confronted with a procedural attack on an Immigration and Naturalization Service policy, remarked that the difference between a legislative rule and a general statement of policy is "enshrouded in considerable smog."[130] The metaphor has frequently been referred to by subsequent courts that have been called upon to distinguish between legislative rules and interpretive

---

125. For example, the Occupational Safety and Health Administration indicated in 2000 that it had issued 3,374 guidance documents since March 1996. *See* U.S. Congress, House Comm. on Gov' Reform, *Non-Binding Legal Effect of Agency Guidance Documents*, 106th Cong., 2d sess., H. Rep. 106-1009 (Washington: GPO, 2000), p.5.

126. *See* Michael Asimow, *Public Participation in the Adoption of Interpretive Rules and Policy Statements*, 75 Mich. L. Rev. 520, 530 (1977) [hereinafter Asimow, *Public Participation*].

127. *See* Richard D. Stoll, Effective EPA Advocacy—Advancing and Protecting Your Client's Interests in the Decision-Making Process 69–83, 131–46 (Oxford Univ. Press 2010) (discussing and strategizing about "sub-regulatory decisions").

128. The APA distinguishes "substantive rules" from other rules. Today the term "legislative rule" is often used in place of "substantive rule." "Substantive" is generally considered the converse of "procedural," yet interpretive rules and policy statements often relate to substance even though they are not "substantive rules" within the meaning of the APA.

129. Attorney General's Manual, *supra* note 4, at 30 n.3 (citations omitted).

130. Noel v. Chapman, 508 F.2d 1023, 1030 (2d Cir. 1975).

rules and policy statements.[131] Indeed, Professor Manning began his comprehensive article on this subject by stating: "Among the many complexities that trouble administrative law, few rank with that of sorting valid from invalid uses of so-called 'nonlegislative rules.'"[132] As he "crisply" puts the issue: "The central inquiry in all nonlegislative rule cases is this: Is the agency document, properly conceived, a legislative rule that is invalid because it did not undergo notice and comment procedures, or a proper interpretive rule or general statement of policy exempt from such procedures?"[133]

Part of the problem is related to the fact that legislative rules, interpretive rules, and policy statements all may involve interpretation of a statute. Therefore, sometimes an agency pronouncement can properly be characterized both as an interpretation and a policy statement.[134] Another problem is that agency actions sometimes do not neatly conform to any of these APA categories of pronouncements.[135]

Finally, it should be noted that the issue of how to categorize an agency statement—as a legislative or non-legislative rule—has important consequences for judicial review, especially with regard to questions of reviewability, timeliness, ripeness, finality, and the level of judicial deference given to such statements. These matters are discussed in detail in Part IV.

   a. *"Substantial impact"*—Dissatisfied with the theoretical distinctions between policy statements, interpretive rules, and legislative rules, some courts in the 1970s decided that the determinative factor for deciding if agencies could dispense with notice and comment in announcing policy or interpretations should be whether the agency pronouncement had a "substantial impact" on the rights or duties of the pub-

---

131. *See, e.g.*, Nat'l Leased Housing Ass'n v. United States, 105 F.3d 1423, 1433 n.13 (Fed. Cir. 1997) (citing *Noel* and describing the line separating those documents covered by the APA and those that are not as "fuzzy," "blurred," "enshrouded by smog," and "baffling"); Cmty. Nutrition Inst. v. Young, 818 F.2d 943, 946 (D.C. Cir. 1987). *See generally* Robert A. Anthony, *"Interpretive" Rules, "Legislative" Rules, and "Spurious" Rules: Lifting the Smog*, 8 Admin. L.J. Am. U. 1, 4 n.13 (1994). For an even pithier summary of his views, *see* Robert A. Anthony, *A Taxonomy of Federal Agency Rules*, 52 Admin. L. Rev. 1045 (2000).

132. John F. Manning, *Nonlegislative Rules*, 72 Geo. Wash. L. Rev. 893, 893 (2004).

133. *Id.* at 917. Professor Gersen described this as "crisply put" in Jacob E. Gersen, *Legislative Rules Revisited*, 74 U. Chi. L. Rev. 1705, 1708 (2007).

134. *See, e.g.*, Presbyterian Med. Ctr. of the Univ. of Pa. v. Shalala, 170 F.3d 1146 (D.C. Cir. 1999) (holding that a Departmental reimbursement guideline concerning how the agency will exercise its discretion in evaluating reimbursement petitions is an interpretive rule); Nat'l Latino Media Coal. v. FCC, 816 F.2d 785, 789 (D.C. Cir. 1987) (holding an FCC order authorizing the use of a tie-breaking lottery where competing applicants for certain licenses were equally qualified was properly labeled an interpretive rule).

135. *See, e.g.*, Cmty. Nutrition Inst. v. Young, *supra* note 131, at 948 (holding informal "action level" for level of aflatoxin in corn was not interpretive rule, policy statement, or "classic legislative rule"), discussed *infra* text accompanying notes 224–29.

lic.[136] As in the case of procedural rules, however, the substantial impact test has been abandoned as the sole criterion for deciding whether notice and comment are required for adoption of interpretive rules and policy statements. The D.C. Circuit explicitly rejected the substantial impact test as an independent basis for distinguishing interpretive and legislative rules in 1982 in *Cabais v. Egger.*[137] The Third Circuit has agreed, stating that "the substantial impact of a rule is relevant to its classification, however, such an impact will not, without more, compel a finding that a rule is legislative."[138] It explained that the "more basic determination, however, involves whether if by its action the agency intends to create new law, rights or duties."[139]

b. The agency's label—Another issue that has been addressed by courts is whether a reviewing court should, or must, accept a contemporaneous agency description of its action as an interpretive rule or policy statement. One commentator states that deference to the agency's description of its intention and desired legal effect of its pronouncement "is and should be of central importance in characterizing its product."[140] According to this view, deference to the agency's label promotes certainty and predictability.[141]

However, courts have shown little enthusiasm for this approach. For example, in *Chamber of Commerce v. OSHA,*[142] the D.C. Circuit rejected OSHA's characterization of its pronouncement as an interpretive rule, stating, "Divining agency intent is rarely a simple matter, for bureaucratic boilerplate often obscures the true purpose. The administrative agency's own label is indicative but not dispositive; we do not classify a rule as interpretive just because the agency says it is."[143]

---

136. *See, e.g.*, Pickus v. U.S. Bd. of Parole, 507 F.2d 1107, 1113–14 (D.C. Cir. 1974); Pharm. Mfrs. Ass'n v. Finch, 307 F. Supp. 858, 863 (D. Del. 1970).

137. 690 F.2d 234 (D.C. Cir. 1982). The court stated, however, that the substantial impact test may be one factor used to determine whether an agency action is a policy statement or exempt from notice-and-comment requirements for good cause. *Id.* at 237. *See also* Am. Postal Workers Union v. U.S. Postal Serv., 707 F.2d 548, 560 (D.C. Cir. 1983) (holding change in retirement benefit calculations for postal workers was interpretive despite substantial impact). Some courts still pay attention to the degree of impact on the parties challenging the policy. *See* Mocanu v. Mueller, 2008 WL 372459 (E.D. Pa. 2008) (concluding that USCIS policy to require name checks for all lawful permanent residents who want to become naturalized citizens, while undoubtedly well-intended, was a substantive change, "which is having a 'substantive adverse impact on [the Plaintiffs].'" In this case the judge enjoined the name checks as a factor in the decision making as to these plaintiffs unless, within 30 days, USCIS initiated a notice-and-comment procedure concerning their use.

138. Dia Nav. Co., Ltd. v. Pomeroy, 34 F.3d 1255, 1265 (3d Cir. 1994) (citations and internal quotation marks omitted).

139. *Id.* at 1264.

140. Michael Asimow, *Nonlegislative Rulemaking and Regulatory Reform*, 1985 Duke L.J. 381, 389–90 [hereinafter Asimow, *Nonlegislative Rulemaking*].

141. *Id.*

142. 636 F.2d 464 (D.C. Cir. 1980).

143. *Id.* at 468 (citations omitted).

A few years later, in *Brock v. Cathedral Bluffs Shale Oil Co.*,[144] the D.C. Circuit considered whether a Department of Labor enforcement policy guideline was a policy statement or a legislative rule. The court responded to the Secretary of Labor's characterization of its pronouncement as a policy statement by stating that "there is deference and there is deference—and the degree accorded to the agency on a point such as this is not overwhelming."[145]

Some reasons have been offered to explain courts' reluctance to defer to an agency's label of its action, including a concern that an agency might label an action an interpretive rule or policy statement to circumvent required notice and comment or to avoid pre-enforcement judicial review.[146] In fact, in *Appalachian Power Co. v. EPA*, the D.C. Circuit flatly rejected EPA's disclaimer that its action was intended solely as non-final, non-binding guidance, finding that the language was "boilerplate."[147]

c. Distinguishing between interpretive rules and legislative rules—Courts have frequently struggled to distinguish between interpretive rules and legislative rules. Judge Wald observed in *American Hospital Ass'n v. Bowen*[148] that distinguishing between interpretive and legislative rules is an "extraordinarily case-specific endeavor" and that "analogizing to prior cases is often of limited utility in light of the exceptional degree to which decisions in this doctrinal area turn on their precise facts."[149]

---

144. 796 F.2d 533 (D.C. Cir. 1986).
145. *Id.* at 537. *See also Cmty. Nutrition Inst., supra* note 131, at 946 ("[C]ourts are to give far greater weight to the language actually used by the agency."); Gen. Motors Corp. v. Ruckelshaus, 742 F.2d 1561, 1565 (D.C. Cir. 1984) (en banc) ("[T]he agency's own label, while relevant, is not dispositive."); Wiggins v. Wise, 951 F. Supp. 614, 619 (S.D. W. Va. 2001) (agency's labeling of a rule as "interpretive" is not determinative and courts may look to other indicators to determine the type of rule). The court found a Bureau of Prisons Program Statement—identified as "interpretive" by the agency—to be a legislative rule when the rule contradicted an already existing regulation and used an existing statutory definition in the Program Statement, thereby importing the case law surrounding that definition. *Id.* at 619. *See also* cases cited *supra* notes 13–16.
146. *See* Asimow, *Nonlegislative Rulemaking, supra* note 140, at 390.
147. 208 F.3d 1015, 1023 (D.C. Cir. 2000) (finding EPA guidance broadened an underlying EPA rule and constituted "marching orders" to the states, thus was improperly issued without notice and comment). *But see* Cement Kiln Recycling Coal. v. EPA, 493 F.3d 207, 228 (D.C. Cir. 2007). The court rejected the claim that the "earlier version [of the guidance docment at issue] contained the language of command" and that "EPA issued the current version after we issued *Appalachian Power*, . . . expressly stat[ing] that it had edited the document's language in response to that decision." The court explained: "But we can hardly fault EPA for responding to an opinion of this court." For a more benign general view as to the utility of guidance documents, see Michael Asimow, *Guidance Documents in the States: Toward a Safe Harbor*, 54 ADMIN. L. REV. 631 (2002).
148. 834 F.2d 1037 (D.C. Cir. 1987).
149. *Id.* at 1045.

(i) *The "legal effect" test.* In a case, from the 1950s, the D.C. Circuit articulated the following test for distinguishing between interpretive and legislative rules:

> Generally speaking, it seems to be established that "regulations," "substantive rules" or "legislative rules" are those which create law, usually implementary to an existing law; whereas interpretative rules are statements as to what the administrative officer thinks the statute or regulation means.[150]

This distinction has come to be referred to as the "legal effect" test. If a rule explaining a statute makes new law, as opposed to merely interpreting existing law or reminding parties of duties under existing law, then the rule is legislative.[151] Rules have been found to make "new law," and thus to be legislative, where they fill a statutory gap by imposing a standard of conduct, create an exemption from a general standard of conduct, establish a new regulatory structure, or otherwise complete an incomplete statutory design.[152]

Agencies need statutorily delegated authority to adopt legislative rules. This authority may be either specifically delegated[153] or derived from a general grant of rulemaking authority.[154] Legislative rules issued under a statutory delegation that have followed section 553 procedures and survived judicial review are later given controlling weight by reviewing courts.[155]

On the other hand, agencies may issue *interpretive* rules without a delegation of rulemaking authority and without following notice-and-comment procedure. Such interpretive rules do not have the "force of law"; that is, their reasonableness is subject to challenge in court when an agency seeks to apply them in an enforcement proceeding. Moreover, in most situations, courts will not give statutory interpretations made in interpretive rules the same degree of deference they give to those made in legislative rules.[156]

---

150. Gibson Wine Co. v. Snyder, 194 F.2d 329, 331 (D.C. Cir. 1952). This statement recognizes that interpretive rules can interpret previously adopted agency rules as well as statutes. *See also* Asimow, *Public Participation, supra* note 126, at 543.

151. *See* Cabais v. Egger, 690 F.2d 234, 239 (D.C. Cir. 1982); Chamber of Commerce v. OSHA, *supra* note 142, at 466–71; Citizens to Save Spencer County v. EPA, 600 F.2d 844, 877–79 (D.C. Cir. 1979).

152. *See* Asimow, *Nonlegislative Rulemaking, supra* note 140, at 394.

153. *See, e.g.,* Batterton v. Francis, 432 U.S. 416, 425–26 (1977).

154. *See, e.g.,* Chrysler Corp. v. Brown, 441 U.S. 281 (1979); Nat'l Petroleum Refiners Ass'n v. FTC, 482 F.2d 672 (D.C. Cir. 1973), *cert. denied,* 415 U.S. 951 (1974). *But see infra* Part II, ch. 2(A)(2) (discussing controversy over delegations of rulemaking authority).

155. *See* Chevron U.S.A. v. Natural Res. Def. Council, 467 U.S. 837, 844 (1984). *See also* Robert A. Anthony, *Which Agency Interpretations Should Bind Citizens and Courts?,* 7 YALE J. ON REG. 1, 44–46 (1990) (discussing *Chevron* deference standard) [hereinafter Anthony, *Agency Interpretations*].

156. *See* Christensen v. Harris Cnty., 529 U.S. 576 (2000) and United States v. Mead Corp., 533 U.S. 218 (2000), discussed *infra* Part IV, ch. 2(A)(4)(d). For most interpretive rules, both cases adopt the level of deference expressed in *Skidmore v. Swift & Co.,* 323 U.S. 134, 140 (1944), which

Application of the legal effect test is illustrated by *General Motors Corp. v. Ruckelshaus*,[157] in which the D.C. Circuit offered "general principles" in defining the difference between interpretations and legislative rules.[158] An interpretive rule, the court said, simply states what the agency thinks the statute means and "only 'reminds' affected parties of existing duties," but with a legislative rule, "the agency intends to create new law, rights or duties."[159] Applying these principles, the court found that EPA's rule on the repair of recalled vehicles was interpretive because the agency so regarded it, EPA's "entire justification" for the rule consisted of "reasoned statutory interpretations," and, most important, the rule "simply restated" the agency's "consistent practice" in conducting recalls under the statute.[160]

(ii) *The "binding norm" test.* Some court decisions have drawn on the "binding norm" language of the D.C. Circuit's 1974 *Pacific Gas & Electric Co. v. Federal Power Commission* decision[161] (involving the similar exemption for "general statements of policy," discussed in the next section) to distinguish interpretive rules from legislative rules. In so doing, however, these decisions do not clearly distinguish or discuss the various ways agency pronouncements can be binding. First, agency pronouncements may have the intent or effect of binding lower-level agency personnel in implementing laws or regulations.[162] Second, agency pronouncements may have

---

states, "We consider that the rulings, interpretations, and opinions of the Administrator under this Act, while not controlling upon the courts by reason of their authority, do constitute a body of experience and informed judgment to which courts and litigants may properly resort for guidance." *See also Nat'l Latino Media Coalition, supra* note 134, at 788 ("[A]n interpretative rule does not have the force of law and is not binding on anyone, including the courts, though the status conferred on an agency as the delegate of Congress and by its expertise often leads courts to defer to the agency's interpretation of its governing statute."). Courts have considered numerous factors in determining how much weight to give to informal interpretations of statutes, including the consistency and duration of the interpretation and the agency's expertise in the matter. *See* Anthony, *Agency Interpretations, supra* note 155, at 13–14 & nn.49–52.

157. 742 F.2d 1561 (D.C. Cir. 1984) (en banc).
158. *Id.* at 1565 (recognizing that the labels agencies put on rules are an important factor but not dispositive).
159. *Id. See also* Chamber of Commerce v. OSHA, *supra* note 142, at 469.
160. 742 F.2d at 1565–66. The principles stated in *General Motors* were followed in *Metropolitan School District of Wayne Township v. Davila*, 969 F.2d 485 (7th Cir. 1992). There, the Seventh Circuit held that even though an agency's interpretation of a statute had a substantial impact, the rule was interpretive rather than legislative and therefore not subject to notice-and-comment procedures. Other courts have relied on the *General Motors* reasoning as well. *See, e.g.,* Jerri's Ceramic Arts, Inc. v. Consumer Prod. Safety Comm'n, 874 F.2d 205, 208 (4th Cir. 1989); Arrow Air, Inc. v. Dole, 784 F.2d 1118, 1122–25 (D.C. Cir. 1986).
161. 506 F.2d 33 (D.C. Cir. 1974).
162. Indeed, Professor Strauss emphasizes that in many situations, regulated parties or the public benefit by having agency staff behavior regularized by interpretations and guidance documents. Peter L. Strauss, *The Rulemaking Continuum*, 41 Duke L.J. 1463 (1992). He finds support

the intent or effect of binding members of the public who are subject to the laws or regulations.[163] Finally, in the case of a validly promulgated legislative rule having the force of law, the agency itself is bound by its terms until it formally amends the rule.

Although it is quite clear that agency policy statements are not supposed to be treated as binding on the public, the analysis is not so simple for interpretive rules. An agency issuing an interpretive rule (that is, an interpretation that merely reminds parties of existing law or interprets a statute without creating new rights and duties) may well intend that its interpretation bind its own personnel and may expect compliance from regulated individuals or entities. Nonetheless, the agency cannot expect the interpretation to be binding in court; because it does not have the force of law, parties can challenge the interpretation. Nor is the agency leadership "bound" by the interpretation, because (except in some cases where a party has relied on a long-standing interpretation, see section iv, below) it can change its interpretation without following notice-and-comment procedures.[164]

---

in the APA for what he calls "publication rules" in § 552(a), which allows such rules to "be relied upon, used, or cited as precedent, if they have been properly published." *Id.* at 1486. Professor Strauss further states:

> [I]t does not follow that the agency or its staff are free to disregard validly adopted publication rules on which a private party may have relied *absent* the demonstration of its inappropriateness. The whole point of the exercise is to structure discretion, to provide warning and context for efficient interaction between the agency and the affected public. This is the plain implication of the rationale for such rules—and, for that matter, the negative pregnant of section 552(a)(2), forbidding the citation of publication rules "against a party other than an agency" unless they have been properly published and indexed.

Id. (emphasis in original). For a judicial affirmation of this view, see *Warder v. Shalala*, 149 F.3d 73 (1st Cir. 1998) ("Of course, a rule with the force and effect of law—binding not only the agency and regulated parties, but also the courts—is by definition a substantive rule. However, a rule may lack this force and still bind agency personnel. Accordingly, '[a]n interpretative rule binds an agency's employees, including its ALJs, but it does not bind the agency itself.'") (citing Davis & Pierce, Administrative Law Treatise, *supra* note 30, § 6.3 at 104 (3d ed. 1994 & Supp. 1997)). *See also* NHTSA's Interpretations Files, available in searchable form *at* http://isearch.nhtsa.gov/. The notice linked to this database states that these opinions by the agency chief counsel "represent the definitive view of the agency on the questions addressed and may be relied upon by the regulated industry and members of the public."

163. This, of course, can cause problems if agencies attempt to or, in effect, bind the public through policy statements without notice and comment. *See* Robert Anthony, *Interpretive Rules, Policy Statements, Guidances, Manuals, and the Like: Should Agencies Use Them to Bind the Public?*, 41 Duke L.J. 1311 (1992) [hereinafter Anthony, *Interpretive Rules*].

164. *See* Flagstaff Med. Ctr., Inc. v. Sullivan, 962 F.2d 879 (9th Cir. 1992) ("[Interpretive rules] are used more for discretionary fine-tuning than for general law making."). The *Flagstaff* court was persuaded by the fact that the shift in enforcement approach was discretionary. *Id.* A new interpretation that turns out to be a major modification, however, might look more like a legislative rule to a reviewing court. *See, e.g.*, Nat'l Family Planning & Reproductive Health Ass'n v.

A case applying the "binding norm" test to distinguish interpretive and legislative rules is *Bellarno Int'l v. Food and Drug Administration.*[165] There the district court reviewed a challenge to a Food and Drug Administration (FDA) import alert, which the FDA maintained was exempt from notice and comment as an interpretive rule or a policy statement.[166] The import alert had the effect of changing the requirements for readmission to the United States of goods originally produced in the United States. The court, also relying on earlier cases interpreting the policy statement exemption, sought to determine whether the FDA import alert was binding on the FDA and the parties. Finding that it was, the court held the action to be invalid for failure to comply with the APA's notice-and-comment requirements.[167]

Cases like this suggest that courts often will look at the practical effect of an agency's pronouncement, rather than theoretical distinctions, to decide whether that pronouncement is an invalidly promulgated legislative rule or a proper interpretive rule.[168] They

---

Sullivan, 979 F.2d 227 (D.C. Cir. 1992). *National Family Planning* involved HHS's new interpretation of its own regulations in response to a presidential directive. The old regulation was a "gag" rule that prevented a woman from receiving medical and abortion information directly from a physician. The new administration's interpretation did not prevent this, and the court held the rule to be legislative. *Cf.* Vietnam Veterans of Am. v. Sec'y of the Navy, 843 F.2d 528, 536–37 (D.C. Cir. 1988) (discussing whether maxim requiring agencies to adhere to their own rules extends to interpretive rules or policy statements).

165. 678 F. Supp. 410 (E.D.N.Y. 1988).
166. *Id.* at 412.
167. *Id.* at 412–16. In July 1990, citing *Bellarno* and other cases, the FDA published a proposed rule rescinding a previously adopted policy that required the agency to follow notice-and-comment procedure when adopting interpretive rules and rules of practice and procedure. Proposed Amendment to 21 C.F.R. § 10.40(d), 55 Fed. Reg. 31,080 (1990). The FDA stated that "it is not feasible for the agency to follow informal rulemaking procedures for all agency pronouncements that a court might find to be interpretative rules or rules of agency practice and procedure." *Id.* The proposal was finalized on April 4, 1991. 56 Fed. Reg. 13,757 (1991). The agency rejected a comment urging the addition of a provision allowing post-promulgation comments. *Id.* at 13,758.
168. *See, e.g.,* Theiss v. Principi, 18 Vet. App. 204 (2004) (holding a change in the definition of educational institution to exclude home-school programs, in opposition to dictionary definition, was invalidly issued without notice and comment); Citizens Awareness Network, Inc. v. NRC, 59 F.3d 284 (1st Cir. 1995) (finding agency interpretation changed policy and was irrational); Malone v. Bureau of Indian Affairs, 38 F.3d 284 (9th Cir. 1994) (finding interpretation articulated "new standard" and foreclosed other options); *Nat'l Family Planning, supra* note 164, at 229 (finding interpretation was "nonobvious and unanticipated reading" of regulation and contradicted prior Supreme Court construction); State of Alaska v. DOT, 868 F.2d 441, 447 (D.C. Cir. 1989) (finding DOT interpretation constituted legislative rule and required notice-and-comment rulemaking because of "mandatory language"). *But see* N.Y. State Elec. & Gas Corp. v. Saranac Power Partners, L.P., 267 F.3d 128, 131–32 (2d Cir. 2001) (agency's reiteration of its "general policy" is "interpretive" rule for the purposes of the APA requirement for notice-and-comment rulemaking); New York City Employees' Retirement Sys. v. SEC, 45 F.3d 7 (2d Cir. 1995) (holding "no-action" letter valid as interpretive despite "sea change" in agency's former policy); Beazer East, Inc. v. EPA, Region III, 963 F.2d 603, 610 (3d Cir. 1992) ("This is

may not accept an agency's characterization of its pronouncement or its disclaimer of the "force of law" effect of the pronouncement. If the pronouncement in fact creates new rights or duties and is binding as a practical matter on those affected, then reviewing courts may well require compliance with notice-and-comment procedures.[169]

Another important but harder to categorize decision is that of Judge Williams in *American Mining Congress v. Mine Safety & Health Administration,*[170] holding that Department of Labor policy letters delineating what type of x-rays' readings qualify for diagnosis of lung disease were interpretive rules. Although the opinion speaks, somewhat confusingly, of using the "legal effect" test, it then goes on to set forth a test composed of four criteria for determining whether a rule is legislative or interpretive. If any one criterion is met, the agency action is a legislative rule subject to the notice-and-comment procedures. The test asks: (1) whether in the absence of the rule there would not be an adequate legislative basis for enforcement action or other agency action to confer benefits or ensure the performance of duties, (2) whether the agency has published the rule in the Code of Federal Regulations, (3) whether the agency has explicitly invoked its general legislative authority, or (4) whether the rule effectively amends a prior legislative rule.[171] I believe the most salient criterion is number (1). The D.C.

---

not a situation where the agency inconsistently interpreted a standard over time or changed its interpretation. . . . Rather, the EPA is making a reasonable attempt to fill the interstices of a complex regulatory scheme by giving meaning to regulatory language entirely within its authority to define."); First Nat'l Bank of Lexington v. Sanders, 946 F.2d 1185 (6th Cir. 1991) (holding Small Business Administration's guideline applying frozen interest rate on defaulted loans not subject to notice-and-comment procedures); Arizona v. Shalala, 121 F. Supp. 2d 40, 50–51 (D.D.C. 2000) (HHS "action transmittal" applying existing government-wide cost allocation principles to the Temporary Assistance for Needy Families (TANF) program was an interpretive rule because it "simply interpret[ed] existing obligations in light of the newly enacted TANF program" and created no new laws or obligations).

169. For an attempt by Congress to grapple with the concept of "binding obligations" in the context of a rulemaking in a major grant program, see a provision buried in the 2005 transportation funding legislation, which provides that the Federal Transit Administration "shall follow applicable rulemaking procedures under section 553" before issuing "a statement that imposes a binding obligation on recipients of Federal assistance." Pub. L. No. 109-59, 119 Stat. 1626, 1627, § 3032 (codified at 49 U.S.C. § 5334(*l*)).

170. 995 F.2d 1106 (D.C. Cir. 1993). *See* Anthony, *Agency Interpretations, supra* note 155, at 15–22. The Ninth Circuit applied the *American Mining Congress* test in *Hemp Industries Ass'n v. DEA,* and invalidated a DEA purported interpretive rule banning the sale of consumable products containing hemp ingredients as an invalidly promulgated legislative rule. 333 F.3d 1082, 1088 (9th Cir. 2003). It stated the test: "[I]f there is no legislative basis for enforcement action on third parties without the rule, then the rule necessarily creates new rights and imposes new obligations. This makes it legislative." *Id. See also* Erringer v. Thompson, 371 F.3d 625 (9th Cir. 2004) (finding a Medicare program manual to be a properly issued interpretive rule because the statutory language provided a sufficient basis for enforcement in the absence of the manual).

171. *Id.* at 1112. *See* Steinhorst Assocs. v. Preston, 572 F. Supp. 2d 112 (D.D.C. 2008) (relying on the *American Mining Congress* test and finding a HUD change in the procedures by which it reviews housing project contracts was not an interpretive rule and was wrongly promulgated without notice and comment).

Circuit has itself subsequently limited its reliance on criterion (2). In *Health Insurance Ass'n of America, Inc. v. Shalala*, it stated that it has not "taken publication in the Code of Federal Regulations, or its absence, as anything more than a snippet of evidence of agency intent," and held that in the case before it "the snippet is not enough."[172]

(iii) *The modern test: Is the rule truly interpretive or does it effect substantive change?* More recent decisions have taken the more literal view, related to criteria (1) and (4) in the *American Mining* test, above, that the test for invoking the interpretive rule exemption is whether the pronouncement really interprets existing legislation (or a pre-existing valid legislative rule). *Shalala v. Guernsey Memorial Hospital*[173] illustrates this approach. The issue in the case was whether HHS's Medicare program was required to reimburse hospitals for losses incurred in refinancing debt in the year the transaction occurs or whether it could "amortize" the losses over a period of years. Generally accepted accounting principles required the former, but HHS adopted a guideline (without notice and comment) requiring amortization. The guideline purported to be an interpretation of HHS regulations adopted under a statute authorizing the secretary to "establish the methods to be used for determining reasonable cost. . . ." The regulations were silent as to the time of reimbursement. The Supreme Court upheld the procedural shortcut, saying, "We can agree that APA rulemaking would still be required if [the guideline] adopted a new position inconsistent with any of the Secretary's existing regulations . . . . [It] does not . . . 'effect a substantive change in the regulations.'"[174] The D.C. Circuit has also pithily stated, "Whereas a clarification may be embodied in an interpretive rule that is exempt from notice-and-comment requirements, new rules that work substantive changes in prior regulations are subject to the APA's procedures."[175]

---

172. 23 F.3d 412, 423 (D.C. Cir. 1994).

173. 514 U.S. 87 (1995).

174. *Id.* at 100 (citation omitted). The four dissenting Justices felt that the guideline did not simply explain existing law, but that its application "contradicted the agency's own regulations." *Id.* at 114 (O'Connor, J., dissenting). The closeness of this question is also shown by the fact that the district court had also initially sustained the secretary's position and the court of appeals reversed. The Sixth Circuit relied heavily on *Guernsey* in *St. Francis Health Care Center v. Shalala*, 205 F.3d 937, 947 (6th Cir. 2000). More recently, the Eleventh Circuit prominently cited *Guernsey* in *Warshauer v. Solis*, 577 F.3d 1330 (11th Cir. 2009), in which the court upheld as an interpretive rule a DOL interpretation, made on a website's "frequently asked questions" page. The answer stated that certain private lawyers recommended to union members were covered by a statutory provision requiring "employers" to file reports disclosing payments made to labor unions. The court said that this guidance was exempt from notice and comment as an interpretive rule because (1) it is relevant that the Secretary characterizes the rule as interpreting the statute; (2) the Secretary's interpretation is drawn directly from the plain language of the statute; and (3) the rule only reminded affected parties of existing duties required by the plain language of the statute. It did not create any new law, right, duty, or have any effect independent of the statute. *Id.* at 1337–38 (citations and quotation marks omitted).

175. Sprint Corp. v. FCC, 315 F.3d 369, 374 (D.C. Cir. 2003) (citations omitted).

Chief Judge Richard Posner of the Court of Appeals for the Seventh Circuit followed this approach in an instructive case involving a quantitative standard. In *Hoctor v. U.S. Department of Agriculture*,[176] the USDA had previously issued a valid legislative regulation after notice and comment, pursuant to the Animal Welfare Act, requiring that structures used for housing wild animals be of sufficient strength and sturdiness for their own protection and containment. The Department subsequently issued an internal memorandum setting a minimum height requirement for perimeter fencing of eight feet. Hoctor, a dealer in wild animals, had built a containment fence and a six-foot perimeter fence and was cited for a violation. The court, per Judge Posner, held that the memorandum that purported to interpret the regulation was legislative rather than interpretive, and therefore was invalid for lack of notice-and-comment procedure. He reasoned that because the change in application of the rule contained a fixed and inflexible numerical component, the agency could not maintain that the new requirement was derived from the underlying statute or regulation. He did, however, leave the door open for agencies to develop nonbinding "rules of thumb" without notice and comment (though for present purposes such issuances are perhaps better classified as policy statements).

In some ways the *Hoctor* case is a blend of two approaches to identifying interpretive rules because Judge Posner not only states the principle that a rule can be an interpretive rule "only if it can be derived from the [earlier law] by a process reasonably described as interpretation,"[177] but he also bases his decision on the "self-contained, unbending, arbitrary" nature of the new rule.[178] Later, in an article, Judge Posner articulated this view more expansively:

> For a rule to be interpretive it is not enough, I believe, that the rule is consistent with the purpose of the statute that it is interpreting; for that is equally true of any valid legislative rule. A valid interpretive rule must in addition be derivable from the statute that it implements by a process fairly to be described as interpretive; that is, there must be a path that runs from the statute to the

---

176. 82 F.3d 165 (7th Cir. 1996). For some interesting background and commentary on this case, see Jacob E. Gersen, *Legislative Rules Revisited*, 74 U. CHI. L. REV. 1705 (2007) (exploring "the legislative rule conundrum through the lens" of Judge Posner's opinion in *Hoctor*).

177. *Id.* at 170. This is basically Professor Anthony's test: "To 'interpret,' as used here, is to derive a proposition from an existing document whose meaning compels or logically justifies the proposition. The substance of the derived proposition must flow fairly from the substance of the existing document." Anthony, *Agency Interpretations*, *supra* note 155, at 6 n.21; *see also* Paralyzed Veterans of Am. v. D.C. Arena L.P., 117 F.3d 579, 588, n.6 (D.C. Cir. 1997) ("[T]he distinction between an interpretative rule and substantive rule . . . likely turns on how tightly the agency's interpretation is drawn linguistically from the actual language of the statute."); Syncor Int'l Corp. v. Shalala, 127 F.3d 90, 95 (D.C. Cir. 1997) (finding that FDA's "guidance" "is not an interpretative rule [because] it does not purport to construe any language in a relevant statute or regulation; it does not interpret anything"); *Wiggins*, *supra* note 145, at 619 (holding Bureau of Prisons Program Statement to be invalid because it was not interpretive).

178. 82 F.3d at 171.

rule, rather than merely consistency between statute and rule.[179]

There is, of course, a risk that this sort of leeway given to agencies to interpret existing language without notice and comment might be too great in the case of very general or vague statutory terms. Professor Anthony addresses this:

> If the relevant language of the existing document consists of vague or vacuous terms—such as "fair and equitable," "just and reasonable," "in the public interest," and the like—the process of announcing propositions that specify applications of those terms is not ordinarily one of interpretation, because those terms in themselves do not supply substance from which the propositions can be derived. The conclusion might be different if the term as enacted has been accompanied by a detailed prior practice, or by a clear legislative history or established usage or the like, to supply substance by which the derived proposition can be justified.[180]

This could also be a problem if the agency is interpreting a vague or vacuous term in a legislative rule. The D.C. Circuit in *Caruso v. Blockbuster-Sony Music Entertainment Centre at the Waterfront* addressed this by stating that an agency cannot "promulgate mush and then give it concrete form only through subsequent less formal 'interpretations.'"[181]

---

179. Richard A. Posner, *The Rise and Fall of Administrative Law*, 72 Chi.-Kent L. Rev. 953, 962 (1997), *as quoted in* Mission Group Kan., Inc. v. Riley, 146 F.3d 775, 883 n.8 (10th Cir. 1998). For an example of the D.C. Circuit's application of this approach, see two related cases decided the same day that reach different results on the question of whether FCC actions were interpretive or legislative rules: *compare* U.S. Telecomm. Ass'n v. FCC, 400 F.3d 29, 30 (D.C. Cir. 2005) ("We conclude that the order is a legislative rule because it constitutes a substantive change in a prior rule.") *with* Cent. Tex. Tel. Co-op., Inc. v. FCC, 402 F.3d 205, 213 (D.C. Cir. 2005) ("We believe the [Order] is fairly characterized as an interpretive rule" and that it "sensibly conforms to the purpose and wording" of [an earlier legislative rule]). In the latter case, Judge Randolph provided a summary of the distinction:

> To fall within [the] category [of interpretive rule], the rule must be interpreting something. It must "derive a proposition from an existing document whose meaning compels or logically justifies the proposition. The substance of the derived proposition must flow fairly from the substance of the existing document." Robert A. Anthony, *"Interpretive" Rules, "Legislative" Rules, and "Spurious" Rules: Lifting the Smog*, 8 Admin. L. J. 1, 6 n. 21 (1994). If, despite an agency's claim, a rule cannot fairly be viewed as interpreting—even incorrectly—a statute or a regulation, the rule is not an interpretive rule exempt from notice-and-comment rulemaking. *E.g., Syncor Int'l Corp. v. Shalala*, 127 F.3d 90, 95 (D.C. Cir. 1997); *Hoctor v. U.S. Dep't of Agric.*, 82 F.3d 165 (7th Cir. 1996); *see* Henry J. Friendly, Benchmarks 144–45 (1967).

180. Anthony, *Agency Interpretations*, *supra* note 155, at 6 n.21. *See also Paralyzed Veterans*, *supra* note 177, at 588.

181. 174 F.3d 166, 174 (3d Cir. 1999) (quoting *Paralyzed Veterans*, 117 F.3d at 584). *See also* Elec. Privacy Info. Ctr. v. U.S. Dep't of Homeland Sec., 653 F.3d 1, 7 (D.C. Cir. 2011) ("[T]he purpose of the APA would be disserved if an agency with a broad statutory command (here, to detect

On the other hand, the agency would not be issuing an interpretive rule without a need to add *some* meaning or gloss to the underlying requirements. As the D.C. Circuit has noted, the agency cannot be said to be amending its earlier rule "merely because it supplies crisper and more detailed lines than the authority being interpreted. If that were so, no rule could pass as an interpretation of a legislative rule unless it were confined to parroting the rule or replacing the original vagueness with another."[182] Two recent cases with opposite results illustrate the need for the agency to show that the purported interpretive rule can be derived from a shared understanding of the underlying statue or regulation. In *Catholic Health Initiatives v Sibelius*,[183] the D.C. Circuit rejected an argument that a Medicare reimbursement manual provision that construed the statutory term "reasonable cost," to require different reimbursement allotments for healthcare providers controlled by offshore companies, an interpretation given "great weight" by the departmental adjudicatory board, could qualify as an interpretive rule. After quoting the language used by Professor Anthony in footnote 182, below, as well as Judge Posner's reasoning in *Hoctor*, the court said, "The short of the matter is that there is no way an interpretation of 'reasonable costs' can produce the sort of detailed-and rigid-investment code set forth in [the manual]."[184]

On the other hand, the Ninth Circuit in *Mora-Meraz v. Thomas*[185] upheld a numerical ("twelve months") requirement derived from a general statutory term. Under the statute at issue in this case, a federal prisoner is eligible for a drug rehabilitation program if he is "determined by the Bureau of Prisons to have a substance abuse problem."[186] The Bureau issued a regulation further requiring that the inmate "must have a verifiable documented drug abuse problem."[187] The Bureau later interpreted this phrase in a program manual as requiring that, to be eligible, "the inmate must show substance dependence or abuse within his last twelve months 'on the street.'"[188]

---

weapons) could avoid notice-and-comment rulemaking simply by promulgating a comparably broad regulation (here, requiring passengers to clear a checkpoint) and then invoking its power to interpret that statute and regulation in binding the public to a strict and specific set of obligations.").

182. Am. Mining Cong. v. MSHA, 995 F.2d 1106, 1112 (D.C. Cir. 1993). For another example (which also contains a useful summary of Seventh Circuit precedent), *see* Novelty, Inc. v. Tandy, 2008 WL 3835655 *16 (S.D. Ind. 2008) ("The tighter enforcement policy set forth in the [agency] letters reflects, in the court's judgment, simply a tighter interpretation of broad existing regulations. DEA was not required to allow any exceptions to those regulations. Its decision to allow some exceptions and to explain them to the regulated industry was not a legislative action subject to the notice-and-comment procedures of the APA.").

183. 617 F.3d 490 (D.C. Cir. 2010). *See also* Natural Res. Def. Council v. EPA. 643 F.3d 311, 321 (D.C. Cir. 2011) ("nothing in the statute, prior regulations, or case law authorizes" the policy EPA set forth in its guidance memo. "Accordingly, the Guidance qualifies as a legislative rule that EPA had no authority to issue without notice and comment.").

184. *Id.* at 496.

185. 601 F.3d 933 (9th Cir. 2010).

186. 18 U.S.C. § 3621(e)(5)(B).

187. 28 C.F.R. § 550.56(a) (2008).

188. 601 F.3d at 937.

The court upheld this as an interpretive rule because the 12-month rule was based on a provision in the *Diagnostic and Statistical Manual of Mental Disorders*, to which the program manual referred.

In his commentary on these two cases, Professor Jordan said that the context of each interpretation was crucial. In *Catholic Health Initiatives* there was "no well recognized understanding that 'reasonable costs' included only charges by companies meeting the various investment restrictions," but in *Mera-Moraz*, the scientific community "had a shared understanding that the meaning of the statutory or regulatory term included particular numerical provisions."[189]

(iv) *Can an agency change a prior interpretive rule without notice and comment?* In a line of cases beginning with *Paralyzed Veterans of America v. D.C. Arena L.P.*,[190] the D.C. Circuit has circumscribed the ability of agencies to significantly modify prior interpretations of their regulations without using notice-and-comment rulemaking— especially if such interpretations are of long standing and have been relied upon. In *Paralyzed Veterans*, the court baldly stated: "Once an agency gives its regulation an interpretation, it can only change that interpretation as it would formally modify the regulation itself: through the process of notice and comment rulemaking." This dictum was not dispositive in that case because the court found that the agency had "never authoritatively adopted a position contrary to its manual interpretation."[191] The dictum was cited in *Caruso v. Blockbuster-Sony Music Entertainment Centre at the Waterfront* in a slightly more expansive way.[192] The *Caruso* court stated that an agency is not free "to make a fundamental change in its interpretation of a substantive regulation without notice and comment rulemaking."[193]

As Professor Seidenfeld remarked, this represented a rather dramatic change to previous understandings of administrative law:

> The traditional view of agency interpretative discretion holds that an agency is free to change an interpretation that is not itself incorporated into a legislative rule either by a subsequent adjudication or a subsequent interpretive rule. This is consistent with the understanding that interpretive rules have no legally binding effect (except on employees of the agency as a matter of agency administration); having no such effect, the agency need not follow them. The

---

189. William S. Jordan, *News from the Circuits*, 36 Admin. & Reg. L. News 22 (Winter 2011). He also pointed to the *American Mining Congress* case, *supra* note 182, as another example of a shared scientific understanding that recognized a "specific x-ray reading as an interpretation of 'diagnosis'"). *Id.*

190. 117 F.3d 579 (D.C. Cir. 1997). *See* Richard J. Pierce, Jr., *Distinguishing Legislative Rules from Interpretive Rules*, 52 Admin. L. Rev. 547 (2000) (praising the approach taken in *American Mining Congress*—*see* note 182, *supra*—and criticizing *Paralyzed Veterans*).

191. *Id.* at 587.

192. 174 F.3d 166 (3d Cir. 1999).

193. *Id.* at 175 (quoting *Paralyzed Veterans*, 117 F.3d at 586).

only limitation on this discretion comes from the arbitrary and capricious standard of review, which requires the agency to explain its change in position. Hence, traditionally, as long as the new interpretation is a reasonable construction of the underlying regulation, and its adoption is adequately justified by the agency, the agency may adopt the new interpretation. *Caruso* and *Paralyzed Veterans* both suggest a very different understanding—that agencies may not use interpretive rules to adopt new constructions of regulations that are fundamentally at odds with prior constructions.[194]

Shortly thereafter, in *Alaska Professional Hunters Ass'n v. FAA*,[195] the D.C. Circuit squarely held that, in the circumstances presented, the agency was precluded from reversing a prior interpretation of a regulation through issuance of another interpretive rule without notice and comment. In a 1963 decision, the Federal Aviation Administration (FAA) had held that its commercial air operations regulations did not apply to hunting and fishing guides who transport patrons in planes if the guides did not charge separately for the air transportation. Since that decision, the Alaska Region of the FAA had consistently exempted such guides from having to comply with the commercial regulations. Prompted by safety concerns, and following five years of studying this issue, the FAA issued a "notice" informing the Alaska guides that the agency had changed its interpretation of its regulations to require the guides to comply with the commercial air service regulations. When this notice was challenged, the court quoted *Paralyzed Veterans*: "Once an agency gives its regulation an interpretation, it can only change that interpretation as it would formally modify the regulation itself: through the process of notice and comment rulemaking."[196] The court emphasized that those regulated by administrative agencies are entitled to know the rules of the game. Asserting that the guide pilots and Alaska lodge operators had relied on the Alaska Region's consistent interpretation, the court invalidated the FAA's reinterpretation for failure to provide notice and comment.

Although the *Alaska Hunters* approach has been roundly criticized by commentators,[197] the Fifth Circuit has agreed with it: "We agree with the reasoning of the D.C.

---

194. Mark Seidenfeld, *Rulemaking Chapter*, DEVELOPMENTS IN ADMINISTRATIVE LAW AND REGULATORY PRACTICE 1998-1999, at 112 (Jeffrey S. Lubbers ed., 2000).
195. 177 F.3d 1030 (D.C. Cir. 1999).
196. 177 F.3d at 1033–34.
197. *See, e.g.*, William S. Jordan III, *News from the Circuits*, 29 ADMIN. & REG. L. NEWS 19, 20 (Fall 2003) (calling this case and its progeny a "virus that . . . continues to mutate doctrinally and expand geographically"); Jon Connolly, Note, Alaska Hunters *and the D.C. Circuit: A Defense of Flexible Interpretive Rulemaking*, 101 COLUM. L. REV. 155 (2001); Peter L. Strauss, *Publication Rules in the Rulemaking Spectrum: Assuring Proper Respect for an Essential Element*, 53 ADMIN. L. REV. 803, 844–47 (2001); Richard J. Pierce, Jr., *Distinguishing Legislative Rules from Interpretive Rules*, 52 ADMIN. L. REV. 547 (2000); Michael Asimow & Robert A. Anthony, *A Second Opinion? Inconsistent Interpretive Rules*, 25 ADMIN. & REG. L. NEWS 16 (Winter 2000) (these decisions "disrespect the [APA's] exemption for interpretative rules"); William Funk, *A Primer on Legislative Rules,* 53 Admin. L. Rev. 1321, 1329–30 (2001) (it violates *Vermont*

Circuit; the APA requires an agency to provide an opportunity for notice and comment before substantially altering a well-established regulatory interpretation."[198] The D.C. Circuit also reaffirmed the decision in 2003 in *CropLife America v. EPA.*[199] In *CropLife*, the court struck down an EPA directive, announced in a press release, that it would no longer rely on or consider third-party human studies, pending review of ethical issues by the National Academy of Sciences. In ruling on an industry challenge to this directive, the court characterized it as a "binding regulation that is directly aimed at and enforceable against petitioners"[200] that required notice and comment. It ordered EPA to continue to consider such studies on a case-by-case ba-

---

Yankee). But it also has its defenders: *see* Richard W. Murphy, Hunters *for Administrative Common Law*, 58 ADMIN. L. REV. 917, 923 (2006) (its reasoning is flawed, but "it may serve some sort of legal and normative values worth enshrining in law"); Ryan DeMotte, Note, *Interpretive Rulemaking and the* Alaska Hunters *Doctrine: A Necessary Limitation on Agency Discretion*, 66 U. PITT. L. REV. 357 (2004). One commentator has argued that the Supreme Court decision in *FCC v. Fox Television Stations, Inc.*, 556 U.S. 502 (2009), discussed *infra* in Part IV, ch. 2(A)(2)(c), has sub silentio overruled *Alaska Hunters*. Brian J. Shearer, Note: Out*Foxing* Alaska Hunters: *How "Arbitrary and Capricious" Review of Changing Regulatory Interpretations Can More Efficiently Restrain Agency Discretion*, 62 AM. U.L. REV. (forthcoming October, 2012).

198. Shell Offshore Inc. v. Babbitt, 238 F.3d 622, 629 (5th Cir. 2001). The Sixth Circuit also announced that it would follow *Alaska Hunters* in cases where agencies modified their previous interpretations of their own regulations, but it did not require notice-and-comment rulemaking when the Office of Legal Counsel modified its previous interpretation of a *statute*. Dismas Charities, Inc. v. U.S. Dep't of Justice, 401 F.3d 666, 682 (6th Cir. 2005). The Third and Eighth Circuits have alluded to the doctrine but without applying it; *see* Minnesota v. CMS, 495 F.3d 991, 996–97 (8th Cir. 2007), SBC Inc. v. FCC, 414 F.3d 486, 498 (3d Cir. 2005). On the other hand the First and Ninth Circuits have not accepted it; *see* Warder v. Shalala, 149 F.3d 73, 81-82 (1st Cir. 1998), and Erringer v. Thompson, 371 F.3d 625, 632 (9th Cir. 2004) ("[N]o notice and comment rulemaking is required to amend a previous interpretive rule" (emphasis omitted)). As the Tenth Circuit noted, "Notably, neither *Warder* nor *Erringer* explicitly analyzes, or even discusses, *Paralyzed Veterans* or *Alaska Professional Hunters*." United States v. Magnesium Corp. of America, 616 F.3d 1129, 1139 n.9 (10th Cir. 2010). Indeed, the Eleventh Circuit, while refraining from taking a position, has counted the First, Second, Fourth, Sixth, Seventh, and Ninth Circuits as agreeing "that changes in interpretations do not require notice and comment because both the original and current positions constitute interpretive rules." *See* Warshauer v. Solis, 577 F.3d 1330, 1338 (11th Cir. 2009).

199. 329 F.3d 876 (D.C. Cir. 2003).

200. *Id.* at 881. Professor Herz criticized this decision as "adopting a strikingly broad understanding of which regulations are 'binding' and 'enforceable' and therefore legislative." Michael Herz, *Rulemaking* chapter, DEVELOPMENTS IN ADMINISTRATIVE LAW AND REGULATORY PRACTICE 2002-2003, at 136 (Jeffrey S. Lubbers ed., 2004). He suggested that the agency's new approach "was a moratorium, pending further investigation and consultation, on a practice that the agency had come to see as highly problematic. Requiring the agency to conduct a notice-and-comment rulemaking before adopting such a policy denies the agency important flexibility." *Id.* He also criticized the court for failing to analyze whether the rule was a procedural rule. *Id.* at 136–37.

sis. Also, in *Iynegar v. Barnhart,*[201] the court rejected an attempt by the government to limit *Alaska Hunters* to situations where the agency has changed its interpretation as a result of a policy change implemented by a new presidential administration.

This line of cases has apparently had a significant effect on party behavior. As two litigators wrote in 2004:

> Cases such as *Appalachian Power and CropLife* have had at least two significant consequences. First, they are emboldening aggressive parties and their counsel to seek judicial relief more frequently whenever there is an agency letter, memorandum, or guidance document they believe may adversely affect them. . . .
>
> Second, and perhaps more troubling, these cases are forcing cautious parties and their counsel to file petitions for judicial review with increasing frequency in situations that *might* be deemed to present a "rule in disguise" when the statute in question specifies deadlines for seeking judicial review of new rules.[202]

But *Alaska Hunters'* importance may be on the wane. The case and its progeny, while clearly making it more difficult for an agency to change its mind, do require the court to find that the agency's interpretation is well established. In *Air Transport Ass'n of America v. FAA,*[203] the D.C. Circuit upheld an FAA interpretation of its regulations governing rest periods for commercial pilots. The regulations were promulgated pursuant to notice-and-comment rulemaking, but the challenged interpretation was set out in a letter responding to an inquiry from a pilot. Among other arguments, the airlines invoked the *Alaska Hunters* principle that a significant change to a settled interpretation is a de facto modification of the underlying rule and requires notice and comment. The court found that there was no firmly settled prior interpretation with which the letter conflicted and, accordingly, no change that would trigger notice-and-comment requirements.[204]

---

201. 233 F. Supp. 2d 5 (D.D.C. 2002) (holding a Social Security Administration reversal of longstanding policy in manual governing issuance of Social Security numbers to non-citizens for the purpose of obtaining a drivers license invalid for failure to follow notice-and-comment procedures).

202. Richard G. Stoll & Katherine M. Lazarski, *Rulemaking* chapter, DEVELOPMENTS IN ADMINISTRATIVE LAW AND REGULATORY PRACTICE 2003-2004, at 147 (Jeffrey S. Lubbers ed., 2005). For a case going the other way, *see* Amoco Prod. Co. v. Watson, 410 F.3d 722, 732 (D.C. Cir. 2005) (letter to gas producers concerning royalty rates that purportedly changed prior policy was not an improperly promulgated legislative rule because signer of letter did not have authority to announce binding rules and because the letter was a common "workaday letter").

203. 291 F.3d 49 (D.C. Cir. 2002).

204. *See also* Ass'n of Am. R.R. v. DOT, 198 F.3d 944, 949 (D.C. Cir. 1999) (finding it "quite clear that the [agency] never adopted a definitive interpretation"). In another case, the D.C. Circuit similarly skirted the *Alaska Hunters* problem by finding that the supposedly contradictory new interpretation merely reflected an earlier clear decision. *See* Darrell Andrews Trucking, Inc. v. Fed. Motor Carrier Safety Admin., 296 F.3d 1120, 1125–30 (D.C. Cir. 2002).

The court must also find some *reliance* on the settled interpretation by the challenging party.[205] Moreover, the interpretation must be an authoritative one. In *Devon Energy Corp. v. Kempthorne*,[206] the D.C. Circuit rejected arguments by a regulated company that the company had relied on interpretive memos by agency officers concerning royalty payment that had then been reversed by another official seven years later when it asked for confirmation that the earlier policy was still in effect. The court rejected the contention that *Alaska Hunters* required the new memorandum to be issued after notice and comment, saying that the earlier memos did not represent policy authoritatively adopted by the agency because they lacked finality in that they were issued by officials who lacked the power to bind the agency.[207] Even more importantly, the court went out of its way to distinguish *Alaska Hunters* "because the disputed agency advice in that case had been upheld in a formal adjudication by the Civil Aeronautics Board, FAA's predecessor agency."[208] This appears to significantly narrow the scope of *Alaska Hunters*.

Shortly thereafter Judge Randolph, the author of *Alaska Hunters*, provided some limits of his own in *MetWest Inc. v. Secretary of Labor*.[209] He declined to hold that an

---

205. *See Ass'n of Am. R.R.*, 198 F.3d at 950 (finding that nothing in the record "suggests that railroads relied on the [supposed prior interpretation] in any [way] comparable [to the hunters in *Alaska Hunters*]").

206. 551 F.3d 1030 (D.C. Cir. 2008). In *United States v. Magnesium Corp. of America*, 616 F.3d 1129, 1141–43 (10th Cir. 2010), the Tenth Circuit, citing *Devon Energy*, also found that EPA had not made a "definitive" interpretation of its earlier ambiguous regulation when it issued a report to Congress and took some other actions that petitioners claimed EPA was now deviating from. The opinion of Judge Gorsuch in this case is a very thoughtful recapitulation of the issues surrounding *Alaska Hunters*, although the court stops short of deciding whether to approve or disapprove of the decision. Similarly, in *LG Electronics U.S.A., Inc. v. U.S. Dep't of Energy*, 679 F. Supp. 2d 18 (D.D.C. 2010), the court rejected a company's argument that the agency's agreement to allow the company to use a certain testing procedure had constituted a definitive interpretation of the underlying regulation, which could not be changed without notice and comment. The court construed the agency's action as allowing an exception to the regulation, rather than constituting an interpretation. Moreover, it found the previous interpretation was not "settled" because the agency's agreement as to the testing procedure had been "*subject to further notice by DOE.*" *Id.* at 28 (emphasis in original). *But see* Montefiore Med. Ctr. v. Leavitt, 578 F. Supp. 2d 129 (D.D.C. 2008) (overturning decision based on a Provider Reimbursement Manual provision that represented a substantial departure from a longstanding interpretation and which therefore should have been subject to notice-and-comment rulemaking, citing *Alaska Hunters*). *See also* an apparently unappealed district court decision in 2008 granting an injunction on the claim that EPA changed its interpretation of its regulations governing the Toxics Release Inventory without notice and comment, citing *Alaska Hunters*. The letters interpreting the regulation were "authoritative" because they appeared in an official agency publication informing regulated entities of the scope of their reporting obligations. Creosote Council v. Johnson, 555 F. Supp. 2d 36 (D.D.C. 2008).

207. *Devon Energy*, 511 F.3d at 1040–41

208. *Id.* at 1041.

209. 560 F.3d 506 (D.C. Cir 2009).

OSHA guidance document and enforcement policy for regulation, governing removal of needles from equipment used to extract blood, effectively amended a previous interpretation of a regulation without notice and comment, as claimed by an employer that received citation for violating the regulation. In so doing, he emphasized that "[a] fundamental rationale of *Alaska Professional Hunters* was the affected parties' substantial and justifiable reliance on a well-established agency interpretation."[210] He took pains to distinguish the high degree of reliance and dislocation that was present in *Alaska Hunters*:

> People in the lower 48 states had pulled up stakes and moved to Alaska. They and others within Alaska had opened hunting and fishing "lodges and built up businesses dependent on aircraft, believing their flights were [not] subject to" certain commercial flight regulations. Forcing guide pilots to comply with regulations developed for commercial airlines would have driven Alaska's hunting and fishing tourism operations out of business. Furthermore, during this 30-year span, the "guide pilots and lodge operators had no opportunity to participate in the development of the . . . regulations" that the FAA had abruptly decided to apply to them. As a result, they were deprived of any opportunity to request changes or exceptions to accommodate the unique circumstances of Alaskan air travel.[211]

These developments may help mollify the critics of *Alaska Hunters* by significantly paring back its scope.

d. Distinguishing between legislative rules and policy statements—Making the distinction between policy statements and legislative rules may be somewhat easier than distinguishing interpretive rules from legislative rules. Policy statements are issued by an agency to advise the public prospectively of the manner in which the agency proposes to exercise a discretionary power in subsequent adjudications or through rulemaking. Often policy statements are issued to guide agency personnel in administering laws, and sometimes they are addressed to the public.[212] "They come with a variety of labels and include guidances, guidelines, manuals, staff instructions, opinion letters, press releases or other informal captions."[213]

---

210. *Id.* at 511. He drove the point home in a footnote, saying "This is a crucial part of the analysis. To ignore it is to misunderstand *Alaska Professional Hunters* to mean that an agency's initial interpretation, once informally adopted, freezes the state of agency law, which cannot subsequently be altered without notice-and-comment rulemaking." *Id.* at 511 n.4 (quoting Strauss, *supra* note 197, at 844 and citing Funk, *supra* note 197, at 1329–30 and Murphy, *supra* note 197, at 921–23).

211. 560 F.3d at 511 (footnotes and citations omitted).

212. *See* Asimow, *Nonlegislative Rulemaking, supra* note 140, at 386–88 (discussing types and uses of policy statements).

213. ACUS Recommendation 92-2, *Agency Policy Statements*, 57 Fed. Reg. 30,103 (July 8, 1992) [hereinafter ACUS Recommendation 92-2].

Perhaps the most concise and clear statement of the attributes of general policy statements was provided in *Pacific Gas & Electric Co. v. Federal Power Commission*,[214] where the court stated:

> A general statement of policy . . . does not establish a "binding norm." It is not finally determinative of the issues or rights to which it is addressed. The agency cannot apply or rely upon a general statement of policy as law because a general statement of policy only announces what the agency seeks to establish as policy.[215]

The D.C. Circuit elaborated upon this test in *American Bus Ass'n v. United States*,[216] stating that a policy statement "genuinely leaves the agency and its decisionmakers free to exercise discretion."[217] The court applied these principles in *Brock v. Cathedral Bluffs Shale Oil Co.*,[218] addressing the question whether certain mine safety enforcement guidelines were "binding norms" to which the Secretary of Labor was required to adhere. In determining that they were policy statements rather than legislative rules, the court focused on the discretion the Secretary retained to apply or not apply the guidelines in particular cases. While stating that the Secretary's characterization of its statement was entitled to some weight, the language used in the statement (for example, use of words of suggestion, such as *may,* rather than inflexible, command words) was far more important.[219] The court concluded that because the guidelines preserved the Secretary's enforcement discretion, they were therefore not "a binding, substantive regulation."[220]

Similarly, in *Mada-Luna v. Fitzpatrick*,[221] the Ninth Circuit expanded upon the policy statement/legislative rule distinction in finding that INS's operating instructions were exempt from notice-and-comment requirements. The court stated that "[t]o the extent that the directive merely provides *guidance* to agency officials in exercising their discretionary powers while preserving their flexibility and their opportunity to make 'individualized determinations,' it constitutes a general statement of policy."[222] In contrast, the court said, a rule is legislative "to the extent that [it] narrowly limits administrative discretion or establishes a *'binding norm'* that 'so fills out the statutory scheme that upon application one need only determine whether a given case is within the rule's criterion.'"[223]

---

214. 506 F.2d 33 (D.C. Cir. 1974).
215. *Id.* at 38 (footnote omitted).
216. 627 F.2d 525 (D.C. Cir. 1980).
217. *Id.* at 529.
218. 796 F.2d 533 (D.C. Cir. 1986).
219. *Id.* at 537–38.
220. *Id.* at 538.
221. 813 F.2d 1006 (9th Cir. 1987).
222. *Id.* at 1013 (citations omitted).
223. *Id.* at 1013–14 (quoting Jean v. Nelson, 711 F.2d 1455, 1481 (11th Cir. 1983) and Guardian Fed. Savings & Loan Ass'n v. Fed. Savings & Loan Ins. Corp., 589 F.2d 658, 666–67 (D.C. Cir. 1978)).

Another example of judicial application of this distinction is the D.C. Circuit's decision in *Community Nutrition Institute v. Young*.[224] *Community Nutrition* involved a challenge to the FDA's decision to allow the marketing of corn containing aflatoxin (a naturally occurring carcinogen) at levels not exceeding 100 parts per billion. The FDA's decision was an exception to a previously established general "action level" of 20 parts per billion. Both the exception and the general action level were adopted under general statutory authority, without notice and comment, and in lieu of establishing tolerance levels under a specific statute requiring use of an elaborate process resembling formal rulemaking.[225]

The Community Nutrition Institute contended in its petition for review that the FDA's action level was a legislative rule and, thus, invalid because FDA failed to follow notice-and-comment procedures.[226] The FDA, however, argued that action levels "represent nothing more than nonbinding statements of agency enforcement policy."[227] The court concluded that the action level was an invalidly promulgated legislative rule, not a policy statement, because the language used by the FDA "suggests that those levels both have a present effect and are binding"[228]—a conclusion supported by the fact that FDA considered it necessary to publish an exception to the aflatoxin action level and by other agency statements.[229]

The flip side of *Community Nutrition* was presented in an unusual Eighth Circuit case, *South Dakota v. Ubbelohde*,[230] where the Army Corps of Engineers had issued a "Master Manual" concerning the water flow of the Missouri River as a policy statement (albeit after some public comment called for by agency regulations). After a drought had led several states to seek or obtain district court injunctions against Corps

---

224. 818 F.2d 943 (D.C. Cir. 1987).
225. *See* Young v. Cmty. Nutrition Inst., 476 U.S. 974 (1986) (upholding an FDA decision to proceed by action levels instead of tolerances and discussing differences between two procedures).
226. 818 F.2d at 945.
227. *Id.* at 946.
228. *Id.* at 947. *See also* McLouth Steel Prods. Corp. v. Thomas, 838 F.2d 1317 (D.C. Cir. 1988) (holding EPA use of a pollution modeling formula issued without notice and comment in ruling on applications "created a norm with 'present day binding effect,'" but allowing the agency to continue using it on condition that it treat it as nonbinding in the future).
229. 818 F.2d at 947–48. Judge Starr dissented, arguing that the determinative factor distinguishing legislative rules from policy statements is "whether the pronouncement has the force of law in subsequent proceedings." *Id.* at 950. Because the FDA disclaimed such effect, he concluded that it could not be a legislative rule. *Id.* at 952. For some critical commentary on Judge Starr's dissent, see David L. Franklin, *Legislative Rules, Nonlegislative Rules, and the Perils of the Short Cut*, 120 YALE L. J. 276, 291–92 (2010). *See also* Syncor Int'l Corp. v. Shalala, *supra* note 177, at 94 (commenting on *Community Nutrition* and stating that "[t]he primary distinction between a substantive rule . . . and a general statement of policy . . . turns on whether an agency intends to bind itself to a particular legal position").
230. 330 F.3d 1014 (8th Cir. 2003), *cert. denied sub nom.*, North Dakota v. Ubbelohde, 541 U.S. 987 (2004).

plans to reduce reservoir levels, the Corps had appealed, arguing that its activities were committed to agency discretion and therefore not reviewable at all. The Eighth Circuit looked to the Manual and determined that there was "law to apply" based on it. This is unexceptionable, but the court then further held that because the Manual used mandatory language and was issued after public comment, it was effectively a legislative rule and was binding on the agency—and the court upheld an injunction sought by the state of Nebraska enforcing the Manual's terms, despite the agency's protest that it was simply a statement of policy. As Professor Jordan has written:

> [D]isputes about the status of a policy statement typically involve arguments that they are invalid for failure to pursue notice and comment. Ironically, in this case the court seems to have accepted the argument that the Manual is effectively a substantive rule and to have enforced the Manual at the behest of Nebraska despite the fact that the Manual was not subjected to [APA] notice and comment.[231]

The agency's practice in applying the policy can be crucial. In an instructive case, the D.C. Circuit examined a policy statement issued by the FCC that provided a fee schedule for monetary forfeitures.[232] Although the FCC repeatedly stated that the statement was not intended to be binding, the court disagreed on the grounds that the framework it provided for the fines was too explicit to allow for discretionary application. The court also noted that, in practice, the FCC had departed from the fee schedule in only eight of 300 cases. In finding that the fee schedule should have been promulgated in accordance with the APA's notice-and-comment provisions, the court also showed its reluctance to defer to the agency's own label of its action.[233]

Nor a does a degree of voluntariness in following the policy necessarily immunize the agency policy statement from notice and comment. In *Chamber of Commerce of the U.S. v. Department of Labor*,[234] OSHA had issued a directive stating that employers in certain industries that participated in a "cooperative compliance program" would have a significantly reduced risk of being subject to an inspection. This cooperative program included some requirements that "exceed[ed] those required by

---

231. William S. Jordan III, *News from the Circuits*, 29 ADMIN. & REG. L. NEWS 19, 21 (Fall 2003).

232. U.S. Tel. Ass'n v. FCC, 28 F.3d 1232 (D.C. Cir. 1994).

233. *But see* Profls. and Patients for Customized Care v. Shalala, 56 F.3d 592, 600 (5th Cir. 1995) (holding that FDA did not treat compliance policy guide as binding in practice, nor did the guide so narrowly constrict the agency's enforcement discretion that it should be deemed to be a substantive rule), and White v. Nicholson, 541 F. Supp. 2d 87, 92–93 (D.D.C. 2008) *vacated on jurisdictional grounds*, 329 Fed. App. 285 (D.C. Cir. 2009) (claim of "one-hundred percent conformance" to the Program Guide not proven, especially since plaintiffs "have not submitted a single decision in which the Board cites or directly refers to" the Guide). *See also* discussion *supra* subsec. (D)(3)(b).

234. 174 F.3d 206 (D.C. Cir. 1999).

law."[235] When challenged by the Chamber, the D.C. Circuit concluded that the directive imposed a "binding norm" because "OSHA admits in its brief that the inspection plan 'leave[s] no room for discretionary choices by inspectors in the field.'"[236] On the other hand, the presence of real discretion points the other way. A straightforward example of this is found in an opinion upholding a Mine Safety and Health Administration policy letter as exempt from notice and comment. The Eleventh Circuit noted that "[B]y its terms, the [letter] . . . addresses the general procedures district managers are to consider when evaluating a discretionary extended cut plan. The agency, through district managers, is therefore 'free to consider the individual facts' when evaluating each specific mine."[237]

In 1992, the Administrative Conference's Recommendation 92-2 summarized the appropriate approach to agency issuance of guidance documents. The Conference recognized the beneficial nature of such policy statements but was concerned "about situations where agencies issue policy statements which they treat or which are reasonably regarded by the public as binding and dispositive of the issues they address."[238]

The main points of the recommendation follow.

1. Agencies should not attempt to bind affected persons through policy statements.

2. When an agency publishes a legislative rule (for example, in the *Federal Register*), the agency should state in the preamble that it is a legislative rule intended to bind affected persons.

3. Policy statements of general applicability should make clear that they are not binding, and agencies should communicate that fact to all agency officials who might apply them.

4. Agencies that issue policy statements should ensure that their procedures allow for an appropriate and effective opportunity to challenge the legality or wisdom of the document and to suggest alternative approaches.

5. When agency policy statements are subject to repeated challenges, agencies should consider initiating legislative rulemaking proceedings on the policy.

6. Agencies should be encouraged to provide guidance to staff in the interest of administrative uniformity or public coherence, provided the staff is advised

---

235. *Id.* at 208. This approach to regulation has been called "administrative arm-twisting." *See* Lars Noah, *Administrative Arm-Twisting in the Shadow of Congressional Delegations of Authority*, 997 WIS. L. REV. 873. *See also* Randolph J. May, *Ruling Without Real Rules—Or How to Influence Private Conduct Without Really Binding*, 53 ADMIN. L. REV. 1303 (2001).

236. *Id.* at 213. This outcome was criticized by Professor Seidenfeld, who argued that the court's expansion of the "binding norm" to rules "backed only by an agency's threat of increased inspection" seems to bar OSHA from exercising the same sort of discretion in a policy statement that it could have exercised through prosecutorial discretion. *See* Seidenfeld, *supra* note 194, at 114–16.

237. Nat'l Mining Ass'n v. Sec'y of Labor, 589 F.3d 1368, 1372 (11th Cir. 2009).

238. ACUS Recommendation 92-2, *supra* note 213.

that such guidance should not be deemed determinative of the public's rights or obligations.

7. Agencies should take care to observe the requirements of 5 U.S.C. § 552(a), which imposes a publication requirement independent of any obligation to employ notice-and-comment procedures.

The D.C. Circuit has reaffirmed this approach to policy statements, finding that an EPA "guidance document" concerning permissible risk assessment techniques for disposal of certain harmful chemicals was a legislative rule, not a statement of policy, and was thus subject to notice-and-comment requirements. In so doing it relied heavily on Professor Robert Anthony's writings:[239]

> Our cases . . . make clear that an agency pronouncement will be considered binding as a practical matter if it either appears on its face to be binding, *Appalachian Power*, 208 F.3d at 1023 ('[T]he entire Guidance, from beginning to end . . . reads like a ukase. It commands, it requires, it orders, it dictates.'), or is applied by the agency in a way that indicates it is binding, *McLouth*, 838 F.2d at 1321.

As Professor Robert A. Anthony cogently comments, the mandatory language of a document alone can be sufficient to render it binding:

> A document will have practical binding effect before it is actually applied if the affected private parties are reasonably led to believe that failure to conform will bring adverse consequences, such as . . . denial of an application. If the document is couched in mandatory language, or in terms indicating that it will be regularly applied, a binding intent is strongly evidenced. In some circumstances, if the language of the document is such that private parties can rely on it as a norm or safe harbor by which to shape their actions, it can be binding as a practical matter.
>
> On the other hand, courts do find that "rebuttable presumptions leave an agency free to exercise its discretion and may therefore properly be announced in policy statements."[240]

---

239. Gen. Elec. Co. v. EPA, 290 F.3d 377, 382–83 (D.C. Cir. 2002) (quoting Anthony, *Interpretive Rules*, *supra* note 163, at 1328–29). *See* note 147, *supra*, for more on *Appalachian Power*.

240. Alliance for Bio-Integrity v. Shalala, 116 F. Supp. 2d 166, 172–73 (D.D.C. 2000) (citing Panhandle Producers v. Econ. Regulatory Admin., 822 F.2d 1105, 1110 (D.C. Cir. 1987)). *See also* Hudson v. FAA, 192 F.3d 1031, 1035 (D.C. Cir. 1999) (FAA policy statement need not go through notice and comment, because "the statement does not cabin agency discretion"); Mada-Luna v. Fitzpatrick, 813 F.2d 1006, 1013 (9th Cir. 1987)); Ryder Truck Lines, Inc. v. United States, 716 F.2d 1369, 1377 (11th Cir. 1983); Broadgate, Inc., v. USCIS, 730 F. Supp. 2d 240, 246 (D.D.C. 2010) (USCIS policy memorandum outlining factors that the agency uses to determine whether an employer's job qualifies under the temporary, skilled worker (H-1B) program does not constitute a legislative rule because it "does not bind USCIS adjudicators" nor does it "amend the [existing] Regulation by repudiating or being irreconcilable with it.").

Finally, it should be noted that Congress and the Office of Management and Budget have shown interest in the issue of how guidance is promulgated. In the Food and Drug Modernization Act of 1997,[241] Congress mandated that the FDA develop a comprehensive regulation on "good guidance practices," containing extensive guidance for the public on how to assess and participate in the development of agency guidance.[242] In January 2007, after receiving public comment, OMB issued a government-wide "Bulletin on Good Guidance Practices" that borrows heavily from the FDA approach.[243] The bulletin requires:

- Approval of significant guidance documents by senior agency officials;
- Standard elements for significant guidance documents, such as identifying the issuing office and who is affected, as well as avoiding unwarranted binding language;

---

241. Pub. L. No. 105-115 § 405, codified at 21 U.S.C. § 371(h).
242. The provision requires the following:
   (1)(A) The Secretary shall develop guidance documents with public participation and ensure that information identifying the existence of such documents and the documents themselves are made available to the public both in written form and, as feasible, through electronic means. Such documents shall not create or confer any rights for or on any person, although they present the views of the Secretary on matters under the jurisdiction of the Food and Drug Administration.
   (B) Although guidance documents shall not be binding on the Secretary, the Secretary shall ensure that employees of the Food and Drug Administration do not deviate from such guidances without appropriate justification and supervisory concurrence. The Secretary shall provide training to employees in how to develop and use guidance documents and shall monitor the development and issuance of such documents.
   (C) For guidance documents that set forth initial interpretations of a statute or regulation, changes in interpretation or policy that are of more than a minor nature, complex scientific issues, or highly controversial issues, the Secretary shall ensure public participation prior to implementation of guidance documents, unless the Secretary determines that such prior public participation is not feasible or appropriate. In such cases, the Secretary shall provide for public comment upon implementation and take such comment into account.
   (D) For guidance documents that set forth existing practices or minor changes in policy, the Secretary shall provide for public comment upon implementation.
   (2) In developing guidance documents, the Secretary shall ensure uniform nomenclature for such documents and uniform internal procedures for approval of such documents. The Secretary shall ensure that guidance documents and revisions of such documents are properly dated and indicate the nonbinding nature of the documents. The Secretary shall periodically review all guidance documents and, where appropriate, revise such documents.
   (3) The Secretary, acting through the Commissioner, shall maintain electronically and update and publish periodically in the Federal Register a list of guidance documents. All such documents shall be made available to the public.
   (4) The Secretary shall ensure that an effective appeals mechanism is in place to address complaints that the Food and Drug Administration is not developing and using guidance documents in accordance with this subsection.
243. Issued January 18, 2007, 72 Fed. Reg. 3432 (Jan. 25, 2007).

- Transparency, including disclosure to the public of significant guidance documents and a comprehensive list of agencies' significant guidance documents;
- Procedures allowing the public to request the creation or modification of significant guidance documents; and
- A presumption for notice and comment for economically significant guidance documents that could lead to a $100 million impact on the economy.[244]

President Bush II then amended E.O. 12,866 to, among other things, require that executive agencies submit significant guidance documents to OMB for review before issuance.[245] President Obama rescinded all of the Bush amendments and reinstated the original Clinton Order;[246] however, the OMB Good Guidance Bulletin was not rescinded, and, more importantly, the Obama Administration "clarified" that significant policy and guidance documents "remain subject to OIRA's review under Executive Order 12,866."[247]

Recently EPA has issued what it has called "interim" guidance and sought comments on it.[248] Industry critics have challenged this practice as a shortcut to issuing binding policies, complaining that, notwithstanding EPA's use of "traditional disclaimers . . . that the guidance is not official EPA policy, EPA transmittal memos to Re-

---

244. *Id.*; *see also* Memorandum for Heads of Executive Departments and Agencies, and Independent Regulatory Agencies (M-07-13), from Rob Portman, Director, OMB, "Implementation of Executive Order 13,422 (amending Executive Order 12866) and the OMB Bulletin on Good Guidance Practices," April 25, 2007, *available at* http://www.whitehouse.gov/sites/default/files/omb/assets/regulatory_matters_pdf/m07-13.pdf.

245. Exec. Order 13,422 (Jan. 18, 2007); 72 Fed. Reg. 2763 (Jan. 23, 2007). For a description of this change and a defense of it by those who were in OMB at the time, see Paul R. Noe & John D. Graham, *Symposium: Due Process and Management for Guidance Documents: Good Governance Long Overdue*, 25 YALE J. ON REG. 103 (2008). *But see* Connor N. Raso, Note, *Strategic or Sincere? Analyzing Agency Use of Guidance Documents*, 119 YALE L. J. 782, 819 (2010) (concluding, after empirical study, that agencies "have issued few significant guidance documents relative to the body of outstanding legislative rules," and that the Bush Administration "chose to revise relatively few of these significant guidance documents").

246. *See* Exec. Order 13,497, "Revocation of Certain Executive Orders Concerning Regulatory Planning and Review" (Jan. 30, 2009), 74 Fed. Reg. 6113 (Feb. 4, 2009).

247. Memorandum for Heads and Acting Heads of Executive Departments and Agencies (M-09-13), from Peter Orszag, Director, OMB, "Guidance for Regulatory Review," March 4, 2009, *available at* http://regs.dot.gov/requirements/m09-13.pdf. For an example of an agency-identified "significant guidance document," see U.S. Dep't of Education, Dear Colleague Letter (Apr. 4, 2011) at 1 n.1, *available at* http://www2.ed.gov/about/offices/list/ocr/letters/colleague-201104.html.

248. *See, e.g.*, "Detailed Guidance: Improving EPA Review of Appalachian Surface Coal Mining Operations under the Clean Water Act, National Environmental Policy Act, and the Environmental Justice Executive Order" (April 1, 2010). In footnote 1, the memo states: "This memo is effective immediately. Concurrent with its release, however, EPA is seeking public comment on this interim final document."

gional offices included instructions for the Regions to object to permits if the state does not include the interim guidance in new [surface coal mining] permits."[249]

e. Summary of the law on non-legislative rules—Professor Manning provides a useful summary of the current state of the law on non-legislative rules in the D.C. Circuit:

> Under the [D.C. Circuit's] framework, an agency may use a "general statement of policy" to announce policymaking initiatives, but only if the resulting document is wholly nonbinding. If an agency wishes to promulgate a more binding directive, it may use an "interpretative rule," but only if the agency's position can be characterized as an "interpretation" of a statute or legislative regulation rather than as an exercise of independent policymaking authority.
>
> * * *
>
> Although there are no fixed criteria for drawing the line [between legislative and interpretative rules], the court of appeals has articulated various tests to assist its determination. For example, if the rule invokes "specific statutory provisions, and its validity stands or falls on the correctness of the agency's interpretation of those provisions," the court may deem it a proper interpretative rule. Similarly, if the rule's justification consists of "reasoned statutory interpretation, with reference to the language, purpose, and legislative history" of the relevant provision, the court is more apt to view it as an interpretative rule. Or, if a rule merely "clarifies a statutory term" or "reminds parties of existing statutory duties," it is an interpretative rule.
>
> Conversely, the court is more likely to deem something a "legislative rule" when it "is based on an agency's power to exercise its judgment as to how best to implement a general statutory mandate." Thus, "an agency can declare its understanding of what a statute requires without providing notice and comment, but an agency cannot go beyond the text of a statute and exercise its delegated powers without first providing adequate notice and comment." In other words, an interpretative rule cannot reflect an agency's exercise of independent policymaking discretion.[250]

---

249. Environmental Council of the States, "ECOS Green Report: Recent U.S. EPA Positions on Interim Guidance, Rules, and Policies" 1–2 (December 2010), *available at* http://www.ecos.org/files/4316_file_December_2010_Green_Report.pdf?PHPSESSID=60c312f35f99e32f83081e33f0d3ae72 (describing other such interim guidance issuances and resulting litigation).
250. Manning, *supra* note 132, at 916, 920 (footnotes omitted). Professor Funk has contributed a series of useful articles as well. *See* William Funk, *Legislating for Nonlegislative Rules*, 56 Admin. L. Rev. 1061 (2004) (proposing a legislative solution to the problems of distinguishing between legislative and interpretive rules and of deciding when an interpretive rule is ripe for

Bottom line:

If filling up the details left blank by a silent or ambiguous statute or legislative rule necessarily entails policymaking or interstitial lawmaking, then the acceptability of an interpretative rule under current law must, in truth, turn on whether the agency has shifted too large a degree of policymaking from the notice-and-comment process to the less formal and often staff-driven process of adopting interpretative rules. If a nonlegislative rule involves policymaking writ small, the court calls it "interpretation"; if such a rule reflects too much policymaking, the court deems it the exercise of delegated lawmaking authority.[251]

f. The intertwining of procedural claims and finality for the purposes of judicial review—It has become increasingly apparent that the inquiries courts use to distinguish properly issued non-legislative rules from improperly issued legislative rules significantly overlap with the question of whether the issuance is final for the purposes of judicial review. Finality is discussed more extensively in Part IV, Chapter 2, but it is appropriate to highlight the issue here. In a case where the D.C. Circuit found that agency policy guidelines do not constitute binding rules, and they do not reflect final agency action, it recognized that intertwining of these issues:

---

review); William Funk, *When Is a "Rule" a Regulation? Marking a Clear Line Between Nonlegislative Rules and Legislative Rules*, 54 ADMIN. L. REV. 659 (2002); William Funk, *A Primer on Nonlegislative Rules*, 53 ADMIN. L. REV. 1321 (2001). Building on the writings of Professors Manning and Funk, Jacob Gersen has suggested that "[r]ather than asking whether a rule is legislative to answer whether notice and comment procedures should have been used, courts should simply ask whether notice and comment procedures were used. If they were, the rule should be deemed legislative and binding if otherwise lawful. If they were not, the rule is nonlegislative" (and more easily challengeable at the enforcement stage). Jacob E. Gersen, *Legislative Rules Revisited*, 74 U. CHI. L. REV. 1705, 1719 (2007).

But this "shortcut" approach has been perceptively criticized in David L. Franklin, *Legislative Rules, Nonlegislative Rules, and the Perils of the Short Cut*, 120 YALE L. J. 276 (2010). Professor Franklin argues that "the shortcut inadequately protects the interests of those persons, particularly regulatory beneficiaries, whose interests are affected by deregulatory or permissive agency pronouncements; [and] it stands in tension with the longstanding principle that agencies may choose to announce new policy through either adjudication or rulemaking. . . ." He admits that the current judicial test is unduly indeterminate and perhaps errs in the direction of "overincentivizing procedural formality by classifying rules as legislative that were never intended to be binding." Yet he concludes that "the lack of a cut-and-dried test for distinguishing between legislative and nonlegislative rules has its advantages, not only for the courts but also for the regulated public. A doctrine with some play in the joints allows courts to tailor the requirement of notice and comment to circumstances in which factors such as technical complexity or significant effects on regulatory beneficiaries make public input more valuable . . . while allowing agencies to dispense with notice and comment when such factors are absent. . . ." *Id.* at 325.

251. Manning, *supra* note 132, at 926.

In order to sustain their position, appellants must show that the [challenged guidelines] either (1) reflect "final agency action," . . . or, (2) constitute a de facto rule or binding norm that could not properly be promulgated absent the notice-and-comment rulemaking required by [the APA]. These two inquiries are alternative ways of viewing the question before the court. Although, if appellants could demonstrate the latter proposition, they would implicitly prove the former, because the agency's adoption of a binding norm obviously would reflect final agency action.[252]

As Judge Walton explained it in a case citing the above language:

In deciding the question of finality, the Court must also assess the question of whether the EPA's actions constitute a de facto legislative rule, promulgated in violation of the APA's notice and comment requirements. This is so given the similarity between the second aspect of the finality assessment—whether the action gives rise to legal obligations or is one from which legal consequences flow—and the standard for determining whether a challenged action constitutes a regulation or a mere statement of policy—"whether the action has binding effects on private parties or on the agency," or, in other words, "whether the agency action binds private parties or the agency itself with the force of law."[253]

g. Post-promulgation comment period—As Judge Wald observed, neither agencies nor affected persons can reliably predict the outcome of a challenge to an agency's use of the APA's exemption for interpretive rules and policy statements.[254] Therefore, agency rulemakers should heed Administrative Conference Recommendation 76-5, which urges use of notice-and-comment procedure where possible if a rule or statement will have a substantial impact on the public.[255]

---

252. Ctr. for Auto Safety v. Nat'l Highway Traffic Safety Admin., 452 F.3d 798, 806 (D.C. Cir. 2006).
253. Nat'l Mining Ass'n v. Jackson, 768 F. Supp. 2d 34, 41 n.6 (D.D.C. 2011) (citations omitted). Another court has taken it to the point of a syllogism, which may go too far in that it implies that non-legislative rules can never be final for the purposes of judicial review:

> If the Memorandum is a legislative rule, then it is final agency action under the APA subject to judicial review, and it is subject to notice and comment rulemaking under § 553. However, as just stated, if the Memorandum is an interpretive rule or general policy statement, the opposite is true: it is not final agency action subject to judicial review under the APA and it is not a "de facto rule or binding norm that could not properly be promulgated absent the notice-and-comment rulemaking required by § 533 of the APA.

Broadgate, Inc., v. USCIS, 730 F. Supp. 2d 240, 245 (D.D.C. 2010).
254. *See supra* text accompanying notes 148–49.
255. ACUS Recommendation 76-5, *Interpretive Rules of General Applicability and Statements of General Policy*, 41 Fed. Reg. 56,769 (Dec. 30, 1976) [hereinafter ACUS Recommendation 76-5]. Some agencies have followed this advice. *See, e.g.*, EPA, *Reporting Requirements for Risk/*

The Conference's recommendation also states that when it is necessary for agencies to make such rules and statements effective immediately, agencies should give the public the opportunity to submit post-promulgation comments.[256] While a post-promulgation comment opportunity is not a *substitute* for pre-promulgation comment where required,[257] it is likely to put the agency in a much better posture on judicial review, especially where it has responded in good faith to post-promulgation comments.[258]

4. *"Good Cause" Exemptions*

Sections 553(b)(B) and 553(d)(3) of the APA authorize agencies to dispense with certain procedures for rules when they find "good cause" to do so. Under section 553(b)(B), the requirements of notice and opportunity for comment do not apply when the agency, for good cause, finds that those procedures are "impracticable, unnecessary, or contrary to the public interest." Section 553(d)(3) allows an agency, upon finding good cause, to make a rule effective immediately, thereby avoiding the 30-day delayed effective date requirement in section 553.

These two exceptions give agencies flexibility by allowing them to dispense with procedures in promulgating rules not otherwise exempted, but like other exemptions, they are to be construed narrowly.[259] Moreover, an agency must give supporting rea-

---

Benefit Information under the Federal Insecticide, Fungicide, and Rodenticide Act (FIFRA), Final Interpretative Rule and Statement of Policy, 50 Fed. Reg. 38,115, 38,119 (Sept. 20, 1985) (requesting public comment although the rule was deemed exempt from public participation requirements of APA as general statement of policy and interpretation of statute).

256. ACUS Recommendation 76-5. *See* Asimow, *Nonlegislative Rulemaking, supra* note 140, at 426 (noting "modest benefit to the public from a post-adoption comment system would outweigh the modest additional costs that it would impose on agency staffs" and questioning the "much costlier requirement" that would add some form of "substantial impact" test into APA).

257. *See* Levesque v. Block, 723 F.2d 175, 188 (1st Cir. 1988) (discussing general rule that a rule found invalid for failure to provide for notice and comment cannot be saved by providing for comment after promulgation, but upholding it because "[w]hen the response suggests that the agency has been open-minded, the presumption against a late comment period can be overcome and a rule upheld"). *See contra* Air Transport Ass'n v. Dep't of Transp., *supra* note 105, at 379–80 (rejecting FAA's contention that its response to comments after promulgation of civil penalty rules cured any noncompliance with section 553). The court stated:

> We strictly enforce this requirement because we recognize that an agency is not likely to be receptive to suggested changes once the agency "put[s] its credibility on the line in the form of 'final' rules. People naturally tend to be more close-minded and defensive once they have made a 'final' determination. . . ." [The FAA] made no changes in the Penalty Rules in response to public comments. Nor did the language of FAA's published replies suggest that the agency had afforded the comments particularly searching consideration.

258. *Levesque*, 723 F.2d at 188. *See also* Asimow, *Nonlegislative Rulemaking, supra* note 140, at 421–24 (discussing benefits of post-promulgation comments).

259. *See* Mobay Chem. Corp. v. Gorsuch, 682 F.2d 419, 426 (3d Cir. 1982) ("In considering whether there was good cause for the agency to adopt the data compensation regulations without prior

sons for invoking the good-cause exemptions.[260] The agency's findings of good cause are judicially reviewable on the same basis as any other findings committed to the agency's judgment.[261] Although the language of the exemption from the delayed effective date requirement is more general than the provision for dispensing with notice and comment, several commentators have concluded that "good cause" under both sections must be predicated on similar findings.[262] The effective date provision also, however, contains an additional exemption for "a substantive rule which grants or recognizes an exemption or relieves a restriction."[263]

The terms "impracticable," "unnecessary," or "contrary to the public interest" used in section 553(b)(B) indicate the circumstances in which the good-cause exemptions may be employed. The APA's legislative history defines each of the terms separately:

> "Impracticable" means a situation in which the due and required execution of the agency functions would be unavoidably prevented by its undertaking public rule-making proceedings. "Unnecessary" means unnecessary so far as the public is concerned, as would be the case if a minor or merely technical amendment in which the public is not particularly interested were involved. "Public interest" supplements the terms "impracticable" or "unnecessary"; it requires that public rule-making procedures shall not prevent an agency from operating and that, on the other hand, lack of public interest in rulemaking warrants an agency to dispense with public procedure.[264]

---

notice-and-comment, we are guided by the principle that the exception is to be narrowly construed."); New Jersey v. EPA, 626 F.2d 1038, 1045 (D.C. Cir. 1980) ("[E]xceptions to the notice and comment provisions of section 553 must be narrowly construed and only reluctantly countenanced."). *See also* Catherine J. Lanctot, Note, *The "Good Cause" Exceptions: Danger to Notice and Comment Requirements Under the Administrative Procedure Act*, 68 GEO. L.J. 765, 773 (1980).

260. *See Legislative History of the APA, supra* note 85 ("The exemption of situations of emergency or necessity is not an 'escape clause' in the sense that any agency has discretion to disregard its terms or the facts. A true and supported or supportable finding of necessity or emergency must be made and published."). 5 U.S.C. § 553(b)(B) requires that the agency incorporate the good-cause finding and a brief statement of reasons therefor in the rules issued.

261. *See* Bonfield, *Military and Foreign Affairs Function Rulemaking, supra* note 60, at 292. Indeed, because public participation has been dispensed with, the courts may scrutinize these rules more carefully than others.

262. *See* Lanctot, *supra* note 259, at 772 n.61. *See* United States v. Gavrilovic, 551 F.2d 1089 (8th Cir. 1977) (strictly construing 30-day period before effectiveness, notwithstanding agency claim of good cause). *See also* Rowell v. Andrus, 631 F.2d 699 (10th Cir. 1980) (holding 30-day requirement runs from publication of final rule, not publication of notice of proposed rulemaking). A later case upheld the agency's invocation of good cause for an immediate effective date but *not* its invocation of good cause for dispensing with notice and comment. Riverbend Farms, Inc. v. Madigan, 958 F.2d 1479 (9th Cir. 1992).

263. 5 U.S.C. § 553(d)(1). *See* Indep. U.S. Tanker Owners Comm. v. Skinner, 884 F.2d 587 (D.C. Cir. 1989) (holding the (d)(1) exemption applies automatically to a rule that relieves a restriction and that it need not be asserted in published notice).

264. *See Legislative History of the APA, supra* note 85, at 200.

The "unnecessary" ground for exemption is usually applied to minor technical amendments or those that involve little exercise of agency discretion.[265] Whatever the agency's basis for the claimed good cause, however, the agency must articulate its "finding and a brief statement of reasons therefore in the rules issued."[266]

In practice, agencies often apply the "impracticable" ground together with the "contrary to the public interest" ground, the two being closely related.[267] Ordinarily, situations potentially covered by these two prongs of the good-cause exemption are those in which advance notice would defeat the agency's regulatory objective; immediate action is necessary to reduce or avoid health hazards or other imminent harm to persons or property; or inaction will lead to serious dislocation in government programs or the marketplace.[268] With the heightened security after September 11, 2001, courts may be more receptive to the invocation of good cause by some agencies.[269]

But in general, reviewing courts have normally applied the section 553(b)(B) good-cause exemption narrowly to prevent agencies using it as an "escape clause" from notice-and-comment requirements. As the D.C. Circuit said in *Action on Smoking and Health v. Civil Aeronautics Board*,[270] "Bald assertions that the agency does not believe comments would be useful cannot create good cause to forgo notice and comment procedures. To hold otherwise would permit the exceptions to carve the heart out of the statute."[271] The court held invalid an agency rule issued without notice

---

265. *See* Juan J. Lavilla, *The Good Cause Exemption to Notice and Comment Requirements Under the Administrative Procedure Act*, 3 ADMIN. L.J. 317, 342 (1989) (finding after empirical survey that "[a]lmost half of all rules adopted pursuant to section 553(b)(B) can be traced to the 'unnecessary' standard; roughly half of those can be deemed 'minor' rules"). *See also* Ellen R. Jordan, *The Administrative Procedure Act's "Good Cause" Exemption*, 36 ADMIN. L. REV. 113, 129–35 (1984).

266. 5 U.S.C. § 553(b)(B). *See* Lanctot, *supra* note 259; Action on Smoking & Health v. Civil Aeronautics Bd., 699 F.2d 1209, 1215–17 (D.C. Cir.), *supplemented by* 713 F.2d 795 (1983).

267. *See, e.g.*, Transportation of Federal Air Marshals, Final Rule with Request for Comments, 50 Fed. Reg. 27,924 (July 8, 1985).

268. *See generally* Lavilla, *supra* note 265; Jordan, *supra* note 265. Some enabling statutes contain parallel provisions authorizing agencies to take "emergency" action without affording the normal opportunity for public participation. *See, e.g.*, OSHA Act, 29 U.S.C. § 655(c) (authorizing OSHA to issue "emergency temporary" occupational safety and health standard where there is "grave danger" to employees and standard is "necessary" to protect employees).

269. *See, e.g.*, Jifry v. FAA, 370 F.3d 1174 (D.C. Cir. 2004) (Agencies had good cause for not engaging in notice-and-comment rulemaking in promulgating regulations requiring automatic revocation by FAA of airman certificates of alien pilots upon notification from Transportation Security Administration that certificate holder posed security threat.).

270. 713 F.2d 795 (D.C. Cir.), *supplementing* 699 F.2d 1209 (1983).

271. *Id.* at 800 (citations omitted). *See also* Natural Res. Def. Council v. Evans, 316 F.3d 904, 906 (9th Cir. 2003) (finding that "good cause requires some showing of exigency beyond generic complexity of data collection and time constraints" and the fact that agency had to issue a new fishery management rule every year was not enough to show good cause); United States v. Picciotto, 875 F.2d 345 (D.C. Cir. 1989) (setting aside Park Service rule seeking to use good-cause exemption to exempt *all future rules* relating to demonstrators in national capital parks).

and comment where the rule was reissued by the agency to correct a different procedural deficiency in an earlier proceeding in which notice and comment had been provided.[272] In an extremely narrow reading of the good-cause exemption, the D.C. Circuit rejected an attempt by EPA to correct an error in a previously promulgated rule caused by an erroneous use of a word-processing "find/replace" command in the drafting of the regulation.[273] On the other hand, in a challenge to amendments made to a regional milk marketing order claiming the improper invocation of emergency rulemaking, the Seventh Circuit upheld the emergency rule, finding that even though there was a "lack of attention to detail" in the agency's explanation, the agency did identify the heart of the problem requiring an emergency rule.[274]

a. Emergency health or safety standards—Courts applying the "contrary to the public interest" ground for exemption have often been inclined to err on the side of public safety and health.[275] At the same time, the fact that an action purports to be protective of the public does not necessarily justify the elimination of public participation, particularly where the regulation has wide impact and is controversial. For example, in the famous Baby Doe case, *American Academy of Pediatrics v. Heckler*,[276] the district court rejected the government's argument that because lives were at stake, good cause existed for HHS to issue its regulation on the treatment of newly born infants with birth defects without notice and comment. The court stated that the argument "could as easily be used to justify immediate implementation of any sort of health or safety regulation no matter how small the risk for the population at large or how long-standing the problem."[277]

---

272. The earlier rule was set aside and remanded in *Action on Smoking and Health, supra* note 266, on the ground that the agency statement of basis and purpose was insufficient under the APA. For a thoughtful opinion reaching the same result in a case where the Department of Labor attempted to issue a revised rule without notice and comment after it was had been vacated by an earlier decision, see *AFL-CIO v. Chao*, 496 F. Supp. 2d 76, 85–86 (D.D.C. 2007) (drawing a distinction between previously remanded and previously vacated rules). *Compare* United Steelworkers v. Pendergrass, 819 F.2d 1263 (3d Cir. 1987) (holding additional notice and comment unnecessary after court remand of rule).
273. Util. Solid Waste Activities Group v. EPA, 236 F.3d 749 (D.C. Cir. 2001) (the court also rejected EPA's argument that it had an inherent power to correct technical errors).
274. White Eagle Co-op Ass'n v. Conner, 553 F.3d 467, 482 (7th Cir. 2009).
275. *See* Jordan, *supra* note 265, at 122–23. *See also* Haw. Helicopter Operators Ass'n v. FAA, 51 F.3d 212, 214 (9th Cir. 1995) ("We perceive no indication in this record that the FAA waived notice and comment for any reasons other than its concern about the threat to public safety reflected in an increasing number of helicopter accidents.").
276. 561 F. Supp. 395 (D.D.C. 1983).
277. *Id.* at 401. The court emphasized there was no indication of "any dramatic change in circumstances that would constitute an emergency justifying shunting off public participation in the rulemaking." *Id.* (footnote omitted). The government's argument that the regulation was "procedural" or "interpretive" was also rejected by the district court, saying that the regulation "was intended . . . to change the course of medical decisionmaking in these cases" and thus was more than a clarification or explanation of an existing rule or statute. *Id.* (quoting Guardian Fed.

In *Asbestos Information Ass'n v. OSHA*,[278] the Fifth Circuit vacated OSHA's asbestos standard issued under a statute authorizing temporary emergency standards where the agency finds that dispensing with notice and comment is "necessary" to protect employees from a "grave danger."[279] The court first agreed that an "emergency" standard may lawfully be issued even though new information on grave danger had not come to the attention of the agency.[280] However, the court concluded that the risk assessment analysis used in the rule, while an "extremely useful tool," is "precisely the type of data that may be more uncritically accepted after public scrutiny, through notice-and-comment rulemaking, especially when the conclusions it suggests are controversial or subject to different interpretations."[281]

b. Congressional deadlines—Another good-cause issue that has arisen with increasing frequency is the extent to which congressionally imposed deadlines justify an agency's issuance of rules without notice and comment. This was addressed in a series of cases challenging EPA's promulgation, without notice and comment, of lists of geographical areas not meeting federal air-quality standards under the Clean Air Act.[282] Courts in five circuits sustained challenges to EPA's action, rejecting its good-cause argument largely on the ground that EPA could have published the lists as a proposal and obtained public comment with little delay.[283] In these and other similar cases, a factor that often surfaces in the judicial analysis is whether or not the agency made a good-faith attempt to comply with the APA's requirements for public participation.[284]

Savings & Loan v. Fed. Savings & Loan Ins. Corp., 589 F.2d 658, 664 (D.C. Cir. 1978)). Apart from its procedural findings, the district court also found the regulation to be invalid as arbitrary and capricious. *Id.* at 399–400, 403. It also expressed concern about the constitutionality of the regulation. *Id.* at 402.

278. 727 F.2d 415 (5th Cir. 1984).

279. 29 U.S.C. § 655(c). OSHA did issue an earlier asbestos emergency temporary standard in 1972 that was not challenged in court.

280. 727 F.2d at 423. The court of appeals added that the agency must offer some explanation of its timing of the emergency standard, "especially when, as here, for years it has known of the serious risk" and "has possessed, albeit in unrefined form, the substantive data forming the basis" of the standard. *Id.*

281. 727 F.2d at 426. The court of appeals also held that the emergency standard was not "necessary" because increased protection of employees could be achieved through more effective enforcement of existing standards. *Id.* at 426–27.

282. Clean Air Act Amendments of 1977, Pub. L. No. 95-95, 91 Stat. 685 (codified at 42 U.S.C. §§ 7401–7431).

283. *See* Jordan, *supra* note 265, at 125–29 (discussing five cases); Lanctot, *supra* note 259. *See also* Sharon Steel Corp. v. EPA, 597 F.2d 377 (3d Cir. 1979). *But see* U.S. Steel Corp. v. EPA, 605 F.2d 283 (7th Cir. 1979) (sustaining good-cause finding).

284. *See, e.g.*, Air Transp. Ass'n v. Dep't of Transp., *supra* note 105, at 379. The court stated:

The agency waited almost nine months before taking action to implement its authority under [the statutory section creating a two-year demonstration program to which the rules were to apply]. At oral argument, counsel for the FAA conceded that the delay was

A similar split in the circuits has emerged in a case involving legislative ambiguity. The Attorney General (AG) attempted to issue a rule without notice and comment and make it immediately effective to implement a statute that requires convicted sex offenders to register before traveling in interstate commerce.[285] In enacting the law, Congress provided that "[T]he Attorney General shall have the authority to specify the applicability of the requirements of this subchapter to sex offenders convicted before [July 27, 2006] . . . ."[286] But it was unclear whether the law applied at all to previously convicted sex offenders under its own terms, or whether the statute's application to such sex offenders depended upon the AG's acting under this provision. The AG sought to avoid any uncertainty by issuing a legislative rule providing that the law applied to those convicted of sex offenses before it was enacted. The AG found good cause in the need to "eliminate any possible uncertainty" about the law's application and in the need to avoid "[impairing] immediate efforts to protect the public from sex offenders who fail to register . . . ."[287]

Several circuits have split both internally and among themselves on the question of whether the AG has demonstrated good cause. In 2009, the Fourth Circuit, over a strong dissent, upheld the AG's actions[288] as did the Eleventh Circuit.[289] On the other hand, the Fifth, Sixth and Ninth Circuits found no good cause.[290]

The judges who found good cause generally rejected the proposition that something like an emergency is necessary to establish good cause, holding that the AG's general assertion of a need for certainty of application of the law and his general

---

largely a product of the agency's decision to attend to other obligations. We are hardly in a position to second-guess the FAA's choices in determining institutional priorities. But insofar as the FAA's own failure to act materially contributed to its perceived deadline pressure, the agency cannot now invoke the need for expeditious action as "good cause" to avoid the obligations of section 553(b).

285. The description in the following three paragraphs is an abridged and updated version of that found in William S. Jordan III, *News from the Circuits*, 35 ADMIN. & REG. L. NEWS 18–19 (Summer 2010).
286. Sex Offender Registration and Notification Act (SORNA), Pub. L. No. 109-248 (2006), § 113, codified at 42 U.S.C. § 16913.
287. Applicability of the Sex Offender Notification and Registration Act, 72 Fed. Reg. 8894, 8896 (Feb. 28, 2007).
288. United States v. Gould, 568 F.3d 459 (4th Cir. 2009), *cert. denied*, 130 S. Ct. 1686 (2010).
289. United States v. Dean, 604 F.3d 1275 (11th Cir. 2010), *cert. denied*, 131 S. Ct. 642 (2010). One judge disagreed with the majority view as to good cause, but concurred in the result because he viewed it as "harmless error."
290. United States v. Johnson, 632 F.3d 912, 927–30 (5th Cir. 2011) (but finding that the error was "harmless in the particular circumstances of this case"); United States v. Valverde, 628 F.3d 1159, 1166 (9th Cir. 2010) ("We strongly disagree with the conclusion reached by the courts that hold that compliance with the APA's notice and comment procedures would have controverted the public interest in this case."); United States v. Cain, 583 F.3d 408 (6th Cir. 2009) (split decision). *See also* United States v. Utesch, 596 F.3d 302, (6th Cir. 2010) (finding error not harmless as to defendant even though Attorney General subsequently properly issued the regulation).

assertion of the "practical danger" of the "threat of additional offenses" was enough to justify his failure to seek notice and comment. By contrast, the judges rejecting the "good cause" claims emphasized the stringency of the good-cause requirement. They argued that agencies may not rely upon generalized assertions of potential harm. Sixth Circuit Judge John Rogers, for example, noted that "the Attorney General gave no specific evidence of actual harm to the public in his conclusory statement of reasons . . . ."[291] Moreover, Judge Rogers emphasized that the AG waited seven months from the effective date of the Act to issue his rule and that an agency may not rely upon its own delay as a basis for asserting good cause to issue a rule without notice and comment. Judge Rogers also emphasized that the effect of the rule in this case is to impose a new criminal liability. This action is so "quintessentially legislative"[292] that it is particularly important to apply the APA's requirements with care.[293]

Courts are more inclined to uphold the agency's action if the agency responds to circumstances beyond its control, if the emergency rule is of limited scope or duration, and if the agency initiates prompt follow-up proceedings allowing for public participation.[294] The Fifth Circuit, in *American Transfer & Food Storage v. Interstate Commerce Commission*,[295] upheld the ICC's good-cause finding that notice and comment was not necessary in issuing rules under the Motor Carrier Act of 1980. The court stated:

> [T]o make the new Act effective and to achieve the goals set by Congress, it was imperative that the Commission, in order to adapt its processes to the new order, adopt almost immediately new rules and procedures with as much notice as was practicable. This it did by issuance of interim rules with invited public input before final regulations were issued.[296]

---

291. *Cain*, 583 F.2d at 422.
292. *Id.* at 420.
293. There are also numerous district court decisions on this issue. The Supreme Court noted this disagreement among the circuits in a related case, but declined to express a view on it. Carr v. United States, 130 S. Ct. 2229, 2234 n.2 (2010).
294. *See, e.g.*, Nat'l Fed'n of Fed. Emps v. Devine, 671 F.2d 607 (D.C. Cir. 1982) (upholding OPM emergency regulations); Council of the Southern Mountains, Inc. v. Donovan, 653 F.2d 573 (D.C. Cir. 1981) (upholding Mine Safety and Health Administration rule delaying effective date without notice and comment); Nw. Airlines, Inc. v. Goldschmidt, 645 F.2d 1309 (8th Cir. 1981) (upholding seven-day comment period and immediate effective date); San Diego Navy Broadway Complex Coal. v. U.S. Coast Guard, 2011 WL 1212888 *6 (S.D. Cal. 2011) (finding good cause for issuance of a "temporary final rule" because agency limited its effect for several months and also explicitly indicated its intent to initiate a notice-and-comment process).
295. 719 F.2d 1283 (5th Cir. 1983).
296. *Id.* at 1294. The Motor Carrier Act became effective immediately and "provided no transition period for developing new procedures to implement the significant legislative changes." *Id.* at 1293. The interim rules were in effect until the final rules were issued.

As this case illustrates, however, rules labeled "interim rules" by an agency are final under the APA, and persons "adversely affected or aggrieved" may challenge the rules in court.[297]

In a number of decisions, reviewing courts have given greater weight to congressional deadlines in justifying lack of notice and comment when the deadlines implemented budget-cutting measures. In *Philadelphia Citizens in Action v. Schweiker*,[298] the Third Circuit held that HHS had "good cause" for not providing notice and comment in issuing rules to implement changes in the Aid to Families with Dependent Children Program (AFDC).[299] The court relied particularly on the fact that Congress imposed substantially shorter deadlines than those involved in the EPA's Clean Air Act cases[300] and that benefit programs, such as the AFDC program, often are statutorily exempt from notice-and-comment requirements.[301]

In *Methodist Hospital of Sacramento v. Shalala*,[302] the D.C. Circuit stated that "[a]s a general matter, strict congressionally imposed deadlines, without more, by no means warrant invocation of the good-cause exception. Nevertheless, deviation from APA requirements has been permitted where congressional deadlines are very tight and where the statute is particularly complicated." In this case, the court pointed out that:

> Between the April 20 enactment and the September 1 deadline, the Secretary faced the daunting task of preparing regulations to implement a complete and radical overhaul of the Medicare reimbursement system. Once published, the interim rules took up 133 pages in the *Federal Register*: 55 pages of explanatory text, 37 pages of revised regulations, and 41 pages of new data tables. . . . [T]his case is different from those where the agency "had a substantial period of time within which to propose regulations, the promulgation of which it knew was both necessary and forthcoming in the future." . . . Nor does this case raise the specter of abuse, where "an agency unwilling to provide notice or an opportunity to comment could simply wait until the eve of a statutory . . . deadline, then

---

297. See discussion in next section and in Part IV, ch. 1(E)(2)(b).

298. 669 F.2d 877 (3d Cir. 1982).

299. The changes were mandated by the Omnibus Budget Reconciliation Act (OBRA) of 1981, Pub. L. No. 97-35, 95 Stat. 357.

300. The OBRA statute was to become effective 49 days after enactment, but in the EPA cases, EPA had three years to promulgate the regulations. 669 F.2d at 883. The court also noted that EPA would have had sufficient time to allow comment on the unreviewed state-submitted plans under the Clean Air Act, an approach that was not available in the AFDC case. *Id.* at 883–84.

301. Notice and comment was required for the regulations involved only because HHS in 1971 waived the exemption in the APA from notice-and-comment requirements for grants and benefits. *Id.* at 881. *See also* Petry v. Block, 737 F.2d 1193, 1201 (D.C. Cir. 1984) (holding USDA regulation promulgated under OBRA of 1981 valid where good-cause exemption was applied); Sepulveda v. Block, 782 F.2d 363 (2d Cir. 1986) (involving OBRA of 1982, Pub. L. No. 97-253, 96 Stat. 772).

302. 38 F.3d 1225, 1236 (D.C. Cir. 1994) (internal quotation marks and footnotes omitted).

raise up the 'good-cause' banner and promulgate rules without following APA procedures."[303]

Judge Freidman's opinion in *Northern Mariana Islands v. United States* sets forth a good summary of the "relevant circumstances" courts look at when deciding whether an "emergency situation" justifies an agency's failure to comply with notice-and-comment requirements: (1) the scale and complexity of the regulatory program the agency was required to implement, (2) any deadlines for rulemaking imposed by the enabling statute, (3) the diligence with which the agency approached the rulemaking process, (4) obstacles outside the agency's control that impeded efficient completion of the rulemaking process, and (5) the harm that could befall members of the public as a result of delays in promulgating the rule in question.[304]

c. *"Interim-final" rules*—As mentioned above, in many cases, agencies issuing rules without notice and comment following a good-cause finding have referred to the rules as "interim final rules" and then modified the rules, as appropriate, following post-promulgation comment.[305] This practice comports with a recommendation of the Administrative Conference adopted in 1995.[306] Congress has also expressly authorized this procedure in specific programs from time to time,[307] and in some cases

---

303. *Id.* at 1237 (footnotes omitted).

304. Northern Mariana Islands v. United States, 686 F. Supp. 2d 7, 14–15 (D.D.C. 2009).

305. *See, e.g.*, Transportation of Federal Air Marshals, Final Rule with Request for Comments, 50 Fed. Reg. 27,924 (July 8, 1985). The FAA emergency rule required "certificate holders" to carry federal air marshals in designated passenger operations. *Id.* Because of the "emergency need for the regulations," including hijackings and terrorist attacks on U.S. aviation, the agency found that notice and comment was "impracticable, and contrary to the public interest." *Id.* at 27,925. However, because under DOT Regulatory Policies and Procedures, 44 Fed. Reg. 11,034 (Feb. 26, 1979), agencies in the Department "should" provide an opportunity for comment on emergency regulations, the notice invited comment on the final rule, which was immediately effective, and stated that the agency would consider the comments and possibly change the rule "in light of the comments received." *Id.*

306. ACUS Recommendation 95-4, *Procedures for Noncontroversial and Expedited Rulemaking*, 60 Fed. Reg. 43,110 (Aug. 18, 1995). The Conference urged agencies to use such procedures whenever they invoked the "impracticable" or "contrary to the public interest" prongs of the good-cause exemption. *Id. See also* Michael R. Asimow, *Interim-Final Rules: Making Haste Slowly*, 51 ADMIN. L. REV. 703 (1999).

307. *See* U.S. GEN. ACCOUNTING OFFICE, SMALL BUSINESS ADMINISTRATION'S ECONOMIC STIMULUS PROVISION (table 1) (GAO-10-298R) (2010) (providing a list of the areas over which the SBA was granted emergency rulemaking authority as part of the stimulus package). The new Patient Protection and Affordable Health Care Act, Pub. L. No. 111-148, 124 Stat. 119 (2010), has several provisions authorizing interim-final rulemaking. *See* 124 Stat. 149 (codified at 42 U.S.C.A. § 1320d-2(g)(4)(C)); 124 Stat. 499 (codified at 42 U.S.C. § 1395kkk(e)(2)(B)); and 124 Stat. 749 (codified at 42 U.S.C. § 1395cc(j)(2)(F)). *See also* OBRA of 1987, Pub. L. No. 100-203, tit. IV, pt. 2, § 4039(g), 101 Stat. 1330, 1330–83 (42 U.S.C. § 1395hh note) (authorizing use of interim-final regulations for Medicare program and placing time limits on their effectiveness). The Magnuson-Stevens (fishery management) Act specifically provides that the Secretary of Commerce may

courts have inferred that the notice-and-comment provisions of § 553 were abrogated by specific statutory provisions authorizing interim final rules.[308] In one unusual case the D.C. Circuit approved a final rule that was issued after three interim final rules.[309] But agencies' proper use of the interim-final rulemaking process depends on whether they have good cause to avoid notice-and-comment rulemaking in the first place.[310] Nor will agency consideration of post-promulgation comments always save a rulemaking where "good cause" does not exist to support exemption from *pre*-promulgation notice-and-comment requirements.[311] Interesting finality and deadline issues can also be raised by interim-final rules.[312] But note that apart from procedural issues, courts tend to be more deferential to agency interim or temporary rules.[313]

promulgate an emergency regulation or interim measure for 180 days without public notice and comment, and that the secretary may extend the interim measure by an additional 180 days, "provided the public has had an opportunity to comment on the emergency regulation or interim measure." 16 U.S.C. § 1855(c)(3)(B), *discussed in* Massachusetts v. Daley, 170 F.3d 23 (1st Cir. 1999).

308. *See* Asiana Airlines v. Fed. Aviation Admin., 134 F.3d 393, 398 (D.C. Cir. 1998) (statute regulating certain flights over the United States and directing FAA to publish "an initial fee schedule and associated collection process as an interim final rule, pursuant to which public comment will be sought and a final rule issued" allows for departure from notice and comment) and Methodist Hosp. of Sacramento v. Shalala, 38 F.3d 1225 (D.C. Cir. 1994) (statutory language directing the Secretary of HHS to publish interim final rules within five months of the statute's effective date, allow for a period of public comment on the interim rules, and publish final rules four months later reflected Congress's "clear intent that APA notice and comment procedures not be followed"). These cases were discussed in *Coalition for Parity, Inc. v. Sebelius*, 709 F. Supp. 2d 10, 18 (D.D.C. 2010) (finding statute at issue unclear, but upholding agencies' invocation of good-cause exemption).

309. *See* Fed. Express Corp. v. Mineta, 373 F.3d 112 (D.C. Cir. 2004) (finding that a series of three interim-final rules with opportunity for after-the-fact comment did not make the fourth "final rule" invalid).

310. *See, e.g.*, Paulsen v. Daniels, 413 F.3d 999 (9th Cir. 2005) (Bureau of Prisons interim-final rule invalid for lack of good cause).

311. In *Paulsen*, agency received 150 comments on the interim final rule. *Id.* at 1003. *See also* the cases cited in note 257 *supra*. For other cases holding final rule invalid, see Natural Res. Def. Council, Inc. v. EPA, 683 F.2d 752, 767–68 (3d Cir. 1982), New Jersey v. EPA, 626 F.2d 1038 (D.C. Cir 1980). Other courts are more open to the argument that the agency seriously considered the comments. *See, e.g.*, Fed. Express Corp. v. Mineta, 373 F.3d 112, 120 (D.C. Cir. 2004), Mortg. Investors Corp. of Ohio v. Gober, 220 F.3d 1375 (Fed. Cir. 2000), Advocates for Highway & Auto Safety v. Fed. Hwy. Admin., 28 F.3d 1288 (D.C. Cir. 1994). *See also* Kristin E. Hickman, *A Problem of Remedy: Responding to Treasury's (Lack of) Compliance with Administrative Procedure Act Rulemaking Requirements*, 76 GEO. WASH. L. REV. 1153, 1191–92 (2008) (collecting cases).

312. *See* discussion *infra* Part IV, ch. 1(E)(2)(b).

313. *See* Rural Cellular Ass'n v. FCC, 588 F.3d 1095 (D.C. Cir. 2009) ("This court has also acknowledged the FCC should be given 'substantial deference' when acting to impose interim regulations. Accordingly, we have repeatedly held that '[a]voidance of market disruption pending broader reforms is, of course, a standard and accepted justification for a temporary rule.'") (citations omitted).

d. *"Direct-final" rulemaking*—Numerous rules issued by agencies are routine or noncontroversial.[314] Nevertheless, agencies are often leery of risking invocation of the good-cause exemption, so they go through the process (with its attendant delays and duplicative publications) even when it is unlikely that any comments will be received. To help obviate this problem, EPA invented a process called "direct-final rulemaking."[315] It was also endorsed as a streamlining approach by the National Performance Review[316] and by the Administrative Conference.

The Administrative Conference described this approach as involving:

> agency publication of a rule in the *Federal Register* with a statement that, unless an adverse comment is received on the rule within a specific time period, the rule will become effective as a final rule on a particular date (at least 30 days after the end of the comment period). However, if an adverse comment is filed, the rule is withdrawn, and the agency may publish the proposed rule under normal notice-and-comment procedures.[317]

The process generally has been used where an agency believes that the rule is noncontroversial and adverse comments will not be received. It allows the agency to issue the rule without having to go through its internal review process twice (that is, at the proposed and final rule stages), while at the same time offering the public the opportunity to challenge the agency's view that the rule is noncontroversial.[318]

Although no legal challenges have been reported,[319] there are strong arguments that this process, which is now being used by several other departments and agencies,[320] complies with the APA and would withstand judicial challenge. The practice would seem to meet the spirit of the notice-and-comment provisions of section 553 because it does allow for public comment, and it also is premised on allowing a single "significant adverse comment"[321] to trigger the regular two-

---

314. One empirical study of all rules published in the *Federal Register* in a six-month period found that approximately one-third (711 of 2,190) dispensed with notice-and-comment procedures expressly or implicitly due to good cause, and about half of those were traced to the "unnecessary" standard. *See* Lavilla, *supra* note 265, at 339 n.86 & 342.

315. It was originally used by EPA to speed up the process for approving revisions to state implementation plans under the Clean Air Act. *See* Ronald M. Levin, *Direct Final Rulemaking*, 64 GEO. WASH. L. REV. 1, 4–6 (1995).

316. *See* OFFICE OF THE VICE PRESIDENT, CREATING A GOVERNMENT THAT WORKS BETTER AND COSTS LESS, NATIONAL PERFORMANCE REVIEW, IMPROVING REGULATORY SYSTEMS 42–44 (1993).

317. ACUS Recommendation 95-4, *supra* note 306.

318. *Id.* (footnotes omitted).

319. Levin, *supra* note 315, at 10. As of July 2010, there had been no reported cases raising the legality of the practice.

320. These include agencies within the Departments of Agriculture and Transportation. *Id.* at 6–10.

321. ACUS Recommendation 95-4, *supra* note 306. ACUS recommended that agencies issue procedural regulations governing their use of direct-final rulemaking and also include a definition of "significant adverse comment." *Id.* ACUS suggests that this be defined as "a comment which

step process.[322] While it is true that the final rule is not republished, and therefore no "statement of basis and purpose" accompanies the rule, this potential objection "seems unduly formalistic."[323] Perhaps a more weighty legal objection might be that the 30-day effectiveness requirement for final rules is illegally circumvented. Professor Levin has suggested that to avoid this argument, agencies using this technique should issue a confirming notice at some point during the process saying that no adverse comments were received and announcing the effective date of the rule in 30 days or more.[324] ACUS urged agencies to state whether they would use that procedure or, alternatively, publish a single notice telling the public to assume it is final no less than 30 days after a specified date unless it is withdrawn by that date.[325]

Direct-final rulemaking for noncontroversial rules is gaining adherents,[326] and if done with proper attention to procedure,[327] it should provide a fair and efficient tech-

---

explains why the rule would be inappropriate, including challenges to the rule's underlying premise or approach, or why it would be ineffective or unacceptable without a change." *Id.*

322. *See* Sw. Pa. Growth Alliance v. Browner, 144 F.3d 984, 987 (6th Cir. 1998) (noting that EPA had withdrawn its original direct-final rule and proceeded to notice-and-comment rulemaking after receiving adverse comment); Sierra Club v. EPA, 99 F.3d 1551, 1554 n.4 (10th Cir. 1996) (same). Note that EPA has a practice of issuing a regular notice of proposed rulemaking simultaneously when proposing the direct-final rule. While this may serve as an "insurance policy" against starting over if an adverse comment is received, it also dilutes the cost savings of the procedure. ACUS did not opine on this strategy.

323. Levin, *supra* note 315, at 17. Professor Levin provides a thorough legal analysis and concludes that "the magnitude of the legal risks involved here should not be overstated." *Id.* at 22.

324. *Id.* at 21.

325. *See supra* note 317.

326. *See* Stuart Shapiro, *Two Months in the Regulatory State*, 30 Admin. & Reg. L. News 12, 13 (Spring 2005) (reporting that 120 of 392 rules issued in two-month period of 2003 were direct-final rules).

327. ACUS recommends that direct-final rulemaking should provide for the following "minimum procedures":

1. The text of the rule and a notice of opportunity for public comment should be published in the final rule section of the *Federal Register,* with a cross-reference in the proposed rule section that advises the public of the comment opportunity.
2. The notice should contain a statement of basis and purpose for the rule which discusses the issues the agency has considered and states that the agency believes the rule is noncontroversial and will elicit no significant adverse comment.
3. The public should be afforded adequate time (at least 30 days) to comment on the rule.
4. The agency's initial *Federal Register* notice should state which of the following procedures will be used if no significant adverse comments are received: (a) the agency will issue a notice confirming that the rule will go into effect no less than 30 days after such notice; or (b) that unless the agency publishes a notice withdrawing the rule by a specified date, the rule will become effective no less than 30 days after the specified date.
5. Where significant adverse comments are received or the rule is otherwise withdrawn, the agency should publish a notice in the *Federal Register* stating that the direct final rulemaking has been terminated.

ACUS Recommendation 95-4, *supra* note 306 (footnotes omitted).

nique for reducing delays in some rulemaking. On the other hand, if it is used by agencies to attempt to issue controversial rules, it will produce delays.[328]

e. Remedies for violations of the good-cause provision—Some disagreement exists about the appropriate remedy for erroneous use of the good-cause exemption from notice and comment. Section 706 of the APA states that "reviewing courts shall . . . hold unlawful and set aside agency action . . . found to be . . . without observance of procedure required by law."[329] Nonetheless, courts sometimes are reluctant to invalidate an otherwise valid rule, especially if it will disrupt ongoing programs.[330] Some courts, therefore, have used their equitable powers to fashion relief that balances the need to uphold procedural values with the need for agencies to carry out important programs. Sometimes courts allow the emergency rules to remain in effect pending completion of new proceedings in accordance with the APA.[331] In one case, the court held the agency's rule was valid but only as an interim measure.[332] On the other hand, courts may well vacate a rule where the good-cause finding is held to be invalid.[333]

As noted above, courts have also often been unwilling to excuse wrongful or erroneous use of the good-cause exemption where the agency sought to "cure" the procedural defect by providing an opportunity for public comment after promulgation.[334]

f. Suspension of effective dates—An issue related to the good-cause exemption is whether an agency may lawfully suspend the effective date of a rule without engaging in notice-and-comment rulemaking.[335] This issue is an outgrowth of the phenomenon known as "midnight rulemaking," whereby outgoing administrations seek to issue rules before leaving office and incoming administrations seek to suspend them, if they can, in order to reconsider or withdraw them.[336] One study has found that in

---

328. *See, e.g.*, Michael Kolber, *Rulemaking without Rules: An Empirical Study of Direct Final Rulemaking*, 72 ALB. L. REV. 79, (2009) (case study of FDA's use of direct-final rulemaking finding that 40% of its "DFRs" have had to be withdrawn due to significant opposing comments).

329. 5 U.S.C. § 706(2)(D). This is qualified by a provision that courts may take due account of the rule of prejudicial error. *Id.* § 706. *See* discussion of courts' power to remand without vacation, *infra* Part IV, ch. 2(C).

330. Jordan, *supra* note 265, at 166–68.

331. *See* W. Oil & Gas Ass'n v. EPA, 633 F.2d 803 (9th Cir. 1980); U.S. Steel Corp. v. EPA, 649 F.2d 572 (8th Cir. 1981).

332. Am. Fed'n of Gov't Emps. v. Block, 655 F.2d 1153, 1157–58 (D.C. Cir. 1981).

333. *See, e.g.*, Union of Concerned Scientists v. NRC, 711 F.2d 370 (D.C. Cir. 1983); Am. Iron & Steel Inst. v. EPA, 568 F.2d 284 (3d Cir. 1977). *Cf.* Air Transport Ass'n v. DOT, *supra* note 105.

334. *See* notes 257 & 311, *supra*.

335. *See also* discussion *infra* Part III, ch. 7(C)(2).

336. Midnight rulemaking has become the subject of a rich new vein of articles and commentary. The Administrative Conference has a research project on the subject at this writing, *see* http://www.acus.gov/research/the-conference-current-projects/midnight-rules/. *See also* Ari Cueni, Note, *Mooting The Night Away: Postinauguration Midnight-Rule Changes and Vacatur for*

election years leading to such changeovers, pages in the *Federal Register* (albeit an admittedly flawed measure) during the post-election quarter increased 27 percent on average as compared to the same periods in non-election years.[337]

The idea of an across-the-board suspension of the effective dates of the outgoing administration's rules first arose in 1981, in connection with the issuance of Executive Order 12,291, when some agencies were required to suspend the effective date of a promulgated rule to reconsider the costs and benefits under the requirements of the new executive order.[338] Two procedural issues were presented: first, whether suspension was rulemaking under the APA; and, second, if so, whether good cause existed for not providing an opportunity for comment. In *Natural Resources Defense Council, Inc. v. EPA*,[339] the Third Circuit specifically addressed whether the indefinite postponement of an EPA rule violated the procedural requirements of the APA. The court expressed concern about the fact that the agency, after a prolonged notice-and-comment period, promulgated a rule in final form with an effective date, and then delayed

---

Mootness, 60 Duke L.J. 453 (2010); Jerry Brito & Veronique de Rugy, *Midnight Regulations & Regulatory Review*, 61 Admin. L. Rev. 163, 163–64 (2009); Jack M. Beermann, *Combating Midnight Regulation*, 103 Nw. U. L. Rev. 352 (2009); Curtis W. Copeland, Midnight Rulemaking: Consideration for Congress and a New Administration, RL34747 (updated Dec. 12, 2008), *available at* http://opencrs.com/document/RL34747/2008-12-12/download/1005; Anne Joseph O'Connell, *Political Cycles of Rulemaking: An Empirical Portrait of the Modern Administrative State*, 94 Va. L. Rev. 889, 967–75 (2008); Jason M. Loring & Liam R. Roth, *After Midnight: The Durability of the "Midnight" Regulations Passed by the Two Previous Outgoing Administrations*, 40 Wake Forest L. Rev. 1441 (2005); Nina A. Mendelson, *Agency Burrowing: Entrenching Policies and Personnel Before a New President Arrives*, 78 N.Y.U. L. Rev. 557 (2003); William M. Jack, *Taking Care That Presidential Oversight of the Regulatory Process Is Faithfully Executed: A Review of Rule Withdrawals and Rule Suspensions under the Bush Administration's Card Memorandum*, 54 Admin. L. Rev. 1479, 1480–81 (2002). *See also* Nina Mendelson, *Midnight Rulemaking and Congress,* in Transitions (Austin Sarat ed., forthcoming 2011). For a critique of a Bush II Administration midnight rule, *see* Alexander Hood, Note, *The Same NEPA Proposal or Connected NEPA Actions?: Why the Bureau of Land Management's New Oil Shale Rules and Regulations Should Be Set Aside*, 37 B.C. Envtl. Aff. L. Rev. 191 (2010) For a critique of the Clinton Administration midnight rules in the context of the mining industry, *see* Andrew P. Morriss, Roger E. Meiners & Andrew Dorchak, *Between a Hard Rock and a Hard Place: Politics, Midnight Regulations and Mining*, 55 Admin. L. Rev. 551 (2003).

337. *See* Jay Cochran III, The Cinderella Constraint: Why Regulations Increase Significantly During Post-Election Quarters (2001), *available at* http://www.mercatus.org/pdf/materials/459.pdf.

338. Exec. Order 12,291, 3 C.F.R. § 127 (1981 compilation), *reprinted in* 5 U.S.C. § 601. Section 7(a) of the Order required agencies, with some exceptions, to "suspend or postpone" the effective dates of major rules that were promulgated in final form but had not yet become effective "to the extent necessary to permit reconsideration" under the Order. *See* Presidential Memorandum Postponing Pending Federal Regulations, 1981 Pub. Papers 63 (Jan. 29, 1981).

339. 683 F.2d 752, 761 (3d Cir. 1982) (concluding that EPA's action postponing the effective date of amendments to regulations relating to toxic pollutants was subject to the APA rulemaking requirements). *See also* Envtl. Def. Fund, Inc. v. Gorsuch, 713 F.2d 802, 814 (D.C. Cir. 1983) (finding EPA's decision not to "call in" permit applications acted as an indefinite suspension).

it.[340] The court said this delay of a duly promulgated rule without notice and comment was a "danger signal," and concluded the indefinite postponement of a final rule is tantamount to a repeal, so as to require rulemaking.[341] Indeed, the court pointed out that without an effective date, a rule "would be a nullity because it would never require adherence."[342] In invalidating the suspension, the court concluded that a justification was not shown for eliminating public participation because the agency could have complied with its obligation under both E.O. 12,291 and the APA by providing a brief public comment period.[343]

Although *Natural Resources Defense Council* focused on the "indefinite" delay of a rule, other courts have found that finite or short-term delays are normally subject to notice-and-comment procedures as well. In *Council of the Southern Mountains v. Donovan*,[344] the D.C. Circuit found that a six-month suspension of a mine safety rule was a rulemaking that would ordinarily be subject to notice and comment but also found that in the circumstances, while a "close case," the agency had good cause to dispense with notice-and-comment rulemaking.[345] Therefore, regardless of the duration of a postponement, a delay of a rule's effective date is normally considered a "rule" within the meaning of the APA so as to require notice-and-comment rulemaking.[346]

The issue of suspension of effective dates also arose in the transitions before and after the Bush II Administration and is likely to arise whenever the White House changes parties.

The Bush Administration's efforts to suspend the effective date of already issued Clinton Administration rules occasioned much controversy in 2001. On January 20, 2001, Andrew H. Card, Jr., President Bush's Chief of Staff, issued a memorandum, which became known as the Card Memorandum, to executive agency

---

340. *See Natural Resources Defense Council*, 683 F.2d at 760 ("By postponing the effective date of the [rules], EPA reversed its course of action up to the postponement. That reversal itself constitutes a danger signal.").

341. *See id.* at 761–64 (finding the effective date is an essential part of any rule).

342. *Id.* at 762 ("If the effective date were not 'part of an agency statement' . . . it would mean that an agency could guide a future rule through the rulemaking process, promulgate a final rule, and then effectively repeal it, simply by indefinitely postponing its operative date.").

343. *Id.* at 766.

344. 653 F.2d 573 (D.C. Cir. 1981).

345. *Id.* at 582.

346. *See* Peter D. Holmes, *Paradise Postponed: Suspensions of Agency Rules*, 65 N.C. L. Rev. 645, 675–76 (1987) (suggesting that agency suspensions are rulemakings and should be subject to APA requirements). *See* N.C. Growers' Ass'n, Inc. v. Solis, 644 F. Supp. 2d 664 (M.D.N.C. 2009) (grant of temporary injunction requiring implementation of a midnight rule after the incoming administration suspended it and reinstated earlier rule after comment period but without permitting comments on the merits of the midnight or earlier rule); N.C. Growers' Ass'n, Inc. v. Solis, slip op., 2011 WL 4708026 (M.D.N.C., Oct. 4, 2011) (granting summary judgment to plaintiffs on same grounds).

heads directing them to withdraw regulations sent to the Office of the Federal Register but not yet published, and to temporarily postpone the effective dates of published regulations not yet in effect.[347] Subsequently many agencies did so, and while a few agencies did go through notice-and-comment rulemaking to do so, most agencies cited the "good cause" and/or the "procedural rule" exemptions from notice and comment in their notices.[348] Most agencies cited the Card Memorandum's directive to reconsider the new regulations and stated something like, given "the imminence of the effective date, seeking prior public comment on this temporary delay would have been impractical, as well as contrary to the public interest in the orderly promulgation and implementation of regulations."[349] These practices tended to evade judicial challenge due to their short time frames, but they did occasion criticism.[350]

This cycle repeated itself on January 20, 2009, when President Obama's Chief of Staff Rahm Emanuel issued a similar memorandum.[351] This memorandum also required all proposed or final regulations that have not been published in the *Federal Register* to be withdrawn from that office so that they can be reviewed and approved by the new administration. But instead of postponing the effective dates of all regulations not in effect, it urged agencies to "consider extending for 60 days

---

347. Memorandum for the Heads and Acting Heads of Executive Departments and Agencies, 66 Fed. Reg. 7702 (Jan. 24, 2001).

348. *See* U.S. GEN. ACCOUNTING OFFICE, REGULATORY REVIEW: DELAY OF EFFECTIVE DATES OF FINAL RULES SUBJECT TO THE ADMINISTRATION'S JANUARY 20, 2001, MEMORANDUM 2 (GAO-02-370R) (Feb. 15, 2002), *available at* http://www.gao.gov/new.items/d02370r.pdf (reporting that 90 of the 371 rules subject to the Card Memorandum were delayed, but that of those 90, 75 were found to have gone into effect one year later). *But see* Nat. Res. Def. Council v. Abraham, 355 F.3d 179, 204–05 (2d Cir 2004) (rejecting DOE attempt to use procedural rule and good-cause exemptions to suspend effective date of energy conservation standards for air conditioners and heat pumps, finding that provisions of Energy Policy and Conservation Act make such a suspension a substantive rule, and "that an emergency of DOE's own making [cannot] constitute good cause").

349. *See* Jack, *supra* note 336, at 1508–09.

350. *See id.* at 1509 (finding that "the repeated explanation that notice and comment would be impracticable or contrary to the public interest is unpersuasive") and at 1517 (urging that "[i]n order to improve the use of rule suspensions in regulatory review plans, incoming administrations should not order the delay of effective dates of rules without directing agencies to evaluate each rule on a case-by-case basis"); *A Rush to Regulate—The Congressional Review Act and Recent Federal Regulations: Hearing Before the Subcomm. on Energy Policy, Natural Res. and Regulatory Affairs of the Comm. on Gov't Reform*, 107th Cong. 116–34 (2001) (prepared statement of Thomas O. McGarity) (analyzing the validity of rule withdrawals and suspensions under the Card Memorandum). For an analysis of the cases involving agency suspensions by the Reagan Administration, *see* Holmes, *supra* note 346.

351. Memorandum for the Heads of Executive Departments and Agencies from Rahm Emanuel, Assistant to the President and Chief of Staff (Jan. 20, 2001), 74 Fed. Reg. 4435 (Jan. 26, 2009).

the effective date of regulations that have been published in the *Federal Register* but not yet taken effect."[352]

5. *Exemptions from Delayed Effective Date Requirement*

Section 553(d) states that "[t]he required publication or service of a substantive rule shall be made not less than 30 days before its effective date." There are three exceptions to this requirement, two of which were discussed earlier in connection with section 553 exemptions from notice-and-comment requirements. Interpretive rules and policy statements[353] are not subject to the delayed effective date requirement, nor are rules for which the agency finds and publishes with the rule good cause for dispensing with the requirement.[354]

The third exception to the delayed effective date requirement is for "a substantive rule which grants or recognizes an exemption or relieves a restriction."[355] This exemption has no direct counterpart in section 553(b)'s exemptions from notice-and-comment requirements. However, it appears to be merely a more particularized statement of when a requirement is "unnecessary," which is one ground for a good-cause finding under section 553(b)(B). The primary purpose of the delayed effective date requirement is to give people a reasonable time to prepare to comply with or take other action with respect to the rule,[356] and one court has recently commented that "[i]t is much easier to demonstrate good cause for the failure to provide a 30-day waiting period, so long as affected parties have time to adjust their behavior before the final rule takes effect."[357]

The D.C. Circuit, upon finding that the Department of Justice had violated the 30-day waiting period, held that the violation is "remedied by denying such a rule effec-

---

352. *Id.* For suggestions as to what President Obama should have done about his predecessor's midnight rules, *see* Reece Rushing, Rick Melberth & Matt Madia, Center for American Progress & OMB Watch, *After Midnight: The Bush Legacy of Deregulation and What Obama Can Do* (2009), *available at* http://www.americanprogress.org/issues/2009/01/pdf/midnight_regulations.pdf.

353. *See supra* subsec. (D)(3).

354. *See supra* subsec. (D)(4). *See also* United States v. Gavrilovic, 551 F.2d 1089 (rejecting agency justification for waiver where consequence of agency rulemaking is to make previously lawful conduct unlawful and to impose criminal sanctions, and placing "heavy burden" on agency to establish "public necessity" for waiver).

355. 5 U.S.C. § 553(d)(1). *See* Indep. U.S. Tanker Owners Comm. v. Skinner, 884 F.2d 587, 591 (D.C. Cir. 1989) (holding where rule relieves restriction, agency need not make explicit claim in published rule of its right to waive 30-day waiting period).

356. *See* ATTORNEY GENERAL'S MANUAL, *supra* note 4, at 37; Jordan, *supra* note 265, at 142 & n.199. *See also* Daniel Int'l Corp. v. OSHRC, 656 F.2d 925 (4th Cir. 1981) (holding OSHA's failure to provide a full 30-day delayed effective date in 1971 did not invalidate rule as applied to corporation six years later).

357. San Diego Navy Broadway Complex Coal. v. U.S. Coast Guard, 2011 WL 1212888 *3 n.3 (S.D. Cal. 2011).

tiveness for the mandated 30 days, allowing it to take effect in full thereafter."[358] It explained that this approach "protects those who are affected by agency action taken during the 30-day waiting period without disturbing later action that is not the product of the violation."[359]

The exemptions from the APA's delayed effective date requirement sometimes have been confused with the exemptions from the APA's notice-and-comment requirements.[360] Therefore, it should be stressed that the exemption for rules granting an exemption or relieving a restriction does *not* apply to section 553's notice-and-comment provisions.[361]

E. Publication Requirements of Section 552 of the APA

While Section 553 of the APA contains most of the procedural requirements imposed on agency rulemaking by the Act, agency rulemakers should not forget that section 552, enacted as part of the Freedom of Information Act (FOIA), also contains certain requirements applicable to agency rules.[362] Subsection 552(a)(1) requires agencies to publish certain items in the *Federal Register* for the "guidance of the public."[363] The items include "rules of procedure"[364] and "substantive rules of general applicability adopted as authorized by law, and statements of general policy or interpretations of general applicability formulated and adopted by the agency."[365] The section also requires publication of "descriptions of [agency] organization"[366] and "statements of the general course and method by which [the agency's] functions are channeled and determined,"[367] which may be rules as defined in 5 U.S.C. § 551(4). Finally, section 552 specifically directs agencies to publish changes in, or repeals of, their rules and policies.[368]

Although the phraseology of section 552 is different from that used in the section 551 definition of *rule*, it appears to encompass almost all of the rules included in

---

358. Prows v. Dep't of Justice, 938 F.2d 274 (D.C. Cir. 1991).
359. *Id.* at 276.
360. Jordan, *supra* note 265, at 141–42.
361. Joseph v. Civil Service Comm'n, 554 F.2d 1140, 1153 n.23 (D.C. Cir. 1977).
362. 5 U.S.C. § 552. Section 552(a) is a revised version of the original section 3 of the APA. FOIA was amended by the Electronic Freedom of Information Act Amendments of 1996, Pub. L. No. 104-231, 110 Stat. 2422, but other than some refinements to the indexing requirements, none of the provisions discussed in this section were affected.
363. 5 U.S.C. § 552(a)(1). Much of the language in this section is carried over from section 3 of the original APA. *See also* Michael J. Kump, Note, *A Model for Determining the Publication Requirements of Section 552(a)(1) of the Administrative Procedure Act*, 13 U. Mich J. L. Reform 515 (1980).
364. 5 U.S.C. § 552(a)(1)(C).
365. *Id.* § 552(a)(1)(D).
366. *Id.* § 552(a)(1)(A).
367. *Id.* § 552(a)(1)(B).
368. *Id.* § 552(a)(1)(E).

section 551, even those exempt from notice-and-comment rulemaking under section 553. The one exception is "rules of particular applicability," which need not be published in the *Federal Register*.[369] Failure to comply with section 552's publication requirements means that a person may not be required to resort to, or be adversely affected by, a matter "required to be published in the *Federal Register* and not so published," unless the person has actual and timely notice of the matter.[370] One court has stated that "[n]onpublication in the *Federal Register* is a strong indication that a rule has not taken effect. . . . We have ruled, however, that a regulation need not necessarily be published in order to be enforced *against* the government."[371]

Subsection 552(a)(2) also requires other agency issuances—including final adjudicative opinions and those documents within the definition of *rule* that are not required to be published in the *Federal Register*—to be made available for public inspection and copying, with similar sanctions for non-adherence.[372] These include rules of *particular* applicability, other statements of policy and interpretations not of general applicability, and "administrative staff manuals and instructions to staff that affect a member of the public." Such issuances are also required to be compiled in publicly available (and, as of the year 2000, computerized) indexes.[373]

---

369. *See* discussion *infra* Part III, ch. 7(C).
370. 5 U.S.C. § 552(a)(1). However, despite the straightforward language, some courts have refused to invalidate agency enforcement actions where the agency failed to publish internal guidelines or policies and the challengers could not show they were adversely affected by nonpublication. *See, e.g.*, New York v. Lyng, 829 F.2d 346, 354 (2d Cir. 1987), where the Second Circuit held that the publication requirement "attaches only to matters which if not published would adversely affect a member of the public." This construction of section 552, the court said, "comports with the stated purpose of providing guidance to the public" and "reconciles the broad language of this provision with the impracticability of publishing all interpretative rulings." *Id. See also* Nguyen v. United States, 824 F.2d 697, 700–02 (9th Cir. 1987) (reiterating requirement that § 552(a)(1)(D) requires agencies to publish in the *Federal Register* all "statements of general policy and interpretations of general applicability," but finding that persons seeking relief from unpublished statements must show that the statement affects their "substantive rights," *i.e.*, that it (1) changes existing rules, policy or practice, (2) deviates from the plain meaning of the statute or regulation at issue, and (3) is of binding force and narrowly limits administrative discretion). The D.C. Circuit has made clear that § 552(a)(1)(D) is not violated unless complaining parties demonstrate that "they have in fact been adversely affected by the lack of notice" of a new standard. Alliance for Cannabis Therapeutics v. Drug Enforcement Admin., 15 F.3d 1131, 1136 (D.C. Cir. 1994). Presumably, this would require a showing that they would have changed their conduct if the matter had been published. *But cf.* Morton v. Ruiz, 415 U.S. 199, 234–36 (1974) (invalidating an interpretation of the Bureau of Indian Affairs adversely affecting the right of needy Indians to federal financial assistance because the interpretation had not been published as required by APA Section 552 and BIA manual of procedures). *See generally* Randy S. Springer, *Gatekeeping and the Federal Register: An Analysis of the Publication Requirement of Section 552(a)(1)(D) of the Administrative Procedure Act*, 41 ADMIN. L. REV. 533 (1989).
371. Zhang v. Slattery, 55 F.3d 732, 748 (2d Cir. 1995) (citation omitted).
372. This is referred to as the "reading room" provision in *Tax Analysts v. IRS*, 117 F.3d 607, 609 (D.C. Cir. 1997).
373. *See* 5 U.S.C. § 552(a)(1)(E).

Chapter 2

Use of Rulemaking or Adjudication for the Setting of Policy: A Comparison

Enabling statutes typically delegate to administrative agencies the central responsibility for policymaking in the area covered by the statute.[1] It is accepted that agencies are generally free to decide whether to formulate policy through rulemaking or adjudication.[2] This principle follows from the structure of the Administrative Procedure Act (APA), whose two main procedural sections are "Rule making" and "Adjudications."[3] Apart from rulemaking and adjudication, there are, of course, a variety of informal means by which administrative agencies articulate policy under a statute. Among these are press releases, speeches, statements, letters, advisory opinions, rulings, negotiation and litigation strategies, and a host of other types of communications.[4] The extent to which these informal means of articulating policy are binding on the public will vary, but their binding effect usually will be significantly less than that

---

1. The constitutionality of Congress's delegation of policymaking authority to administrative agencies has been frequently questioned. However, not since the 1930s, when the Supreme Court invoked the so-called nondelegation doctrine to strike down portions of the New Deal legislation (*e.g.*, Schechter Poultry Corp. v. United States, 295 U.S. 495 (1935)), has the Court relied on this principle to invalidate a statutory delegation. *See* Indus. Union Dep't AFL-CIO v. Am. Petroleum Inst., 448 U.S. 607, 674–75 (1980) (Rehnquist, J., concurring); Am. Textile Mfrs. Inst. v. Donovan, 452 U.S. 490, 543–44 (1981) (Burger, C.J., dissenting). *See also* Mistretta v. United States, 488 U.S. 361 (1989) (finding that a statute delegating authority to issue sentencing guidelines to the United States Sentencing Commission does not violate the nondelegation doctrine) and most recently, and definitively, Whitman v. Am. Trucking Ass'ns, 531 U.S. 457, 474 (2001) (unanimously reversing a D.C. Circuit decision that Environmental Protection Agency (EPA) standard-setting violated the nondelegation doctrine).
2. The first major case enunciating this principle was *SEC v. Chenery Corp.*, 332 U.S. 194 (1947) [hereinafter *Chenery II*]. *See* Russell L. Weaver, Chenery II*: A Forty-Year Retrospective*, 40 Admin. L. Rev. 161 (1988) (discussing *Chenery II* and its impact on agency decisionmaking); *see also* Roy A. Schotland, *A Sporting Proposition*, SEC v. Chenery, *in* Administrative Law Stories 168 (Peter L. Strauss ed., 2006) (providing historical account of case).
3. 5 U.S.C. §§ 553–554.
4. *See generally* Andrew P. Morriss, Bruce Yandle & Andrew Dorchak, *Choosing How to Regulate*, 29 Harv. Envtl. L. Rev. 179 (2005).

of a "rule" issued after rulemaking or an "order" after adjudication.[5] As a matter of practice, most significant agency policy decisions are formulated as either rulemaking or adjudication.[6] This chapter discusses the considerations, legal and other, that typically enter into an agency's deliberations in deciding whether to develop policy through rulemaking or adjudication.

Some agencies charged with enforcing regulatory statutes rely almost exclusively on decisions made in adjudicative proceedings for making policy to be applied in future cases. The National Labor Relations Board (NLRB) has traditionally been considered the best example. Over the years, the NLRB was widely criticized by courts and commentators for its failure to use rulemaking.[7] In one notable but isolated instance, the NLRB did utilize rulemaking to develop policy on appropriate collective bargaining units for certain facilities in the health-care industry.[8] Twenty years later, in late 2010, the Board again began to engage in rulemaking.[9]

Most other agencies routinely use rulemaking to develop "legislative" policy. These rulemaking agencies are typically also charged with bringing administrative or judicial enforcement actions against those who violate the agency's statute or rules issued

---

5. *See* ACUS Recommendation 89-5, *Achieving Judicial Acceptance of Agency Statutory Interpretations*, 54 Fed. Reg. 28,972 (July 10, 1989). *See also infra* subsec. (B)(1) for a discussion of the binding effects of rules.

6. *But see* Elizabeth Magill, *Agency Choice of Policymaking Form*, 71 U. Chi. L. Rev. 1383, 1384 (2004) (pointing out that "agencies have a range of policymaking forms to address problems within its purview," most notably legislative rulemaking, guidance, administrative enforcement actions, and judicial enforcement actions). This thoughtful and comprehensive article explores the "puzzle" presented by the doctrine that:

   [A]n agency can choose among its available policymaking tools and a court will not require it to provide an explanation for its choice. This judicial reaction is out of step with the rest of the law of judicial review of agency action. Courts usually demand that agencies provide reasoned explanations for their discretionary choices, but there is no such reason-giving requirement when agencies select their preferred policymaking form.

   Id. at 1385. *See also* Jeffrey J. Rachlinski, *Rulemaking Versus Adjudication: A Psychological Perspective*, 32 Fla. St. L. Rev. 529 (2005) (decrying the unwillingness of courts to review this policy choice).

7. My own contribution to this literature is Jeffrey S. Lubbers, *The Potential of Rulemaking by the NLRB*, 5 FIU L. Rev. 411 (2010). *See also* Samuel Estreicher, *Policy Oscillation at the Labor Board: A Plea for Rulemaking*, 37 Admin. L. Rev. 163 (1985). In *NLRB v. Wyman-Gordon Co.*, 394 U.S. 759 (1969), a majority of Justices criticized the Board for not using rulemaking.

8. *See* Mark H. Grunewald, *The NLRB's First Rulemaking: An Exercise in Pragmatism*, 41 Duke L.J. 274 (1991). The Supreme Court ultimately upheld the rule in *American Hospital Ass'n v. NLRB*, 499 U.S. 606 (1991). *See also* ACUS Recommendation 91-5, *Facilitating the Use of Rulemaking by the National Labor Relations Board*, 56 Fed. Reg. 33,851 (1991).

9. *See* Notification of Employee Rights Under the National Labor Relations Act, 76 Fed. Reg. 54,006 (Aug. 30, 2011); Representation—Case Procedures, 76 Fed. Reg. 80,138 (Dec. 22, 2011). The former rule was upheld (except for the remedy provision) in *National Ass'n of Manufacturers v. NLRB*, 2012 WL691535 (D.D.C. Mar. 2. 2012), but invalidated in *Chamber of Commerce v. NLRB,* 2012 WL1245677 (D.S.C. Apr. 13, 2012).

under its authority. These enforcement proceedings, although adjudicative, frequently also make policy, filling in the interstices of a statute and agency rules. Thus, many agencies regularly make policy through both rulemaking and adjudication and are confronted with the problem of choosing the more appropriate route in a particular situation. In this connection, note that the increasing complexity of rulemaking may result in more policy being made through enforcement proceedings and less through rulemaking. Few observers would applaud such a result.[10]

A. Legal Constraints on Choosing Rulemaking or Adjudication

1. *Statutory Requirements*

Some agencies have their discretion limited by a statutory mandate requiring them to issue rules on a particular issue. Environmental law provides numerous examples.[11] In such situations, the agency must use rulemaking, although the content, timing, and procedures used may involve significant opportunities for the exercise of agency discretion.[12]

2. *Statutory Authority*

"It is axiomatic that an administrative agency's power to promulgate legislative regulations is limited to the authority delegated by Congress."[13] Many statutes contain

---

10. *But see* Katie R. Eyer, *Administrative Adjudication and the Rule of Law*, 60 Admin. L. Rev. 647, 651 (2008) ("[P]osit[ing] that this apathetic (or sometimes hostile) attitude toward adjudicative lawmaking may not be as unambiguously appropriate as the current literature would seem to suggest.").

11. For example, under the Resource Conservation and Recovery Act of 1976, EPA was required to promulgate performance standards for the treatment, storage, or disposal of certain hazardous wastes within 18 months of the statute's enactment, following opportunity for public hearing and consultation with appropriate federal and state agencies. 42 U.S.C. § 6924(a). *See also* 42 U.S.C. § 7409 (requiring EPA to adopt national ambient air quality standards under the Clean Air Act). In one case, the D.C. Circuit rebuked EPA for attempting to use adjudication instead of rulemaking. *See* Michigan v. EPA, 268 F.3d 1075 (D.C. Cir. 2001) (holding that EPA could not determine jurisdictional issues over Indian country relating to federal operating permits under the Clean Air Act on an adjudicative case-by-case basis, where Clean Air Act required it to follow notice-and-comment rulemaking).

12. The statute limits EPA discretion on the contents of the rules by listing seven types of requirements that must be included in the standards. 42 U.S.C. § 6924(a)(1)–(7). Time limits for completion of agency rulemaking action are common but controversial. *See* discussion *supra* Part I(C).

13. Bowen v. Georgetown Univ. Hosp., 488 U.S. 204, 208 (1988). In turn, Congress must have the constitutional authority to regulate. The Supreme Court suggested limits on Congress's powers to enact extensive federal regulatory measures in *United States v. Morrison*, 529 U.S. 598 (2000) and *United States v. Lopez*, 514 U.S. 549 (1995). *Morrison* held that the civil rights

explicit authority for the agency to promulgate "legislative" rules. Thus, for example, the Occupational Safety and Health Administration (OSHA) is authorized to issue "occupational safety and health standard[s]."[14] The National Highway Traffic Safety Administration (NHTSA) is directed to issue motor vehicle safety standards that "shall be practicable, shall meet the need for motor vehicle safety and shall be stated in objective terms."[15] Other statutes, while not explicitly authorizing legislative rules, contain language authorizing agencies to "make such rules and regulations as may be necessary to carry out the provisions" of the Act.[16] Such an authorization clearly enables an agency to promulgate procedural, organizational, or other "housekeeping" rules[17] and probably also enables an agency to issue nonbinding guidelines or interpretations of its statutory authority. These powers are now quite widely accepted and may even be deemed within an agency's "inherent" authority. Moreover, decisions of the Supreme Court and the D.C. Circuit indicate judicial willingness to find legislative rulemaking authority in such language.[18]

---

remedy of the Violence Against Women Act of 1994 exceeded Congress's power under the Interstate Commerce Clause, and *Lopez* struck down federal regulation of guns near schools as an unconstitutional exercise of Congress's powers under the Commerce Clause. *But see* Gonzales v. Raich, 545 U.S. 1 (2005) (holding that the Controlled Substance Act's criminalization of purely intrastate activity, specifically the growing and consumption of medical marijuana, did not violate the Commerce Clause); Gibbs v. Babbitt, 214 F.3d 483 (4th Cir. 2000), *cert. denied sub nom.* Gibbs v. Norton, 531 U.S. 1145 (2001) (upholding a Fish and Wildlife Service regulation under the Endangered Species Act limiting the taking of red wolves on private land as constitutional under the Interstate Commerce Clause). *See also* United States v. Comstock, 130 S. Ct. 1949 (2010) (upholding, under the Necessary and Proper Clause, a federal civil-commitment statute that authorizes the Department of Justice to detain a mentally ill, sexually dangerous federal prisoner beyond the date the prisoner would otherwise be released if a state will not receive and incarcerate the prisoner). The Supreme Court has also, pursuant to the Tenth Amendment, struck down federal laws requiring states to enact or administer regulatory programs. *See* Printz v. Ravalli County, 521 U.S. 898 (1997) (finding portions of Brady handgun law requiring local officials to run background checks to be unconstitutional); New York v. United States, 505 U.S. 144 (1992) (striking down a law requiring states to "take title" of toxic waste sites or to enact legislation providing for disposal). Courts have also held that an agency's rule has extraterritorial effect only if Congress has indicated its intent to give the agency such authority and the agency has clearly exercised it. *See* Nieman v. Dryclean U.S.A. Franchise Co., 178 F.3d 1126 (11th Cir. 1999).

14. Occupational Health and Safety Act of 1970, 29 U.S.C. § 655(b).
15. National Traffic and Motor Vehicle Safety Act of 1966, 15 U.S.C. § 1392.
16. *See, e.g.*, Labor Management Relations Act, 29 U.S.C. § 156.
17. *See* 5 U.S.C. § 301 for specific authority for agency adoption of "housekeeping rules."
18. *See* Mayo Found. for Med. Educ. & Research v. United States, 131 S. Ct. 704, 713–14 (2011) (stating that the question of whether Congress "'delegated authority to the agency generally to make rules carrying the force of law' . . . does not turn on whether Congress's delegation of authority was general or specific" (quoting United States v. Mead Corp., 533 U.S. 218, 226–27 (2001))); Thorpe v. Housing Auth., 393 U.S. 268, 277 n.28 (1969) (interpreting HUD's statute granting it the power to "make, amend, and rescind such rules and regulations as may be neces-

One of the most significant early cases on this issue is *National Petroleum Refiners Ass'n v. FTC*,[19] in which the D.C. Circuit construed the Federal Trade Commission's enabling statute giving the agency only general "rules and regulations" authority as authorizing legislative rulemaking by the agency. The court, relying largely on Congress's concern with the "judicial delay, inefficiency and uncertainty" involved in the adjudicatory process, concluded that the "broad undisputed policies" that motivated the framers of the Federal Trade Commission Act of 1914[20] would be furthered by assigning substantive rulemaking authority to the agency.[21]

This issue has taken on added importance after the Supreme Court's decisions in *Christensen v. Harris County*[22] and *United States v. Mead Corp.*,[23] which held that

---

sary to carry out the provisions of this Act" as giving it the power to make regulations with the force of law, and stating that "[s]uch broad rule-making powers have been granted to numerous other federal administrative bodies in substantially the same language"); Am. Paper Inst. v. Am. Elec. Power Co., 461 U.S. 402, 419 (1983); E.I. du Pont de Nemours & Co. v. Train, 430 U.S. 112, 132 (1977); Mourning v. Family Publications Serv., Inc., 411 U.S. 356, 372–73 (1973); *In re* Permanent Surface Mining Regulation Litig., 653 F.2d 514, 522–24 (D.C. Cir. 1981) (en banc); Citizens to Save Spencer County v. EPA, 600 F.2d 844, 873 (D.C. Cir. 1979); Nat'l Petroleum Refiners Ass'n v. FTC, 482 F.2d 672 (D.C. Cir 1973), *cert. denied*, 415 U.S. 951 (1974). *See also* Michael J. Burstein, *Rules for Patents*, 52 Wm. & Mary L. Rev. 1747 (2011) (arguing that the Patent and Trademark Office (PTO) should be granted substantive rulemaking authority). In inconclusive litigation over whether the PTO already has rulemaking authority, a district court ruled that the PTO only had procedural rulemaking authority. *See* Tafas v. Dudas, 541 F. Supp. 2d 805 (E.D. Va. 2008), *aff'd in part and vacated in part by* Tafas v. Doll, 559 F.3d 1345 (Fed. Cir. 2009), *vacated*, 328 Fed. App'x. 658 (Fed. Cir. 2009), *appeal dismissed*, Tafas v. Kappos, 586 F.3d 1369 (Fed. Cir. 2009). For a strongly stated alternate view, *see* Thomas W. Merrill & Kathryn Tongue Watts, *Agency Rules with the Force of Law: The Original Convention*, 116 Harv. L. Rev. 467 (2002). *Cf.* Michigan v. EPA, 268 F.3d 1075, 1082 (D.C. Cir. 2001) ("Mere ambiguity in a statute is not evidence of congressional delegation of authority.").

19. 482 F.2d 672 (D.C. Cir. 1973), *cert. denied*, 415 U.S. 951 (1974).
20. 38 Stat. 717 (codified as amended in scattered sections of 15 U.S.C.).
21. *Nat'l Petroleum Refiners Ass'n*, 482 F.2d at 683–87. Two years later Congress confirmed the FTC's authority to issue legally binding trade regulation rules, albeit with additional procedural requirements, by enacting the Magnuson-Moss Warranty–Federal Trade Commission Improvement Act, Pub. L. No. 93-637, 88 Stat. 2183 (1975) (codified at 15 U.S.C. § 57a). The GAO has weighed in recently on several other issues concerning the breadth of agency rulemaking authority. *See, e.g.*, U.S. Gov't Accountability Office, Credit Cards: Fair Debt Collection Practices Act Could Better Reflect the Evolving Debt Collection Marketplace and Use of Technology 49–51 (GAO-09-748, 2009) (describing the FTC's lack of rulemaking authority to administering the Fair Debt Collection Practices Act and suggesting that Congress remedy this); U.S. Gov't Accountability Office, Consumer Safety: Better Information and Planning Would Strengthen CPSC's Oversight of Imported Products 16 (GAO-09-803, 2009) (describing the CPSC's mandate to conduct more than 40 rulemakings under its new legislation and the delays in completing them).
22. 529 U.S. 576 (2000) (discussed *infra* Part IV, ch. 2, text at notes 207–15).
23. 533 U.S. 218 (2001) (discussed *infra* Part IV, ch. 2, text at notes 216–23). *See also* Gonzales v. Oregon, 546 U.S. 243, 258 (2006) (to be entitled to *Chevron* deference, "the rule must be

agency interpretations should receive *Chevron* deference only when Congress has delegated power to the agency to make rules with the force of law and the agency has
rendered its interpretation in the exercise of that power. Professor Thomas Merrill and
Kathryn Watts have provocatively argued that the original (and better) understanding is
that only those rulemaking grants that are "coupled with a statutory provision imposing
sanctions on those who violate the rules" should be understood to authorize rules with
the force of law, and that "rulemaking grants not coupled with any provision for sanctions should be understood to authorize only interpretive and procedural rules."[24]

3. *Judicial Constraints*

The Supreme Court in *SEC v. Chenery Corp. (Chenery II)*[25] first enunciated the
general rule that the choice between rulemaking and adjudication is primarily the
agency's to make. The case involved the Securities and Exchange Commission's (SEC's)
disapproval of a public utility holding company's reorganization on the ground that
the reorganization violated standards of fairness derived from the SEC's interpretation of the relevant Act. In effect, the Commission both formulated a rule and applied
it in the adjudication before it. The Supreme Court, although observing that "[t]he
function of filling in the interstices of the Act should be performed, as much as possible, through the quasi-legislative promulgation of rules to be applied in the future,"[26]
ultimately gave the agency the option: "the choice made between proceeding by general rule or by individual, ad hoc litigation," the Court said, "is one that lies primarily
in the informed discretion of the administrative agency."[27]

The Supreme Court gave a bigger boost to policymaking by rulemaking in *United
States v. Storer Broadcasting Co.*[28] In that case, the Federal Communications Commission (FCC) issued a notice of proposed rulemaking to amend its rules limiting the
number of radio and television stations an entity could own or control. After the
notice, but before the adoption of the amendment, Storer Broadcasting Company,
which already held the maximum number allowed under the new proposal, applied
for an additional station. Storer also participated in the rulemaking proceeding by
opposing the proposal, but the Commission adopted the rule and simultaneously dismissed Storer's application for the new station as violative of the new rule. Storer, on
judicial review, claimed it was deprived of a "full hearing," which the Commission's

---

promulgated pursuant to authority Congress has delegated to the official" (citing *Mead*, 533
U.S. at 226–27)). In *Gonzales*, the Court found that Congress had granted the Attorney General narrowly limited authority to issue rules under the Controlled Substances Act. *Id.* at 917.
24. Merrill & Watts, *supra* note 18, at 469 (2002) (opining that "courts held that some agencies,
such as the FTC, FDA, and NLRB, had legislative rulemaking powers that Congress almost
certainly had not intended").
25. *Chenery II*, 332 U.S. 194 (1947).
26. *Id.* at 202.
27. *Id.* at 203.
28. 351 U.S. 192 (1956).

rules made a prerequisite to the denial of applications. The Supreme Court upheld the Commission's power to issue such rules and to deny the application without hearing on the basis of the rule. The Court did, however, caution that the rules must be flexible enough to permit applicants to seek amendments or waivers.[29]

Storer did not result in any rush by agencies to employ rulemaking, but other agencies and courts did slowly follow its lead. The Federal Power Commission began to use rulemaking to set gas rates, an action previously undertaken through individual trial-type proceedings, and the Supreme Court approved this development in *Federal Power Commission v. Texaco, Inc.*[30] and *In re Permian Basin Area Rate Cases.*[31] The Civil Aeronautics Board's move toward rulemaking was upheld by the courts despite claims that the rules, in effect, modified existing certificates without adjudicatory hearings. Especially influential was *American Airlines, Inc. v. CAB*, where Judge Harold Leventhal wrote that "rulemaking is a vital part of the administrative process . . . and . . . is not to be shackled, in the absence of clear and specific congressional require-ment, by importation of formalities developed for the adjudicatory process and basi-cally unsuited for policy rulemaking."[32]

As rulemaking became more and more pervasive, the issue no longer was whether rulemaking was a proper mechanism for policymaking. Rather, the arguments fo-cused on whether formulating general policy rules through adjudication constituted a circumvention of the notice-and-comment provisions of § 553 of the APA.[33] This criticism was particularly leveled at the NLRB, whose refusal to employ rulemaking was well known.

However, in *NLRB v. Bell Aerospace Co.*,[34] the Supreme Court reaffirmed *Chenery II*'s rule that the choice between rulemaking and adjudication is generally the agency's to make. The Supreme Court asserted:

> [T]he Board is not precluded from announcing new principles in an adjudica-tive proceeding and . . . the choice between rulemaking and adjudication lies

---

29. The Supreme Court relied on *Storer* in *Heckler v. Campbell*, 461 U.S. 458 (1983), which upheld HHS's reliance on "medical vocational guidelines" in an adjudicatory proceeding to determine a claimant's right to Social Security benefits. *See* discussion *infra* subsec. (B)(1). However, in *FCC v. WNCN Listeners Guild*, 450 U.S. 582 (1981), the Court upheld an FCC rule that provided that waiver requests would not be considered.
30. 377 U.S. 33 (1964).
31. 390 U.S. 747 (1968).
32. 359 F.2d 624, 629 (D.C. Cir. 1966), *cert denied*, 385 U.S. 843 (1966).
33. One challenge of this type, in an enforcement context, is *Kaspar Wire Works, Inc. v. Sec'y of Labor*, 268 F.3d 1123, 1131, 1132 (D.C. Cir. 2001) (rejecting the claim that the Secretary of Labor's decision to impose a per instance penalty on petitioner must be done through rulemaking: "The Secretary's decision to assess per instance penalties reflects use of an enforcement tool within her authority," and "because the statutory authorization of per in-stance penalties is so clear from the statutory language, publication in the Federal Register was not required").
34. 416 U.S. 267 (1974).

in the first instance within the Board's discretion. Although there may be situations where the Board's reliance on adjudication would amount to an abuse of discretion or violation of the Act, nothing in the present case would justify such a conclusion."[35]

The doctrine that agencies may choose between rulemaking and adjudication has been reaffirmed in a number of court decisions.[36] Challenges, however, continue to come from a variety of directions.

Some petitions for review, rather than challenging agency policymaking made through adjudication, sought to *force* the agency to use adjudicatory procedures to determine the rights of a party. A typical example is *Wisconsin Gas Co. v. FERC*,[37] where sellers of natural gas challenged certain FERC orders involving the rights of sellers to recover variable costs, on the ground, among others, that they were based on informal rulemaking. The sellers claimed that because their individual rights were being affected by the orders, they "merited individualized case-by-case adjudication."[38] The D.C. Circuit rejected the argument, emphasizing "the breadth and complexity of the Commission's responsibilities" and the "intensely practical difficulties" involved in natural gas regulation.[39] It reaffirmed the principle in *Chenery II* that the choice between proceeding either by general rule or by individual ad hoc litigation lies primarily in the "informed discretion of the agency."[40] The court said: "[N]otice and comment rulemaking, particularly appropriate for determination of legislative

---

35. *Id.* at 294. This case eliminated much of the confusion created by *NLRB v. Wyman-Gordon, Inc.*, 394 U.S. 759, where the Court, in a badly split decision, suggested disapproval of the NLRB's practice of promulgating general rules through adjudication, although it did approve the agency's application of the rule in the instant case. *See also* Morton v. Ruiz, 415 U.S. 199 (1974) (criticizing agency policymaking in an adjudicatory context as ad hoc); Weaver, *supra* note 2, at 186.

36. *See, e.g.*, Qwest Services Corp. v. FCC, 509 F.3d 531 (D.C. Cir. 2007) ("[Petitioner] argues that such a broadly applicable order as in fact came forth . . . can only take the form of a rule, and thus must be prospective only. There is no such general principle. Most norms that emerge from a rulemaking are equally capable of emerging (legitimately) from an adjudication, and accordingly agencies have very broad discretion whether to proceed by way of adjudication or rulemaking." (citing *Bell Aerospace*, 416 U.S. 267, 294–95 (1974), other citations and internal quotation marks omitted)); Panhandle E. Pipe Line Co. v. FERC, 907 F.2d 185 (D.C. Cir. 1990) ("It is far too late in the day to claim that an agency may not simplify adjudications by resolving issues in a rulemaking." (citing Heckler v. Campbell, 461 U.S. 458, 467 (1983)). *See also* Tearney v. NTSB, 868 F.2d 1451 (5th Cir. 1989); Quivira Mining Co. v. NRC, 866 F.2d 1246 (10th Cir. 1989); Anaconda Co. v. Ruckelshaus, 482 F.2d 1301, 1306 (10th Cir. 1973) (upholding EPA's denial of an adjudicatory hearing in the context of an emission standard rulemaking for sulfur oxide even though it only applied to a single entity).

37. 770 F.2d 1144 (D.C. Cir. 1985).

38. *Id.* at 1165. *See also* Anaconda Co. v. Ruckelshaus, *supra* note 36 (upholding EPA's use of rulemaking procedures to issue a general rule that, in practice, covered only one company).

39. *Wisconsin Gas Co.*, 770 F.2d at 1166 (quoting *In re* Permian Basin Area Rate Cases, 390 U.S. 747, 790 (1968)).

40. *Id.*

facts and policy of general, prospective applicability, was a manifestly reasonable method of addressing the systemic problems of the natural gas market."[41]

The principle that an agency is free to choose rulemaking or adjudication has also arisen in the context of court suits to compel an agency to institute rulemaking proceedings. In *Arkansas Power & Light Co. v. ICC*,[42] the court, after noting that courts will compel rulemaking only in "extremely rare instances," asserted that an even stronger case for deference to the agency determination exists where the selected alternative to rulemaking is not maintenance of the status quo but "formulation of standards through case-by-case adjudication."[43]

There are times, however, when courts have found that an agency abused its discretion in choosing to make law by order rather than by rule. For example, agencies are not free to overrule one of their legislative rules in an adjudication.[44]

In other cases, it may be an abuse of discretion for an agency to announce a new ruling in an adjudication to parties who had justifiably relied on the law as it was when they undertook their conduct.[45] A more controversial broadside was issued in

---

41. *Id.* Indeed, in the view of the court, case-by-case adjudication in these circumstances "may have been entirely inappropriate," because the agency, by applying an adjudicatory order to the individual seller, would be subjecting that seller to unfair competition from other sellers not yet the subject of agency orders. *Id.* at 1166–67 n.36. The court further stated that case-by-case adjudication would open the agency to the objection that it was "unfairly effectuating a general policy change without the necessary industry-wide data and commentary." *Id. See also* Mobil Oil Exploration & Producing Se., Inc. v. United Distrib. Cos., 498 U.S. 211, 227–28 (1991) (sustaining FERC rulemaking on abandonment of gas supply contracts that eliminated the need for individualized hearings on such abandonments); Quivira Mining Co. v. NRC, 866 F.2d 1246, 1261 (10th Cir. 1989); Hercules Inc. v. EPA, 598 F.2d 91 (D.C. Cir. 1978).

42. 725 F.2d 716 (D.C. Cir. 1984).

43. *Id.* at 723. *See also* British Caledonia Airways Ltd. v. Civil Aeronautics Bd., 584 F.2d 982 (D.C. Cir. 1978) (upholding the agency's choice of declaratory order procedure under § 554(d) of the APA instead of rulemaking, despite the industry-wide impact of the order).

44. *See, e.g.*, Tunik v. Merit Sys. Prot. Bd., 407 F.3d 1326, 1341–42, 1345–46 (Fed. Cir. 2005) (citing United States v. Nixon, 418 U.S. 683, 695–96 (1974)) (finding that the Board erred in reversing an earlier holding because it had, in the intervening time, codified the earlier decision in a rule issued after notice and comment). The dissenting judge argued that the earlier decision, and thus the rule, were both ultra vires. *Id.* at 1346–52 (Schall, J., dissenting). *See also* Am. Fed'n of Gov't Emps., AFL-CIO v. Fed. Labor Relations Auth., 777 F.2d 759 (D.C. Cir. 1985) ("[A]n agency seeking to repeal or modify a legislative rule promulgated by means of notice and comment rulemaking is obligated to undertake similar procedures to accomplish such modification or repeal . . . .").

45. The Supreme Court has described this as "the doctrine that an administrative agency may not apply a new rule [announced in an adjudication] retroactively when to do so would unduly intrude upon reasonable reliance interests." Heckler v. Cmty. Health Servs. of Crawford Cnty., Inc., 467 U.S. 51, 60 n.12 (1984) (citing *Bell Aerospace, supra* note 34, at 295). This issue had earlier been thoroughly plumbed in *Retail, Wholesale & Dep't Store Union, AFL-CIO v. NLRB*, 466 F.2d 380 (D.C. Cir. 1972), *cert. denied*, 459 U.S. 999 (1982), where the NLRB had relied on one of its recently decided cases that had reversed an earlier case, thus making the employer's conduct—which was legal at the time it occurred—an unfair labor practice. In the circumstances, the court found this to be an abuse of discretion. The court listed the following consid-

Ford Motor Co. v. FTC,[46] where the Ninth Circuit set aside an FTC cease-and-desist order against a car dealer because the credit practice rule announced in that adjudication should have been promulgated through rulemaking. The court's use of broad language, stating that because "this adjudication changes existing law and has widespread application . . . the matter should have been addressed by rulemaking,"[47] led to extensive criticism of the decision,[48] and the Ninth Circuit has subsequently "refrained from striking down adjudications on the ground that the agency should have proceeded instead by rulemaking."[49]

---

erations in determining whether agency policymaking by adjudication is an abuse of discretion: (1) whether the particular case is one of first impression, (2) whether the new rule represents an abrupt departure from well-established practice or merely attempts to fill a void in an unsettled area of law, (3) the extent to which the party against whom the new rule is applied relied on the former rule, (4) the degree of the burden that a retroactive order imposes on a party, and (5) the statutory interest in applying a new rule despite the reliance of a party on the old standard. *Id.* at 390. *See also* Stoller v. Commodity Futures Trading Comm'n, 834 F.2d 262, 265–66 (2d Cir. 1987) (holding that while an agency may change existing policy through adjudication, it may not retroactively "charge a knowing violation of that revised standard and thereby cause undue prejudice to a litigant who may have relied on the agency's prior policy or interpretation").

46. 673 F.2d 1008 (9th Cir. 1981).
47. *Id.* at 1009.
48. 1 Kenneth Culp Davis & Richard J. Pierce, Jr., Administrative Law Treatise § 6.6, 13.2 (3d ed. 1994); Richard K. Berg, *Re-examining Policy Procedures: The Choice Between Rulemaking and Adjudication*, 38 Admin. L. Rev. 149, 151 n.21 (1986).
49. William D. Araiza, *Agency Adjudication, the Importance of Facts and the Limitations of Labels*, 57 Wash. & Lee L. Rev. 351, 370 (2000). Professor Manning suggests that "[m]ore typically, post-*Bell Aerospace* decisions have relied on rather idiosyncratic grounds to reject an agency's procedural choice." John F. Manning, *Nonlegislative Rules*, 72 Geo. Wash. L. Rev. 893, 909 n.96 (2004). He characterizes *Ford Motor Co.* as "holding that the agency improperly proceeded by adjudication where the order has 'general application' and adopts 'the precise rule that the [agency] has proposed, but not yet promulgated' in a notice-and-comment proceeding." *Id.* (quoting *Ford*, 673 F.2d at 1010). He also mentions two other cases:

Matzke v. Block, 732 F.2d 799, 802 (10th Cir. 1984) (concluding that rulemaking was required where Congress had indicated "an urgent need for relief" from farm foreclosures and where "it seem[ed] a bit late to begin the accumulation of decisional guides" under a new statute passed for that purpose) . . . and Patel v. INS, 638 F.2d 1199, 1202 (9th Cir. 1980) (holding that an agency may not use adjudication to add a regulatory requirement that "had been expressly discarded during . . . rule-making proceedings").

Id. He concludes that:

Such decisions do not establish a meaningful general restriction on the procedural discretion established by *Chenery II* and confirmed by *Bell Aerospace*. Indeed, the Ninth Circuit, which had taken the lead in developing post–*Bell Aerospace* limits on agency choice, subsequently suggested that its (non-reliance-based) limits apply only when an agency employs adjudication to "amend a recently adopted rule" or "to supplant a pending rule-making proceeding."

Id. (quoting Cities of Anaheim, Riverside, Banning, Colton & Azusa v. FERC, 723 F.2d 656, 659 (9th Cir. 1984)).

In *Independent U.S. Tanker Owners Committee v. Lewis,*[50] the court addressed the following issue: "What is the effect of an invalidly promulgated rule upon an adjudicative decision that relies on that rule when the decision, without any rule, would have been within the discretion of the agency?" Or, as the court bluntly rephrased the question: "MarAd having botched the rulemaking, the question is whether the subsequent adjudication . . . can still be upheld in its own right."[51] The answer apparently depends on the nature of the rule and its impact on the challenger; in this case, the court refused to invalidate the decision.[52]

B. Practical Considerations in Choosing Rulemaking or Adjudication

Rulemaking and adjudication both can be used to establish standards of conduct for those who are regulated. Both types of decisionmaking can be used to create the necessary predicate for penalizing violators of those standards. They both require the assembly of sufficient factual information to support wise policy judgments. Nevertheless, various advantages are associated with each procedure.

1. Advantages of Rulemaking

In the last two decades, most commentators have espoused the benefits of rulemaking over adjudication for policymaking. A former ACUS General Counsel summarized these benefits as follows:[53]

1. A rule formulated after rulemaking, "with its wider notice and broader opportunities for participation[,] is fairer to the class of persons who would be affected by a new 'rule' than" a rule announced in an adjudication. "Such broader participation also makes rulemaking more efficient as an information-gathering technique for the agency."[54]
2. "Rulemaking is superior to adjudication as a means of making new law because rulemaking is normally prospective while adjudication normally involves prescribing consequences for past conduct or present status."[55]

---

50. 690 F.2d 908 (D.C. Cir. 1982).
51. *Id.* at 920.
52. *Id.* at 922.
53. Berg, *supra* note 48, at 163. *See also* Arthur Earl Bonfield, *State Administrative Policy Formulation and the Choice of Lawmaking Methodology*, 42 ADMIN. L. REV. 121, 122–36 (1990). *But see* Glen O. Robinson, *The Making of Administrative Policy: Another Look at Rulemaking and Adjudication and Administrative Procedure Reform*, 118 U. PA. L. REV. 485, 508–13 (1970).
54. Berg, *supra* note 48, at 163.
55. *Id.*

3. "The articulation of a generally applicable rule provides greater clarity to those affected as well as greater uniformity in enforcement."[56]

4. "Rulemaking is more efficient from the agency's point of view because its procedures offer more flexibility, at least when the choice is between the notice-and-comment requirements of section 553 of the APA and the formal adjudicatory procedures of sections 554, 556, and 557 of the APA. Two of the most significant elements of this flexibility are the agency's broad control over the procedure for the presentation of information and argument and the agency's freedom to resort to its staff expertise without the inhibitions of separation of functions requirements."[57]

5. "Since the agency is better able to control the scope and the pace of a rulemaking proceeding, use of rulemaking to formulate policy gives the agency better control of its agenda and enables it to define and to focus on the policy issues without the distractions of individual adjudicative issues" or the need to wait for issues to arise in a case.[58]

6. "Rulemaking is also more efficient for the agency because it can result in the adoption of a general principle which can thereafter be applied without reexamination," thereby eliminating the need for many case-by-case adjudications.[59]

Another major advantage of policymaking through rulemaking is the broader binding effect of rules. Valid legislative rules are binding and enforceable on the public; that is, they have the force and effect of law.[60] Adjudicatory decisions and orders, on the other hand, are typically binding only on the parties involved, and the rule stated in the proceeding would have precedential effect only in subsequent adjudications.[61] This principle was stated by the D.C. Circuit in *National Petroleum Refin-*

---

56. *Id.*

57. *Id. See infra* Part III, ch. 6(E) (discussing separation of functions).

58. Berg, *supra* note 48, at 163.

59. *Id.* at 163–64.

60. Great N. Ry. Co. v. Washington, 300 U.S. 154 (1937).

61. *See, e.g.,* NLRB v. St. Francis Hosp., 601 F.2d 404 (9th Cir. 1979) (holding that NLRB could announce a prospective policy in an adjudication, but had to allow parties in subsequent enforcement actions to challenge application of the policy to them). This should not be read to require the agency to re-decide these issues de novo every time, but the agency would need to entertain arguments and explain why they are unavailing. After a while, litigants might give up on finding new arguments, but the main difference is that if it were a "rulemaking rule," the agency would not have to entertain arguments. (With one caveat—if a party seeks a waiver from a rulemaking rule and can make a good argument, the agency would have to respond to it—but courts have also allowed agencies to respond that they have a policy of denying all requests for waivers from a particular rule, *cf.* the FAA's long-standing age-60 rule for pilots. *See, e.g.,* Yetman v. Garvey, 261 F.3d 664 (7th Cir. 2001). The current FAA pilot age rule is at 14 C.F.R. §121.383 (2010), but the age limit is now 65.

ers Ass'n v. FTC,[62] a case upholding the FTC's authority to define violations of the FTC Act through regulations. The court noted that one benefit of rulemaking was that the principal issue in future enforcement cases would simply be whether the defendant in fact violated the rule. In that case, the FTC had issued a rule requiring posting of gasoline octane ratings. It therefore would only have to prove that a defendant's gasoline pumps were not properly marked with octane ratings. Had no rule requiring postings of octane ratings been promulgated, the FTC would have been obliged to prove that the failure to post was an unfair trade practice, a "laborious process" that might well have to be repeated each time a new enforcement case was brought.[63]

This principle, based on the Supreme Court holding in *Storer Broadcasting,* that an agency may rely on a rule promulgated under the notice-and-comment procedures of the APA to limit the issues to be litigated in a subsequent adjudicative proceeding, was reaffirmed by the Supreme Court in *Heckler v. Campbell.*[64] In that case, the Secretary of Health and Human Services (HHS), after notice-and-comment rulemaking, promulgated a medical-vocational "grid" to be applied in disability hearings under the Social Security Act. A claimant's qualifications for work were determined on an individual basis, but the guidelines directed the conclusion whether work existed in the national economy that the claimant could perform.[65] The Supreme Court upheld government reliance on the guidelines, saying that although the Social Security Act requires an individualized trial-type determination of the claimant's disability, HHS may resolve a "general factual issue," such as the question of the availability of jobs in the national economy, "as fairly through rulemaking as by introducing the testimony of vocational experts at each disability hearing."[66] The Court reaffirmed this decision in 2001 in a case involving the Bureau of Prisons.[67]

---

62. 482 F.2d 672 (D.C. Cir. 1973), *cert. denied,* 415 U.S. 951 (1974).
63. 482 F.2d at 690–91. But note that policy statements have their advantages too. As the D.C. Circuit stated in upholding the agency's explanation for why it declined to apply a revised policy statement to a case that was pending when a policy was revised: "When an agency hears a case under an established policy statement, it may decide the case using that policy statement if the decision is not otherwise arbitrary and capricious. If, however, the agency changes its policy statement before the case is complete, it must explain why the pending case should be decided on the basis of the old versus the new policy." Consol. Edison Co. of N.Y., Inc. v. FERC, 315 F.3d 316, 323 (D.C. Cir. 2003).
64. 461 U.S. 458 (1983).
65. *Id.* at 460–62.
66. *Id.* at 468. *But see* Broz v. Heckler, 711 F.2d 957 (11th Cir. 1983), *modified,* 721 F.2d 1297 (11th Cir. 1983) (holding that in disability hearings, the effect of claimant's age on his or her ability to work must be determined on a case-by-case basis).
67. Lopez v. Davis, 531 U.S. 230 (2001) (holding that the Bureau of Prisons had discretion, under the governing statute, to promulgate regulation categorically denying early release to prisoners whose felonies involved use of a firearm). *See also* Munoz v. Sabol, 517 F.3d 29 (1st Cir. 2008). For affirmation of this principle in another regulatory setting, *see* Massachusetts v. United

126   *A Guide to Federal Agency Rulemaking*

2. Advantages of Adjudication

Among the advantages of adjudication and the disadvantages of rulemaking are the following:

1. Rulemaking's increasing procedural complexity can be avoided. New statutes and executive orders have imposed many additional requirements on the rulemaking process. Whatever their benefits in other respects, clearance provisions (OMB review, paperwork reduction provisions), impact statements (regulatory impact analyses, regulatory flexibility analyses), statutes requiring more cumbersome hybrid procedures, and "hard look" judicial review tend to make rulemaking by some agencies a more difficult and protracted venture.[68] If an area is equally susceptible to regulation by adjudication or rulemaking—where, for example, a small number of firms are engaged in the regulated activity—policymaking through adjudication may be seen as more efficient.[69]

2. Modifications can be made more easily. Specific rules may become obsolete more quickly than more general statutory standards. However, modifications or repeal of rules for policy or technical reasons may be difficult or protracted because a new rulemaking has to be conducted. This may be especially difficult for agencies governed by "hybrid" rulemaking statutes or for rules defined as "major rules" under E.O. 12,866. Changing policy established by adjudication may, therefore, consume much less time.

3. Conflict can be minimized. At least one commentator has explained the NLRB's previously steadfast reluctance to abandon the making of policy through adjudication as based on a desire to avoid political conflicts with congressional oversight committees and other overseers.[70] The premise is that the slow, case-

---

States, 522 F.3d 115, 120 (1st Cir. 2008) (finding that because certain environmental issues concerning spent nuclear fuel "have already been addressed globally by [a regulation], they cannot be litigated in individual adjudications, such as license renewal proceedings for individual plants").

68. See *infra* Part II, ch. 3, Part III, ch. 2, and Part IV, ch. 2, for a discussion of these requirements. *See also* E. Donald Elliott, *Re-Inventing Rulemaking*, 41 DUKE L.J. 1490 (1992).

69. In 1981, Professor (now Justice) Scalia suggested that increased procedural burden on rulemaking might lead agencies to rely more on adjudication for development of policy. Antonin Scalia, *Back to Basics: Making Law Without Making Rules*, REGULATION MAG., July/ Aug. 1981, at 25; *see also* JERRY L. MASHAW & DAVID L. HARFST, THE STRUGGLE FOR AUTO SAFETY (1990) (providing an account of the administration of national highway safety laws and concluding that the National Highway Traffic Safety Administration retreated from rulemaking after repeated reversals of its rules in court). *But see* Berg, *supra* note 48, at 178 (foreseeing no "broad movement away from rulemaking toward adjudication").

70. *See* Note, *NLRB Rulemaking: Political Reality Versus Procedural Fairness*, 89 YALE L.J. 982 (1980). A more pragmatic reason may be that the agency's organic statute fails to provide for direct court-of-appeals review of its rules, thus allowing challengers to forum shop among district courts around the country.

by-case accretion of policy is less dramatic or visible, easier to modify, and yet also more impregnable to political attack.[71]

4. Adjudicatory decisions can be situation-specific, thus potentially avoiding overinclusiveness or underinclusiveness. Rules may unintentionally be overinclusive, reaching unanticipated fact situations, thereby deterring socially desirable behavior or imposing unnecessary costs on society. On the other hand, a rulemaking intended to create a predicate for regulatory sanctions may lead to rules whose terms miss some of the conduct sought to be affected.[72] Subsequent enforcement adjudications may be more easily rebuffed as a result. A related advantage of adjudication is that it may permit a better targeting of resources. Enforcement against egregious violators of statutory standards is thought by some to be more cost-effective, less cumbersome, and more politically palatable than attempting to promulgate an industry-wide standard.[73]

The Supreme Court in *NLRB v. Bell Aerospace Co.*[74] focused on a somewhat different reason why some agencies use adjudications for certain types of policymaking activity. In concluding that it would have been difficult or impossible for the NLRB to issue a general rule on the determination of managerial status of "buyers" under the National Labor Relations Act for the purpose of determining appropriate units, the Supreme Court said:

> There must be tens of thousands of manufacturing, wholesale and retail units which employ buyers, and hundreds and thousands of the latter. Moreover, duties of buyers vary widely depending on the company or industry. It is doubtful whether any generalized standard could be framed which would have more than marginal utility. The Board thus has reason to proceed with caution, developing its standards in a case-by-case manner with attention to the specific character of the buyers' authority and duties in each company.[75]

Finally, it should be noted that the APA does contain an often overlooked provision[76] permitting agencies "to issue a declaratory order to terminate a controversy or remove uncertainty." A few agencies have taken advantage of this provision to an-

---

71. *Id.*
72. *See* ACUS Statement 9, *Statement on Guidelines for Choosing the Appropriate Level of Agency Policy Articulation,* 48 Fed. Reg. 31,181 (1983) (discussing the over- and underinclusiveness of rules); *see also* Colin S. Diver, *The Optimal Precision of Administrative Rules,* 93 YALE L.J. 65 (1983).
73. *See also* Eyer, *supra* note 10, at 660–63 (touting the benefits of adjudicative lawmaking in producing consistency).
74. 416 U.S. 267 (1974).
75. *Id.* at 294–95 (citation omitted).
76. 5 U.S.C. § 554(d).

nounce a policy as a declaratory order after giving what amounts to notice and comment, and the courts have upheld them.[77]

3. Summary

Clearly, an interplay between rulemaking and adjudication exists under the APA. Rules issued after public participation in notice-and-comment proceedings establish general principles that will be binding on the public and can be applied to individual parties in adjudicatory proceedings. Rulemaking may not ordinarily be used as a substitute for individualized adjudication without implicating due process considerations; however, rules issued after informal proceedings may limit the issues to be adjudicated in subsequent proceedings and reduce the agency burden in establishing statutory violations. Ultimately, unless the statute requires otherwise,[78] however, it is up to the agency to determine which method of policymaking it wishes to use in a particular context.[79]

---

77. *See* Jeffrey S. Lubbers & Blake D. Morant, *A Reexamination of Federal Agency Use of Declaratory Orders*, 56 ADMIN. L. REV. 1097 (2004); *see also supra* note 43. In *Qwest Services Corp. v. FCC*, 509 F.3d 531, 536 (D.C. Cir. 2007), the D.C. Circuit made clear that "a declaratory ruling can be a form of adjudication" and that the FCC's use of a declaratory order was allowable even though the Commission's "process started out as a rulemaking," but later was "split" "into a dual one, half rulemaking and half adjudication."
78. *See, e.g.*, Michigan v. EPA, *supra* note 11.
79. *See* Araiza, *supra* note 49, stating:

> Unless the agency's choice violates a constitutional guarantee (i.e., the fair notice requirement of the non-retroactivity principle), or unless the agency's choice reflects an internal inconsistency in how the agency uses that discretion (i.e., if it tries to circumvent its own decision that rulemaking is the appropriate modality), the choice between "adjudication" and "rulemaking" must be left with the agency.

Chapter 3

Other Procedural Statutes Affecting Rulemaking

Previous chapters have described the trend toward imposing procedural requirements on agency rulemaking in addition to those in the Administrative Procedure Act
(APA). In some laws Congress has required a "hybrid" form of rulemaking procedure
for particular agencies or agency programs. In other laws, Congress has imposed
additional procedural requirements through government-wide statutes on agencies
conducting rulemaking.[1] This chapter summarizes these government-wide procedural
requirements.[2]

A. The Federal Register Act

Recognizing the need for a uniform system for handling the publication of federal
regulations, Congress in 1935 passed the Federal Register Act.[3] The Act requires the
filing of certain documents with the Office of the Federal Register, the availability of
documents for public inspection, the publication of documents in the *Federal Register*, and the permanent codification of rules in the *Code of Federal Regulations*. Publication of a document in the *Federal Register* has certain important legal effects; in
particular, it provides official notice of the document's existence and contents.[4] The
APA gave added importance to the *Federal Register* by requiring publication of agency
statements of organization, procedural rules, and the public notices mandated for
agency rulemaking.[5]

The Office of the Federal Register, together with the Public Printer, is responsible
for printing and distributing the *Federal Register*.[6] Under the Federal Register Act, the

---

1. The texts and commentary on these and other cross-cutting government procedural statutes
   are available in William F. Funk, Jeffrey S. Lubbers & Charles Pou, Jr., Federal Administrative
   Procedure Sourcebook (4th ed. 2008).
2. Additional requirements imposed on a general basis through presidential executive orders
   are discussed in Part III, ch. 2(A) & (H).
3. 49 Stat. 500 (1935) (codified at 44 U.S.C. §§ 1501–1511). The Act has been amended several
   times, most recently in 1984. *See* National Archives and Records Administration Act of 1984,
   Pub. L. No. 98-497, 98 Stat. 2280, 2286. *See generally* Note, *The Federal Register and the
   Code of Federal Regulations—A Reappraisal*, 20 Harv. L. Rev. 439 (1966).
4. 44 U.S.C. § 1507.
5. The APA requirements are discussed throughout the *Guide* and, in particular, in Part III, chs. 3,
   4, & 7.
6. 44 U.S.C. § 1502.

Administrative Committee of the Federal Register is required to prescribe, with the approval of the President, regulations for carrying out the Act.[7] These regulations appear in 1 C.F.R. Chapter 1 and deal with, among other things, the format, distribution, and special editions of the *Federal Register* and the preparation, transmittal, and processing of documents.[8] The Office of the Federal Register's website contains a wealth of useful information about its activities and documents.[9] The Office also publishes a *Document Drafting Handbook,* which explains in some detail how to prepare documents for *Federal Register* publication.[10] The Office also works with the Plain Language Action & Information Network, a government-wide group of volunteers, which has developed guidance for preparing documents in plain English.[11]

B. The National Environmental Policy Act

The National Environmental Policy Act (NEPA)[12] originated the "impact statement" as a technique for directing agencies to give special attention to certain values during the decisionmaking process. Under NEPA, the potential impact on the environment of federal agency action, including regulations, must be considered. NEPA directs all agencies of the federal government to include in proposals for "major Fed-

---

7. *Id.* § 1506.
8. 1 C.F.R. pts. 1–22. The Administrative Committee of the Federal Register included in its regulations provisions concerning, for example, reinstatement of expired regulations, effective dates and time periods, and incorporation by reference.
9. *See* http://www.archives.gov/federal-register/index.html. Another good source is the revamped Government Printing Office website, http://www.gpo.gov/fdsys.
10. National Archives of the United States, Office of the Federal Register, Document Drafting Handbook (Oct. 1998 revision, with supplements) [hereinafter Document Drafting Handbook], *available at* http://www.archives.gov/federal-register/write/handbook/ddh.pdf.
11. This guidance document, *Federal Plain Language Guidelines* (March 2011, rev'd May 2011), is *available at* http://www.plainlanguage.gov/howto/guidelines/FederalPLGuidelines/FederalPLGuidelines.pdf. The main page is http://www.plainlanguage.gov. President Clinton also issued a Memorandum for the Heads of Executive Departments and Agencies on "Plain Language in Government Writing" (June 1, 1998) requiring the use of plain language in all proposed and final rules issued after January 1, 1999, *available at* http://www.plainlanguage.gov/whatisPL/govmandates/memo.cfm. *See also* the Plain Writing Act of 2010, Pub. L. No. 111-274. The law requires that federal agencies use "clear Government communication that the public can understand and use." *Id.* § 2. "Regulations" are not covered by this law. *Id.* § 3(2)(C). However, an implementing memo from OIRA Director Sunstein emphasized that "rulemaking preambles are not exempted, and long-standing policies currently in effect require regulations to be written in a manner that is 'simple and easy to understand.'" Memorandum for the Heads of Executive Departments and Agencies, and Independent Regulatory Agencies from Cass R. Sunstein, OIRA Administrator, *Final Guidance on Implementing the Plain Writing Act of 2010,* at 5 (April 13, 2011), *available at* http://www.whitehouse.gov/sites/default/files/omb/memoranda/2011/m11-15.pdf.
12. 42 U.S.C. §§ 4321–4347d.

eral actions significantly affecting the quality of the human environment" a detailed environmental impact statement (EIS) addressing certain listed subjects and applying substantive criteria set forth in the Act.[13]

To comply with NEPA, all federal agencies with legislative rulemaking authority should have regulations establishing the procedures for assessing the need for an EIS and for preparing and obtaining comment on the statement.[14] The Council on Environmental Quality (CEQ) has adopted regulations binding upon all agencies that set forth uniform standards for conducting environmental reviews.[15] The CEQ's regulations are codified at 40 C.F.R. Parts 1500–1508.[16]

For proposals where the disposition of available resources is an issue—which would include many rulemakings—a discussion of alternatives is required.[17] This would generally be part of either an EIS or an environmental assessment (EA), which is used when a full EIS is not required.[18] The Act requires that agencies consult with, and solicit comments from, agencies with jurisdiction or expertise on the particular

---

13. *Id.* § 4332(C).
14. *See, e.g.*, Food and Drug Administration, Environmental Impact Considerations, 21 C.F.R. pt. 25 (illustrating agency regulations describing procedures for conducting environmental reviews); Regulations for Implementation of the National Environmental Policy Act (NEPA), 22 C.F.R. pt. 161; Federal Communications Commission, Procedures Implementing the National Environmental Policy Act, 47 C.F.R. ch. 1, subch. A, pt. 1, subpt. 1.
15. These regulations were issued pursuant to Exec. Order 11,991, 3 C.F.R. § 123 (1977 compilation). The Supreme Court has treated these regulations as deserving substantial deference. *See* Andrus v. Sierra Club, 442 U.S. 347 (1979); Note, *NEPA After* Andrus v. Sierra Club: *The Doctrine of Substantial Deference to the Regulations of the Council on Environmental Quality*, 66 VA. L. REV. 843, 849–55 (1980) (discussing background and legal effect of CEQ's regulations). *See also* the CEQ's Guidance Memorandum, *Forty Most Asked Questions Concerning CEQ's National Environmental Policy Act Regulations*, 46 Fed. Reg. 18,026 (Mar. 23, 1981).
16. For some analyses of the state of NEPA, see NEPA TASK FORCE, REPORT TO THE COUNCIL ON ENVIRONMENTAL QUALITY; MODERNIZING NEPA IMPLEMENTATION (Sept. 2003), *available at* http://ceq.hss.doe.gov/ntf/report/finalreport.pdf; Bradley C. Karkkainen, *Toward a Smarter NEPA: Monitoring and Managing Government's Environmental Performance*, 102 COLUM. L. REV. 903 (2002). For a classic look at the role of judicial review under NEPA, see Harold Leventhal, *Environmental Decisionmaking and the Role of the Courts*, 122 U. PA. L. REV. 509 (1974).
17. 42 U.S.C. § 4332(E).
18. Where "no significant impact" on the environment would result from the action, neither an environmental impact statement nor an environmental assessment is necessary. *See* 40 C.F.R. § 1508.4. Some federal agencies have classified rulemakings for NEPA purposes as normally requiring only an environmental assessment. *See id.* § 1507.3(b); 18 C.F.R. § 380.5(b)(12); 21 C.F.R. § 25.22(a)(6); 49 C.F.R. § 1105.6(b)(6). *But see* Ill. Commerce Comm'n v. ICC, 848 F.2d 1246, 1257 (D.C. Cir. 1988) ("[I]t is not at all apparent that a change in procedure alone will not affect the environment—the new procedure may, for example, lessen the opportunity for environmental groups to influence the agency's final decision. The procedural nature of a regulation does not, therefore, exempt an agency from complying with NEPA and preparing an environmental assessment (EA) or environmental impact statement (EIS) where appropriate.").

environmental impacts at issue.[19] Although there is no statutory requirement for agencies to obtain *public* comment on an EA, some agencies have established such requirement by regulation.[20]

In addition, the EIS or EA and any agency comments must be made available as part of the public rulemaking record,[21] and several statutes require that EISs be made available online over the Internet.[22] The adequacy of an EIS is subject to judicial review.[23] For an exhaustive review of an agency's compliance with NEPA in connection with a rulemaking, see the recent decision in *Wyoming v. U.S. Department of Agriculture*, upholding the Forest Service's compliance with NEPA regarding its roadless rule.[24]

Under the CEQ regulations, a "programmatic EIS" should be prepared when federal actions are connected or cumulative, or when actions are similar, and a single statement is the best vehicle for assessing environmental effects.[25]

On the other hand, the regulations also provide that when an agency identifies certain actions that do not have any significant effect on the environment, the agency

19. The CEQ regulations specify that "[I]n the case of an action with effects of national concern notice shall include publication in the Federal Register and notice by mail to national organizations reasonably expected to be interested in the matter . . . . An agency engaged in rulemaking may provide notice by mail to national organizations who have requested that notice regularly be provided. Agencies shall maintain a list of such organizations." 40 C.F.R § 1506.6(b)(2).
20. *See, e.g.*, the Department of Transportation's regulation, 23 C.F.R § 771.119(f).
21. 42 U.S.C. § 4332(C); 40 C.F.R. § 1505.1(c). *See, e.g.*, Kootenai Tribe of Idaho v. Veneman, 313 F.3d 1094 (9th Cir. 2002) (reversing the district court's preliminary injunction based on an inadequate EIS on the Forest Service's roadless rule and finding the 69-day period was substantially longer than the minimum 45 days required, that the Forest Service held over 400 public meetings and received over 1,150,000 written comments, and that the draft and final EIS analyzed an adequate range of alternatives).
22. *See generally* Michael B. Gerrard & Michael Herz, *Harnessing Information Technology to Improve the Environmental Impact Review Process*, 12 N.Y.U. ENVTL. L.J. 18 (2003) (arguing that NEPA itself, the Paperwork Reduction Act, the Electronic Freedom of Information Act Amendments, and the E-Government Act of 2002 all require online availability of EISs).
23. *See, e.g.*, Valley Citizens for a Safe Env't v. Aldridge, 886 F.2d 458, 459–60 (1st Cir. 1989) ("In a typical challenge to the adequacy of such a statement, a reviewing court will apply a 'reasonableness standard . . . aimed at insuring a good faith effort by the Agency.'").
24. 661 F.3d 1209 (10th Cir. 2011). In this decision, the court reiterated that "[w]e consider [the CEQ Forty Questions Guidance] 'persuasive authority offering interpretive guidance' regarding the meaning of NEPA and the implementing regulations." *Id.* at 1260, n.36. *See* note 15, *supra*.
25. 40 C.F.R. §§ 1508.7, 1508.25(a)(1)–(3). *See* Nat'l Wildlife Fed'n v. Appalachian Reg'l Comm'n, 677 F.2d 883, 888 (D.C.Cir.1981) (explaining requirement and describing it as a programmatic EIS). *See also* Piedmont Envtl. Council v. FERC, 558 F.3d 304 (4th Cir. 2009) (programmatic EIS not required in connection with issuance of new regulations detailing information requirements for permit applications for construction or modification of electric transmission facilities, but FERC should have consulted with CEQ before revising its own NEPA regulations).

may classify those actions as categorical exclusions.[26] If an action falls within a particular categorical exclusion, the agency need prepare neither an EIS nor an EA. It has been held that neither NEPA nor CEQ regulations required the Forest Service to conduct an EA or an EIS prior to the promulgation of a rule setting forth its procedures for creating categorical exclusions.[27] In addition to NEPA, agency rules might also implicate the Endangered Species Act.[28]

C. The Regulatory Flexibility Act

The Regulatory Flexibility Act (RFA)[29] adopted the NEPA impact-statement approach by directing agencies to consider the potential impact of regulations on small business and other small entities. Originally enacted in 1980, it mandates consideration of regulatory alternatives that would accomplish the stated objectives of the proposed rule and that minimize any significant economic impact on such entities. In follow-up legislation in 1996, Congress enacted the Small Business Regulatory Enforcement Fairness Act (SBREFA),[30] which strengthened the RFA, required agencies to produce regulatory compliance guides and guidance materials,[31] and added addi-

---

26. *See* 40 C.F.R. § 1508.4.
27. *See* Heartwood, Inc. v. U.S. Forest Serv., 230 F.3d 947 (7th Cir. 2000); *see also* New Jersey v. U.S. Nuclear Regulatory Com'n, 526 F.3d 98, 103 (3d Cir. 2008) (categorical exclusion from NEPA covered nonbinding guidance document). *But see* Kevin H. Moriarty, *Circumventing the National Environmental Policy Act: Agency Abuse of the Categorical Exclusion*, 79 N.Y.U. L. Rev. 2312 (2004); California *ex rel.* Lockyer v. Dept. of Agriculture, 575 F.3d 999, 1004-05 (9th Cir. 2009) (rejecting Forest Service's use of a categorical exemption to repeal the nationwide protections of the its roadless rule and to invite states to pursue varying rules for roadless area management).
28. *See Lockyer*, 575 F.3d at 1019 (finding that repeal of roadless rule may have affected listed species and their critical habitats under the Endangered Species Act (ESA), and thus agency was required to engage in consultation under the ESA).
29. Pub. L. No. 96-354, 94 Stat. 864 (1980) (codified as amended at 5 U.S.C. §§ 601–612).
30. Pub. L. No. 104-121, Title II, 110 Stat. 847, 857 (1996) (codified as amended at 5 U.S.C. §§ 601–612, 801–808). *See generally* Jennifer A. Smith, U.S. Small Business Administration, *Squeezing Back: Making Federal Agencies Measure Their Economic Impact on Small Entities* (2007), *available at* http://archive.sba.gov/advo/laws/rfa_impact07.pdf; Thomas O. Sargentich, *The Small Business Regulatory Enforcement Fairness Act*, 49 Admin. L. Rev. 123 (1997). A key change was the addition of judicial review of compliance with the RFA. SBREFA § 242, 110 Stat. at 865. See *infra* Part IV, ch. 2(A)(5)(b), for a discussion of judicial review under the RFA.
31. 110 Stat. at 858 (codified at 5 U.S.C. § 601 note). The compliance guides are to be issued with each rule having a significant economic impact on a substantial number of small entities and are to assist small entities in complying with the rule. For a critical review of agency activities under this requirement, see U.S. Gen. Accounting Office, Regulatory Reform: Compliance Guide Requirement Has Had Little Effect on Agency Practices (GAO-02-172) (Dec. 2001). For an example of an agency that takes this mandate seriously, see the Department of Labor's website, http://www.dol.gov/compliance.

tional consultation requirements for "covered agencies" (only EPA, OSHA, and, added in 2010, the newly created Consumer Financial Protection Bureau (CFPB) of the Federal Reserve System).[32] The Regulatory Flexibility Act incorporates the APA's broad definition of "agency,"[33] making it applicable to independent regulatory agencies as well as executive agencies.[34] Despite the significant strengthening amendments in SBREFA, the RFA's coverage still has a few important limitations. First, it applies only to rules for which an agency publishes a notice of proposed rulemaking, pursuant to either the APA or some other law, and it does not apply to ratemaking.[35] The RFA's

---

32. *See* 5 U.S.C.A. § 609(d). The CFPB was added by Pub. L. No. 111-203, § 1100G(a) (2010). SBREFA also created a Small Business and Agriculture Regulatory Enforcement Ombudsman and the congressional review process. 15 U.S.C. § 657; 5 U.S.C. §§ 801–808. *See also* discussion of congressional review in section J of this chapter. The amendment adding the CFPB added some additional requirements to that agency's regulatory flexibility analyses. In addition to the regular requirements of the initial regulatory flexibility analysis (IRFA) found in 5 U.S.C. § 603, a CFPB IRFA must include:

> a description of . . . (A) any projected increase in the cost of credit for small entities; (B) any significant alternatives to the proposed rule which accomplish the stated objectives of applicable statutes and which minimize any increase in the cost of credit for small entities; and (C) advice and recommendations of representatives of small entities relating to issues described in subparagraphs (A) and (B) and subsection (b).

Pub. L. No. 111-203, § 1100G(b), 124 Stat. 1375, 2112 (2010).

Moreover, when the Bureau produces a final regulatory flexibility analysis, it must include "a description of the steps the agency has taken to minimize any additional cost of credit for small entities." *Id.* § 1100G(c), 124 Stat. 2113.

33. 5 U.S.C. § 601(1).

34. *See also* Memorandum for the Heads of Executive Departments and Agencies, *Regulatory Flexibility, Small Business, and Job Creation* (Jan. 18, 2011), 76 Fed. Reg. 3827 (Jan. 21, 2011) (reinforcing the Act's requirements).

35. *Id.* § 601(2). *Compare* Nat'l Ass'n of Home Builders v. U.S. Army Corps of Eng'rs, 417 F.3d 1272, 1284–85 (D.C. Cir. 2005) (requiring the Corps to conduct regulatory flexibility analyses before issuing nationwide dredge-and-fill permits because that action was rulemaking and the binding nature of rule made it a legislative rule that should have required notice of proposed rulemaking) *with* Am. Moving & Storage Ass'n, Inc. v. U.S. Dep't of Def., 91 F. Supp. 2d 132 (D.D.C. 2000) (holding that a DOD change in procurement policies was not a "rule" under RFA, notwithstanding a DOD statute requiring an opportunity for comment on such changes; alternatively, the nature of the change amounted to "ratemaking" and was therefore not within RFA definition of rule for that reason).

This provision in the RFA also makes the Act inapplicable to final (and interim-final) rules issued pursuant to an exemption from notice and comment. *See also* Nat'l Ass'n for Home Care v. Shalala, 135 F. Supp. 2d 161, 165–66 (D.D.C. 2001) (Act does not apply to interpretive rules; finding HHS's rule to be interpretive because HHS was interpreting the Balanced Budget Act of 1997, which was itself written with "remarkable specificity"). *Compare* U.S. Telecom Ass'n v. FCC, 400 F.3d 29 (D.C. Cir. 2005) (finding that Act applies because the challenged action was a legislative rule) *with* Cent. Texas Tel. Co-op., Inc. v. FCC, 402 F.3d 205, 213 (D.C. Cir. 2005) (finding the Act did not apply because the challenged action was an interpretive rule). For an early case finding an exemption from the RFA due to the foreign affairs exemption from notice and comment, see *In re* Sealed Case, 666 F. Supp. 231 (D.D.C. 1987).

flexibility analysis requirements are limited to rulemaking for which the agency "is *required* by section 553 . . . or any other law, to publish general notice of proposed rulemaking for any proposed rule or publishes a notice of proposed rulemaking for an interpretative rule involving the internal revenue laws of the United States. . . ."[36] Thus, technically the flexibility analysis requirements do not apply where the agency voluntarily follows notice-and-comment procedure, although they may well be found to apply to rulemaking where the agency has, by regulation, subjected itself to notice-and-comment procedure.[37]

Through requirements for notice and analysis, the RFA requires agencies to consider the impact of proposed rules on "small entities"—including "small businesses," "small (not-for-profit) organizations," and "small governmental jurisdictions."[38] The Act does not, however, mandate any particular outcome in rulemaking. It only requires consideration of alternatives that are less burdensome to small entities and an agency explanation of why alternatives were rejected.[39] Four regulatory alternatives

---

36. *Id.* § 603(a) (emphasis added). The language pertaining to IRS interpretive rules was added by SBREFA. *Id.* § 604(a).
37. This interpretation is suggested in Paul R. Verkuil, *A Critical Guide to the Regulatory Flexibility Act*, 1982 DUKE L.J. 213, 240.
38. The Act contains definitions of these terms, but they are open-ended in the sense that agencies can establish alternative definitions appropriate to their activities. 5 U.S.C. § 601(3)–(5). The Department of Commerce also provides the following definitions:

   > A *small business* is any business that meets the size standards set forth in part 121 of Title 13, Code of Federal Regulations (CFR). Part 121 sets forth, by the North American Industry Classification System (NACIS), the maximum number of employees or maximum average annual receipts a business may have to be considered a small entity. Provision is made for an agency to develop industry-specific definitions. The NACIS is available at http://www.sba.gov/size/sizetable2002.html. A *small organization* is any not-for-profit enterprise that is independently owned and operated and not dominant in its field. A *small government jurisdiction* is any government or district with a population of less than 50,000.

   GUIDELINES FOR PROPER CONSIDERATION OF SMALL ENTITIES IN AGENCY RULEMAKING, *available at* http://www.ogc.doc.gov/ogc/legreg/zregs/guidelines.htm.
39. 5 U.S.C. § 603(a)(3). The declaration of purpose in the note accompanying 5 U.S.C. § 601 states in part:

   > It is the purpose of this Act to establish as a principle of regulatory issuance that agencies shall endeavor, consistent with the objectives of the rule and of applicable statutes, to fit regulatory and informational requirements to the scale of the businesses, organizations, and governmental jurisdictions subject to regulation. To achieve this principle, agencies are required to solicit and consider flexible regulatory proposals and to explain the rationale for their actions to assure that such proposals are given serious consideration.

   It should be pointed out that the agency's explanation, as set forth in any regulatory flexibility analysis, will be part of the "whole record of agency action" if judicial review of a final rule is sought. *Id.* § 611(b). *See infra* Part IV, ch. 2(A)(5)(b), for a discussion of the judicial review requirements in the Regulatory Flexibility Act.

are included in the Act as examples of alternatives to be considered in rulemaking: (1) "tiering," (2) clarification and simplification, (3) performance rather than design standards, and (4) exemptions.[40]

The RFA charges the Chief Counsel for Advocacy of the Small Business Administration with overseeing agency compliance with the flexibility analysis requirements.[41] The Office of Advocacy's chief enforcement weapons are publicity (through the requirement of reporting at least annually on agency compliance to the President and Congress)[42] and amicus ("friend-of-the-court") appearances in court proceedings involving agency rules.[43] For example, in one case the chief counsel submitted an amicus brief supporting a small business's claim that the RFA exception under section 605—waiving RFA analyses when the head of the agency believes the rule would not have a "significant economic impact on a substantial number of small entities"— should not apply. The court agreed with the chief counsel that in defining *small entity*, agencies should use the SBA's definition. In this case the rulemaking agency did not, and therefore did not comply with RFA.[44]

The Regulatory Flexibility Act operates on the APA rulemaking process in the following fashion:[45] Unless the agency head certifies to the Chief Counsel for Advocacy and publishes such certification in the *Federal Register* that the rule will not have a "significant economic impact on a substantial number of small entities,"[46]

---

40. 5 U.S.C. § 603(c).

41. *Id.* § 612(a). The Small Business Administration's website is located at http://archive.sba.gov/advo.

42. 5 U.S.C. § 612(a). *See also, e.g.,* SBA Office of Advocacy, Report on the Regulatory Flexibility Act, FY 2010 (Jan. 2011), *available at* http://www.sba.gov/sites/default/files/files/10regflx_rs379.pdf; Cindy Skrzycki, *Small Business Advocate Plays a Big Role in Rulemaking*, Wash. Post, Jan. 11, 2005, at E-1 (describing the increasing clout of this office).

43. 5 U.S.C. § 612(b).

44. Nw. Mining Ass'n v. Babbitt, 5 F. Supp. 2d 9 (D.D.C. 1998).

45. In addition, SBREFA added a provision requiring a "covered agency," prior to issuance of the initial regulatory flexibility analysis, to convene a special review panel consisting of agency, Office of Management and Budget, and Small Business Administration officials and representatives of affected small entities. 5 U.S.C. § 609(b)(5). The panel must file a public report on the impacts of the proposal within 60 days. However, only three agencies (EPA, OSHA, and the new Consumer Financial Protection Bureau of the Federal Reserve System) are included in the definition of "covered agency" for the purposes of this provision. *Id.* § 609(d). As of March 17, 2012, EPA reported that it had convened 42 such panels, with seven to be scheduled, *see* http://www.epa.gov/sbrefa/sbar-panels.html; SBA reports that OSHA had convened 10, *see* http://archive.sba.gov/advo/laws/is_oshapanel.html. For an assessment of the implementation of this requirement, see U.S. Gen. Accounting Office, Regulatory Reform: Implementation of the Small Business Advocacy Review Panel Requirements (GAO-GGD-98-36) (Mar. 1998). *See infra* Part III, ch. 2(C), for additional discussion of the analysis requirements of the Act.

46. 5 U.S.C. § 605(b). *See* Verkuil, *supra* note 37, at 241 (discussing certification procedure and criteria). The GAO has for a long time suggested that Congress needs to clearly delineate "what is meant by the terms 'significant economic impact' and 'substantial number of small entities.'"

the agency must prepare an initial regulatory flexibility analysis (IRFA). The IRFA, or a summary thereof, must be published in the *Federal Register* along with the proposed rule. Courts now regularly review such certifications.[47] And an agency's failure to comply can be a real setback. For a classic example of a thwarting of an agency program in part due to a failure to comply with the RFA, see *American*

See CURTIS W. COPELAND, CONG. RESEARCH SERV., RL34355, THE REGULATORY FLEXIBILITY ACT: IMPLE-MENTATION ISSUES AND PROPOSED REFORMS (updated Feb. 12, 2008), *available at* http://opencrs.com/document/RL34355/2008-02-12/download/1005 (citing numerous GAO reports). For one agency's guidelines for defining "small entities," "significant impact," and for preparing IRFAs and FRFAs, *see* Lewis E. Queirolo, *Conducting Economic Impact Analyses for NOAA Fisheries Service* 10–17 (Feb. 23, 2011), *available at* http://alaskafisheries.noaa.gov/analyses/RIR_RFAAguidance.pdf.

47. For cases upholding the agency's certification, *see* Envtl. Def. Ctr., Inc. v. EPA, 344 F.3d 832, 878–79 (9th Cir. 2003) and Cement Kiln Recycling Coal. v. EPA, 255 F.3d 855, 869 (D.C. Cir. 2001) (holding that under RFA, an agency need not consider impacts on small businesses indirectly affected by the regulation of other entities; EPA certification upheld where it concluded that only six directly affected facilities met the definition of a "small business" and that only two of these would experience compliance costs in excess of 1% of annual sales). *See also* Sw. Pa. Growth Alliance v. Browner, 121 F.3d 106, 123 (3d Cir. 1997) (alternate holding); Colo. State Banking Bd. v. Resolution Trust Corp., 926 F.2d 931 (10th Cir. 1991); Mid-Tex Elec. Coop., Inc. v. FERC, 773 F.2d 327 (D.C. Cir. 1985). *But see* N.C. Fisheries Ass'n, Inc. v. Daley, 27 F. Supp. 2d 650, 659–60 (E.D. Va. 1998) (setting aside the annual fishing quota rule where the secretary "did not consider a community any smaller than the entire state of North Carolina," "ignored readily available data which would have shown the number of fishing vessels impacted by the agency's regulatory actions," "disregarded the distinction between a license holder and a fisherman who actually fishes for flounder," and "improperly maintained that any present economic losses are alleviated by past revenues earned by overfishing"). *See also* S. Offshore Fishing Ass'n v. Daley, 995 F. Supp. 1411, 1434–37 (M.D. Fla. 1998) (rejecting the Commerce Department's certification of no significant impact on shark fishermen of a 50% quota cut and granting summary judgment under RFA); S. Offshore Fishing Ass'n v. Daley, 55 F. Supp. 2d 1336 (M.D. Fla. 1999) (granting an injunction against the following year's quota after remand); Ocean Conservancy v. Evans, 260 F. Supp. 2d 1162 (M.D. Fla. 2003) (upholding the settlement of shark fishermen's suit after it was challenged by environmentalists).

There is also a standing aspect to these challenges. *Compare* Aeronautical Repair Station Ass'n, Inc. v. FAA, 494 F.3d 161 (D.C. Cir. 2007) (FAA drug and alcohol testing rule did directly affect contractors and subcontractors who therefore could challenge the agency RFA analysis or certification) *with* White Eagle Co-op Ass'n v. Conner, 553 F.3d 467 (7th Cir. 2009) (finding that petitioner who challenged milk marketing order amendment was a dairy producer who was only indirectly affected by the order and thus lacked standing to bring a challenge to the RFA analysis). However, such review may be sought only "during the period beginning on the date of final agency action and ending one year later," unless a different provision of law specifies a shorter period. 5 U.S.C. § 611(a)(3)(A). Valentine Props. Assocs., LP v. U.S. Dept. of Hous. & Urban Dev., 785 F. Supp. 2d 357, 369 (S.D.N.Y. 2011) (finding claim time-barred). *See also* State v. Ctrs. for Medicare & Medicaid Servs., 2010 WL 1268090 *7–*8 (M.D. Ala. 2010) (holding that only small entities may bring actions for judicial review under the Act and that therefore the state of Alabama is barred from doing so).

Federation of Labor v. Chertoff,[48] where Judge Charles Breyer enjoined the Department of Homeland Security from enforcing its rule mandating employers to implement procedure to match employees with Social Security records within 90 days. The court found that plaintiffs "raised serious doubts about the veracity of DHS's prediction that the rule will 'not impose any new or additional costs'" on small businesses.[49]

The IRFA or the certification must be sent to the Chief Counsel for Advocacy. When a rule will have a significant economic impact, the agency, in addition to publishing the proposed rule and IRFA, or summary, in the *Federal Register*, "shall assure that small entities have been given an opportunity to participate in the rulemaking for the rule through the reasonable use of techniques" such as advance notice of proposed rulemaking, publication of notice in specialized publications, direct notification of small entities, the holding of public conferences or hearings, or use of simplified or modified procedures that make it easier for small entities to participate.[50] After the comment period on the proposed rule is closed, the agency must either certify a lack of impact or prepare a final regulatory flexibility analysis (FRFA), which, among other things, responds to issues raised by public comments on the IRFA.[51] The agency is not required to send the FRFA to the Chief Counsel for Advocacy, but it must make it available to the public on request and publish the analysis or a summary of it in the *Federal Register*.[52]

In addition, the Small Business Jobs Act of 2010 further amended the FRFA section of the RFA.[53] It struck the word "succinct" from the Section 604(a)(1) requirement that the agency provide "a succinct statement of the need for, and objectives of, the rule." It also substituted the word "statement" for the word "summary" in section 604(a)(2), which requires agencies to address public comments to the IRFA. Furthermore, section 1601 of the Small Business Jobs Act requires agencies to respond to any comments filed by the Chief Counsel for Advocacy in response to a proposed rule and a detailed statement of any changes made in response to the comments.

The Regulatory Flexibility Act also requires agencies to publish and implement a plan for reviewing (within 10 years) existing (and subsequently issued) rules that have a significant economic impact on a substantial number of small entities.[54] The

---

48. 552 F. Supp. 2d 999 (N.D.Cal. 2007). In another case, the Eastern District of California overturned a final rule allowing an importation of citrus fruits due to an agency certification that was based on a flawed risk assessment. Harlan Land Co. v. U.S. Dep't. of Agriculture, 186 F. Supp. 2d 1076, 1096–98 (E.D. Cal 2001).

49. 552 F. Supp. 2d at 1013.

50. 5 U.S.C. § 609.

51. *Id.* § 604(a). *See also* Grand Canyon Air Tour Coal. v. FAA, 154 F.3d 455, 470–71 (D.C. Cir. 1998) (accepting FAA's responses to comments on IRFA).

52. *Id.* § 604(b).

53. Pub. L. No. 111-240, § 1601, 124 Stat. 2504, 2551 (2010).

54. *Id.* § 610(a). The period for review may be extended in one-year increments for up to five additional years. *Id.* For critical reviews of agency activities under this requirement, see Michael R. See, *Willful Blindness: Federal Agencies' Failure to Comply with the Regulatory Flexibility Act's Periodic Review Requirement—and Current Proposals to Invigorate the Act*, 33 Fordham Urb. L.J. 1199 (2006); U.S. Gen. Accounting Office, Regulatory Flexibility Act: Agencies' Interpretations of Review Requirements Vary (GAO-GGD-99-55) (Apr. 1999).

agency is to review existing rules to minimize "any significant economic impact of the rule on a substantial number of small entities . . . ."[55] This review should consider the continued need for the rule; the nature of complaints or comments received concerning the rule; the complexity of the rule; the extent of duplication or conflict with other federal, state, or local regulation; and any relevant economic or technological changes that have occurred since the rule was issued.[56]

Finally, the Act requires each agency to prepare a regulatory flexibility agenda of rules under development that may have a significant economic impact on a substantial number of small entities.[57] The agenda must be published in the *Federal Register* semiannually, in October and April, and is to be transmitted to the Office of Advocacy for comment and brought to the attention of small entities or their representatives.[58] In practice, this agenda is incorporated into the *Unified Agenda of Federal Regulatory and Deregulatory Actions*, published semiannually by the Regulatory Information Service Center in the General Services Administration.[59] The SBA Office of Advocacy has also issued a lengthy guide for agencies on compliance with the RFA.[60]

Ultimately, though, the D.C. Circuit has explained that the Act is fundamentally a procedural one: "Though it directs agencies to state, summarize, and describe, the Act in and of itself imposes no substantive constraint on agency decisionmaking. In effect, therefore, the Act requires agencies to publish analyses that address certain legally delineated topics."[61]

---

55. 5 U.S.C. § 610(b). Throughout the Act, the goal of minimizing the impact on small entities is always understood to be considered in the context of achieving objectives of the relevant statute underlying the regulation in question. 5 U.S.C. §§ 603(c), 604(a)(3), 606.

56. *Id.* § 610(b).

57. *Id.* § 602(a).

58. *Id.* § 602(b), (c); *see also infra* Part III, ch. 2(I) (discussing coordination in implementation of RFA and Exec. Order 12,866).

59. *See, e.g.*, the Department of Agriculture's Unified Agenda entry, 75 Fed. Reg. 79,710 (Dec. 20, 2010) (describing regulations affecting small entities as required by section 602 of the RFA, and identifying regulatory actions that are being reviewed in compliance with section 610(c) of the RFA).

60. *See* SBA Office of Advocacy, A Guide for Government Agencies—How to Comply with the Regulatory Flexibility Act (June 2010), *available at* http://www.sba.gov/advo/laws/rfaguide.pdf; *see also* EPA, Final Guidance for EPA Rulewriters: Regulatory Flexibility Act as Amended by the Small Business and Regulatory Enforcement Fairness Act (Nov. 2006), *available at* http://www.epa.gov/rfa/documents/rfaguidance11-00-06.pdf; and Department of Commerce, Guidelines for Proper Consideration of Small Entities in Agency Rulemaking, *supra* note 38.

61. National Telephone Co-op. Ass'n v. FCC, 563 F.3d 536, 540 (D.C. Cir 2009) (finding that "[b]ecause the analysis at issue here undoubtedly addressed all of the legally mandated subject areas, it complies with the Act").

D. The Paperwork Reduction Act

The Paperwork Reduction Act (PRA)[62] assigns to the Office of Management and Budget (OMB) the role of coordinating federal information policy. Among the statute's principal purposes are minimization of the federal paperwork burden for individuals, small businesses, and state, local, and tribal governments; minimization of the cost to the federal government of collecting and disseminating information; and maximization of the usefulness to the federal government of the information collected.[63] The Act was amended in 1986[64] and again in 1995[65] in several important respects. OMB has issued revised regulations that, among other things, incorporate the statutory modifications.[66] In 2000, the Information Quality Act was added as an amendment to the PRA (see Section H, below).

The PRA's coverage is extremely broad. With a few narrow exceptions, it applies to virtually the entire executive branch.[67] The breadth of the Act's coverage also is

---

62. Pub. L. No. 96-511, 94 Stat. 2812 (1980) (current version codified at 44 U.S.C. §§ 3501–3520), *superseding* Federal Reports Act, Pub. L. No. 77-381, 56 Stat. 1078 (1942); *see also* William F. Funk, *The Paperwork Reduction Act: Paperwork Reduction Meets Administrative Law*, 24 Harv. J. Legis. 1 (1987) (discussing the legislative histories of the Federal Reports Act and Paperwork Reduction Act of 1980). For a concise overview of the Act, *see* Esa L. Sferra-Bonistalli, *The Paperwork Reduction Act: Collecting Information, Collecting Your Input, Protecting You*, Proceedings, Spring 2010, at 21, *available at* http://www.uscg.mil/proceedings/spring2010/articles/21_SferraBonistalli_ThePaperworkReductionAct.pdf.

63. 44 U.S.C. § 3501.

64. One important change in 1986 provided that the Administrator of OMB's Office of Information and Regulatory Affairs (OIRA), which was formally established in 1980 by the Act and which has lead responsibility for implementing the Act, be confirmed by the Senate. 44 U.S.C. § 3503(b). The 1986 amendments also eliminated the confusion that arose in the 1980 Act in connection with the definition of the terms *collection of information* and *information collection request. Id.* § 3502(3). Congress made it clear that "collection of information" requirements resulting from agency rules are treated in the same manner under the PRA as other collection of information requirements, except as expressly provided under 44 U.S.C. § 3506(c). *See* Control of Paperwork Burdens on the Public, Regulatory Changes Reflecting Amendments to the Paperwork Reduction Act, 53 Fed. Reg. 16,618 (May 10, 1988). Congress in 1986 also added a provision requiring that all communications between the OIRA Administrator, agency staff, and nongovernment personnel concerning collection of the information request must be made public, with a limited exception. 44 U.S.C. § 3507(e).

65. The main change was a clarification that agency rules requiring businesses or individuals to maintain information for the benefit of third parties or the public (rather than the government) were covered. This overruled the contrary decision by the Supreme Court in *Dole v. United Steelworkers of America*, 494 U.S. 26 (1990). *See generally* Jeffrey S. Lubbers, *Paperwork Redux: The (Stronger) Paperwork Reduction Act of 1995*, 49 Admin. L. Rev. 111 (1997).

66. 60 Fed. Reg. 44,978 (Aug. 29, 1995) (codified at 5 C.F.R. pt. 1320); *see also* discussion *infra* Part III, ch. 2(B).

67. The PRA's definition of "agency" excludes only the Government Accountability Office; the Federal Election Commission; the governments of the District of Columbia, U.S. territories and possessions; and government-owned contractor-operated facilities. 44 U.S.C. § 3502(1). *But see* Kuzma v. U.S. Postal Serv., 798 F.2d 29 (2d Cir. 1986) (holding postal service regulations are not subject to PRA review).

apparent from the narrowness of the agency functions that are exempted from it. Specific exemptions are provided for (1) federal criminal matters or actions; (2) civil actions and agency litigation or investigation; (3) compulsory process issued in connection with antitrust proceedings; and (4) federal intelligence activities carried out under presidential executive order.[68] The PRA does apply to "general investigations" (other than antitrust investigations) that are "undertaken with reference to a category of individuals or entities such as a class of licensees or an entire industry."[69]

A significant limitation of the PRA is that it has been held to bar judicial review of agency failure to comply with the Act's procedural requirements.[70]

1. The OMB Clearance Requirements

The Paperwork Reduction Act assigns the OMB Director numerous functions, including information collection clearance and paperwork control functions.[71] These functions can significantly affect agencies engaged in rulemaking.

The Act provides that agencies "shall not conduct or sponsor the collection of information"[72] without first obtaining the approval of OMB (in practice, the Office of Information and Regulatory Affairs (OIRA)). The Act defines collection of information as follows:

> the obtaining, causing to be obtained, soliciting, or requiring the disclosure to third parties or the public, of facts or opinions by or for an agency, regardless of form or format, calling for either—
>
>> (i) answers to identical questions posed to, or identical reporting or recordkeeping requirements imposed on, ten or more persons, other than agencies, instrumentalities, or employees of the United States;[73] or

---

68. 44 U.S.C. § 3518(c)(1).
69. *Id.* § 3518(c)(2). Through subsequent legislation, Congress has granted narrow exemptions to the Act. *See, e.g.*, Amendment to the Marine Mammal Protection Act of 1972, Pub. L. No. 97–58, § 4, 95 Stat. 979, 984 (codified at 16 U.S.C. § 1379(d)(2)).
70. *See* Sutton v. Providence St. Joseph Med. Ctr., 192 F.3d 826, 844 (9th Cir. 1999) ("the Act authorizes its protections to be used *as a defense.* The Act does not authorize a private right of action."); Ass'n of Am. Physicians & Surgeons, Inc. v. U.S. Dep't of Health and Human Servs., 224 F. Supp. 2d 1115 (S.D. Tex. 2002) (same); Tozzi v. EPA, 148 F. Supp. 2d 35 (D.D.C. 2001) (same).
71. *See* 44 U.S.C. § 3504.
72. *Id.* § 3507(a). The PRA does not define *sponsor*, but OMB has defined the term to apply "if the agency collects the information, causes another agency to collect the information, contracts or enters into a cooperative agreement with a person to collect the information, or requires a person to provide information to another person." 5 C.F.R. § 1320.3(d). This provision also defines the circumstances in which an agency is considered the sponsor of a collection of information undertaken by the recipient of a federal grant. *Id.*
73. 44 U.S.C. § 3502(3)(A)(i). OMB has explained that "[F]or the purpose of counting the number of respondents, agencies should consider the number of respondents within any 12 month period." 2010 OMB Memorandum on "Information Collection under the Paperwork Reduction Act," *infra* note 88, at 2.

  (ii) answers to questions posed to agencies, instrumentalities, or employees of the United States which are to be used for general statistical purposes.[74]

  OMB has interpreted its authority expansively. OMB's regulations define *collection of information* and expand upon the list of methods and formats encompassed by the term.[75] The regulations also make clear that voluntary surveys, etc., are covered.[76] In addition the law now makes clear that collections of information "requiring the disclosure to third parties or the public" are covered and must be cleared by OIRA. This provision overruled the contrary Supreme Court decision *Dole v. United Steelworkers of America*,[77] which had interpreted the 1986 version of the PRA.

  The Act forbids OMB to approve any information collection for a period of more than three years.[78] Failure to obtain OMB approval of a collection of information triggers operation of the Act's public protection provision, which provides that "no person shall be subject to any penalty for failing to comply with a collection of information that is subject to this [Act] if—(1) the collection of information does not display a valid control number assigned by the Director [of OMB], or (2) the agency fails to inform the person who is to respond . . . that such person is not required to respond . . . unless it displays a valid control number."[79]

---

74. 44 U.S.C. § 3502(3)(A)(ii). Inclusion of the language pertaining to "disclosure to third parties or the public" was added in the 1995 amendments.
75. The statutory definition is interpreted by the OMB to include:

> report forms; application forms; schedules; questionnaires; surveys; reporting or recordkeeping requirements; contracts; agreements; policy statements; plans; rules or regulations; planning requirements; circulars; directives; instructions; bulletins; requests for proposals or other procedural requirements; interview guides; oral communications; posting, notification, labeling, or similar disclosure requirements; telegraphic or telephonic requests; automated, electronic, mechanical, or other technological collection techniques; standard questionnaires used to monitor compliance with agency requirements; or any other technological collection techniques or technological methods used to monitor compliance with agency requirements.

> 5 C.F.R. § 1320.3(c)(1). But see *id.* § 1320.3(h) for a list of items not considered to be "information collections" under the PRA, including hosting public meetings and certain types of *Federal Register* solicitations.

76. 5 C.F.R. § 1320.3(c).
77. 494 U.S. 26 (1990).
78. 44 U.S.C. § 3507(g).
79. *Id.* § 3512; *see also* Funk, *supra* note 62, at 70–78 (discussing potential pitfalls of the public protection provision). At least two criminal prosecutions have been dismissed due to violations of this provision. *See* United States v. Hatch, 919 F.2d 1394 (9th Cir. 1990); United States v. Smith, 866 F.2d 1092 (9th Cir. 1989). Moreover, the D.C. Circuit has confirmed that "adversely affected person [may] raise PRA violations without limitation, so long as the administrative or judicial process in connection with a particular license or with a particular application continues." Saco River Cellular Inc. v. FCC, 133 F.3d 25, 30 (D.C. Cir. 1998); *see also* Ctr. for Auto Safety v. NHTSA, 244 F.3d 144 (D.C. Cir. 2001).

2. Clearance Procedure

The Paperwork Reduction Act sets out a general set of clearance procedures for approving agency collections of information, with specific clearance procedures prescribed for collections imposed through notice-and-comment rulemaking.[80]

Section 3507(d) of the PRA prescribes the following procedure for clearance of collection of information contained in rules promulgated following notice and comment:

1. No later than publication of the notice of proposed rulemaking (NPRM), the agency must submit the proposed rule and preamble to OMB along with any background information OMB needs to conduct its review.[81]

2. OMB has 60 days after publication of the NPRM to either approve or file comments on the collections of information.[82] If OMB does not file comments, OMB forfeits its right to disapprove of the requirement.[83]

3. When publishing its final rule, the agency must explain how its rule responds to OMB's comments or why it rejected the comments.[84]

4. If OMB has not approved the proposed collection of information and instead filed comments, the agency must resubmit it at the final stage of rulemaking.

---

80. There are similar requirements for freestanding collections of information (*e.g.*, surveys, questionnaires, forms):

   1. Agencies must provide 60-day notice in the *Federal Register* and consult with the public and affected agencies for each new proposed collection. After this is done, the agencies submit their paperwork clearance package (including a certification as to burdens, etc., and comments received) to OIRA for clearance. 44 U.S.C. § 3506(c).

   2. On or before the day an information collection proposal is submitted to OMB for clearance, the agency must send a notice to the *Federal Register*, in which the agency advises the public that OMB approval has been requested and that the public may submit comments on the request to the OMB desk officer for the agency. A copy of the notice, and the expected date of its publication in the *Federal Register*, are to be included in the submission to OMB. *Id.* § 3507(a).

   3. OMB shall provide at least 30 days for public comment on the submission. *Id.* § 3507(b).

   4. Within 60 days after receipt of the agency's submission, OMB will notify the agency of its decision to approve or disapprove, in whole or part, the information collection. *Id.* § 3507(c).

   5. If OMB does not act within the 60-day review period, the agency can ask OMB to assign the required control number, and OMB must do so without delay. *Id.* § 3507(c)(3).

   In addition, OMB provided a 99-page guidance document, *Questions and Answers When Designing Surveys for Information Collections*, *see* http://www.whitehouse.gov/sites/default/files/omb/inforeg/pmc_survey_guidance_2006.pdf.

81. 44 U.S.C. § 3507(d)(1).

82. *Id.* § 3507(d)(3).

83. *Id.* Of course, for most executive agencies, OIRA also has independent authority to review the rule itself under Exec. Order 12,866, 58 Fed. Reg. 51,735 (Sept. 30, 1993), *reprinted in* Appendix B.

84. 44 U.S.C. § 3507(d)(2).

OMB has 60 days from publication of the final rule to disapprove the collection of information provision. Disapproval may be because (a) the agency failed to comply with the submission requirements; (b) the agency substantially modified the collection of information in the final rule without giving OMB 60 days to review the modified requirement; or (c) the agency's response to OMB's comments is found to be "unreasonable."[85]

5. OMB's decision to disapprove the collection of information in the rule, and its reasons for that decision, must be made publicly available.[86] Such decisions, however, are not judicially reviewable.[87]

OMB's regulations implementing the Paperwork Reduction Act have added certain requirements to the clearance procedure for collection of information provisions contained in proposed agency rules.[88] Agencies must use OMB Form 83-1.[89] OMB requires the following, among other things:

1. The public must always be given a chance to comment on proposed collections of information. In rulemaking, this is accomplished by including in the notice of proposed rulemaking reference to the fact that the rule has been submitted to OMB for review and that comments may be sent to the OMB desk officer for the agency.[90] The rules also require that the agency include in the preamble to the NPRM information on the reasons for the requirement, an estimate of the total annual reporting and record-keeping burden that will result from each collection of information, and other information.[91] At the final rulemaking stage, no additional public notice and opportunity for com-

85. *Id.* § 3507(d)(4).
86. *Id.* § 3507(e)(1).
87. *Id.* § 3507(d)(6). There is no such preclusion of review of OMB's review of freestanding collections of information. *See* Funk, *supra* note 62, at 79–80 (discussing preclusion-of-review provision).
88. The Obama Administration has provided a concise summary of the Act's requirements: Memorandum for the Heads of Executive Departments and Agencies, and Independent Regulatory Agencies, from Cass R. Sunstein, Administrator, *Information Collection under the Paperwork Reduction Act* (April 7, 2010), *available at* http://www.whitehouse.gov/sites/default/files/omb/assets/inforeg/PRAPrimer_04072010.pdf. For a more comprehensive description of the entire Act's requirements, as interpreted by OIRA, *see* OMB/OIRA, THE PAPERWORK REDUCTION ACT OF 1995: IMPLEMENTING GUIDANCE (Draft, Aug. 16, 1999), *available at* http://www.thecre.com/pdf/PRAguidenew.pdf [hereinafter DRAFT IMPLEMENTING GUIDANCE]. This document, which is still being finalized as of March 2012, discusses the clearance process for collections of information in proposed and current rules. *Id.* at 88–98. For helpful agency guidance on following the PRA (with related exhibits), *see* IRS CHIEF COUNSEL REGULATION HANDBOOK, § 32.1.2.5, *Applicability of the Paperwork Reduction Act* (last revised April 2009), *available at* http://www.irs.gov/irm/part32/irm_32-001-002.html#d0e384.
89. Paperwork Reduction Act Submission, *available at* http://www.fws.gov/forms/83i.pdf.
90. 5 C.F.R. § 1320.11(a).
91. *Id.* §§ 1320.8(a), 1320.8(c)(iii).

ment is required, although OMB may direct the agency to publish a notice in the *Federal Register* notifying the public of OMB review.[92]

2. OMB comments on collection of information provisions in rules shall be placed in the agency's rulemaking record.[93]

3. All collections of information in rules must display an OMB control number; OMB may assign this number when it approves a collection of information provision even if this occurs prior to publication of the final rule.[94]

OMB has established a separate procedure for clearance of information collections in *existing* rules.[95] The purpose of this procedure is to prevent the expiration of OMB's approval for a collection of information before the agency has undertaken the necessary administrative procedure to repeal or amend the rule containing the collection requirement.[96] The agency is supposed to initiate the OMB review process not later than 90 days before the expiration of OMB approval.[97] The agency may still enforce the rule during the review period, but if OIRA disapproves the requirement, then the agency is required, consistent with the APA or other applicable requirements, to initiate and complete a rulemaking within 120 days to amend or rescind the collection of information.[98]

The Paperwork Reduction Act contains several variations from the general review procedure for agency information collections. First, the Act establishes a "fast-track" review procedure for emergency situations. Agency heads can request emergency processing under section 3507(j) of the Act.[99] OMB has also provided by regulation that agencies may request expedited processing of collections of information even though the request does not qualify for emergency processing under the statute.[100]

---

92. DRAFT IMPLEMENTING GUIDANCE, *supra* note 88, at 90. *See also* Chamber of Commerce of U.S. v. SEC, 443 F.3d 890, 901 (D.C. Cir. 2006) (requiring another round of notice and comment after agency reaffirmed remanded rule based on extra-record materials, because those materials "did not merely supplement the rulemaking record without prejudice to the Chamber, and the public availability of those materials, in this instance, does not merit an exception to the comment requirement of section 553(c)").

93. 5 C.F.R. § 1320.11(c).

94. *Id.* § 1320.11(g).

95. *See id.* § 1320.12; 44 U.S.C. § 3507(h)(2).

96. 5 C.F.R. § 1320.14(a).

97. *Id.*

98. *Id.* § 1320.12(f). Any amended requirements are also subject to OMB approval. *Id.*

99. This section requires that the collection of information be essential to the mission of the agency and that the agency "cannot reasonably comply" with the normal procedure because (1) public harm is reasonably likely to result, (2) an unanticipated event has occurred, or (3) the normal procedure is reasonably likely (a) to prevent or disrupt the collection of information, or (b) cause a statutory or court deadline to be missed. 44 U.S.C. § 3507(j). This test was loosened significantly in the 1995 amendments.

100. 5 C.F.R. § 1320.18(g). If the agency requests expedited review, it is required to publish in the *Federal Register* notice of the time period within which it is requesting OMB to approve or disapprove the collection of information. *Id.* § 1320.13(b). OMB may also waive any of the Act's requirements, to the extent permitted by law. *Id.* § 1320.18(d).

The PRA also authorizes the OMB Director, following notice and comment, to delegate his or her approval authority to an agency senior official who "is sufficiently independent of program responsibility to evaluate fairly whether proposed information collection requests should be approved and has sufficient resources to carry out this responsibility effectively."[101] Of course, the agency's senior official must comply with OMB's regulations in reviewing agency information collection requests.[102]

It should be noted that OMB's general clearance procedure is subject to the PRA's provision that independent regulatory agencies[103] may, by majority vote of their members, override an OMB decision disapproving a proposed information collection.[104]

3. PRA and the Internet

The Obama Administration has recognized that some adjustments to PRA implementation are necessitated by the growth of new media such as blogs, wikis, and social networks. Most significantly, it issued a guidance document on the use of "Social Media, Web-based Interactive Technologies, and the Paperwork Reduction Act" that describes the relationship between the PRA and modern technologies.[105] This memorandum explains how agencies may (and in some cases may not) use social media to engage with the public without seeking OMB approval under the PRA. It followed this up with guidance to the agencies outlining the availability and uses of "generic" Information Collection Requests.[106] These are to be used to provide a streamlined process for OMB's approval especially for voluntary, low-burden, and uncontroversial collections. The memo suggests that this process can be used for certain collections, "including methodological testing, customer satisfaction surveys, focus groups, contests, and website satisfaction surveys."[107] In June 2011, OMB pro-

---

101. 44 U.S.C. § 3507(i).
102. *Id.* As of March 2012, OMB has delegated review authority only to the Board of Governors of the Federal Reserve System and, more narrowly, to the managing director of the Federal Communications Commission. 5 C.F.R. § 1320.16(d); Appendix A to 5 C.F.R. pt. 1320.
103. The PRA contains a definition of "independent regulatory agency" and enumerates existing ones. 44 U.S.C. § 3502(5). The provision was amended in 2010 to add the Office of the Comptroller of the Currency, and the Bureau of Consumer Financial Protection, the Office of Financial Research. Pub. L. No. 111-203, §§ 315, 1100(D(a).
104. *Id.* § 3507 (f).
105. Memorandum for the Heads of Executive Departments and Agencies, and Independent Regulatory Agencies, from Cass R. Sunstein, OIRA Administrator, *Social Media, Web-Based Interactive Technologies, and the Paperwork Reduction Act* (April 7, 2010), *available at* http://www.whitehouse.gov/sites/default/files/omb/assets/inforeg/SocialMediaGuidance_04072010.pdf.
106. Memorandum for the Heads of Executive Departments and Agencies, and Independent Regulatory Agencies, from Cass R. Sunstein, OIRA Administrator, *Paperwork Reduction Act— Generic Clearances* (May 28, 2010), *available at* http://www.whitehouse.gov/sites/default/files/omb/assets/inforeg/PRA_Gen_ICRs_5-28-2010.pdf.
107. *Id.* at 1.

vided more detail about this "fast track" method of obtaining customer feedback and a list of a large group of agencies that are participating in this process.[108] It also added a feature to its "regulatory dashboard" (www.reginfo.gov) it calls the "ICR Dashboard"—information on all the Paperwork Reduction Act Information Collection requests under review by OIRA.[109] At this writing, the Administrative Conference has a study of the PRA that examines whether the Act needs updating.[110]

4. Standard of Review

Agencies must provide a certification (and a record supporting such certification) that, among other things, shows that their proposed information collection is "necessary for the proper performance of the functions of the agency, including that the information has practical utility"; "is not unnecessarily duplicative of information otherwise reasonably accessible to the agency"; "reduces to the extent practicable and appropriate the burden on persons who shall provide information to or for the agency"; "is written using plain, coherent, and unambiguous terminology, and is understandable to those who are to respond"; "is to be implemented in ways consistent . . . with . . . existing reporting and recordkeeping requirements"; and "to the maximum extent practicable, uses information technology to reduce burden."[111]

The backdrop to these requirements was the PRA's requirement that overall information collection burdens be reduced annually by a specified percentage for each fiscal year from 1996 to 2001.[112]

---

108. Memorandum for the Heads of Executive Departments and Agencies, and Independent Regulatory Agencies, from Cass R. Sunstein, OIRA Administrator & Jeffrey D. Zients, Deputy Director, Management and Federal Chief Performance Officer, *New Fast-Track Process for Collecting Service Delivery Feedback Under the Paperwork Reduction Act* (June 15, 2010), *available at* http://www.whitehouse.gov/sites/default/files/omb/memoranda/2011/m11-26.pdf.

109. *See* http://www.reginfo.gov/public/jsp/PRA/praDashboard.jsp.

110. *See* http://www.acus.gov/research/the-conference-current-projects/paperwork-reduction-act/.

111. 44 U.S.C. § 3506(c)(3)(A). OMB regulations also warn that it will not approve a collection of information that requires respondents to report more often than quarterly, requires a response in fewer than 30 days after receipt, requires respondents to submit more than an original and two copies, requires retention of records (other than health, medical, government contract, grant-in-aid, or tax records) for more than three years, contains a poorly designed survey, or contains a pledge of confidentiality that cannot be backed up or might lead to disclosure of trade secret information. 5 C.F.R. § 1320.5(d)(2). *See* DRAFT IMPLEMENTING GUIDANCE, *supra* note 88, at 63–78, for a detailed discussion of these requirements.

112. 44 U.S.C. § 3505(a)(1). *See* Office of Management and Budget, Information Collection Budget of the United States Government (2010), *available at* http://www.whitehouse.gov/sites/default/files/omb/inforeg/icb/icb_2010.pdf at 1–9 (detailing 1% rise in information collection burden in FY 2009). But note that the Act has not been revised to add goals beyond FY 2001.

Also pertinent to OMB's authority is section 3518(e), which states the following:

Nothing in [the PRA] shall be interpreted as increasing or decreasing the authority of the President, the Office of Management and Budget or the Director thereof, under the laws of the United States, with respect to the substantive policies and programs of departments, agencies and offices, including the substantive authority of any Federal agency to enforce the civil rights laws.[113]

5. *The Small Business Paperwork Relief Act*

Another law, the Small Business Paperwork Relief Act of 2002,[114] requires agencies to give special attention to the paperwork burden on small businesses. It requires agencies to establish one "point of contact . . . to act as a liaison between the agency and small business concerns"[115] with respect to information collections and the control of paperwork, and exhorts agencies to "make efforts to further reduce the information collection burden for small business concerns with fewer than 25 employees."[116] Pursuant to the law, a task force was established, which reported on "the feasibility of streamlining requirements with respect to small business concerns regarding the collection of information and strengthening dissemination of information."[117]

E. The Federal Advisory Committee Act

The Federal Advisory Committee Act (FACA)[118] regulates the formation and operation of advisory committees by federal agencies. The Administrator of the General Services Administration (GSA) has authority for guiding and coordinating the admin-

---

113. 44 U.S.C. § 3518(e). This provision was added to make clear that, although Congress intended paperwork reduction review to complement substantive review pursuant to existing executive orders, the Paperwork Reduction Act should not be used for general substantive regulatory reform. *See* S. Rep. No. 96-930 at 8–9 (1980). This was partly out of concern that paperwork and information policy concerns would be subordinated to substantive review. *Id.* at 9.

114. Pub. L. No. 107-198 (codified at 44 U.S.C. § 101 note).

115. Pub. L. 107-198, § 2(b) (amending 44 U.S.C. § 3506 by adding a new subsection (i)). The list of contacts is maintained at SBA.gov, Federal Compliance Contacts and Resources, http://www.sba.gov/category/navigation-structure/starting-managing-business/starting-business/business-law-regulations/contact-government-agency/fe.

116. Pub. L. No. 107-198 § 2(c) (amending 44 U.S.C. § 3506(c) by adding a paragraph 3(J)(4)).

117. *Id.* § 3 (amending 44 U.S.C. to add a new § 3520 (and redesignating former § 3520 as § 3521)). The Task Force Report was issued on June 28, 2004. *See* Report of the Small Business Paperwork Relief Act Task Force (June 28, 2004), *available at* http://www.whitehouse.gov/sites/default/files/omb/assets/omb/inforeg/sbpr2004.pdf.

118. Pub. L. No. 92-463, 86 Stat. 770 (1972) (codified at 5 U.S.C. App. 2); *see also* Steven P. Croley & William F. Funk, *The Federal Advisory Committee Act and Good Government*, 14 Yale J. Reg. 451 (1997); Steven P. Croley, *Practical Guidance on the Applicability of the Federal Advisory Committee Act*, 10 Admin. L.J. Am. U. 111 (1996).

istration of the Act[119] and has issued regulations for agencies on management of advisory committees.[120]

FACA defines "advisory committee" to include any committee or similar group (1) established or utilized in the interest of obtaining advice or recommendations for the President or one or more federal agencies and (2) that is not composed wholly of full-time federal officers or employees.[121] Among FACA's requirements, new advisory committees may be established by agencies only after public notice and a determination that the establishment will be in the public interest.[122] Each advisory committee must have a clearly defined purpose, and its membership must be fairly balanced in terms of the points of view represented and the functions to be performed.[123] Meetings of the advisory committees must be open to public observation, subject to the same exceptions as provided in the Government in the Sunshine Act.[124] But note that FACA contains an exception for discussions with state and local officials.[125] Nor is a committee formed by an agency contractor covered by the Act, even if the agency played a big role in forming the committee.[126]

---

119. This role was originally performed by OMB but was transferred to GSA by Exec. Order 12,024, 3 C.F.R. § 158 (1977 compilation).

120. 41 C.F.R. pts. 102–103, issued 66 Fed. Reg. 37,728 (July 19, 2001).

121. 5 U.S.C. App. 2, § 3.

122. *Id.* § 9(a). President Clinton also added another requirement in Executive Order 12,838, which instructed agencies to eliminate one-third of their existing advisory committees and to create new committees only if "compelling considerations" so require. 58 Fed. Reg. 8207 (Feb. 10, 1993). The order created apparent tensions with the Administration's previously stated support of negotiated rulemaking, which requires advisory committees. *See* Croley, *supra* note 118, at 112–14 (discussing this Executive Order). OMB then reiterated its support for negotiated rulemaking, although the Executive Order was not formally amended. Memorandum for the Heads of Executive Departments and Agencies, *Guidance on Establishing Negotiated Rulemaking Advisory Committees*, from Alice Rivlin, OMB Director, December 12, 1995 [hereinafter Rivlin Memorandum]. A subsequent OMB memo, dated April 8, 1996, exempted negotiated rulemaking committees from the OMB ceiling on advisory committees. ACUS has recommended that the cap be abolished. *See* ACUS Recommendation 2011-7, *The Federal Advisory Committee Act—Issues and Proposed Reforms* ¶ 4 (Dec. 9, 2011), 77 Fed. Reg. 2261 (Jan. 17, 2012).

123. 5 U.S.C. App. 2 § 5; *see also* Pub. Citizen v. Nat'l Advisory Comm. on Microbiological Criteria for Foods, 886 F.2d 419 (D.C. Cir. 1989) (dismissing, by a divided panel, a public interest group challenge under FACA to the composition of a Department of Agriculture advisory committee); Claybrook v. Slater, 111 F.3d 904 (D.C. Cir. 1997) (dismissing suit against Federal Highway Administrator for failing to prevent an advisory committee from taking allegedly harmful and *ultra vires* action).

124. 5 U.S.C. App. 2 § 10(d); Government in the Sunshine Act, Pub. L. No. 94-409, 90 Stat. 1241 (codified at 5 U.S.C. § 552b).

125. Section 4(c) of FACA states: "Nothing in this Act shall be construed to apply to . . . any State or local committee, council, board, commission, or similar group established to advise or make recommendations to State or local officials or agencies." 5 U.S.C. App. 2, §4(c).

126. *See* Byrd v. EPA, 174 F.3d 239 (D.C. Cir. 1999).

Advisory committees can play an important role in federal agency rulemaking. These committees, normally composed of experts in the regulatory field involved, representatives of affected interest groups, and federal and state agencies, typically counsel agencies on the advisability or content of rulemaking or on issues while the rulemaking is in progress. Some statutes require the agency to utilize an advisory committee, and others authorize but do not require their use.[127] In some cases, the enabling statute will contain procedural and composition requirements for the advisory committee operating in a particular arena.[128] Many federal agencies have issued their own regulations on advisory committee management and procedures.[129]

The breadth of the definition of "advisory committee" has provoked uncertainty and a spate of litigation.[130] The relationship between FACA issues and negotiated

---

127. The OSHA Act, for example, authorizes, but does not require, the use of advisory committees for the bulk of OSHA safety and health standards. 29 U.S.C. § 656. *See also* Part III, ch.1(A)(4).

128. *See, e.g.*, OSHA Act, 29 U.S.C. § 656. The courts sometimes construe these procedural requirements strictly. In one case, the Third Circuit vacated an OSHA standard regulating a carcinogen because the agency had failed to follow the procedures governing the sequence of advisory committee participation in the rulemaking. Synthetic Organic Chem. Mfrs. Ass'n v. Brennan, 506 F.2d 385 (3d Cir. 1974).

129. *See, e.g.*, Nuclear Regulatory Commission, 10 C.F.R. pt. 7; Consumer Product Safety Commission, 16 C.F.R. pt. 1018; Department of Transportation, 49 C.F.R. pt. 95.

130. *See* Croley, *supra* note 118. The leading case is still *Pub. Citizen v. Dep't of Justice*, 491 U.S. 440 (1989), in which the Supreme Court held that the President did not "utilize" advisory committee within terms of the FACA when he consulted with a standing American Bar Association committee concerning nominees for federal judgeships. This case has been read to limit the term "utilized" "to apply only to committees that are under the actual management or control of the agency." Town of Marshfield v. FAA, 552 F.3d 1, 5–6 (1st Cir. 2008). *See also In re* Cheney, 406 F.3d 723, 728 (D.C. Cir. 2005) (holding that a committee is composed wholly of federal officials, and thus outside FACA, if the President has given no one other than a federal official a vote in or (if the committee acts by consensus) a veto over the committee's decisions); Animal Legal Def. Fund, Inc. v. Shalala, 104 F.3d 424 (D.C. Cir. 1997) (holding that National Academy of Sciences research committees are "utilized"); Ass'n of Am. Physicians & Surgeons, Inc. v. Clinton, 997 F.2d 898 (D.C. Cir. 1993) (holding the presence of the First Lady did not render the Health Care Task Force an advisory committee, though working groups may be); Nat. Res. Def. Council v. Herrington, 637 F. Supp. 116 (D.D.C. 1986) (holding DOE-appointed safety panel was not advisory committee because scientists' individual views were sought).

Some debate in the courts concerns whether information generated by an advisory committee that failed to meet FACA's procedural requirements can still be used by the government. *See, e.g.*, Cal. Forestry Ass'n v. U.S. Forest Serv., 102 F.3d 609 (D.C. Cir. 1996) (remanding the case to the district court for consideration of injunctive relief); Alabama-Tombigbee Rivers Coal. v. Dep't of Interior, 26 F.3d 1103 (11th Cir. 1994) (enjoining use of advisory committee's report because of failure to follow requirements of FACA); *but see* Nat. Res. Def. Council v. Peña, 147 F.3d 1012, 1025 (D.C. Cir. 1998) ("a use injunction should be the remedy of last resort"); *accord*, Cargill, Inc. v. United States, 173 F.3d 323, 342 (5th Cir. 1999); Nw. Forest Res. Council v. Espy, 846 F. Supp. 1009 (D.D.C. 1994) (allowing the government to use report produced by advisory committee despite a FACA violation).

rulemaking is discussed in the next section. Moreover, just as with the Paperwork Reduction Act, the rise of electronic communications has produced new uncertainties as to the coverage of FACA.[131]

F. The Negotiated Rulemaking Act

The Negotiated Rulemaking Act of 1990 (NRA)[132] established a statutory framework for agency use of negotiated rulemaking to formulate proposed regulations. The NRA supplements the rulemaking provisions of the APA, clarifying the authority of federal agencies to conduct negotiated rulemaking. It largely codifies the practice of those agencies that had previously used the procedure and incorporates relevant recommendations of the Administrative Conference.[133] The NRA does not require use of the technique, allowing each agency the discretion whether to employ it.

Negotiated rulemaking emerged in the 1980s as an alternative to traditional procedures for drafting proposed regulations. The essence of the procedure is that in certain situations it is possible to bring together representatives of the agency and the various affected interest groups to negotiate the text of a proposed rule. If they do achieve consensus, the resulting rule is likely to be easier to implement and the likelihood of subsequent litigation is diminished. Even in the absence of consensus on a draft rule, the process may be valuable as a means of better informing the regulatory agency of the issues and the concerns of the affected interests.

The NRA was intended to clarify agency authority and to encourage agency use of the process. Although the Act sets forth some basic public notice requirements, most of the language is permissive.[134] Congress intended that it not impair any rights otherwise retained by agencies or parties, expressly providing that nothing in the Act

---

131. *See* discussion of PRA in section D.3 of this chapter. *See also* ACUS Recommendation 2011-7, *supra* note 122, at ¶ 6 (urging GSA to amend its FACA implementing regulations "to clarify that, in addition to holding teleconferenced or webconferenced meetings, agencies also may host virtual meetings that can occur electronically in writing over the course of days, weeks or months on a moderated, publicly accessible web forum. Agencies with advisory committees should be aware that they have the option of holding committee meetings via such online forums."). *See generally* Reeve T. Bull, *The Federal Advisory Committee Act: Issues and Proposed Reforms*, Report to ACUS, (Sept. 12, 2011), *available at* www.acus.gov.

132. Pub. L. No. 101-648, 104 Stat. 4969 (codified at 5 U.S.C. §§ 561–570). The NRA was permanently reauthorized by the Administrative Dispute Resolution Act of 1996, Pub. L. No. 104-320, § 11, 110 Stat. 2870, 3873. *See infra* Part III, ch. 1(B)(2), for a general discussion of the negotiated rulemaking process.

133. ACUS Recommendation 82-4, *Procedures for Negotiating Proposed Regulations*, 47 Fed. Reg. 30,708 (July 15, 1982); ACUS Recommendation 85-5, *Procedures for Negotiating Proposed Regulations*, 50 Fed. Reg. 52,895 (Dec. 27, 1985); *see also* Administrative Conference of the U.S., Negotiated Rule-making Sourcebook (David M. Pritzker & Deborah Dalton eds., 2d ed. 1995); discussion *infra* Part III, ch. 1(B)(2).

134. *See* Texas Office of Pub. Util. Counsel v. FCC, 265 F.3d 313, 327 (5th Cir. 2001) ("The plain language of the statute undermines the notion that the NRA's procedures are mandatory.").

"should be construed as an attempt to limit innovation and experimentation with the negotiated rulemaking process or with other innovative rulemaking procedures otherwise authorized by law."[135] Although the NRA plainly permits an agency to publish as its own the consensus proposal adopted by the negotiating committee, the Act does not require the agency to publish either a proposed or final rule merely because a negotiating committee proposed it.[136]

The NRA lists a number of criteria that are to be taken into account when an agency considers whether to use negotiated rulemaking in any particular instance.[137] Use of a convener to report on the feasibility of undertaking a negotiated rulemaking is authorized.[138] The public notice announcing the agency's intent to use the procedure should provide an opportunity, for at least 30 days, for members of the public who believe they are inadequately represented on the negotiating committee to apply for membership or better representation, though the agency retains discretion as to whether to grant such requests.[139] If, after considering the public responses to the published notice of intent to establish a negotiating committee, the agency determines not to do so, the agency should publish a notice of that fact and the reasons for the decision.[140]

The agency must comply with the Federal Advisory Committee Act in establishing and administering the negotiating committee.[141] To avoid creating new sources of potential litigation, other agency procedural actions relating to establishing, assisting, or terminating the committee are not subject to judicial review.[142] However, otherwise available judicial review of a rule resulting from negotiated rulemaking is not affected

---

135. 5 U.S.C. § 561.
136. *See* USA Group Loan Servs. v. Riley, 82 F.3d 708 (7th Cir. 1996) (rebuffing the complaint that the Department of Education breached promises made in negotiated rulemaking proceeding and rejecting a request for discovery of department officials). For a critical commentary on the reasoning (but not the result) in this case, see Philip J. Harter, *First Judicial Review of Reg Neg a Disappointment*, 22 ADMIN. & REG. L. NEWS 1 (Fall 1996). *See also* Jody Freeman, *Collaborative Governance in the Administrative State*, 45 UCLA L. REV. 1, 87–91 (1997) (discussing the case).
137. *Id.* § 563(a).
138. *Id.* § 563(b). For a good example of such a report, see EPA, Final Convening Report on the Feasibility of a Negotiated Rulemaking Process to Develop the All Appropriate Inquiry Standard Required under the Small Business Liability Relief and Brownfields Revitalization Act (Dec. 17, 2002) (prepared for EPA by Susan Podziba & Associates), *available at* http://podziba.com/supporting%20docs/AAI_Final_Report.pdf.
139. *Id.* § 564.
140. *Id.* § 565(a).
141. *Id. See supra* subsec. (E).
142. 5 U.S.C. § 570. *See* Ctr. for Law and Educ. v. Dep't of Education, 396 F.3d 1152 (D.C. Cir. 2005) (denying an advocacy group standing to challenge final rule on the basis of an alleged defect in the composition of a negotiated rulemaking committee).

by the Negotiated Rulemaking Act, and a reviewing court is not to accord such a rule any greater deference merely because of the procedure followed.[143]

It is assumed that the agency will be represented on the committee, but committee meetings are to be chaired by an impartial "facilitator" or mediator who assists the committee in its deliberations.[144] If the committee reaches consensus on a proposed rule, it transmits to the agency a report containing the proposal.[145] Consensus is defined as unanimous concurrence among the interests represented unless the committee agrees on a different definition.[146] If the committee does not reach consensus on a rule, it may transmit to the agency whatever information, recommendations, or other material it considers appropriate.[147] The agency may keep a negotiating committee in existence until promulgation of the final rule, but earlier termination is permitted if the agency or the committee so chooses.[148]

Agencies may contract with private parties or may use government employees to act as facilitators or mediators, or to assist the agency in the "convening" process— that is, the initial determination of the feasibility of negotiating a rule and the assem-

---

143. 5 U.S.C. § 570. *See generally* Michael Herz, *Some Thoughts on Judicial Review and Collaborative Governance*, 2009 J. Disp. Resol. 361 (2009). Courts obviously know that a rule has been a product of negotiated rulemaking. *See, e.g.*, Fort Peck Housing Auth. v. U.S. Dep't of Hous. & Urban Dev., 367 Fed. App'x 884, 886 (10th Cir. 2010) (upholding a rule and noting it was the product of a negotiated rulemaking); United Keetoowah Band of Cherokee Indians of Okla. v. U.S. Dep't of Hous. & Urban Dev., 567 F.3d 1235, 1246 (10th Cir. 2009) (overturning a rule after *Chevron* step one analysis and stating: "The fact that the regulatory scheme was developed through a negotiated rulemaking procedure is of no relevance to this determination."); Steel Joist Inst. v. Occupational Safety & Health Admin., 287 F.3d 1165, 1166 (D.C. Cir. 2002) (upholding a rule and noting that it was "based on a consensus document submitted by a rulemaking advisory committee in a negotiated rulemaking"); Cent. Ariz. Water Conservation Dist. v. EPA, 990 F.2d 1531, 1544 (9th Cir. 1993) (upholding a negotiated sulfur dioxide emission rule designed to improve visibility at the Grand Canyon). *See also* City of Portland, Ore. v. EPA. 507 F.3d 706, 715 (D.C. Cir. 2007) (upholding a rule and rejecting claim that Negotiated Rulemaking Act "requires an agency to provide more detailed notice of possible changes in its draft rules just because they evolve from negotiated rulemaking"). The court added, "Indeed, adopting the cities' suggestion would make it easier for disappointed parties to overturn negotiated rules than non-negotiated rules, thus discouraging agencies from engaging in negotiated rulemaking—exactly the opposite of what Congress intended." *Id.*

144. *Id.* §§ 565(b), 566.

145. *Id.* § 566(f).

146. *Id.* § 562(2).

147. *Id.* § 566(f).

148. *Id.* § 567. *But see* Jody Freeman & Laura I. Langbein, *Regulatory Negotiation and the Legitimacy Benefit*, 9 N.Y.U. Envtl. L.J. 60, 135 (2000) (recommending "that agencies maintain negotiating committees through rule promulgation, rather than disbanding them upon reaching consensus," and suggesting "that agencies experiment with keeping committees intact, or recalling them periodically, for post-promulgation consultation, perhaps through the implementation period").

bly of an appropriate committee membership.[149] Agencies are authorized to pay expenses of certain committee members in accordance with FACA, and agencies are authorized to accept outside funds and use them in planning or conducting negotiated rulemakings if no conflict of interest is created.[150] The provisions of the NRA originally were to terminate after six years, but this sunset provision was eliminated in 1996.[151]

President Clinton also exhorted agencies to use negotiated rulemaking. Executive Order 12,866 directs agencies to, "where appropriate, use consensual mechanisms for developing regulations, including negotiated rulemaking."[152] He followed that with a memorandum urging agencies to "negotiate, don't dictate" and "to expand substantially . . . efforts to promote negotiated rulemaking."[153] Neither the Bush II nor the Obama Administration has taken an active role to either promote or discourage the use of negotiated rulemaking.

In the last decade, Congress has increasingly mandated the use of negotiated rulemaking in connection with specific programs, even as agency voluntary use of it is waning.[154]

---

149. 5 U.S.C. § 568.
150. *Id.* § 569, *amended*, Administrative Dispute Resolution Act of 1996, Pub. L. No. 104-320, § 11, 110 Stat. 3870, 3873. This provision was modified to take account of the 1995 closure of ACUS, which previously was authorized to accept and pay out such funds. *See* ADMINISTRATIVE CONFERENCE OF THE UNITED STATES, BUILDING CONSENSUS IN AGENCY RULEMAKING: IMPLEMENTING THE NEGOTIATED RULEMAKING ACT—A REPORT TO CONGRESS (1995), *available at* http://ftp.resource.org/acus.gov/gov.acus.1995.consensus.pdf. With ACUS's re-establishment, this may be revisited in the future.
151. *See supra* note 132.
152. Exec. Order 12,866 § 6(a), *supra* note 83.
153. Memorandum on Regulatory Reform, 1 PUB. PAPERS 304 (1995); *see also* OFFICE OF THE VICE PRESIDENT, CREATING A GOVERNMENT THAT WORKS BETTER AND COSTS LESS, NATIONAL PERFORMANCE REVIEW, IMPROVING REGULATORY SYSTEMS 29–33 (1993); Rivlin Memorandum, *supra* note 122.
154. *See* Jeffrey S. Lubbers, *Achieving Policymaking Consensus: The (Unfortunate) Waning of Negotiated Rulemaking*, 49 S. TEX. L. REV. 987, app. (2008) (listing negotiated rulemakings and indicating those that were congressionally mandated), *e.g.*, Intelligence Reform and Terrorism Prevention Act of 2004, Pub. Law No. 108-458, § 7212, 118 Stat. 3829 (requiring the Secretary of Transportation to convene a negotiated rulemaking concerning driver's licenses and personal identification cards); Carl D. Perkins Vocational and Applied Technology Education Act Amendments of 1990, 104 Stat. 753 (codified in scattered sections of 20 U.S.C.); Hawkins-Stafford Elementary and Secondary School Improvements Amendments of 1988, Pub. L. No. 100-297, 102 Stat. 130 (codified in scattered sections of 20 U.S.C.); Price-Anderson Amendments Act of 1988, Pub. L. No. 100-408, 102 Stat. 1066 (codified in scattered sections of 42 U.S.C.). The 1992 amendment to the Higher Education Act mandated the use of negotiated rulemaking. Pub. L. No. 102-325, 106 Stat. 448. *See* USA Group Loan Servs. v. Riley, *supra* note 136, at 714.

G. The Unfunded Mandates Reform Act

This legislation (UMRA), enacted in 1995 with broad, bipartisan support,[155] requires Congress and the agencies[156] to give special consideration to proposed legislation and regulations imposing mandates[157] on state, local, and tribal entities.[158] It also contains a special provision requiring agencies to prepare a statement, in the nature of a regulatory impact analysis, for any proposed rulemaking that is likely to result in an expenditure by the private sector in excess of $100 million (adjusted annually for inflation). The Act thus contains the only broad regulatory impact analysis requirement currently mandated by statute.[159] The UMRA's impact is, however, somewhat lessened because its provisions for judicial review of agency compliance with the Act are quite limited.[160]

The UMRA's purpose was to help reveal, and ultimately limit, the high (and often hidden) costs of federal mandates on state and local governments to undertake regulatory activity without sufficient federal compensation for this activity. It enacted into legislation some requirements that were already required by executive order.[161]

Title I of the Act modifies the legislative process by requiring any congressional authorizing committee that approves a bill containing a federal mandate to identify that mandate in its committee report.[162] The Congressional Budget Office (CBO) must

---

155. Pub. L. No. 104-4, 109 Stat. 48 (1995) (codified at 2 U.S.C. chs. 17A, 25). *See* Note, *Recent Legislation: Unfunded Mandates Reform Act of 1995*, 109 HARV. L. REV. 1469 (1996); Daniel E. Troy, *The Unfunded Mandates Reform Act*, 49 ADMIN. L. REV. 139 (1997); *see also* OMB, AGENCY COMPLIANCE WITH TITLE II OF UNFUNDED MANDATES REFORM ACT OF 1995: A REPORT TO CONGRESS (1996).

156. The Act does not cover "independent regulatory agencies." 2 U.S.C. § 658(1).

157. The term *mandates* is carefully defined in the Act. *Id.* § 658 (5)–(7).

158. OFFICE OF INFORMATION AND REGULATORY AFFAIRS, OMB, 2011 REPORT TO CONGRESS ON THE BENEFITS AND COSTS OF FEDERAL REGULATIONS AND UNFUNDED MANDATES ON STATE, LOCAL, AND TRIBAL ENTITIES (2011), *available at* http://www.whitehouse.gov/sites/default/files/omb/inforeg/2011_cb/2011_cba_report.pdf (providing the fourteenth report issued by OMB summarizing estimates by federal regulatory agencies of the monetized benefits and costs of federal regulations reviewed by OMB).

159. In effect, it codifies many of the provisions of Exec. Order 12,866. *See* discussion *infra* Part III, ch. 2(A), (D).

160. *See infra* text accompanying notes 173–74. Early reviews of the effect of the Act were critical. *See* U.S. GEN. ACCOUNTING OFFICE, UNFUNDED MANDATES: REFORM ACT HAS HAD LITTLE EFFECT ON AGENCIES' RULEMAKING ACTIONS (GAO-GGD-98-30) (Feb. 1998).

161. *See* Exec. Order 12,875, 3 C.F.R. § 669 (1993 compilation) (requiring consultation with state and local officials before imposing unfunded mandates); Memorandum for the Heads of Executive Departments and Agencies, and Independent Regulatory Agencies, *Guidance for Implementing E.O. 12,875, "Reduction of Unfunded Mandates,"* from Leon E. Panetta, OMB Director (Jan. 11, 1994) (with attached memorandum from OIRA Administrator Sally Katzen). The Order was later revoked by Exec. Order 13,132, § 10, 64 Fed. Reg. 43,255 (Aug. 4, 1999).

162. 2 U.S.C. § 658b(b). Certain bills are excluded from coverage. *Id.* § 1503. According to GAO, "the CBO estimates that about 2 percent of the bills that it reviewed from 1996 to 2004 contained

then estimate the overall impact of such mandates, and state whether the bill contains an unfunded mandate imposing a $50 million or greater burden on state, local, and tribal governments or $100 million on the private sector.[163] Points of order are in order for unfunded mandates exceeding $50 million on state, local, and tribal governments.[164] All of these amounts are to be adjusted annually for inflation.[165]

Title II of the Act addresses agency regulations containing regulatory mandates of state, local, and tribal governments and on the private sector.[166] The key requirement is for a "statement to accompany significant regulatory actions."[167] The statement is required in "any general notice of proposed rulemaking that is likely to result in the . . . expenditure by State, local, and tribal governments, in the aggregate, or by the private sector, of $100 million or more (adjusted annually for inflation) in any 1 year."[168]

The statement must include (1) citation to the law under which the rule is being promulgated; (2) "a qualitative and quantitative assessment of the anticipated costs and benefits of the Federal mandate . . . as well as the effect of the Federal mandate on health, safety, and the natural environment," along with an analysis of the availability of federal funds to help governments pay for the mandate; (3) estimates of future compliance costs and of disproportionate budgetary effects on regions or particular governments or segments of the private sector; (4) estimates of the effect on aspects of the national economy; and (5) a summary of the agency's consultations with elected representatives.[169] A summary of this statement must appear in the notice of proposed

provisions that fit within UMRA's exclusions." Government Accountability Office, Unfunded Mandates: Opinions Vary About Reform Act's Strengths, Weaknesses, and Options for Improvement 10 (GAO-05-454) (Mar. 31, 2005).

163. *Id.* § 658c(a) & (b).

164. *Id.* § 658d(a)(2). No such points of order lie for private sector burdens, unless CBO fails to do the report.

165. *Id.* § 568c. The inflation-adjusted amount on the original $100 million amount would be approximately $148.72 million as of February 17, 2012. *See* U.S. Inflation Calculator, http://www.usinflationcalculator.com/ (calculated by entering $100 million in the "amount of money" field, the year "1995" in the initial year field, and "2012" in the final year field).

166. *See* Memorandum for the Heads of Executive Departments and Agencies, *Guidance for Implementing Title II of S. 1,* from Alice Rivlin, OMB Director (Mar. 31, 1995) (with attached memorandum from OIRA Administrator Sally Katzen).

167. 2 U.S.C. § 1532.

168. *Id.* § 1532(a). *See supra* note 165, concerning inflation adjustment.

169. *Id.* The agency must also develop a plan to specially notify small governments of such requirements and develop a process to receive meaningful and timely input from elective officials. *Id.* §§ 1533, 1534. In that connection, an exemption from the Federal Advisory Committee Act is carved out for such consultations. *Id.* § 1534. See Memorandum for the Heads of Departments and Agencies, *Guidelines and Instructions for Implementing Section 240, 'State, Local, and Tribal Government Input,' of Title II of P.L. 104-4,* from Alice Rivlin, OMB Director (Sept. 21, 1995), *reprinted in* 60 Fed. Reg. 50,651 (Sept. 29, 1995) (providing OMB Guidance on these consultations); *see also* Memorandum for Committee Management Officers, *Application of the*

rulemaking.[170] However, the Act does allow agencies to prepare the statement "in conjunction with or as a part of any other statement or analysis . . . ."[171]

Before issuing a final rule that was subject to the above requirements, the agency must "identify and consider a reasonable number of regulatory alternatives and from those alternatives, select the least costly, most cost-effective or least burdensome alternatives that achieve the objectives of the rule."[172]

Judicial review of agency compliance with the UMRA is limited. The Act provides that agency statements accompanying significant regulatory actions are subject to review only under 5 U.S.C. § 706(1)—which allows courts to "compel agency action unlawfully withheld or unreasonably delayed."[173] This means that courts may compel the production of such agency statements but cannot review the contents of them. In fact, the Act makes clear that "the inadequacy or failure to prepare such statement (including the inadequacy or failure to prepare any estimate, analysis, statement or description) or written plan shall not be used as a basis for staying, enjoining, invalidating or otherwise affecting such agency rule."[174]

The Act requires OMB to submit annual reports to Congress on agency compliance with Title II of the Act.[175]

H. The Information Quality Act

The Information Quality Act (IQA),[176] enacted in 2000 as an undebated amend-

---

Federal Advisory Committee Act (FACA) to Intergovernmental Contacts, from James L. Dean, director, [GSA] committee management secretariat (Mar. 21, 1994); Department of Commerce, Proposed Statement of Policy on Intergovernmental Consultation under the Unfunded Mandates Reform Act of 1995, 61 Fed. Reg. 5531 (Feb. 13, 1996) (providing an example of an agency plan).

170. 2 U.S.C. § 1532(b).
171. *Id.* § 1532(c).
172. *Id.* § 1535(a).
173. *Id.* § 1571.
174. *Id.* § 1571(a)(3). However, the statements are to be considered as part of the record for judicial review. *Id.* § 1571(a)(4). Thus, an agency's admission that the least burdensome alternative was not chosen may catch a reviewing court's notice. *See* Troy, *supra* note 155, at 146–47.
175. Now the report is subsumed into OMB's *Report to Congress on the Costs and Benefits of Federal Regulations. See* 2011 REPORT TO CONGRESS ON THE BENEFITS AND COSTS OF FEDERAL REGULATIONS AND UNFUNDED MANDATES ON STATE, LOCAL, AND TRIBAL ENTITIES 91–98, *available at* http://www.whitehouse.gov/sites/default/files/omb/inforeg/2011_cb/2011_cba_report.pdf (Fifteenth Annual Report to Congress on Agency Compliance with the Unfunded Mandates Reform Act).
176. Sometimes referred to as the Data Quality Act. The most complete source of information on the Act is found on the website of the Center for Regulatory Effectiveness, http://www.thecre.com/quality/index.html. CRE's founder, James Tozzi, acting as a lobbyist, was responsible for the drafting of the Act. See Annamaria Baba, Daniel M. Cook, Thomas O. McGarity & Lisa A. Bero, *Legislating "Sound Science": The Role of the Tobacco Industry,* 95 AM J. PUB. HEALTH S20 (2005), *available at* http://ajph.aphapublications.org/cgi/content/full/95/S1/S20?view=long&pmid=16030333 (detailing Mr. Tozzi's role).

ment of the Paperwork Reduction Act inserted into an omnibus appropriations bill,[177] has quickly become one of the more noteworthy statutes affecting the rulemaking process. The IQA requires every agency[178] to issue guidelines, with OMB oversight, to ensure and maximize the quality, objectivity, utility, and integrity of information disseminated by the agency. Agencies must also establish administrative mechanisms allowing affected persons to seek and obtain correction of information maintained and disseminated by the agency. Additionally, agencies are required to post such requests and their responses on their websites.[179]

The IQA (in its entirety) provides:

> (a) In General—The Director of the Office of Management and Budget shall, by not later than September 30, 2001, and with public and Federal agency involvement, issue guidelines under sections 3504(d)(1) and 3516 of title 44, United States Code, that provide policy and procedural guidance to Federal agencies for ensuring and maximizing the quality, objectivity, utility, and integrity of information (including statistical information) disseminated by Federal agencies in fulfillment of the purposes and provisions of . . . the Paperwork Reduction Act.
>
> (b) Content of Guidelines—The guidelines under subsection (a) shall—

---

177. Consolidated Appropriations Act of 2001, Pub. L. No. 106-554, § 515, 114 Stat. 2763, 2763A154 (2000) (codified at 44 U.S.C.A. § 3516 Note). For commentary on the Act, see Stephen M. Johnson, *Junking the "Junk Science" Law: Reforming the Information Quality Act*, 58 Admin. L. Rev. 37, 78–80 (2006); Alexander Nathan Hecht, *Administrative Process in an Information Age: The Transformation of Agency Action under the Data Quality Act*, 31 J. Legis. 233 (2005); Karl S. Bourdeau, *Information Quality Act Challenges to Flawed Use of Science*, 19 Nat. Res. & Envt. 41 (Spring 2005); Mark A. Greenwood, *The Information Quality Act: How a Sunshine Statute Brought a Perfect Storm,* Daily Env't Rep. (BNA) No. 57 (Mar. 25, 2005); Michelle V. Lacko, Comment, *The Data Quality Act: Prologue to a Farce or a Tragedy?*, 53 Emory L. J. 305 (2004); Sidney A. Shapiro, *The Information Quality Act and Environmental Protection: The Perils of Reform by Appropriations Rider*, 28 Wm. & Mary Envtl. L. & Pol'y Rev. 339 (2004); James T. O'Reilly, *The 411 on 515: How OIRA's Expanded Information Roles in 2002 Will Impact Rulemaking and Agency Publicity Actions*, 54 Admin. L. Rev. 835, 846 (2002). *See also* National Academy of Science, Workshop: Ensuring the Quality of Data Disseminated by the Federal Government (May 21–22, 2002), transcript, *available at* http://www.nap.edu/books/0309088577/html.

178. Because the Act applies to every agency subject to the Paperwork Reduction Act, this includes independent regulatory agencies as well as executive agencies. In fact, independent agencies did comply with the OMB directives under the IQA. For a list of agency rules, see http://www.thecre.com/quality/agency-database.html.

179. Memorandum from John D. Graham, OIRA Administrator, for the President's Management Council Regarding Posting of Information Quality Act Requests and Responses (Mar. 2, 2004), *available at* http://www.whitehouse.gov/sites/default/files/omb/assets/regulatory_matters_pdf/memo_pmc_a4.pdf. Some agencies also post third-party comments on such requests. *See, e.g.*, http://www.epa.gov/quality/informationguidelines/thirdparty.htm.

(1) apply to the sharing by Federal agencies of, and access to, information disseminated by Federal agencies; and

(2) require that each Federal agency to which the guidelines apply—

(A) issue guidelines ensuring and maximizing the quality, objectivity, utility, and integrity of information (including statistical information) disseminated by the agency, by not later than 1 year
after the date of issuance of the guidelines under subsection (a);

(B) establish administrative mechanisms allowing affected persons
to seek and obtain correction of information maintained and
disseminated by the agency that does not comply with the
guidelines issued under subsection (a); and

(C) report periodically to the Director—(i) the number and nature
of complaints received by the agency regarding the accuracy
of information disseminated by the agency and; (ii) how such
complaints were handled by the agency.[180]

After OMB issued its guidance to the agencies,[181] each agency then subsequently
issued proposed and final guidelines that were vetted by OMB.[182]

The IQA does not, by its terms, specifically apply to rulemaking, and there was
some debate over its applicability. OMB has taken the position that the IQA applies to
information that an agency cites in its notice of proposed rulemaking because the
agency is thereby endorsing the reliability of that information.[183]

Professor Sidney Shapiro, while recognizing that courts might defer to OMB's
interpretation of the ambiguous term *dissemination*,[184] argued that Congress could
not have intended that the IQA apply to rulemaking because the rulemaking process
accomplishes the same goal as the Act's requirement that each agency establish an
"administrative mechanism" to hear information quality complaints, and that "information receives far more scrutiny in rulemaking than it receives under IQA."[185] He

---

180. For citation, *see supra* note 177.
181. Guidelines for Ensuring and Maximizing the Quality, Objectivity, Utility, and Integrity of
Information Disseminated by Federal Agencies; Republication, 67 Fed. Reg. 8452 (Feb. 22,
2002) [hereinafter OMB Guidelines].
182. *See* Office of Mgmt. & Budget, Office of Information & Regulatory Affairs, OIRA Review of
Information Quality Guidelines Drafted by Agencies at 15–16, 32–35 (June 10, 2002) (detailing
an attachment to a memo from John D. Graham to the President's Management Council). For
a detailed compilation of agency guidelines, petitions, and other matters related to the Information Quality Act, see the CRE Web site, *supra* note 176.
183. OMB Guidelines, *supra* note 181, at 8460, § V(8). *See also* James W. Conrad, Jr., *The Information Quality Act: Antiregulatory Costs of Mythic Proportions?*, 12 Kan. J. L. & Pub. Pol'y 521,
539–46 (2003) (agreeing that rulemaking is included). Apparently, however, EPA's policy is
that if an IQA petition is related to an ongoing rulemaking (or risk assessment) proceeding,
the EPA defers to the ongoing proceeding. Same for ongoing litigation. (Remarks by an EPA
official at an ABA meeting attended by author.)
184. Shapiro, *supra* note 177, at 363.
185. *Id.* at 365.

also argued that "prior to the enactment of IQA, industry groups were complaining about the lack of a process to challenge information in reports and on the Internet, not in rulemaking."[186]

In rebuttal, Jamie Conrad, of the American Chemistry Council, argued that "the much greater—and potentially infinite—delays associated with rulemaking are [hardly] equivalent to the shorter and more dependable deadlines in the agency [IQA] guidelines,"[187] and that it is also "difficult to see how the rulemaking process would provide any sort of administrative appeal mechanism."[188] He also made an efficiency argument: "What if the affected person did not care about the substance of the rule, only the information issued with the proposal—do we want people who otherwise would not do so challenging rules for essentially ancillary reasons?"[189]

We have not had a definitive resolution of this issue, since the courts have so far ruled that the Act does not allow for a private right of action in federal court to enforce its provisions.[190] But one review of the experience under the Act has concluded that:

> [A]lthough the limited experience to date with the IQA makes definitive conclusions difficult, the Act appears to be working largely as intended and with-

---

186. *Id.* at 365–66.
187. Conrad, *supra* note 183, at 542.
188. *Id.* at 543.
189. *Id.*
190. The judicial review issue is becoming more complicated. Because the IQA is silent on judicial review, some courts have held that there is no private right of action under it. *See, e.g.*, *In re* Operation of the Missouri River, 363 F. Supp. 2d 1145, 1174–75 (D. Minn. 2004) (holding that judicial review of agency compliance with the IQA is foreclosed by the APA exception for action "committed to agency discretion by law"); *accord* Salt Inst. v. Thompson, 345 F. Supp. 2d 589, 602–03 (E.D. Va. 2004) (also finding a lack of standing, finality, and no private right of action), *aff'd on standing grounds*, Salt Inst. v. Leavitt, 440 F.3d 156 (4th Cir. 2006). But in two recent cases the courts have at least entertained the idea of judicial review. In *Americans for Safe Access v. Department of Health & Human Services*, 399 Fed. App'x 314 (9th Cir. 2010), a case brought by a pro-marijuana group challenging HHS's refusal to correct statements made concerning the efficacy of marijuana for medicinal purposes, the court found the agency's decision to defer consideration of the request until it completed its comprehensive review of marijuana's medical uses in conjunction with a petition for rescheduling of the drug filed with the Drug Enforcement Administration was not final action under the APA. It is notable, however, that the court did not simply affirm the district court's decision that the Act did not provide for any judicial review. Perhaps more significantly, in *Prime Time Int'l Co. v. Vilsack*, 599 F.3d 678 (D.C. Cir. 2010), the court did reach the merits of the IQA claim, but found that the relief sought by the petitioner was barred by the OMB's interpretation of the Act in its Guidelines, to which the court gave deference. Thus, the court implicitly found the agency's failure to respond to the petition for correction under the IQA to be reviewable—even though no relief was granted. For an argument against judicial review, see Sidney A. Shapiro, Rena Steinzor & Margaret Clune, *Ossifying Ossification: Why the Information Quality Act Should Not Provide for Judicial Review*, Center for Progressive Reform White Paper 601 (Feb. 2006), *available at* http://www.progressivereform.org/articles/CPR_IQA_601.pdf.

out the dire repercussions predicted by opponents of the law. Moreover, correction requests have come from a broad cross-section of affected parties representing an extensive array of interests and political viewpoints.[191]

Another key rulemaking issue presented by the IQA is whether agencies will also have to ensure the quality and objectivity of studies on which they rely—including those submitted by outside commenters—in the rulemaking process. OMB's guidelines establish a distinction between information that the agency adopts or endorses as its own, which is subject to the Act, and "opinions, where the agency's presentation makes it clear that what is being offered is someone's opinion rather than fact or the agency's views."[192] But as Professor Herz has written:

> Under prevailing administrative law standards, agencies must make available outside studies on which they rely in promulgating a rule. However, they need not obtain, make available, or independently assess the underlying data contained in those studies [citing *American Trucking Associations v. EPA*, 283 F.2d 355, 372 (D.C. Cir. 2002)]. A strong reading of the [IQA] would require the agency to assess the raw data underlying scientific studies before "disseminating" them so as to ensure the "quality" and "objectivity" of the studies. While the [IQA] applies only to dissemination, not other uses of information, general rulemaking principles require an agency to disseminate studies on which it relies. The combination might mean that a rulemaking agency could not rely on an outside study without undertaking the herculean, indeed impossible, task of obtaining, evaluating, and vouching for the data underlying such a study. The OMB Guidelines seem to stake out a middle ground on this issue. "Influential" analytic *results* contained in disseminated information must be "capable of be-

---

191. Bourdeau, *supra* note 177, at 47. *See also* Jamie Conrad, DEVELOPMENTS IN ADMINISTRATIVE LAW AND REGULATORY PRACTICE 2003-2004, at 131–32 (Jeffrey S. Lubbers ed., 2004) ("[A]vailable data tend to suggest that the IQA is not living up to the predictions of either its proponents or its detractors. It does not appear to be producing significant, widespread changes in the quality of agency information, or to be inhibiting those agencies from issuing rules or publishing information. Rather, it appears to be offering a limited opportunity for affected persons to request, and in some cases obtain, correction of information with respect to which, in many cases, no such opportunity existed prior to the IQA's enactment." (citing CRS Report for Congress, "The Information Quality Act: OMB's Guidance and Initial Implementation" (Order Code RL32532) (updated Sept. 17, 2004), *available at* http://www.ombwatch.org/info/dataquality/RL32532_CRS_DQA.pdf)). For another view, see Thomas O. McGarity et al., *Truth and Science Betrayed: The Case Against the Information Quality Act*, CENTER FOR PROGRESSIVE REGULATION (Mar. 2005), *available at* http://www.progressiveregulation.org/articles/iqa.pdf; *see also* Rick Weiss, *'Data Quality' Law Is Nemesis of Regulation*, WASH. POST, Aug. 16, 2004, at A6; Chris Mooney, *Paralysis by Analysis*, WASH. MONTHLY, May 2004, *available at* http://www.washingtonmonthly.com/search.html#2004 (May 2004 link).

192. OMB Guidelines, *supra* note 181, at 8460, § V(5).

ing substantially reproduced," but this requirement does not apply to the original or supporting *data*, since those are not being disseminated.[193]

President Obama has signed on to the goals of the IQA. His March 9, 2009, Memorandum on Scientific Integrity, among other things, refers to the need for each agency to "have appropriate rules and procedures to ensure the integrity of the scientific process within the agency" and "make available to the public the scientific or technological findings or conclusions considered or relied upon in policy decisions."[194] It was followed by a December 17, 2010, Memorandum by the Director of the Executive Office's Office of Science and Technology Policy that provides further guidance.[195]

In conclusion, this short piece of legislation has already produced a considerable amount of commentary and debate over its ramifications on the regulatory activities of the federal government, and specifically on agency rulemaking processes. The IQA has also provided the foundation for OMB's Information Quality Bulletin for Peer Review (described in Part III, Chapter 2(E)).[196] It is still too early to make many definitive judgments about the IQA or its progeny, but the IQA is certainly a law that federal rulemakers must take seriously.

I.   The E-Government Act of 2002[197]

This bipartisan legislation was intended to further the federal government's approach to information dissemination in the Internet Age. It contains many requirements for the government, but of most impact on the rulemaking process are the following requirements:[198]

---

193. MICHAEL HERZ, DEVELOPMENTS IN ADMINISTRATIVE LAW AND REGULATORY PRACTICE 2001-2002, at 179–80 (Jeffrey S. Lubbers ed., 2003) (citing OMB Guidelines, *supra* note 181, at §§ V.3(b), V.9, V.10); *see also* NAS Workshop (May 21, 2002), *supra* note 177, at 24 (remarks of Alan Morrison) ("[I]f the agency refers to, incorporates, or relies on studies in its notice of proposed rulemaking it is only the most artificial of determinations that could possibly say that is it not a dissemination of government information.").

194. White House Office of the Press Secretary, Memorandum for Heads of Departments and Agencies, *Scientific Integrity* (Mar. 9, 2009), *available at* http://www.whitehouse.gov/the_press_office/Memorandum-for-the-Heads-of-Executive-Departments-and-Agencies-3-9-09.

195. White House Office of the Press Secretary, Memorandum for Heads of Executive Departments and Agencies, *Scientific Integrity* (Dec. 17, 2010), *available at* http://www.whitehouse.gov/sites/default/files/microsites/ostp/scientific-integrity-memo-12172010.pdf.

196. *See* Patrick A. Fuller, Note, *How Peer Review of Agency Science Can Help Rulemaking: Enhancing Judicial Deference at the Frontiers of Knowledge*, 75 GEO. WASH. L. REV. 931 (2007) (describing the nexus between the IQA and the Peer Review Bulletin).

197. Pub. L. No. 107-347, 116 Stat. 2899 (2002) (codified as 44 U.S.C. § 3501 note). The provisions with special importance to regulatory agencies are in § 206, 116 Stat. 2915–16, and § 208, 116 Stat. 2921–23.

198. This summary draws from Neil Eisner's valuable annual compilation of "Rulemaking Requirements," prepared while Assistant General Counsel for Regulation and Enforcement at the U.S.

- *Public Information.* To the extent practicable, agencies must provide a website that includes all information about that agency required to be published in the *Federal Register* under 5 U.S.C. § 552(a)(1) and (2).[199]
- *Electronic Submission.* To the extent practicable, agencies must accept electronically those submissions made in rulemaking under 5 U.S.C. § 553(c).[200]
- *Electronic Dockets.* To the extent practicable, agencies must have an Internet-accessible rulemaking docket that includes all public comments and other materials that by agency rule or practice are included in the agency docket, whether or not electronically submitted.[201]
- *Privacy Impact Assessments.* OMB is required to develop guidelines for privacy notices on agency websites, and agencies must conduct "privacy impact assessments" before collecting information that will be collected, maintained, or disseminated using information technology and that "includes any information in an identifiable form permitting the physical or online contacting of a specific individual, if identical questions have been posed to, or identical reporting requirements imposed on, 10 or more persons, other than" federal agencies or employees.[202] It should be noted here that a number of agencies are also required by a recent appropriations act to do a special privacy assessment for proposed rules "on the privacy of information in an identifiable form, including the type of personally identifiable information collected and the number of people affected."[203]

For further discussion of electronic rulemaking, see Part III, Chapter 1(C).

J. Congressional Review of Rules

In 1996, an important requirement was added to the rulemaking process. The Small Business Regulatory Enforcement Fairness Act of 1996 added a new chapter to

---

Department of Transportation, Neil Eisner, *U.S. Department of Transportation Rulemaking Requirements* 21 (April 2011), *available at* http://regs.dot.gov/docs/Rulemaking_Requirements_05312011.pdf.

199. Pub. L. No. 107-347 § 206(b). But note that subsection 552(a)(2) of Title 5 does not, by its terms, require publication of any documents, only that specified documents be available for public inspection and copying. Of course, many agencies now publish these materials on their websites.

200. *Id.* at § 206(c).

201. *Id.* at § 206(d).

202. *Id.* at § 208.

203. Consolidated Appropriations Act, 2005 Pub. L. No. 108-447, 118 Stat. 2809, 3268 division H, § 522(a)(5) (codified at 5 U.S.C.A. § 552a note) (covering agencies within the Transportation, Treasury, Independent Agencies, and General Government Appropriations Act). *See also* OMB Memorandum (M-03-22) on the privacy impact assessments required under the E-Government Act, *available at* http://regs.dot.gov/requirements/m03-22.pdf.

Title 5 of the United States Code, establishing a requirement for congressional review of agency rules.[204] This title became commonly known as the Congressional Review Act (CRA). Under this process, all federal agencies, including independent regulatory agencies, are required to submit each "rule" to both houses of Congress and to the Government Accountability Office (GAO)[205] before it can take effect.

For the purpose of the CRA, "rule" is defined similarly to the basic APA definition in 5 U.S.C. § 551(4) with minor exceptions.[206] This means that a large volume of rules that fit the APA's definition, but are exempted from notice-and-comment rulemaking procedures (for example, interpretive rules, statements of policy, rules within the "proprietary" or military/foreign affairs exemptions), are subject to congressional review.[207]

For each such rule, agencies must submit (1) a report containing "a concise general statement relating to the rule" and the rule's proposed effective date;[208] (2) a copy of any cost-benefit analysis and descriptions of the agency's actions under the Regulatory Flexibility Act and Unfunded Mandates Reform Act; and (3) any other information or statements required by relevant executive orders.[209]

The CRA makes a critical distinction between "major" rules, which are subject to a delayed effective date requirement, and other rules, which are not. *Major rules* are defined in a similar fashion to the operative definition of what are called "economically significant rules" under Executive Order 12,866 (the word "major" is taken

---

204. Pub. L. No. 104-121, Title II, subtitle E, 110 Stat. 856 (codified at 5 U.S.C. §§ 801–808). The following description draws heavily from Daniel Cohen & Peter L. Strauss, *Congressional Review of Agency Regulations*, 49 ADMIN. L. REV. 95 (1997); *see also* Morton Rosenberg, *Congressional Review of Agency Rulemaking: An Update and Assessment of The Congressional Review Act after a Decade*, CRS Report RL30116 (updated May, 8, 2008), *available at* http://www.fas.org/sgp/crs/misc/RL30116.pdf.
205. The GAO was formerly known as the General Accounting Office. The name was changed by Pub. L. 108-271, effective July 7, 2004.
206. 5 U.S.C. § 804. The following types of rules are exempted from congressional review: (1) rules of particular applicability; (2) rules relating to agency management or personnel; and (3) rules of agency organization, procedure, or practice that do not substantially affect the rights or obligations of nonagency parties. *Id.* § 804(3). *See, e.g.*, U.S. Gen. Accounting Office, Letter B-292045 to Rep. Lane Evans (May 19, 2003) (concluding that a DVA memorandum terminating a discretionary loan program was not a covered "rule" under the CRA because it was a "rule relating to 'agency management' or 'agency organization, procedure, or practice that does not substantially affect the rights or obligations of non-agency parties'"). Certain rules of the Federal Reserve Board are also exempted. *Id.* § 807.
207. *See Oversight Hearings on the Congressional Review Act Before the House Subcomm. on Commercial and Administrative Law of the Comm. on the Judiciary*, 104th Cong. 3–4 (1997) (statement of Richard J. Pierce, Jr.) (decrying "extreme overbreadth" of definition and urging that review be limited to major rules) [hereinafter *Oversight Hearing*]; *accord, id.* at 2 (statement of Peter L. Strauss).
208. 5 U.S.C. § 801(a)(1). The effective date requirement may be problematic for interpretive rules and policy statements because agencies ordinarily intend them to be effective immediately, and sometimes retroactively. *See* Cohen & Strauss, *supra* note 204, at 106–07.
209. *Id.*

from the predecessor order, E.O. 12,291); this makes the determination of the OIRA Administrator controlling.[210] Under the complex language of section 801, a major rule's effective date is automatically delayed for at least 60 days[211] while it is reviewed by Congress.[212]

Non-major rules can go into effect without delay, although Congress may, of course, still review them. The GAO is required to submit a report to the congressional committees with jurisdiction on each major rule within 15 calendar days.[213]

The CRA also contains complicated provisions on how days are counted for the purposes of the expedited legislative process for considering joint resolutions of disapproval.[214] For example, as long as a resolution of disapproval is introduced within 60 calendar days (but not counting periods when either house is adjourned for longer than three days) of receipt of the rule and report, there is no time limit on congressional action on that resolution during that Congress. There is also a provision allowing for expedited action in the Senate (limited debate, no filibuster) during the period

---

210. 5 U.S.C. § 804(2). Rules adopted under the Telecommunications Act of 1996 are excepted. *Id.*
211. A major rule takes effect, unless disapproved, on the *latest* of three possible dates: (1) 60 calendar days after Congress receives the report or the rule is published in the *Federal Register*; (2) where Congress has passed a joint resolution of disapproval of the rule, subsequently vetoed by the President, 30 session days after Congress receives the veto, or if earlier, the date on which either House of Congress votes and fails to override the veto; or (3) the date on which the rule would otherwise go into effect, if not for this review requirement. *Id.* § 801(a)(3). If either House votes to reject a joint resolution of disapproval, the rule goes into effect at that time. *Id.* § 801(a)(5). Note that supporters of a popular rule can engineer such a vote early in the 60-day period to hasten the rule's effective date. *See, e.g.,* S. J. Res. 60, 104th Cong. (1996) (disapproving Medicare rule) (rejected).
212. More specifically, the Court of Appeals for the Federal Circuit has held that the CRA does not *alter* major rules' effective dates, but simply suspends their operation pending the outcome of congressional review. *See* Part III, ch. 7(A)(6)(b). There are also exceptions to the delayed effective date provision. Major rules relating to hunting, fishing, and camping can be made effective immediately. 5 U.S.C. § 808(1). There is also a "good cause" exception in § 808(2), similar to that in 5 U.S.C. § 553(b). Finally, the President may personally make a rule immediately effective by issuing an Executive Order that the rule is necessary due to an imminent threat to health, safety, or other emergency; necessary for the enforcement of criminal laws; necessary for national security; or issued pursuant to any statute implementing an international trade agreement. *Id.* § 801(c).
213. These major rule reports are available on the Internet within 24 hours of transmittal to the committees. *Oversight Hearing, supra* note 207, at 4 (statement of Robert P. Murphy, General Counsel, GAO).
214. The CRA's drafters met the dictates of *INS v. Chadha*, 462 U.S. 919 (1983), by requiring that rules could only be rejected through joint resolutions, which require passage by both Houses and "presentment" to the President for signature or veto. *See* Part I(C).
215. 5 U.S.C. § 802(c)–(e). A "session" day (sometimes called a "legislative" day) "is the period of time following an adjournment of the Senate until another adjournment. A recess (rather than an adjournment) in no way affects a legislative day. Therefore, one legislative day may consume a considerable period of time—days, weeks, even months." ROBERT B. DOVE, ENACTMENT OF A LAW (1997), *available at* http://thomas.loc.gov/home/enactment/enactlaw.pdf.

of 60 "session" days after the rule's submission or publication date.[215] This means that a major rule could easily go into effect after the 60-calendar-day period, only to be subject to disapproval much later in the session.[216]

The CRA provides for this scenario by stipulating that if a resolution is enacted, the rule is immediately deprived of any effect. If it had already gone into effect, either because the deadline had expired for a major rule or because the rule was a non-major rule, it "shall be treated as though such rule had never taken effect."[217] This could obviously cause problems if the agency or regulated parties had acted pursuant to the later overturned rule.[218] And it may make agencies unwilling and other parties reluctant to rely on the rule until the period for review is terminated.

Moreover, if a resolution of disapproval is enacted, the CRA provides that the disapproved rule "may not be reissued in substantially the same form, and a new rule that is substantially the same as such a rule may not be issued" unless specifically authorized by a subsequent law.[219]

Other aspects of the law worth noting are that the courts are directed to attach no significance to congressional action or inaction with respect to a rule under review[220] and that the Congress does not need to explain why it has disapproved a rule.[221]

While a large number of rules are sent to Congress each week,[222] the impact of the CRA on the rulemaking process has been slight. Obviously, it gives interested parties another "bite at the apple" after the agency's process is complete. It also gives Congress another weapon in its oversight arsenal. But so far, only one rule has been disapproved, and few resolutions of disapproval have even passed a single House of

---

216. Or even into the *next* session, because the Act also provides that any rule submitted in the last 60 session/legislative days of the current session (a period that is almost impossible to forecast) is treated for review (though not effective-date) purposes as if it were submitted on the fifteenth session/legislative day of the next session. 5 U.S.C. § 801(d)(1). This provision of the law was crucial to the one successful disapproval that has taken place, discussed below. For an explanation of how this provision works, see Curtis W. Copeland, Cong Research Serv., RL34633, Congressional Review Act: Disapproval of Rules in a Subsequent Session of Congress, (updated Sept. 3, 2008), *available at* http://assets.opencrs.com/rpts/RL34633_20080903.pdf.

217. *Id.* § 801(f). *See* Adam M. Finkel & Jason W. Sullivan, *A Cost-Benefit Interpretation of the "Substantially Similar" Hurdle in the Congressional Review Act: Can OSHA Ever Utter the E-Word (Ergonomics) Again?*, 63 Admin. L. Rev. 707 (2011) (urging a narrow interpretation of the "substantially similar" provision).

218. Cohen and Strauss illustrate this problem by positing that (1) a rule has gone into effect requiring fishermen to cut holes into their nets for conservation purposes, and (2) after the fishermen comply, the rule is overturned. Cohen & Strauss, *supra* note 204, at 109.

219. 5 U.S.C. § 801(b)(2).

220. *Id.* § 801(g). *See* Cohen & Strauss, *supra* note 204, at 105–06.

221. Cohen and Strauss are critical of this: "Under this procedure, however, a simple and unelaborated 'No!' withdraws from agencies a range of substantive authority that cannot be determined without subsequent litigation." Cohen & Strauss, *supra* note 204, at 104.

222. As of March 31, 2008, the Comptroller General had submitted reports on 731 major rules under section 801(a)(2)(A) and GAO had cataloged the submission of 47,540 non-major rules as required by section 801(a)(1)(A). Rosenberg, note 204, at 6.

Congress.[223] The disapproval occurred in March 2001 when the congressional leadership, supported by the Bush Administration, successfully used the CRA to overturn OSHA's controversial ergonomic regulations.[224] President Clinton had issued final ergonomic regulations in November 2000 but the rules did not take effect until January 16, 2001, four days before Clinton left office.[225] After the inauguration of President Bush, the Republican-controlled Senate and House voted to approve the Joint Resolution of Disapproval and President Bush signed it into law.[226]

This was an unusual circumstance because the rule in question was a rule approved by a previous administration and, due to the holdover provision in the law,[227] was subject to review by a Congress and new President controlled by the other party. It should be remembered that enactment requires either signing (normally) by the same President whose OMB has already cleared the rule or a very rare veto override—so the number of rules to be overturned through this mechanism will likely be low.[228] Indeed, even when President Obama's inauguration created the same situation (in reverse) as led to the one successful disapproval of the ergonomics rule, the Democrats refrained from seeking to employ this tactic.[229]

---

223. *Id.* (reporting that as of March 31, 2008, "47 joint resolutions of disapproval had been introduced relating to 35 rules"). Morton Rosenberg, Powerpoint presentation in Symposium, *Interbranch Control of Regulation: Executive, Legislative and Judicial Influence, and Agency Response*, Washington College of Law, American University (Feb. 17, 2012), provided updated numbers, as follows: Since April 1996 to February 15, 2012, there have been 60,031 rules reported, 1,085 major rules reported, 72 resolutions of disapproval introduced respecting 49 rules, 3 disapprovals passed by the Senate, 2 disapprovals passed by the House, 1 disapproval (OSHA's ergonomics rule) passed and signed by the President.

224. The ergonomics regulations issued after 10 years of development by OSHA addressed the concerns that surround repetitive lifting and motions in the workplace. These regulations would have mandated standards for employers to promote ergonomics, buy specific equipment, and reduce workplace injuries. *See* Ergonomics Program, 66 Fed. Reg. 20,403 (Apr. 23, 2001) (providing official notice of withdrawal of the regulation).

225. *See* 65 Fed. Reg. 68,262 (Nov. 14, 2000).

226. For House and Senate votes on Pub. L. 107-5, see Cong. Rec. H684, Mar. 7, 2001, roll call no. 33, Cong. Rec. S51888, Cong. Rec. H684, roll call no. 33 (Mar. 7, 2001), and Cong. Rec. S51888, vote no. 15 (Mar. 6, 2001).

227. *See* note 216, *supra.*

228. Of course, the rules of independent agencies are not reviewed by OMB and are less controllable by the President. So it is more likely perhaps that a rule from such an agency might be made subject to such a resolution. *See, e.g.,* H. J. Res. 72 & S. J. Res. 17, 108th Cong., 1st Sess. (disapproving a rule submitted by the Federal Communications Commission with respect to broadcast media ownership). The matter was subsequently addressed in an appropriations rider instead.

229. *See* Note, *The Mysteries of the Congressional Review Act*, 122 Harv. L. Rev. 2162, 2164 (2009) (suggesting that "the experiences at the beginning and end of the Bush Administration [show] that even in times of presidential transitions, when the CRA might be most effective, the Act is little needed"). The Note also explained, "The requirement that each disapproval resolution come to the floor in a separate vehicle—and for up to ten hours of debate in the Senate—ensures that Congress can only use the disapproval procedure for the most problematic rules." *Id.* at 2176.

As an authoritative 2008 study by the Congressional Research Service summarized the situation regarding the CRA:

> [A] number of critical interpretive issues remain to be resolved, including the scope of the provisions' coverage of rules; whether an agency failure to report a covered rule is subject to court review and sanction; whether a joint resolution of disapproval may be utilized to veto parts of a rule or only may be directed at the rule in its entirety; and what is the scope of the limitation that precludes an agency from promulgating a "substantially similar" rule after disapproval of a rule. Of a total of 47 joint resolutions of disapproval that have been introduced to date since April 1996, only one has passed and that one may have been sui generis because of the unique circumstances accompanying its passage. During that period some 47,540 major and non-major rules have been reported and become effective.[230]

One of the problems has received some attention—the reported failure of agencies to submit numerous covered rules to GAO as is required by the CRA.[231] The government has so far argued successfully that the language of section 805 precluding judicial review is so clear that it prevents judicial review of an agency's failure to report a covered rule.[232] As the D.C. District Court said in the most recent decision on this issue, "There is limited case law interpreting Section 805, but what is available supports the plain reading of the statute [that judicial review is barred]."[233]

Nevertheless, despite its almost nonexistent success rate, the Congressional Review Act created additional responsibilities for agencies and Congress, new waiting

---

230. Rosenberg, *supra* note 204, at "summary."
231. *See* Sean D. Croston, *Congress and the Courts Close Their Eyes: The Continuing Abdication of the Duty to Review Agencies' Noncompliance with the Congressional Review Act*, 62 ADMIN. L. REV. 907 (2010); CURTIS W. COPELAND, CONG RESEARCH SERV., R40997, CONGRESSIONAL REVIEW ACT: RULES NOT SUBMITTED TO GAO AND CONGRESS (Dec. 29, 2009), *available at* http://assets.opencrs.com/rpts/R40997_20091229.pdf.
232. For a thorough legal analysis of this issue, see Rosenberg, *supra* note 204, at 28–34.
233. Montanans for Multiple Use v. Barbouletos, 542 F. Supp. 2d 9, 20 (D.D.C. 2008). Judge Hogan cited *Texas Savings & Community Bankers Ass'n v. Federal Housing Finance Board*, 1998 WL 842181 (W.D. Tex. June 25, 1998) (rejecting plaintiffs' allegation that FHFB's failure to submit new rules to Congress violated SBREFA and holding "the language [805] could not be plainer" and "the statute provides for no judicial review of any 'determination, finding, action, or omission under this chapter'"), *aff'd*, 201 F.3d 551 (5th Cir. 2000); United States v. Am. Elec. Power Serv., 218 F. Supp. 2d 931 (S.D.Ohio 2002) (holding that "the language of § 805 is plain" and that an agency's failure to submit a rule to Congress is not judicially reviewable); *In re* Operation of the Missouri River System Litig., 363 F. Supp. 2d 1145, 1173 (D. Minn. 2004) (holding that section 805 precluded judicial review of the U.S. Fish and Wildlife's decision that the designation of certain critical habitat was not a major rule), *vacated in part on other grounds*, 421 F.3d 618 (8th Cir. 2005).

periods, and new pressure points in the process. Moreover, it created tracking responsibilities for the agencies.[234]

K. Miscellaneous Other Statutes Affecting Rulemaking

Over the years, Congress has also enacted various provisions in either appropriations or substantive legislation that affect the rulemaking process. In addition to the privacy impact assessment requirement discussed above,[235] there are three other laws that agency rulemakers should be aware of:

1. The Trade Agreements Act

The Trade Agreements Act of 1979[236] provides a number of government-wide requirements concerning the adoption of standards.[237] As a threshold matter, it prohibits agencies from setting standards that create "unnecessary obstacles to the foreign commerce" of the United States.[238] The statute is primarily concerned with products, and the Act makes clear that legitimate domestic objectives are not considered unnecessary obstacles.[239] The Act also generally requires the use of performance rather than design standards, where appropriate. Finally it also requires that when agencies develop domestic standards, they consider international standards and, where appropriate, that they be used as the basis for the U.S. standards.[240]

Note also that Executive Order 12,889, "Implementation of the North American Free Trade Agreement," requires that agencies subject to the APA must provide at

---

234. *Oversight Hearings, supra* note 207, at 3–4 (statement of Jon Cannon, General Counsel, EPA) (describing the centralization of the submittal and tracking function at EPA and the need for a daily messenger to deliver rules to three required offices); *id.* at 2–3 (statement of Nancy McFadden, General Counsel, Department of Transportation) (describing the computer tracking system and messenger system used by the Department).

235. *See supra*, text accompanying notes 202–03.

236. Pub. L. No. 96-39, 93 Stat. 144 (1979) (codified at 19 U.S.C. §§ 2531–2533).

237. The term "standard" for the purpose of this Act was later defined to mean "a document approved by a recognized body that provides, for common and repeated use, rules, guidelines, or characteristics for products or related processes and production methods, with which compliance is not mandatory. Such term may also include or deal exclusively with terminology, symbols, packaging, marking, or labeling requirements as they apply to a product, process, or production method." Uruguay Round Agreements Act, Pub. L. No. 103-465, § 351(e) (1994) (codified at 19 U.S.C. § 2571).

238. Pub. L. No. 96-39, § 402 (codified at 19 U.S.C. § 2532).

239. Listed legitimate objectives include: (1) national security requirements, (2) the prevention of deceptive practices, (3) the protection of human health or safety, animal or plant life or health, or the environment, (4) fundamental climatic or other geographical factors, or (5) fundamental technological problems. *Id.*

240. *Id.*

least a 75-day comment period for "any proposed Federal technical regulation or any Federal sanitary or phytosanitary measure of general application."[241]

2. *The National Technology Transfer and Advancement Act*

Another law that bears on the development of standards is the National Technology Transfer and Advancement Act.[242] Under this Act, agencies are required to "use technical standards that are developed or adopted by voluntary consensus standards bodies" to carry out policy objectives determined by the agencies, unless they are "inconsistent with applicable law or otherwise impractical." There is also a waiver provision authorizing an agency to waive this provision if doing so would be "inconsistent with applicable law or otherwise impractical," and if the head of each such agency or department transmits to the OMB an explanation of the reasons for not using such standards. In general, however, agencies are required to consult with and—if compatible with agency missions, authority, priorities, and resources—participate with voluntary, private-sector, consensus standards bodies.

These provisions are implemented by OMB Circular A-119.[243]

3. *Assessment of Federal Regulations and Policies on Families*[244]

An omnibus appropriations act is the basis for a statutorily required "family policymaking assessment" to be performed by agencies before implementing policies and regulations that may affect family well-being. Most of these requirements call for extremely subjective judgments on the part of the agency.[245]

The provision requires agency heads to submit a written certification to OMB and Congress that the assessment has been done. OMB also must compile, index, and submit annually to Congress the written certifications it receives.[246] Agencies are specifically required to conduct assessments in accordance with this section's criteria when requested by a Member of Congress.[247] Agency actions or inactions under this

---

241. Exec. Order 12,889, § 4 (Dec. 27, 1993). 58 Fed. Reg. 69,681 (Dec. 30, 1993).
242. Pub. L. No. 104-113, § 12(d) (1996) (codified at 15 U.S.C.A. § 272 note).
243. OMB Circular No. A-119, Federal Participation in the Development and Use of Voluntary Consensus Standards and in Conformity Assessment Activities (revised Feb. 10, 1998), 63 Fed. Reg. 8546 (1998). *See also* NAT'L INST. OF STANDARDS AND TECH., THIRTEENTH ANNUAL REPORT ON FEDERAL AGENCY USE OF VOLUNTARY CONSENSUS STANDARDS AND CONFORMITY ASSESSMENT, *available at* https://standards.gov/NTTAA/resources/nttaa_ar_2009.pdf.
244. Omnibus Consolidated and Emergency Supplemental Appropriations Act, 1999. Pub. L. No. 105-277, (1998), § 654 (codified at 5 U.S.C.A. § 601 note).
245. *See infra*, Part III, ch. 2(F).
246. Pub. L. No. 105-277, § 654(d)(2) (codified at 5 U.S.C.A. § 601 note).
247. *Id.* § 654(e).

law are not subject to judicial review; the law states that it is not intended to create any right or benefit enforceable against the United States.[248]

248. *Id.* § 654(f). This law appears to have had a negligible impact on the rulemaking process. A Westlaw search on March 30, 2012, turned up only one rule in which the agency issued an impact statement, an INS rule affecting family reunification. See 65 Fed. Reg. 43,677, 43,679 (July 14, 2000). There were numerous statements of no impact.

PART III

INFORMAL RULEMAKING IN PRACTICE

As explained in Part II, informal or "notice-and-comment" rulemaking is the predominant form of federal agency rulemaking. This Part examines in more detail the notice-and-comment requirements of section 553 of the Administrative Procedure Act (APA). It also discusses the relationship between informal rulemaking procedure and the additional analysis and procedures imposed by presidential executive orders and government-wide procedural statutes.

Chapter 1 covers the initiation of the rulemaking process, including procedural and substantive considerations and the emergence of "electronic" rulemaking. Chapter 2 discusses the regulatory and related analyses that have become such a central part of rulemaking. Chapter 3 looks closely at the notice requirements stemming from the APA and court decisions interpreting the APA. Chapter 4 looks at public participation and hearings in rulemaking. Chapter 5 covers the developing concept of the "rulemaking record." Chapter 6 examines the related principles covering the ex parte communications in rulemaking. Chapter 7 discusses the many requirements that agencies must consider in drafting and promulgating final rules. And, finally, Chapter 8 raises issues concerning agency review of existing rules.

Chapter 1

Beginning the Process

Because the courts, Congress, and the President have increasingly required that agencies demonstrate the need for, and rationality of, the rules they adopt, the agency process that precedes rulemaking has become significantly more important. This chapter will discuss a number of preliminary legal and policy considerations that should be taken into account before an agency begins a rulemaking following the APA procedures.[1] This assumes, of course, that an agency has rulemaking authority[2] and has decided, as a matter of strategy, to issue a regulation instead of a more informal and nonbinding type of guidance document,[3] or to make an "incremental adjustment" via a waiver, exception, or variance.[4] It also assumes that the agency has considered alternative approaches to the regulatory problem at hand, such as market-based or economic-incentive instruments, some of which will still require rulemaking.[5]

---

1. For an excellent overview of the *management* aspects of rulemaking, see CORNELIUS M. KERWIN, THE MANAGEMENT OF REGULATION DEVELOPMENT: OUT OF THE SHADOWS, (IBM Center for The Business of Government, 2007), *available at* http://www.businessofgovernment.org/sites/default/files/ KerwinReport.pdf.
2. *See supra*, Part II, ch. 2(A)(2).
3. *See generally* M. Elizabeth Magill, *Agency Choice of Policymaking Form,* 71 U. CHI. L. REV. 1383 (2004). *See also* James T. Hamilton & Christopher H. Schroeder, *Strategic Regulators and the Choice of Rulemaking Procedures: The Selection of Formal vs. Informal Rules in Regulating Hazardous Waste*, 57 LAW & CONTEMP. PROBS. 185 (1994) (discussing a case study of one agency's strategic choices). For one of the few examinations of agencies' pre-notice-of-proposed-rulemaking activity, see Blair P. Bremberg, *Pre-Rulemaking Regulatory Development Activities and Sources as Variables in the Rulemaking Fairness Calculus: Taking a Soft Look at the Ex-APA Side of Environmental Policy Rulemakings*, 6 J. MIN. L. & POL'Y 1 (1990–1991). *See also* Richard Williams, *Regulation Checklist: Common Pitfalls in Regulations* (Mercatus Center, Working Paper No. 10-01, 2010), *available at* http://mercatus.org/sites/ default/files/publication/Common%20Pitfalls%20in%20Regulations.pdf.
4. *See* Robert L. Glicksman & Sidney A. Shapiro, *Improving Regulation Through Incremental Adjustment*, 52 U. KAN. L. REV. 1179 (2004). The procedural and accountability issues associated with back-end adjustments have taken on much more salience after Hurricane Katrina.
5. *See, e.g.*, Dennis D. Hirsch, *Project XL and the Special Case: The EPA's Untold Success Story*, 26 COLUM. J. ENVTL. L. 219 (2001); Nathaniel O. Keohane, Richard L. Revesz & Robert Stavins, *The Choice of Regulatory Instruments in Environmental Policy*, 22 HARV. L. REV. 313 (1998). For a more critical view, see Rena I. Steinzor, *Regulatory Reinvention and Project XL: Does the Emperor Have Any Clothes?*, 26 Envtl. L. Rep. (Envtl. L. Inst.) 10,527 (1996). For more recent

A. External Considerations

Rulemakings vary significantly in their manner and pace of development, and the events or external interests that "trigger" a rulemaking may be a major factor influencing the way the rulemaking is conducted. Congress, the courts, OMB, the public, and other entities may be instrumental in causing an agency to undertake a rulemaking.[6]

Of course, whatever triggers an agency's interest in developing a proposed rule, the agency's activities during the time between the trigger and the issuance of the notice of proposed rulemaking (NPRM) is not regulated by the APA or other statute—other than perhaps the general requirements for registration of lobbyists.[7] Yet this "drafting" period can obviously be quite important to the eventual outcome of the rulemaking. This is not lost on sophisticated interested parties.[8] Some agencies docket all meetings related to rulemakings, even those held before the NPRM.[9]

---

thoughts on these issues, see Kristin E. Hickman & Claire A. Hill, *Concepts, Categories, and Compliance in the Regulatory State*, 94 Minn. L. Rev. 1151 (2010); George B. Wyeth, *"Standard" and "Alternative" Environmental Protection: The Changing Role of Environmental Agencies*, 31 Wm. & Mary Envtl. L. & Pol'y Rev. 5 (2006).

6. For example, a political scientist found that the Environmental Protection Agency's (EPA's) rulemaking agenda was primarily set by statutes or court orders and consent decrees. She found one exception where an EPA administrator initiated a rulemaking on product labeling after "being frustrated by the quality of the labels" on products at the local hardware store. The National Highway Safety Administration's rulemaking agenda, on the other hand, was "technology driven" by staff scientists, public petitions, and the National Transportation Safety Board. At a third agency, the Administration for Families and Children (within the Department of Health and Human Services), both the career staff and political officers "consciously try to avoid rulemaking unless explicitly ordered by Congress" to do so. Marissa Martino Golden, "Diverse Paths: The Multiple Routes to Federal Agencies' Rulemaking Agendas," 9–18 (Dec. 3–4, 1999) (paper presented at the Fifth National Public Management Research Conference, College Station, Texas) (on file with author).

7. *But see* President Obama's Executive Order 13,563 § 2(c), urging agencies to seek public input from affected persons "[b]efore issuing a notice of proposed rulemaking," 76 Fed. Reg. 3821, 3822 (Jan. 21, 2011).

8. *See, e.g.*, Richard G. Stoll, Effective EPA Advocacy (2010) 85–116 (describing and advocating "early advocacy" in the pre-proposal process). *See also* Wendy Wagner, et al., *Rulemaking in the Shade: An Empirical Study of EPA's Air Toxic Emission Standards*, 63 Admin. L. Rev. 99, 110–113, 124–28 (2011) (discussing results of study that showed that EPA engaged in an average of 178 contacts with interest groups per rule in the pre-NPRM phase of hazardous air pollution rulemaking). The study also found that such meetings were "almost completely monopolized by regulated parties." *Id.* at 125.

9. Wagner, et al., *supra* note 8, at 125, n.100 (suggesting that EPA's recording of such contacts "may be a wise move" because "evidence of extensive industry communications should help buffer the agency against accusations of sloppy or incomplete analysis, at least when the industry is the legal challenger").

1. Congressional and Judicial Pressure

Congress operates in several ways to bring about agency rulemaking. Most directly, an agency's enabling statute may require an agency to undertake specific rulemaking actions, frequently within a particular time frame. In some cases, Congress, in the exercise of its oversight function, will hold hearings and issue a congressional report "recommending" or "urging" agency rulemaking action.[10] There are also frequent informal contacts between agency officials and individual members of Congress or their staff members on specific rulemaking projects.[11] These often result in the agency giving greater or lesser priority to a rulemaking project or otherwise affect the agency decisionmaking process. A good example of a congressional directive occurred in the Transportation Equity Act for the 21st Century, which mandated that "the Secretary of Transportation shall issue a notice of proposed rulemaking to improve occupant protection for occupants of different sizes, belted and unbelted . . . , while minimizing the risk to infants, children, and other occupants from injuries and deaths caused by air bags, by means that include advanced air bags."[12]

The judiciary too has had an increasing role in triggering rulemaking activity.[13] As discussed later,[14] there have been an increasing number of cases in which litigants have sought court enforcement of statutory rulemaking deadlines or otherwise challenged agency failure to act. Agencies often must adjust their priorities to comply with court orders issued in such cases. The public response to a court decision ordering agency action, or the court's criticism of the agency in a decision, may bring about a new agency rulemaking action, even where avenues of legal appeal are available to the agency. Indeed, on occasion, the mere filing of a lawsuit may lead to agency action.[15]

---

10. *See* discussion of legislative deadlines *supra* Part I (C).
11. *See, e.g.*, the discussions between EPA officials and Senator Robert Byrd and his staff regarding EPA's standard under the Clean Air Act for sulfur dioxide. *See* Sierra Club v. Costle, 657 F.2d 298, 408–10 (D.C. Cir. 1981), discussed *infra* ch. 6. For a comprehensive look at Congress's involvement in agency activity, see Jack M. Beermann, *Congressional Administration*, 43 SAN DIEGO L. REV. 61 (2006).
12. Pub. L. No. 105-178, § 7103(a)(1), 112 Stat. 107, 466 (1998) (codified at 49 U.S.C. § 30127 note). DOT's advanced airbags rule was upheld in *Public Citizen, Inc. v. Nat'l Hwy. Traffic Safety Admin.*, 374 F.3d 1251 (D.C. Cir. 2004).
13. This is particularly true with respect to EPA. A study of EPA hazardous air pollution rulemaking (which is under tight statutory deadlines) showed that 73% (66 rules) were promulgated under court order. Wendy Wagner, et al., *supra* note 8, at 137.
14. *See infra* Part IV, ch. 3.
15. For example, OSHA issued a temporary emergency occupational health standard on certain pesticides a month after a public interest group brought an action in a federal district court to compel issuance of the standard even though no court order was issued. *See* BENJAMIN W. MINTZ, OSHA: HISTORY, LAW AND POLICY 99 n.5 (1984).

2. Public Petitions for Rulemaking

The public too may provide the impetus for rulemaking. Section 553(e) of the APA provides that "[e]ach agency shall give an interested person the right to petition for the issuance, amendment, or repeal of a rule."[16] This requirement applies "not only to substantive [legislative] rules but also to interpretations and statements of general policy, and to organizational and procedural rules. It applies both to existing rules and to proposed or tentative rules."[17] While the APA itself does not contain any specific procedural requirements concerning agency responses to rulemaking petitions, some statutes mandate certain procedures.[18] In addition, the *Attorney General's Manual on the APA* advised that every agency with rulemaking authority should establish and publish procedural rules governing the receipt, consideration, and disposition of rulemaking petitions.[19] A number of agencies have issued such rules.[20]

In 1986, the Administrative Conference completed a study of agencies' handling of rulemaking petitions.[21] The Conference's recommendation based on this report noted that while most agencies have established some procedures governing petitions for rulemaking, "few agencies have established sound practices in dealing with petitions or responded promptly to such petitions."[22] The Conference, therefore, recommended the adoption of basic procedures for the receipt, consideration, and prompt disposition of petitions for rulemaking, including specifications for the address for filing petitions and their contents, maintenance of a public petition file, and provision for prompt notification to petitioners of the disposition, including "a summary explanatory statement."[23]

---

16. 5 U.S.C. § 553(e).
17. Attorney General's Manual on the Administrative Procedure Act 38 (1947), *reprinted in* William F. Funk, Jeffrey S. Lubbers & Charles Pou, Jr., Federal Administrative Sourcebook 39, 75 (4th ed. 2008).
18. *See, e.g.*, Toxic Substance Control Act, 15 U.S.C. § 2620 (authorizing citizens to petition for rulemaking, requiring EPA to either grant or deny a petition within 90 days, and if granted, promptly commence rulemaking, and if denied, publish reasons in the *Federal Register*, and allowing petitioner to seek de novo review in federal district court if the petition is denied or if no response is made within a specified period); Envtl. Def. Fund v. Thomas, 657 F. Supp. 302 (D.D.C. 1987).
19. Attorney General's Manual, *supra* note 7, at 38.
20. *See, e.g.*, Nuclear Regulatory Commission, 10 C.F.R. §§ 2.802–2.803; Department of Energy Regulations Implementing 42 U.S.C. § 6297(b), 10 C.F.R. §§ 430.41–430.49; Consumer Product Safety Commission, 16 C.F.R. §§ 1051.1–1051.11; *see also* William Luneburg, *Petitioning Federal Agencies for Rulemaking: An Overview of Administrative and Judicial Practice and Some Recommendations for Improvement*, 1988 Wis. L. Rev. 1 (1988) (containing discussion of agency regulations implementing 5 U.S.C. § 553(e)).
21. *See* Luneburg, *supra* note 20.
22. ACUS Recommendation 86-6, *Petitions for Rulemaking*, 51 Fed. Reg. 46,988 (1986).
23. *Id.* This recommendation was echoed by the National Performance Review. *See* Office of the Vice President, Creating a Government That Works Better and Costs Less, National Performance Review, Improving Regulatory Systems 44 (1993) [hereinafter National Performance Review, Improving Regulatory Systems]. For an example of a good explanatory statement, see Department of

The Conference additionally suggested that agencies, among other things, "develop effective methods for providing notice to interested persons that a petition has been filed"[24] and establish "internal management controls to assure the timely processing of petitions," which might include deadlines for completing interim actions and reaching decisions on petitions.[25] In 1995 the Conference urged that, "if necessary, the President by executive order or Congress should mandate that petitions be acted upon within a specified time."[26] Agencies as a matter of practice often invite comment on petitions for rulemaking, either directly[27] or as a part of a more general notice of proposed rulemaking.[28]

Indeed, the Supreme Court has advised that when a challenger's complaint concerns an agency's failure to revisit a regulatory policy, "the proper procedure . . . is set forth explicitly in the APA: a petition to the agency for rulemaking, § 553(e), denial of which must be justified by a statement of reasons, § 555(e), and can be appealed to the courts, §§ 702, 706."[29]

---

the Interior, Office of Surface Mining Reclamation & Enforcement, Petition to Initiate Rulemaking; Surface Coal Mining and Reclamation Operations; Permanent Regulatory Program Federal Inspection and Enforcement Authority, 52 Fed. Reg. 21,598–603 (1987) (containing text of the agency's letter to petitioner advising that petition had been granted in part, with the enclosed statement of reasons for agency's decision). *See also* 30 C.F.R. § 700.12.

24. *But see* Alternative Res. & Dev. Found. v. Veneman, 262 F.3d 406, 407–08 (D.C. Cir. 2001) (stating that an association was not allowed to intervene in a rulemaking petition while the petitioner and agency entered into a stipulation of dismissal containing an agreement by the agency to conduct rulemaking on the petition). The court denied the association's intervention request because the association's interests were not harmed by the agency's agreement to conduct rulemaking. *Id.* at 411.

25. ACUS Recommendation 86-6, *supra* note 22, at 29.

26. ACUS Recommendation 95-3, *Review of Existing Agency Regulations*, 60 Fed. Reg. 43,109 (1995). Congress has done so with respect to the Federal Aviation Administration (FAA), which is directed by statute to "act upon all petitions for rulemaking no later than 6 months after the date such petitions are filed by dismissing such petitions, by informing the petitioner of an intention to dismiss, or by issuing a notice of proposed rulemaking or advanced notice of proposed rulemaking." 49 U.S.C. § 106(f)(3)(A).

27. *See, e.g.*, Eipper Aircraft, Inc.; Regulation of Ultralight Vehicles, Petition for Rulemaking, 50 Fed. Reg. 6312 (1985). The *Federal Register* notice stated that the agency was publishing the "substantive parts of the petition for rulemaking" and inviting the public to comment and "assist the FAA in determining the need, if any, for additional rules governing the operation of ultralight vehicles." *Id.*

28. *See, e.g.*, Occupational Exposure to Hepatitis B Virus and Human Immunodeficiency Virus, Advance Notice of Proposed Rulemaking, 52 Fed. Reg. 45,438 (1987). The notice, referring to two petitions for rulemaking on this subject that had been filed with the agency, concluded that the "appropriate course of action" would be for the Occupational Safety and Health Administration (OSHA) to collect further information through the publication of an advance notice of proposed rulemaking (ANPRM). *Id.* at 45,438–39. ANPRMs are discussed *infra* subsec. (B)(1).

29. Auer v. Robbins, 519 U.S. 452, 459 (1997).

Whether or not an agency has issued regulations on petitions for rulemaking, petitioners would be well advised to support requests for the initiation of rulemaking with data and legal and policy arguments. These petitions are more likely to result in a favorable response, and court decisions reversing agency refusals to initiate rulemaking have typically occurred in the context of the agency having denied a petition for rulemaking.[30]

3. *Agency Priority Setting*

Agencies in most cases have insufficient resources to undertake all of the rulemakings that demand attention. As an Administrative Conference report concluded, for example, the Occupational Safety and Health Administration (OSHA) can undertake only a small number of new rulemaking projects a year from among the thousands of hazardous conditions that warrant attention.[31] Although an agency has a

---

30. The leading case is now *Massachusetts v. EPA*, 549 U.S. 497 (2007) (holding that the Clean Air Act authorizes federal regulation of emissions of carbon dioxide and other greenhouse gases, and that EPA had misread the Act when it denied a rulemaking petition seeking controls on greenhouse gas emissions from new motor vehicles). Recent cases upholding denials of petitions include *Preminger v. Sec'y of Veterans Affairs*, 632 F.3d 1345 (Fed. Cir. 2011) (holding that the Court of Appeals for the Federal Circuit did have jurisdiction to review denials of petitions for rulemaking under APA § 553 but that the Secretary's reasons for denying the petition were not arbitrary and capricious); *Public Citizen v. NRC*, 573 F.3d 916 (9th Cir. 2009) (upholding the NRC's denial of a petition to amend its nuclear facility safeguard regulations against "attacking forces equal to those of 9/11," including air-based threats, ruling that they were outside the scope of threats that the agency could be expected to reasonably defend); *Spano v. NRC*, 293 F. App'x 91 (2d Cir. 2008) (rejecting petitioners' argument that NRC should have afforded them an opportunity to provide supplementary information and hold hearings after the NRC determined that the rulemaking petition did not provide a sufficient factual or technical basis in support of the action requested where issues raised by the petition had already been "considered at length" in a separate rulemaking); *Defenders of Wildlife v. Gutierrez*, 532 F.3d 913 (D.C. Cir. 2008) (upholding the denial of an environmental group's petition to National Marine Fisheries Service (NMFS) to undertake emergency rulemaking aimed at reducing the risk of ships striking right whales where NMFS was in the process of conducting full notice-and-comment rulemaking on the subject). *See also, e.g.*, Am. Horse Prot. Ass'n, Inc. v. Lyng, 812 F.2d 1 (D.C. Cir. 1987) (finding reasons given for refusal to grant rulemaking petition were insufficient); Pub. Citizen Health Res. Grp. v. Auchter, 702 F.2d 1150 (D.C. Cir. 1983) (ordering OSHA to propose rule regulating ethylene oxide after agency failed to respond promptly to a petition for emergency standard); Families for Freedom v. Napolitano, 628 F. Supp. 2d 535 (S.D.N.Y. 2009) (holding the Department of Homeland Security's two-and-a-half year delay in responding to rulemaking petition addressing defects in the immigrant detention system as unreasonable and ordering that the agency either accept or deny the petition within 30 days of the judgment).

31. Thomas O. McGarity & Sidney A. Shapiro, *OSHA Rulemaking Procedures*, 1987 ACUS 79, 83 (1987). One study in 2000 noted that OSHA promulgated only two contested standards substantially revising exposure limits between 1992 and 1999, that it takes between four and seven years to complete most rules, that its inflation-adjusted budget had remained constant since

great deal of discretion in how it sets priorities in rulemaking,[32] how an agency chooses the projects to pursue—that is, its priority system—"is a matter of no small importance to the agency, the regulated industries, and workers [the protected group]."[33]

Some enabling statutes establish a priority by mandating agency action within a specific time period. Other statutes only give the agency general directions in setting priorities.[34] Court orders, individually or taken together, may effectively establish priorities for agency activity by directing action in specific rulemaking proceedings.[35] Indeed, court-directed rulemaking action has been criticized on the ground that the court, arguably without sufficient expertise, sets the agency's rulemaking agenda. Cognizant of this limitation, courts have often accorded agencies considerable deference in their priority setting and resource allocation.[36] Under Executive Order 12,866's regulatory planning process, the role of the President and OMB in reviewing agency rulemaking priorities has continued to be important.[37] From 2001 to 2006 OIRA used a system of "prompt letters." The letters had no legal weight but were used to notify agencies that they should consider creating or modifying rulemaking on certain issues.[38] This practice was discontinued in 2006.

Priority setting thus falls largely on the agency itself; this is not, however, an easy task. The Administrative Conference addressed the issue of setting priorities in the context of carcinogen regulation in Recommendation 82-5, Federal Regulation of Cancer-Causing Chemicals. Recognizing that estimates of the number of carcinogens describe a universe "larger than government agencies can evaluate or regulate," the Conference concluded that a "prioritization system" is necessary to ensure that the chemicals posing the greatest risk and the ones that can be controlled the most eco-

---

1982, and that it had 200 fewer employees than in 1971, its first year in existence, and almost 800 fewer employees than in 1980. *See* Sidney A. Shapiro & Randy Rabinowitz, *Voluntary Regulatory Compliance in Theory and Practice: The Case of OSHA*, 52 ADMIN. L. REV. 97 (2000).

32. *See* Am. Iron & Steel Inst. v. Occupational Safety & Health Admin., 182 F.3d 1261, 1269 (11th Cir. 1999) (while the "agency's chosen scope of rulemaking is a matter subject to judicial review, . . . such review is rather limited and deferential in nature").

33. McGarity & Shapiro, *supra* note 31, at 124.

34. *See* OSH Act, 29 U.S.C. § 655(g) (stating the agency should give "due regard to the urgency of the need for mandatory safety and health standards for particular industries, trades, crafts, occupations, businesses, workplaces or work environments").

35. Court orders requiring agency rulemaking actions are discussed *infra* Part IV, ch. 3. *See also* discussion of consent decrees, *infra* subsec. 5.

36. *See* Nat'l Congress of Hispanic Americans v. Marshall, 626 F.2d 882, 889 (D.C. Cir. 1979) ("With its broader perspective, and access to a broad range of undertaking . . . the agency has a better capacity than the court to make the comparative judgments involved in determining priorities [in rulemaking] and allocating resources.").

37. Exec. Order 12,866 is discussed *supra* Part I(D). *See also* Exec. Order 12,498, 3 C.F.R. § 323 (1985), *superseded by* Exec. Order 12,866, 3 C.F.R. 638 (1994).

38. *See* OIRA Prompt Letters, *available at* http://www.reginfo.gov/public/jsp/EO/promptLetters.jsp. OIRA issued 13 such letters.

nomically get the most attention.[39] The Clinton Administration's National Performance Review also urged agencies to (1) rank the seriousness of environmental, health, or safety risks and (2) develop long-range future plans and anticipatory approaches to regulatory problems.[40]

In addition, agencies, especially those engaged in health and safety regulation, need to be aware of the possibility that voluntary standards prepared by nongovernmental organizations might be relevant. Given appropriate safeguards, agencies should cooperate with private standards-developing organizations and evaluate whether standards issued by such groups might be incorporated.[41] Indeed, a 1995 law requires that the National Institute of Standards and Technology "coordinate the use by Federal agencies of private sector standards, emphasizing where possible the use of standards

---

39. ACUS Recommendation 82-5, *Federal Regulation of Cancer-Causing Chemicals*, 47 Fed. Reg. 30,710 (1982). It suggested that the priority-setting procedure should permit interested members of the public to submit their views and information. *Id. See also* ACUS Recommendation 87-1, *Priority Setting and Management of Rulemaking by the Occupational Safety and Health Administration*, 52 Fed. Reg. 23,629 (1987).

40. *See* NATIONAL PERFORMANCE REVIEW, IMPROVING REGULATORY SYSTEMS, *supra* note 23, at 55.

41. *See* ACUS Recommendation 78-4, *Federal Agency Interaction with Private Standard-Setting Organizations in Health and Safety Regulation*, 44 Fed. Reg. 1357 (1979); Robert W. Hamilton, *Role of Nongovernment Standards in the Development of Mandatory Federal Standards Affecting Safety or Health*, 56 TEX. L. REV. 1329 (1978). An early book-length treatment is PHILIP J. HARTER, REGULATORY USE OF STANDARDS (1979) (Report to Natural Bureau of Standards). For more recent appraisals, see John S. Moot, *When Should the FERC Defer to the NERC?* 31 ENERGY L.J. 317 (2010); Kevin Werbach, *Higher Standards: Regulation in the Network Age*, 23 HARV. J.L. & TECH. 179 (2009); Stacy Baird, *The Government at the Standards Bazaar*, 18 STAN. L. & POL'Y REV. 35 (2007) (suggesting principles that should guide the willingness of government to impose standards); Sidney A. Shapiro, *Outsourcing Government Regulation*, 53 DUKE L.J. 389, 405 (2003) ("Although relying on private actors can save the government money, this choice can also increase the government's transaction costs when a transaction involves significant opportunistic behavior, incomplete contracting, and hold-up problems."). *See also* Robert H. Heidt, *Damned for Their Judgment: The Tort Liability of Standards Development Organizations*, 45 WAKE FOREST L. REV. 1227 (2010); Tyler R.T. Wolf, Note, *Existing in a Legal Limbo: The Precarious Legal Position of Standards-Development Organizations*, 65 WASH. & LEE L. REV. 807 (2008).

Congress occasionally requires agencies to use consensus standards. *See, e.g.*, the American Homeownership and Economic Opportunity Act of 2000, Pub. L. No. 106-569, § 604, 114 Stat. 2944, 2999–3006 (2000) (amending 42 U.S.C. § 5403), requiring the development of Federal Manufactured Home Construction and Safety Standards through a competitively procured, contract-based consensus committee; 42 U.S.C. §§ 6291–6320 (Energy Conservation Program for Consumer Products Other Than Automobiles, incorporating over 80 different private standards). For a recent example of an agency-updated consensus standard, see Updating OSHA Standards Based on National Consensus Standards; Personal Protective Equipment, 74 Fed. Reg. 46,350 (Sept. 9, 2009). For an interesting case in which an Energy Department rule construing the meaning of a statute incorporating a standard developed by an industry association was unsuccessfully challenged by that very association, see *National Electrical Mfrs. Ass'n v. U.S. Dep't of Energy*, 654 F.3d 496 (4th Cir. 2011).

developed by private, consensus organizations."[42] Agencies are also required to give consideration to international standards under international trade legislation.[43] Another important international body that issues standards that are increasingly finding their way into U.S. law is the International Organization for Standardization (ISO).[44] When incorporating consensus standards, agencies must be careful to follow the rules and policies governing "incorporation by reference."[45]

4. Other Influences on an Agency's Decision to Begin Rulemaking

Other entities may also play a role in agency rulemaking activity. Under some regulatory statutes, the agency is required to conduct a negotiated rulemaking (see Section B(2)) or a joint rulemaking,[46] or consult with an advisory committee or panel before initiating its rulemaking proceeding.[47] In other instances, the statute authorizes

---

42. National Technology Transfer and Advancement Act of 1995, Pub. L. No. 104-113, § 12(a)(3), amending 15 U.S.C. § 272(b). For an overview, see NATIONAL SCIENCE AND TECHNOLOGY COUNCIL, SUBCOMMITTEE ON STANDARDS FEDERAL ENGAGEMENT IN STANDARDS ACTIVITIES TO ADDRESS NATIONAL PRIORITIES—BACKGROUND AND PROPOSED POLICY RECOMMENDATIONS (Oct. 2011), *available at* http://standards.gov/upload/Federal_Engagement_in_Standards_Activities_October12_final.pdf. *See also supra* Part II, ch. 3(K)(2).

43. 19 U.S.C. § 2531. For discussion of international standards, *see infra* ch. 7(A)(3).

44. *See* Int'l Organization for Standardization, http://www.iso.org/iso/about.htm. For commentary, see David A. Wirth, *The International Organization for Standardization: Private Voluntary Standards as Swords and Shields*, 36 B.C. ENVTL. AFF. L. REV. 79, 81, 88 (2009).

45. *See infra*, chs. 3(C) & 7(C)(2).

46. For the first in-depth look at this, building on the short discussion in the 4th edition of this *Guide*, see Jody Freeman & Jim Rossi, *Agency Coordination in Shared Regulatory Space* 31–39, *available at* http://papers.ssrn.com/sol3/papers.cfm?abstract_id=1778363## (forthcoming 125 HARV. L. REV.) (describing examples of joint rulemaking). For a comprehensive account of an apparently successful joint rulemaking, see Jody Freeman, *The Obama Administration's National Auto Policy: Lessons from the "Car Deal,"* 35 HARV. ENVTL. L. REV. 343 (2011) (detailing the joint rulemaking between EPA and NHTSA concerning greenhouse gas emissions and fuel efficiency economy standards). Another important example of joint rulemaking is the Federal Acquisition Regulations (FAR) System, which comprehensively describes the federal government acquisition system. Its regulations are codified at Title 48 of the Code of Federal Regulations. The government-wide acquisition regulations in Chapter 1 of Title 48 are jointly issued by the General Services Administration, the Department of Defense, and the National Aeronautics and Space Administration. For more information on the Defense FAR system, see http://www.acq.osd.mil/dpap/dars/index.html; for the Civilian FAR, see https://www.acquisition.gov/comp/caac/index.html.

47. *See* Consumer Product Safety Act, 15 U.S.C. § 2080(b)(l) (holding the Commission may not issue an advance notice of proposed rulemaking or proposed consumer product safety rule relating to the risk of cancer or birth defects unless it has received a report from the Chronic Hazard Advisory Panel as to whether the substance contained in the product is a carcinogen, mutagen, or teratogen); *see also* Medical Device Amendments of 1976, 21 U.S.C. §§ 360c(f)(2)(A)–(B) (stating that an agency must refer a petition found not to be deficient to an appropriate classification panel under 21 U.S.C. § 360c(b)).

but does not require the use of an advisory committee in rulemaking.[48] And, of course, one should never discount the influence of politics and the changes in policy that occur due to changes in administrations.[49] These changeovers also produce midnight rules by outgoing administrations and attempts to withdraw them by incoming administrations.[50]

5. *Litigation Settlements and Consent Decrees*

Litigation settlements (sometimes reflected in consent decrees) that bind agencies to undertake rulemaking have become an increasingly important influence. A significant example was a 2006 consent decree binding the Department of Energy to promulgate separate energy-efficiency rules covering 22 appliances in 30 months.[51]

---

48. *See* Occupational Safety and Health (OSH) Act, 29 U.S.C. § 656 (authorizing OSHA to establish an advisory committee to assist the agency in its standard-setting functions under the Act). When an advisory committee is established by statute, its composition is typically regulated. *See* 15 U.S.C. § 2077 (regulating the composition of the Consumer Product Safety Commission's Chronic Hazard Advisory Panels). Advisory committees usually must be chartered under the Federal Advisory Committee Act (FACA), which imposes certain requirements for the functioning of covered advisory committees. 5 U.S.C. App. 2. *See supra* Part II, ch. 3(E), for a discussion of FACA. Committee action may be subject to time limitations as part of the rulemaking process.

49. *See* OSH Act, 29 U.S.C. § 655(b)(1) (requiring an advisory committee to submit its recommendation within 90 days, or longer or shorter period as prescribed by OSHA, but in no event longer than 270 days). The FAA established an Aviation Rulemaking Advisory Committee (ARAC), a formal standing committee comprising representatives of aviation associations and industry, consumer groups, and interested individuals. It tasked ARAC with providing recommended rulemaking actions dealing with specific areas and problems. *See* 14 C.F.R. § 11.27. The FAA has recently announced a plan to revise the ARAC's structure. *See* FAA, Notice of Intent to Review Structure of the Aviation Rulemaking Advisory Committee, 76 Fed. Reg. 11,845 (Mar. 3, 2011). Since 1996, the Federal Railroad Administration has also had a similar committee, the Railroad Safety Advisory Committee. *See* Railroad Safety Advisory Committee; Establishment, 61 Fed. Reg. 9740 (Mar. 11, 1996).

50. *See supra* Part II, ch. 1(D)(4)(f).

51. *See* Consent Decree in *State of New York v. Bodman*, dckt. nos. 05 Civ. 7807 & 05 Civ. 7808 (S.D.N.Y) (signed Nov. 3, 2006) (on file with author) (settling litigation between a group of environmental, consumer, and state plaintiffs and the Department of Energy (DOE), and requiring that DOE complete energy-efficiency rulemakings on 22 categories of appliances by a date certain preceded by advance notices of proposed rulemaking and notices of proposed rulemaking). *See also* New York *ex rel.* Lockyer v. Bodman, 2007 WL 3238763 *2 (S.D.N.Y. 2007) (describing the consent decree). For an example of a case where the industry was unhappy with the actions taken by the Bush Administration in the aftermath of a 2002 settlement with the Administration in a challenge to a Clinton Administration midnight rule, see *National Mining Ass'n v. Mine Safety and Health Administration,* 599 F.3d 662, 670 (D.C. Cir. 2010) (upholding the agency's decision to withdraw a rule it had agreed to propose as part of the settlement and to instead enforce a variation of it, finding that the industry parties had "repudiated" the settlement by challenging interim actions taken by the agency in 2007 that the court considered to be in accordance with the settlement).

More controversial are consent decrees that bind future administrations to issue rules. Although Attorney General Meese addressed this issue in a policy statement in 1986 that prohibits an agency from entering a consent decree "that divests a [government official] of discretion" or "that converts into a mandatory duty the otherwise discretionary authority [of an official] to revise, amend, or promulgate regulations,"[52] the interplay of settlements and rulemaking authority has been "remarkably uncontroversial" until an ensuing case raised the issue in a way that "may augur greater disputes to come."[53]

The case, *Save the Manatee v. Ballard*,[54] involved a lawsuit brought at the end of the Clinton Administration challenging the government's failure to adequately protect the endangered Florida manatee. Various industry organizations intervened as defendants, and the parties ultimately reached a settlement in January 2001 obliging the Fish & Wildlife Service (FWS) to commence a rulemaking concerning the "incidental taking" of manatees. The agreement also required the FWS to propose by April 2001, and promulgate in final form by September 2001, new manatee refuges and sanctuaries in Florida. Early in 2002, FWS published a final rule that designated only two refuges and no sanctuaries. The plaintiffs returned to the district court, which ruled in July 2002 that the defendants were in violation of the settlement agreement, but the Justice Department attorneys representing FWS argued that the underlying agreement was invalid. They argued that if the agreement really committed the Service to a particular rulemaking outcome—numerous protective areas throughout the state—it violated the APA, because it would make the notice-and-comment process a sham. The district court rejected the government's argument and ordered FWS to issue final regulations by November 1, 2002, and scheduled a show-cause proceeding on whether to hold the Secretary of the Interior in contempt for failing to carry out the agreement.[55]

As Professor Herz noted,

---

52. Memorandum from Edwin Meese III, Attorney General, to All Assistant Attorneys General and All United States Attorneys 3, 4 (Mar. 13, 1986). The Meese memo is discussed in Timothy Stoltzfus Jost, *The Attorney General's Policy on Consent Decrees and Settlement Agreements*, 39 ADMIN. L. REV. 101 (1987). The Clinton Office of Legal Counsel offered its commentary on this issue in a Memorandum from Randolph D. Moss, Acting Assistant Attorney General, Office of Legal Counsel, for Raymond C. Fisher, Associate Attorney General (June 15, 1999), *available at* http://www.usdoj.gov/olc/consent_decrees2.htm. *See also* 28 C.F.R. § 0.160(d)(3) (2010) (requiring assistant attorneys general to refer to the deputy attorney general or the associate attorney general a "proposed settlement [that] converts into a mandatory duty the otherwise discretionary authority of a department or agency to promulgate, revise, or rescind regulations").

53. Michael Herz, *Rulemaking Chapter, in* DEVELOPMENTS IN ADMINISTRATIVE LAW AND REGULATORY PRACTICE 2001–2002, at 164 (Jeffrey S. Lubbers ed., 2003). The following discussion of this case is entirely based on Prof. Herz's insightful analysis.

54. 215 F. Supp. 2d 88 (D.D.C. 2002), *appeal dismissed*, No. 02-5318, 2003 WL 1873852 (D.C. Cir. Apr. 11, 2003).

55. *Id.* For another denial of a motion to vacate a consent decree involving a rulemaking, see *Conservation Law Fed'n of New England v. Franklin*, 989 F.2d 54 (1st Cir. 1993).

[T]his ruling may be correct, and the struggle in this case is wrapped up in political considerations, but the legal issue here is much more substantial than it seemed to the district court. Rulemaking settlements *do* have the potential to conflict with substantive requirements or short-circuit procedural ones.[56]

Of course, most civil litigation ends in settlements, and consent decrees are a common way to enforce those settlements. But there are special considerations where the government is a party, and where the settlement addresses future rulemaking. This subject was recently the subject of an illuminating presentation by Russell S. Frye at an ABA Administrative Law Section Institute.[57]

Some settlements in rulemaking cases "may require the agency to reconsider a rule in broad terms, or may commit the agency to consider or propose detailed changes to regulations or to issue specific guidance concerning application of the rule." Others "may establish timelines and deadlines for proposal and promulgation of regulations, may commit the agency to conducting certain studies to support rulemaking, may specify criteria the agency will apply in developing regulations, or may commit the agency to broad policy directions or new regulatory programs."[58]

---

56. Herz, *supra* note 53, at 166. He also referred readers to Jim Rossi's "illuminating general discussion of the problems posed by rulemaking settlements" in *Bargaining in the Shadow of Administrative Procedure: The Public Interest in Rulemaking Settlement*, 51 DUKE L.J. 1015 (2001). He added, "Rossi's particular concern is that the public interest and subsequent administration's prerogatives may get short shrift when courts enforce essentially private bargains between an agency and one interested party concerning the scope, content, or timing of rulemaking." Herz, *supra*, at 166 n.61. Many of the consent decree controversies involve EPA. *See* Wendy Wagner, Katherine Barnes, & Lisa Peters, *Rulemaking in the Shade: An Empirical Study of EPA's Air Toxic Emission Standards*, 63 ADMIN. L. REV. 99 (2011); Robert V. Percival, *The Bounds of Consent: Consent Decrees, Settlements and Federal Environmental Policy Making*, 1987 U. CHI. LEGAL F. 327 (1987); Jeffrey M. Gaba, *Informal Rulemaking by Settlement Agreement*, 73 GEO. L.J. 1241, 1253 n.73 (1985). *See also* Peter M. Shane, *Federal Policy Making by Consent Decree: An Analysis of Agency and Judicial Discretion*, 1987 U. CHI. LEGAL F. 241 (1987).
57. Much of the following discussion is drawn from the outline of this presentation. Russell S. Frye, "The Role of Judicial Settlements in Driving Rulemaking—Overview," ABA Administrative Law Section Institute, 7th Annual Administrative Law and Regulatory Practice Institute (May 3, 2011) (outline on file with author) [hereinafter Frye Outline]. As Mr. Frye pointed out, settlement agreements may be used to try to insulate a policy against a change in administration, or to try to effectuate change in a policy adopted under a previous administration. *See, e.g.*, Michael W. McConnell, *Why Hold Elections? Using Consent Decrees to Insulate Policies from Political Change*, 1987 U CHI. LEGAL F. 295, 315–17 (1987). *But see* Citizens for a Better Environment v. Gorsuch, 718 F.2d 1117, 1134 (D.C. Cir. 1983) (Wilkey, J., dissenting) (questioning whether an agency head, by consenting to limit her discretion in a consent decree, can bind the discretion of future heads of that agency); Jeremy A. Rabkin & Neal E. Devins, *Averting Government by Consent Decree: Constitutional Limits on the Enforcement of Settlements with the Federal Government*, 40 STAN. L. REV. 203, 204 (1987). *See also* Environmental Defense Fund, Inc. v. Costle, 636 F.2d 1229 (D.C. Cir. 1980) (modification of a settlement does not require APA rulemaking procedures).
58. Frye Outline, *supra* note 57, at 5.

The procedural aspect of the settlement is partly controlled by whether the review is in the district court or court of appeals. District courts can incorporate the settlement into a consent decree. In courts of appeals, "typically a settlement agreement is accompanied by a motion for the court to hold the case in abeyance, dismiss the case, or remand the rule to the agency (with or without vacating the rule). . . . If the court retains jurisdiction, a stay pending appeal may include the time of implementation of a settlement agreement."[59]

Another issue he recognizes is whether the consent decree is enforceable through contempt of court proceedings or other equitable relief, pointing out that some consent decrees provide that they are "not enforceable in contempt or that the only remedy for an agency's non-compliance is reactivation of the lawsuit. This may give the settling party limited leverage."[60]

In a court of appeals review, or a district court case without a consent decree, a dismissal or stay of a pending legal action may have a similar effect. As Mr. Frye points out, "If accompanied by a judicial stay, or especially by judicial vacatur of the rule, the effect may be to negate a rule arrived at after notice-and-comment rulemaking, based on private negotiations and without any public notice and comment."[61] This can allow an agency to reconsider a rule.[62] Of course, this happens more frequently and more controversially when a new administration agrees with previous challengers.[63]

---

59. *Id.* He notes, however, that an agency cannot indefinitely suspend regulations by agreeing not to enforce them, citing *Natural Resources Defense Council, Inc. v. EPA*, 683 F.2d 752, 766 (3d Cir. 1982). *Id.* at 6.

60. *Id.* at 6. He points to "a particularly striking example" in which "EPA agreed, in a 1982 settlement of a Clean Air Act petition for review in the D.C. Circuit, to propose major changes to the New Source Review program, but ignored its commitment for 14 years and then 'proposed' the agreed changes but said in the same notice that it did not favor adopting the changes." See explanation at 67 Fed. Reg. 80,186, 80,204–206 (Dec. 31, 2002). *Id.*

61. *Id.* at 7.

62. *See* Macktal v. Chao, 286 F.3d 822, 826 (5th Cir. 2002) ("An agency's inherent authority to reconsider its decisions is not unlimited. An agency may not reconsider its own decision if to do so would be arbitrary, capricious, or an abuse of discretion."). Courts are more receptive when both the plaintiffs/petitioners and the government jointly ask for a remand, but not always. *See* Nat'l Parks Conservation Ass'n v. Salazar, 660 F. Supp. 2d 3, 5 (D.D.C. 2009) ("[G]ranting vacatur here would allow the Federal defendants to do what they cannot do under the APA, repeal a rule without public notice and comment, without judicial consideration of the merits."); *see also* Sears, Roebuck & Co. v. EPA, 543 F.2d 359 (D.C. Cir. 1976) (suspending proceedings without remanding and retaining jurisdiction over the groups of petitions to review EPA regulations which, inter alia, were subject to reconsideration or suspension by EPA).

63. *See* Alexander L. Merritt, Note, *Confessions of Error by Administrative Agencies*, 67 WASH. & LEE L. REV. 1197, 1227 (2010) ("[A]n agency may use confession of error as a strategic device to undo final regulations issued by the previous presidential administration while avoiding lengthy Administrative Procedure Act requirements.").

Another potential problem is that it can be difficult for third parties to challenge or seek changes to settlements. Mr. Frye suggests that:

> The criteria the district court should apply in deciding whether to enter a consent decree are not well-defined. There are few cases discussing those criteria for a settlement agreement involving future rulemaking (there are more where the settlement is of an enforcement action). . . . For example, what is the administrative record for a consent decree? Is one required? If EPA's agreement to propose changes to a rule is based on new information, then does that create an obligation to provide notice and opportunity for comment on that new information, as in cases such as *Weyerhaeuser Co. v. Costle*, 590 F.2d 1011, 1030 (D.C. Cir. 1978)?

Other tricky questions involving rights of intervenors include the standing of others to challenge settlements, agency duties to complete otherwise required rulemaking analyses, payment of attorney fees, and ethics considerations presented in such cases.[64]

Finally, one thing the agency should *not* have to worry about is being sued under the Federal Tort Claims Act for alleged negligence in its rulemaking.[65]

B. Procedural Decisions

Once the agency has determined that it will undertake a rulemaking, some preliminary procedures may simplify the process in the long run. The increasing usefulness of information technology to manage rulemakings and increase public participation must be considered. Agencies should also consider whether it might be useful to seek preliminary views from the public on issues before they formulate a definite agency approach by use of such techniques as hearings, forums, and advance notices of proposed rulemaking.[66] Negotiated rulemaking is also a technique to consider when developing certain types of proposed rules.

1. Advance Notice of Proposed Rulemaking

The APA does not provide for the publication by an agency of an advance notice of proposed rulemaking (ANPRM).[67] However, some regulatory statutes, such as the

---

64. *See* Frye Outline, *supra* note 57, at 15–22.
65. *See* C.P. Chem. Co. v. United States, 810 F.2d 34 (2d Cir. 1987) (holding the Consumer Product Safety Commission could not be liable under FTCA for "negligent" rulemaking); Jayvee Brand v. United States, 721 F.2d 385 (D.C. Cir. 1983) (same).
66. As urged by President Obama's Executive Order 13,563, see *supra* note 7.
67. In 1976, the Administrative Conference recommended that agencies consider, in appropriate circumstances, voluntarily publishing an ANPRM in order to "solicit comments and suggestions with respect to the contents" of the forthcoming notice of proposed rulemaking. ACUS Recommendation 76-3, *Procedures in Addition to Notice and the Opportunity for Comment in Informal Rulemaking*, 41 Fed. Reg. 29,654 (1976).

Federal Trade Commission Improvements Act,[68] Consumer Product Safety Act,[69] and the Energy Policy and Conservation Act,[70] require that rulemaking begin with an ANPRM.[71] An ANPRM notifies the public that an agency is considering an area for rulemaking and usually requests written comments on the appropriate scope of the rulemaking or on specific topics.

An ANPRM may be useful to the agency in a variety of circumstances. For example, an agency may seek public comment on what its regulatory response should be to a petition for rulemaking or other "triggering" events. In such circumstances, the *Federal Register* notice is often titled "Request for Comment on Petition for Rulemaking" or "Receipt of Petition" or a similar title.[72] In other circumstances, the agency has decided (or been required) to undertake rulemaking but seeks information from the public to assist it in framing the notice of proposed rulemaking.[73] This latter type of advance notice of proposed rulemaking can be extremely helpful in narrowing the issues during the public comment period on the proposed rule, with obvious advantages to both the public and the agency.[74]

Although the value of the ANPRM as a preliminary step in rulemaking is suggested by its frequent use by some agencies, it is potentially subject to overuse, or even abuse. In several cases, OSHA's use of an ANPRM in a particular situation was viewed by the court as evidence of agency procrastination in the face of its obligation to proceed quickly with important rulemaking activity.[75] A report to the Administra-

---

68. 15 U.S.C. § 57a(b)(2)(A). Under this provision, the advance notice must contain a brief description of the "area of inquiry under consideration," the "objectives" FTC seeks to achieve, and possible regulatory alternatives. *Id.* The notice must also invite a response from interested parties, including suggestions or alternative methods to achieve the regulatory alternatives. The FTC must submit the advance notice to the appropriate Senate and House committees. *Id.* § 57a(b)(2)(B).

69. 15 U.S.C. § 2058(a).

70. 42 U.S.C. § 6295(p)(1) (also requiring a 60-day comment period on the ANPRM), *discussed in* Nat. Res. Def. Council v. Abraham, 355 F.3d 179, 196 (2d Cir. 2004).

71. *See also* Medicare and Medicaid Patient and Program Protection Act, Pub. L. 100-93, § 14, 101 Stat. 680 (1987) (requiring an ANPRM for Medicare anti-kickback regulations).

72. *See, e.g.*, Eipper Aircraft, Inc.; Regulation of Ultralight Vehicles, Petition for Rulemaking, 50 Fed. Reg. 6312 (1985).

73. *See* Occupational Exposure to Hepatitis B Virus and Human Immunodeficiency Virus, Advance Notice of Proposed Rulemaking, 52 Fed. Reg. 45,438 (1987); Request for Comments on Developing Regulations for Anti-Kickback Provisions, 52 Fed. Reg. 38,794 (1987).

74. Thus, the OSHA notice requested comments on 14 specific issues. *See* Occupational Exposure to Hepatitis B Virus and Human Immunodeficiency Virus, Advance Notice of Proposed Rulemaking, 52 Fed. Reg. 45,438 (1987).

75. United Steelworkers of Am. v. Pendergrass, 819 F.2d 1263, 1268 (3d Cir. 1987) (criticizing OSHA's publication of ANPRM to supplement original record, stating that "[s]ome of the questions [in the ANPRM] could hardly have been posed with the serious intention of obtaining meaningful information since the answers are self-evident"). Neither the OSH Act, 29 U.S.C. § 655(b), nor OSHA's regulations on rulemaking procedures, 29 C.F.R. §§ 1911.10–1911.19, require advance notices of proposed rulemaking.

tive Conference on OSHA rulemaking noted that there was "a general feeling among agency staff and outside petitioners that [the ANPRM] rarely results in the production of useful information for OSHA. Outside parties are simply unwilling to scour their files for information at this [pre-notice of proposed rulemaking] stage," and if the information is available, the parties are unwilling to make it public and "incur the risk of revealing or foreclosing later strategies."[76]

2. *Negotiated Rulemaking*

In 1990, Congress endorsed the use by agencies of an alternative procedure known as "negotiated rulemaking."[77] This procedure, sometimes called "regulatory negotiation," or "reg-neg," has been used by a fair number of agencies to bring interested parties into the rule-drafting process at an early stage, under circumstances that foster cooperative efforts to achieve solutions to regulatory problems. Where successful, negotiated rulemaking can lead to better, more acceptable rules, based on a clearer understanding of the concerns of all affected interests. Negotiated rules may be easier to enforce and less likely to be challenged in litigation.

Absent special circumstances, the APA requires an agency planning to adopt a rule on a particular subject to publish a proposed rule in the *Federal Register* and to offer the public an opportunity to comment.[78] However, the APA does not specify who is to draft the proposed rule nor any particular procedure to govern the drafting process. Ordinarily, agency staff performs this function, with discretion to determine how much opportunity for public input to allow. Any agency contacts with regulated parties or the general public while the agency is considering or drafting a proposed rule are usually informal and unstructured. Typically, there is no opportunity for interchange of views among potentially affected parties, even where an agency chooses to conduct a hearing.

The dynamics of the rulemaking process tend to encourage interested parties to take extreme positions in their written and oral statements—in pre-proposal contacts as well as in comments on any published proposed rule. They may choose to withhold information that they view as damaging. A party may appear to put equal weight on every argument, giving the agency little clue as to the relative importance it places

---

76. Thomas O. McGarity & Sidney A. Shapiro, *OSHA Regulation: Regulatory Alternatives and Legislative Reform,* 1987 ACUS 999, 1046 (1987). The Administrative Conference recommended that the agency not routinely use ANPRMs as an information-gathering technique and that they be used only when information not otherwise available "is likely to be forthcoming" in response to the ANPRM. ACUS Recommendation 87-10, *Regulation by the Occupational Safety and Health Administration,* 52 Fed. Reg. 49,147 (1987).

77. Negotiated Rulemaking Act of 1990, Pub. L. No. 101-648, 104 Stat. 4969 (codified at 5 U.S.C. §§ 561–570). The Act was permanently reauthorized by the Administrative Dispute Resolution Act of 1996, Pub. L. No. 104-320 § 11. *See supra* Part II, ch. 3(F), for a discussion of the Act.

78. *See* discussion *infra* Part III, chs. 3, 4.

on the various issues. There is usually little willingness among commenters to recognize the legitimate viewpoints of others. The adversarial atmosphere often contributes to the expense and delay associated with regulatory proceedings, as parties try to position themselves for the expected litigation. What is lacking is an opportunity for the parties to exchange views and to focus on finding constructive, creative solutions to problems.[79]

In negotiated rulemaking, the agency, with the assistance of one or more neutral advisers known as "convenors," assembles a committee of representatives of all affected interests to negotiate a proposed rule. The goal of the process is to reach consensus on a text that all parties can accept. The agency should be represented at the table by an official who is sufficiently senior to be able to speak authoritatively on behalf of the agency. Negotiating sessions, however, are chaired not by the agency representative, but by a neutral mediator or facilitator skilled in assisting in the resolution of multiparty disputes.

Negotiated rulemaking is clearly not suitable for all agency rulemaking.[80] The Negotiated Rulemaking Act sets forth several criteria to be considered when an agency determines whether to use reg-neg.[81] These include (1) whether there are a limited number of identifiable interests—usually not more than 25, including any relevant government agencies—that will be significantly affected by the rule; (2) whether a balanced committee can be convened that can adequately represent the various interests and negotiate in good faith to reach consensus on a proposed rule; (3) whether

---

79. For a seminal discussion of the dynamics of "traditional" notice-and-comment rulemaking that provided the basis for the Administrative Conference's original recommendation in support of negotiated rulemaking, see Philip J. Harter, *Negotiating Regulations: A Cure for Malaise*, 71 GEO. L.J. 1 (1982). Much later, Professor Harter confided that the title was supposed to read "A Cure for the Malaise?," Philip J. Harter, *Collaboration: The Future of Governance*, 2009 J. DISP. RESOL. 411, 414 & n.5 (2009).

80. Numerous commentators, however, have suggested using negotiated rulemaking in specific contexts. *See, e.g.*, Julia Kobick, *Negotiated Rulemaking: The Next Step in Regulatory Innovation at the Food and Drug Administration?*, 65 FOOD & DRUG L.J. 425, 425 (2010) (reporting that Secretary of HHS Leavitt opposed a bill to create a reg-neg committee to develop a Clinical Trial Registry Data Bank, quoting a letter stating that HHS and FDA "have concerns with the mandated negotiated rulemaking process, which is time consuming and resource intensive"); Sarah Devlin, Comment, *"I Lost My Home, Don't Take My Voice!" Ensuring the Voting Rights of the Homeless Through Negotiated Rulemaking*, 2009 J. DISP. RESOL. 175 (2009); Danielle Holley-Walker, *The Importance of Negotiated Rulemaking to the No Child Left Behind Act*, 85 NEB. L. REV. 1015 (2007) (arguing that the Department of Education is improperly implementing the statutorily mandated reg-neg procedures); Michael O. Spivey & Jeffrey G. Micklos, *Developing Provider-Sponsored Organization Solvency Standards Through Negotiated Rulemaking*, 51 ADMIN. L. REV. 261 (1999); Troy M. Yoshino, *Still Keeping the Faith?: Asian Pacific Americans, Ballot Initiatives, and the Lessons of Negotiated Rulemaking*, 6 ASIAN L.J. 1, 13 (1999) (preferring reg-neg to ballot initiatives); Timothy L. Skelton, *Internet Copyright Infringement and Service Providers: The Case for a Negotiated Rulemaking Alternative*, 35 SAN DIEGO L. REV. 219 (1998).

81. *See* 5 U.S.C. § 563.

the negotiation process will not unreasonably delay issuance of the rule; (4) whether the agency has adequate resources to support the negotiating committee; and (5) whether the agency—to the maximum extent consistent with its legal obligations—will use a committee consensus as the basis for a proposed rule. These criteria are based on recommendations of the Administrative Conference and actual agency experience using the process.[82]

In addition, there should be a number of diverse issues that participants can rank according to their own priorities, so that each of the participants may be able to find room for compromise on some of the issues as an agreement is sought. However, it is essential that the issues to be negotiated not require compromise of principles so fundamental to the parties that meaningful negotiations are impossible. Parties must indicate a willingness to negotiate in good faith, and no single interest should be able to dominate the negotiations.

The goal of the committee is to reach consensus on a draft rule. The word "consensus" is usually understood in this context to mean that each interest represented, including the agency, concurs in the result, unless all members of the committee agree at the outset to a different meaning. Negotiators try to reach consensus through a process of evaluating their own priorities and making trade-offs to achieve an acceptable outcome on the issues of greatest importance to them. The existence of a deadline for completing negotiations, whether imposed by statute, by the agency, or by other circumstances, has been found to impart a degree of urgency that can aid the negotiators in reaching consensus on a proposed rule. On the other hand, where the participants feel that they have a strong "BATNA" (best alternative to a negotiated agreement),[83] such as hope of obtaining a better result from the agency or Congress through the political process, the chances of an agreement are reduced.

If consensus is achieved by the committee, the agency ordinarily would publish the draft rule based on that consensus in a notice of proposed rulemaking—and the agency would have committed itself in advance to doing so. Such a commitment is not an abdication of the agency's statutory responsibility, for there would not be consensus without the agency's concurrence in the committee's proposed rule.[84] Even negotiations that result in less than full consensus on a draft rule can still be very useful to the agency by narrowing the issues in dispute, identifying information necessary to resolve issues, ranking priorities, and finding potentially acceptable solutions.[85]

---

82. *See* ACUS Recommendation 82-4, *Procedures for Negotiating Proposed Regulations*, 47 Fed. Reg. 30,708 (1982); ACUS Recommendation 85-5, *Procedures for Negotiating Proposed Regulations*, 50 Fed. Reg. 52,895 (1985).

83. *See* Roger Fisher, William Ury & Bruce Patton, Getting to Yes 97–106 (2d ed. 1991) (describing the concept of BATNA).

84. Nor would such an agreement undercut the agency's authority to make changes at the final rule stage. *See* Nat. Res. Def. Council v. EPA, 859 F.2d 156, 194–95 (D.C. Cir. 1988).

85. There remains a lively debate on the pros and cons of negotiated rulemaking. *See generally* Curtis W. Copeland, *Negotiated Rulemaking*, CRS Report RL32452 (updated Sept. 18, 2006),

Negotiated rulemaking should be viewed as a supplement to the rulemaking provisions of the APA. This means that the negotiation sessions generally take place prior to issuance of the notice and the opportunity for the public to comment on a proposed rule. In some instances, negotiations may be appropriate at a later stage of the proceeding. But it should be emphasized that negotiated rulemaking does not in any way

---

available at http://opencrs.com/document/RL32452/2006-09-18/download/1005/; Symposium, Twenty-Eighth Annual Administrative Law Issue, 46 DUKE L.J. 1255 (1997). Several critics have argued that negotiated rulemaking allows agencies to transfer too much control to private parties. *See* Michael McCloskey, *Problems with Using Collaboration to Shape Environmental Public Policy*, 34 VAL. U. L. REV. 423 (2000); William Funk, *Bargaining Toward the New Millennium: Regulatory Negotiation and the Subversion of the Public Interest*, 46 DUKE L.J. 1351 (1997); Susan Rose-Ackerman, *Consensus Versus Incentives: A Skeptical Look at Regulatory Negotiation*, 43 DUKE L.J. 1206 (1994); William Funk, *When Smoke Gets in Your Eyes: Regulatory Negotiation and the Public Interest—EPA's Woodstove Standards*, 18 ENVTL. L. 55 (1987) (arguing that EPA's negotiated woodstove emissions rule went beyond the bounds of the Clean Air Act). Cary Coglianese has challenged empirically the basic assumption that regulatory negotiation has produced faster and less litigated rules. *See* Cary Coglianese, *Assessing the Advocacy of Negotiated Rulemaking: A Response to Philip Harter*, 9 N.Y.U. ENVTL. L.J. 386 (2001); Cary Coglianese, *Assessing Consensus: The Promise and Performance of Negotiated Rulemaking*, 46 DUKE L.J. 1255 (1997).

On the other hand, the authors of several empirical studies have strenuously rebutted the critics. *See* Philip J. Harter, *Collaboration: The Future of Governance*, 2009 J. DISP. RESOL. 411, 419 n.31 (2009) (responding for a second time to Professor Coglianese); Philip J. Harter, *A Plumber Responds to the Philosophers: A Comment on Professor Menkel-Meadow's Essay on Deliberative Democracy*, 5 NEV. L.J. 379 (2004–05) (summarizing his arguments in response to critics of regulatory negotiation); Philip J. Harter, *Assessing the Assessors: The Actual Performance of Negotiated Rulemaking*, 9 N.Y.U. ENVTL. L.J. 32 (2000) (rebutting Professor Coglianese); Laura I. Langbein & Cornelius M. Kerwin, *Regulatory Negotiation Versus Conventional Rule Making: Claims, Counterclaims, and Empirical Evidence*, 10 J. PUB. ADMIN. RES. & THEORY 599 (2000) (finding that participants felt negotiated rules were superior and more likely to be implemented than conventional rules); Jody Freeman & Laura I. Langbein, *Regulatory Negotiation and the Legitimacy Benefit*, 9 N.Y.U. ENVTL. L.J. 60 (2000) (finding significant legitimacy benefit); *see also* Andrew P. Morriss, Bruce Yandle & Andrew Dorchak, *Choosing How to Regulate*, 29 HARV. ENVTL. L. REV. 179, 195–202 (2005) (finding good arguments on both sides, but generally siding with Coglianese on empirical debate with Harter); Mark Seidenfeld, *Empowering Stakeholders: Limits on Collaboration as the Basis for Flexible Regulation*, 41 WM. & MARY L. REV. 411, 458 (2000) ("The collaborative process is most promising, however, if used as a tool to guide agency discretion, rather than as an alternative mechanism to promulgate regulations backed by the coercive power of the state."). For specific commentary on EPA negotiated rulemakings, see E. Donald Elliott, *Lessons From Implementing the 1990 CAA Amendments*, 40 Envtl. L. Rep. News & Analysis 10,592, 10,594 (June 2010) ("Some of the subsequent academic literature has questioned the benefits of formal 'reg negs,' but we had a positive experience with negotiated rulemaking."); Jody Freeman, *Collaborative Governance in the Administrative State*, 45 UCLA L. REV. 1, 33–55 (1997); Siobhan Mee, Comment, *Negotiated Rulemaking and Combined Sewer Overflows (CSOs): Consensus Saves Ossification?*, 25 B.C. ENVTL. AFF. L. REV. 213 (1997) (lauding the success of this particular negotiated rulemaking).

reduce the agency's obligations to follow the APA process, to produce a rule within its statutory authority, or to adequately explain the result.

As described in Part II, the Negotiated Rulemaking Act was intended to clarify agency authority to use the process. The Act establishes basic public notice requirements, including providing for an opportunity for members of the public who believe they are inadequately represented on a negotiating committee to apply for membership or better representation. The Act also clarifies the applicability of the Federal Advisory Committee Act to reg-neg.[86]

For a detailed discussion of all aspects of negotiated rulemaking, the reader is referred to the Administrative Conference's 1995 *Negotiated Rulemaking Sourcebook*.[87] The *Sourcebook* contains a step-by-step guide for the conduct of reg-neg proceedings, with samples of necessary *Federal Register* notices and other relevant documents. The volume also contains a number of analytical articles that examine the experiences of several federal agencies that have used the process, including EPA, OSHA, and the Department of Transportation.[88]

Finally, it should be noted that although negotiation seems to be catching on in the states,[89] its use seems to be waning in the federal government. In my own review of the state of negotiated rulemaking in 2008, I found that:

> from the beginning of 1991 (the year after the NRA was enacted) through the end of 1999, sixty-three separate such committees were created, while from 2000 to the end of 2007, there were only twenty-two. Thus, the number went from about seven per year to about three per year. More tellingly, the number

---

86. *See* 5 U.S.C. § 565; *see also supra* Part II, ch. 3(E)–(F). The applicability of FACA to negotiated rulemaking, and the Clinton Administration's directive to reduce the number of advisory committees, produced some conflict with its similar desire to increase the use of negotiated rulemaking. *See* Steven P. Croley, *Practical Guidance on the Applicability of the Federal Advisory Committee Act*, 10 ADMIN. L.J. AM. U. 111, 112–14 (1996).

87. ADMINISTRATIVE CONFERENCE OF THE U.S., NEGOTIATED RULEMAKING SOURCEBOOK (David M. Pritzker & Deborah S. Dalton eds., 2d. ed. 1995).

88. *See also* ADMINISTRATIVE CONFERENCE OF THE UNITED STATES, BUILDING CONSENSUS IN AGENCY RULEMAKING: IMPLEMENTING THE NEGOTIATED RULEMAKING ACT, REPORT TO CONGRESS (1995).

89. *See* Ronald M. Levin, *Rulemaking Under the 2010 Model State Administrative Procedure Act*, 20 WIDENER L.J. 855, 874 & n.89 (2011) (reporting that the 2010 MSAPA added a provision "similar to the federal Negotiated Rulemaking Act," that "[t]hree states have adopted statutes that are actually labeled 'negotiated rulemaking acts,'" and that "[m]easures that authorize or encourage the process have also been adopted in at least six other states"). *See also* Daniel P. Selmi, *The Promise and Limits of Negotiated Rulemaking: Evaluating the Negotiation of a Regional Air Quality Rule*, 35 ENVTL. L. 415, 469 (2005) ("[T]he present [California] rulemaking does indicate one set of circumstances where the [reg-neg] process was quite beneficial. Furthermore, by its detailed description of the actual negotiations, this article shows how the dynamics of regulatory negotiation are very different from those in a notice and comment rulemaking. It demonstrates how, in one situation, regulatory negotiation can help parties with very different interests reach creative solutions to regulatory problems.").

of statutorily mandated committees was only twenty-three of sixty-three (36.5%) in the first period but fifteen of twenty-two (68%) in the most recent period.[90]

I tried to explain the reasons for this "waning" of negotiated rulemaking, suggesting the following reasons:[91]

(1) The disbanding of ACUS in 1995. ACUS not only produced the recommendations that led to agency experimentation with reg-neg and the eventual enactment of the NRA, Congress also gave ACUS a series of official responsibilities pertaining to the technique: to compile data, serve as a clearinghouse of information, report to Congress, provide training, and even pay the expenses of agencies in conducting a reg-neg (including paying the expenses of the convenors, facilitators, and committee members). When ACUS lost its funding in 1995, this function went unassigned. A year later the NRA was amended to require the President to "designate an agency or . . . interagency committee to facilitate and encourage agency use of negotiated rulemaking." President Clinton then designated the Regulatory Working Group, which he had previously established under Section 4(d) of Executive Order 12,866, as the lead agency. However, it appears that the Regulatory Working Group is no longer a functioning entity and, in any event, does not engage in support of negotiated rulemaking. With the return of ACUS in 2010, there is some hope that it can re-acquire its responsibilities in this regard.

(2) Budgetary reasons.

    (a) Convening and conducting a reg-neg involves a greater cost than organizing a notice-and-comment process. These up-front costs are supposed to be more than cancelled out, when the process works effectively, by cost savings at the end of the proceeding that result from having fewer comments to consider and fewer challenges in court. The relevant data is disputed,[92] but, even if these effects are present, budget officers tend to have a short-term perspective—"what resources do we have this fiscal year?" And the costs described above will be incurred immediately, while any savings are not only speculative, they will be accrued next year. Moreover some of the biggest savings—created by fewer court challenges—will tend to be pocketed more by the Department of Justice—the litigators—rather than the agency's own legal office. And, of course, overall agency resources at many agencies have seriously eroded in recent years.

    (b) Another budgetary issue concerns the demands that reg-neg places on the stakeholders: attending a series of negotiating sessions can involve a de-

---

90. Jeffrey S. Lubbers, *Achieving Policymaking Consensus: The (Unfortunate) Waning of Negotiated Rulemaking*, 49. S. Tex. L. Rev. 987, 996 (2008).

91. This is condensed from *id.* at 996–1004 (footnotes omitted).

92. *See* note 85, *supra*.

votion of considerable resources. This can be especially problematic for environmental and other public interest groups. Funding was provided in the original Negotiated Rulemaking Act, but it has dried up.

(3) Key staff within the OIRA, the office entrusted to carry out the President's regulatory review program, are distinctly unenthusiastic about it. Executive Order 12,866 is officially supportive of the reg-neg process (see § 6(a)), but career officers of OIRA dislike it.[93] I believe that OIRA should welcome a well-done reg-neg—the affected industry parties have by definition signed on to a successfully negotiated proposed rule, and, if the final rule changes, the normal review process is still available.

(4) The applicability of FACA to the process. The NRA makes clear that FACA is broadly applicable to reg-neg. One obvious problem occurred in the 1990s when the Clinton Administration's directive to reduce the number of advisory committees produced some conflict with its stated desire to increase the use of negotiated rulemaking. This conflict was subsequently redressed when reg-neg committees were exempted from the ceiling on FACA committees. But beyond mere numbers, FACA's requirements of chartering, balance, and openness may discourage agencies from undertaking reg-negs.

(5) This in turn has led to a related fifth reason for the demise of negotiated rulemaking—the emergence of "reg-neg lite."[94] Of course, there is nothing wrong with agencies using techniques other than "formal" reg-neg to learn the views of affected stakeholders, and it may even be preferable when consensus seems impossible, but they are less likely to produce consensus-based rule texts. Moreover, such meetings should not be seen as a substitute for achieving negotiated consensus where possible.

(6) Criticism by several respected scholars (as discussed above). The criticism has two main tenets. The first set of concerns suggest that reg-neg leads agencies to too easily shirk their responsibilities to uphold the public interest by accepting the consensus rule—thus turning the regulatory responsibility to the regulated, sometimes leading to results that are outside the agency's legal authority. The second strain of criticism suggests that the reg-neg's purported savings of time and litigation costs are illusory. I believe that the first set of

---

93. *See* Donald R. Arbuckle, *Collaborative Governance Meets Presidential Regulatory Review*, 2009 J. Disp. Resol. 343, 351 (describing OIRA participation in reg-neg committees as "unsatisfactory from OIRA's point of view because it (1) required a substantial time commitment by an OIRA staff member . . . and (2) required OIRA to agree to accede to a group decision").

94. *See* Charles Pou, Jr., *Federal Agency ADR: Turning Square Corners to Meet Real Challenges*, 49 S. Tex. L. Rev. 1019, 1027 (2008) (describing agency request that he undertake the facilitation of a version of negotiated rulemaking that was explained as "'mediation lite,' i.e., 'We really don't want you to get with the parties between the meetings and spend lots of time with them seeing if the whole group can come up with an agreement. We really just want you to facilitate these four meetings, get as far as possible, and then let the agency take the drafting forward from there.'").

concerns are largely theoretical, and that if the convening stage is done correctly, the right stakeholders and agency representatives are all around the table. Moreover, if the resulting rule somehow strays outside of the agency's statutory authority, an adversely affected person can challenge it in court. As for the empirical debate concerning time savings and reduced court challenges, I would say that it misses the point to some degree. Even if reg-neg does take longer than paper rulemaking (which I do not concede), a large but hard-to-measure benefit of the process is the buy-in of the stakeholders in the rulemaking and eventual implementation of the rule. Thus, even a longer process would be worth it if the resulting rule proved to be more durable and easier to implement because of the reg-neg process.

I concluded that while I did not "discount the possibility that other types of agency facilitation of public meetings may be useful, the waning of the use of negotiated rulemaking is unfortunate. Not because it is a panacea, but because when used in a properly targeted way, it can be very effective."[95]

C. Electronic Rulemaking

Although the possibilities of "e-rulemaking" began to be apparent to those with an aptitude and interest in computerized database management in the early 1990s,[96] the use of electronic "bulletin boards" on the Internet to conduct rulemaking proceedings was still a novelty as recently as 1994,[97] and the third edition of this *Guide*

---

95. Lubbers, *supra* note 90, at 1005–06.
96. Henry H. Perritt, Jr., *The Electronic Agency and the Traditional Paradigms of Administrative Law*, 44 ADMIN. L. REV. 79, 84 (1992) [hereinafter *The Electronic Agency*]. *See also* Henry H. Perritt, Jr., *Electronic Dockets: Use of Information Technology in Rulemaking and Adjudication*, Report to the Administrative Conference (Oct. 19, 1995), *available at* http://www.kentlaw.edu/faculty/rstaudt/classes/oldclasses/internetlaw/casebook/electronic_dockets.htm. This report contained case studies of the Nuclear Regulatory Commission's and Department of Transportation's pioneering electronic-docketing initiatives. It also addressed emerging legal issues such as authentication, public access, confidentiality, copyright issues, and rulemaking-record concerns, and technological issues such as public access technology, choosing between open versus closed systems, keeping information current, limiting paper filings, image-based versus character-based systems, vendor-neutral citation systems, and archiving concerns. Another early review of many of these issues is Stephen M. Johnson, *The Internet Changes Everything: Revolutionizing Public Participation and Access to Government Information Through the Internet*, 50 ADMIN. L. REV. 277 (1998). For a survey of agency e-rulemaking efforts, see Curtis W. Copeland, *Electronic Rulemaking in the Federal Government*, CRS Report RL34210 (updated May 16, 2008), *available at* http://opencrs.com/document/RL34210/2008-05-16/download/1005.
97. *See, e.g.*, Cindy Skrzycki, *Modem Times: OSHA to Try Writing Rules in Cyberspace*, WASH. POST, Feb. 8, 1994, at D1.

contained only a brief section on the topic in 1998.[98]

By 2005, however, the age of e-rulemaking was upon us,[99] and now in 2012, with the many refinements to the government's central rulemaking portal, www.regulations.gov, most rulemaking takes place electronically.[100] In 1994 the Office of the Federal Register led the way by making the daily *Federal Register* and the *Code of Federal Regulations* available online for free.[101] Agencies followed by making their websites increasingly informative and sophisticated. Some agencies now maintain listservs for people to join for announcements of regulatory actions.[102] Even more dramatically, government-wide Internet portals have been established, which allow the public to search for government documents generally[103] and find thousands of datasets provided by agencies,[104] and file comments on any pending rule.[105] Some of these activities started in the Clinton Administration,[106] but the Bush II and Obama

---

98. It referenced several early agency uses of e-rulemaking. *See, e.g.*, Animal and Plant Health Inspection Service, Proposed Rule, Importation of Logs, Lumber, and Other Unmanufactured Wood Articles, 59 Fed. Reg. 3002 (1994) (permitting comments to be filed on electronic bulletin board); EPA, National Capacity Assessment Report: Availability of Draft, 59 Fed. Reg. 59,226 (1994) (permitting comments through Internet and announcing experiment in electronic comments).

99. For some early commentary on the "rise of e-rulemaking," see Cary Coglianese, *E-Rulemaking: Information Technology and the Regulatory Process*, 56 ADMIN. L. REV. 353, 363–66 (2004). *See also* STUART W. SHULMAN, THE INTERNET STILL MIGHT (BUT PROBABLY WON'T) CHANGE EVERYTHING: STAKEHOLDER VIEWS ON THE FUTURE OF ELECTRONIC RULEMAKING 21 (2004), *available at* http://erulemaking.ucsur.pitt.edu/doc/reports/e-rulemaking_final.pdf [hereinafter SHULMAN, STAKEHOLDER VIEWS]; Stuart W. Shulman, *E-Rulemaking: Issues in Current Research and Practice*, 28 INT'L J. PUB. ADMIN. 621 (2005); Beth Simone Noveck, *The Electronic Revolution in Rulemaking*, 53 EMORY L.J. 433 (2004); Barbara H. Brandon & Robert D. Carlitz, *Online Rulemaking and Other Tools for Strengthening Our Civil Infrastructure*, 54 ADMIN. L. REV. 1421 (2002); Stephen Zavestoski & Stuart W. Shulman, *The Internet and Environmental Decision Making: An Introduction*, 15 ORG. & ENV'T 323, 326 (2002). Links to some of these and many other related papers and studies are available on the comprehensive list posted on the University of Pennsylvania's "E-Rulemaking.org" website, http://www.law.upenn.edu/academics/institutes/regulation/erulemaking/papersandreports.html.

100. The National Archives and Records Administration maintains a list with links to agency e-rulemaking websites. *See* http://www.archives.gov/federal-register/public-participation/rulemaking-sites.html.

101. *See infra* notes 128–29.

102. A list of these is available at the NARA website, *supra* note 100.

103. *See* http://www.usa.gov/.

104. *See* http://www.data.gov/.

105. *See* http//:www.regulations.gov.

106. *See, e.g.*, NATIONAL PERFORMANCE REVIEW, IMPROVING REGULATORY SYSTEMS, REG04: ENHANCE PUBLIC AWARENESS AND PARTICIPATION, Recommendation 3, "Increase use of Information Technology" (Sept. 1993), *available at* http://govinfo.library.unt.edu/npr/library/reports/reg04.html. The recommendation stated:

> The application of information technology in rule development and implementation should be explored by agencies individually, through the [Regulatory Coordinating

Administrations have accelerated them as part of their overall E-Government strategies.[107]

These developments have also been spurred by the enactment of the E-Government Act of 2002,[108] as discussed in Part II, Chapter 3(I). Among its requirements are that "to the extent practicable," agencies should accept electronic submissions in rulemaking[109] and create "an internet-accessible rulemaking docket that includes all public comments and other materials that by agency rule or practice are included in the agency docket, whether or not electronically submitted."[110] The "E-Rulemaking Initiative," spearheaded by EPA, was made one of the Bush Administration's 24 "e-gov" projects.[111] Its first task was to establish the Regulations.gov portal, which has been up and running since January 2003.[112] Its second task, the development of a single electronic rulemaking docket known as the Federal Docket Management System (FDMS), took longer to achieve, due to the many different agency docketing practices,[113] but it is now a reality.[114]

Group] and in coordination with existing information resources management groups. At a minimum, agencies should explore computerization of rulemaking dockets. DOT found that the cost savings in storage space would exceed the costs of implementing such a program. It would also give the public easier and more meaningful access to rulemaking and policy guidance documents. Agencies also should consider establishing computer bulletin boards or automated systems that could be accessed by interested parties.

   Id.; *see also* REENGINEERING THROUGH INFORMATION TECHNOLOGY, IT03: DEVELOP INTEGRATED ELECTRONIC ACCESS TO GOVERNMENT INFORMATION AND SERVICES (Sept. 1993), *available at* http://govinfo.library.unt.edu/npr/library/reports/it03.html.

107. *See* http://www.whitehouse.gov/omb/egov. The original *E-Government Strategy*, issued on February 27, 2002, by OMB and the President's Management Council, at 27, listed "online rulemaking management" as one of its 24 e-government projects, *available at* http://www.usa.gov/Topics/Includes/Reference/egov_strategy.pdf.

108. Pub. L. No. 107-347, 116 Stat. 2899 (2002) (codified as 44 U.S.C. § 3501 note). The provisions with special importance to regulatory agencies are in § 206, 116 Stat. 2915–16, and § 208, 116 Stat. 2921–23.

109. *Id.* at § 206(c).

110. *Id.* at § 206(d).

111. *See supra* note 107.

112. Http://www.regulations.gov. For a somewhat critical review of its first few months of operation, see U.S. GEN. ACCOUNTING OFFICE, ELECTRONIC RULEMAKING: EFFORTS TO FACILITATE PUBLIC PARTICIPATION CAN BE IMPROVED (GAO-03-901) (Sept. 2003). The report notes that while the portal had millions of hits, few visitors used it to comment on proposed rules.

113. As Oscar Morales, the then-director of the interagency e-rulemaking team, put it, "The serious problems that we encountered trying to implement this initiative really rested on a pretty common characteristic—the governmental cultural insensitivity and sometimes frustrating and impenetrable agency-specific business processes." Statement at AU State of Rulemaking Conference, *infra* note 116, at panel 4, p. 19.

114. For an authoritative history of the project, see COMM. ON THE STATUS & FUTURE OF FED. E-RULEMAKING, ACHIEVING THE POTENTIAL: THE FUTURE OF FEDERAL E-RULEMAKING 21–32 (ABA Admin. L. & Reg. Prac. Sec.) (2008), *available at* http://ceri.law.cornell.edu/documents/report-web-version.pdf [here-

For its part, the ABA has formally advocated increased government use of e-rulemaking and sponsored a special committee to review its progress in 2008.[115] Several major forums were held on the subject as well.[116] These conferences have provided much food for thought on the potential benefits of e-rulemaking as well as the legal and technological challenges that face policymakers in this area.

1. Potential Benefits

The main touted benefits from e-rulemaking, of course, are increased opportunities for information dissemination, public participation, and governmental transparency, along with better outcomes and greater trust in government. Commenters can now e-mail their comments to the agency with just a keystroke, and agencies can post all comments on their websites for everyone in cyberspace to read and react to. The days of having to travel to Washington to physically visit a dusty records repository are over. Possibilities abound for enhancing the entire notice-and-comment process.[117]

Notices can be improved and more widely disseminated.[118] Automatic notices can be generated by request to individuals who have requested them. Notices can be made word-searchable, and alternative or revised drafts can be posted with the changes clearly designated. Moreover, related studies, required draft regulatory analyses, and other information can be linked to the notices to provide easier public access. The comment process can also be made much more user-friendly and responsive to agency

---

inafter Future of Federal e-Rulemaking]. *See also* Cynthia R. Farina, *Achieving the Potential: The Future of Federal E-Rulemaking*, 62 ADMIN. L. REV. 279 (2010) (providing a summary and update).

115. *See id. See also* Recommendation 107C on More Effective Public Participation in Significant Agency Dissemination Efforts, approved at the ABA Annual Meeting in August 2001. The recommendation was sponsored by the Section of Administrative Law and Regulatory Practice and the Government and Public Sector Lawyers' Division.

116. The National Science Foundation (NSF) provided seed money for an early workshop on e-rulemaking in May 2001 at the Council for Excellence in Government, which led to a series of other workshops, including those organized by Harvard University's Regulatory Policy Program in 2002–2004, and another one with a set of focus groups in June 2004 by NSF, along with the George Washington University School of Public Policy and Public Administration. *See* resulting report, SHULMAN, STAKEHOLDER VIEWS, *supra* note 99. American University's Center for Rulemaking also sponsored an E-rulemaking Conference on January 8, 2004, *see* transcript *at* http://www.american.edu/academic.depts/provost/rulemaking/transcripts.pdf [hereinafter AU E-Rulemaking Conference] and a follow-up Conference on the State of Rulemaking in the Federal Government on March 16, 2005, *see* http://www.thecre.com/pdf/20050428 _kerwin.pdf [hereinafter AU State of Rulemaking Conference].

117. Note, however, that the APA's notice requirement is not met if an agency gives notice of a proposed rule on the Internet instead of in the *Federal Register*. Util. Solid Waste Activities Group v. EPA, 236 F.3d 749, 754 (D.C. Cir. 2001).

118. Many of the ideas in this paragraph for enhanced citizen participation through e-rulemaking are discussed more fully in Noveck, *supra* note 99, at 471–94.

needs through the use of request-for-comments forms, segmentation of proposed rules for comments, and opportunities to file reply comments[119]—even producing "threads" of comments on particular issues. And the final stage of rulemaking can be enhanced though new publication techniques, such as linking all other related regulatory documents and final regulatory analyses, and grouping comments and the agency's response. And there are other potential benefits:

> With increased transparency, [commenters] may learn from earlier submissions and refine their views accordingly. In smaller rulemakings, some set of participants may reach a partial consensus on an issue that the agency can incorporate into the final rule. Online interchanges may further benefit the judiciary, because the rulemaking record could provide more insights into how a regulation will work in practice. This increase in transparency could also minimize concerns about the impact that ex parte communications have on decisionmakers. Prompt docketing of summaries allows others monitoring a particular docket to stay abreast of matters.[120]

Others have focused on the possibilities of using these electronic tools for more *interactive* rulemaking.[121] Suggestions for "deliberative dialogues,"[122] "online chat rooms,"[123] or "electronic negotiated rulemaking" concerning proposed regulations have proliferated, but so far this potential is relatively untapped.[124]

It still remains to be seen whether e-rulemaking will revolutionize public participation. As one leading commentator has concluded, "Electronic rulemaking may transform the process fundamentally or it may simply digitize established paper-based processes."[125] How well the questions raised below[126] can be answered may determine its fate.

---

119. As one agency expert described it, "We can say the comment period ends on November 1st. From November 1st, for example, to December 1st, we're going to allow anybody to come back and reply to what someone else has said. Not say something new, but reply to what others said. It will help the agency, at least theoretically, more efficiently address the comments that they've received." Neil Eisner, Department of Transportation, comments at AU E-Rulemaking Conference, *supra* note 116, transcript at 77. *See also* ACUS Recommendation 2011-2 *Rulemaking Comments* ¶ 6 (June 16, 2011), 76 Fed. Reg. 48,791 (Aug. 9. 2011) (recommending agency use of reply comments).

120. Brandon & Carlitz, *supra* note 99, at 1442.

121. *See, e.g.*, THOMAS C. BEIERLE, DISCUSSING THE RULES: ELECTRONIC RULEMAKING AND DEMOCRATIC DELIBERATION (2003) (Resources for the Future Discussion Paper 03–22), *available at* http://www.rff.org/rff/Documents/RFF-DP-03-2.pdf.

122. Noveck, *supra* note 99, at 499.

123. Johnson, *supra* note 96, at 321–24 (discussing early experiments by the Nuclear Regulatory Commission).

124. *See* BEIERLE, *supra* note 121, at 8 (discussing some agency attempts to use dialogues in rulemaking). *See also* the discussion of the "Regulation Room," *infra* text at note 187.

125. SHULMAN, STAKEHOLDER VIEWS, *supra* note 99, at 35.

126. The following discussion is adapted from Jeffrey S. Lubbers, *The Future of Electronic Rulemaking: A Research Agenda*, Regulatory Policy Program Paper RPP-2002-04 (Mar. 2002),

2. *Legal and Technical Issues*

In 1996, in a symposium about the administrative law agenda for the next decade, I cited what was then called the "Information Revolution" and said the following:

> As the Internet washes over us all, what will this mean for agency proceedings? Electronic rulemaking has already begun. Will we be shortly seeing global rulemaking complete with chat rooms and word searches of all records?

Agencies are beginning to computerize their documents as well. What new problems likely will be caused by this? Issues include security, confidentiality, hacking, authentication, need for backups, and access to hard copies of documents for those who do not know how to get onto the information highway. Moreover, how does our increasing reliance on e-mail fit into our conceptions of the Freedom of Information Act, not to mention, of course, the Paperwork Reduction Act? This area is going to require some enlightened and balanced policymaking mixed with technical expertise. We all know that lawyers and techies often do not get along; however, this is one area where communication across the professions is necessary.[127]

We have come a long way since then. Government websites have become enormously useful. The online *Federal Register*,[128] *Code of Federal Regulations*,[129] and *Unified Agenda of Federal Regulatory and Deregulatory Actions*[130] have eclipsed the paper versions in a few short years. And the Electronic Freedom of Information Act Amendments of 1996[131] have geometrically increased the amount of information provided proactively by agencies.

Kennedy School of Government, Harvard University, *available at* http://www.hks.harvard.edu/m-rcbg/research/rpp/RPP-2002-04.pdf, *reprinted in* 27 ADMIN. & REG. L. NEWS 6 (Summer 2002).

127. Jeffrey S. Lubbers, *The Administrative Law Agenda for the Next Decade*, 49 ADMIN. L. REV. 159, 165–66 (1997) (in *Symposium: The Future of the American Administrative Process*).

128. *See* http://www.gpo.gov/fdsys/browse/collection.action?collectionCode=FR (containing electronic archives of the *Federal Register* going back to 1994). The paper *Federal Register* is no longer produced.

129. *See* http://www.gpo.gov/fdsys/browse/collectionCfr.action?collectionCode=CFR (containing electronic archives of the C.F.R. going back to 1996, and an unofficial version that is updated daily).

130. *See* http://www.reginfo.gov/public/do/eAgendaHistory (containing electronic archives of the *Unified Agenda* and *Regulatory Plan* going back to 1995).

131. Pub. L. No. 104-231, 110 Stat. 3049 (1996). An important addition to the Act was a requirement that the agencies affirmatively make available documents that have been requested frequently in the past or are likely to be in the future. 5 U.S.C. § 552(a)(2)(D). Most agencies have chosen to make these available on their websites.

Technology is moving at its usual rapid clip. But legal developments are still moving more slowly, and there is still a wealth of e-rulemaking issues for lawyers, administrators, and their technologically adept colleagues to study. The goal for the future is how to design a transformation of the rulemaking process as a whole while maintaining the features that have made it such a successful procedure for the past 65 years. Of course, some transformations have occurred already. As Michael Herz has observed, e-rulemaking has "helped to entrench the idea of an informal rulemaking docket."[132] He points out that:

> The APA does not provide for such a thing, and historically it was an incoherent concept since notice-and-comment was not an on-the-record proceeding. Over the last generation—largely as a result of the reconception of notice and comment as involving a "paper hearing," both by courts and in some specific statutes such as the Clean Air Act—it has become more common to think of informal rulemaking as involving a docket and a record. That language and that conception run through and through the world of e-rulemaking. Thus, the E-Rulemaking Act [§ 206(d)(2)(B)] requires agencies to "make publicly available online . . . materials that by agency rule or practice are included in the rulemaking docket under section 553(c)" (even though there is no such thing as a "rulemaking docket under section 553(c))."

One may view this transformation of the rulemaking (and docketing) process as having two main purposes. The first is an *informational* one of providing a global, seamless view of each rulemaking. "Global" in this sense means both a "horizontal" view—meaning access to every meaningful step in the generation of a rule—from the statute enacted by Congress that authorizes the rule to the earliest agency action (perhaps an "advance notice of proposed rulemaking"), to the last step in the process—whether it be the final rule, a decision in a court challenge, or later agency amendments, interpretations, guidelines, or enforcement actions. This view, at a minimum, requires proper docket definition and numbering so that agencies can properly catalog these actions and so that interested viewers can be sure that everything is there. Ideally, this would include not just the text of the proposed and final rules, but the public comment files, preambles, ex parte communications, videotaped or audiotaped public hearings, OMB review documents,[133] SBREFA review panel documents,[134] relevant impact statements, models, risk assessments, peer review information, congressional

---

132. Michael Herz, *Rulemaking Chapter, in* DEVELOPMENTS IN ADMINISTRATIVE LAW AND REGULATORY PRACTICE 2002–2003, at 148 (Jeffrey S. Lubbers ed., 2004).

133. For example, section 6 of Exec. Order 12,866 requires disclosure by OMB and agencies of information about communications between OMB and outside parties, and between OMB and the agency, concerning rulemakings under review by OMB. *See infra* ch. 6(C)(2).

134. This refers to special review panels, required by the Small Business and Regulatory Enforcement Fairness Act of 1996, 5 U.S.C. § 609, convened for rulemakings conducted by EPA and OSHA. *See infra* ch. 4(B).

review documents,[135] relevant court proceedings, etc. But a good first step is to at least make sure that proposed and final rules are linked.

What constitutes a "meaningful step" in each rulemaking should ideally be determined by the user as much as possible. Since many new rulemakings grow out of older rulemakings, or have implications for other concurrent rulemakings, a truly seamless view should permit users to search across past or current rulemakings to find connections, analogies, and consistencies (or inconsistencies).[136]

In addition to this chronological view, the public should be provided a "vertical" view of pending or final rules—what might be called "drilling down" into the meaningful agency and outside studies and analyses that are now found in the docket, along with the public comments, for any significant proposed and final rule—and, where possible through links, into those secondary studies and analyses referenced in the primary studies.

To fully implement this vision, it would be helpful for agencies to place archival records online. ACUS has recommended that agencies take steps to ensure access to material from completed rulemakings.[137]

The second purpose of the transformation of rulemaking is a *participatory* one— making it possible for participants to participate in real time with other stakeholders in a rulemaking process (an idealized "chat room") that will allow a more rational, interactive, and less adversarial path to an optimum final rule. And as information-filtering technologies become more sophisticated and allow more tailoring for individualized needs, commenters will also be able to zero in on their particular interests and contribute more targeted comments.[138]

Both the informational and the participatory goals raise issues that require further research and experimentation. Fortunately, the revived Administrative Conference has taken up this challenge and begun to provide some guidance.[139]

a. Questions about the informational goal

(i) How should we best integrate existing sources of information? The Office of the Federal Register now is able to constantly update the electronic *Code of*

---

135. Pursuant to 5 U.S.C. §§ 801–808.
136. I am indebted to Professor Cary Coglianese for this early insight.
137. ACUS Recommendation 2011-8, *Agency Innovations in E-Rulemaking* (Dec. 9, 2011), 77 Fed. Reg. 2264 ¶ 7(Jan. 17, 2012) ("Agencies should develop systematic protocols to enable the online storage and retrieval of materials from completed rulemakings. Such protocols should, to the extent feasible, ensure that website visitors using out-of-date URLs are automatically redirected to the current location of the material sought.").
138. Professor Stuart Shulman persuasively illustrated this last point in a presentation to the Fall 2005 meeting of the ABA Section of Administrative Law and Regulatory Practice.
139. ACUS Recommendation 2011-1, *Legal Considerations in E-Rulemaking* (June 16, 2011), 76 Fed. Reg. 48,789 (Aug. 9. 2011); ACUS Recommendation 2011-2, *Rulemaking Comments* (June 16, 2011), 76 Fed. Reg. 48,791 (Aug. 9. 2011).

Federal Regulations (CFR)—which in itself is a great boon to anyone who needs to know what government regulations are in effect at the moment. As Regulations.gov evolves, it should become a one-stop shop for all agency rules and related documents. This should include non-legislative rules as well. Some years ago Professors Hamilton and Schroeder catalogued all of EPA's hazardous waste regulations under the Resource Conservation and Recovery Act that appeared in the CFR by counting each CFR decimal point number as a separate rule.[140] This yielded 697 separate rules. Then they examined all of the related agency guidance documents (office directives, guidance memos, and hotline responses) since the beginning of the program and matched them with the appropriate CFR rule. Some rules, they discovered, had many associated guidances; some had none. This was done by a consulting firm, by hand, and it must have been a tedious task in the early 1990s. But it could be done fairly easily now—leading to a sort of "CFR Annotated."

(ii) Docketing issues. The importance of the docketing issues was demonstrated by a letter sent to OMB concerning the implementation of the FDMS, signed by 55 academic students of the rulemaking process.[141] The letter, which was well received by OMB,[142] made three primary recommendations regarding the design of the FDMS:[143]

(1) Consistency in Data. It urged the OMB and EPA to work to keep data fields consistent, both across agencies and over time.[144]

---

140. *See* James T. Hamilton & Christopher H. Schroeder, *Strategic Regulators and the Choice of Rulemaking Procedures: The Selection of Formal vs. Informal Rules in Regulating Hazardous Waste*, 57 LAW & CONTEMP. PROBS. 111 (Spring 1994); Jeffrey S. Lubbers, *Anatomy of a Regulatory Program: Comment on "Strategic Regulators and the Choice of Rulemaking Procedures,"* 57 LAW & CONTEMP. PROBS. 161 (Spring 1994).

141. The letter is reprinted in Cary Coglianese, Stuart Shapiro & Steven J. Balla, *Unifying Rulemaking Information: Recommendations for the New Federal Docket Management System*, 57 ADMIN. L. REV. 621, 634–45 (2005). It should be noted that the author of this *Guide* signed the letter.

142. *See id.* at 633–34 (reporting that OMB had pledged to "design FDMS in a manner consistent with our recommendations").

143. *Id.* at 632.

144. The authors of the letter explained:

> We have noticed over the years that agency dockets and rulemaking filings do not often have a one-to-one relationship, as agencies sometimes open dockets for non-rulemaking activities and other times open multiple dockets for a single rulemaking. Unless the correspondence between agency dockets and rulemakings is addressed, users of the new FDMS will face considerable confusion. We recommend that the OMB consider designing the FDMS so that users will be able to search the system for a particular Federal Register notice and then easily find all other documents associated with that notice. Toward this end, it will be crucial to develop a system for coding Federal Register documents in a consistent way across agencies.

> *Id.* at 632.

(2) Flexibility of Search. It recommended that the FDMS be designed so that users will be able to define their own searches using any of the fields within the docket system.[145]

(3) Ease of Downloading. It stressed that users should be able to download and export search results in large batches and in commonly used formats.[146]

The Obama Administration has been very responsive to these concerns and has significantly upgraded Regulation.gov's capabilities.[147]

Other docketing issues include:

- *Scanning issues.* Scanning issues have faded in importance as agencies have access to efficient scanners and paper comments have become relatively rare.[148]
- *Archiving issues.* While there was some initial question about whether agencies need to keep redundant paper copies of electronic comments, the answer appears to be no.[149] Another question posed in a recent ACUS study is "How do

---

145. The authors explained, "We strongly urge the OMB to ensure that the move to the new FDMS results in no loss of information currently available to the public." *Id.* at 633. OMB's response specifically agreed to this. *See supra* note 142.

146. The authors added:

> The ability of researchers to undertake such studies depends on the ease and flexibility of searching the FDMS. We urge the OMB and the EPA to ensure that users will be able to generate their own searches of any data field or combination of fields contained in the system. Users should also be able to easily download batches of data, not just individual documents, from these searches in any of several commonly used formats.

> *Id.* at 633.

147. *See* Gregory D. Jones, Comment, *Electronic Rulemaking in the New Age of Openness: Proposing a Voluntary Two-Tier Registration System for Regulations.gov*, 62 ADMIN. L. REV. 1261, 1271 (2010) (footnotes omitted):

> After soliciting public feedback on proposed changes to the system through the Regulations.gov Exchange and brainstorming ways to improve e-rulemaking, the eRulemaking Program released an upgraded version of Regulations.gov that included the following innovations: advanced search options that allow users to apply filters or search within results; labels for documents on the system (called "topics") designed to make searches easier; and various visual upgrades, such as a list of proposed rules that are expiring soon and visual graphics with Web site statistics.

148. *See* Steven J. Balla, *Public Commenting on Federal Agency Regulations: Research on Current Practices and Recommendations to the Administrative Conference of the United States* 15 (March 15, 2011 draft), *available at* http://www.acus.gov/wp-content/plugins/download-monitor/download.php?id=168 (reporting that DOT and FCC interviewees said that most paper comments were scanned and uploaded within 24 hours, partly because such paper comments have become infrequent).

149. *See* Bridget C.E. Dooling, *Legal Issues in e-Rulemaking*, 63 ADMIN. L. REV. 893, 922 (2011). (concluding that "[w]hile there may be lingering reluctance to destroy paper documents that have been scanned into the electronic docket, . . . [f]rom a legal perspective, . . . agencies may rely on the electronic version to preserve the rulemaking record"). Ms. Dooling was on detail from OIRA when she wrote this report for ACUS.

the requirements of the Federal Records Act intersect with e-Rulemaking activities? For example, might an agency official's tweet about a rulemaking, or a public comment submitted on a blog entry about the rule, trigger the requirements of the Federal Records Act?"[150] That Act, enacted in 1950, generally defines a federal record as "documentary materials, regardless of physical form or characteristics, made or received by an agency of the United States Government . . . and . . . appropriate for preservation . . . as evidence of the . . . policies, decisions, procedures, operations, or other activities . . . or because of the informational value of data in them."[151] Thus many rulemaking documents would appear to be covered, requiring agencies to establish and maintain schedules for their disposition that must be approved by the National Archives and Records Administration (NARA). These issues get even trickier with respect to information acquired through blogs, tweets, and other social media. NARA has recognized this and provided some guidance.[152]

- *Attachments.* Attachments can pose a risk of viruses and of overloading systems, and electronic technology makes it all too easy for commenters to "dump" huge files or links within their electronic comments.[153] Should it be the agency's responsibility to sift through everything that is "sent over the transom"? How should exhibits, forms, photographs, and other physical objects be dealt with? ACUS has recommended that "[A]gencies should include in the electronic docket a descriptive entry or photograph for all physical objects received during the comment period."[154]

---

150. *See id.* at 31. This discussion is derived from *id.* at 31–34.

151. 44 U.S.C. § 3301.

152. *See* National Archives and Records Administration, Guidance on Managing Records in Web 2.0/Social Media Platforms (Oct. 20, 2010), http://www.archives.gov/records-mgmt/bulletins/2011/2011-02.html. The guidance states:

> When using web 2.0/social media platforms, the following non-exhaustive list of questions may help determine record status:
>
> - Is the information unique and not available anywhere else?
> - Does it contain evidence of an agency's policies, business, mission, etc.?
> - Is this tool being used in relation to the agency's work?
> - Is use of the tool authorized by the agency?
> - Is there a business need for the information?
>
> If the answers to any of the above questions are yes, then the content is likely to be a Federal record.

> *Id.* at #4. The guidance has an expiration date of October 31, 2013.

153. Agency rulemakers did express some concern about acquiring viruses in attachments. See Jeffrey S. Lubbers, *A Survey of Federal Agency Rulemakers' Attitudes About E-Rulemaking,* 62 ADMIN. L. REV. 451, 482 (2010).

154. ACUS Recommendation 2011-1, *supra* note 139, at ¶ 5; *see also* Dooling, *supra* note 149, at 922–23.

• *Copyright concerns.* As public comments have been transformed from easily controlled physical files in Washington, D.C. to Internet-accessible digitized documents, copyright issues have arisen—both where the submitter is the copyright holder of the comments and where the submitter includes someone else's copyrighted work without permission.[155] The former situation seems to be relatively unproblematic because the government can take the position that "submittal of one's own copyrighted material comes with an implied grant that it may use these materials in its internal deliberations."[156] The submission of others' materials raises more difficult issues.[157] The 2011 ACUS study suggests: "[A] good practice is to share only the pertinent portions of copyrighted material in the online docket. For example, if a commenter sends a book, the

---

155. *See* Brandon & Carlitz, *supra* note 99, at 1472–74; *see also* Perritt, *The Electronic Agency*, *supra* note 96, pt. G; Noveck, *supra* note 99, at 487–88.

156. *See* Dooling, *supra* note 149, at 913 ("It would be peculiar for a commenter to complain of a copyright violation upon seeing his or her comment posted to Regulations.gov, because by submitting the comment to a public docket the commenter was on notice that the material would be shared with the public. If challenged, an agency could assert that it had an implied license to post the material, especially if the preamble or the proposed rule explained that comments will be shared online" (citing 3–10 MELVILLE B. NIMMER & DAVID NIMMER, NIMMER ON COPYRIGHT § 10.03 (2010)).).

157. However, see section 107 of the Copyright Act, which provides that "the fair use of a copyrighted work . . . for purposes such as . . . comment . . . is not an infringement of the copyright." 17 U.S.C. § 107. It is also certainly arguable that Congress did not intend to prohibit, as "reproduction," the scanning of comments containing copyrighted materials into a comment file for the purpose of increased public access or archiving. Nor does copyright protection extend to the facts themselves in the submissions. *See* Feist Publ'ns v. Rural Tel. Serv. Co., 499 U.S. 340, 350–51 (1991) (holding that a "factual compilation is eligible for copyright if it features an original selection or arrangement of facts, but the copyright is limited to the particular selection or arrangement. In no event may copyright extend to the facts themselves"). There are several other considerations that bear on the issue of submission of third-party works, and I am grateful to Professor Josh Sarnoff for sharing his thoughts on this matter. First, there may be First Amendment protection under an analogy to the Noerr-Pennington doctrine in antitrust law, which immunizes activity directed to influencing government action under a right-to-petition-the-government theory. *See* Mine Workers v. Pennington, 381 U.S. 657 (1965); Eastern R.R. Presidents Conference v. Noerr Motor Freight, Inc., 365 U.S. 127 (1961). Second, in regard to copying and distribution by the U.S. government, it may be that these actions are privileged under a "necessary to governmental operations" theory. The analogy might be to the acts of members of Congress inserting newspaper articles into the *Congressional Record* or judges publishing copyrighted materials as part of judicial opinions. *See, e.g.,* Hannibal Travis, Comment, *Pirates of the Information Infrastructure: Blackstonian Copyright and the First Amendment*, 15 BERKELEY TECH. L.J. 777, 859 (2000) (highlighting this practice). In addition, if necessary, the agency could seek to limit any liability by indicating clearly that any submission to the docket would constitute a waiver of owned copyrights (where the submitter has authority to make such a waiver) and a warranty of non-infringing fair use for third-party copyrights.

agency could merely scan and share the relevant pages or a table of contents, rather than uploading the entire volume." And that: "If an agency is approached by someone asserting to be copyright holder who is concerned about the amount of his or her work that is included in the docket, [the agency should] consider the copyright holder's request to display less material."[158] In addition, various technological fixes have been suggested, such as software controls that would code such documents so that downloading and copying can be regulated (as is now being done with digital music and films).[159] Professor Noveck suggests that a "simple innovation is to amend the comment interface to allow the user to designate an attachment as nonpublic [confidential business information] or critical infrastructure information by means of a drop-down menu. Once designated, that data could be encrypted and transmitted to the relevant official but not made available to the public."[160] She suggests that in that way "transparency in the process would be maintained while safeguarding confidentiality."[161] Also, "A user could further specify the copyright treatment that should apply to a given work by identifying the holder of the copyright and the name and e-mail address to which one must apply for permission to redistribute the information."[162]

- *Different levels of user classifications.* In some circumstances might it be appropriate for one type of participants (like agency staff) to see everything, while others have more limited access? Should agencies be allowed to ask viewers to register?[163]

- *Authentication issues.* As Professor Noveck points out:

> Nothing in the APA or any other source of law mandates either anonymous or accountable comment. Agencies lack resources to authenticate paper-based signatures in any case. If, for example, the DOT receives a comment on the letterhead of the General Counsel's office of General Motors, it must take the signature at face value. Since it is fraud to forge the signature, the risk of criminal penalty creates a disincentive to lying, as does the work involved in perpetrating the forg-

---

158. *See* Dooling, *supra* note 149, at 914.
159. Brandon & Carlitz, *supra* note 99, at 1473–74.
160. Noveck, *supra* note 99, at 487.
161. *Id.*
162. *Id.* at 487–88. She also suggests that copyright clearinghouses such as the Creative Commons system could be used to obtain appropriate clearances. *See, e.g.*, Creative Commons Home Page, http://www.creativecommons.org. See the discussion of the handling of confidential business information in the rulemaking record in Chapter 5(B)(4), *infra*.
163. *See, e.g.*, Jones, *supra* note 147 (suggesting a voluntary two-tiered registration system, based in part on the European Commission's process of conducting stakeholder consultations, differentiating between private individuals and registered interest groups and organizations).

ery. However, when the comment is submitted through the equivalent of an electronic "suggestion box" on the Web, those authenticity safeguards are diluted.

However, she suggests that:

[I]nterfaces can be designed to permit both anonymous and accountable participation, or to make one or the other mandatory. Commenters should have the option to authenticate postings with digital signatures verified by digital certificates. Alternatively, and more simply, the system might require a verification of return address by sending a confirming e-mail to the address indicated by the commenter, requesting confirmation that the person at this address, in fact, wished to post the stated comment.

Agencies now have some benchmarks on this subject because, as required by the Government Paperwork Elimination Act, in 2003, OMB and the National Institute for Standards and Technology issued extensive guidance concerning authentication issues, including digital signatures, presented by electronic communications to the government.[164]

- *Security issues.* In a post-9/11 world, security issues have become of heightened concern—both in terms of preventing unauthorized tampering and in making sure that sensitive information is not made available to potential terrorists.
- *Privacy issues.* Agency rulemakers ranked "[e]nsuring the protection of the privacy of commenters" as one of their biggest concerns with e-rulemaking in my survey.[165] Agencies have different policies on allowing anonymous comments.[166] But there are clearly privacy concerns in allowing commenters to be identified, or searchable, by name. Professor Noveck observed that:

[I]f we want to encourage more deliberative responses to other comments, this raises the question of how the new ability to search comments easily by author will impact privacy and how, in turn, that will impact participation. . . . The fact that comments can be searched by author does not mean such a capability is necessarily desirable. Does designing for participation mean that the general public should know my views on a particular topic or those of General Motors or the

---

164. *See* OMB, *E-Authentication Guidance for Federal Agencies* (M-04-04), *available at* http://www.whitehouse.gov/sites/default/files/omb/memoranda/fy04/m04-04.pdf, and National Institutes of Standards and Technology (NIST), Special Publication 800-63-1, Electronic Authentication Guidelines (Draft 3, June 2011), *available at* http://csrc.nist.gov/publications/drafts/800-63-rev1/SP800-63-Rev1-Draft3_June2011.pdf.
165. Lubbers, *supra* note 153, at 464.
166. *See* Future of Federal e-Rulemaking, *supra* note 114, at 25 (noting that "Agencies have emphatically different views on this.").

> Audubon Society? When my name is "googled," should my response to an open rulemaking be the first item returned for the world to see? . . . Accountability is desirable in order to foster responsible participation, yet the overwhelmingly public nature of open comment on the Internet may undermine informational self-determination.[167]

She suggested that a solution was to create "a two-tier authentication system whereby the participant's e-mail address is registered as part of the user profile and is accessible to the agency without being available to the public."[168]

ACUS has acknowledged that privacy concerns need more attention. Its study pointed to the fact that "agency staff might screen comments because they are concerned that posting a commenter's personal information or that of another individual discussed in a comment on Regulations.gov is an unlawful disclosure or otherwise violates a policy of protecting personal information."[169] It also suggested the need for the eRulemaking Program Management Office[170] to review the Privacy Act System of Records Notice for its uses on the FDMS, and the privacy warning currently used on the Regulations.gov webpage where comments are submitted.[171] ACUS formally recommended that "[A]gencies should assess whether the [FDMS] System of Records Notice provides sufficient Privacy Act compliance for their uses of Regulations.gov. This could include working with the eRulemaking [Program Management Office] to consider whether changes to the FDMS System of Records Notice are warranted."[172]

- *Mandating e-comments.* What legal impediments prevent agencies from *requiring* e-comments to the exclusion of paper comments? The "digital divide" continues to exist—not everyone owns or is comfortable using a computer, so agencies continue to accept mailed, messengered, or hand-delivered comments. On the other hand, problems caused by the need to screen regular mail to the government after 9/11 and the anthrax scare have made e-mail even more effective by comparison.[173] We may be nearing the point that agencies

---

167. Noveck, *supra* note 99, at 488.
168. *Id.* at 488–89.
169. Dooling, *supra* note 149, at 909.
170. *Id.* at 15. The PMO is housed at the Environmental Protection Agency and funded by contributions from partner federal agencies.
171. *See* http://www.regulations.gov/#!privacyNotice.
172. ACUS Recommendation 2011-1, *supra* note 139, at ¶ 2.
173. See comment by John Morrall from OMB that "[o]ne of the reasons digitized submissions increased, of course, was because after 9/11 we couldn't get any mail at the White House complex. I just got one dated two years ago." AU E-Rulemaking Conference, *supra* note 116, transcript at 84. Ten years after 9/11, this continues to be a concern. *See, e.g.,* NLRB, Representation—Case Procedures, 76 Fed. Reg. 36,812 (proposed June 22, 2011) ("Because of security precautions, the Board continues to experience delays in U.S. mail delivery. You should take this into consideration when preparing to meet the deadline for submitting comments.").

could require that comments be filed electronically *unless* a filer can show hardship in his or her paper filing.

b. Questions concerning the participatory goal

(i) How can we best reach the goal of better, more targeted notices?[174] As noted, agencies are increasingly offering an opportunity to join listservs.[175]

(ii) Can we also provide easier, more convenient comment opportunities? Professor Noveck suggests that:

> [A]gencies should be able to segment a rule to allow for comment on a specific part as well as on the whole. . . . In that way, rule writers can get a sense of which parts of the rule are provoking the greatest ire. They can review comments on a particular part and reserve reading of other comments for later. Citizens can also limit their reading of comments to those on a particular part of the rule. This kind of segmentation makes particularly good sense when the rule is long, complicated, technical, and involves diverse issues. The rule writer should be able to segment the rule, labeling individual sections for comment. When reading the rule, these sections would be clearly delineated for the viewer, and she can select the subsection to which her comment applies.[176]

Other commentators have suggested that agencies use numbered questions or numbered issues to help organize the comments.[177]

ACUS has suggested a number of things that agencies can do to increase the visibility of rulemakings, including (1) designing and managing their "presence on the Web (including the Web as accessed by mobile devices) with rulemaking participation in mind," (2) providing a "one-stop location, which should be easily reachable from its home page, for all of its pending rulemakings," and (3) "using social media tools" with "clear notice as to whether and how it will use the discussion in the rulemaking proceeding."[178]

iii. What rules should govern rulemaking "chat rooms"? Brandon and Carlitz have noted how easily online discussions can be disrupted by anonymous posters who operate in an unfettered manner. The most common problems are incivility, aim-

---

174. For a discussion of the usefulness of listservs, see statement of Professor Peter Strauss at AU E-Rulemaking Conference, *supra* note 89, transcript at 31–32.
175. For a list of agency listservs, see the website cited at *supra* note 100.
176. Noveck, *supra* note 99, at 484.
177. *See* Fred Emery & Andrew Emery, *A Modest Proposal: Improve E-Rulemaking by Improving Comments*, 31 Admin. & Reg. L. News 8 (2005).
178. ACUS Recommendation 2011-8, *supra* note 137, at ¶¶ 1–3.

lessness, anonymity, the dominance of some high-volume posters, and the failure to set clear procedural and behavioral norms. Many experienced observers of online discussions believe that online discourse works best when the discussion includes a moderator.[179]

They suggest that First Amendment issues are tricky in this area and "turn on public forum analysis and how one characterizes asynchronous discussions."[180] But "[i]f a dialogue is viewed as an online public hearing, and the software controls are transparent and administered in a content-neutral manner, the constitutional concern should be lessened."[181]

What rules should pertain to archiving of chats? To be consistent with the above informational goals, this should be done, but how much flexibility should there be, opportunity for correction, disclaimers, etc.? Another potential problem is whether participants should be permitted to send attachments in such chat rooms.

Interactive rulemaking also poses bureaucratic challenges for the agency. As Thomas Beierle observes, "Dialogues also present bureaucratic challenges in real time. The participating public doesn't necessarily make fine distinctions about the roles of various offices within an agency, the boundaries of particular policies, or other bureaucratic distinctions. Questions, complaints, and demands may well arise that are outside the jurisdiction of a sponsoring office."[182] He also points out that when EPA organized a regulatory dialogue, its lawyers' interpretation of the Paperwork Reduction Act and the Privacy Act "prevented organizers from collecting demographic data and interest group affiliations on each participant via the dialogue's registration form. In order not to violate the Privacy Act, [the office of general counsel] advised project staff against allowing an index of messages sorted by author and rejected the idea of voluntarily submitted biographies of participants."[183]

Finally, what about electronic "negotiated rulemaking"? Would this just become a more formalized, more highly moderated version of regular electronic rulemaking? Or would it add value by liberating negotiated rulemaking from the up-front cost concerns (of convening meetings) that seem to be holding it back now?[184]

All of these participatory issues have come into greater focus with the rise of what has been called "rulemaking 2.0,"[185] building on blogs, twitter, social networks, and

---

179. Brandon & Carlitz, *supra* note 99, at 1474.
180. *Id.*
181. *Id.* at 1474–75.
182. Beierle, *supra* note 121, at 15.
183. *Id.* at 15–16.
184. *See, e.g.*, Matthew J. McKinney, *Negotiated Rulemaking: Involving Citizens in Public Decisions*, 60 Mont. L. Rev. 499, 511 (1999) (citing as a reason for not using negotiated rulemaking "the costs to an agency, in both time and money").
185. Cynthia R. Farina et al., *Rulemaking 2.0*, 65 U. Miami L. Rev. 395 (2011) [hereinafter *Rulemaking 2.0*]. For more emphasis on possible use of social networks in rulemaking, see Cynthia R. Farina et al., *Rulemaking in 140 Characters or Less: Social Networking and Public Participation in Rulemaking*, 31 Pace L. Rev. 382 (2011) [hereinafter *Rulemaking in 140 Characters*].

other so-called Web 2.0 technology. At first, these technological developments seemed to provide the perfect platform for e-rulemaking, but it has not proven to be so easy to merge them with the traditional rulemaking process.[186]

The most significant and promising experiment with e-participation has been the "Regulation Room" project based on an agreement between the U.S. Department of Transportation (DOT) and the Cornell eRulemaking Initiative (CeRI).[187] In this experiment, Cornell researchers and students organize a moderated online discussion forum to discuss proposed rules provided by DOT.[188] As part of the arrangement, DOT does not want the entire file of individual Regulation Room comments submitted to the rulemaking record, so the Regulation Room team creates a draft and, after a comment period of its own, a final summary of the discussion, which is then submitted to DOT.[189]

While only two rules have been subjected to the Regulation Room treatment, as of this writing the team leaders have tentatively concluded the following:

> In describing early experience with the Regulation Room project, we have argued that rulemaking is in fact an extremely challenging process for e-government innovation. The electronic docket concept of Regulations.gov can increase transparency by making the formal documents of rulemaking more broadly and readily accessible. Taking the next step—achieving more and better public participation—will be considerably more difficult. No existing, commonly used and understood Web services or applications are good analogies for what a Rulemaking 2.0 site has to do to lower the barriers to effective public engagement in rulemaking. New methods and applications will have to be developed. More deeply, a culture of effective public participation in rulemaking will emerge only if users acquire new expectations about how they engage information on the Web—and, perhaps, about what is required for civic participation.[190]

---

186. *See Rulemaking 2.0, supra* note 185, at 395 (2011) ("Early results give some cause for optimism about the open-government potential of Web 2.0-supported rulemaking. But significant challenges remain. Broader, better public participation is hampered by 1) ignorance of the rulemaking process; 2) unawareness that rulemakings of interest are going on; and 3) information overload from the length and complexity of rulemaking materials.").

187. Http://www.regulationroom.org. *See* Federal Motor Carrier Safety Administration, Proposed Rule, Limiting the Use of Wireless Communication Devices, 75 Fed. Reg. 16,391, 16,391–92 (Apr. 1, 2010) (describing the Regulation Room project from the DOT perspective, strongly encouraging commenters to participate, but also making clear that it is not an official DOT website and that commenters can also comment directly to DOT).

188. *See Rulemaking 2.0* at 398 (describing the two DOT rulemakings that had been presented in Regulation Room: a Federal Motor Carrier Safety Administration proposal to ban texting by commercial motor vehicle drivers and the second round of airline passenger rights regulations proposed by the Office of the Secretary).

189. *Id.* at 414. The Regulation Room process and the technology used is described at 410–15.

190. *Id.* at 447.

3. The Impact of E-Rulemaking on the Rulemaking Process

The flip side of increased public participation, of course, is increased responsibilities on agencies to digest and react to a higher volume of comments. Blizzards of comments have become increasingly common in controversial rulemakings, and e-rulemaking can only further this trend. Professor Strauss has warned of some of the problems this might cause:

> I think we're going to see an enormous explosion in the volume of rulemaking comments, and some of them will be quite manipulative. And it will be a challenge for the agencies receiving these comments to tell the one from the other, the valid from the invalid. And then, once they have received hundreds of thousands, tens of thousands of comments, the impulse to treat them as a reflection of e-democracy—we're hearing from the people, and what we do ought to reflect the people, rather than we are collecting information and what we ought to do ought to reflect the outcome of that information—is going to be quite strong.[191]

Professor Herz concurs that this may be a problem:

> What can realistically be expected of an agency dealing with a million comments, thousands of which duplicate one another? The old model of careful individual consideration is inapplicable. Unavoidably, the agency will start to do what, for example, Members of Congress do: avoid the subtleties and keep a running tally with the grossest sort of division—basically "for" or "against."[192]

This, he cautions, may not only lead to information overload[193] (although here it should be pointed out that technology may also make it possible for agencies to efficiently sort and categorize voluminous comments),[194] it might also lead to a gen-

---

191. Peter Strauss, comments at AU E-Rulemaking Conference, *supra* note 116, transcript at 28.
192. Herz, *supra* note 132, at 148–49. He also points out, "There is one important caveat, however. To the extent that the comments are duplicative, the burden of responding is not increased." *Id.* at 149 n.78.
193. *Id.* at 149. *See also* Wendy E. Wagner, *Administrative Law, Filter Failure, and Information Capture*, 59 Duke L.J. 1321, 1431 (2010) ("There are no provisions in administrative law for regulating the flow of information entering or leaving the system, or for ensuring that regulatory participants can keep up with a rising tide of issues, details, and technicalities."); Randolph J. May, *Under Pressure: Campaign-Style Tactics Are the Wrong Way to Influence Agency Decisions*, Legal Times, July 7, 2003, at 44; Jim Rossi, *Participation Run Amok: The Costs of Mass Participation for Deliberative Agency Decisionmaking*, 92 Nw. L. Rev. 173, 224–28 (1997).
194. This technology, the "Public Comment Analysis Toolkit," created to search, sort, and analyze data, such as a large volume of public comments, was demonstrated by its leading proponent, Professor Stuart Shulman of University of Massachusetts at the ABA's Administrative Law and Regulatory Practice Institute on Rulemaking on June 10, 2010. *See* Scott D. Rafferty, *Proceedings of the Sixth Annual Administrative Law and Regulatory Practice Institute on Rulemaking,*

eral politicization of the rulemaking process—away from the technocratic model of rulemaking, where the substance of the comment is more important than who submitted it or how many times it was repeated—to a type of referendum.[195] "In short," he notes, rather disquietingly, "the new technology is forcing agencies toward a particular model of the process and function of rulemaking, as opposed to enabling agencies better to function under the model chosen independent of that technology."[196] Other researchers have found a proliferation of "form comments,"[197] making Professor Noveck's concern about the use of robot programs to generate "notice and spam" all the more plausible.[198]

> 35 ADMIN. & REG. L. NEWS 20 (Summer 2010). The technology can be viewed at the website for Texifter, LLC, http://pcat.qdap.net (not intended as an endorsement). See also comments by Stuart Shulman at AU's State of Rulemaking Conference, *supra* note 116, Panel 4 at 18: "Part of what we're doing with the computer scientists is developing tools for dealing with this information flood, and we're making some progress on developing the computer science side where we'll be able to deliver a tool to agency personnel who want to identify quickly as possible those clusters of duplicate and near-duplicate e-mails." For a technical paper describing these techniques for sorting comments, see Hui Yang, Jamie Callen & Stuart Shulman, *Next Steps in Near-Duplicate Detection for eRulemaking*, *in* Proceedings of the Fifth National Conference on Digital Government Research (2006), *available at* http://www.cs.cmu.edu/~callan/Papers/dgo06-huiyang.pdf.

195. Prof. Herz points to the example of the "roadless rule," a heavily litigated rule issued in the waning days of the Clinton Administration, which attempted to restrict road construction in large parts of Forest Service land.

> The rule has generated a number of legal challenges, with several district judges finding defects in the process, and the Bush Administration is considering diluting its protections in Alaska. Comments on the proposed rule and/or the Draft EIS, and on the current Alaska proposals, numbered in the millions and have been overwhelmingly in favor of stringent protections. Press coverage has overwhelmingly treated the comment process as a sort of vote. This conception can also be seen in an amicus brief submitted to the 9th Circuit in *Kootenai Tribe* by the Montana attorney general. The brief's basic point had nothing to do with legality, but came down to this: "Hey, Montanans overwhelmingly support this rule, as shown by tabulating our comments during the process." Emphasizing that 67 percent of commenters in Montana (and 96 percent nationwide) favored stronger protections than were anticipated in the Draft EIS, and that the Forest Service responded by strengthening protections, the brief concludes that the rule is "the product of public rulemaking at its most effective." What's more, the Ninth Circuit placed some weight on this argument.

Herz, *supra* note 132, at 150–51 (footnotes omitted).

196. *Id.* at 151.

197. *See* David Schlosberg, Stephen Zavetoski & Stuart Shulman, *To Submit a Form or Not to Submit a Form, That Is the (Real) Question: Deliberation and Mass Participation in U.S. Regulatory Rulemaking* (2005), *available at* http://erulemaking.ucsur.pitt.edu/doc/papers/SDEST_Western_05.pdf (finding significant differences between respondents who submitted original comments and those who submitted form letters).

198. Noveck, *supra* note 99, at 441.

Finally, another aspect of the possible increased politicization of rulemaking due to the new technology is the potential for even greater White House control of the process. Professor Strauss has suggested that not only is OMB playing a central role in "creating this new apparatus," "to have all information travel through their gateway only adds to the possibilities of their influence."[199] "As agencies become more transparent, they become more transparent to the President as well as to the public. . . . Now the docket is immediately available on equal and easy terms to all who want it, including the President, and politics will give him the incentive to attend to it."[200] This is a potentially profound development that deserves more debate and consideration.

In closing, a preliminary survey I conducted on agency rulemakers concluded that:

[A]gency rulemakers are generally receptive to e-rulemaking, although a common theme of their early evaluations was that the new system is a "boon for the public but a bane for the agency." Indeed, a large majority of respondents reported a general increase in rulemaking efficiency and a smaller majority reported a general increase in rulemaking quality. They said this even though they were also generally dubious about the usefulness of the resulting additional comments. In addition, a series of questions asked whether e-rulemaking has made it more or less easy to undertake some positive rulemaking activities, and in each case the answer was that it was easier.

On the other hand, another series of questions asked whether e-rulemaking has increased the level of concern about some of the worries hypothetically associated with e-rulemaking, and in the case of eight of them, the answer was that their worries had increased.

Thus, the early picture is still mixed—no one doubts that the new system is better at engendering more public participation, although most agency rulemakers did not report receiving a concomitant increase in useful information or arguments among the additional comments. Moreover, while rulemakers *are* quite impressed with the internal administrative and coordination benefits provided by the new technology, they also have heightened concerns about hacking and the potential problems of inappropriate worldwide exposure of certain information in their electronic dockets.[201]

---

199. Richard G. Stoll & Katherine Lazarski, *Rulemaking Chapter*, DEVELOPMENTS IN ADMINISTRATIVE LAW AND REGULATORY PRACTICE 2003–2004, at 160 (Jeffrey S. Lubbers ed., 2004) (attributing this portion of the chapter to Professor Peter Strauss). *See also* Evan J. Criddle, *Fiduciary Administration: Rethinking Popular Representation in Agency Rulemaking*, 88 TEX. L. REV. 441 (2010) (arguing that federal administrative law should seek to promote popular representation in agency rulemaking through "fiduciary representation," as opposed to allowing the President to serve as a proxy for the will of the people).

200. *Id.*

201. Lubbers, *supra* note 153, at 474.

Other acute observers, the Regulation Room team leaders, also project a cautious optimism:

> Based on early Regulation Room experience, we believe that [helping those who have a stake in regulation (but do not know it) understand why they should make the considerable investment in time and effort that meaningful participation requires] is a far more challenging undertaking than e-rulemaking proponents have imagined. At the same time, the experience also gives us reason to believe that Rulemaking 2.0 can indeed be the vehicle through which some portion of the public—certainly not all, probably not most, but *some* portion—chooses to move from a state of civic ignorance and uninvolvement to a state of understanding and perhaps even empowerment.[202]

Now that the attention of the Administrative Conference is focused on addressing the legal concerns, and if the progress made by the Obama Administration in refining FDMS and Regulation.gov continues, the capacity of the "e-rulemaking revolution" to actually become revolutionary may be realized.

---

202. *Rulemaking in 140 Characters, supra* note 185, at 462–63. *But see* Stuart M. Benjamin, *Evaluating E-Rulemaking: Public Participation and Political Institutions*, 55 Duke L.J. 893 (2006) (considering e-rulemaking in a broader institutional context and finding that there are good reasons to believe that e-rulemaking initiatives' costs outweigh their benefits, but that it would be premature to settle on that conclusion); Cary Coglianese, *Citizen Participation in Rulemaking: Past, Present, and Future*, 55 Duke L.J. 943, 949 (2006) (comparing empirical observations on citizen participation in the past, before e-rulemaking, with more recent data on citizen participation afterwards and finding that e-rulemaking made little difference with citizen input remaining typically sparse).

Chapter 2

Regulatory Analysis and Review

Regulatory analysis and review requirements derive from several different statutes and executive orders, which are discussed in Parts I and II. This chapter summarizes their practical effects for agency rulemakers.

For "significant regulatory actions" subject to Executive Order 12,866,[1] rules containing information-collection requirements, rules likely to have significant economic impact on small businesses or state and local governments, and rules implicating certain other policy interests, an agency must be prepared, when it authorizes publication of a notice of proposed rulemaking (NPRM), to explain and provide support for its choice of a preferred regulatory approach to a problem. Where such analyses are required, an initial or preliminary report must generally be prepared in conjunction with the NPRM, and a final report, responding to comments on the earlier report, must be prepared with the final rule.[2]

Executive Order 12,866 requires, unless prohibited by law,[3] a cost-benefit assessment of "economically significant rules" that evaluates the potential costs and benefits of the proposed rule. It also requires a description of alternative approaches that could substantially achieve the same regulatory goal at a lower cost and a brief explanation of the legal reasons why such alternatives could not be adopted.[4] The Paperwork Reduction Act[5] requires an agency to justify the burdens imposed by information collection requirements. The Regulatory Flexibility Act[6] requires the agency's initial analysis accompanying an NPRM to describe in detail the expected impact of the proposed rule on small entities and to evaluate significant alternatives to the proposed rule. The Unfunded Mandates Reform Act[7] essentially codified E.O. 12,866's analy-

---

1. Exec. Order 12,866 § 3(f), 58 Fed. Reg. 51,735 (Sept. 30, 1993), *reprinted in* Appendix B.
2. For a discussion of the requirements associated with the final rule, *see infra* Part III, ch. 7.
3. Exec. Order 12,866 § 6(a)(3)(C). Some statutes prohibit agencies from using cost-benefit analysis. *See e.g.*, City of Portland, Ore. v. EPA, 507 F.3d 706, 710–13 (D.C. Cir. 2007) (holding that while the Safe Drinking Water Act requires EPA to conduct cost-benefit analysis when issuing regulations, it prohibits EPA from using cost-benefit analysis to set a standard other than the most stringent feasible for cryptosporidium).
4. Exec. Order 12,866 § 3(f).
5. 44 U.S.C. §§ 3501–3520. *See* discussion *supra* Part II, ch. 3(D).
6. 5 U.S.C. §§ 601–612. *See* discussion *supra* Part II, ch. 3(C).
7. Pub. L. No. 104-4, 109 Stat. 48 (1995) (codified at 2 U.S.C. chs. 17A, 25). *See* discussion *supra* Part II, ch. 3(G).

sis requirements and extended them to rules having a special impact on state, local, or tribal governments, as well as on the private sector. In addition, executive orders on federalism, tribal governments, takings of private property, energy effects, and the protection of children from environmental health risks may require analysis of a rulemaking's impacts in particular areas.[8]

For each of these statutes and executive orders, this chapter will discuss (1) the rules subject to the analysis requirements; (2) generally, the applicable requirements; and (3) the review process.[9]

A. Executive Order 12,866

Executive Order 12,866 is intended to minimize duplication and conflict in federal regulation and to ensure that agencies "promulgate only such regulations as are required by law, are necessary to interpret the law, or are made necessary by compelling public need."[10] The order sets forth certain policy requirements that, "to the extent permitted by law,"[11] a federal agency[12] is required to follow in promulgating new

---

8. *See* discussion *infra* sec. H.
9. It should be noted that some individual agency statutes require preparation of some types of analysis, or to consider the impacts of their rules on the public or particular segments of the public in rulemaking. See discussion and examples in Curtis Copeland, *Regulatory Analysis Requirements: A Review and Recommendations for Reform* 29–32, draft report to the Administrative Conference of the U.S. (Apr. 23, 2012), *available at* http://www.acus.gov/wp-content/uploads/downloads/2012/04/CDR-Final-Reg-Analysis-Report-for-5-3-12-Mtg.pdf. One example is the CFTC's statute, 7 U.S.C. § 19, added by Pub. L. No. 106-554 (2000), § 1(a)(5) [Title I, § 119], 114 Stat. 2763, 2763A-403 ("Before promulgating a regulation under this chapter or issuing an order . . . , the Commission shall consider the costs and benefits of the action of the Commission."). On the other hand, the NLRB's statute contains a curious provision *barring* the Board from "appoint[ing] individuals for the purpose of . . . economic analysis." 29 U.S.C. § 154(a).
10. Exec. Order 12,866, *supra* note 1, § 1(a).
11. *Id.* § 1(b). Note that in *Entergy Corp. v. Riverkeeper, Inc.*, 556 U.S. 208 (2009), the Supreme Court ruled that a "best available technology" requirement for effluent limitations under the Clean Water Act did not preclude the use of cost-benefit analysis by EPA, reversing a contrary ruling by the Second Circuit.
12. As with similar orders issued by previous presidents, the "centralized review of regulations" portion, section six, of Executive Order 12,866 is made applicable only to executive departments and agencies and not to independent agencies. However, in a break from the past, portions of Executive Order 12,866 pertaining to regulatory planning, in section four, are made applicable to independent regulatory agencies as well. The President's authority over independent agencies has been frequently debated. See discussion *supra* Part I(D)(2). Numerous small agencies are completely exempt from the order. *See* OFFICE OF MGMT. & BUDGET, REPORT ON EXECUTIVE ORDER NO. 12,866, 59 Fed. Reg. 24,276, 24,293 (May 10, 1994). President Obama's OMB also issued a special memorandum urging independent agencies to comply. *See* OMB Memorandum M-11-28 from OIRA Administrator Cass Sunstein for the Heads of Independent Agen-

regulations, reviewing existing regulations, and offering legislative proposals.[13] It was reaffirmed by President Obama in Executive Order 13,579.[14]

1. Rules Covered by Executive Order 12,866 Review

Executive Order 12,866 requires executive branch agencies to periodically prepare and send to OMB's Office of Information and Regulatory Affairs (OIRA) a list of all planned regulatory actions, noting those that the agency believes to be "significant" within the meaning of the order. Section 3(f) defines *significant regulatory action* to be one that is likely to result in a rule that may:

1. have an annual effect on the economy of $100 million or more or adversely affect in a material way the economy, a sector of the economy, productivity, competition, jobs, the environment, public health or safety, or State, local, or tribal governments or communities;
2. create a serious inconsistency or otherwise interfere with an action taken or planned by another agency;
3. materially alter the budgetary impact of entitlements, grants, user fees, or loan programs or the rights and obligations of recipients thereof; or
4. raise novel, legal or policy issues arising out of legal mandates, the President's priorities, or the principles set forth in this Executive Order.[15]

If the matter is determined by the agency or OIRA Administrator to be "economically significant" (that is, within the scope of Section 3(f)(1)),[16] the agency must undertake an assessment in the nature of a cost-benefit analysis.[17] Provision is made for emergency situations and for those actions "governed by a statutory or court-imposed deadline," although agencies are required to comply with the order's provisions "to the extent practicable."[18] The order also allows the Administrator to exempt any category of regulations from review.[19]

---

cies (July 22, 2011), *available at* http://www.whitehouse.gov/sites/default/files/omb/memoranda/2011/m11-28.pdf (providing non-binding guidance to independent agencies in carrying out E.O. 13,579, and stating that "the key principles of Executive Order 13563 [are] designed to promote public participation, improve integration and innovation, promote flexibility and freedom of choice, and ensure scientific integrity.").

13. Exec. Order 12,866 § 1.
14. Exec. Order 13,579, 76 Fed. Reg. 41,587 (July 11, 2011).
15. Exec. Order 12,866, *supra* note 1, § 3(f).
16. A similar definition for "major" rules is included in the Congressional Review Act, 5 U.S.C. § 804(2). *See* Part II, ch. 3(J).
17. Exec. Order 12,866, *supra* note 1, § 6(a)(2)(C). The section delineates the types of benefits and costs to be assessed and also requires that "potentially effective and reasonably feasible alternatives to the planned regulation" be assessed as well. *Id.* § 6(a)(2)(C)(iii).
18. *Id.* § 6(a)(2)(D).
19. *Id.* § 3(d). The definition of "rule" operates to exempt rules of particular applicability and also specifically exempts other narrow categories of rules from coverage: (1) rules issued through

The Clinton Administration consciously sought to make the OIRA review process more selective than it had been under the Reagan-Bush order,[20] although OIRA retains the final say on whether a proposed or final rule on the agency's list is "significant" and therefore subject to review.[21] Regulatory actions deemed not to be significant may go forward without OIRA review, although agencies are still supposed to uphold the 12 "principles of regulation" in Section 1(b) of the order. Naturally, agencies must be forthright about the potential significance of the rules on their lists submitted to OIRA; agencies that underestimate the later significance (or controversiality) of their rules will likely be subject to more frequent and intensive OIRA review.

Executive Order 12,866 also requires agencies to participate in the *Unified Agenda of Federal Regulatory and Deregulatory Actions*[22] by publishing information on all regulations under development or review; it requires that agencies develop an annual "Regulatory Plan" to be forwarded to OIRA by June of each year for review by the OMB Director and other "Advisors";[23] and it requires that the plan include the agency's plans to review *existing* regulations.[24] Moreover, it created a Regulatory Working Group, chaired by the OIRA Administrator, to coordinate regulatory approaches and develop innovations.[25]

---

formal rulemaking; (2) rules pertaining to a military or foreign affairs function (other than those involving procurement or import/export of nondefense articles); and (3) rules limited to agency organization, management, or personnel. *Id.*

20. *See Clinton Regulation Will Be "Rational": Interview with Sally Katzen, the New OIRA Administrator,* 3 REGULATION MAG. 36 (1993), *available at* http://www.cato.org/pubs/regulation/regv16n3/v16n3-4.pdf. The number of rules reviewed by OIRA fell significantly from the Reagan Administration to the Clinton Administration. Since then it has stayed about the same. *See* figures in Part I, note 140. For an illuminating article on the Bush Administration's OIRA Administrator, see Rebecca Adams, *Regulating the Rule-Makers: John Graham at OIRA,* CQ WEEKLY 520 (Feb. 23, 2002).

21. OIRA reported that in the first six months under the order, it had received lists designating 1,624 regulatory actions as significant or nonsignificant. *See* Office of Mgmt. & Budget, *Report on Executive Order No. 12,866,* 59 Fed. Reg. 24,276, 24,276–77 (May 10, 1994). Specifically, the agencies and OIRA agreed that 64 percent were nonsignificant and that 19 percent were significant. *Id.* The remaining 16 percent were initially listed as nonsignificant by the agencies but redesignated as significant by OIRA. *Id.* As of May 1994, OIRA listed about 30 agencies as exempt from centralized review. *Id.* at 24,293.

22. The title was changed to add "Deregulatory" in 1996. For online versions of the Agenda from 1995 to the present, see http://www.reginfo.gov/public/do/eAgendaHistory.

23. Exec. Order 12,866, *supra* note 1, § 4(c). The "Advisors" are top regulatory policy officials of the Administration. *Id.* § 3(a). The plan is published each year in the October Unified Agenda. *See also* Memorandum for Designated Agency Heads, Guidance for Preparing 1994 Regulatory Plan, from Sally Katzen, OIRA Administrator (Apr. 4, 1994). For a recent commentary on the effectiveness of the Unified Agenda, see CURTIS W. COPELAND, CONG. RESEARCH SERV., RL 40713, THE UNIFIED AGENDA: IMPLICATIONS FOR RULEMAKING TRANSPARENCY AND PARTICIPATION (2009), *available at* http://www.fas.org/sgp/crs/secrecy/R40713.pdf.

24. Exec. Order 12,866, *supra* note 1, § 5.

25. *Id.* § 4(d). This was in response to a recommendation by the National Performance Review. *See* OFFICE OF THE VICE PRESIDENT, CREATING A GOVERNMENT THAT WORKS BETTER AND COSTS LESS, NATIONAL

2. Content of the Regulatory Analysis

For over 30 years executive agencies have been required by executive order to undertake some form of regulatory impact analysis for their "major" or "significant" rules. Executive Order 12,866 uses the term "assessment,"[26] but this *Guide* will use the more all-purpose term "regulatory analysis." Under E.O. 12,866, the regulatory analysis must contain (1) an assessment (quantitative where feasible) of the anticipated benefits, "such as, but not limited to, the promotion of the efficient functioning of the economy and private markets, the enhancement of health and safety, the protection of the natural environment, and the elimination of discrimination or bias"; (2) a similar assessment of the anticipated costs, "including, but not limited to, the direct cost both to the government in administering the regulation and to businesses and others in complying with the regulation, and any adverse effects on the efficient functioning of the economy, private markets . . . , health, safety and the natural environment"; and (3) an assessment of the costs and benefits of "reasonably feasible" alternative approaches and an explanation of why the planned action is preferable to the identified potential alternatives.[27]

In 1996, a task force of the Regulatory Working Group reviewed the state of the art for regulatory analyses and prepared a "best practices" guide for preparing the economic analysis of a significant regulatory action called for by the executive order.[28] On September 17, 2003, OMB, after an outside peer review, issued Circular A-4, "Regula-

---

PERFORMANCE REVIEW, IMPROVING REGULATORY SYSTEMS 17–22 (1993). The members of the Regulatory Working Group are listed in Office of Mgmt. & Budget, *Report on Executive Order No. 12,866*, App. B, 59 Fed. Reg. 24,276, 24,293 (1994). However, according to informal interviews with OIRA staff, the RWG was inactive during the Bush II Administration and has not been prominent in the Obama Administration.

26. Exec. Order 12,866, *supra* note 1, § 6(a)(3)(C)(i).

27. *Id.* § 6(a)(3)(C). With respect to the requirement for assessing alternatives, it should be noted that in some situations, the agency's discretion is constrained. *See* U.S. GEN. ACCOUNTING OFFICE, REGULATORY BURDEN: SOME AGENCIES' CLAIMS REGARDING LACK OF RULEMAKING DISCRETION HAVE MERIT 10 (GAO/GGD-99-20) (Jan. 8, 1999), *available at* http://www.gpo.gov/fdsys/pkg/GAOREPORTS-GGD-99-20/pdf/GAOREPORTS-GGD-99-20.pdf (examining 27 of the most problematic regulatory concerns of surveyed companies, and concluding that the statutory provisions underlying 13 of the 27 company concerns "provided the agencies with no discretion in how the relevant regulatory provisions could be developed," that the statutory provisions underlying 12 of the remaining 14 concerns "permitted the agencies some discretion in establishing regulatory requirements," and that the provisions related to two concerns "allowed the agencies broad rulemaking discretion").

28. *Id.* The report, *Economic Analysis of Federal Regulations Under Executive Order 12,866*, is *available at* http://www.whitehouse.gov/omb/inforeg_riaguide. It was then issued as OMB Guidance in March 2000. *See* OMB Memorandum M-00-08, *Guidelines to Standardize Measures of Costs and Benefits and the Format of Accounting Statements* (Mar. 22, 2000), available in *OMB Report to Congress on the Costs and Benefits of Federal Regulations* (2000) at p.60, http://clinton4.nara.gov/media/pdf/2000fedreg-report.pdf. *See also* EPA's *Guidelines for Preparing Regulatory Analyses* (2000), *available at* http://yosemite.epa.gov/ee/epa/eed.nsf/pages/Guidelines.html.

tory Analysis,"[29] which refines and replaces refines OMB's "best practices" document of 1996 and the 2000 guidance that followed. According to OIRA Administrator John Graham's March 4, 2004, memorandum to the President's Management Council, the OMB guidance embodied in Circular A-4 contains several significant changes from previous OMB guidance, including "(1) more emphasis on cost-effectiveness analysis, (2) formal probability analysis for rules with more than a billion-dollar impact on the economy, and (3) more systematic evaluation of qualitative as well as quantified benefits and costs."[30] In 2011, the Obama Administration issued a checklist to help agencies comply with the Circular[31] and an FAQ on Regulatory Impact Analysis.[32]

The headings in Circular A-4 illustrate some of the considerations that agencies must ponder in the preparation of regulatory analyses:

A. Introduction[33]
B. The Need for Federal Regulatory Action[34]
C. Alternative Regulatory Approaches[35]
D. Analytical Approaches[36]
E. Identifying and Measuring Benefits and Costs[37]

---

29. *Available at* http://www.whitehouse.gov/omb/circulars_a004_a-4/.
30. *Available at* http://www.whitehouse.gov/omb/inforeg/memo_pmc_a4.pdf. For an interesting intensive review of a single EPA regulatory analysis, see U.S. GEN. ACCOUNTING OFFICE, DRINKING WATER: REVISIONS TO EPA'S COST ANALYSIS FOR THE RADON RULE WOULD IMPROVE ITS CREDIBILITY AND USEFULNESS (GAO-02-333) (Feb. 2002).
31. OMB, OIRA, 2011 REPORT TO CONGRESS ON THE BENEFITS AND COSTS OF FEDERAL REGULATIONS AND UNFUNDED MANDATES ON STATE, LOCAL, AND TRIBAL ENTITIES 147–51, Appendix I: Agency Checklist: Regulatory Impact Analysis, *available at* http://www.whitehouse.gov/sites/default/files/omb/inforeg/2011_cb/2011_cba_report.pdf.
32. *Available at* http://www.whitehouse.gov/sites/default/files/omb/circulars/a004/a-4_FAQ.pdf.
33. Subheadings include "The Need for Analysis of Proposed Regulatory Actions," and "Key Elements of a Regulatory Analysis."
34. Subheadings include "Market Failure or Other Social Purpose, "Showing That Regulation at the Federal Level Is the Best Way to Solve the Problem," and "The Presumption Against Economic Regulation."
35. Subheadings include "Different Choices Defined by Statute," "Different Compliance Dates," "Different Enforcement Methods," "Different Degrees of Stringency," "Different Requirements for Different Sized Firms," "Different Requirements for Different Geographic Regions," "Performance Standards Rather than Design Standards," "Market-Oriented Approaches Rather than Direct Controls," and "Informational Measures Rather than Regulation."
36. Subheadings include "Benefit-Cost Analysis," "Cost-Effectiveness Analysis," "The Effectiveness Metric for Public Health and Safety Rulemakings," and "Distributional Effects."
37. Subheadings include "General Issues" [1. Scope of Analysis, 2. Developing a Baseline, 3. Evaluation of Alternatives, 4. Transparency and Reproducibility of Results]; "Developing Benefit and Cost Estimates" [1. Some General Considerations, 2. The Key Concepts Needed to Estimate Benefits and Costs, 3. Revealed Preference Methods, 4. Stated Preference Methods, 5. Benefit-Transfer Methods, 6. Ancillary Benefits and Countervailing Risks, 7. Methods for Treating Non-Monetized Benefits and Costs, 8. Monetizing Health and Safety Benefits and Costs]; "Discount Rates" [1. The Rationale for Discounting, 2. Real Discount Rates of 3 Percent and 7 Percent, 3. Time Preference for Health-Related Benefits and Costs, 4. Intergenerational Dis-

F. Specialized Analytical Requirements[38]

G. Accounting Statement[39]

Circular A-4 offers this general advice:

To evaluate properly the benefits and costs of regulations and their alternatives, you will need to do the following:

- Explain how the actions required by the rule are linked to the expected benefits. For example, indicate how additional safety equipment will reduce safety risks. A similar analysis should be done for each of the alternatives.
- Identify a baseline. Benefits and costs are defined in comparison with a clearly stated alternative. This normally will be a "no action" baseline: what the world will be like if the proposed rule is not adopted. Comparisons to a "next best" alternative are also especially useful.
- Identify the expected undesirable side-effects and ancillary benefits of the proposed regulatory action and the alternatives. These should be added to the direct benefits and costs as appropriate.[40]

Of special importance is the supplementary guidance on calculating benefits and costs. The Circular fleshes out the terms of the order by stating the following:

You should monetize quantitative estimates whenever possible. Use sound and defensible values or procedures to monetize benefits and costs, and ensure that key analytical assumptions are defensible. If monetization is impossible, explain why and present all available quantitative information. For example, if you can quantify but cannot monetize increases in water quality and fish populations resulting from water quality regulation, you can describe benefits in terms of stream miles of improved water quality for boaters and increases in game fish populations for anglers.[41]

---

counting, 5. Time Preference for Non-Monetized Benefits and Costs, 6. The Internal Rate of Return]; "Other Key Considerations" [1. Other Benefit and Cost Considerations, 2. The Difference between Costs (or Benefits) and Transfer Payments]; and "Treatment of Uncertainty" [1. Quantitative Analysis of Uncertainty, 2. Economic Values of Uncertain Outcomes, 3. Alternative Assumptions].

38. Subheadings include "Impact on Small Businesses and Other Small Entities," "Analysis of Unfunded Mandates," "Information Collection, Paperwork, and Recordkeeping Burdens," "Information Quality Guidelines," "Environmental Impact Statements," "Impacts on Children," and "Energy Impacts."

39. Subheadings include "Categories of Benefits and Costs"; "Quantifying and Monetizing Benefits and Costs"; "Qualitative Benefits and Costs"; "Treatment of Benefits and Costs over Time"; "Treatment of Risk and Uncertainty"; "Precision of Estimates"; "Separate Reporting of Transfers"; and "Effects on State, Local, and Tribal Governments, Small Business, Wages and Economic Growth."

40. Circular A-4, *supra* note 29.

41. *Id.*

The Circular also recognizes that in some situations, quantification of the effects of the regulation is difficult:

> If you are not able to quantify the effects, you should present any relevant quantitative information along with a description of the unquantified effects, such as ecological gains, improvements in quality of life, and aesthetic beauty. You should provide a discussion of the strengths and limitations of the qualitative information. This should include information on the key reason(s) why they cannot be quantified.[42]

Several approaches for the valuation of reduction in fatality risks are also offered, including the "willingness to pay" approach and the "value of statistical life."[43] In addition, agencies are advised how to handle uncertainty and to make assumptions explicit.[44] Guidance is also given on cost-effectiveness analysis[45] and discounting future costs and benefits to their present values.[46]

---

42. *Id.* For a suggestion that the effect of a rule on "happiness" should be a factor in regulatory analysis, see Anthony Vitarelli, *Happiness Metrics in Federal Rulemaking*, 27 YALE L.J. 115 (2010).

43. Circular A-4, *supra* note 29. This topic was addressed by the Administrative Conference in ACUS Recommendation 88-7, *Valuation of Human Life in Regulatory Decisionmaking*, 53 Fed. Reg. 39,585 (Oct. 11, 1988). The Conference recommended that agencies "should disclose the dollar value per statistical life used" for determining whether compliance costs to reduce the risk to human life are justified. *Id.* The Conference concluded that it would be useful if the agencies "would reveal publicly the processes through which they have determined the valuation of life incorporated in policy decisions," thus "provid[ing] useful clarification and exposition of the unavoidable trade-offs in regulating hazards" and permitting agency practice to be measured against valuation techniques used elsewhere. *Id.* at 39,587. The recommendation is based on Clayton P. Gillette & Thomas D. Hopkins, *Federal Agency Valuations of Human Life*, 1988 ACUS 367. For an example of one Department's treatment of valuation of a statistical life, see Department of Transportation Memorandum (Mar. 18, 2009), *available at* http://regs.dot.gov/docs/VSL%20Guidance%202008%20and%202009rev.pdf (raising the value from $5.8 million to $6.0 million). *See also* Binyamin Appelbaum, *As U.S. Agencies Put More Value on a Life, Businesses Fret*, N.Y. TIMES (Feb. 16, 2011) (reporting that EPA's value was $9.1 million, and FDA's $7.9 million). *See generally* CASS R. SUNSTEIN, THE COST-BENEFIT STATE: THE FUTURE OF REGULATORY PROTECTION (2002); Thomas O. McGarity, *A Cost-Benefit State*, 50 ADMIN. L. REV. 7 (1998).

44. OMB Circular A-4, *supra* note 29. An especially difficult issue is presented in calculating the benefits of regulations concerning homeland security. In a speech to the ABA, OIRA Administrator John Graham mentioned the following "perplexing issues": (1) how to identify targets of potential terrorist attacks, the probability of attacks and associated damages, and the effectiveness of various countermeasures; and (2) how to respect the need for secrecy in discussing such issues. John D. Graham, *The Smart Regulation Agenda: Progress and Challenges*, speech summarized in 31 ADMIN. & REG. L. NEWS 11 (Winter 2006).

45. *Id.*

46. *Id.* The Administrative Conference addressed procedural and managerial issues relating to the preparation of regulatory analyses in ACUS Recommendation 85-2, *Agency Procedures for Performing Regulatory Analysis of Rules*, 50 Fed. Reg. 28,363 (July 12, 1985). Recommendation 85-2 contains advice on the use and limits of regulatory analysis and on integration of

Since 1995, OMB has also been submitting a report to Congress attempting to provide an overall look at the costs and benefits of regulation.[47] This is now done to implement Section 624 of the Treasury and General Government Appropriations Act of 2001, commonly known as the Regulatory Right-to-Know Act.[48] These reports have regularly estimated high aggregate net benefits for the rules OMB reviews.[49]

Some efforts have been made to evaluate the quality of regulatory analyses. The Mercatus Center at George Mason University has issued several critiques of recent regulatory analyses.[50] OIRA Administrator Cass Sunstein has also publicly praised

---

regulatory analysis into the agency rulemaking process. It stresses that the regulatory analysis process must be integrated into the agency's decisionmaking process from the beginning and not "used to produce post hoc rationalizations for decisions already made." The analysis should discuss its major assumptions and explain why the agency selected a particular set of assumptions, inferences, or models. This recommendation was based on Thomas O. McGarity, *The Role of Regulatory Analysis in Regulatory Decisionmaking*, 1985 ACUS 107. *See also* Thomas O. McGarity, *Regulatory Analysis and Regulatory Reform*, 65 Tex. L. Rev. 1243 (1987); Thomas O. McGarity, Reinventing Rationality (1991). For an interesting article on developments in agency discounting policies, see Ben Trachtenberg, *Tinkering with the Machinery of Life*, 59 UCLA L. Rev. Discourse 128 (describing changes in EPA's and DOT's discounting policies in calculating the value of a statistical life).

47. *See, e.g.*, Office of Mgmt. & Budget, Office of Information and Regulatory Affairs, Progress in Regulatory Reform: 2011 Report to Congress on the Costs and Benefits of Federal Regulations and Unfunded Mandates on State, Local, and Tribal Entities (2011), *available at* http://www.whitehouse.gov/sites/default/files/omb/inforeg/2011_cb/2011_cba_report.pdf. For early commentary on this effort, see Robert W. Hahn & Mary Beth Muething, *The Grand Experiment in Regulatory Reporting*, 55 Admin. L. Rev. 607 (2003).
48. Pub. L. No. 106-554 (codified at 31 U.S.C. § 1105 note). For a critical review of OMB's early reports (1997–98), see U.S. Gen. Accounting Office, Regulatory Accounting: Analysis of OMB's Reports on the Costs and Benefits of Federal Regulation (GAO-GGD-99-59) (Apr. 1999).
49. *See* 2011 Report to Congress, *supra* note 47, at 19–20 (table 1-3), noting that from 2000 to 2010 at least, "the benefits exceed the costs in every fiscal year." *Id.* at 20.
50. *See* Jerry Ellig & John Morrall, *Assessing the Quality of Regulatory Analysis: A New Evaluation and Data Set for Policy Research*, working paper No. 10-75 (December 2010) *available at* http://mercatus.org/sites/default/files/publication/wp1075-assessing-the-quality-of-regulatory-analysis.pdf. The study examines the regulatory analyses used in all economically significant regulations proposed in 2009 against a set of criteria, and finds the quality to be low. The highest-scoring analysis was for the joint EPA and DOT proposed rule on Greenhouse Gases from Light-Duty Vehicles, 74 Fed. Reg. 51,249 (Oct. 6, 2009). *See also* Patrick McLaughlin & Jerry Ellig, *Does Haste Make Waste in Regulatory Analysis?*, working paper No. 10-57 (November 2010), *available at* http://mercatus.org/sites/default/files/publication/wp1057-does-haste-make-waste-in-federal-regulations.pdf. For a critical review of agency performance in this area covering all economically significant rules issued from July 1996 to March 1997, *see generally* U.S. Gen. Accounting Office, Regulatory Reform: Agencies Could Improve Development, Documentation, and Clarity of Regulatory Economic Impact Analyses (GAO-GGD-99-59) (May 1998); U.S. Gen Accounting Office, Cost-Benefit Analyses Can Be Useful in Assessing Environmental Regulations Despite Limitations (GAO/RCED-84-62) (Apr. 6, 1984), *available at* http://archive.gao.gov/d5t1/123970.pdf. *See also* U.S. Gov't Accountability Office, GAO-05-252, Clean Air Act—Observations on EPA's Cost-Benefit Analysis of Its Mercury Control Options (Feb. 2005) (discussing

three regulatory analyses that he considered to be exemplary.[51] Nevertheless, the costs and benefits of cost-benefit analysis continue to be debated.[52]

3. *OIRA Review*[53]

With limited exceptions, all planned regulatory actions by executive branch agencies that may lead to a proposed or final rule must be reported to OIRA, and an action may be subject to review and clearance if it is deemed to be significant. Rules issued by independent regulatory agencies are exempt from review under the Executive Order but not from OMB review of information-collection provisions contained in rules.[54] OIRA must waive or finish its review of certain preliminary actions (for example, notices of inquiry, advance notices of proposed rulemaking) within 10 working days of submission.[55] For proposed or final rules, OIRA has 90 calendar days

---

shortcomings); W. Norton Grubb, Dale Whittington & Michael Humphries, *The Ambiguities of Benefit-Cost Analysis: An Evaluation of Regulatory Impact Analyses under Executive Order* 12291, chapter in V. Kerry Smith, ed., Environmental Policy under Reagan's Executive Order: The Role for Benefit-Cost Analysis 121, 154–59 (1984) (discussing the quality of cost-benefit analyses from the early 1980s).

51. Speech at Washington College of Law, American University, sponsored by the *Administrative Law Review*, on Feb. 16, 2010. His three exemplars were U.S. Dep't of Transportation, Final Regulatory Impact Analysis of Rulemaking on Enhanced Airline Passenger Protections, Final Regulatory Evaluation (Dec. 17, 2009), *available at* http://www.regulations.gov/#!documentDetail;D=DOT-OST-2007-0022-0265 (final rule issued at 74 Fed. Reg. 68,983 (Dec. 30, 2009); Dep't of Health & Human Servs., Ctrs. for Disease Control and Prevention, final rule, Medical Examination of Aliens—Removal of Human Immunodeficiency Virus (HIV) Infection From Definition of Communicable Disease of Public Health Significance, 74 Fed. Reg. 56,547, 56,554–61 (Nov. 2, 2009) ("Required Regulatory Analyses Under Executive Order 12866"); Dep't of Labor, Occupational Safety & Health Admin., proposed rules, Hazard Communication, 74 Fed. Reg. 50,280, 50,307–55 (Sept. 30, 2009) ("Preliminary Economic Analysis and Initial Regulatory Flexibility Screening Analysis"). Interestingly, the DOL proposed rule was rated as slightly below average by the Mercatus study.

52. The extensive debate on the uses and abuses of cost-benefit analysis is beyond the scope of this book. But one useful balanced commentary and collection of references on this debate is Shi-Ling Hsu, *On the Role of Cost-Benefit Analysis in Environmental Law: A Book Review of Frank Ackerman and Lisa Heinzerling's "Priceless: On Knowing the Price of Everything and The Value of Nothing,"* 35 Envtl. L. 135 (2005). Two well-considered but opposing views are Rena Steinzor, et al., *A Return to Common Sense: Protecting Health, Safety, and the Environment Through 'Pragmatic Regulatory Impact Analysis,'* Center for Progressive Reform White Paper #909 (October 2009), *available at* http://www.progressivereform.org/articles/PRIA_909.pdf, and John D. Graham, *Saving Lives Through Administrative Law and Economics*, 157 U. Pa. L. Rev. 395 (2008). A middle-ground inquiry is David M. Driesen, *Is Cost-Benefit Analysis Neutral?*, 77 U. Colo. L. Rev. 335 (2006).

53. *See also* the discussion in Part I (D).

54. *See infra* Part III, ch. 2(B) (discussing the Paperwork Reduction Act).

55. Exec. Order 12,866, *supra* note 1, § 6(b)(2)(A).

from submission to complete the review.[56] This limit is subject to a 30-day extension if the agency head so requests[57] and the OIRA Administrator approves the request in writing. Of course, the administrator may in effect "remand" the matter back to the agency for further consideration.[58] During the pendency of the review (or until the expiration of applicable time periods), the agency ("except to the extent required by law") is prohibited from publishing in the *Federal Register* or otherwise issuing an action under review.[59]

OIRA maintains a website that provides the contents of all of its "return letters" from July 2001 to the present.[60] The site explains:

> During the course of OIRA's review of a draft regulation, the Administrator may decide to send a letter to the agency that returns the rule for reconsideration. Such a return may occur if the quality of the agency's analyses is inadequate, if the regulatory standards adopted are not justified by the analyses, if the rule is not consistent with the regulatory principles stated in EO 12866 or with the President's policies and priorities, or if the rule is not compatible with other Executive Orders or statutes. Such a return does not necessarily imply that either OIRA or OMB is opposed to the draft rule. Rather, the return letter explains why OIRA believes that the rulemaking would benefit from further consideration by the agency.

Section 7 of the order spells out a procedure for presidential resolution of any conflicts that might arise between the agency and OMB. Such a process can be initiated only by the OMB Director or agency head, and the order contains a time limit of 60 days for the Vice President to develop recommendations on the matter.[61]

---

56. *Id.* § 6(b)(2)(B). If OIRA has previously reviewed the submission and there has "been no material change in the facts and circumstances," the limit is reduced to 45 days. *Id.*

57. *Id.* § 6(b)(2)(C).

58. *Id.* § 6(b)(3).

59. *Id.* § 8. *See* Envtl. Def. Fund v. Thomas, 627 F. Supp. 566 (D.D.C. 1986) (holding an agency may proceed if regulatory review will delay promulgation of rule beyond statutory deadline).

60. OIRA, REGINFO.GOV, http://www.reginfo.gov/public/do/eoReturnLetters. As of March 17, 2012, there were 28 such letters. None were posted by the Obama Administration, but OIRA Administrator Cass Sunstein did send a letter returning an important draft final rule to EPA, Letter to the Environmental Protection Agency on "Reconsideration of the 2008 Ozone Primary and Secondary National Ambient Air Quality Standards" (Sept. 2, 2011), *available at* http://www.whitehouse.gov/sites/default/files/ozone_national_ambient_air_quality_standards_letter.pdf. Why it was not posed on the list is unclear. In addition, there were 16 "review" letters. *See* http://www.reginfo.gov/public/jsp/EO/postReviewLetters.jsp.

61. Exec. Order 12,866 § 7. Reported instances of this presidential resolution process are rare. *But see* 62 Fed. Reg. 38,421 (July 18, 1997) (providing a Memorandum for the Administrator [of EPA], signed by President Clinton, announcing that "I have approved the issuance of new air quality standards"). The ozone regulation's pullback mentioned in the previous note is the only other reported instance.

The order also includes broad disclosure requirements pertaining to agency regulatory analyses, changes in the rules made after OIRA review, communications between OIRA and the agencies, and any communications received by OIRA from persons "not employed by the executive branch."[62]

The OIRA review process seems well entrenched, given its support among Presidents of both parties, but it still receives criticism from some commentators.[63]

B. The Paperwork Reduction Act

Originally enacted in 1980, with significant amendments in 1986 and 1995,[64] the Paperwork Reduction Act is intended to minimize the federal paperwork burden for individuals, small businesses, and state, local, and tribal governments; to minimize the cost to the federal government of collecting and disseminating information; and to maximize the usefulness to the federal government of the information collected.[65] The Act statutorily established OIRA within OMB and assigned OIRA responsibility for reviewing agency information-collection requirements. The Act contains clearance procedures, which have been supplemented in detailed regulations issued by OMB.[66] Later legislation has added a requirement that "privacy impact assessments" be undertaken when new collections of information are collected, maintained, or disseminated using information technology.[67]

---

62. *Id.* §§ 6(a)(3)(E), 6(b)(4). *See infra* Part III, ch. 6(C) (discussing openness requirements and "ex parte communications").

63. *See, e.g.,* GOV'T ACCOUNTABILITY OFFICE, FEDERAL RULEMAKING—IMPROVEMENTS NEEDED TO MONITORING AND EVALUATION OF RULES DEVELOPMENT AS WELL AS TO THE TRANSPARENCY OF OMB REGULATORY REVIEWS, GAO-09-205 (April 2009), *available at* http://www.gao.gov/new.items/d09205.pdf; Nicholas Bagley & Richard L. Revesz, *Centralized Oversight of the Regulatory State*, 106 COLUM. L. REV 1260, 1263 (2006) (urging "a reconsideration of the foundational role that centralized review should play in our regulatory state, and a revival and reconceptualization of the neglected principles of harmonization that once ostensibly animated the call for centralized review of administrative action."). See also the many commentaries in the public comments made in response to President Obama's request for comments on E.O. 12,866, http://www.reginfo.gov/public/jsp/EO/fedRegReview/publicComments.jsp. There is also a fear that the "costs" of OIRA review is causing agencies to use avoidance strategies. *See* Note, *OIRA Avoidance*, 124 HARV. L. REV. 994 (2011).

64. *See supra* Part II, ch. 3(D) for a more extensive analysis of the Paperwork Reduction Act.

65. 44 U.S.C. § 3501.

66. 5 C.F.R. pt. 1320.

67. *See* the E-Government Act, § 208, 44 U.S.C.A. § 3601 note. Extensive guidance on this and other privacy-related provisions of the Act is provided in *OMB Guidance for Implementing the Privacy Provisions of the E-Government Act of 2002* (Sept. 26, 2003), *available at* http://www.whitehouse.gov/omb/memoranda_m03-22.

1. Coverage

The Act's clearance requirements apply to agency rules that contain "collections of information" as well as to other types of information collection.[68] The Act requires an agency to justify to OMB its proposed collection of information and to show that it is the least burdensome possible, that it is not duplicative of other federal information collections, and that the collected information will have practical utility.[69] Although the Act covers virtually all federal agencies, independent agencies may by majority vote overrule OMB's determinations.[70]

2. Content of the Analysis

Proposed rules that contain collections-of-information requirements must be submitted for review to OMB, along with supporting documents, no later than the date of publication of the NPRM in the *Federal Register*. As a practical matter, the procedures for review under E.O. 12,866 take precedence for all rules but those of independent regulatory agencies.[71] In addition to copies of documents to be used in the information collection, the agency must also submit a certification that, among other things, the information to be collected is necessary, is not unnecessarily duplicative, minimizes to the extent practicable the burden on respondents, is understandable to respondents, and uses effective statistical survey methodology.[72] The agency must also, in its NPRM, notify the public that the rule has been sent to OMB and that the public may file comments on the information-collection provisions with OMB.[73] The preamble to the NPRM must also include a brief statement on the need to collect the particular information, a description of the likely respondents, and an estimate of the annual recordkeeping and reporting burden.[74]

3. OIRA Review

Under the Act, OMB/OIRA has 60 days from the date the NPRM is published in

---

68. *See* 44 U.S.C. § 3502(3) for definition of "collections of information"; *see also supra* Part II, ch. 3(D)(1).
69. 44 U.S.C. § 3506(c)(3)(A).
70. *Id.* § 3507(f). *See supra* Part II, ch. 3(D) for a more detailed discussion of the Act's coverage, including its limited exemptions.
71. *See* William Funk, *The Paperwork Reduction Act: Paperwork Reduction Meets Administrative Law*, 24 HARV. J. LEGIS. 1, 85–93 (1987) (discussing the interplay between the Act and the Order's predecessor, Exec. Order 12,291).
72. 5 C.F.R. § 1320.9.
73. *Id.* § 1320.11(a).
74. *Id.* § 1320.8(b)(3). The notice should also indicate whether the responses are voluntary and to what extent confidentiality will be provided. *Id.* Note also that section 208 of the E-Government Act requires agencies to conduct a "privacy impact assessment."

the *Federal Register* to file comments on the information-collection provisions.[75] The agency must demonstrate to OMB through a series of certifications that, among other considerations, it has taken every reasonable step to ensure that the information collection is the least burdensome necessary, that it is not duplicative of information otherwise accessible to the agency, and that the information has practical utility.[76]

C. The Regulatory Flexibility Act

1. Coverage

The Regulatory Flexibility Act directs all agencies to give particular attention to the potential impact of regulation on small businesses and other small entities and requires consideration of regulatory alternatives that are less burdensome to small entities.[77] Under the Act, the agency may have to prepare an initial regulatory flexibility analysis of the proposed rule's economic impact upon small entities whenever the agency must publish an NPRM pursuant to the APA.[78] The analysis requirement may be avoided if the head of the agency certifies in the NPRM that the proposed rule will not "have a significant economic impact on a substantial number of small entities" and sends the certification and supporting statement of reasons to the Chief Counsel for Advocacy of the Small Business Administration.[79] In addition, the 1996 amendments in SBREFA added a provision requiring a "covered agency," prior to issuance of the initial regulatory flexibility analysis, to convene a special review panel consisting of agency, OMB and SBA officials, and representatives of affected small entities.[80] The panel must file a public report on the impacts of the proposal within 60 days (however, only three agen-

---

75. 44 U.S.C. § 3507(d)(3). OMB also has 60 days following publication of the final rule to approve or disapprove the final provisions. *Id.* § 3507(d)(4)(C).

76. For a comprehensive discussion of these certifications, see OMB/OIRA, *The Paperwork Reduction Act of 1995: Implementing Guidance* (preliminary draft, Feb. 3, 1997), *available at* http://www.thecre.com/pdf/THE%20PAPERWORK%20REDUCTION%20ACT%20OF% 201995.pdf. *See also* U.S. Gov't Accountability Office, Paperwork Reduction Act: New Approach May be Needed to Reduce Government Burden on Public (GAO-05-424) (May 2005) (discussing these certifications and arguing for the need for improved compliance through adequate support for certifications). If OMB does comment on the information collection, the agency must explain, in conjunction with the final rule, how it has responded to OMB's comments. 44 U.S.C. § 3507(d)(2).

77. *See supra* Part II, ch. 3(C) for a more detailed analysis of the Regulatory Flexibility Act.

78. 5 U.S.C. § 603(a). See cases mentioned in Part II, ch. 3(C).

79. *Id.* § 605(b). The Regulatory Flexibility Act does not require an agency to conduct small-entity impact analysis when the agency does not regulate affected entities. *See* Michigan v. EPA, 213 F.3d 663, 688–89 (D.C. Cir. 2000) (finding EPA's regulations for state implementation plans under the Clean Air Act did not need to include RFA analysis for small entities creating emissions because the regulation did not intend to regulate small entities).

80. *Id.* § 609(b)–(e).

cies, EPA, OSHA, and the new Consumer Financial Protection Bureau, are included in the definition of "covered agency" for the purposes of this provision).[81] Even more important, SBREFA made this certification decision subject to judicial review.[82] If a regulatory flexibility (reg-flex) analysis is required, the initial analysis or a summary must be published in the NPRM,[83] and the final analysis or a summary of it must accompany the final rule in the *Federal Register.*[84]

2. *Content of the Analysis*

The Regulatory Flexibility Act requires that a reg-flex analysis be submitted for review by the Chief Council for Advocacy of the Small Business Administration. The reg-flex analysis is in some ways similar to the regulatory analysis required under Executive Order 12,866. The initial analysis must include a description and estimate of the number of affected small entities, a description of the compliance requirements, and identification—to the extent practicable—of federal rules that may duplicate, overlap, or conflict with the rule. It must also discuss significant alternatives that minimize economic impacts on small entities, including "tiering" (that is, non-uniform requirements that take account of small business concerns), use of performance standards, and exemptions.[85] The final reg-flex analysis (FRFA) must respond to comments and explain why each significant alternative was rejected.[86] The agency need not present its FRFA in any "particular mode of presentation," as long as the FRFA "compiles a meaningful, easily understood analysis that covers each requisite component dictated by the statute and makes the end product—whatever form it reasonably may take—readily available to the public."[87] Moreover, agencies may incorporate into a reg-flex analysis "any data or analysis contained in any other impact statement or analysis required by law."[88] One court has, in fact, upheld as adequate a final RFA

---

81. As of March 17, 2012, EPA reported that it had convened 42 such panels, with 7 to be scheduled, *see* http://www.epa.gov/sbrefa/sbar-panels.html; SBA reports that OSHA had convened 10, *see* http://archive.sba.gov/advo/laws/is_oshapanel.html. For an assessment of the implementation of this requirement, see U.S. GEN. ACCOUNTING OFFICE, REGULATORY REFORM: IMPLEMENTATION OF THE SMALL BUSINESS ADVOCACY REVIEW PANEL REQUIREMENTS (GAO-GGD-98-36) (MAR. 1998).
82. *Id.* § 611(a). *See supra* Part II, ch. 3(C).
83. *Id.* § 603(a).
84. 5 U.S.C. § 604(b).
85. *Id.* § 603(b)–(c). Both the Unfunded Mandates Reform Act, discussed below, and Exec. Order 12,866 require similar information for "significant regulatory actions." The laws permit these analyses to be combined. *See* 2 U.S.C. § 1532(c); 5 U.S.C. § 605(a).
86. 5 U.S.C. § 604. The agency must make copies of the final analysis available to the public and publish it, or a summary thereof, in the *Federal Register. Id.*
87. Associated Fisheries of Me., Inc. v. Daley, 127 F.3d 104, 115 (1st Cir. 1997).
88. *See id.* at 115. Yet another executive order requiring cost-benefit analysis in a non-rulemaking context is Exec. Order No. 12,893, "Principles for Federal Infrastructure Investments," 3 C.F.R. 854 (1993 compilation).

that consisted *only* of the initial reg-flex analysis and the agency's response to comments on it.[89]

3. *Review by the Small Business Administration*

The authority of the Chief Counsel for Advocacy of the Small Business Administration is limited to reviewing the analyses and filing comments on the rulemaking; he or she cannot prevent the promulgation of a rule—although the added judicial review provisions have provided a boost to the Chief Counsel's practical authority. The Regulatory Flexibility Act also requires at least annual reporting on agency compliance with the Act to both the President and Congress, and the Chief Counsel is specifically authorized to appear as amicus curiae (friend of the court) in actions brought to review a final agency rule.[90]

D. Unfunded Mandates Reform Act

1. *Coverage*

This legislation (UMRA), enacted in 1995,[91] requires Congress and executive agencies[92] to give special consideration to proposed legislation and regulations imposing mandates[93] on state, local, and tribal entities. It also contains a provision requiring agencies to prepare a written statement, in the nature of a regulatory analysis, for any proposed rulemaking that may result in an expenditure by state, local, or tribal governments in the aggregate, or by the private sector, in excess of $100 million (adjusted for infla-

---

89. *Id.* The court added, "Section 604 prescribes the content of an FRFA, but it does not demand a particular mode of presentation." *But see* Nat'l Ass'n of Psychiatric Health Sys. v. Shalala, 120 F. Supp. 2d 33, 43 (D.D.C. 2000) ("Secretary did not obtain data or analyze available data on the impact of the final rule on small entities, nor did she properly assess the impact the final rule would have on small entities.") However, in that case, the court permitted the rule to stay in effect while the agency completed a new FRFA. On the other hand, in *North Carolina Fisheries Ass'n v. Daley*, 27 F. Supp. 2d 650 (E.D. Va. 1998), the court set aside a portion of the fishing quota for a repeated violation of the RFA.

90. *Id.* § 612. For a defense of this provision's constitutionality despite a challenge from the Department of Justice, see John Contrubis, *Constitutional Analysis of Sec. 612(b) of the Regulatory Flexibility Act Authorizing the Chief Counsel for Advocacy of the Small Business Administration to Appear as Amicus Curiae in Any Court Action to Review an Agency Rule*, Memorandum of the American Law Division (Cong. Research Serv.) (Oct. 22, 1993); Appendix D of House Report 104-49, Regulatory Flexibility Act Amendments, pt. 1, 104th Cong. 1st Sess., *available at* http://www.gpo.gov/fdsys/pkg/CRPT-104hrpt49/html/CRPT-104hrpt49-pt1.htm.

91. *Supra* note 7. *See supra* Part II, ch. 3(G) for a more extensive analysis of the UMRA.

92. The Act does not cover "independent regulatory agencies." 2 U.S.C. § 658(1).

93. The term *mandates* is carefully defined in the Act. *Id.* § 658 (5)–(7).

tion) in any one year. This Act thus contains the only broad regulatory analysis requirement currently mandated by statute; however, its impact is lessened because its provisions for judicial review of agency compliance with the Act are limited.[94]

Interestingly, a Congressional Research Service study reports that from 1995 to
2010 agencies completed written mandate cost estimate statements for only nine pub-
lic-sector rules with costs of more than $100 million per year (adjusted for inflation)
on state, local, and tribal governments, while during the same period they did so for
183 private-sector rules because they required this level of expenditures by the private sector.[95]

2. *Content of the Analysis*

Statements prepared under UMRA must include (1) citation to the law under which
the rule is being promulgated; (2) "a qualitative and quantitative assessment of the
anticipated costs and benefits of the Federal mandate . . . as well as the effect of the
Federal mandate on health, safety, and the natural environment," along with an analysis
of the availability of federal funds to help governments pay for the mandate; (3) estimates of future compliance costs and of disproportionate budgetary effects on regions
or particular governments or segments of the private sector; (4) estimates of the effect
on aspects of the national economy; and (5) a summary of the agency's consultations
with elected representatives.[96] A summary of this statement must appear in the notice of
proposed rulemaking.[97] However, UMRA does allow agencies to prepare the statement
"in conjunction with or as a part of any other statement or analysis."[98]

Before issuing a final rule that was subject to the above requirements, the agency
must "identify and consider a reasonable number of regulatory alternatives and from
those alternatives, select the least costly, most cost-effective or least burdensome alternative that achieves the objectives of the rule," or explain why it did not do so.[99]

---

94. *See supra* Part II, ch. 3(G).
95. *See* Robert Jay Dilger & Richard S. Beth, Cong. Research Serv., R40957, Unfunded Mandates
    Reform Act: History, Impact, and Issues 29 (2011), *available at* http://assets.opencrs.com/rpts/
    R40957_20110419.pdf.
96. 2 U.S.C. § 658 (5)–(7). The agency must also develop a plan to specially notify small govern-
    ments of such requirements and develop a process to receive meaningful and timely input
    from elected officials. *Id.* §§ 1533, 1534. In that connection, an exemption from the Federal
    Advisory Committee Act is carved out for such consultations. *Id.* § 1534.
97. *Id.* § 1532(b).
98. *Id.* § 1532(c).
99. *Id.* § 1535(a), (b). *See generally* Memorandum from Alice Rivlin, OMB Director, for the Heads
    of Executive Departments and Agencies, Guidance for Implementing Title II of S. 1 (Mar. 31,
    1995), *available at* http://www.whitehouse.gov/sites/default/files/omb/memoranda/m95-
    09.pdf (attaching a Memorandum from OIRA Administrator Sally Katzen). Examples of agency
    rulemakings meeting these requirements can be found in OMB, OIRA, 2011 Report to Con-
    gress on the Benefits and Costs of Federal Regulations and Unfunded Mandates on State, Local,
    and Tribal Entities 94–98, *available at* http://www.whitehouse.gov/sites/default/files/omb/
    inforeg/2011_cb/2011_cba_report.pdf.

3. *Review of the Analyses*

UMRA is not very prescriptive with respect to the review of agency statements prepared under the Act. It simply provides that the OMB Director "collect from the agencies the statements prepared"[100] and periodically forward copies of such statements to the Director of the Congressional Budget Office on a reasonably timely basis.[101] The Act further requires the OMB Director to submit annual "certification[s]" to Congress concerning agency compliance with the Act.[102]

A GAO study issued shortly after its passage found that the Act had "only limited direct impact on agencies' rulemaking in the first 2 years since its implementation."[103] The study found that of the 110 economically significant rules promulgated during that period, 78 did not require written statements for various reasons,[104] and most other such rules were accompanied by information that met UMRA's requirements.[105] A more recent GAO study found decidedly mixed reviews of the effectiveness of both the legislative and rulemaking review provisions.[106]

E. OMB Peer Review Bulletin

On December 16, 2004, OMB issued an Information Quality Bulletin for Peer Review.[107] The Bulletin requires administrative agencies[108] to conduct a peer review

---

100. 2 U.S.C. § 1536 (1).

101. 2 U.S.C. § 1536 (2).

102. 2 U.S.C. § 1535(c).

103. U.S. Gen. Accounting Office, Unfunded Mandates Reform Act Has Had Little Effect on Agencies' Rulemaking Actions 3 (GAO/GGD-98-30) (Feb. 1998), *available at* http://www.gao.gov/archive/1998/gg98030.pdf (report to the Sen. Comm. on Governmental Affairs).

104. *Id.* at 12–15.

105. *Id.* at 18–20.

106. Gov't Accountability Office, Unfunded Mandates: Opinions Vary About Reform Act's Strengths, Weaknesses, and Options for Improvement 13 (GAO-05-454) (Mar. 31, 2005), *available at* http://www.gao.gov/new.items/d05454.pdf. *See also* Curtis Copeland, *Regulatory Analysis Requirements: A Review and Recommendations for Reform, supra* note 9, at 33–34. Copeland reported that executive agencies mentioned the Unfunded Mandates Reform Act in 77 of the 83 major rules issued in 2010; however, the agencies prepared a written statement pursuant to Section 202 of UMRA in only 4 of the 77 rules. In the remaining 73 rules, the agencies either referred to another analysis as satisfying the requirements of UMRA (9 rules) or cited one of the many exemptions and exceptions to UMRA coverage, such as no "expenditures" of at least $100 million in a year (30 rules), no UMRA "mandate" as defined in the Act (16 rules), or no prior notice of proposed rulemaking (9 rules).

107. Executive Office of the President, Office of Mgmt. & Budget, Final Information Quality Bulletin for Peer Review, 70 Fed. Reg. 2664 (Jan. 14, 2005). For the history of the public comment process on this Bulletin, see Part I (D)(3), *supra.*

108. The Bulletin applies to "agencies," as defined in the Paperwork Reduction Act, 44 U.S.C. § 3502(1). *See* Section I(2), *id.* at 2674. This definition in the Paperwork Reduction Act encompasses "any executive department, military department, Government corporation, Government-

of "scientific information disseminations that contain findings or conclusions that represent the official position of one or more agencies of the federal government."[109] It was "issued under the Information Quality Act and OMB's general authorities to oversee the quality of agency information, analyses, and regulatory actions."[110] It "establishes minimum standards for when peer review is required for scientific information and the types of peer review that should be considered by agencies in different circumstances."[111]

The Bulletin provides agencies with broad discretion in implementation:

> The purpose of the Bulletin is to enhance the quality and credibility of the government's scientific information. We recognize that different types of peer review are appropriate for different types of information. Under this Bulletin, agencies are granted broad discretion to weigh the benefits and costs of using a particular peer review mechanism for a specific information product. The selection of an appropriate peer review mechanism for scientific information is left to the agency's discretion. Various types of information are exempted from the requirements of this Bulletin, including time-sensitive health and safety determinations, in order to ensure that peer review does not unduly delay the release of urgent findings.[112]

The requirements in the Peer Review Bulletin specifically apply to agency rulemaking. In fact, OMB makes clear that:

> Peer review should not be confused with public comment and other stakeholder processes. The selection of participants in a peer review is based on expertise, with due consideration of independence and conflict of interest. Furthermore, notice-and-comment procedures for agency rulemaking do not provide an adequate substitute for peer review, as some experts—especially those most knowledgeable in a field—may not file public comments with federal agencies.[113]

---

controlled corporation or other establishment in the executive branch (including the Executive Office of the President) or any independent regulatory agency [except the Federal Election Commission]."

109. 70 Fed. Reg. at 2664.
110. *Id.* at 2666. See Part II, ch. 3(H) for an analysis of the Information Quality Act.
111. 70 Fed. Reg. at 2666.
112. *Id.* at 2665.
113. *Id.* In addition, the Bulletin states that:

> [T]he Bulletin does not directly cover information supplied to the government by third parties (e.g., studies by private consultants, companies and private, non-profit organizations, or research institutions such as universities). However, if an agency plans to disseminate information supplied by a third party (e.g., using this information as the basis for an agency's factual determination that a particular behavior causes a disease), the requirements of the Bulletin apply, if the dissemination is "influential."

Id. at 2667.

Moreover, rulemaking agencies must conduct any required peer reviews early enough to allow the agency to plan its regulatory approaches accordingly:

> When an information product is a critical component of rule-making [sic], it is important to obtain peer review before the agency announces its regulatory options so that any technical corrections can be made before the agency becomes invested in a specific approach or the positions of interest groups have hardened. If review occurs too late, it is unlikely to contribute to the course of a rulemaking. Furthermore, investing in a more rigorous peer review early in the process "may provide net benefit by reducing the prospect of challenges to a regulation that later may trigger time-consuming and resource-draining litigation."[114]

The result of the peer review is a report—

> an evaluation or critique that is used by the authors of the draft to improve the product. Peer review [reports] typically evaluate[] the clarity of hypotheses, the validity of the research design, the quality of data collection procedures, the robustness of the methods employed, the appropriateness of the methods for the hypotheses being tested, the extent to which the conclusions follow from the analysis, and the strengths and limitations of the overall product.[115]

Rulemaking agencies must consider the need to make these peer review reports available to potential commenters in the rulemaking: "If the scientific information is used to support a final rule then, where practicable, the peer review report shall be made available to the public with enough time for the public to consider the implications of the peer review report for the rule being considered."[116] And when issuing the final rule,

> [I]f an agency relies on influential scientific information or a highly influential scientific assessment subject to the requirements of this Bulletin in support of a regulatory action, the agency shall include in the administrative record for that action a certification that explains how the agency has complied with the requirements of this Bulletin and the Information Quality Act. Relevant materials are to be placed in the administrative record.[117]

The Bulletin also contains a series of other requirements for agencies, including "a systematic process of peer review planning for influential scientific information

---

114. *Id.* at 2668 (citing Fred Anderson et al., *Regulatory Improvement Legislation: Risk Assessment, Cost-Benefit Analysis, and Judicial Review*, 11 Duke Envtl. L. & Pol'y F. 132 (2000)).

115. *Id.* at 2665.

116. *Id.* at 2672.

117. *Id.* at 2673. But note that this Bulletin, like the executive orders discussed in this Part, also provides that it is not intended to create any private rights of enforcement of judicial review. *See* Section XII, *id.* at 2677.

(including highly influential scientific assessments) that the agency plans to dissemi-
nate in the foreseeable future."[118] This includes a "web-accessible listing of forthcoming influential scientific disseminations (i.e., an agenda) that is regularly updated by
the agency."[119] For each entry on the agenda, the agency shall describe the peer review plan, including a specifically prescribed series of entries, and a link from the
agenda to each document made public pursuant to this Bulletin.[120] These peer review
agendas must be updated at least every six months. Agencies must also submit an
annual report on these activities to OIRA.[121] OMB now regularly reports on agency
peer review activities.[122]

The draft versions of this Bulletin occasioned considerable criticism—including
its potential for increasing the ossification of rulemaking,[123] and the final version
addressed many of the concerns.[124] There is no question, however, that these additional requirements do add procedural complications to rulemakings that are based
on scientific information.[125]

F. Assessment of Federal Regulations and Policies on Families

An omnibus appropriations act is the basis for a statutorily required "family
policymaking assessment" to be performed by agencies before implementing policies and regulations that may affect family well-being. Most of these requirements
call for extremely subjective judgments on the part of the agency.[126]

---

118. *Id.* at 2672.
119. *Id.*
120. *See* Section V, *id.* at 2676–77.
121. *See* Section VI, *id.* at 2677.
122. *See* 2011 REPORT TO CONGRESS, *supra* note 99, at 86–90 (finding 193 total peer reviews and 31
     reviews of "highly influential scientific assessments" in FY 2010).
123. *See, e.g.*, Randolph J. May, *OMB's Peer Review Proposal—Swamped by Science?*, 29 ADMIN.
     & REG. L. NEWS 4 (Spring 2004); Sidney A. Shapiro, *OMB's Dubious Peer Review Procedures*,
     34 Envtl. L. Rep. (Envtl. L. Inst.) 10,064 (2004).
124. *See* Sarah Grimmer, Note, *Public Controversy Over Peer Review*, 57 ADMIN. L. REV. 275, 283
     (2005) (commenting that although some former critics approve of the final bulletin, others
     remain critical).
125. For a positive review of the Bulletin, see Patrick A. Fuller, Note, *How Peer Review of Agency
     Science Can Help Rulemaking: Enhancing Judicial Deference at the Frontiers of Knowl-
     edge*, 75 GEO. WASH. L. REV. 931 (2007). For a broader look at peer review in regulation,
     written before the drafting of the OMB Bulletin, see Lars Noah, *Peer Review and Regulatory
     Reform*, 30 ENVTL. L. REP. (Envtl. L. Inst.) 10,606 (2000). *See also* Louis J. Virelli III, *Scientific
     Peer Review and Administrative Legitimacy*, 61 ADMIN. L. REV. 723 (2009) (suggesting the
     importance of peer review for administrative legitimacy).
126. Specifically, the agency should consider whether:
     (1) the action strengthens or erodes the stability or safety of the family and, particu-
     larly, the marital commitment;
     (2) the action strengthens or erodes the authority and rights of parents in the educa-
     tion, nurture, and supervision of their children;

The provision requires agency heads to submit a written certification to OMB and Congress that the assessment has been done. In doing so, agency heads must provide an "adequate rationale" for implementing actions that may negatively affect family well-being.[127] OMB is required to ensure that policies and regulations are implemented consistent with these requirements. It also must compile, index, and submit annually to Congress the written certifications it receives.[128] Agencies are specifically required to conduct assessments in accordance with this section's criteria when requested by a Member of Congress.[129] Agency actions or inactions under this law are not subject to judicial review—the law states that it is not intended to create any right or benefit enforceable against the United States.[130]

This law appears to have had a negligible impact on the rulemaking process. A Westlaw search on September 11, 2011, turned up only three rules in which the agency issued a family impact assessment: an INS rule affecting family reunification, and two similar "head start" rules.[131] There were numerous statements of no impact.

G. Privacy Assessments

Another omnibus appropriations act requires agencies to have a chief privacy officer who is supposed to conduct "a privacy impact assessment of proposed rules" "including the type of personally identifiable information collected and the number of people affected."[132]

---

(3) the action helps the family perform its functions, or substitutes governmental activity for the function;

(4) the action increases or decreases disposable income or poverty of families and children;

(5) the proposed benefits of the action justify the financial impact on the family;

(6) the action may be carried out by State or local government or by the family; and

(7) the action establishes an implicit or explicit policy concerning the relationship between the behavior and personal responsibility of youth, and the norms of society.

Omnibus Appropriations Act FY 99, Pub. L. No. 105-277 § 654(c) (1998).

127. *Id.* § 654(d)(1).
128. *Id.* § 654(d)(2).
129. *Id.* § 654(e).
130. *Id.* § 654(f).
131. *See, e.g.,* Head Start Program, 73 Fed. Reg. 1285, 1295 (Jan. 8, 2008); Implementation of *Hernandez v. Reno* Settlement Agreement, 65 Fed. Reg. 43,677, 43,679 (July 14, 2000).
132. Consolidated Appropriations Act of 2005, § 522(a)(5), Pub. L. No. 108-447, 5 U.S.C § 552a note. The Act requires "each agency" to do this, but confusingly refers to "proposed rules of the Department."

H. Other Executive Orders

Other executive orders require analysis of particular regulations. These orders are relevant only to certain regulatory topics and cover only executive departments and agencies, not independent regulatory agencies. There are no specific time frames associated with OMB review under these executive orders. They are presented in chronological order, not necessarily in order of importance.[133]

(1) Executive Order 12,630, "Governmental Actions and Interference with Constitutionally-Protected Property Rights," requires agencies to limit interference with private property rights protected under the Fifth Amendment to the Constitution.[134] The order requires agencies to consider certain criteria when considering policies with takings implications[135] and to include an analysis of the impact of proposed regulations on such property rights in its submissions to OMB.[136] A 2003 GAO report on the experience under this order in four agencies showed that there had been relatively little impact on the rulemaking process. Of the 375 *Federal Register* notices issued by those agencies that mentioned the EO in 1989, 1997, and 2002, only 50 specified that an assessment of the rule's potential for takings implications was prepared, and of these, only 10 noted that the rule had the potential for "significant" takings implications.[137] In addition, GAO added:

---

133. ACUS observed that the profusion of these analytical requirements has become a problem: "While these analytical emphases can be rationalized individually, in the aggregate, they can result in redundant requirements, boilerplate-laden documents, circumvention, delays, and clutter in the Federal Register." ACUS Recommendation 93-4 (part I of preamble). *See also* Stuart Shapiro, *Defragmenting the Regulatory Process*, 31 RISK ANALYSIS 893 (2011). The ABA has also urged that Congress and the President show restraint in establishing analytical requirements. ABA House of Delegates Recommendation on Rulemaking Impact Analyses (Feb. 1992); *see also* U.S. GEN. ACCOUNTING OFFICE, FEDERAL RULEMAKING: PROCEDURAL AND ANALYTICAL REQUIREMENTS AT OSHA AND OTHER AGENCIES (GAO-01-852T) (June 14, 2001), *available at* http://www.gao.gov/new.items/d01852t.pdf (testimony of Victor Rezendes, Managing Director, Strategic Issues Team, before the House Comm. on Education and the Workforce) (describing the many requirements and their impact on OSHA rulemaking).
134. Exec. Order 12,630, 3 C.F.R. 554 (1988 compilation). The Department of Justice issued guidelines for the order. DEPARTMENT OF JUSTICE, ATTORNEY GENERAL'S GUIDELINES FOR THE EVALUATION OF RISK AND AVOIDANCE OF UNANTICIPATED TAKINGS (1988) [hereinafter GUIDELINES FOR THE EVALUATION OF RISK]. Some agencies have their own supplemental guidelines, which must be approved by the Department of Justice.
135. Exec. Order 12,630, *supra* note 134, § 4.
136. *Id.* § 5.
137. *See* U.S. GEN. ACCOUNTING OFFICE, REGULATORY TAKINGS: IMPLEMENTATION OF EXECUTIVE ORDER ON GOVERNMENT ACTIONS AFFECTING PRIVATE PROPERTY USE 19 (GAO-03-1015) (Sept. 2003).

Agencies provided us a few written examples of takings implication assessments. Agency officials said that these assessments are not always documented in writing, and, because of the passage of time, those assessments that were put in writing may no longer be on file. They also noted that these assessments are internal, predecisional documents that generally are not subject to the Freedom of Information Act or judicial review; thus they are not typically retained in a central file for a rulemaking or other decision, and therefore they are difficult to locate.[138]

(2) Executive Order 12,898, "Federal Actions to Address Environmental Justice in Minority Populations and Low-Income Populations,"[139] requires each agency to develop an "environmental justice strategy . . . that identifies and addresses disproportionately high and adverse human health or environmental effects of its programs, policies, and activities on minority populations and low-income populations,"[140] and identify, among other things, rules that should be revised to meet the objectives of the order. Each agency must ensure any such activities "that substantially affect human health or the environment" do not exclude persons (including populations) from participating in or getting the benefits of, or subject them to discrimination under, such programs, policies, and activities.[141] An agency's public documents, notices, and hearings relating to human health and the environment must be "concise, understandable, and readily accessible."[142] This order was accompanied by a Presidential Memorandum on Environmental Justice that "underscore[s] certain provisions of existing law that can help ensure that communities have a safe and healthful environment."[143]

(3) Executive Order 12,988, "Civil Justice Reform,"[144] requires agencies to conduct reviews on civil justice and litigation impact issues before proposing legislation or issuing proposed regulations. With respect to regulations, the order requires agencies to "make every reasonable effort to ensure":

> that the regulation, as appropriate—(A) specifies in clear language the preemptive effect, if any, to be given to the regulation; (B) specifies in clear language the effect on existing Federal law or regula-

---

138. *Id.* at 17.
139. Issued Feb. 11, 1994, 59 Fed. Reg. 7629 (Feb. 16, 1994).
140. *Id.* § 1-103.
141. *Id.* § 2-2.
142. *Id.* § 5-5(c).
143. Also issued Feb. 11, 1994, and *available at* http://govinfo.library.unt.edu/npr/library/direct/memos/21a6.html.
144. Issued Feb. 5, 1996, 61 Fed. Reg. 4729 (Feb. 7, 1996).

tion, if any, including all provisions repealed, circumscribed, displaced, impaired, or modified; (C) provides a clear legal standard for affected conduct rather than a general standard, while promoting simplification and burden reduction; (D) specifies in clear language the retroactive effect, if any, to be given to the regulation; (E) specifies whether administrative proceedings are to be required before parties may file suit in court and, if so, describes those proceedings and requires the exhaustion of administrative remedies; (F) defines key terms, either explicitly or by reference to other regulations or statutes that explicitly define those items; and (G) addresses other important issues affecting clarity and general draftsmanship of regulations. . . .[145]

(4) Executive Order 13,045, "Protection of Children from Environmental Health Risks and Safety Risks,"[146] requires that agencies issuing "economically significant"[147] rules that also concern an environmental health risk or safety risk that an agency has reason to believe may disproportionately affect children must include an evaluation of the environmental health or safety effects of the planned regulation on children. Agencies must also include an explanation of why the planned regulation is preferable to other potentially effective and reasonably feasible alternatives considered by the agencies. Provision is made for emergency rules and for inclusion of this analysis "as part of any other required analysis." This order revoked the Reagan-era Executive Order 12,606, "The Family."[148]

(5) Executive Order 13,132, "Federalism,"[149] requires consideration of issues of federalism by executive departments and agencies. Its purpose is "to ensure that the principles of federalism established by the Framers [of the Constitution] guide the Executive departments and agencies in the formulation and implementation of policies."[150] Under the order, the head of each executive department or agency is required to appoint an official who is responsible for the order's implementation. It also provides that "no agency shall promulgate any regulation that has federalism implications, that imposes

---

145. *Id.* § 3(b)(2).
146. *See* U.S. Gov't Accountability Office, Environmental Health: High-Level Strategy and Leadership Needed to Continue Progress Toward Protecting Children from Environmental Threats (GAO-10-205) (January 2010), *available at* http://www.gao.gov/new.items/d10205.pdf.
147. *See supra* text accompanying notes 15–16.
148. *But see* the statutory family-impact-analysis requirement discussed above in section F.
149. Issued Aug. 4, 1999, 64 Fed. Reg. 43,255 (Aug. 10, 1999). It was preceded by an earlier Clinton Order on Federalism, Exec. Order 13,083, 63 Fed. Reg. 27,651 (May 19, 1998), which was withdrawn by Exec. Order 13,095, 63 Fed. Reg. 42,565 (Aug. 7, 1998) to allow for more consultation with affected groups.
150. *Id.*

substantial direct compliance costs on State and local governments, and that is not required by statute," unless the agency (1) has consulted with state and local officials early in the process, (2) submits to OMB copies of any written communications from such officials, and (3) published in the pre-amble of the rule "a federalism summary impact statement" describing the consultations, "a summary of the nature of their concerns and the agency's position supporting the need to issue the regulation, and a statement of the extent to which the concerns of State and local officials have been met."[151]

Among other things, this order contains direction to the agencies that they construe a statute to be preemptive of state regulations "only where the statute contains an express preemption provision or there is some other clear evidence that the Congress intended preemption of State law, or where the exercise of State authority conflicts with the exercise of Federal authority under the Federal statute."[152] In addition, agencies are directed to "review the processes under which State and local governments apply for waivers of statutory and regulatory requirements and take appropriate steps to streamline those processes."[153] OMB is made responsible for coordinating and reviewing agency actions so that they are consistent with the requirements of the executive order,[154] and it issued guidance in 1999.[155] It should be noted that the previous version, Executive Order 12,612, issued in 1987 by President Reagan, had very little impact on the rulemaking process.[156]

(6) Executive Order 13,175, "Consultation with Indian Tribal Governments,"[157] requires the same sorts of consultations and considerations as does the "Federalism" order, described above.

---

151. Exec. Order 13,132, *supra* note 149, § 6(b). *See also* Cal. Wilderness Coal. v. U.S. Dep't of Energy, 631 F.3d 1072 (9th Cir. 2011) (enforcing requirement under Energy Policy Act for DOE to undertake study of electric transmission congestion "in consultation with affected States" by finding that failure of DOE to consult with affected states regarding study of electric transmission congestion was not harmless error and that entire study had to be vacated).

152. Exec. Order 13,132, *supra* note 149, § 4(a).

153. *Id.* at § 7(a).

154. *Id.* § 8. The designated agency official is directed to certify that all applicable requirements of this order are met as part of OMB's review process under Executive Order 12,866. In addition, independent regulatory agencies are "encouraged" to comply with the provisions of this order. *Id.* § 9.

155. Memorandum for Heads of Executive Departments and Agencies, and Independent Regulatory Agencies, from Jacob J. Lew, OMB Director, Guidance for Implementing E.O. 13,132, "Federalism" (M-00-02, Oct. 28, 1999), *available at* http://www.whitehouse.gov/sites/default/files/omb/assets/regulatory_matters_pdf/m00-02.pdf.

156. *See* U.S. GEN. ACCOUNTING OFFICE, FEDERALISM: PREVIOUS INITIATIVES HAVE HAD LITTLE EFFECT ON AGENCY RULEMAKING (GAO/T-GGD-99-31) (June 30, 1999), *available at* http://www.gao.gov/archive/1999/gg99131t.pdf (finding that only five of the more than 11,000 final rules that federal agencies issued between April 1996 and December 1998 indicated that the agencies had conducted a federalism assessment).

(7) Executive Order 13,211, "Actions Concerning Regulations That Significantly Affect Energy Supply, Distribution, or Use,"[158] requires agencies to prepare and submit to OMB a "Statement of Energy Effects" for significant energy actions, to the extent permitted by law. The statements must cover "any adverse effects on energy supply, distribution, or use (including a shortfall in supply, price increases, and increased use of foreign supplies)" for the action and reasonable alternatives and their effects.[159] They must be published (or summarized) in the related NPRM and final rule. A "significant energy action" is one that is "significant" under E.O. 12,866 and is likely to have a significant adverse energy effect, or is designated by the OMB. OMB also issued a memorandum on "Guidance for Implementing E.O. 12,311."[160]

(8) Executive Order 13,272, "Proper Consideration of Small Entities in Agency Rulemaking,"[161] requires agencies to notify the Small Business Administration's Office of the Chief Counsel for Advocacy of draft rules that may have a significant economic impact on a substantial number of small entities when the draft rule is submitted to the OIRA or, if submission to OIRA is not required, "at a reasonable time prior to publication of the rule."[162] The Chief Counsel is authorized to submit comments on the draft rule. Agencies must give "every appropriate consideration" to any Chief Counsel comments on a draft rule.[163] If consistent with legal requirements, agencies must include in final rule preambles their response to any such comments, unless the agency head certifies that the public interest is not served by such action.[164] OIRA and the Office of Advocacy issued a Memorandum of Understanding on improving their working relationship to achieve better compliance with the Regulatory Flexibility Act.[165] However, it should be noted that this particular Executive Order merely underlines the agencies' responsibilities under the Regulatory Flexibility Act.[166]

---

157. Issued Nov. 6, 2000, 65 Fed. Reg. 67,249 (Nov. 9, 2000).
158. Issued May 18, 2001, 66 Fed. Reg. 28,355 (May 22, 2001).
159. *Id.* § 2(b).
160. Memorandum for Heads of Executive Departments and Agencies, and Independent Regulatory Agencies, from Mitchell E. Daniels, Director, Guidance for Implementing E.O. 13,211 (M-01-27, July 13, 2001), *available at* http://regs.dot.gov/requirements/Memoranda%2001-27.pdf.
161. Issued Aug. 13, 2002, 67 Fed. Reg. 53,461 (Aug. 16, 2002).
162. *Id.* § 3(b).
163. *Id.* § 3(c).
164. *Id.*
165. Signed March 19, 2002, *available at* http://www.sba.gov/advo/laws/law_mou02.pdf.
166. *See* Michael Herz, *Rulemaking Chapter*, DEVELOPMENTS IN ADMINISTRATIVE LAW AND REGULATORY PRACTICE 2001-2002, at 172 (Jeffrey S. Lubbers ed., 2003) ("[T]he order adds nothing substantively and little procedurally to existing requirements. In essence it is a reminder to agencies of the existence of the Regulatory Flexibility Act.").

The Office of Advocacy has also issued a lengthy guide for agencies on compliance with that Act.[167]

(9) Executive Order 13,563, "Improving Regulation and Regulatory Review,"[168]
represents an elaboration on the primary rulemaking review Executive Order
12,866. It is reproduced in Appendix B and discussed at Part I(D)(4).

(10) Executive Order 13,609, "Promoting International Regulatory Cooperation,"[169]
requires that for significant regulations with significant international impacts,
executive agencies should consider regulatory approaches of foreign governments where consistent with a plan developed by the government under this
order.

I. Coordination of Analysis Requirements

Both the initial regulatory flexibility analysis and the preliminary regulatory
analysis involve specific calculation or assessment of the economic impact of the
proposed rule, as well as analysis of alternative regulatory approaches to addressing the problem. This kind of analysis requires that the agency have both a thorough understanding of the nature of the problem and data that can be used to estimate
the effects of alternative courses of action. Therefore, where these requirements
apply, agencies must allocate relatively large amounts of resources to preparing the
NPRM and supporting documents.[170]

The contents of the various required regulatory analyses may overlap sufficiently to
permit collapsing them into a single document or incorporating them by reference to
minimize redundancy. Both the Regulatory Flexibility Act and the Unfunded Mandates
Reform Act specifically provide that agencies may perform regulatory analyses in conjunction with or as a part of any other analysis required by law, as long as the analysis
satisfies each Act's requirements.[171] The Council on Environmental Quality's (CEQ's)
regulations governing agency preparation of environmental impact statements (EISs)
require that any cost-benefit analysis being considered for a proposed action "be incorporated by reference or appended to the [EIS] as an aid in evaluating the environmental
consequences."[172] Executive Order 12,866 also makes specific reference to the require-

---

167. *See* SBA Office of Advocacy, A Guide for Government Agencies—How to Comply with the Regu-
     latory Flexibility Act (June 2010), *available at* http://www.sba.gov/advo/laws/rfaguide.pdf.
168. Issued Jan. 18, 2011, 76 Fed. Reg. 3821 (Jan. 21, 2011).
169. Issued May 1, 2012, 77 Fed. Reg. 26,413 (May 4, 2012). *See also* Part II, ch.7 (A)(3).
170. *See* Thomas O. McGarity, *The Role of Regulatory Analysis in Regulatory Decisionmaking*,
     1985 ACUS 107 (providing study of agencies' regulatory analysis activities). For an ex-
     panded version of this report, see Thomas O. McGarity, Reinventing Rationality: The Role of
     Regulatory Analysis in the Federal Bureaucracy (1991).
171. *See supra* note 88 and accompanying text. As of this writing, ACUS is considering whether
     additional consolidation might be possible, based on the Copeland study cited in note 9, *supra*.
172. 40 C.F.R. § 1502.23. *See supra* Part II, ch. 3(B) (discussing EIS requirements).

ments of the Regulatory Flexibility Act and Paperwork Reduction Act.[173]

If a proposed rule is subject to all these requirements, it would generally make sense to make the regulatory flexibility analysis, as well as any required paperwork burden analysis, part of the regulatory analysis required by E.O. 12,866. However, where an EIS has been prepared, it would ordinarily be separate, or at least severable, from the regulatory analysis, even though the substance of each may overlap. This is because CEQ's regulations for preparing and circulating an EIS are quite specific and differ from the requirements for regulatory impact analysis.[174] Agencies may, however, include the EIS as an appendix to the regulatory impact statement.

The regulatory agendas required by E.O. 12,866 and the Regulatory Flexibility Act are intended to be coordinated.[175] In fact, the two agendas are issued together, as the *Unified Agenda of Federal Regulatory and Deregulatory Actions*, by the Regulatory Information Service Center.[176]

The rulemaking staff can refer to several sources for guidance on the substance of or criteria for completing the various analyses. The staff preparing a regulatory flexibility analysis may refer to a guide to the Regulatory Flexibility Act prepared for the Administrative Conference by Professor Verkuil[177] and a guide prepared by the SBA Office of Advocacy.[178] OMB has issued guidance on the Paperwork Reduction Act.[179]

---

173. Exec. Order No. 12,866, *supra* note 1, § 6(a)(3). Although the order, unlike its predecessor, does not otherwise address the possibility of consolidation of analyses, there is no reason to think that the policy has changed. Other executive orders expressly contemplate that agency analyses under those orders will be incorporated with existing submissions to OMB. *See, e.g.,* Exec. Order No. 12,630, 3 C.F.R. § 554 (1988 compilation); GUIDELINES FOR THE EVALUATION OF RISK, *supra* note 134, at ¶ 5(b).

174. *See* 40 C.F.R. §§ 1502.7, 1502.10, 1502.11 (providing page limit and format); 40 C.F.R. pt. 1503 (providing opportunity to comment on environmental impact statements).

175. *See* Exec. Order No. 12,866, *supra* note 1, § 4(b).

176. *See, e.g., Regulatory Information Service Center: Introduction to the Unified Agenda of Federal Regulatory and Deregulatory Actions* (June 1, 2011), *available at* http://www.reginfo.gov/public/jsp/eAgenda/StaticContent/201104/Preamble_8888.html. The Unified Agenda also incorporates the publication requirement for certain information relating to procurement regulations. *Id.*

177. *See* Paul R. Verkuil, *A Critical Guide to the Regulatory Flexibility Act*, 1982 DUKE L.J. 213.

178. *Supra* note 164.

179. *See* OMB/OIRA, THE PAPERWORK REDUCTION ACT OF 1995: IMPLEMENTING GUIDANCE (Draft, Aug. 16, 1999), *available at* http://www.thecre.com/pdf/PRAguidenew.pdf. This document, which was still being finalized as of September 2011, discusses the "supporting statement that the agency must provide in its certification under the Act." *Id.* at 63–78.

Chapter 3

The Notice of Proposed Rulemaking

Issues relating to the notice of proposed rulemaking (NPRM)[1] itself are covered in this chapter. The adequacy of the NPRM is closely related to the question of whether the public was afforded a meaningful opportunity to participate in the rulemaking. The public's right to participate in the rulemaking proceedings, which is triggered by the publication of the NPRM, is discussed in the next chapter.[2]

A. Publication Requirements[3]

For informal rulemaking not otherwise exempt from the APA's requirements, the Act requires that "general notice of proposed rulemaking shall be published in the Federal Register."[4] Publication in the *Federal Register* is referred to as "constructive notice" and is considered legally sufficient to give affected persons notice of the NPRM's contents.[5] Failure to publish a *Federal Register* notice of a proposed rule may result in the court setting aside the rule or remanding it to the agency for further proceedings.[6] The APA does provide, however, that *Federal Register* notice is not required if persons subject to the rule "are named and either personally served or otherwise have actual notice [of the rulemaking] in accordance with law."[7]

The prudent rulemaking staff should, however, view the "actual notice" substitute for the *Federal Register* notice with caution. Although there may be cases where other

---

1. This acronym reflects the fact that "rulemaking" is "rule making" in the Administrative Procedure Act. Some agencies now use the acronyms "NPR" or "NOPR."
2. *See infra* Part III, ch. 4.
3. For a discussion of publication of *final* rules under 5 U.S.C. § 552, see *infra* Part III, ch. 7(C).
4. 5 U.S.C. § 553(b). An agency's enabling statute or the statute authorizing the rulemaking may have other requirements that must be considered.
5. *See* Fed. Crop Ins. Corp. v. Merrill, 332 U.S. 380, 385 (1947) ("Congress has provided that the appearance of rules and regulations in the *Federal Register* gives legal notice of their contents.").
6. *See, e.g.*, PPG Indus. Inc. v. Costle, 659 F.2d 1239, 1249–51 (D.C. Cir. 1981). The rule may also be set aside where the NPRM is published in the *Federal Register,* but its contents are determined to be inadequate to afford a meaningful opportunity to comment on the issues in the rulemaking. *See infra* subsecs. (D) & (E).
7. 5 U.S.C. § 553(b).

forms of notice are equal or even superior to *Federal Register* notice, there simply is too much at stake in most rulemakings to not also publish an NPRM in the *Federal Register*.[8] Where interested persons can be readily identified, and more effective notice can be given by means other than the *Federal Register*,[9] many agencies both publish the proposal in the *Federal Register* and utilize other means of notice to better inform the affected public of the rulemaking.

The rulemaking staff should thus consider the advantages of other, supplementary methods of giving notice of the rulemaking in addition to that provided in the *Federal Register*.[10] General notice may be accomplished by means such as press releases to general, trade, or other specialized publications. The rulemaking staff also may "target" notice to persons most likely to be affected by the rule or to persons likely to have information needed to develop the rule. For example, notice may be sent to relevant trade associations or other membership organizations. The staff may also give notice through paid advertisements in the media or directly to individuals or groups concerned with the subject matter of the rule. The advent of the Internet and social media has obviously also opened up many new opportunities for electronic publication of notices.[11] However, agency attempts to use press releases or Internet publication of the notices in lieu of publication in the *Federal Register* do not suffice.[12] Nor is it enough for an agency to modify an existing rule

---

8. The APA's "actual notice" provision may aid agencies defending rules in court if the party challenging the rule had actual notice of an issue but, nevertheless, claims the *Federal Register* notice was inadequate. *See, e.g.*, Lloyd Noland Hosp. & Clinic v. Heckler, 762 F.2d 1561, 1565–66 (11th Cir. 1985); Water Transport Ass'n v. ICC, 684 F.2d 81, 84–85 (D.C. Cir. 1982); Conservation Law Found. of New England, Inc. v. Clark, 590 F. Supp. 1467, 1475–76 (D. Mass. 1984). But the provision of "actual notice" may be of little help where the agency fails to publish any NPRM in the *Federal Register*. *See, e.g.*, Rodway v. Dep't of Agric., 514 F.2d 809, 815 (D.C. Cir. 1975).

9. Proceedings to establish utility rates fall in this category. A combination of personal service, circulation with utility bills, posting, and so on might give notice of the proceeding to all affected persons.

10. *See* ACUS Recommendation 71-6, *Public Participation in Administrative Hearings*, 38 Fed. Reg. 19,789 (July 23, 1973).

11. *See* the discussion and the sources cited, *supra* in Chapter 1(C)(3) of this Part.

12. *See* Util. Solid Waste Activities Group v. EPA, 236 F.3d 749 (D.C. Cir. 2001) (rejecting EPA's argument that petitioners received "actual notice" when EPA published a change to a rule on its website and when it held a meeting attended by counsel for petitioners). "This court has never found that Internet notice is an acceptable substitute for publication in the Federal Register, and we refuse to do so now. . . . In any event, EPA has not even alleged that the petitioners were 'named' in the Internet publication, as APA § 553(b) would require if this sort of notice were sufficient." *Id.* at 754. *See also* Sugar Cane Growers Coop. of Fla. v. Veneman, 289 F.3d 89, 95–96 (D.C. Cir. 2002) (agency did not comply with APA notice requirements when it released a press release and "notice of program implementation" detailing guidelines for program participants even though the agency maintained the program was voluntary and not rulemaking). The agency's argument that the lack of notice-and-comment rulemaking was a "harmless error" was without merit because it was unclear to what extent the omission might cause harm. *Id.* at 96–97 (citing Sheppard v. Sullivan, 906 F.2d 756, 761–62 (D.C. Cir. 1990)).

through a "reconsideration" order without publishing it or an NPRM in the *Federal Register*.[13]

B. Contents of the Notice of Proposed Rulemaking

Section 553 of APA provides that the NPRM must state the "time, place, and nature" of the public proceedings.[14] The generality of this requirement may stem from the fact that section 553's notice provision applies both to formal rulemaking (where an oral trial-type hearing is required) and to notice-and-comment rulemaking. In the context of notice-and-comment rulemaking, this language requires the agency to specify the type of rule involved; the time during which the agency will receive comments on the proposal; and instructions regarding the manner of filing comments.[15]

The APA does not specify a minimum period for comment.[16] A common misconception is that the APA prescribes a 30-day minimum comment period, a belief that may derive from the APA's requirement that final rules be published 30 days prior to their effective date.[17] A reasonable time should be allowed for comment, with "reasonableness" judged in relation to the particular facts of each rulemaking. Executive Order 12,866 provides that most rulemakings "should include a comment period of not less than 60 days."[18] In addition, Executive Order 12,889, implementing the North

---

13. *See* Sprint Corp. v. FCC, 315 F.3d 369 (D.C. Cir. 2003). *See also* Atl. Urological Assocs., P.A. v. Leavitt, 549 F. Supp. 2d 13, 19 (D.D.C. 2008), *vacated on other grounds*, 549 F. Supp. 2d 20 (granting injunction because "while the Secretary admits that [the agency] issued the Final Rule pursuant to 'informal' comment, no record indicating the nature and substance of such comments has been presented to the Court for review").

14. 5 U.S.C. § 553(b)(1).

15. The rules of the Administrative Committee of the Federal Register contain more specific requirements for the contents of the "formal" portions of the *Federal Register* notice. See the discussion in the next section of this chapter.

16. In 1993, ACUS recommended that Congress amend the APA to "specify a comment period of 'no fewer than 30 days,' provided that a good-cause provision allowing shorter comment periods or no comment period is incorporated." ACUS Recommendation 93-4, *Improving the Environment for Agency Rulemaking*, 58 Fed. Reg. 4670 (1994).

17. 5 U.S.C. § 553(d). The 30-day period following publication is not intended to provide an opportunity for comment; it is a grace period for coming into compliance with the rule and, consequently, may be omitted when the rule grants an exemption or relieves a restriction. *Id.* § 553(d)(1). *See* discussion *supra* Part II, ch. l(D)(5).

18. *See* Exec. Order No. 12,866 § 6(a). President Obama issued an order reaffirming this. *See* Exec. Order 13,563, "Improving Regulation and Regulatory Review" § 2(b) (Jan. 18, 2011), 76 Fed. Reg. 3821 (Jan. 21, 2011) ("To the extent feasible and permitted by law, each agency shall afford the public a meaningful opportunity to comment through the Internet on any proposed regulation, with a comment period that should generally be at least 60 days."). ACUS revisited this issue in 2011. *See* ACUS Recommendation 2011-2, *Rulemaking Comments* ¶ 2 (June 16, 2011), 76 Fed. Reg. 48,791 (Aug. 9. 2011):

> Agencies should set comment periods that consider the competing interests of promoting optimal public participation while ensuring that the rulemaking is conducted

American Free Trade Agreement, requires that a proposed "Federal technical regulation or any Federal sanitary or phytosanitary measure of general application" be subject to a comment period of not less than 75 days.[19]

As a practical matter, most agencies do provide 60 or more days for complex or controversial rules.[20] Even when a shorter comment period is allowed, the agency may extend the period for comment where a legitimate request for extension has been received. In such a case, of course, notice of the extension should be published in the *Federal Register* to give all members of the public an equal opportunity to comment. Some enabling statutes expressly provide for a specific minimal period for public comment.[21]

Agencies also have the discretion to accept late comments,[22] but a recent ACUS study identified some inconsistencies in agency practices in this regard[23] and recommended:

> Agencies should adopt and publish policies on late comments and should apply those policies consistently within each rulemaking. Agencies should determine whether or not they will accept late submissions in a given rulemaking and should announce the policy both in publicly accessible forums (*e.g.*, the agency's Web site, Regulations.gov) and in individual Federal Register notices including requests for comments. The agency may make clear that late comments are disfavored and will only be considered to the extent practicable.[24]

---

efficiently. As a general matter, for "[s]ignificant regulatory action[s]" as defined in Executive Order 12,866, agencies should use a comment period of at least 60 days. For all other rulemakings, they should generally use a comment period of at least 30 days. When agencies, in appropriate circumstances, set shorter comment periods, they are encouraged to provide an appropriate explanation for doing so.

19. Exec. Order 12,889 § 4, 58 Fed. Reg. 69,681 (Dec. 30, 1993).
20. *See, e.g.*, Motor Carrier Safety Standards: Controlled Substances, Notice of Proposed Rulemaking, 53 Fed. Reg. 22,268 (1988) (providing 90-day comment period). The NPRM also stated that the agency was considering holding a public hearing on the proposal and that the hearing, if held, would be announced later in the *Federal Register.*
21. *See, e.g.*, Safe Water Drinking Act, 42 U.S.C. § 300g-l(b)(2)(B); 42 U.S.C. § 1395hh(b)(1) (requiring a 60-day comment period for most Medicare rulemaking).
22. *See, e.g.*, Highway-Rail Grade Crossing; Safe Clearance, 76 Fed. Reg. 5120, 5121 (Jan. 28, 2011) (Department of Transportation notice of proposed rulemaking announcing that "[c]omments received after the comment closing date will be included in the docket, and we will consider late comments to the extent practicable") (cited in ACUS Recommendation 2011-2, *supra* note 18, at n.5).
23. *See* Memorandum to Committee on Regulation, from Reeve T. Bull (Staff Counsel) (Apr. 18, 2011) at 3, *available at* http://www.acus.gov/wp-content/uploads/downloads/2011/04/COR-Research-for-Mtg-2-v.41.pdf (detailing the "disparity of agency practices regarding announcement of the acceptance *vel non* of late comments").
24. ACUS Recommendation 2011-2, *Rulemaking Comments, supra* note 18, at ¶ 5.

Agencies are making increasing use of "reply comment" periods as well. Public comments are much more likely to be focused and useful if the commenters have access to the comments of others. This can be thwarted when significant comments are submitted at the very end of the comment period.[25] To address this concern, several hybrid rulemaking statutes require agencies to receive rebuttal comments,[26] and some agencies, although not required to do so, voluntarily give interested persons the opportunity to submit "reply comments."[27] ACUS has recommended that, "[W]here appropriate, agencies should make use of reply comment periods or other opportunities for receiving public input on submitted comments, after all comments have been posted."[28] Replying to comments is, of course, much more feasible now that public comments are available on the Internet through Regulations.gov.

Section 553 requires the notice of proposed rulemaking to contain a "reference to the legal authority under which the rule is proposed."[29] Although this requirement is fairly straightforward, it has occasionally been an issue on judicial review, and courts have invalidated rules for failure to comply with it.[30]

The APA also requires the NPRM to include "either the terms or substance of the proposed rule or a description of the subjects and issues involved."[31] The *Attorney*

---

25. A recent study of comments filed in rulemaking by DOT and the Animal and Plant Health Inspection Service found that 25% of comments filed by individuals and 50% of comments filed by organizations were submitted in the last three days of the comment period. *See* Steven J. Balla, *Public Commenting on Federal Agency Regulations: Research on Current Practices and Recommendations to the Administrative Conference of the United States* 32 (draft report, March 15, 2011), *available at* http://www.acus.gov/wp-content/uploads/downloads/2011/04/COR-Balla-Report-Circulated.pdf.

26. *See, e.g.*, Clean Air Act, 42 U.S.C. § 7607(d)(5) (requiring EPA to keep rulemaking record open for an additional 30 days after completion of proceeding to allow submission of rebuttal comments); *see also* Toxic Substances Control Act, 15 U.S.C. § 2605(c)(3)(A).

27. *See* FCC Practice and Procedure, Comments and Replies, 47 C.F.R. § 1.415(c). A study of reply comments found that over half of the examples indentified in recent years were from the FCC. *See* Balla, *supra* note 25, at 10. For an example from another agency, see NLRB, Proposed Rule, Representation—Case Procedures, 76 Fed. Reg. 36,812 (proposed June 22, 2011) ("Comments regarding this proposed rule must be received by the Board on or before August 22, 2011. Comments replying to comments submitted during the initial comment period must be received by the Board on or before September 6, 2011. Reply comments should be limited to replying to comments previously filed by other parties.").

28. ACUS Recommendation 2011-2, *Rulemaking Comments*, *supra* note 18, at ¶ 6.

29. 5 U.S.C. § 553(b)(2). Indeed, the Office of the Federal Register requires that agencies cite the authority in virtually every rulemaking document submitted for publication. *See* DOCUMENT DRAFTING HANDBOOK, *infra* note 43, at 1-18, 2-24, & 3-5.

30. *See, e.g.*, Nat'l Tour Brokers Ass'n v. United States, 591 F.2d 896, 900 (D.C. Cir. 1978).

31. 5 U.S.C. § 553(b)(3). *But see* the Federal Coal Mine Health and Safety Act, 30 U.S.C. § 811(a)(2) (requiring MSHA to publish "the text of such rules proposed in their entirety"), *discussed in* Nat'l Mining Ass'n v. Mine Safety and Health Admin., 512 F.3d 696, 699 & n.3 (D.C. Cir. 2008). In that case the court permitted the agency to treat a statutorily authorized "emergency temporary standard" as the proposed final rule.

General's Manual on the Administrative Procedure Act recommended that agencies include in the proposal only a description of the subjects and issues of the rulemaking, rather than the terms of a proposed rule, if "publication . . . in full would unduly burden the *Federal Register* or would in fact be less informative to the public."[32] Today, however, most agencies publish the text of the proposed rule when commencing rulemaking, and some enabling statutes expressly require that the agency do so.[33] The heightened scrutiny given agency rules by courts is an incentive for prior agency consideration and publication of specific proposals.[34] Specific proposals help focus public comment, and that, in turn, assists reviewing courts in deciding whether interested persons were given a meaningful opportunity to participate in the rulemaking.

The NPRM must also describe compliance with the Regulatory Flexibility Act, the Paperwork Reduction Act, the Unfunded Mandates Reform Act, Executive Order 12,866, and other applicable analytical requirements.[35] For example, the preamble of a regulation containing a collection of information must notify the public that the proposal was sent to OMB for review and that the public may file comments with OMB.[36]

C. *Federal Register* Requirements and Incorporation by Reference

In 1934, Congress enacted the Federal Register Act, establishing a uniform system for the handling of federal agency regulations through the filing of documents with the Office of the Federal Register, placement of documents for public inspection, publication of documents in the *Federal Register,* and codification of rules in the *Code of Federal Regulations.*[37] The Administrative Committee of the Federal Register has

---

32. ATTORNEY GENERAL'S MANUAL ON THE ADMINISTRATIVE PROCEDURE ACT 29 (1947), *reprinted in* WILLIAM F. FUNK, JEFFREY S. LUBBERS & CHARLES POU, JR., FEDERAL ADMINISTRATIVE SOURCEBOOK 39, 66 (4th ed. 2008).

33. *See, e.g.,* Federal Trade Commission Act, 15 U.S.C. § 57a(b)(1)(A) (stating an agency must "publish a notice of proposed rulemaking including with particularity the text of the rule including any alternatives which the Commission proposes to promulgate; and the reasons for the proposed rule") One glaring exception is the FCC, *see* U.S. GOV'T ACCOUNTABILITY OFFICE, FCC MANAGEMENT: IMPROVEMENTS NEEDED IN COMMUNICATION, DECISION-MAKING PROCESSES, AND WORKFORCE PLANNING 27 (GAO-10-79) (December 2009), www.gao.gov/new.items/d1079.pdf (criticizing the FCC for "rarely include[ing] the text of the proposed rule in the notice, which may limit the effectiveness of the public comment process," and finding that from 1990 through 2007, the Commission "issued approximately 3,408 NPRMs, 390 (or 11.4 percent) of which contained the text of proposed rules").

34. *See infra* Part IV, ch. 2. Advance notices of proposed rulemaking, discussed *supra* Part III, ch. 1(B)(1), may further assist the agency in preparing a specific proposal for publication.

35. *See supra* Part III, ch. 2, for a description of the scope of these requirements.

36. 44 U.S.C. § 3507(a).

37. *Id.* §§ 1501–1511. The Federal Register Act is also discussed *supra* Part II, ch. 3(A).

issued regulations under the statute.[38] Subchapter E of its rules deals particularly with the preparation, transmitting, and processing of documents.[39]

Particularly relevant to both proposed and final rules is 1 C.F.R. § 18.12, titled "Preamble requirements," which sets forth minimum requirements for the form and substance of agency preambles that are to be published in the *Federal Register*. Agency staff should pay particular attention to these requirements because the Director of the Office of the Federal Register may return to the issuing agency any document submitted for publication in the *Federal Register* that does not comply with the publication requirements.[40] One general requirement is that every proposed or final rule must include a "preamble which will inform the reader, who is not an expert in the subject area, of the basis and purpose for the rule or proposal."[41] Additionally, the preamble must follow a set format, or the Office of the Federal Register will not print the rule document.[42] The Office of the Federal Register's *Document Drafting Handbook*[43] provides detailed instructions for drafting rules and proposed rules. The Office's staff also may be consulted for additional assistance.

An agency wishing to incorporate material into a rule by reference must also comply with relevant *Federal Register* requirements.[44] Generally, any published data, criteria, standards, and similar material may be incorporated by reference into a rule if it is reasonably available to and usable by the class of persons affected by the agency's rule.[45] However, material published previously in the *Federal Register*, or in the *U.S. Code*, will not be approved for incorporation by reference, and there is a presumption that a publication produced by the same agency that is seeking its approval will not be approved.[46]

Incorporation by reference in the modern Internet era raises a variety of complicated legal and policy issues, which are the subject of a recent ACUS recommendation.[47] For example, the "reasonably available" requirement may raise questions with

38. 1 C.F.R. ch. I, pts. 1–22. In 1989 the Administrative Committee of the Federal Register amended and consolidated these rules. 54 Fed. Reg. 9670 (1989).
39. 1 C.F.R. pts. 15–22.
40. 1 C.F.R. § 2.4(b).
41. *See id.* § 18.12(a). This provision is cited and enforced in *Kooritzky v. Reich*, 17 F.3d 1509, 1513 (D.C. Cir. 1994).
42. *See* 1 C.F.R. § 18.12(b).
43. NAT'L ARCHIVES & RECORDS ADMIN., OFFICE OF THE FEDERAL REGISTER, DOCUMENT DRAFTING HANDBOOK (October 1998 revision, with supplements), on the Office of the Federal Register website, *available at* http://www.archives.gov/federal-register/write/handbook/.
44. *See* 1 C.F.R. pt. 51; *see also* DOCUMENT DRAFTING HANDBOOK, *supra* note 43, at ch. 6; Appalachian Power Co. v. Train, 566 F.2d 451, 455–56 (4th Cir. 1977).
45. 1 C.F.R. § 51.7.
46. *Id.*
47. ACUS Recommendation 2011-5, *Incorporation by Reference* (Dec. 8, 2011), 77 Fed. Reg. 2257 (Jan. 17, 2012). *See* Emily Schleicher Bremer, *Incorporation by Reference in Federal Regulations*, revised draft report to the Administrative Conference of the United States (Oct. 19, 2011),

respect to copyrighted materials, such as technical standards developed by private entities.[48] These entities often sell such materials to fund their activities, so they are only available for a price. ACUS has recommended ways in which agencies and such organizations can work to increase access to such materials.[49]

Another difficult issue is how to update regulations that incorporate by reference, since "dynamic" incorporations that would update the regulation automatically when the referenced material was updated is not permissible.[50] ACUS has suggested strategies for agencies to use in updating such regulations or using enforcement discretion when they cannot be readily updated.[51] Agencies should also be careful, when they incorporate a document that itself incorporates other documents, to clarify their position on the legal effect of these secondary documents.[52]

Furthermore, when incorporating documents by reference, agencies should be mindful of the effect the incorporation has on the intelligibility of the notice. In *PPG Industries, Inc. v. Costle*,[53] EPA referenced internal agency guidelines on acceptable test methods for ensuring air quality in a footnote in the NPRM but did not indicate that it intended the guidelines to be legally incorporated by reference.[54] The referenced guidelines were meant to change the monitoring requirements for regulated industries. When EPA sought to enforce the guidelines, the reviewing court held them invalid because the agency had not given the public sufficient notice and opportunity to comment on this aspect of the NPRM. Further, EPA had failed to give adequate notice in the final rule of the change because it had neither published the guidelines nor formally incorporated them by reference.[55]

---

available at http://www.acus.gov/wp-content/uploads/downloads/2011/10/Revised-Draft-IBR-Report-10-19-11.pdf. *See also* Rebecca Day & Tom Mielke, *Incorporation by Reference: Using External Expertise to Make Coast Guard Regulations More Efficient*, PROCEEDINGS, Spring 2010, at 26, *available at* http://www.uscg.mil/proceedings/spring2010/articles/26_Mielke,Day_IncorporationByReference.pdf.

48. *See* Veeck v. S. Building Code Congress Int'l, Inc., 293 F.3d 791 (5th Cir. 2002) (en banc) (holding that a model building code lost its copyright protection when the author promoted it for use as legislation and it was then adopted wholesale by several Texas municipal governments).

49. ACUS Recommendation 2011-5, *supra* note 47, at ¶¶ 1–5. *See also* OMB, Request for Information and Notice of Public Meeting, Federal Participation in the Development and Use of Voluntary Consensus Standards and in Conformity Assessment Activities, 77 Fed. Reg. 19,357 (Mar. 30, 2012).

50. *See* Bremer, *supra* note 47, at 33–34. *See also* City of Idaho Falls, Idaho v. FERC, 629 F.3d 222 (D.C. Cir. 2011) (finding an APA notice violation when FERC attempted to adopt updates in a Forest Service fee schedule that it had originally incorporated by reference in its own regulations, without reopening its regulation for notice and comment).

51. ACUS Recommendation 2011-5, *supra* note 47, at ¶¶ 6–11.

52. *Id.* at ¶ 17.

53. 659 F.2d 1239, 1250 (D.C. Cir. 1981).

54. It should be emphasized that the Office of the Federal Register usually will not approve agency incorporation by reference of a publication of the same agency. 1 C.F.R. § 51.5(b).

55. 659 F.2d at 1249–50.

D. Adequacy of the Notice[56]

The notice-and-comment procedures of the APA are intended to encourage public participation in the administrative process, to help educate the agency, and, thus, to produce more informed agency decisionmaking.[57] To obtain "meaningful" participation from the public, it has been consistently held that the NPRM must "fairly apprise interested persons" of the issues in the rulemaking.[58] The Seventh Circuit has said that "notice is adequate if it apprises interested parties of the issues to be addressed in the rulemaking proceeding with sufficient clarity and specificity to allow them to participate in the rulemaking in a meaningful and informed manner."[59]

The factual basis for agency rules frequently is subject to close judicial scrutiny. As discussed in more detail below, the more closely courts have reviewed the data supporting rules, the more sensitive they have become to the fact that meaningful comment on proposed rules can be precluded by the failure of agencies to disclose especially relevant information. In a leading early example, *Portland Cement Association v. Ruckelshaus*,[60] Judge Leventhal stated that:

> [I]t is not consonant with the purpose of a rule-making proceeding to promulgate rules on the basis of inadequate data or data that [in] critical degree, is known only to the agency . . . . In order that rule-making proceedings to determine standards be conducted in orderly fashion, information should generally be disclosed as to the basis of a proposed rule at the time of issuance. If this is not feasible, . . . information that is material to the subject at hand should be disclosed as it becomes available. . . .[61]

In another memorable turn of phrase, Judge Mikva agreed, saying:

---

56. *See also infra* Part III, ch. 4.
57. Chocolate Mfrs. Ass'n v. Block, 755 F.2d 1098, 1103 (4th Cir. 1985).
58. United Steelworkers v. Marshall, 647 F.2d 1189, 1221 (D.C. Cir. 1980) (quoting Am. Iron & Steel Inst. v. EPA, 568 F.2d 284, 293 (3d Cir. 1977)). *MCI Telecomm. Corp. v. FCC*, 57 F.3d 1136 (D.C. Cir. 1995) provides a pointed example of inadequate notice. The FCC, as part of its plan to require unbundling in telecommunications services offered by local exchange carriers, instituted a rulemaking to develop an Open Network Architecture (ONA) so that enhanced service providers (ESPs) could purchase services on an unbundled basis. The FCC issued an NPRM on the ONA plan, in which it mentioned in a footnote in the background section that long-distance carriers would also have to purchase services from local exchange carriers under the ONA plan. The NPRM was otherwise devoted entirely to how the ONA plan would affect ESPs. The D.C. Circuit held that a footnote in the background section was not adequate notice to long-distance carriers affected by the rulemaking. *But see* U.S. Telecom Ass'n v. FCC, 400 F.3d 29, 40 (D.C. Cir. 2005) (FCC's labeling of its notice as a request for comment on a "Petition for Declaratory Ruling," rather than as a "Notice of Proposed Rulemaking," was a harmless error).
59. Am. Med. Ass'n v. United States, 887 F.2d 760, 767 (7th Cir. 1989).
60. 486 F.2d 375 (D.C. Cir. 1973).
61. *Id.* at 393–94.

In order to allow for useful criticism, it is especially important for the agency to identify and make available technical studies and data that it has employed in reaching the decisions to propose particular rules. To allow an agency to play hunt the peanut with technical information, hiding or disguising the information that it employs, is to condone a practice in which the agency treats what should be a genuine interchange as mere bureaucratic sport. An agency commits serious procedural error when it fails to reveal portions of the technical basis for a proposed rule in time to allow for meaningful commentary.[62]

This development requiring agencies to disclose relevant information is described more fully in the next chapter,[63] but it is mentioned here because of its obvious implications for the contents of the agency's NPRM.[64]

E. Need for a Second Cycle of Notice and Comment ("Logical Outgrowth" Test)

A second round of notice and comment (sometimes called a "supplemental notice of proposed rulemaking") may be required or useful in a number of circumstances. It may well avoid agency vulnerability in court on the issue of the adequacy of the notice, especially where it appears during the course of the rulemaking that the final rule will materially differ from the proposal. If the final rule differs to such a great extent from the agency's proposal that it can be said that the public was not apprised of the issues in the proceeding, the court may vacate the final rule for inadequate notice.

---

62. Conn. Light & Power Co. v. NRC, 673 F.2d 525, 530–31 (D.C. Cir. 1982). *But see* Tex. Office of Pub. Util. Counsel v. FCC, 265 F.3d 313, 326 (5th Cir. 2001) (stating that "while interested parties should be able to participate meaningfully in the rulemaking process, the public need not have an opportunity to comment on every bit of information influencing an agency's decision" (internal quotation omitted)).

63. It should be noted that one D.C. Circuit judge has recently expressed the opinion that *Portland Cement*, while still binding Circuit precedent, "stands on a shaky legal foundation." Am. Radio Relay League, Inc. v. FCC, 524 F.3d 227, 246 (D.C. Cir. 2008) (Kavanaugh, J., concurring). And another panel has required challengers making such an argument to "indicate with reasonable specificity what portions of the documents it objects to and how it might have responded if given the opportunity." Owner-Operator Indep. Drivers Ass'n, Inc. v. Fed. Motor Carrier Safety Admin., 494 F.3d 188, 202 (D.C. Cir. 2007) (citing Gerber v. Norton, 294 F.3d 173, 182 (D.C. Cir. 2002). *See infra* Part III, ch. 4(A)(2).

64. The Conference recommended public disclosure of relevant data in several contexts. *See* ACUS Recommendation 76-3, *Procedures in Addition to Notice and the Opportunity for Comment in Informal Rulemaking*, ¶ 1(c), 41 Fed. Reg. 29,654, 29,655 (1976) (advising agencies to consider including in the NPRM a summary of current agency attitudes toward critical issues in proceedings and description and location of data on which agency relied; suggesting including description of scientific tests and other procedures used by agency and significance agency has attached to them); *see also* ACUS Recommendation 88-7, *Valuation of Human Life in Regulatory Decisionmaking*, 53 Fed. Reg. 39,586 (1988); ACUS Recommendation 79-4, *Public Disclosure Concerning the Use of Cost-Benefit and Similar Analyses in Regulation*, 44 Fed. Reg. 38,826 (1979).

This does not mean that the agency may not alter the proposal in its final rule. Indeed, the final rule "must so differ [from the proposal] when the record evidence warrants the change."[65] As the Seventh Circuit has cautioned:

> The law does not require that every alteration in a proposed rule be reissued for notice and comment. If that were the case, an agency could "learn from the comments on its proposals only at the peril of subjecting itself to rulemaking without end." The purpose of a rulemaking proceeding is not merely to vote up or down the specific proposals advanced before the proceeding begins, but to refine, modify, and supplement the proposals in the light of evidence and arguments presented in the course of the proceeding. If every modification is to require a further hearing at which that modification is set forth in the notice, agencies will be loath to modify initial proposals, and the rulemaking process will be degraded.[66]

However, an agency does not have complete discretion to radically change a proposed rule simply because it is doing so in response to adverse comments.[67] The issue thus becomes whether the notice adequately alerted the interested parties of the possibility of the changes that were eventually adopted. In one case, for example, EPA attempted to justify the inclusion of administrative exemptions in a final rule by arguing that the proposed rule discussed statutory exemptions.[68] The court rejected this argument, saying, "Such reasoning, accepted by the court, would turn notice and comment rulemaking into a guessing game in which the inclusion of one subject indicates that a distant cousin of that subject might be addressed."[69]

The prevailing test devised by the courts to help them decide whether notice in the NPRM was adequate is whether the final rule was a "logical outgrowth" of the proposal and comments.[70] In an early case, the D.C. Circuit stated, "A final rule is

---

65. United Steelworkers v. Marshall, 647 F.2d 1189, 1221 (D.C. Cir. 1980). *See also* Kooritzky v. Reich, 17 F.3d 1509, 1513 (D.C. Cir. 1994) ("It is an elementary principle of rulemaking that a final rule need not match the rule proposed, indeed must not if the record demands a change. The reason is plain enough. Agencies should be free to adjust or abandon their proposals in light of public comments or internal agency reconsideration without having to start another round of rulemaking." (citations omitted))

66. Alto Dairy v. Veneman, 336 F.3d 560, 569–70 (7th Cir. 2003) (citing First Am. Discount Corp. v. CFTC, 222 F.3d 1008, 1015 (D.C. Cir. 2000)).

67. Chocolate Mfrs Ass'n v. Block, 755 F.2d 1098, 1104 (4th Cir. 1985).

68. Fertilizer Inst. v. EPA, 935 F.2d 1303 (D.C. Cir. 1991).

69. *Id.* at 1311.

70. *See generally* Philip M. Kannan, *The Logical Outgrowth Doctrine in Rulemaking*, 48 ADMIN. L. REV. 213 (1996); Arnold Rochvarg, *Adequacy of Notice of Rulemaking Under the Federal Administrative Procedure Act—When Should a Second Round of Notice and Comment Be Provided?*, 31 AM. U. L. REV. 1 (1981). See *Small Refiner Lead Phase-Down Task Force v. EPA*, 705 F.2d 506, 547 (D.C. Cir. 1983) and *S. Terminal Corp. v. EPA*, 504 F.2d 646, 659 (1st Cir. 1974) for early statements of the "logical outgrowth" test. In the former case, the court said that the task of the court is fundamentally one of balancing the advantages of additional comment

considered the 'logical outgrowth' of the proposed rule if at least the 'germ' of the outcome is found in the original proposal."[71] This test was further explicated by the court in the leading 1997 *National Mining* case as follows:

> Our cases offer no precise definition of what counts as a "logical outgrowth." We ask "whether 'the purposes of notice and comment have been adequately served.'" *American Water Works Ass'n v. EPA*, 40 F.3d 1266, 1274 (D.C. Cir. 1994) (quoting *Fertilizer Inst. v. EPA*, 935 F.2d 1303, 1311 (D.C. Cir. 1991)). Notice was inadequate when "the interested parties could not reasonably have 'anticipated the final rulemaking from the draft [rule].'" *Id.* at 1275 (quoting *Anne Arundel County v. EPA*, 963 F.2d 412, 418 (D.C. Cir. 1992)). "We inquire whether the notice given affords 'exposure to diverse public comment,' 'fairness to affected parties,' and 'an opportunity to develop evidence in the record.'" *Association of Am. Railroads v. Dep't of Transp.*, 38 F.3d 582, 589 (D.C. Cir. 1994) (quoting *Small Refiner Lead Phase-Down Task Force v. EPA*, 705 F.2d 506, 547 (D.C. Cir. 1983)).[72]

A later decision summarized the D.C. Circuit case law on this issue as follows:

A final rule qualifies as a logical outgrowth "if interested parties 'should have anticipated' that the change was possible, and thus reasonably should have filed their comments on the subject during the notice-and-comment period." *Ne. Md. Waste Disposal Auth. v. EPA,* 358 F.3d 936, 952 (D.C. Cir. 2004) (citations omitted). By contrast, a final rule fails the logical outgrowth test and thus violates the APA's notice requirement where "interested parties would have had to 'divine [the agency's] unspoken thoughts,' because the final rule was surprisingly distant from the proposed rule." *Int'l Union, United Mine*

(improving the quality of rules, fairness, and facilitating judicial review) against the burden on "the public interest in expedition and finality." *Id. See also* Kooritzky v. Reich, 17 F.3d 1509, 1513–14 (D.C. Cir. 1994); Am. Med. Ass'n v. United States, 887 F.2d 760, 767–69 (7th Cir. 1989); City of Stoughton v. EPA, 858 F.2d 747, 751, 753 (D.C. Cir. 1988); Action Alliance of Senior Citizens v. Bowen, 846 F.2d 1449, 1455 (D.C. Cir. 1988); Natural Res. Def. Counsel v. Thomas, 838 F.2d 1224, 1242 (D.C. Cir. 1988); Career College Ass'n v. Duncan, 796 F. Supp. 2d 108 (D.D.C. 2011) (lack of logical outgrowth). For a discussion on whether the final rule may be based on the public comments rather than the proposed rule, see *infra* text accompanying notes 83–96.

71. *NRDC v. Thomas*, 838 F.2d at 1242.
72. Nat'l Mining Ass'n v. MSHA, 116 F.3d 520, 531 (D.C. Cir. 1997) (upholding the agency's rule except for one provision which failed the logical outgrowth test); *see also* Natural Res. Def. Counsel v. EPA, 279 F.3d 1180, 1187–88 (9th Cir. 2002) (finding EPA's notice-and-comment procedure was inadequate when the permit notice referred to a "one-acre zone of deposit" and the final permit allowed a greater use than the one-acre zone, even though draft permit referred to the fact that the proposed zones of deposit might exceed the one-acre zone). The court reasoned that because the public could not have reasonably anticipated the increased zone, agency notice was inadequate; Horsehead Res. Dev. v. Browner, 16 F.3d 1246, 1266–68 (D.C. Cir. 1994) (vacating the portion of EPA rule not properly noticed).

Workers of Am. v. Mine Safety & Health Admin., 407 F.3d 1250, 1259–60 (D.C. Cir. 2005) (internal citations omitted).[73]

A straightforward application of the test was presented in *Owner-Operator Independent Drivers Ass'n, Inc. v. Federal Motor Carrier Safety Administration*,[74] in which a truck drivers' organization challenged a Federal Motor Carrier Safety Administration (FMCSA) rule that changed its ten-hour rest period rule to require at least one eight-hour segment in a sleeper berth. One of the drivers' contentions was that FMCSA violated the APA because the NPRM did not give interested parties adequate notice that the agency was considering such a modification, claiming that the NPRM "was too broad and unfocused to provide adequate notice[,] thus precluding meaningful comment."[75] The court rejected that argument, pointing to language in the NPRM stating that "FMCSA will consider a variety of possible changes to the sleeper-berth provisions, including but not limited to . . . establishing a minimum time for one of the two 'splits,' such as 5 hours, 8 hours, or some other appropriate level . . . ."[76]

The drivers also paradoxically argued that the NPRM was "too specific" because it listed "virtually every option for changing the sleeper berth exception" and thus "really proposed nothing." But the court determined "there was no 'needle in a haystack' quality to the NPRM."[77]

After this long gestation period in the lower courts, the Supreme Court finally adopted the test, albeit in a relatively undemanding way, in *Long Island Care at Home, Ltd. v. Coke*.[78] The Court first described the object of the test as "fair notice."[79] It upheld a Department of Labor rule that applied an exemption from the Fair Labor Standards Act minimum wage and maximum hours requirements for "companionship services" to such services rendered by persons not employed by the household itself, but employed by third-party agencies. The workers argued that because the Department originally proposed a rule that would have limited the exemption to household-

---

73. CSX Transp., Inc. v. Surface Transp. Bd., 584 F.3d 1076, 1079–80 (D.C. Cir. 2009). This decision applied the test quite strictly, finding that the Board's switch from a one-year in the NPRM to a four-year data sample failed the logical outgrowth test. The court said: "In essence, the Board contends that the mere mention of the release of one-year data for comparison groups gave notice that the amount of data available for that purpose might change. . . . Although the NPRM proposed several revisions to the existing system, it nowhere even hinted that the Board might consider expanding the number of years from which comparison groups could be derived." *Id.* at 1082. The court also mentioned that "that not one commenter indicated that it understood the proposal to mean that the Board might consider using more than one year's worth of private data." *Id.* at 1080.

74. 494 F.3d 188 (D.C. Cir. 2007).

75. *Id.* at 209 (alteration in original).

76. *Id.* at 209 (emphasis omitted) (quoting Hours of Service of Drivers, 70 Fed. Reg. 3339, 3349–50 (proposed Jan. 24, 2005) (to be codified at 49 C.F.R. pts. 385, 390, 395)).

77. *Id.* at 209 n.6 (quoting Owner-Operator Independent Drivers Ass'n, Inc. Br. 32).

78. 551 U.S. 158 (2007).

79. *Id.* at 174.

employed workers, this deprived them of fair notice that the Department would issue the opposite rule. The Court rejected this argument, saying the opposite proposal "meant that the Department was *considering* the matter; after that consideration the Department might choose to adopt the proposal or to withdraw it," and "We do not understand why such a possibility was not reasonably foreseeable."[80]

This is a rather undemanding application of the test—in a sense, the agency's final rule was the opposite of the proposal. Lower court cases had found a violation of the test where an agency neglected to mention in its proposal a key part of the ultimate final rule, see *Chocolate Manufacturers Ass'n v. Block.*[81] So it seems odd that in *Long Island Care*, an agency that proposed the reverse of the final rule should pass the test. On the other hand, in the latter case the commenters' antennae should have been more attuned to this possibility than had the agency been silent.

In a brief colloquy on this point during the oral argument, Justice Scalia foreshadowed the Court's undemanding application of the test by comparing the NPRM to "floating an idea" by "run[ning] it up the flagpole."[82]

In determining the adequacy of notice, some courts have attempted to determine whether changes in the final rule were in fact made in response to comments received during the rulemaking. In *United Steelworkers of America v. Schuylkill Metal Corp.*,[83] the Fifth Circuit rejected a claim that OSHA's proposal did not adequately alert the public that the scope of medical removal benefits under the OSHA occupational health standard for lead was at issue in the rulemaking. Noting that public comments received by the agency expressly raised the medical removal issue, the court concluded that "it was readily apparent to interested parties that the scope of . . . [removal] benefits was in dispute," and therefore these comments provided "additional support

---

80. *Id.* at 175. To some extent, this result seems inconsistent with *Environmental Integrity Project v. EPA*, 425 F.3d 992, 995–96 (D.C. Cir. 2005), where the court rejected EPA's defense that it had negatively mentioned the final interpretation in the preamble to the proposed rule, finding that EPA had violated the logical outgrowth test when it "pull[ed] a surprise switcheroo on regulated entities" and adopted a rule that was the "inverse interpretation" of the policy it had proposed to codify.

81. *Supra* note 67.

82. *Long Island Care at Home*, Transcript of Oral Argument 12–13:

> JUSTICE SCALIA: Well, wait. Does the notice of proposed rulemaking set forth the agency's position?
> MR. FARR: No, it does not.
> JUSTICE SCALIA: I didn't think it did. They're just floating an idea. You know—
> MR. FARR: That's correct.
> JUSTICE SCALIA: Run it up the flagpole, see if—
> MR. FARR: Well, that it solicited comments on that proposal. And after the comments, it changed its position to say no, in fact, all third-party employers will be exempt.

83. 828 F.2d 314 (5th Cir. 1987).

for the broad, final rule."[84] Furthermore, "petitioners must show how they were preju-diced by the [agency's] failure to solicit additional comments, and how they would have responded had they been given the opportunity to submit additional responses."[85]

In *National Mining Ass'n v. Mine Safety and Health Administration*,[86] the court rejected a "logical outgrowth" challenge, emphasizing that the court does not simply compare the final rule to the proposed rule, it also considers "the comments, state-ments and proposals made during the notice-and-comment period."[87] In fact it re-stated the test to say that the question is not simply whether the final rule is a logical outgrowth of the proposed rule, but also whether it is a logical outgrowth "'of the hearing and related procedures' during the notice and comment period."[88] The court noted that several parties (although not the petitioner) had submitted comments con-cerning the possibility of the alternative ultimately chosen.[89] As Professor Jordan noted in writing about this case, "To some extent, this analysis suggests that the more an agency leaves issues inherently open at the proposal stage, the less vulnerable it may be to a 'logical outgrowth' challenge, particularly if participants happen to file com-ments related to matters that show up in the final rule."[90]

Some other courts, although now seemingly in the minority, have refused to use public comments on an issue as the basis for a finding that the notice was adequate. In

---

84. *Id.* at 318. The court of appeals also found that the NPRM "more than adequately sufficed to apprise fairly an interested party that there was an issue regarding the breadth of . . . [medical] benefits." *Id.* The court added that it was not necessary to apprise parties "such as these sophisticated industry members," who had challenged the standard a number of times to "spell out with particularity" the proposed meaning of the medical benefits. *Id.* In *Associated Builders & Contractors v. Brock*, 862 F.2d 63, 67 (3d Cir. 1988), the court relied in part on an ANPRM in holding that the proposal provided adequate notice of the agency's consideration of the issue of industry-wide coverage of hazard communication standard. *See also* Rybachek v. EPA, 904 F.2d 1276 (9th Cir. 1990).

85. Tex. Office of Pub. Util. Counsel v. FCC, 265 F.3d 313, 326 (5th Cir. 2001). *See also* CSX Transp., Inc. v. Surface Transp. Bd., 584 F.3d 1076, 1080 (D.C. Cir. 2009); Int'l Union, United Mine Workers of Am. v. Mine Safety and Health Admin., 626 F.3d 84 (D.C. Cir. 2010) (reject-ing a "logical outgrowth" challenge where a final rule had changed the amount of space required in a mine refuge because the proposal had specifically called for comments on space and volume requirements in such circumstances, and where union could not show that it was prejudiced because it had already discussed the same basic issue in its comments).

86. 512 F.3d 696 (D.C. Cir. 2008).

87. *Id.* at 699.

88. *Id.* (quoting S. Terminal Corp. v. EPA, 504 F.2d 646, 659 (1st Cir. 1974)).

89. *See also* Council Tree Communications, Inc. v. FCC, 619 F.3d 235, 256 (3d Cir. 2010) (ac-cepting a "logical outgrowth" challenge to part of the FCC rule because the final rule con-tained a change in the proposal that was only claimed to be impliedly inferable from the language of the proposal, and "no commenter manifested an understanding that the FCC was considering" such a change).

90. William S. Jordan III, *Rulemaking, in* DEVELOPMENTS IN ADMINISTRATIVE LAW AND REGULATORY PRAC-TICE 2007-2008, at 138 (Jeffrey S. Lubbers ed., 2009)

AFL-CIO v. Donovan,[91] a case involving the Department of Labor's revision of its regulations under the Service Contract Act, the court said, "Neither can we properly attribute notice to the other appellants on the basis of an assumption that they would have monitored the submission of comments."[92] The court relied on its earlier statement that "notice necessarily must come—if at all—from the agency"[93] and vacated a portion of the rules as violative of APA notice-and-comment requirements.[94] In another case the court said, "While we have noted that insightful comments may be reflective of notice and may be adduced as evidence of its adequacy, we have rejected bootstrap arguments predicating notice on public comments alone."[95] In *National Mining* the court explained, "Even if a party knows that a commenter has made some novel proposal to an agency during a rulemaking, the party cannot be expected to respond unless it has some reason to believe the agency will take the proposal seriously."[96]

Thus, the issue whether, and in what circumstances, a court will find agency notice to be adequate is a fact-driven inquiry. In some cases the courts have struggled to find, and have found, adequacy of notice,[97] while in others courts have vacated rules

---

91. 757 F.2d 330 (D.C. Cir. 1985).
92. *Id.* at 340. Of course, now that comments are readily available online, it is more difficult for challengers to plead ignorance of comments that addressed the supposedly unanticipatable issue.
93. *Id.* (quoting Small Refiner Lead Phase-Down Task Force v. EPA, 705 F.2d 506, 549 (D.C. Cir. 1983).
94. The court stated that the principle that comments should not be relied on to provide notice was "particularly appropriate" in that case, because only two comments had been received on the issue in a rulemaking of "broad scope" in which some 1,600 comments were received. *Id.* The court in this connection quoted *Wagner Electric Corp. v. Volpe*, 466 F.2d 1013, 1019 (3d Cir. 1972), which held that the fact that "some knowledgeable manufacturers" responded is not relevant because "others possibly not so knowledgeable" had a right to adequate notice. *Id.*
95. Horsehead Res. Dev. v. Browner, 16 F.3d 1246, 1268 (D.C. Cir. 1994) (citation omitted).
96. Nat'l Mining Ass'n v. MSHA, 116 F.3d 520, 531 (D.C. Cir. 1997); *see also* Shell Oil Co. v. EPA, 950 F.2d 741, 751 (D.C. Cir. 1991) (finding that "the ambiguous comments and weak signals from the agency gave petitioners no such opportunity to anticipate and criticize the rules or to offer alternatives. Under these circumstances, the mixture and derived-from rules exceed the limits of a 'logical outgrowth'"). In that case the court invalidated a rule that had been issued 13 years earlier. In *Int'l Union, United Mine Workers v. Mine Safety and Health Admin.*, 407 F.3d 1250 (D.C. Cir. 2005), the court found a logical outgrowth violation and did not accept the argument that the comments provided notice because no comment suggested the air flow limit ultimately required in the final rule.
97. *See, e.g.*, United Steelworkers v. Marshall, 647 F.2d 1189 (D.C. Cir. 1980). In that case, OSHA had proposed a permissible exposure limit for lead of 100 micrograms; in its final rule, it reduced the permissible level to 50 micrograms. *See also* Nat'l Ass'n of Psychiatric Health Sys. v. Shalala, 120 F. Supp. 2d 33, 41 (D.D.C. 2000) (finding commenters' "failure to anticipate the exact contours of the Secretary's final rule does not compel the conclusion that the final rule is not a logical outgrowth of the proposed rule. 'They cannot now complain because they misread

because, as the court in *Chocolate Manufacturers Ass'n v. Block* stated, the notice did "not serve the policy underlying the notice requirement."[98] Because courts may be strict in insisting that notice be adequate, and because policy considerations strongly favor full and meaningful public participation, it is essential that agency officials, in drafting the NPRM and during the rulemaking proceeding, give special attention to the potential vulnerability of a final rule on adequacy-of-notice grounds.[99] In particular, the rulemaking staff must be aware of the importance of the wording of the proposed rule and the language of the preamble to the proposal.

Although specific proposals are valuable in focusing comment, they may ultimately place the agency at a disadvantage, in that the proposal's very specificity might limit the options available in the final rule.[100] On the other hand, although a generally worded proposal may well avoid some of the restrictive effects of a too-specific proposal,[101] an agency must be careful that such a proposal is not so general that it affords inadequate notice of particular issues in the proceeding.[102] In general, agencies should, to the extent possible, make clear which issues are "on the table."

---

the regulatory waters, incorrectly anticipated how [the agency] would react to their criticisms, and, consequently, submitted comments that left some things unsaid'" (quoting BASF Wyandotte Corp. v. Costle, 598 F.2d 637, 643 (1st Cir. 1979)). The district court noted that the agency "listed a number of prescriptive requirements as examples of the types of standards it had considered adopting," and also noted that it had "requested comments on whether additional prescriptive requirements were necessary." *Id.* at 36. *See also* La. Fed. Land Bank Ass'n, FLCA v. Farm Credit Admin., 336 F.3d 1075, 1081–82 (D.C. Cir. 2003).

98. 755 F.2d 1098 (4th Cir. 1985). *See, e.g.*, DeBraun v. Meissner, 958 F. Supp. 227, 231 (E.D. Pa. 1997) (finding that INS provided notice of the *subject* involved—regulation of the fingerprinting process—but it did not fairly apprise interested parties that it also intended to address other material *issues*—those of the permanency and physical structure of the provider's fingerprinting location).

99. As discussed *infra* Part III, ch. 7(B), the preamble to the final rule must carefully address discrepancies between the proposal in the NPRM and the final rule. A well-reasoned explanation of how the final rule derived from (or is the "logical outgrowth" of) the NPRM can be extremely useful if a rule is challenged.

100. *See* comments of Professor Jordan, text at note 90. *But see* City of Portland, Ore. v. EPA, 507 F.3d 706 (D.C. Cir. 2007) (rejecting "logical outgrowth" challenge to a final rule issued after a negotiated rulemaking proceeding that deviated from the negotiated proposed rule text).

101. *See* Am. Med. Ass'n v. United States, 887 F.2d 760, 767 (7th Cir. 1989).

102. *See, e.g.*, Envtl. Integrity Project v. EPA, 425 F.3d 992, 998 (D.C. Cir. 2005) (rejecting EPA's argument that it met its notice-and-comment obligations because its final interpretation was also mentioned (albeit negatively) in the agency's proposal). The court explained:

> A contrary rule would allow an agency to reject innumerable alternatives in its Notice of Proposed Rulemaking only to justify *any* final rule it might be able to devise by whimsically picking and choosing within the four corners of a lengthy "notice." Such an exercise in "looking over a crowd and picking out your friends" does not advise interested parties how to direct their comments and does not comprise adequate notice under APA § 553(c).

Id. (citing Exxon Mobil Corp. v. Allapattah Servs., Inc., 125 S. Ct. 2611, 2626 (2005)).

One way an agency can both set forth specific proposals in an NPRM and retain flexibility in fashioning the final rule is to include in the NPRM several alternatives that are under consideration. Thus, for example, the National Highway Traffic Safety Administration's proposed rule on passive restraints in automobiles, issued after remand from the Supreme Court,[103] contained several options that the agency was considering.[104] Similarly, EPA's NPRM for regulating benzene exposure under the Clean Air Act contained four alternative proposed rules, each containing significantly different permissible exposure levels.[105]

A related approach would be for the agency, in addition to its specific proposal, to pose a series of questions going beyond the terms of the proposal on which it seeks comment. OSHA used this strategy in its proposed standard on ethylene oxide,[106] and as it developed, the major issue in the rulemaking—whether a short-term exposure limit should be established—was raised not in the proposed rule itself but in one of the questions in the preamble. This technique may be even more necessary as agencies begin to receive large numbers of electronic comments."[107]

This discussion suggests that the rulemaking staff should routinely give serious consideration to going beyond the minimum legal requirements in giving notice. A focused and well-explained NPRM can educate the public and generate more helpful information from interested persons. From a purely tactical viewpoint, it is desirable to find out earlier rather than later about views and information adverse to the agency's proposal or bearing on its practicality.[108]

---

103. Motor Vehicle Mfrs. Ass'n v. State Farm Mut. Auto. Ins. Co., 463 U.S. 29 (1983).

104. Federal Motor Vehicle Safety Standards; Occupant Crash Protection, 48 Fed. Reg. 48,622 (proposed Oct. 19, 1983). The proposal suggested a range of alternatives and proposed other actions that could be taken in conjunction with, or as a supplement to, those alternatives. The agency then held public meetings in three cities and received more than 6,000 comments on the NPRM.

105. EPA Proposed Rule and Notice of Public Hearing, National Emission Standards for Hazardous Air Pollutants, Benzene, 53 Fed. Reg. 28,496, 28,497 (proposed July 28, 1988). EPA took this approach in part because of the court of appeals decision on the agency's vinyl chloride standard. Nat. Resources. Def. Council v. EPA, 824 F.2d 1146 (D.C. Cir. 1987). The final rule took pieces from each alternative. 54 Fed. Reg. 38,044, 38,045 (1988).

106. Occupational Exposure to Ethylene Oxide, 49 Fed. Reg. 25,734 (June 22, 1984).

107. *See* Fred Emery & Andrew Emery, *A Modest Proposal: Improve E-Rulemaking by Improving Comments*, 31 ADMIN. & REG. L. NEWS 8 (2005). See Part III, ch. 1(C) for a discussion of "e-rulemaking." The European Union makes great use of this technique in its "stakeholder engagement" process for issuing legislation. *See* Better Regulation Task Force, Get Connected: Effective Engagement in the EU (Sept. 2005), *available at* http://www.brtf.gov.uk/reports/getconnectedentry.asp. The EU's primary comment portal is http://europa.eu.int/yourvoice. *See also* Peter Strauss, *Rulemaking in the Ages of Globalization and Information: What America Can Learn From Europe, and Vice Versa*, unpublished paper prepared for ABA Section of Administrative Law and Regulatory Practice's EU Administrative Law project (2005), on file with author.

108. *See generally* ACUS Recommendation 76-3, *supra* note 64. ACUS also recommended that Congress codify the logical outgrowth test in the APA. ACUS Recommendation 93-4, *supra* note 16.

More generally, the Administrative Conference recommended that agencies consider providing for two cycles of notice and comment where comments bring new issues to the attention of the agency, as well as for rulemakings where from the outset the agency anticipates that the issues will be unusually complex or where the first notice contains only a general description of the subject and issues.[109] Other circumstances that might support a second cycle include the availability of new studies or experiments while the rulemaking is in progress; supervening legal developments such as statutes, regulations, or court decisions that significantly affect the rulemaking; or any other important change in the framework of agency analysis of the rulemaking. Agencies often resort to a second cycle of notice and comment in these types of situations, and courts have expressed their approval of the technique and disapproval of its non-use.[110] Indeed, agencies that voluntarily use a second cycle bear little risk of a procedural violation during that cycle.[111]

---

109. ACUS Recommendation 76-3, *supra* note 64; *see also* Appalachian Power Co. v. EPA, 251 F.3d 1026, 1032–33 (D.C. Cir. 2001) (when EPA allowed additional comments on data methodology to create state budgets and its public notice was ambiguous, it implicitly opened up a second round of public comments on the budgets themselves).

110. In *United Steelworkers v. Marshall*, 647 F.2d 1189, 1222 n.41 (D.C. Cir. 1980), the court referred approvingly to OSHA's use of a supplemental notice on the medical removal protection issue and critically to the agency's failure expressly to mention in that supplemental notice the issue of an "obviously anticipated" lowering of the permissible exposure limit. The court nonetheless held that the proposal was adequate on the issue of the permissible exposure limit because it contained sufficient suggestion of the possibility of a lower permissible exposure limit, even though "OSHA would have served the parties far better" had it listed in the proposed rule two or more alternative permissible limits. *Id. See also* Envtl. Defense, Inc. v. EPA, 509 F.3d 553, 561–62 (D.C. Cir. 2007) (EPA supplemental NPRM provided sufficient notice-and-comment opportunities).

Note that an agency notice of proposed rulemaking may become "too old" at some point anyway, at least without an additional opportunity to comment. *See* Idaho Farm Bureau Fed'n v. Babbitt, 58 F.3d 1392, 1404 (9th Cir. 1995) (upholding a Fish and Wildlife Service rule originally proposed in 1985 and issued in 1992 but only because FWS allowed a second round of comments on new studies in 1992). *See* ACUS Recommendation 2011-2, *supra* note 18, at ¶ 7:

> Although agencies should not automatically deem rulemaking comments to have become stale after any fixed period of time, agencies should closely monitor their rulemaking dockets, and, where an agency believes the circumstances surrounding the rulemaking have materially changed or the rulemaking record has otherwise become stale, consider the use of available mechanisms such as supplemental notices of proposed rulemaking to refresh the rulemaking record.

111. *See* Tex. Office of Pub. Util. Counsel v. FCC, 326 ("Even if we assume that the abbreviated second round of notice-and-comment did not fully meet the APA requirements, it would not undermine the validity of the [rule] because the FCC was not legally required to offer an additional period of notice-and-comment." The court also found that the final rule issued after the second cycle was a logical outgrowth of the original proposal, so petitioners could not have complained if the agency had not offered a second cycle.).

To be sure, a second cycle will delay completion of the rulemaking, but the delay may be legally necessary or desirable from a policy point of view.[112] In any event, a decision on the second cycle will involve balancing fairness and the need for expedition. In one rulemaking, EPA attempted to inoculate itself from a "logical outgrowth" challenge by placing a draft final rule on its website, publishing a notice in the *Federal Register* that it was accepting comments for 30 days before promulgating the final rule.[113] In this instance, however, the agency was persuaded by the comments to undertake a second round of notice and comment, so it is unclear whether this strategy would have worked had the agency proceeded directly to a final rule.[114] On the other hand, merely responding to comments should not in and of itself trigger the need for a second round of notice and comment.[115]

It should also be noted that an agency cannot use the logical outgrowth theory to modify an existing legislative rule without going through a new notice-and-comment rulemaking procedure.[116]

F. Dissents

Members of agency boards or commissions may wish to dissent from the proposed rule. The APA is silent on this matter, so how the dissent is published or otherwise publicized is a matter for the agency (majority) to decide. Agencies typically allow the dissenting member to publish his or her dissent in the NPRM, but occasionally the dissent is paraphrased or published elsewhere.[117]

---

112. *But see* Pub. Citizen Health Res. Grp. v. FDA, 724 F. Supp. 1013, 1022 (D.D.C. 1989).
113. *See* Environmental Protection Agency, Notice of Availability of Draft Rules and Accompanying Information, Operating Permits Program, 62 Fed. Reg. 30,289 (June 3, 1997) ("The draft placed in the docket is styled as a draft 'final' rule because EPA does not anticipate substantial additional changes. However, EPA is accepting comments on revisions to the draft final rule that have changed since the earlier proposals.").
114. *See* Environmental Protection Agency, Notice to Defer Comments on Draft Part 70 Revisions, Operating Permits Program, 62 Fed. Reg. 36,039 (July 3, 1997). An e-mail from Professor Craig Oren brought this to my attention.
115. *See* Natural Res. Def. Council v. Jackson, 650 F.3d 662 (7th Cir. 2011) ("Unless the revisions materially change the text, adding features that the commentators could not have anticipated, there's no need for another round of public comments.").
116. *See* Sprint Corp. v. FCC, 315 F.3d 369, 376 (D.C. Cir. 2003) ("Suffice it to say, there can be no 'logical outgrowth' of a proposal that the agency has not properly noticed.").
117. *See, e.g.*, National Mediation Board, Proposed Rule, Representation Election Procedure, 74 Fed. Reg. 56,750, 56,752–54 (Nov. 3, 2009) (dissenting statement); NLRB, Proposed Rule, Representation—Case Procedures, Notification of Employee Rights Under the National Labor Relations Act, 75 Fed. Reg. 80,410, 80,415 (Dec. 22, 2010) (dissenting statement); Proposed Rule Representation—Case Procedures, 76 Fed. Reg. 36,812, 36,829–33 (June 22, 2011) (containing dissenting view of one member—and a preceding response by the majority); Railroad Retirement Board, Proposed Rule, Recovery of Overpayments, 60 Fed. Reg. 67,108, 67,109 (Dec. 28, 1995) (stating that the Labor Member of the Board dissented from the action of the

majority of the Board in approving this proposed rule" and paraphrasing the Member's reasons); FCC, Proposed Rule Correction, 50 Fed. Reg. 11,188 (Mar. 20, 1985) (stating that "Commissioner Henry Rivera's dissenting statement, inadvertently omitted in the original, is included here"); NRC, Proposed Rule, 49 Fed. Reg. 31,700 (Aug. 8, 1984) (containing separate views of Former Commissioner Gilinsky [who had voted on the rule but left office before it was published]); FCC, Notice of Proposed Rulemaking, 75 F.C.C.2d 138, 1979 WL 43947 (Dec. 19, 1978) (listing the separate views of all five Commissioners).

Chapter 4

Public Participation

Section 553 of the APA provides that "the agency [in informal rulemaking] shall give interested persons an opportunity to participate in the rulemaking through submission of written data, views, or arguments *with or without opportunity for oral presentation.*"[1] The APA thus mandates that rulemaking include an opportunity for written comment but leaves to agencies the decision whether to allow oral presentation of data and views. Some enabling statutes specify a minimum comment period or mandate that public hearings be held; these statutes may also contain other requirements for participation by the public or other groups.[2] This chapter discusses public participation in the rulemaking process, focusing particularly on the general function of written comments in rulemaking.[3] The role of oral hearings in rulemaking is then considered.[4]

A. Opportunity for Written Comment[5]

Although the notice-and-comment process has been criticized as providing an inadequate forum for the public to participate in the rulemaking process,[6] there is little

---

1. 5 U.S.C. § 553(c) (emphasis added).
2. *See, e.g.*, Resource Conservation and Recovery Act of 1976, 42 U.S.C. § 6924(a) (requiring EPA, within specified time limit, to promulgate regulations for treatment, storage or disposal of hazardous waste, "after opportunity for public hearings and after consultation with appropriate Federal and State agencies").
3. For some helpful hints for commenters, see Richard G. Stoll, *Effective Written Comments in Informal Rulemaking*, 32 ADMIN. & REG. L. N. 15 (Summer 2007). *See generally* RICHARD D. STOLL, EFFECTIVE EPA ADVOCACY—ADVANCING AND PROTECTING YOUR CLIENT'S INTERESTS IN THE DECISION-MAKING PRACTICE (Oxford Univ. Press 2010).
4. For a good contemporary commentary on many of the issues covered in this chapter, see Cary Coglianese, Heather Kilmartin & Evan Mendelson, *Transparency and Public Participation in the Federal Rulemaking Process: Recommendations for the New Administration*, 77 GEO. WASH. L. REV. 924 (2009).
5. It should be noted that in some situations, filing a comment may be a prerequisite to judicial review. *See* discussion *infra* Part IV, ch. 1(E)(2).
6. *See, e.g.*, David Barron & Elena Kagan, Chevron*'s Nondelegation Doctrine*, 2001 SUP. CT. REV. 201, 231–32 (calling the process "a charade" that serves as a "forum for competition among

question that agencies must and do take comments seriously and often modify the
final rule as a result of them.[7]

1. *Minimum Time*

The previous chapter's discussion of notices of proposed rulemaking noted that
the APA does not specify a minimum time for submission of written comments.[8] Little
case law exists relating specifically to the length of the comment period. Reviewing
courts apparently are more concerned with the overall adequacy of the opportunity to
comment; the length of the comment period is only one factor to be considered.[9] The
adequacy of the opportunity to comment often turns on steps the agency took, or

---

interest groups rather than as a means to further the public interest"); Jody Freeman, *Collaborative Governance in the Administrative State*, 45 UCLA L. Rev. 1, 12 (1997) (notice and
comment "fail[s] to encourage dialogue and deliberation among the parties most affected by
[the rules]"); E. Donald Elliott, *Re-Inventing Rulemaking*, 41 Duke L.J. 1490, 1492 (1992)
("Notice-and-comment rulemaking is to public participation as Japanese Kabuki theater is to
human passions—a highly stylized process for displaying in a formal way the essence of
something which in real life takes place in other venues."). For interesting broader commentary on public participation in agency proceedings, see Nina A. Mendelson, *Rulemaking,
Democracy, and Torrents of E-Mail*, 79 Geo. Wash. L. Rev. 1343 (2011); Steven P. Croley,
Theories of Regulation: Incorporating the Administrative Process, 98 Colum. L. Rev. 1 (1998);
Jim Rossi, *Participation Run Amok: The Costs of Mass Participation for Deliberative Agency
Decisionmaking*, 92 Nw. U. L. Rev. 173 (1997).

There is also a significant body of literature, mostly published by political scientists,
questioning whether the comment process has been "captured" by "a narrow group of well-
financed stakeholders." Wendy Wagner, et al., *Rulemaking in the Shade: An Empirical Study
of EPA's Air Toxic Emission Standards*, 63 Admin. L. Rev. 99, 106 (2011). This article cites
several studies that seem to show a relative lack of participation by public interest groups, *id.*
at 106–08, and found a significant imbalance in its own study of commenters in EPA hazardous air pollution rulemaking, *id.* at 128–32.

7. *See* ch. 7(B) *infra* for a discussion of the agency's obligation to respond to comments. *See also*
Mariano-Florentino Cuéllar, *Rethinking Regulatory Democracy*, 57 Admin. L. Rev. 411, 414 &
n.6 (2005) (finding public administration literature to be mixed on this subject, but concluding after three of his own agency case studies that agencies did make significant changes in
proposed rules); Cass R. Sunstein, Administrator, Office of Information and Regulatory Affairs, *Humanizing Cost-Benefit Analysis*, Remarks prepared for American University's Washington College of Law, Administrative Law Review Conference 21–22, Feb. 2010, *available
at* http://www.whitehouse.gov/sites/default/files/omb/assets/inforeg/cost_benefit_analysis_
02172010.pdf ("In numerous cases, you will see significant differences from rules as proposed and rules as finalized; the reason is that public comment has pointed the way toward
major improvements.").
8. *See* discussion *supra*, ch. 3(B).
9. *See, e.g.*, Fla. Power & Light Co. v. United States, 846 F.2d 765, 772 (D.C. Cir. 1988) (holding
a 15-day comment period not unreasonable in circumstances); Conn. Light & Power Co. v.
NRC, 673 F.2d 525, 534 (D.C. Cir. 1982) (holding 30 days not unreasonable in light of
industry familiarity with problem).

failed to take, to apprise interested persons of important data or information in its possession.[10]

The fact that reviewing courts have not focused specifically on the time allowed for comment does not mean that agency practice is always sufficient to permit the submission of informed comment. As noted earlier, there is a misconception that the APA establishes a minimum comment period of 30 days. But even assuming interested persons receive notice the day it is published in the *Federal Register*, 30 days may be an inadequate period of time for people to respond to proposals that are complex or based on scientific or technical data.[11] "Interested persons" often are large organizations, which may need time to coordinate an organizational response or to authorize expenditure of funds to do the research needed to produce informed comments.

The APA's legislative history indicates that the notice of proposed rulemaking "must be sufficient to fairly apprise interested parties of the issues involved, so that they may present responsive data or argument."[12] This language was not intended to require an agency, in informal rulemaking, to give interested persons an opportunity to attack the agency's factual basis or to develop "evidence" countering that of the agency. Rules developed through notice-and-comment procedure were supposed to be rational, but the agency had no duty to produce "substantial evidence" in support of its rule.[13] Consequently, it was not envisioned at the time the APA was enacted that interested persons must be given significant time to generate contrary factual information during the public rulemaking proceeding. Rather, the section 553 notice-and-comment opportunity was intended to give interested persons a chance to submit

---

10. *See infra* subsec. A(2); *see also* Omnipoint Corp. v. FCC, 78 F.3d 620 (D.C. Cir. 1996). The FCC responded to the Supreme Court's decision in *Adarand Constructors v. Pena*, 515 U.S. 200 (1995), which applied strict scrutiny to federal programs granting minority preferences, by postponing an auction and quickly proposing its own rule to eliminate sections of its bidding rules that were based on gender or race. The FCC made its final rule immediately effective and only allowed two weeks for comments. Parties who did not have enough time to take advantage of the previous rule's gender and race preferences sued to enjoin the revised rule on the basis that the extremely short comment period did not allow for sufficient public participation. In *Omnipoint*, the D.C. Circuit nevertheless upheld the rule.

11. Note that Executive Order 12,889, "Implementation of the North American Free Trade Agreement," requires that agencies subject to the APA must provide at least a 75-day comment period for "any proposed Federal technical regulation or any Federal sanitary or phytosanitary measure of general application." *Id.* § 4, 58 Fed. Reg. 69,681, 69,681 (Dec. 27, 1993). Also, Exec. Order 12,866 provides that each "agency should afford the public a meaningful opportunity to comment on a proposed regulation, which in most cases should include a comment period of not less than 60 days." Exec. Order 12,866, § 6(a), 58 Fed. Reg. 51,735, 51,735 (Sept. 30, 1993), *reprinted in* Appendix B of this GUIDE.

12. ADMINISTRATIVE PROCEDURE ACT: LEGISLATIVE HISTORY, S. DOC. NO. 248 79-258 (1946).

13. *See* Daniel J. Gifford, *Rulemaking and Rulemaking Review: Struggling Toward a New Paradigm*, 32 ADMIN. L. REV. 577, 588–89 (1980); *see also infra* Part IV, ch. 2(A)(6).

available information to the agency to enhance the agency's knowledge of the subject matter of the rulemaking.[14] Along these lines, one court has pointed out that:

> [T]he APA does not expressly require agencies to keep an "open" mind, whatever such a subjective term might mean [when reviewing public comments]. Rather, section 553(c) requires agencies to afford interested persons an opportunity to participate in public rule making through submission of written data, views, or arguments. Section 553 requires consideration of whatever data and views are submitted. Such consideration has been considered to demonstrate an "open mind."[15]

2. Agency Disclosure of Important Data or Information

The traditional view of section 553 procedure as a process for educating the agency has, however, been gradually replaced, in practice if not in theory, by the belief that informal rulemaking procedure should provide interested persons an opportunity to "challenge the factual assumptions on which [the agency] is proceeding and to show in what respect such assumptions are erroneous."[16] In other words, the public must be informed of the data and assumptions on which the agency's proposal is based.[17]

This change stems largely from courts that have been called upon to review, often in a pre-enforcement setting,[18] complex, scientifically based agency rules. The lead-

---

14. *See* Carl A. Auerbach, *Informal Rule Making: A Proposed Relationship Between Administrative Procedures and Judicial Review*, 72 Nw. L. Rev. 15, 21–23 (1977).
15. Mortg. Investors Corp. of Ohio v. Gober, 220 F.3d 1375, 1379 (Fed. Cir. 2000) (citing Advocates for Highway & Auto Safety v. Fed. Highway Admin., 28 F.3d 1288, 1293 (D.C. Cir. 1994)) ("A review of comments submitted and the responses made persuades us that the agency approached the post-promulgation comments with the requisite open mind.")); *see also* Grand Canyon Air Tour Coal. v. FAA, 154 F.3d 455, 467–68 (D.C. Cir. 1998) (holding that the petitioner's argument that it was not allowed to "comment meaningfully" on an FAA proposed rule did not present a violation of APA opportunity-to-comment requirements when the FAA maintained the enabling statute *required* the FAA to use the Park Service's definition and therefore to ignore petitioner's comments). *But see* Prometheus Radio Project v. FCC, 652 F.3d 431, 453 (3d Cir. 2011) (finding that the FCC failed "to remain 'open-minded' because the timeline of the rulemaking reveals" that two weeks before the comment "period closed and before most of the responses were received, a draft of the [final rule] was circulated internally. The final vote occurred within a week of the response deadline. This is not the agency engagement the APA contemplates.").
16. Magnuson-Moss Warranty–Federal Trade Commission Improvement Act, H. Conf. Rep. No. 1606, 93rd Cong., 2d Sess. 33 (1974).
17. It should be noted that, by and large, pre-proposal drafts of agency rules are considered exempt from disclosure under the Freedom of Information Act's exemption 5 (intra-agency memoranda). This has been criticized. *See, e.g.*, James T. O'Reilly, *Let's Abandon Regulatory Creationism: The Case for Access to Draft Agency Rules*, 28 Admin. & Reg. L. News 4 (Spring 2003).
18. *See infra* Part IV, ch. 1(E)(3), for a discussion of pre-enforcement judicial review.

ing case in this area is *Portland Cement Ass'n v. Ruckelshaus.*[19] In adopting new source performance standards for portland cement plants under the Clean Air Act, EPA published a statement with its final rule indicating that the agency relied on test results that had not been made available for public comment. The D.C. Circuit held there was "a critical defect in the decision-making process in arriving at the standard . . . in the initial inability of petitioners to obtain—in timely fashion—the test results and procedures used . . . [in determining the final standard]."[20] The court went on to state that "[i]t is not consonant with the purpose of a rule-making proceeding to promulgate rules on the basis of inadequate data, or on data that, [in] critical degree, is known only to the agency."[21] Later cases involving EPA rules followed the reasoning of *Portland Cement,*[22] as have cases involving other agencies.[23]

In a 1985 case involving Medicare rules, *Lloyd Noland Hospital and Clinic v. Heckler,*[24] the Eleventh Circuit reaffirmed the principle that "[w]hen a proposed rule is based on scientific data, the agency should identify the data and methodology used to obtain it."[25] The court, citing *Portland Cement,* held that the original agency notice, which cited only a "study conducted by an [agency] consultant . . . ," standing alone, was legally inadequate where the specific study was not identified until the final rule.[26] However, because a copy of the study was sent to three affected hospital associations, and many individual members of the associations submitted comments on it, the court, "[b]ased on the number and relative uniformity of responses," held that there was sufficient "actual notice" to cure any defects in the original notice.[27]

---

19. 486 F.2d 375 (D.C. Cir. 1973), *cert. denied,* 417 U.S. 921 (1974); *see also* discussion *supra* Part III, ch. 3(D).
20. *Id.* at 392.
21. *Id.* at 393.
22. *See, e.g.,* Ethyl Corp. v. EPA, 541 F.2d 1, 48–49 (D.C. Cir. 1976).
23. The court in *United States v. Nova Scotia Food Products Corp.,* 568 F.2d 240 (2d Cir. 1977), focused on the need for full disclosure by the Food and Drug Administration of scientific research being relied on in order to generate meaningful public comment. *Id.* at 252; *see also* Connecticut Light & Power Co., 673 F.2d at 531. Nor will it be enough in most circumstances for the agency to claim that the relied-upon materials were widely available on the Internet. *See* Chamber of Commerce of U.S. v. SEC, 443 F.3d 890, 906–07 (D.C. Cir. 2006). In *Chamber of Commerce,* the court required another round of notice and comment after the agency reaffirmed the remanded rule based on extra-record materials, because those materials "did not merely supplement the rulemaking record without prejudice to the Chamber, and the public availability of those materials, in this instance, does not merit an exception to the comment requirement of section 553(c)"). *Id.* at 901.
24. 762 F.2d 1561 (11th Cir. 1985).
25. *Id.* at 1565.
26. *Id.*
27. *Id.* at 1565–66; *see also* City of Stoughton v. EPA, 858 F.2d 747 (D.C. Cir. 1988) (upholding an EPA rule against challenge that EPA had not made consultant's report available to public, saying that the agency had adequately set forth its theory on issue in question early in proceeding, and that commenters had the opportunity to, and in fact did, specifically address the issues raised); *supra* Part III, ch. 3(E) (discussing the existence of public comments on a particular issue as evidence of adequate notice).

The court decisions suggest that an agency that discovers new and important factual information—or new methods of analyzing the data—that is relevant to the rulemaking and does not notify interested persons of its availability and allow comment on it is running a risk of reversal if the rule is challenged in court.[28] Moreover, when the agency does provide its underlying analysis for a proposed rule, it must be intelligible. For example in *Engine Manufacturers Ass'n v. EPA,*[29] the association was challenging an EPA rule assessing engine manufacturers for the cost of the agency's engine-testing program under the Clean Air Act. In the rulemaking, EPA prepared a 30-page cost analysis that it made available on request during the period for public comment upon the proposed fee schedule. However, the D.C. Circuit said that this was inadequate because it was not something that "the concerned public could understand, at least with the aid of other information that was also reasonably available to the public during the time for public comment."[30] In remanding the rule, the court scathingly criticized the analysis:

> In this case the EPA cost analysis contains page after page of impressive looking but utterly useless tables that appear to have been prepared for internal agency use. Only four of the 30 pages contain any text, and one of those is a rather cursory introduction. The text on each of the other three pages consists primarily of a list of assumptions used in the cost study. Many of those assumptions are complete gibberish to anyone on less than intimate terms with the inner workings of the agency.[31]

---

28. *See* Owner-Operator Indep. Drivers Ass'n, Inc. v. Fed. Motor Carrier Safety Admin., 494 F.3d 188, 201–03 (D.C. Cir. 2007) (holding that FMCSA failed to provide opportunity for comment on methodology of operator-fatigue model for calculating crash risks used to determine benefits and costs of options considered for final rule revising hours of service of long-haul truck drivers, and petitioners were prejudiced by this failure); Penobscot Indian Nation v. U.S. Dep't of Hous. & Urban Dev., 539 F. Supp. 2d 40, 47–51 (D.D.C. 2008) (vacating and remanding HUD rule because HUD relied on its own internal analysis of its loan portfolio without having referred to analysis in proposed regulation and without providing at least a summary of specific data and methodology upon which analysis relied). *But see* Mtg. Investors Corp. of Ohio v. Gober, 220 F.3d at 1379–80 (finding that the Department of Veterans Affairs had not withheld any key data in its notice of proposed rulemaking); Air Transp. Ass'n of Am. v. FAA, 169 F.3d 1, 7–8 (D.C. Cir. 1999) (explaining that in rulemaking an agency can rely on supplemental data not disclosed in a proposed rule) (citing Solite Corp. v. EPA, 952 F.2d 473, 485 (D.C. Cir. 1991) (no procedural error where the agency used supplementary data, not disclosed during the notice-and-comment period, which expanded on and confirmed information in the proposed rulemaking)); Air Transp. Ass'n of Am. v. CAB, 732 F.2d 219, 224 (D.C. Cir. 1984) (no procedural error where the agency relied on internal staff studies, not disclosed during the notice-and-comment period, where the methodology *was* disclosed and the agency made no major changes in the final rule).
29. 20 F.3d 1177 (D.C. Cir. 1994) (R. Ginsburg, J.).
30. *Id.* at 1181.
31. *Id.* It should be noted that one D.C. Circuit judge has recently expressed the opinion that *Portland Cement*, while still binding Circuit precedent, "stands on shaky legal foundation."

These cases raise the question to what extent agencies should routinely make information in their files, or information submitted by interested persons, available to the public for comment during rulemaking. As a matter of sound rulemaking practice, the agency should consider making all information generated during a pre-notice of proposed rulemaking investigation available for comment by interested persons early in the rulemaking, unless it is exempt from disclosure under the Freedom of Information Act.[32] Similarly, all written comments submitted by interested persons should promptly be placed in the rulemaking docket, so that persons who later submit comments can refer to them. This, of course, extends to electronic dockets. OMB has told agencies that it "expects agencies to post public comments and public submissions to the electronic docket on Regulations.gov in a timely manner, regardless of whether they were received via postal mail, email, facsimile, or web form documents submitted directly via Regulations.gov."[33] As noted above, a second cycle of notice and comment may be desirable or necessary in certain circumstances.[34] But the opportunity for comment has to end sometime, and the agencies may have to make hard judgments about the need to reopen the record to receive additional comment.

It should also be noted here that a post-promulgation comment opportunity will not normally serve as an adequate substitute where an agency has not provided opportunity for comment before issuing a rule subject to notice-and-comment requirements.[35] Courts have voiced concerns that an agency will be less likely to change its

---

Am. Radio Relay League, Inc. v. FCC, 524 F.3d 227, 245 (D.C. Cir. 2008) (Kavanaugh, J., concurring) (arguing that the requirement violates *Vermont Yankee's* strictures against mandated procedures not required by the APA). And another panel has required challengers making such an argument to "indicate with reasonable specificity what portions of the documents it objects to and how it might have responded if given the opportunity." Owner-Operator Indep. Drivers Ass'n, Inc. v. Fed. Motor Carrier Safety Admin., 494 F.3d at 202.

32. The Freedom of Information Act (FOIA) exemptions are provided in 5 U.S.C. § 552(b)(1)–(9). Following this advice will consume time and resources, but if the rulemaking is at all controversial, FOIA requests for this material are to be expected. Therefore, the question becomes one of timing, and agency staff may ultimately benefit from not having to divert their efforts to do this work midway through a rulemaking proceeding. Use of the Internet and other information technologies can facilitate this effort. *See supra* Part III, ch. 1(C).

33. Office of Information & Regulatory Affairs, Memorandum for the President's Management Council on Increasing Openness in the Rulemaking Process—Improving Electronic Dockets 2 (May 28, 2010), *available at* http://www.whitehouse.gov/sites/default/files/omb/assets/inforeg/edocket_final_5-28-2010.pdf. ACUS has echoed this: "Agencies should adopt stated policies of posting public comments to the Internet within a specified period after submission. Agencies should post all electronically submitted comments on the Internet and should also scan and post all comments submitted in paper format." ACUS Recommendation 2011-2, *Rulemaking Comments*, ¶ 3 (June 16, 2011), 76 Fed. Reg. 48,791 (Aug. 9, 2011).

34. ACUS Recommendation 76-3, *Procedures in Addition to Notice and the Opportunity for Comment in Informal Rulemaking*, ¶¶ 1(a) and (b), 41 Fed. Reg. 29,653, 29,654 (July 19, 1976). *See* discussion *supra* Part III, ch. 3(E).

35. Air Transport Ass'n v. DOT, 900 F.2d 369 (D.C. Cir. 1990), *remanded*, 498 U.S. 1077 (1991), *vacated as moot*, 933 F.2d 1043 (D.C. Cir. 1991); *see supra* Part II, ch. 1(D)(3)(f) & (D)(4)(c).

mind after a rule is in place, and the public is less likely to participate in what appears to be a *fait accompli*. Courts have, however, sometimes taken into account an agency's response to post-promulgation comments in deciding whether to uphold a rule that should have been issued after notice and comment. Where an agency's response suggests that it has been open-minded in considering comments, "the presumption against a late comment period can be overcome and a rule upheld."[36]

B. Special Consultation Requirements

Under the Regulatory Flexibility Act, as strengthened by the Small Business Regulatory Enforcement Fairness Act of 1996 (SBREFA),[37] agencies are subject to additional consultation requirements when they are proposing a rule that "will have a significant economic impact on a substantial number of small entities."[38] In such instances, agencies are directed to "assure that small entities have been given an opportunity to participate in the rulemaking" through techniques such as (1) use of advance notices of proposed rulemaking to broadcast the potential impact, (2) publication of the notice in specialized publications, (3) direct notification of small entities, (4) conduct of open conferences and public hearings and use of computer networks, and (5) procedures to make participation easier and less costly for small entities.[39] However,

---

36. Levesque v. Block, 723 F.2d 175, 188 (1st Cir. 1983); *cf. Air Transport Ass'n*, 900 F.2d at 369. Where notice and comment is not required, such as in cases involving interpretive rules or "good cause," the Administrative Conference recommended providing opportunity for post-promulgation comment to identify shortcomings in the rule and to assist a reviewing court in determining the reasonableness of the agency's position. ACUS Recommendation 76-5, *Interpretive Rules of General Applicability and Statements of General Policy*, 41 Fed. Reg. 56,769 (Dec. 30, 1976); ACUS Recommendation 83-2, *The 'Good Cause' Exemption from APA Rulemaking Requirements*, 48 Fed. Reg. 31,180 (July 7, 1983); ACUS Recommendation 95-4, *Procedures for Noncontroversial and Expedited Rulemaking*, ¶ II, 60 Fed. Reg. 43,110 (Aug. 18, 1995); *see also* Michael R. Asimow, *Interim-Final Rules: Making Haste Slowly*, 51 ADMIN. L. REV. 703 (1999); Part II, ch. 1(D)(2)–(3), *supra*.

37. Pub. L. No. 104-121, Title II, 110 Stat. 857 (1996) (codified in scattered sections of 5 U.S.C.). The amendments to the Regulatory Flexibility Act are in Subtitle D, 104 Stat. 864–68. *See generally* Thomas O. Sargentich, *The Small Business Regulatory Enforcement Fairness Act*, 49 ADMIN. L. REV. 123 (1997). The most important change was the addition of judicial review of compliance with the Act. The SBREFA also created a Small Business and Agriculture Regulatory Enforcement Ombudsman, 15 U.S.C. § 657, and the congressional review process, 5 U.S.C. §§ 801–808, discussed *supra* Part II, ch. 3(J).

38. 5 U.S.C. § 609(a).

39. *Id*; *see also* Unfunded Mandates Reform Act, Pub. L. No. 104-4, § 202, 109 Stat. 48, 64 (1995) (codified at 2 U.S.C. § 1532(a)(5)) (requiring agencies to describe their consultations with elected representatives of state, local, and tribal governments); Exec. Order No. 12,866, §§ 1(b)(9), 4(e) (mandating consultations with state, local, and tribal officials). *See* discussion *supra* Part II, ch. 3(G).

while section 609 instructs the agency to assure participation, the method and manner of doing so is left primarily to the agency's discretion.[40]

For "covered agencies" (currently only EPA, OSHA, and the Consumer Financial Protection Bureau of the Federal Reserve System),[41] additional consultation requirements were added, requiring them, prior to issuance of the initial regulatory flexibility analysis, to convene a special review panel consisting of OMB and representatives of affected small entities. The panel must file a public report on the impacts of the proposal within 60 days. The agency, upon receiving the report, shall, as appropriate, modify the proposed rule or the analysis.[42]

Also, several Executive Orders require special requirements for consultation with state and local governments and Indian tribes.[43]

C. Oral Hearings in APA Rulemakings

The APA gives agencies the discretion whether to hold oral hearings in informal rulemaking. However, some specific statutes require that agencies provide an opportunity for oral presentation of data or views or a public hearing,[44] and a few statutes require agencies to provide an opportunity for cross-examination in informal rulemaking.[45]

1. The Administrative Procedure Act

As noted at the beginning of this chapter, section 553 of the APA requires agencies to give the public notice and an opportunity to comment on a proposed rule "with or without opportunity for oral presentation."[46] The APA does not mandate an oral hearing in *informal* rulemaking. However, section 553(c) provides that for *formal* rulemaking, that is, "[w]hen rules are required by statute to be made *on the record after opportunity for an agency hearing*, sections 556 and 557 of this title apply. . . ."[47] Sections 556 and 557 contain requirements for "trial-type," or evidentiary, hearings, including the right of interested parties to present evidence, conduct cross-examination of witnesses who introduce opposing evidence, and submit rebuttal evidence—and the rulemaking record

---

40. *See* Associated Fisheries of Me., Inc. v. Daley, 127 F.3d 104, 117 (1st Cir. 1997) ("While section 609 instructs the Secretary to assure participation, the method and manner of doing so is left primarily to the Secretary's sound discretion. In this situation, we are satisfied that the Secretary provided adequate participatory opportunities for small businesses.").

41. 5 U.S.C. § 609(d). See discussion, *supra* Part III, ch. 2(C).

42. *Id.*

43. *See* Executive Order 13,132 ("Federalism") and Executive Order 13,175 ("Consultation with Indian Tribal Governments"). These orders are discussed *supra* in Part III, ch. 2(H).

44. *See, e.g.*, Resource Conservation and Recovery Act, 42 U.S.C. § 6924(a); Occupational Safety and Health Act, 29 U.S.C. § 655(b).

45. *See infra* subsec. (C)(2).

46. 5 U.S.C. § 553(c).

47. *Id.* (emphasis added).

is the exclusive basis for the decision.[48]

In the early 1970s, the Supreme Court issued two important decisions concerning the application of these APA rulemaking provisions. In *United States v. Allegheny-Ludlum Steel Corp.*,[49] the Supreme Court held that even though section 1(14)(a) of the Interstate Commerce Act provided that rules must be adopted "after hearing," the Interstate Commerce Commission (ICC) did not violate the APA when it promulgated freight-car service rules under that section without holding a trial-type hearing in accordance with the formal rulemaking provisions of the APA. The Court read section 553(c) narrowly and concluded that because the Interstate Commerce Act did not require rules to be made *on the record* after a hearing, sections 556 and 557 did not apply. Therefore, a requirement for a hearing in a statute does not, by itself, trigger the APA's formal rulemaking requirements.[50]

In *United States v. Florida East Coast Railway*,[51] the Court went even further. In that case, a subsequent ICC rule was challenged on the ground that the ICC's rulemaking procedure was deficient because it did not afford affected persons any oral hearing opportunity. Appellants argued that even if the formal rulemaking provisions of the APA were not triggered, the Interstate Commerce Act gave them a right to something like a trial-type hearing. The Supreme Court rejected the appellants' contention that they were entitled to present evidence orally, cross-examine opposing witnesses, and present oral argument to the agency decisionmaker. The Court concluded that a statutory requirement of a hearing may, in some circumstances, be satisfied by procedures that meet only the standards of section 553.[52] In other words, notice-and-comment procedure may satisfy a "hearing" requirement.[53]

Although the petitioners in *Florida East Coast Railway* did not claim they were denied constitutional due process by the ICC's procedures, the Supreme Court made clear that in legislative rulemaking, notice-and-comment procedure ordinarily comports with due process.[54] Only when a rulemaking singles out a particular person for

---

48. *See* discussion *supra* Part II, ch. 1(B), for a brief summary of procedural requirements for formal rulemaking.

49. 406 U.S. 742 (1972).

50. *Id.* at 757.

51. 410 U.S. 224 (1973).

52. *Id.* at 240–41.

53. Because this case involved ratemaking, which traditionally has been conducted using formal procedures, some observers agreed with the Court's dissenters that *Florida East Coast Railway* was a "sharp break with traditional concepts of procedural due process." 410 U.S. at 246 (Douglas, J., dissenting). *See* KENNETH CULP DAVIS & RICHARD J. PIERCE, JR., ADMINISTRATIVE LAW TREATISE § 7.2 (3d ed. 1994); *cf.* Nathaniel L. Nathanson, *Probing the Mind of the Administrator: Hearing Variations and Standards of Judicial Review Under the Administrative Procedure Act and Other Federal Statutes*, 75 COLUM. L. REV. 721 (1975).

54. 410 U.S. at 242–46; *see also* Ernest Gellhorn & Glen O. Robinson, *Rulemaking "Due Process": An Inconclusive Dialogue*, 48 U. CHI. L. REV. 201 (1981).

special consideration based on individualized facts at issue will an oral hearing be required.[55]

In most rulemakings those conditions are not present, and the Supreme Court has ruled that in the absence of other statutory requirements, courts normally are limited in requiring additional procedures beyond those mandated by the APA's notice-and-comment rulemaking procedures.[56] However, the Court also was careful to point out that:

> [I]n prior opinions we have intimated that even in a rulemaking proceeding when an agency is making a "quasi-judicial" determination by which a very small number of persons are "exceptionally affected, in each case upon individual grounds," in some circumstances additional procedures may be required in order to afford the aggrieved individuals due process.[57]

This principle was recognized by Judge Posner in *United Airlines, Inc. v. CAB.*[58] In that case, he first made it clear:

> [That] an agency is not allowed to conduct what is in fact an adjudicative proceeding without giving the affected parties an opportunity for an evidentiary hearing, just by calling the proceeding informal rulemaking. That would be too facile an evasion of the procedures that the Administrative Procedure Act requires for adjudicative proceedings. . . .[59]

After finding that the CAB did not do this, although "[a]dmittedly it came close," the court found that even in a legitimate rulemaking, *Vermont Yankee* did not prevent the "judicial importation of cross-examination requirements, where an ancient and well-established adjudicatory issue has been kidnapped into rulemaking."[60]

In the end, the court upheld the rulemaking process because:

> In the face of [the precedents cited], United [Airlines], to show entitlement to an evidentiary hearing in this matter, would have to show with some particularity that cross-examination or other procedures that only such a hearing would enable was necessary to resolve specific factual disputes that are critical to the soundness of the Board's rules. It has not attempted to show this.[61]

---

55. *Fla. East Coast Ry.*, 410 U.S. at 245–46; *cf.* Pickus v. U.S. Bd. of Parole, 543 F.2d 240, 244–45 (D.C. Cir. 1976). The Supreme Court has long recognized the need for an individualized hearing where adjudicative facts are in issue, and "a relatively small number of persons" are "exceptionally affected" by the government's action. *See* Bi-Metallic Inv. Co. v. State Bd. of Equalization, 239 U.S. 441, 446 (1915) (Holmes, J.).

56. Vt. Yankee Nuclear Power Corp. v. Natural Res. Def. Council, 435 U.S. 519 (1978).

57. *Id.* at 542 (citing *Bi-Metallic* and *Fla. East Coast Ry.*, 410 U.S. at 242–45).

58. 766 F.2d 1107 (7th Cir. 1985).

59. *Id.* at 1116.

60. *Id.* at 1118 (citing Antonin Scalia, Vermont Yankee: *The APA, the D.C. Circuit, and the Supreme Court*, 1978 Sᴜᴘ. Cᴛ. Rᴇᴠ. 345, 395).

61. *Id.* at 1121.

2. Hearing Requirements in Hybrid Rulemaking Statutes

Although the APA does not contain an oral hearing requirement for informal rulemaking, some laws enacted in the 1970s do contain requirements that the agency hold a "public hearing" or provide interested persons "an opportunity for the oral presentation of data, views, or arguments" in rulemaking. Such statutes became known as "hybrid" rulemaking statutes because they combined elements of formal and informal rulemaking.[62] Statutes calling for a legislative-type hearing include the Occupational Safety and Health Act (1970),[63] the Consumer Product Safety Act (1972),[64] the Safe Drinking Water Act (1974),[65] the Energy Policy and Conservation Act (1975),[66] the Clean Water Act (1977),[67] the Federal Mine Safety and Health Amendment Act (1977),[68] and the Endangered Species Act Amendments (1978).[69]

A few of these hybrid rulemaking statutes require not only a legislative-type hearing but also an opportunity for interested persons to question or cross-examine opposing witnesses. These include the Magnuson-Moss Warranty–Federal Trade Commission Improvement Act (1975),[70] the Securities Acts Amendments (1975),[71] and the Toxic Substances Control Act (1976).[72] Some agencies have provided by regulation for questioning of witnesses.[73]

The enactment of statutes requiring an oral hearing likely reflected the growing complexity of the issues involved in informal rulemaking, the perceived need to probe the accuracy of public comments on these issues, and the strong belief among legislators in the value of oral communication between regulators and the regulated. However, few such statutes have been enacted since the 1970s.[74]

---

62. *See supra* Part I, n.2.
63. 29 U.S.C. § 655.
64. 15 U.S.C. §§ 2056, 2058.
65. 42 U.S.C. § 300g–l(d).
66. *Id.* §§ 6295, 6306.
67. *Id.* § 7606(d).
68. 30 U.S.C. § 811.
69. 16 U.S.C. § 1533.
70. 15 U.S.C. § 57a. *See* Harry and Bryant Co. v. FTC, 726 F.2d 993 (4th Cir 1984) (upholding FTC funeral industry rule over challenge that plaintiffs were denied due process in rulemaking).
71. 15 U.S.C. § 78f(e).
72. *Id.* § 2605.
73. *See, e.g.*, OSHA, Nature of a Hearing, 29 C.F.R. § 1911.15(a)(3) ("The oral hearing shall be legislative in type. However, fairness may require an opportunity for cross-examination on crucial issues.").
74. As discussed in Part I, the trend toward court-imposed additional rulemaking was halted in 1978 by the Supreme Court decision in *Vermont Yankee*. The strong emphasis on deregulation after 1981 sharply reduced the number of regulatory statutes enacted and thus the use of hybrid rulemaking. *But see* 20 U.S.C.A. § 1028 (2002) (requiring use of negotiated rulemaking by Department of Education).

3. *The Position of the Administrative Conference on Hearings in Rulemaking*

The Administrative Conference addressed the issue of hearings in informal rulemaking in several recommendations. In Recommendation 72-5,[75] the Conference recommended that (1) Congress ordinarily should not impose mandatory procedures beyond those required by section 553;[76] (2) Congress should never require trial-type procedures for resolving questions of policy or general fact (in contrast to "specific" or "adjudicative" fact);[77] and (3) agencies should decide in light of the needs of particular proceedings whether to employ additional procedures, including "a public-meeting type of hearing, or trial-type hearing for issues of specific fact."[78]

Although opposing across-the-board, statutorily mandated additions to section 553 procedure, the Conference did recommend that agencies, in appropriate circumstances, enlarge the opportunity for public participation in informal rulemaking by employing procedures beyond a single round of notice and comment. It recommended such mechanisms as providing for a second cycle of notice and comment, holding public conferences where allowing participants to question each other would be effective in clarifying or narrowing the disputed issues, providing a fuller statement of issues in the proposal, and allowing oral argument or other oral presentations at which the presiding official could ask questions.[79]

In a 1982 statement, "Views of the Administrative Conference on Proposals Pending in Congress to Amend the Informal Rulemaking Provisions of the Administrative Procedure Act,"[80] the Conference reiterated that "an opportunity for oral presentation of data and views should not be a mandatory requirement in rulemaking under section 553 even if the requirement is limited, . . . to 'major' rulemakings."[81] The Conference reaffirmed its earlier position that agencies should use oral hearings in appropriate circumstances but concluded that "agencies should have discretion to decide when and to whom the presentations are made."[82] Finally, the Conference advised Congress not to enact provisions in the bills that would require cross-examination in rulemaking,

---

75. ACUS Recommendation 72-5, *Procedures for the Adoption of Rules of General Applicability*, 38 Fed. Reg. 19,792 (July 23, 1973).
76. *Id.* ¶ 2.
77. *Id.* ¶ 3. The distinction has often been drawn between the type of "factual" questions that arise in rulemaking proceedings, that is, questions of "policy," "general fact," or "legislative fact," and those that arise in adjudication, referred to as questions of "adjudicative" fact. On this distinction, see Davis & Pierce, *supra* note 53, at § 10.5.
78. ACUS Recommendation 72-5, *supra* note 75, at ¶ 5.
79. ACUS Recommendation 76-3, *supra* note 34.
80. ACUS Statement 7, *Views of the Administrative Conference on Proposals Pending in Congress to Amend the Informal Rulemaking Provisions of the APA*, 47 Fed. Reg. 30,715 (July 15, 1982).
81. *Id.* at ¶ 2.
82. *Id.*

even though these bills would have required cross-examination only as a "last resort" procedure.[83]

4. *Agency Oral Hearing Procedures*

Agencies have adopted several procedural approaches in determining whether and when to hold legislative-type hearings in rulemakings under section 553. Where the statute requires the agency to hold a hearing upon request,[84] the agency may publish a proposal, request written comments, and wait until one or more requests are received and evaluated before directing a hearing.[85] Where the statute requires an oral hearing, or the issues are such that a hearing clearly will be needed, an agency may set the hearing date in the initial proposal in anticipation of requests for a hearing,[86] especially where time is a factor—for example, when there is a judicial deadline.[87] An agency may announce in its NPRM that a hearing is being considered and then await public reaction before making its decision on the hearing.[88] Where the statute does

---

83. *Id.* ¶ 3. The FTC is one of the few agencies with extensive experience using cross-examination in rulemaking. 15 U.S.C. 57a(c)(2)(B). At Congress's request, the Administrative Conference studied the FTC's experience. *See* ACUS Recommendation 79-1, *Hybrid Rulemaking Procedures of the Federal Trade Commission*, 44 Fed. Reg. 38,817 (July 3, 1979); ACUS Recommendation 80-1, *Trade Regulation Rulemaking Under the Magnuson-Moss Warranty FTC Improvement Act*, 45 Fed. Reg. 46,772 (July 11, 1980). After analyzing the FTC procedure, the Conference reaffirmed its view that "Congress should not ordinarily require, for agency rulemaking, procedures in addition to those specified by section 553 of the [APA], although the agencies should have the discretion to utilize them." *Id.* ¶ B.2.
84. *See, e.g.*, OSH Act, 29 U.S.C. § 655(b)(3) ("[A]ny interested persons may file with the Secretary [of Labor] written objections to the proposed rule, stating the grounds therefor and requesting a public hearing on such objections."); *see also* 29 C.F.R. §§ 1911.11(b)(4), 1911.11(c).
85. *See, e.g.*, OSHA, Notice of Proposed Rulemaking, Explosive and Other Dangerous Atmospheres in Vessels and Vessel Sections, 53 Fed. Reg. 48,092, 48,105 (Nov. 29, 1988) (inviting written comments on proposal and advising that interested persons may file objections to proposal and request informal hearing).
86. *See* EPA, Proposed Rule and Notice of Public Hearing, National Emission Standard for Hazardous Air Pollutants, Benzene Emissions from Various Sources, 53 Fed. Reg. 28,496, 28,571 (July 28, 1988) (setting public hearing in accordance with § 112(b)(1)(B) and § 307(d)(5) of Clean Air Act); OSHA, Proposed Rule, Air Contaminants, 53 Fed. Reg. 20,960, 21,262 (June 7, 1988) (setting informal hearing under § 6(b)(3) of OSH Act).
87. *See, e.g.*, OSHA, Proposed Rule, Occupational Exposure to Ethylene Oxide, 48 Fed. Reg. 17,284 (Apr. 21, 1983). The D.C. Circuit had ordered OSHA to issue a proposed standard within 30 days and strongly urged that a final standard be issued within a year. Pub. Citizen Health Res. Group v. Auchter, 702 F.2d 1150 (D.C. Cir. 1983).
88. *See, e.g.*, Federal Highway Administration, Notices of Proposed Rulemaking, Motor Carrier Safety Standards; Controlled Substances, 53 Fed. Reg. 22,268, 22,268 (June 14, 1988) (allowing 90 days for written comments and indicating that FHA is "also considering holding a public hearing on this proposal, and if so, will announce the time and place of the hearing in the Federal Register").

not require a hearing, the agency may exercise its discretion to call the hearing at any stage of the process.[89]

Where a legislative-type rulemaking hearing will be conducted, the agency must determine the specific procedures that will be followed. In some cases, the enabling statute will stipulate the procedures that must be followed.[90] In others, agency rulemaking regulations may establish general procedures.[91] In any event, the agency will usually state the procedural ground rules in its notice of the hearing.[92] An innovation used by the Department of Agriculture was to hold a "scoping" meeting in which interested parties were invited to discuss the agenda and the format for a scheduled public hearing on a proposed rule to revise regulations concerning genetically engi-

---

89. Agencies sometimes set a series of hearings either because they wish to facilitate nationwide participation or because the issues involved are of special interest to particular parts of the country. *See, e.g.*, NLRB, Second Notice of Proposed Rulemaking, Collective-Bargaining Units in the Health Care Industry, 53 Fed. Reg. 33,900 (Sept. 1, 1988) (requesting second cycle of public comments and describing first round of public hearings held in various cities); *see also* Office of the Secretary, Department of Transportation, denial of petition for fact hearing, Computer Reservations System Regulations; Statements of General Policy, 68 Fed. Reg. 12,883 (Mar. 18, 2003) (denying petition for "fact hearing" that would give each commenter the opportunity to interrogate Department staff members about the basis for the notice of proposed rulemaking's tentative findings and proposals and to cross-examine representatives from the other commenters, but allowing an oral hearing where commenters could present their factual and legal arguments).

90. *See, e.g.*, FTC Improvements Act of 1980, 15 U.S.C. § 57a(c)(2); 16 C.F.R. § 1.14. For an application of these procedures, see FTC, Notice of Proposed Rulemaking, Funeral Industry Practices Trade Regulation Rule, 53 Fed. Reg. 19,864, 19,871–72 (May 31, 1988) (setting public hearing and specifying procedures).

91. *See, e.g.*, 29 C.F.R. § 1911.15–17 (describing OSHA procedures).

92. Among the procedural issues that may need to be addressed are (1) who will preside at the hearing; (2) any requirements individuals wishing to testify at the hearing must satisfy; (3) whether cross-examination will be permitted; (4) what will be the agency's role at the hearing, including whether it will present witnesses in support of its proposal; and (5) what post-hearing procedures will be provided. *See, e.g.*, OSHA, Proposed Rule, Air Contaminants, 53 Fed. Reg. 20,960, 21,262 (June 7, 1988) (setting informal hearing under § 6(b)(3) of OSH Act); FTC, Funeral Industry Practices Trade Regulation Rule, 53 Fed. Reg. 19,864, 19,872 (May 31, 1988); EPA, National Emission Standards for Hazardous Air Pollutants, Benzene Emissions, 53 Fed. Reg. 28,496, 28,571 (July 28, 1988) (requiring that persons desiring to appear at hearing must contact EPA; oral statements limited to 10 minutes; written statements may be filed before, during, or within 30 days of hearing). *See also* FTC, ADMINISTRATIVE STAFF MANUAL: OPERATING MANUAL, RULEMAKING ch. 7, *available at* http://www.ftc.gov/foia/ch07rulemaking.pdf.

neered organisms.[93] Agencies now commonly webcast these public hearings and sometimes allow remote public participation.[94]

93. *See* Animal & Plant Health Inspection Serv., Proposed Rule; notice of public scoping session and extension of public comment period, Introduction to Organisms and Products Altered or Produced Through Genetic Engineering, 74 Fed. Reg. 10,517 (Mar. 11, 2009).

94. For examples of recent federal agency use of webcasts in rulemaking, see, *e.g.*, FTC "Appliance Labeling Rule," 73 Fed. Reg. 40,988 (July 17, 2008) (public roundtable made available via live webcast at http://www.ftc.gov/bcp/ workshops/lamp/index.shtml); SSA, ANPRM on Compassionate Allowances for Cancers, 73 Fed. Reg. 10,715 (Feb. 28, 2008) (public hearing available for viewing live via webcast at http://www.socialsecurity.gov/ compassionateallowances/hearings0407.htm; DHS, final rule, Minimum Standards for Driver's Licenses and Identification Cards Acceptable by Federal Agencies for Official Purposes, 73 Fed. Reg. 5272 (Jan. 29, 2008) (indicating that DHS held several public meetings "with participation also available via webcast"); DOE, final rule, Distribution Transformers, Energy Conservation Standards, 72 Fed. Reg. 58,190 (Oct. 12, 2007) ("In preparation for the September 28, 2004, ANOPR public meeting, DOE held a Webcast to acquaint stakeholders with the analytical tools and with other material DOE had published the previous month.").

Chapter 5

The Rulemaking Record

The development of the concept of the rulemaking record or file has been one of the most significant changes in informal rulemaking procedure since the APA was enacted. Although debate remains about its function, a consensus has emerged that a rulemaking record or file (now typically called a "docket") should be created in informal rulemaking.

A. The Evolution of the "Rulemaking Record" Concept

When the APA was enacted, it was not generally thought that agencies needed to develop factual support for legislative rules.[1] Of course, agencies frequently would have developed factual support for a rule in anticipation of a court challenge, if not simply as a matter of sound agency practice.[2] In fact, the legislative history of section 553 indicates that the Act's drafters expected agencies to use their discretion to develop supporting records if the nature of the particular proceeding required it.[3]

---

1. Professor Kenneth Culp Davis described the original understanding as follows:

   In making rules of general applicability, agencies were generally free, in absence of special statute, to develop factual materials or not to develop them, as they saw fit, unless a party subject to a rule attempted to rebut the presumption [of the existence of facts justifying the rule] on judicial review. Such freedom of agencies was understood and accepted at the time of enactment of the [APA] in 1946. Nothing in the APA changed the presumption.

   KENNETH CULP DAVIS, ADMINISTRATIVE LAW TREATISE § 6:1 (2d ed. 1978).

2. *See* REPORT OF THE ATTORNEY GENERAL'S COMMITTEE ON ADMINISTRATIVE PROCEDURE IN GOVERNMENT AGENCIES, S. DOC. NO. 77-8 111-14 (1941) (describing agency investigation practices).

3. The legislative history provides:

   The first sentence [of § 4 of the APA, now 5 U.S.C. § 553] states the minimum requirements of public rulemaking procedure short of statutory hearing. Under it agencies might in addition confer with industry advisory committees, consult organizations, hold informal "hearings," and the like. Open proceedings may be aided by the submission of reports or summaries of data by agency representatives. . . . Considerations of practicality, necessity, and public interest as discussed in connection with section 4(a) will naturally govern the agency's determination of the extent to which public proceedings may be carried. *Matters of great import, or those where the public submission of facts will be either useful to the agency or a protection to the public, should naturally be accorded*

One reason the APA drafters were content to give agencies discretion to develop record support for legislative rules was that when the APA was enacted, the validity of rules generally was determined on judicial review of an agency enforcement action. A record for review could thus be developed either in the agency proceeding or de novo in the reviewing court.[4]

Another reason for the latitude given agencies to produce factual support for rules was the presumption in favor of the existence of facts supporting a rule. This presumption was established by *Pacific States Box & Basket Co. v. White*,[5] a 1935 decision in which the Supreme Court applied to a rulemaking something like the "rational basis" test used in review of statutes. The Court labeled the regulation involved as "general legislation."[6] The effect of this presumption was to place upon a rule challenger the burden of disproving supporting factual premises and rationales for the rule, at least as applied to the challenger. The agency had no burden to show, in the first instance, factual support for the rule.[7]

Around 1970, reviewing courts, especially in the environmental area, began to back away from *Pacific States Box & Basket*'s deferential review of informal rulemaking. In *Citizens to Preserve Overton Park, Inc. v. Volpe*,[8] the Supreme Court stated that although agency action is entitled to a presumption of regularity, "that presumption is not to shield [the] action from a thorough, probing, in-depth review."[9] In rejecting the argument that the case be remanded to the agency for formal findings, the Court stated that the delay involved in the remand would be unnecessary because

---

> *more elaborate public procedures. The agency must keep a record of and analyze and consider all relevant matter presented prior to the issuance of rules. The required statement of the basis and purpose of rules issued should not only relate to the data so presented but with reasonable fullness explain the actual basis and objectives of the rule.*

Report on the Administrative Procedure Act, H.R. Rep. No. 1980, 79th Cong., 2d Sess. 259 (1946) (emphasis added).

4. *See* Carl A. Auerbach, *Informal Rule Making: A Proposed Relationship Between Administrative Procedures and Judicial Review*, 72 Nw. U. L. Rev. 15, 24–25 (1977).

5. 296 U.S. 176 (1935).

6. *Id.* at 186.

7. *See* Daniel J. Gifford, *Rulemaking and Rulemaking Review: Struggling Toward a New Paradigm*, 32 Admin. L. Rev. 577, 582–90 (1980) (discussing the presumption of validity). It should be noted that the APA's provisions for formal rulemaking, required to be conducted under the procedures in §§ 556 and 557, stand in sharp contrast with those required for informal rulemaking under § 553. In formal rulemaking, the proponent of a rule has the burden of proof, and the final rule must be supported by "reliable, probative, and substantial evidence." 5 U.S.C. § 556(d). The "transcript of testimony and exhibits, together with all papers and requests filed in the proceeding, constitutes the exclusive record for decision" in such rulemaking. 5 U.S.C. § 556(e). Formal rulemaking is often called "on-the-record" rulemaking because of these requirements.

8. 401 U.S. 402 (1971); *see also* discussion *supra* Part I(B).

9. 401 U.S. at 415.

"there is an administrative record that allows the full, prompt review of the Secretary [of Transportation]'s action."[10] However, the Court refused to accept as the record in the proceeding the agency's "'post hoc' rationalizations" of the decision in the form of litigation affidavits. The Court therefore remanded the case to the district court for "plenary review," which was to be "based on the full administrative record that was before the Secretary at the time he made his decision."[11]

Although *Overton Park* itself did not involve agency rulemaking,[12] it has been a major influence on the standard of court review of agency rulemaking and of the requirement for a record as a basis for court review.[13] Cases such as *Portland Cement Ass'n v. Ruckelshaus*[14] and *United States v. Nova Scotia Food Products*[15] further promoted the growth of "records" in informal proceedings by requiring agencies to make available for public comment important studies and other data on which they rely in determining the final rule.[16]

The rulemaking record's importance in the review process was articulated by the D.C. Circuit in 1977 in *Home Box Office, Inc. v. FCC*[17] as follows: "Whatever the law may have been in the past, there can now be no doubt that implicit in the decision to treat the promulgation of rules as a 'final' event in an ongoing process of administration is an assumption that an act of reasoned judgment has occurred, an assumption which further implicates the existence of a body of material—documents, comments, transcripts, and statements in various forms declaring agency expertise or policy—with reference to which such judgment was exercised."[18] It is "against this material,"

---

10. *Id.* at 419.
11. *Id.* at 420–21.
12. The action in *Overton Park* was an informal adjudication because it involved the Secretary's determination to release federal funds to a state highway department for highway construction through a public park. The story is well told in Peter L. Strauss, Citizens to Preserve Overton Park v. Volpe—*of Politics and Law, Young Lawyers and the Highway Goliath, in* ADMINISTRATIVE LAW STORIES 258 (Peter L. Strauss ed., 2006).
13. *Overton Park* was cited in more than 650 federal court opinions just in the period between March 1971, when the case was decided, and December 1978. *See* William H. Rodgers, Jr., *A Hard Look at* Vermont Yankee*: Environmental Law Under Close Scrutiny*, 67 GEO. L.J. 699, 716 n.126 (1979); *see also* James V. DeLong, *Informal Rulemaking and the Integration of Law and Policy*, 65 VA. L. REV. 257, 262–76 (1979).
14. 486 F.2d 375 (D.C. Cir. 1973).
15. 568 F.2d 240 (2d Cir. 1977).
16. *Nova Scotia* involved a challenge to an FDA rule in the context of an enforcement proceeding. The rule was challenged on the grounds that FDA had failed to follow proper notice-and-comment procedures in promulgating the rule. The court upheld the challenge, in part on the basis that the agency had failed to make or certify a "contemporaneous record," which included certain scientific studies relied on in promulgating the rule at the time of the original rulemaking agency proceeding. *Id.* at 249.
17. 567 F.2d 9 (D.C. Cir. 1977), *cert. denied*, 434 U.S. 829 (1977).
18. *Id.* at 54 (citations omitted). See also the Supreme Court's assumption of the existence of a rulemaking record in *Vermont Yankee*, 435 U.S. at 547 ("Thus, the adequacy of the 'record' in

the court in *Home Box Office* said, that it is "the obligation of this court to test the actions of the agency for arbitrariness or inconsistency with delegated authority."[19]

Congress, in enacting hybrid rulemaking statutes, has specifically required agencies to have record support for final rules, and some of these statutes explicitly require the agency to maintain a rulemaking record or file for judicial review.[20] The Clean Air Act has particularly detailed record requirements.[21]

Comprehensive regulatory reform bills considered by Congress in 1982, and again in 1995, would have required agencies to maintain a rulemaking file and to include certain material in the file.[22] The Administrative Conference reacted to these proposals by supporting a rulemaking file requirement in the APA, although the Conference's recommended language differed somewhat from the bill provisions.[23]

---

this type of proceeding is not correlated directly to the type of procedural devices employed, but rather turns on whether the agency has followed the statutory mandate of the Administrative Procedure Act or other relevant statutes.").

19. *Id.* (citing *Overton Park*). As discussed *infra* in Part III, ch. 6, *Home Box Office* also involved issues of ex parte communications. While the case's holding on that issue has been limited, such limitations would not appear to affect the principle cited here.

20. *See, e.g.*, Magnuson-Moss Warranty–Federal Trade Commission Improvement Act, 15 U.S.C. § 57a(e)(1)(B); Consumer Product Safety Act, 15 U.S.C. § 2060(a); Toxic Substances Control Act, 15 U.S.C. § 2618 (1976); OSH Act, 29 U.S.C. § 655(f); Clean Air Act, 42 U.S.C. § 7607(d)(7)(A).

21. 42 U.S.C. § 7607(d)(2)–(4). It requires EPA to establish a "docket" no later than the date on which the NPRM is published. The Act expressly requires EPA to promptly place all written comments and documentary information received in the docket. EPA must also place in the docket "as soon as possible after their availability" all documents that became available after the proposed rule has been published and that "the Administrator [of EPA] determines are of central relevance to the rulemaking . . . ." *Id.* § 7607(d)(4)(B)(i). *See* Sierra Club v. Costle, 657 F.2d 298 (D.C. Cir. 1981). The statute also requires that EPA place in the record drafts of proposed and final rules and accompanying documents submitted to OMB for review, written comments by other agencies, and the EPA administrator's written responses. *Id.* § 7607(d)(4)(B)(ii). Requirements for disclosure of drafts and other documents involved in the OMB review process are discussed below. *See infra* Part III, ch. 6(C).

22. *See* S. 1080, Regulatory Reform Act, § 3 (passed by the Senate on Mar. 24, 1982); H.R. 746, Regulatory Procedure Act, § 201 (reported by the House Judiciary Committee on Feb. 25, 1982); S. 343, Comprehensive Regulatory Reform Act of 1995, CONG. REC. S. 9542 (June 30, 1995) (proposed section 553(j)—"rulemaking file").

23. ACUS Recommendation 93-4, *Improving the Environment for Agency Rulemaking*, 59 Fed. Reg. 4670 (Feb. 1, 1994). The Conference recommended that Congress consider amending § 553 of the APA to "require establishment of a public rulemaking file beginning no later than the date on which an agency publishes an advance notice of proposed rulemaking or notice of proposed rulemaking, whichever is earlier." *Id.* ¶ IV(C). The Conference also suggested that agencies manage their files so that a "usable and reliable file is available for purposes of judicial review." *Id.* ¶ V(E). *See also* ACUS Statement 7, *Views of the Administrative Conference on Proposals Pending in Congress to Amend the Informal Rulemaking Provisions of the Administrative Procedure Act*, ¶¶ 4–5, 47 Fed. Reg. 30,715 (July 15, 1982) (urging creation of, and opportunity to comment on, rulemaking file).

The development of the concept of a "rulemaking record" for informal rulemaking is also reflected in the Regulatory Flexibility Act, which requires that reports of review panels "be made public as part of the rulemaking record."[24]

And, in the age of the Internet, the E-Government Act of 2002 requires that "[t]o the extent practicable, agencies must have an internet-accessible rulemaking docket that includes all public comments and other materials that by agency rule or practice are included in the agency docket, whether or not electronically submitted."[25] This has been largely accomplished with the development of the Federal Docket Management System (FDMS), as described in Chapter 1(C) of this Part.

B. The Importance of the Rulemaking Record in Informal Rulemaking

Deciding what to include in the rulemaking record, and when, requires an understanding of the functions the record serves. A rulemaking record (1) aids public participation in the rulemaking; (2) provides the basis for the agency's decision whether to adopt a rule and, if so, what provisions the rule should include; and (3) assists judicial review of the final rulemaking decision.

1. The Rulemaking Record as an Aid to Public Participation

The existence of a public rulemaking record is a critical factor in making public participation in the rulemaking meaningful. Public comments are much more likely to be focused and useful if the commenters have access to the comments of others. More ample comments benefit the agency, the public, and ultimately the reviewing courts. Issues not otherwise raised by the agency's proposal may arise in the comments. There is, as noted earlier,[26] a difference of views among courts as to whether issues raised in the comments but not in the notice of proposed rulemaking (NPRM) provide adequate notice to other members of the public. In any event, the exchange of views and new information in the comments may, in the agency's discretion, serve as a basis for additional rulemaking proceedings by the agency on new issues. Finally, it is noted that several hybrid rulemaking statutes require agencies to receive rebuttal comments.[27] Other agencies, although not required to do so, voluntarily give interested persons the opportunity to submit "reply comments" in rulemaking.[28] This exchange

---

24. 5 U.S.C. § 609 (b)(5).
25. Pub. L. No. 107-347, 116 Stat. 2899 (2002) (codified at 44 U.S.C. § 3501 note). The e-docketing provision is at § 206(d).
26. *See* discussion *supra* Part III, ch. 3(E).
27. *See, e.g.*, Clean Air Act, 42 U.S.C. § 7607(d)(5) (requiring EPA to keep rulemaking record open for an additional 30 days after completion of proceeding to allow submission of rebuttal comments); *see also* Toxic Substances Control Act, 15 U.S.C. § 2605(c)(3)(A).
28. FCC Rules of Practice, 47 C.F.R. § 1.415(c). *See also* ACUS Recommendation 2011-2, *Rulemaking Comments*, at ¶ 6. Agencies often extend comment periods (after public notice in the *Federal Register*), raising new issues or announcing the availability of new data. Informa-

of comments becomes part of the rulemaking record. The public's overall access to the rulemaking record has been enhanced dramatically by the advent of electronic docketing, described above in Part III, Chapter 1(C).

2. *The Rulemaking Record as the Basis for the Agency's Rulemaking Decisions*

A second and related function of the rulemaking record is to provide the agency decisionmaker with enough information to decide whether a final rule is warranted, and if so, what provisions it should contain. Structuring the record or file to serve both the needs of interested persons and the agency decisionmaker may be difficult in complex rulemaking proceedings. To avoid delay in a rulemaking, the agency staff should index and organize the record in a way that will enable both agency staff and interested parties to use the rulemaking record during the rulemaking. In major rulemakings, this can be an onerous task. The FDA's controversial proposed rule on tobacco sales and advertising generated more than 700,000 comments, including 250,000 postcards alone opposing one part of the rule and a 2,000-page comment from the industry with 45,000 pages of supporting documents.[29] The agency developed a sophisticated computerized sorting system that enabled it to digest the comments and issue the final rule in one year.[30]

Of course, as sorting technology improves, the agency will be more able to cope with a large volume of comments. See the discussion in Chapter 1(C)(3) of this Part.

The Administrative Conference, in recognizing the importance of agency management of the rulemaking process, urged agencies to develop the following techniques:

> Managing rulemaking files, so that maximum disclosure to the public is achieved during the comment period and so that a usable and reliable file is available for purposes of judicial review. The rulemaking file should, insofar as feasible, include (1) all notices pertaining to the rulemaking, (2) copies or an index of all written factual material, studies, and reports substantially relied on or seriously considered by agency personnel in formulating the proposed or final rule (except insofar as disclosure is prohibited by law), (3) all written comments submitted to the agency, and (4) any other material required by statute, executive order, or agency rule to be made public in connection with the rulemaking.[31]

---

tion in the agency files pertinent to the rulemaking would normally also be available to members of the public under the Freedom of Information Act, 5 U.S.C. § 552; however, there is no assurance that interested persons would know of its existence or could obtain the information before the end of the rulemaking comment period.

29. John Schwartz, *Comments Couldn't Kill Tobacco Rule Process*, WASH. POST, Feb. 19, 1997, at A19.

30. *Id.* The final rule was published at 61 Fed. Reg. 44,396–45,318 (Aug. 28, 1996).

31. ACUS Recommendation 93-4, *supra* note 23, at ¶ V(E). The recommendation notes that "written" documents include those in electronic form. *Id.*

Agency practices in compiling rulemaking files have sometimes been criticized for incompleteness, inaccessibility, or a lack of indexing.[32]

3. The Rulemaking Record as the Basis for Judicial Review

Agencies must anticipate that courts will conduct "thorough, probing, in-depth review" of informal rulemaking,[33] and that they will require the agency to produce an administrative record to support its final rule. The power to require submission of a record for judicial review purposes is inherent in the review function. If a reviewing court is not given the reasoning and factual justification needed to support the rationality of the rule, the court has no choice, absent a statutory provision for de novo review, but to remand the matter to the agency for further proceedings.

Judges have been somewhat perplexed and unhappy about some of the rulemaking records they have been called upon to review. One court described the record before it as "a sump in which the parties have deposited a sundry mass of materials that have neither passed through the filter of rules of evidence nor undergone the refining fire of adversarial presentation."[34] And at the close of a 100-plus-page rulemaking review decision, a weary D.C. Circuit panel concluded, "We reach our decision after interminable record search (and considerable soul searching). We have read the record with as hard a look as mortal judges can probably give its thousands of pages."[35] The author of that decision, Judge Wald, stated in another forum that

> [a]t times it is hard not to feel that no one seriously expects the judge to look at, let alone understand, the record. Weighing the substantiality of the evidence is perceived more as a quantitative than a qualitative exercise. Since a record search in a lengthy agency proceeding—time constraints aside—too often resembles a safari through uncharted lands without benefit of a guide, it is not recommended for amateurs.[36]

Several factors account for the difficulties the courts confront in examining rulemaking records. Rulemaking is essentially a legislative process, encompassing

---

32. *See* U.S. GEN. ACCOUNTING OFFICE, COMMENTS ON S. 981, THE REGULATORY IMPROVEMENT ACT OF 1997, SEN. COMM. ON GOVERNMENTAL AFFAIRS 4–6 (GAO/T-GGD/RCED-97-250) (Sept. 12, 1997) (providing the testimony of L. Nye Stevens, Director, Federal Management and Workforce Issues); *see also* Hanover Potato Prods., Inc. v. Shalala, 989 F.2d 123 (3d Cir. 1993) (holding FDA's failure to include 63% of rulemaking record in the public file at the agency was prejudicial and an adequate basis for attorney fee award under Equal Access to Justice Act).
33. Citizens to Preserve Overton Park, Inc. v. Volpe, 401 U.S. 402, 415 (1971) (informal adjudication). This dictum has also been regularly applied to the review of rulemaking. *See, e.g.,* Simms v. Nat'l Highway Traffic Safety Admin., 45 F.3d 999, 1003 (6th Cir. 1995).
34. Natural Res. Def. Council v. SEC, 606 F.2d 1031, 1052 (D.C. Cir. 1979).
35. Sierra Club v. Costle, 657 F.2d at 410 (footnote omitted); *see also* Ethyl Corp. v. EPA, 541 F.2d 1, 49 n.102 (D.C. Cir. 1976).
36. Patricia M. Wald, *Judicial Review of Complex Administrative Agency Decisions*, 462 ANNALS AM. ACAD. POL. & SOC. SCI. 72 (1982).

value and policy judgments as well as factual material. Even the "facts" on which the agency relies include accumulated expertise and experience of the agency and others, which are difficult if not impossible to package in the record of the proceeding. Thus, it is the nature of the proceeding itself that determines the kind of record that will reach the court. As the D.C. Circuit said in one of its early hybrid rulemaking decisions, "The record resembles nothing so much as that of a typical legislative committee hearing."[37]

A major issue regarding judicial review of rulemaking is whether the record on review should consist only of materials that were before the agency when it made its final decision or whether the agency may augment the record with additional facts or arguments before the reviewing court.

The Administrative Conference, in a 1974 recommendation that addressed issues raised by pre-enforcement judicial review of informal rulemaking, recommended that certain basic rulemaking documents be included in the record before the court.[38] However, by suggesting that the agency include in the record "factual information . . . that is proffered by the agency as pertinent to the rule," the recommendation clearly did not intend to limit review to materials that were before the agency when it made its final rulemaking decision. The Conference also did not assume that the court was "invariably confined" to the materials the agency placed in the record.[39]

---

37. Indus. Union Dep't v. Hodgson, 499 F.2d 467, 471 n.9 (D.C. Cir. 1974). The court described the "testimonial pattern" in the record as follows: witnesses generally read "long statements" followed by "cross-examination"; the questions asked "tended to be few, sporadic, and perfunctory." *Id.* The case involved OSHA's rulemaking leading to the issuance of a standard regulating asbestos.

38. ACUS Recommendation 74-4, *Pre-enforcement Judicial Review of Rules of General Applicability*, 39 Fed. Reg. 23,044 (June 26, 1974). These included the notice, comments, transcripts of testimony, "factual information not included in the foregoing that was considered by the authority responsible for promulgation of the rule or that is proffered by the agency as pertinent to the rule," advisory committee reports, the statement of basis and purpose, and any documents referred to therein. *Id.* ¶ 1.

39. *Id.* For a judicial affirmation of this view, see *San Diego Navy Broadway Complex Coalition v. U.S. Coast Guard*, 2011 WL 1212888 *6 (S.D. Cal. Mar. 30, 2011). ("An agency need not provide all explanation for its action within the *Federal Register* notice or the rule itself. Nothing within the APA or case law requires an agency to provide the explanation for its action in the *Federal Register*. The court may allow supplementation of the record where 'necessary to explain agency decisions.'") (citing Midwater Trawlers Co-op. v. Dep't of Commerce, 393 F.3d 994, 1006 (9th Cir. 2004)). *See also* Ad Hoc Metals Coal. v. Whitman, 227 F. Supp. 2d 134, 140–42 (D.D.C. 2002) (supplementation of administrative record was appropriate in actions seeking judicial review of final EPA rule to include comments submitted by industry representatives at meeting with EPA officials critical of human health data relied upon by EPA in formulating rule, even though meeting took place eight months after close of comment period where final rule was not issued until more than four months later, and EPA considered comments prior to issuance of final rule, and where EPA did include comments from another group made at similar meeting).

Some commentators criticize Recommendation 74-4 for not confining judicial review to the rulemaking record or file that was before the agency when it made its final rulemaking decision. They argue that confining review to an "exclusive" rulemaking record would have a salutary disciplining effect on agencies and would aid courts in performing their review function.[40]

Congress has taken both approaches in enacting statutes containing definitions of the "rulemaking record" for judicial review purposes. In the Consumer Product Safety Act and the Federal Trade Commission Improvements Act, Congress adopted the "open-ended" definitional approach recommended by the Conference.[41] In other instances, Congress has specified that the record for review shall include only information that was before the agency when it made its final decision.[42]

The Department of Justice, which represents most agencies in court defenses of rules, has also provided guidance on the assembling of rulemaking records.[43]

Regardless of whether or not a statute requires that judicial review be limited to the administrative record that was before the agency when it made its decision, the rulemaking staff should anticipate court rejection of "post-hoc rationalizations" for rules[44] and close judicial scrutiny of reliance on data obtained after the public stage of rulemaking.[45] Accordingly, the agency would be well advised, except in unusual cir-

---

40. *See* William F. Pedersen, Jr., *Formal Records and Informal Rulemaking*, 85 YALE L.J. 38, 73 (1975); DAVIS, *supra* note 1, at § 6:5 (1982 Supp.) (expressing a preference for confining review to a record that was before the agency when it made its decision); Ober v. EPA, 84 F.3d 304 (9th Cir. 1996) (requiring a new round of notice and comment after a commenter added 300 pages of critical material after the comment period closed); Idaho Farm Bureau Fed'n v. Babbitt, 58 F.3d 1392 (9th Cir. 1995) (overturning an agency rule after the agency added a new government report to record after the comment period and relied on the report in its explanation for the rule). *But see* Rybachek v. EPA, 904 F.2d 1276 (9th Cir. 1990) (approving EPA's addition of 6,000 pages into record following close of comments, saying that agency could use what it needed to support its rule).

41. The Federal Trade Commission Improvements Act defines the "rulemaking record" as including the rule, the statement of basis and purpose, the transcript of the hearing, written submissions, and "any other information which the Commission considers relevant to such rule." 15 U.S.C. § 57a(e)(1)(B); *see also* Consumer Product Safety Act, 15 U.S.C. § 2060(a).

42. Under the Clean Air Act, the record for judicial review consists "exclusively" of "written comments and documentary information" on the proposed rule received during the comment period, transcript of the public hearing, all documents that "become available" after the proposed rule has been published that EPA "determines are of central relevance to the rulemaking," and the statement accompanying the promulgated rule. 42 U.S.C. § 7607(d)(4)(B)(i), 7607(d)(6)(A),(B), 7607(d)(7)(A); *see also* Toxic Substances Control Act, 15 U.S.C. § 2618.

43. Env't and Natural Res. Div., U.S. Dep't of Justice, Guidance to Federal Agencies on Compiling the Administrative Record (1999), *available at* http://environment.transportation.org/pdf/programs/usdoj_guidance_re_admin_record_prep.pdf.

44. Post-hoc rationalizations are those marshaled by attorneys in a court review proceeding to justify agency actions that were not accompanied by adequate explanation of the reason for the action. *See* discussion *infra* ch. 7(B)(1).

45. *See, e.g., Ad Hoc Metals*, 227 F. Supp. 2d at 138–41 (addressing data obtained after the close of the comment period.

cumstances, to include in the public file all materials on which it relies in making final rulemaking decisions and to provide an opportunity for public comment in appropriate circumstances.

Although there is a "presumption of regularity" as to the agency's compilation of the rulemaking record,[46] courts do retain some discretion to supplement the record. As one district court judge wrote: "For a court to supplement the record, the moving party must rebut the presumption of administrative regularity and show that the documents to be included were before the agency decisionmaker. On the other hand, for a court to review extra-record evidence, the moving party must prove applicable one of the eight recognized exceptions to the general prohibition against extra-record review."[47]

On the other hand, courts are reluctant to require internal agency memoranda to be placed in the record. As one court stated:

> Judicial review of agency action should be based on an agency's stated justifications, not the predecisional process that led up to the final, articulated decision. To require the inclusion in an agency record of documents reflecting internal agency deliberations could hinder candid and creative exchanges regarding proposed decisions and alternatives, which might, because of the chilling effect on open discussion within agencies, lead to an overall decrease in the quality of decisions.[48]

The overall burden on judges reviewing rulemaking has increased along with the increase in the volume, importance, and complexity of rulemaking. The agency rulemaking staff cannot do much to relieve this burden in many instances. However,

---

46. Ronald Levin, *Rulemaking Under the 2010 Revised Model State Administrative Procedure Act*, 20 Widener L.J. 855, 861 (2011). He explains:

    The presumption is well recognized in the extant case law. *See* Bar MK Ranches v. Yuetter, 994 F.2d 735, 740 (10th Cir. 1993) (citing Wilson v. Hodel, 758 F.2d 1369, 1374 (10th Cir. 1985)) ("[T]he designation of the Administrative Record, like any established administrative procedure, is entitled to a presumption of administrative regularity. The court assumes the agency properly designated the Administrative Record absent clear evidence to the contrary."); Amfac Resorts, LLC v. U.S. Dep't of Interior, 143 F. Supp. 2d 7, 12 (D.D.C. 2001) ("[A] party must provide good reason to believe that discovery will uncover evidence relevant to the Court's decision to look beyond the record. Thus, a party must make a significant showing—variously described [in case law] as a 'strong', 'substantial', or 'prima facie' showing—that it will find material in the agency's possession indicative of bad faith or an incomplete record.").

47. Pac. Shores Subdivision, Cal. Water Dist. v. U.S. Army Corps of Eng'rs, 448 F. Supp. 2d 1, 6 (D.D.C. 2006) (citing Fund for Animals v. Williams, 391 F. Supp. 2d 191, 197–98 (D.D.C. 2005).

48. *Id.* at 143 (citations omitted). *But see* James N. Saul, Comment, *Overly Restrictive Records and the Frustration of Judicial Review*, 38 ENVTL. L. 1301 (2008) (describing some agencies' practice of withholding "allegedly deliberative documents from the record without following the minimal procedures required to assert the deliberative process privilege").

it can take measures to facilitate judicial review of rulemaking records and avoid complaints like the following in 1977 by Judge Wright of the D.C. Circuit:

> Today's informal rulemaking proceedings do not provide a proper record . . . . The result is that courts spend an inordinate amount of time in review of informal rulemaking cases attempting to find documents that presumably are in the record but which are somehow unavailable. Often there is not even a list of the documents that make up the record. Perhaps the most distressing aspect of such reviews is that documents seem to surface one at a time, first from one party, then from another. And one understandably gets the uneasy feeling that the whole record is not really before the court.[49]

Despite the "formalization" of records in informal rulemaking, courts continue to recognize the "informality" of these proceedings.[50] In *Association of Data Processing Service Organizations v. Board of Governors*,[51] the D.C. Circuit, after concluding that the differences between the "arbitrary and capricious" and "substantial evidence" tests were "largely semantic,"[52] made it clear that there remained one important difference between the two types of reviews. Where a statute requires that "substantial evidence" support agency decisions,[53] substantial evidence must "be found *within*

---

49. J. Skelly Wright, *New Judicial Requisites for Informal Rulemaking: Implications for the Environmental Impact Statement Process*, 29 ADMIN. L. REV. 59, 61–62 (1977). Judge Wald of the D.C. Circuit also criticized agency failure to make records accessible to reviewing courts as follows:

> [I]t is only in recent years that many agencies have indexed the thousands of pages that compose a rulemaking "record." Even now, the agency seldom, if ever, organizes the mass of information in a way that allows reviewing judges quick access to supporting material for particular propositions. Yet the physical impossibility of a single judge—and law clerk—reading every page of a 10,000-page rulemaking record five years in the making puts a high priority on the organization and detailed indexing of the record. To be of greatest assistance, the record should be organized in terms of the major attacks upon the rule, preferably with summaries of the evidence or documents contained therein. But this is certainly not the usual practice.

Wald, *supra* note 36, at 80.
50. This principle has been recognized by the courts of appeals, particularly the D.C. Circuit, in deciding rulemaking issues such as ex parte communications, decisionmaker bias, and separation of functions. *See* Home Box Office, Inc. v. FCC, 567 F.2d 9 (D.C. Cir. 1977); Ass'n of Nat'l Advertisers v. FTC, 627 F.2d 1151 (D.C. Cir. 1979); United Steelworkers of Am. v. Marshall, 647 F.2d 1189 (D.C. Cir. 1980); *see also* discussion *infra* Part III, chs. 6, 7.
51. 745 F.2d 677 (D.C. Cir. 1984).
52. *Id.* at 684. The *Data Processing* decision and the standards for judicial review are discussed below. *See infra* Part IV, ch. 2.
53. Under the applicable statute, the "substantial evidence" test applied to all actions of the Board of Governors of the Federal Reserve System. 745 F.2d at 685. The issue in the case was the meaning of that standard of review in the context of that statute.

the record of closed-record proceedings to which it exclusively applies."[54] With respect to the "arbitrary and capricious" standard applicable to informal rulemaking, however, the court stated that the "'administrative record' might well include crucial material that was neither shown to nor known by the private parties in the proceeding."[55] While conceding that in informal rulemaking, "at least the most critical factual material that is used to support the agency's position on review must have been made public in the proceeding and exposed to refutation,"[56] the court concluded that the requirement does not extend to all data.[57]

The uncertainty concerning the required contents of the record before the court in informal rulemaking is related to the treatment of off-the-record communications[58] and the requirements for public comment in informal rulemaking.[59] A court decision reflecting these complex relationships is *Community Nutrition Institute v. Block*,[60] in which the D.C. Circuit rejected a procedural challenge to a Department of Agriculture regulation based on the agency's reliance on two scientific studies completed by agency staff after the close of the rulemaking record and on which no opportunity for public comment had been provided. The court noted that these studies did not provide "entirely new information" but only expanded on and confirmed studies mentioned in the NPRM.[61] "Rulemaking proceedings would never end if an agency's response to comments must always be made the subject of additional comment," the court said, concluding that an agency's response to public comment may take the form of a new scientific study without requiring public comment, "unless prejudice is shown."[62] On the other hand, in *National Coalition Against the Misuse of Pesticides v. Thomas*,[63] the D.C. Circuit concluded that EPA should have included in the public file a memorandum explaining the agency's position on a central issue in the proceeding because it "clearly supplied information critical to informed comment on EPA's proposal to reestablish the 30 [parts per billion] tolerance, and, for that matter, to review by the court."[64]

---

54. *Id.* at 684 (emphasis in original). Then-Judge Scalia noted that although the substantial evidence test under the APA has traditionally applied to adjudicatory proceedings, some statutes attached substantial evidence review to informal rulemaking. *Id.* at 685.

55. *Id.* at 684.

56. *Id.*

57. *Id.* (citing ACUS Recommendation 74-4, *supra* note 38).

58. *See infra* Part III, ch. 6.

59. *See supra* Part III, ch. 4.

60. 749 F.2d 50 (D.C. Cir. 1984).

61. *Id.* at 58. The court distinguished *Portland Cement*, where the agency relied on entirely new information that was "critical" to the determination. *Id. See supra* Part III, ch. 4, for a discussion of agency reliance in rulemaking on information known only to the agency.

62. 749 F.2d at 58.

63. 809 F.2d 875 (D.C. Cir. 1987). In this case, petitioners challenged EPA's reinstatement of a 30 part per billion tolerance level for ethylene dibromide in imported mangoes. The court held the action arbitrary and capricious. *Id.*

64. *Id.* at 884 n.10.

The court held, however, that the omission from the public record was harmless as to petitioners because they obtained the memorandum in question in time to comment on it.[65]

A difficult issue arises respecting the record where the court reviews an agency action that did not involve a "proceeding" in the usual sense of the term. This issue may arise, for example, where the agency issues a rule that it believes is exempt from notice-and-comment requirements, perhaps because it is an interpretive rule or falls within the "good cause" exception. Because neither a proposal nor public comments would ordinarily exist in such a situation, the agency's rulemaking docket or file would be skimpy at best. A similar circumstance may arise where a party challenges an agency's refusal to commence rulemaking after a petition for rulemaking has been filed or even without having filed a petition.[66] In those circumstances, there also may be no "file" or "record" to present to the court.

In such cases, the agency may establish a file after the fact and present it to the court as a basis for review. This practice obviously is problematic, because the agency's judgment on which documents should be included is likely to be self-serving and challenged by opposing parties. This may lead to controversy over what constitutes the record.[67]

The Administrative Conference addressed this issue indirectly in its 1986 Recommendation, "Petitions for Rulemaking."[68] In recommending certain "basic procedures" for the consideration and disposition of petitions for rulemaking, the Conference suggested the "maintenance of a publicly available petition file." It recommended that an agency maintain a file of all pertinent documents that it considers whenever it undertakes a rulemaking action, including decisions not to commence rulemaking and regardless of whether the rulemaking action is taken after notice and comment. Whether the file will be entirely public or some documents will be maintained as confidential is a separate issue to be discussed next.[69] However, the critical point is that the agency, in the event of a court challenge, would be in a position to offer this "record" to the court as historical rather than manufactured.

---

65. *Id.* The issue of what should be in the record is also complicated by contact between OMB and agencies. *See infra* Part III, ch. 6(C).
66. *See infra* Part IV, ch. 3 (discussing judicial review of agency inaction).
67. This occurred, for example, in connection with court review of an OSHA emergency temporary standard. *See* Asbestos Info. Ass'n v. OSHA, 727 F.2d 415 (5th Cir. 1984) (staying OSHA's asbestos emergency standard). In this case, the court considered unfavorable peer reviews even though the agency originally included in the record only favorable peer reviews on which it relied in issuing the emergency standard. *Id.* at 420 n.12. To do otherwise, the court said, "would convert the reviewing process into an artificial game." *Id.* (quoting Amoco Oil Co. v. EPA, 501 F.2d 722, 729 n.10 (D.C. Cir. 1974)).
68. ACUS Recommendation 86-6, *Petitions for Rulemaking*, 51 Fed. Reg. 46,988 (Dec. 30, 1986).
69. Certain internal documents that are part of the deliberative process may well be exempt from public disclosure. *See* Wolfe v. Dep't of Health & Human Servs., 839 F.2d 768 (D.C. Cir. 1988) (en banc).

4. Treatment of "Confidential" Comments

In some rulemakings, commenters may wish to submit information to the agency that they consider to be confidential business information (CBI).[70] The agency could benefit from learning about this information but may be constrained in placing it in the rulemaking record, responding to it, or relying on it as a basis for the final rule.[71] Some agencies have therefore developed procedures for handling confidential comments in rulemaking.[72]

Although FOIA does not directly address the issue of CBI submitted via comments in an agency rulemaking, the Act may still govern in some respects. Generally speaking, if a third party requests disclosure of submitted CBI, the agency can either deny the request because the information is covered by Exemption Four of FOIA or release it after determining that it is not.[73] Executive Order 12,600[74] provides some pre-submission procedures that are designed to regularize practice in this regard. This order requires agencies to issue FOIA rules that allow submitters to designate their information as confidential at the time of submission to the agency. For such designated submissions, agencies must afford submitters a series of rights, most notably a chance to object if a request is made for that information. However, because E.O. 12,600's restrictions apply only after a party files an FOIA request, they do not cover an agency's handling or release of information prior to an FOIA request, for example, in a rulemaking docket or record.

According to a review by the editor-in-chief of the *Administrative Law Review* done in 2004, agencies have developed various ways of managing CBI during informal rulemaking.[75] For example, the FTC does not include comments containing CBI

---

70. This is a term borrowed from the Freedom of Information Act case law in defining what information is exempt from disclosure under exemption 4 of the Act, 5 U.S.C. § 552(b)(4). *See, e.g.*, Critical Mass Energy Project v. NRC, 975 F.2d 871 (D.C. Cir 1992).

71. One of the few cases discussing CBI in the context of rulemaking is Ass'n of Nat'l Advertisers, Inc. v. FTC., 617 F.2d 611, 624 (D.C. Cir. 1979) (Wright, J., concurring) (discussing the FTC's changes to its comment submission rules during the pendency of this litigation). *See also* U.S. Gov't Accountability Office, Anti-Money Laundering: Improved Communication Could Enhance the Support FinCEN Provides to Law Enforcement (GAO-10-141, 2009) (observing that the Financial Crimes Enforcement Network (FinCEN) within the Department of the Treasury lacks and needs a mechanism to collect law enforcement sensitive information in a nonpublic rulemaking docket that could be pertinent to making decisions regarding proposed changes).

72. *See generally* Heather E. Kilgore, Comment, *Signed, Sealed, Protected: Solutions to Agency Handling of Confidential Business Information in Informal Rulemaking*, 56 Admin. L. Rev. 519 (2004); *see also* P. Stephen Gidiere III, *Protecting Confidential Business Information in the Hands of Environmental Regulators*, 14-SPR Nat. Resources & Env't 262 (2000).

73. *See also* Chrysler Corp v. Brown, 441 U.S. 281 (1979) (interpreting interaction of APA and Trade Secrets Act, 18 U.S.C. § 1905, to require that agencies have a mandatory obligation to withhold CBI, unless authorized by law to release).

74. Exec. Order 12,600, 52 Fed. Reg. 23,781 (June 23, 1987).

75. Kilgore, *supra* note 72. *See also* Bridget C.E. Dooling, *Legal Issues in e-Rulemaking*, 63 Admin. L. Rev. 893, 911–13 (2011), quoting the language used by EPA and NHTSA in their joint

301

in the public rulemaking record, nor does it make clear whether it has excluded information from the rulemaking record. But where a rulemaking record that contains an omitted section of CBI is subject to review by a court or administrative law judge, the FTC allows the submitter to obtain either a protective or in camera order.[76]

The NRC and the FAA maintain more transparent procedures that indicate when such information is deleted from the record. The NRC also deletes CBI from the public rulemaking file, but publicizes the fact that the agency omitted information from the record as well as the amount of information deleted from the file. Similarly, although the FAA places submitted CBI into a non-public file, it also places a note in its docket stating that it received the information.[77]

Other agencies have addressed this transparency problem by establishing procedures requiring submission of both a non-public and a public version of the documents. For example, the Department of the Interior, Federal Maritime Commission, and National Highway Traffic Safety Administration (NHTSA) all require submission of both public and non-public versions of confidential documents.[78] On the other hand, the IRS takes the position that it will not accept any comments containing CBI.[79]

Another issue is when the confidential status of submitted CBI should be determined—when the information is first provided to the agency, or only if and when an FOIA disclosure request is filed. The NRC, Department of Labor, and NHTSA and are all examples of agencies that immediately decide whether information labeled "confidential" deserves confidential treatment.[80] Both the EPA and the FAA afford immediate confidential status to submitted information that is marked "confidential" regardless of whether the information actually constitutes CBI.[81]

---

rulemaking on fuel economy standards, Revisions and Additions to Motor Vehicle Fuel Economy Label, 75 Fed. Reg. 58,078, 58,080 (proposed Sept. 23, 2010) (to be codified at 40 C.F.R. pts. 85, 86, 600 & 49 C.F.R. pt. 575) (footnotes omitted).

76. See id. at 526–27 (citing 16 C.F.R. § 4.10(a)(2)). EPA's NPRMs also provide quite categorically that "[a]lthough a part of the official docket, the public docket does not include Confidential Business Information (CBI) or other information whose disclosure is restricted by statute." Environmental Protection Agency, Proposed Rules, Control of Emissions of Air Pollution From New Motor Vehicles: In-Use Testing for Heavy-Duty Diesel Engines and Vehicles, 69 Fed. Reg. 32,804, 32,805 (June 10, 2004).

77. See Kilgore, supra note 72, at 527 (citing 10 C.F.R. § 9.19(a) (NRC); 14 C.F.R. § 11.35 (FAA)).

78. See id. at 527 (citing 43 C.F.R. § 4.31 (DOI); 46 C.F.R. § 502.119(b) (FMC); 49 C.F.R. § 512.5 (NHTSA)).

79. See id. at 528 (citing 26 C.F.R. § 601.601(b)(1)) (opining that that such a limitation "infringes on § 533 of the APA, which allows for any person to comment during an informal rulemaking").

80. See id. at 528–29 (citing 10 C.F.R. § 2.790(c) (NRC); 29 C.F.R. § 90.33(c) (DOL); 49 C.F.R. § 512.17 (NHTSA)).

81. See id. at 529 (citing 40 C.F.R. § 2.204(a) (EPA) & 14 C.F.R. § 11.35(b) (FAA)). Ms. Kilgore comments that:

This means that agencies forego substantiating the sufficiency of confidential documents unless a third party files a FOIA disclosure request for the information. Although this approach may save agencies from assessing the adequacy of all confidentially sub-

Finally, there is a disparity among agency practices with regard to the return of submitted confidential documents. Some agencies that conduct immediate confidentiality checks on submitted documents return the documents to a submitter if the agency denies confidential protection, while others forbid the return of any information received by the agency.[82]

As a concluding observation, I note that Professor Levin has pointed out that the 2010 Model State APA contains a concise provision that may serve as a good basis for agency posting of comments online with respect to "copyrighted comments as well as comments that are tasteless, scurrilous, or worse."[83] Section 302 of the MSAPA provides, "If an agency determines that any part of the rulemaking record cannot be displayed practicably or is inappropriate for public display on the Internet website, the agency shall describe the part and note that the part is not displayed."[84]

---

mitted information, it creates a presumption of confidentiality for information designated as "confidential" by businesses, thereby making the record less transparent. This method, therefore, requires the public to assume the burden of making FOIA requests in order to force agency review of the designations. *Id.*

82. *See id.* at 530–31 & n.56, *citing* 47 C.F.R. § 0.459(e) (FCC's policy to return documents to submitters upon request), and 49 C.F.R. § 512.21(a) (NHTSA's procedure to disclose documents to the public upon a negative confidentiality determination, unless the agency receives a "timely petition for reconsideration").

83. *See* Ronald M. Levin, *Rulemaking Under the 2010 Model State Administrative Procedure Act*, 20 WIDENER L.J. 855, 861 (2011).

84. *See* Revised Model State Administrative Procedure Act (2010) § 302, *available at* http://www.law.upenn.edu/bll/archives/ulc/msapa/2010_final.htm.

Chapter 6

"Off-the-Record" or "Ex Parte" Communications in Rulemaking

The emergence of the rulemaking record concept led to criticism of "off-the-record" or "ex parte" communications between agency decisionmakers and other persons during informal rulemaking. While most of the uncertainty about the law in this area has been removed by court decisions, the treatment of such communications in informal rulemaking raises complex issues and conflicting considerations that the agency rulemaker should be aware of during rulemaking.

A. Summary of the Law

The APA places no restrictions on ex parte communications made in informal rulemaking.[1] Indeed, the notions of "parties" and "off-the-record" contacts do not really apply in informal rulemaking under section 553, because participation in informal rulemaking is not limited to named parties and the agency decision need not be based exclusively on the record produced during the rulemaking. However, the term *ex parte communications* is used throughout this chapter simply to mean off-the-record, private communications between agency decisionmakers and other persons concerning the substance of the agency's proposed rule.

Early cases, such as *Sangamon Valley Television Corp. v. United States*, held that ex parte communications in informal rulemaking were improper where conflicting private claims to a valuable privilege were involved.[2] In 1977, the D.C. Circuit, in *Home Box Office, Inc. v. FCC*,[3] issued an opinion with language suggesting a much broader prohibition on ex parte communications in informal rulemakings:

> Once a notice of proposed rulemaking has been issued, . . . any agency official or employee who is or may reasonably be expected to be involved in the decisional process of the rulemaking proceeding, should refus[e] to discuss matters relating to the disposition of a [rulemaking proceeding] with any in-

---

1. The APA does prohibit ex parte contacts between outsiders and the decisionmaker in formal rulemaking and formal adjudication. 5 U.S.C. § 577(d)(1); *see also id.* § 551(14) (defining ex parte communication).
2. 269 F.2d 221 (D.C. Cir. 1959).
3. 567 F.2d 9 (D.C. Cir. 1977).

terested private party, or an attorney or agent for any such party, prior to the [agency's] decision.[4]

The court proceeded to set aside the FCC's revision of its cable television rules, based on the existence of heavy ex parte lobbying of individual commissioners during the deliberative stage of the rulemaking proceeding.

The *Home Box Office* decision's apparent broad prohibition sparked a debate within the D.C. Circuit, and the decision was soon limited significantly.[5] The debate was effectively ended by two later decisions that rejected its sweeping generalizations. In *United Steelworkers of America v. Marshall*,[6] the court, in an opinion written by Judge J. Skelly Wright, author of the *Home Box Office* opinion, rejected claims that an OSHA rule was procedurally defective because the agency decisionmaker engaged in ex parte communications with the rulemaking staff.[7] The court's opinion in *Steelworkers* was predicated primarily on the view that neither constitutional concerns[8] nor the principle on which cases like *Home Box Office* were based applied to the staff contacts that were challenged in the case.[9] The court went out of its way to distinguish the OSHA rulemaking from proceedings, such as those involved in *Sangamon* and *Home Box Office*, that resolve "conflicting private claims to a valuable privilege" and from

---

4. *Id.* at 57 (citations omitted). Judge Wright stated that "agency secrecy stands between us and fulfillment of our obligation" to "test the actions of the Commission for arbitrariness and inconsistency with delegated law." *Id.* at 54. "Equally important," he said, was the "inconsistency of secrecy with fundamental notions of fairness implicit in due process and with the idea of reasoned decisionmaking on the merits which undergirds all our administrative law." *Id.* This case has been the subject of extensive scholarly comment. *See, e.g.*, Ernest Gellhorn & Glen O. Robinson, *Rulemaking "Due Process": An Inconclusive Dialogue*, 48 U. Chi. L. Rev. 201 (1981).

5. Less than four months after *Home Box Office* was decided, a different panel of the D.C. Circuit rejected the reasoning of the *Home Box Office* majority. In *Action for Children's Television v. FCC*, the court, agreeing with the concurrence in *Home Box Office* that the ex parte communications ban in *Home Box Office* was justified only because the rulemaking involved competing private claims to a valuable interest, ruled that in any event, *Home Box Office* should not be applied retroactively. 564 F.2d 458, 474 (D.C. Cir. 1977); *see also* Tex. Office of Pub. Util. Counsel v. FCC, 265 F.3d 313, 327 (5th Cir. 2001) (rejecting petitioners' "speculative and perhaps sinister scenario imputed to the *ex parte* communication between the FCC and the interested parties"); Iowa State Commerce Comm'n v. Office of the Fed. Inspector of the Alaska Natural Gas Transp. Sys., 730 F.2d 1566, 1576 (D.C. Cir. 1984) ("[T]his court has not interpreted *Home Box Office* to apply to all informal rulemaking proceedings."); Hercules, Inc. v. EPA, 598 F.2d 91 (D.C. Cir. 1978) (refusing to invalidate EPA rule because of ex parte communications between agency presiding officer and rulemaking staff).

6. 647 F.2d 1189 (D.C. Cir. 1980) (upholding, in most respects, OSHA's lead standard).

7. For a discussion of contacts between decisionmakers and rulemaking staff, see *infra* subsec. (E).

8. The court in *Steelworkers* restated the principle that, as a general rule, due process imposes no constraints on informal rulemaking beyond those imposed by statute. 647 F.2d at 1215 n.28 (citing Willapoint Oysters, Inc. v. Ewing, 174 F.2d 676, 694 (9th Cir. 1949)).

9. *Id.* at 1215–16.

"quasi-adjudicatory" proceedings in which the "potential for bias [was] as great as that in a case of competing claims."[10]

Any doubts about the D.C. Circuit's refusal to apply the *Home Box Office* rationale to informal rulemaking were removed by *Sierra Club v. Costle*.[11] *Sierra Club* involved an EPA rulemaking under the Clean Air Act, and, on review, an environmental group alleged that the final air pollution standard was the product of an "ex parte blitz" that began after the close of the comment period.[12] The challenged communications were of various sorts: late comments entered in the record and meetings between the agency and private persons, executive branch officials, and elected officials.[13] With respect to the oral communications with outsiders, the court, per Judge Wald, stated:

> Oral face-to-face discussions are not prohibited anywhere, anytime, in the Act. The absence of such prohibition may have arisen from the nature of the informal rulemaking procedures Congress had in mind. Where agency action resembles judicial action, where it involves formal rulemaking, adjudication, or quasi-adjudication among "conflicting private claims to a valuable privilege," the insulation of the decisionmaker from ex parte contacts is justified by basic notions of due process to the parties involved. But where agency action involves informal rulemaking of a policymaking sort, the concept of ex parte contacts is of more questionable utility.
>
> Under our system of government, the very legitimacy of general policymaking performed by unelected administrators depends in no small part upon the openness, accessibility, and amenability of these officials to the needs and ideas of the public from whom their ultimate authority derives, and upon whom their commands must fall. As judges we are insulated from these pressures because of the nature of the judicial process in which we participate; but we must refrain from the easy temptation to look askance to all face-to-face lobbying efforts, regardless of the forum in which they occur, merely because we see them as inappropriate in the judicial context. Furthermore, the importance to effective regulation of continuing contact with a regulated industry, other affected groups, and the public cannot be underestimated. Informal contacts may enable the agency to win needed support for its program, reduce future enforcement requirements by helping those regulated to anticipate and shape their plans for the future, and spur the provision of information which the agency needs.[14]

---

10. *Id.* As an example of a quasi-adjudicatory proceeding, the court of appeals cited *U.S. Lines v. FMC*, 584 F.2d 519, 536–43 (D.C. Cir. 1978), where a hearing was statutorily required; in the OSHA "hybrid" rulemaking context, a hearing is required only if requested. *Id.* at 1214.
11. 657 F.2d 298 (D.C. Cir. 1981).
12. *Id.* at 386.
13. *Id.* at 387–91
14. *Id.* at 400–01 (footnotes omitted). *Sierra Club* also involved the question whether, under the Clean Air Act, EPA was required to put into the rulemaking docket memoranda on its post-

Thus, neither the APA nor the case law establishes a broad ban on off-the-record communications in rulemaking.[15]

B. Agency Practices for Handling Ex Parte Communications

1. *Policy Considerations*

Although *Home Box Office*'s holding has subsequently been read narrowly, the concerns expressed by Judge Wright and in the literature that followed in its wake do raise issues that agencies should consider. One major concern of critics of ex parte communications in informal rulemaking is that decisionmakers may be influenced by communications made privately, which runs counter to the need for accountable government.[16] Another concern is that interested persons may be unable to reply effectively to information, proposals, or arguments presented off the record. It also has been suggested that participants may have little incentive to submit thoughtful comments or carefully prepared supporting data if they believe that other interests have privileged access to decisionmakers. Assuring interested persons a chance to comment and respond to others' comments may reduce the influence of "insiders," yield new sources of information for the agency to consider in drafting the rule, and improve acceptance of the final rule. There is also concern that ex parte communications may increase the likelihood that crucial information influencing the agency decision will not be available to the reviewing court.[17]

Agencies should consider these issues in determining their policy on ex parte communications. While courts under existing case law are not likely, except in egregious situations, to set aside rules because ex parte contacts took place, agencies must still be

---

comment meetings with the President and Members of Congress on issues involved in the rulemaking. *See* discussion *infra* subsecs. (C), (D).

15. The D.C. Circuit later explained: "*Home Box Office*, which was sharply limited by *Sierra Club v. Costle*, could be thought to be undermined by *Vermont Yankee Nuclear Power Corp. v. Natural Resources Defense Council*. If *ex parte* material were to lead to an unanticipatable change in the final rule, that would be, of course, objectionable." Air Transp. Ass'n of Am. v. FAA, 169 F.3d 1, 7 n.5 (D.C. Cir. 1999). For a critical report on an EPA rulemaking that was influenced by industry ex parte comments, see EPA, Office of Inspector General, Rulemaking on Solvent-Contaminated Industrial Wipes, Evaluation Report No. 2006-P-00001 at 13 (Oct. 4, 2005), *available at* www.epa.gov/oig/reports/2006/20051004-2006-P-00001.pdf (finding that the "'reusable wipes industry' influenced EPA's rulemaking but that this is allowable," although "appearances of favoritism contributed to perceptions of impropriety").

16. *See, e.g.*, Thomas Patterson, Note, *Judicial Control of Ex Parte Contacts in Informal Rulemaking Proceedings*—Home Box Office v. FCC, 27 DePaul L. Rev. 489 (1977).

17. *See* Home Box Office, Inc. v. FCC, 567 F.2d 9, 54 (D.C. Cir. 1977); *but see Sierra Club*, 657 F.2d at 408 ("[W]e do not believe that Congress intended that the courts convert informal rulemaking into a rarefied technocratic process, unaffected by political considerations or the presence of Presidential power.").

sensitive to the concerns raised and to the understandably unfavorable public reaction when the agency receives information in private discussions with persons outside the agency. On the other hand, non-public candid contacts between the agency and interested parties can be useful in working out tentative and compromise positions.[18]

2. The Administrative Conference's Recommendation

Shortly after *Home Box Office* was decided, the Administrative Conference reviewed the problem and concluded that a general prohibition in informal rulemaking of private contacts, or a requirement that every such communication be summarized and exposed on the public record, was undesirable. In Recommendation 77-3,[19] the Conference counseled that a general prohibition "would deprive agencies of the flexibility needed to fashion rulemaking procedures appropriate to the issues involved, and would introduce a degree of formality that would, at least in most instances, result in procedures that are unduly complicated, slow and expensive, and, at the same time, perhaps not conducive to developing all relevant information."[20] Recognizing the valid concerns of critics of ex parte contacts, however, the Conference called on agencies to (1) promptly place in a public file all written comments addressed to the merits of a proposed rule received after issuance of a notice of proposed rulemaking, and (2) experiment with procedures, including use of summaries and public meetings, to disclose oral communications that contain significant information or argument respecting the merits of a proposed rule.[21] This transparency might also inhibit those who desire secret meetings from even making such requests.

3. Agency Practice

Agencies take various approaches in handling ex parte communications, and the independent regulatory agencies appear to have the most restrictive policies regarding

---

18. *See, e.g.*, Nathaniel L. Nathanson, *Report to the Select Committee on Ex Parte Communications in Informal Rulemaking Proceedings*, 30 ADMIN. L. REV. 377 (1978); Glenn T. Carberry, *Ex Parte Communications in Off-the-Record Administrative Proceedings: A Proposed Limitation on Judicial Innovation*, 1980 DUKE L.J. 65; *see also Sierra Club*, 657 F.2d at 408. A similar approach to informal rulemaking was expressed by the D.C. Circuit in *Association of National Advertisers v. FTC*, a case involving allegations of prejudgment by an agency decisionmaker of one of the major issues in a hybrid rulemaking proceeding. 627 F.2d 1151 (D.C. Cir. 1979).
19. ACUS Recommendation 77-3, *Ex Parte Communications in Informal Rulemaking Proceedings*, 42 Fed. Reg. 54,253 (Oct. 5, 1977). This recommendation was based on the Nathanson report, *supra* note 18.
20. *Id.*
21. *Id.* The Conference's recommendation recognized that Congress or the courts might conclude that greater restrictions are appropriate in limited categories of agency proceedings in the interests of fairness or adequate judicial review. *Id.* at ¶ 5. The Conference's approach was cited with approval in *Sierra Club*, 657 F.2d at 403 n.513.

such contacts in rulemaking. The Federal Trade Commission is required by the 1980 amendments to the FTC Act to place a verbatim record or summary of ex parte contacts in the rulemaking record.[22] The Consumer Product Safety Commission has stringent requirements for openness of agency meetings and disclosure of communications with interested persons. Notice must be given of virtually all meetings between agency employees and outside persons; the public may attend any meeting; and summaries are kept of all meetings and telephone conversations between agency employees and interested persons.[23] The independent regulatory agencies' policies may reflect experience with the open-meeting requirements of the Government in the Sunshine Act,[24] as well as reaction to the D.C. Circuit's *Home Box Office* decision, which involved the FCC. Interestingly, the FCC itself seems to have the most developed policy on ex parte communications, allowing them in most informal rulemaking on a "permit-but-disclose" basis.[25]

---

22. 15 U.S.C. § 57a(j) (requiring the FTC to publish a rule (1) authorizing FTC or its commissioners to meet with "any outside party concerning any rulemaking proceeding" and (2) requiring that a notice of meeting be included in any FTC weekly calendar and that a verbatim record or summary of meeting or "any communication relating to any such meeting" be kept, made available to the public, and included in the record). *See* 16 C.F.R. § 1.13(c)(6) (prohibiting any presiding officer from consulting with any person or party respecting "a fact in issue" without notice and opportunity for all parties to participate); *see also* 16 C.F.R. § 1.18 (imposing requirements for including in the rulemaking record ex parte oral and written communications).

23. *See* 16 C.F.R. pt. 1012.

24. 5 U.S.C. § 552b (requiring that federal agencies headed by a collegial body, a majority of whose members are appointed by the President with the advice and consent of the Senate, shall be open to public observation).

25. *See* 47 C.F.R. § 1.1206. They are not allowed in rulemakings involving the allotment of a broadcast channel, the type of rulemaking in *Home Box Office*. The FCC's more liberal policy has been criticized. *See* Harvey Reiter, *The Contrasting Policies of the FCC and FERC Regarding the Importance of Open Transmission Networks in Downstream Competitive Markets*, 57 FED. COMM. L.J. 243, 319–20 n.392 (2005) (internal citation omitted):

> The FCC, as contrasted with the FERC, has a remarkably indifferent attitude towards the impact that its liberal ex parte rules have on smaller entities. A quick perusal of a typical FCC rulemaking order indicates that the comments only really begin *after* the comment period ends. Ex parte submissions sometimes account for more than half the record citations in an FCC order. It is certainly true that any party can submit an ex parte presentation, but it is also true that the squeaky wheel gets the grease. Only the largest participants can afford the substantial expense of the face-to-face meetings with decision makers. The notices of ex parte communications are hardly informative to the smaller user. A letter describing a long meeting with key decisionmaking personnel might say no more than that the named participants "met today with the [named FCC staff] to discuss the comments filed." Such contacts are not entertained by FERC.

See also GOV'T ACCOUNTABILITY OFFICE, FCC MANAGEMENT: IMPROVEMENTS NEEDED IN COMMUNICATION, DECISION-MAKING PROCESSES, AND WORKFORCE PLANNING 31–36 (GAO-10-79) (December 2009), www.gao.gov/new.items/d1079.pdf (describing weaknesses in the FCC's enforcement of its disclosure policies).

Executive agencies having formal policies governing ex parte communications include the Department of Transportation,[26] EPA,[27] and the Federal Emergency Management Agency.[28] The Department of Agriculture requires all timely written submissions made after publication of a notice of proposed rulemaking to be made available for public inspection, unless the submitter has requested confidentiality and a determination is made that the records can be withheld under the Freedom of Information Act.[29] If they cannot be withheld, the submitter is given an opportunity to withdraw the submission. It is the agency's policy to avoid ex parte communications during the rulemaking process; if they do occur, the agency official is to draft a memorandum detailing the communication for inclusion in the rulemaking record.

C. Executive Branch Communications in Rulemaking

Off-the-record communications from within the government—that is, from the President, the President's staff, the Office of Management and Budget (OMB), or other agencies—became an issue as the process of OMB review of rules became more entrenched.[30] While the analogy between private communications and presidential or other intragovernmental contacts is far from exact, off-the-record communications even among agencies raise concerns about fairness to rulemaking participants and the integrity of the rulemaking record. There is concern that behind-the-scenes intervention by a President or presidential advisors may frustrate congressional mandates, reduce incentives for regulators to act independently, undermine the APA's

---

26. Dep't of Transp. Order No. 2100.2 (1970). Ex parte communications are discouraged after the end of the comment period. After the NPRM is published, all communications must be reduced to writing and promptly placed in the public docket. Summaries should include list of participants, summary of discussion, and statement of commitments made by Department of Transportation personnel. *See also* the FAA's policy at 14 C.F.R. pt. 11 (App. I), published with explanation at 65 Fed. Reg. 50,850, 50,852–53 (Aug. 21, 2000).

27. Administrator's Memorandum of May 31, 1985, *available at* http://www.regulationwriters.com/downloads/EPA-Fishbowl-Memo-05-19-1983-Ruckelshaus.pdf (instructing agency employees to "be certain (1) that all written comments received from persons outside the Agency (whether during or after the comment period) are entered in the public record for the rulemaking, [and] (2) that a memorandum summarizing any significant new factual data or information likely to affect the final decision received during a meeting or other conversations is placed in the public record").

28. 44 C.F.R. § 1.6 (requiring written summary of all outside communications with "significant information and argument respecting the merits of the proposed rule" to be placed in the informal rulemaking file). The Solicitor of Labor also announced a policy on the handling of ex parte communications in a memorandum to departmental staff. *See Hearings on the Use and Control of Ethylene Oxide Before the Subcomm. on Labor Standards of the House Comm. on Education and Labor*, 98th Cong. 237–42 (1983).

29. 7 C.F.R. § 1.27. It is the Department's policy to exclude any late comments from the rulemaking record, although they remain available under the Freedom of Information Act.

30. *See supra* Part I(D) for a discussion of this development.

rulemaking process, and serve as undisclosed conduits for information supplied by interested private groups.[31] These concerns led to a series of steps that have regularized and increased the transparency of the OMB review process.[32]

1. The Administrative Conference's Recommendations

In 1980, the Administrative Conference first considered the issue of communications between agencies and other executive branch personnel. The Conference adopted a recommendation that sought to accommodate the need for internal policy debate with the demands for public participation and requirements of judicial review. First, the Conference concluded that executive departments and agencies should be free to receive written or oral *policy* advice from other executive personnel without having to publicize these contacts.[33] However, when an executive communication contains material *factual* information on a proposed rule, the Conference called on agencies to promptly place copies of documents received (or summaries of oral communications) in the public rulemaking file/docket and to consider giving interested persons an opportunity to respond if the factual material presents important new issues or creates serious conflicts of data.[34] In addition, the Conference advised agencies to alleviate "conduit" concerns by identifying and making public every communication that contains or reflects comments from persons outside the government, regardless of content.[35]

In 1988, the Administrative Conference again addressed the question of executive branch communications during informal rulemaking. In Recommendation 88-9,[36] the Conference concluded that:

> 1. When an agency submits a draft proposal or final rule for presidential review, the submissions and any additional formal analysis submitted should be made public when the proposal or final rule is published or the rulemaking is terminated.[37]

---

31. *See* discussion *supra* Part I(D)(2).
32. *See id.*
33. ACUS Recommendation 80-6, *Intragovernmental Communications in Informal Rulemaking Proceedings*, 45 Fed. Reg. 86,407 (Dec. 31, 1980). In the preamble, the Conference stated that agencies other than the one conducting the rulemaking "may have perspectives or expertise not readily available to the rulemaking agency that would enhance the quality of internal debate." *Id.* at 86,408.
34. *Id.* at 86,408.
35. *Id. See generally* Paul R. Verkuil, *Jawboning Administrative Agencies: Ex Parte Contacts by the White House*, 80 Colum. L. Rev. 943, 944–47 (1980).
36. ACUS Recommendation 88-9, *Presidential Review of Agency Rulemaking*, 54 Fed. Reg. 5207 (Feb. 2, 1989). The recommendation is based on Harold H. Bruff, *Presidential Management of Agency Rulemaking*, 57 Geo. Wash. L. Rev. 533 (1989). *See also supra* Part I(D) (discussing ACUS Recommendation 88-9).
37. ACUS Recommendation 88-9, ¶ 4(a), *supra* note 36. The recommendation also calls for the disclosure of agendas and summaries of pending or planned rulemaking and supporting statements submitted for review. *Id.* ¶ 4(b).

2. An agency should not be required to place in the public file "policy guidance concerning the rulemaking" received from the President or the Executive Branch; however, "official written policy guidance from the officer responsible for presidential review of rulemaking" should be placed in the file once the proposed or final rule is published or the rulemaking is terminated.[38]

3. If an agency receives a communication with new factual information in the presidential review process, the agency should promptly place the communication (or a summary if oral) in the public file.[39]

4. If the agency receives a communication with factual submissions or the views or positions of persons outside the government, the agency should promptly place the communication (or a summary if oral) in the public file.[40]

2. *The Transparency of OMB's Review of Agency Rules*

To accommodate concerns about its communications with agencies during review of agency rulemaking, the Reagan Administration issued a memorandum stating:

> Both the public and the agencies should understand that the primary forum for receiving factual communications regarding proposed rules is the agency issuing the proposal, not the Task Force [on Regulatory Relief] or OMB. Factual materials that are sent to the Task Force or OMB regarding proposed regulations should indicate that they have also been sent to the relevant agency.[41]

The memorandum also stated that, where the President's Task Force on Regulatory Relief or OMB receives or develops factual material that is submitted for agency consideration, it "will be identified as material appropriate for the whole record of the agency rulemaking."[42] The memorandum did not indicate whether the directive applied to oral, as well as written, communications.

---

38. *Id.* ¶ 5(a).

39. *Id.* ¶ 5(b).

40. *Id.* ¶ 5(c). The recommendation states that the official responsible for presidential review "should not allow the process of review to serve as a conduit to the rulemaking agency for unrecorded communications from persons outside the governments." *Id.* ¶ 6. The responsible official should take appropriate steps to guard against this, such as inviting agency representatives to meetings with persons outside the government; in that case, the agency official should prepare a summary of the discussion and promptly place it in the rulemaking file. *Id.* ¶ 6(d).

41. Memorandum from David Stockman, OMB Director, to Heads of Executive Departments and Agencies, June 11, 1981, *reprinted in* OFFICE OF MGMT. & BUDGET, REGULATORY PROGRAM OF THE UNITED STATES GOVERNMENT 618 (1990–1991); *see also* Memorandum, Dep't of Justice, Office of Legal Counsel to OMB, Contacts Between OMB and Executive Branch Agencies Pursuant to Executive Order No. 12,291 (Apr. 24, 1981), *reprinted in part in* Bruff, *supra* note 36, at 580.

42. Memorandum from David Stockman, *supra* note 41.

The role of OMB in agency rulemaking remained a source of controversy, however, and in 1986, Congress began to consider legislation to restrict OMB's monitoring role.[43] In June 1986, OMB responded to this pressure by reaffirming certain previously established procedures and by establishing additional transparency procedures for reviews by OIRA.[44] This accommodation with Congress later formed the basis for the Administrative Conference's Recommendation 88-9, which in turn was implemented by the Clinton Administration's inclusion of strict openness provisions in E.O. 12,866.

The Order provides that after the agency has concluded its rulemaking, it should make available to the public all submissions to OIRA and identify all substantive changes made in the rule, noting those made at the behest of OIRA.[45] In addition, OIRA, for its part, must regularize the way it receives any outside communications concerning an agency rule that is subject to review. Only the Administrator or his/her designee may receive such communications. OIRA must forward any such communications to the agency within 10 days, invite agency officials to any meetings held with outsiders, and maintain a public log of all such contacts. At the end of the proceeding, OIRA must also make available all documents exchanged with the agency.[46]

---

43. *See* Bruff, *supra* note 36, at 582–83 (describing the proposed legislation).

44. Memorandum from Wendy A. Gramm, OIRA Administrator, Additional Procedures Concerning OIRA Reviews Under Executive Order Nos. 12,291 and 12,498 [Revised] (June 13, 1986), to Heads of Departments and Agencies Subject to Executive Orders 12,291 and 12,498, *reprinted in* OFFICE OF MGMT. & BUDGET, REGULATORY PROGRAM OF THE UNITED STATES GOVERNMENT 605–07 (1990–1991).

45. *But see* GOV'T ACCOUNTABILITY OFFICE, FEDERAL RULEMAKING: IMPROVEMENTS NEEDED TO MONITORING AND EVALUATION OF RULES DEVELOPMENT AS WELL AS TO THE TRANSPARENCY OF OMB REGULATORY REVIEWS 39 (GAO-09-205) (April 2009), www.gao.gov/new.items/d09205.pdf (urging, among other things, that OMB "define in guidance what types of changes made as a result of the OIRA review process are substantive and need to be publicly identified," and "direct agencies to clearly state in final rules whether they made substantive changes as a result of the OIRA reviews").

46. *See* Exec. Order 12,866 §§ 6(a)(3)(E), 6(b)(4), 58 Fed. Reg. 51,735 (Oct. 4, 1993), *reprinted in* Appendix B of this GUIDE. These provisions are necessary in part because the courts have held that Freedom of Information Act exemptions protect from disclosure these interagency communications. *See, e.g.*, Wolfe v. Dep't of Health & Human Servs., 839 F.2d 768 (D.C. Cir. 1988) (en banc). In *Wolfe*, the D.C. Circuit held that a public interest group was not entitled access under the Freedom of Information Act (FOIA) to HHS records showing the dates on which regulatory proposals of the Food and Drug Administration (FDA) were forwarded from FDA to the Secretary of HHS and from there to OMB. *Id.* Concluding that the requested records were protected by the FOIA exemption for inter- and intra-agency memoranda, the court stated that the "information sought will generally disclose the recommended outcome of the consultative process at each stage of the process, as well as the source of any decision not to regulate." *Id.* at 773–76. This disclosure, the court held, could reveal policies "prematurely," "chill discussion at a time when agency opinions are fluid and tentative," and "force officials to punch a public time clock." *Id. See also* Pub. Citizen Health Res. Group v. Tyson, 796 F.2d 1479 (D.C. Cir. 1986) (avoiding the issue of OMB involvement in rulemaking and disposing of case on other grounds).

3. The Judicial Perspective

Although questions concerning OMB's involvement in informal rulemaking and its off-the-record contacts with agencies during rulemaking have been raised in several cases, courts have thus far declined to deal explicitly with either the statutory or constitutional issues raised by critics of OMB review.[47]

The policy reasons for the courts' reluctance to interfere with intragovernmental communications were forcefully stated by the D.C. Circuit in *Sierra Club v. Costle*:[48]

> The authority of the President to control and supervise executive policymaking is derived from the Constitution; the desirability of such control is demonstrable from the practical realities of administrative rulemaking. Regulations such as those involved here demand a careful weighing of cost, environmental, and energy considerations. They also have broad implications for national economic policy. Our form of government simply could not function effectively or rationally if key executive policymakers were isolated from each other and from the Chief Executive. Single mission agencies do not always have the answers to complex regulatory problems. An overworked administrator exposed on a 24-hour basis to a dedicated but zealous staff needs to know the arguments and ideas of policymakers in other agencies as well as in the White House.[49]

The court accordingly held that it was not unlawful for EPA to omit from the rulemaking file a summary of a policy session involving the President and EPA officials that occurred in the post-comment period, because EPA did not base its rule on "information or data" arising from that meeting.[50] In reaching this conclusion, the court referred favorably to the Administrative Conference recommendation that distinguished policy advice from communications containing material factual information.[51] The court noted that a rule must have factual support in the rulemaking record, and though recognizing the possibility that "Presidential prodding" could produce a different result that was based on information already in the rulemaking record, the court did not "believe that Congress intended that the courts convert informal rulemaking into a rarefied technocratic process, unaffected by political considerations or the presence of political power."[52]

---

47. *See supra* Part I(D)(3).
48. 657 F.2d 298, 404–08 (D.C. Cir. 1981) (internal footnotes omitted).
49. *Id.*
50. *Id.* at 407–08.
51. *Id.* at 407; ACUS Recommendation 80-6, *supra* note 33.
52. 657 F.2d at 408. For a continuation of the debate over the place politics should have in rulemaking and judicial review of rules, see Kathryn A. Watts, *Proposing a Place for Politics in Arbitrary and Capricious Review*, 119 YALE L.J. 2 (2009), and Enrique Armijo, *Politics, Rulemaking, and Judicial Review: A Response to Professor Watts*, 62 ADMIN. L. REV. 573 (2010). *See also* Kevin M. Stack, *Agency Statutory Interpretation and Policymaking Form*, 2009 MICH. ST. L. REV. 225 (2009) (suggesting that when an agency engages in notice-and-comment rulemaking, it is appropriately influenced by political directions and internal management considerations).

In 1988, the Fifth Circuit, in *National Grain & Feed Ass'n v. OSHA*,[53] rejected a union contention that OSHA's grain-handling standard should be remanded because OMB "displaced the Secretary's congressionally authorized role" by its alleged "off-the-record coercion" of OSHA.[54] Characterizing the unions' brief as telling a "colorful tale of 'the behind-the-scenes evolution of the OSHA standard,'" the court concluded that the record did not support the unions' contention and ruled that the final rule must "stand or fall on the basis of the record before the agency, not on the basis of some 'secret record' of OMB's."[55] However, it is important that the agency give the public a chance to comment on significant data or information supplied by other agencies after the comment period. As the D.C. Circuit cautioned while upholding an EPA rule:

> The main sources of petitioners' concern are several EPA memoranda recording meetings with DOE and OMB . . . , which occurred after the close of the period for public comments. EPA placed the memos in the open public docket. If these showed that DOE had supplied EPA with additional data, on which EPA relied in the final rule and on which others had no chance to comment, we would have cause for concern.[56]

D. Congressional Communications in Rulemaking

Occasionally, parties challenging agency rules have alleged that ex parte communications between members of Congress and agency decisionmakers constituted procedural error justifying invalidation of the rules. However, while courts have held that congressional[57] or presidential[58] interference in agency *adjudication* can cause a denial of procedural due process, courts have not found congressional contacts in informal rulemaking to be improper.

In *Sierra Club v. Costle*,[59] the D.C. Circuit refused to invalidate an EPA rule because of off-the-record meetings between agency personnel and a U.S. Senator.

---

53. 866 F.2d 717 (5th Cir. 1989).
54. *Id.* at 729 n.22.
55. *Id.*
56. New Mexico v. EPA, 114 F.3d 290, 295 (D.C. Cir. 1997).
57. *See, e.g.*, Pillsbury Co. v. FTC, 354 F.2d 952 (5th Cir. 1966). Judge Crabb's opinions in *Sokaogon Chippewa Cmty. v. Babbitt* provide an excellent review of the cases involving political pressure (by Congress or the President) on agency adjudications or rulemakings. 929 F. Supp. 1165, 1173–76 (W.D. Wis. 1996), *op. on recons.*, 961 F. Supp. 1276 (W.D. Wis. 1996) (permitting extra-record discovery on issue of political pressure); *see also* Ronald M. Levin, *Congressional Ethics and Constituent Advocacy in an Age of Mistrust*, 95 MICH. L. REV. 1 (1996); MORTON ROSENBERG & JACK H. MASKELL, CONGRESSIONAL INTERVENTION IN THE ADMINISTRATIVE PROCESS: LEGAL AND ETHICAL CONSIDERATIONS (Cong. Res. Serv. Report for Congress, 1990).
58. *See, e.g.*, Portland Audubon Soc'y v. Endangered Species Comm., 984 F.2d 1534, 1543–49 (9th Cir. 1993).
59. 657 F.2d 298, 404–08 (D.C. Cir. 1981).

Even though the Clean Air Act requires creation of an exclusive record for judicial review, the court concluded that the meetings were not improper:

> The meetings did underscore [the Senator's] deep concerns for EPA, but there is no evidence he attempted actively to use "extraneous" pressures to further his position. Americans rightly expect their elected representatives to voice their grievances and preferences concerning the administration of our laws. We believe it entirely proper for Congressional representatives vigorously to represent the interests of their constituents before administrative agencies engaged in informal general policy rulemaking, so long as individual Congressmen do not frustrate the intent of Congress as a whole as expressed in statute, nor undermine applicable rules of procedure . . . .[60]

The court held that to upset a rule based on such ex parte contacts, the challenging party would have to demonstrate that the agency's decision was based upon factors introduced by the ex parte communications that are not relevant to decision under the applicable statute.[61]

The advent of congressional review of agency regulations[62] may "cut both ways" on this issue. On the one hand, it may make such communications more troubling because of the extra amount of potential leverage individual members of Congress may have or may be perceived to have by agency officials. On the other hand, because members now also have increased leverage after the agency action, it may make substantive communications less frequent and even less relevant.

E. Intra-agency Communications in Rulemaking

Nothing in the APA bars agency personnel from advising the decisionmaker in informal rulemaking. This contrasts with agency adjudication, in which agency administrative law judges are barred from off-the-record consultations with anyone, and agency heads may not be advised by agency investigators or prosecutors, on

---

60. *Id.* at 409.
61. *Id.* In *Sierra Club*, the court did not accept a newspaper article account of extraneous pressure by the senator as evidence of "unlawful congressional interference." *Id.* at 409 n.539. In *Federation of Civic Associations v. Volpe*, the agency's decision to approve construction of a bridge across the Potomac River was influenced by a congressman's threats to withhold appropriations for the Washington, D.C., area subway system. 459 F.2d 1231 (D.C. Cir. 1971). The court found the subway appropriations factor was "extraneous" to the statutory criteria that applied to construction of the bridge and thus not properly considered. *Id.* For a similar decision in the context of a congressionally mandated National Oceanic and Atmospheric Administration determination as to whether tuna-fishing practices were affecting the dolphin population, see *Earth Island Institute v. Hogarth*, 494 F.3d 757, 768 (9th Cir. 2007) ("We agree with the district court's conclusion that this record demonstrates the Secretary was improperly influenced by political concerns.").
62. *See supra* Part II, ch. 3(J); *infra* Part III, ch. 7(A)(5)(b).

facts in issue.[63] The *Attorney General's Manual on the APA* explains this different treatment as follows:

> Not only were the draftsmen and proponents of the bill aware of this realistic distinction between rulemaking and adjudication, but they shaped the entire Act around it. . . . Even in formal rulemaking proceedings subject to sections 7 and 8 [now §§ 556 and 557], the Act leaves the hearing officer entirely free to consult with any other member of the agency's staff. In fact, the intermediate decision may be made by the agency itself or by a responsible officer other than the hearing officer. This reflects the fact that the purpose of the rulemaking proceeding is to determine policy. Policy is not made in federal agencies by individual hearing examiners; rather it is formulated by the agency heads relying heavily upon the expert staffs which have been hired for that purpose. And so the Act recognizes that in rulemaking the intermediate decisions will be more useful to the parties in advising them of the real issues in the case if such decisions reflect the views of the agency heads or of their responsible officers who assist them in determining policy.[64]

In *United Steelworkers of America v. Marshall,*[65] the D.C. Circuit relied on the distinction between adjudication and rulemaking in refusing to invalidate an OSHA rule because of ex parte communications between the head of OSHA and attorneys on the agency's rulemaking staff. Finding no statutory basis for restricting such communications, the court rejected the petitioners' claim of procedural error, stating:

> Rulemaking is essentially an institutional, not an individual, process, and it is not vulnerable to communication within an agency in the same sense as it is to communication from without. In an enormously complex proceeding like an OSHA standard setting, it may simply be unrealistic to expect an official facing a massive, almost inchoate, record to isolate herself from the people with whom she worked in generating the record.[66]

---

63. 5 U.S.C. § 554(d). Although the APA does prohibit ex parte communications with persons outside the agency in formal rulemaking, it does not bar communications between the decisionmaker and agency personnel. *Id.* § 557(d). However, inasmuch as in all formal proceedings the testimony, exhibits, and other papers filed in the proceeding constitute the exclusive record for decision, no extra-record information may be received in either formal adjudication or formal rulemaking. *Id.* § 556(e); *see also* Hercules, Inc. v. EPA, 598 F.2d 91, 123–24 (D.C. Cir. 1978).

64. ATTORNEY GENERAL'S MANUAL ON THE ADMINISTRATIVE PROCEDURE ACT 38 (1947), *reprinted in* WILLIAM F. FUNK, JEFFREY S. LUBBERS & CHARLES POU, JR., FEDERAL ADMINISTRATIVE SOURCEBOOK 39, 75 (4th ed. 2008); *see also* Michael Asimow, *When the Curtain Falls: Separation of Functions in the Federal Administrative Agencies,* 81 COLUM. L. REV. 759 (1981) (providing an excellent treatment of separation of functions in agency proceedings).

65. 647 F.2d 1189 (D.C. Cir. 1980).

66. *Id.* at 1216.

The D.C. Circuit again confronted the issue of staff communications with the agency rulemaking decisionmaker in *National Small Shipments Traffic Conference, Inc. v. ICC.*[67] The court refused to invalidate a rule on the basis that staff that had conducted an underlying study supportive of the rule had also been actively involved in the decisionmaking process, emphasizing that neither a federal statute nor due process "imposes a general separation-of-function requirement on informal rulemaking by an agency."[68] The ICC was therefore free to lift its restrictions on staff participation.

The court also addressed the issue of the agency's handling of staff recommendations. Petitioners argued that staff evaluations critical of the study relied on by the ICC in its decision had been "suppressed." The court rejected this contention, stating:

> [P]etitioners do have a legal right that their comments reach Commission members in at least summary form, and that those comments be considered before final action is taken. Neither the APA nor the due process clause, however, accords similar treatment to staff evaluations that move beyond a mere summary of record comments to express the independent judgments of subordinate agency personnel. An agency is free to structure its internal policy debate in any manner it deems appropriate. Mid-level managers may therefore filter out the evaluations of lower-level personnel if they so choose, so long as relevant record comments are not eliminated in the process as well.[69]

To assure itself of the accuracy or completeness of rulemaking staff representations, as well as to increase public confidence in the fairness of the process, an agency should consider placing in the record any documents written by the staff that summarize or characterize the information in the rulemaking record. This procedure can provide a check to minimize the chances of distortion of public comments and other information in the record by staff members who may have become unduly committed to a particular point of view.

F. Communications with Consultants

Agencies sometimes use the services of outside consultants in developing rules or supporting analyses, particularly in rulemakings involving questions of science or technology for which the agency needs added expertise. The tasks consultants are asked to perform vary, but they include testifying as witnesses, conducting research,

---

67. 725 F.2d 1442 (D.C. Cir. 1984).
68. *Id.* at 1448.
69. *Id.* at 1451 (footnote omitted). In any event, the court rejected the argument on the merits, finding that the evidence established that the Commission members were made fully aware of the comments, particularly those criticizing the agency's proposed action. *Id.*

summarizing and evaluating data in the record, and helping to draft portions of the final rule and its rationale.[70]

Decisionmakers' use of consultants' reports and analyses that were not placed in the rulemaking record was challenged in *United Steelworkers of America v. Marshall*.[71] The D.C. Circuit concluded that even though the consultants had testified publicly in favor of the proposed rule and later analyzed the public record for the agency decisionmaker, they were the "functional equivalent" of agency staff and, therefore, not subject to ex parte or separation-of-function restraints.[72] The opinion intimated, however, that had the consultants introduced significant new information in their reports, the court would have had greater difficulty upholding the rule.[73]

In *National Small Shipments*,[74] the court, again relying on *Steelworkers*, held that "in the informal rulemaking context private technical consultants may assist the agency in analyzing the record without running afoul of the prohibition on ex parte contacts."[75] Although some bureaucratic "disarray" surrounded the individual's contract with the agency in that case, the court held that a consultancy did exist, thus making the individual "an insider" for purposes of the ex parte contacts rule.[76]

---

70. *Id. See also* ACUS Recommendation 85-2, *Agency Procedures for Performing Regulatory Analysis of Rules*, ¶ 6, 50 Fed. Reg. 28,364 (July 12, 1985) for a discussion of the use of consultants in the preparation of regulatory analysis documents. *See also* U.S. GEN. ACCOUNTING OFFICE, OCCUPATIONAL SAFETY AND HEALTH: OSHA CONTRACTING FOR FEDERAL RULEMAKING ACTIVITIES (GAO-HRD-89-102 BR) (June 1989) (discussing the use of consultants by federal agencies in rulemaking activity in a briefing book for congressional requestors).

71. 647 F.2d 1189, 1218 (D.C. Cir. 1980).

72. *Id.* at 1218–20.

73. *Id.* at 1220. In a related case, *Lead Industries Ass'n v. OSHA*, 610 F.2d 70 (2d Cir. 1979), the Second Circuit held that consultants' reports in the lead rulemaking were exempt from disclosure under the Freedom of Information Act as internal agency communications.

74. 725 F.2d at 1442.

75. *Id.* at 1449–50.

76. *Id.*

Chapter 7

The Final Rule

Between the end of the comment period and a final rule's publication in the *Federal Register*, there are some issues that an agency may need to consider in addition to decisions on the substance of the rule. Topics discussed in the first section of this chapter include the importance of time limits, interagency coordination where necessary, effective dates for rules, and disqualification of decisionmakers.

The chapter then addresses the statement of basis and purpose (commonly referred to as the "preamble") required by the APA for a final rule. The courts have underscored the necessity that such a statement adequately articulates the reasons for the agency's decisions.

Finally, this chapter discusses several technical steps, including those required by the Office of the Federal Register, that must be complied with in publishing the rule.

A. Issues for Agency Consideration

1. *Time Limits for Agency Action*

The APA does not require agencies to act on rulemaking proposals within a prescribed time after the end of public proceedings.[1] Agency rulemaking activities are, however, often subject to deadlines. Enabling statutes have, with increasing frequency, imposed deadlines for issuing rules and, in some cases, for completing various rulemaking steps.[2] In addition, courts have issued orders containing rulemaking deadlines based either on the enabling statute or on a finding that the agency has not completed rulemaking "within a reasonable time."[3] An agency should, therefore, be keenly aware of the importance of prompt completion of rulemaking, both for good management and in view of legal constraints imposed on agencies.

---

1. 5 U.S.C. § 555(b) does require agencies to conclude matters "within a reasonable time," and courts are authorized to compel agency action "unreasonably delayed." 5 U.S.C. § 706(1). *See* discussion *infra* Part IV, ch. 3.
2. *See* discussion *supra* Part I(C) for examples of these enabling statutes.
3. Court suits to compel agency actions are discussed more fully *infra* Part IV, ch. 3.

Numerous delays can occur in the latter stages of rulemaking. The record, often lengthy, must be assessed by the staff and summarized for decisionmaking. Recommendations must be prepared. Different disciplines may become involved, and coordination with other agencies and OMB review will typically take place. Sometimes, internal policy disputes arise at the deliberative stage. All of these, as well as other factors, may delay the issuance of a final rule.[4]

Where the enabling statute imposes a time limit on agency action, the agency should obviously strive to meet the congressional deadline.[5] However, even in the absence of a statutory time limit, many agencies find it helpful to set their own schedules for completion of the various rulemaking steps, including the deliberative process. Not only do these schedules provide the agency a practical yardstick for determining whether its rulemaking is making satisfactory progress toward completion,[6] but in some cases courts have accepted such schedules as representing good-faith efforts by the agency to complete its rulemaking within a "reasonable" time.[7] Some federal agencies have established formal case-tracking systems and set time limits to speed up their adjudicative proceedings.[8] Similar "milestones" and tracking systems are now in use for agency rulemaking.[9]

---

4. *See, e.g.*, U.S. GEN. ACCOUNTING OFFICE, AVIATION SAFETY—PRELIMINARY INFORMATION ON AIRCRAFT ICING AND WINTER OPERATIONS 13–14 (GAO-10-441T, Feb. 2010), *available at* http://www.gao.gov/new.items/d10441t.pdf (testimony describing the FAA's 15-year struggle to issue standards for transport-category airplanes to address a certain type of icing conditions, and identifying the following issues: (1) inadequate early involvement of key stakeholders, (2) inadequate early resolution of issues, (3) inefficient review process, (4) inadequate selection and training of personnel involved in rulemaking, and (5) inefficient quality guidance).

5. However, if the agency misses the statutory deadline, it does not void a subsequent rule (unless the statute so provides). *See* Newton Cnty. Wildlife Ass'n v. U.S. Forest Serv., 113 F.3d 110, 112 (8th Cir. 1997).

6. The Administrative Conference recommended that agencies adopt time limits in agency proceedings, either by announcing schedules for particular agency proceedings or by adopting general timetables for dealing with categories of the agency's proceedings. ACUS Recommendation 78-3, *Time Limits on Agency Actions*, 43 Fed. Reg. 27,509 (June 26, 1978); *see also Study on Federal Regulation, IV: Delay in the Regulatory Process*, Senate Comm. on Governmental Affairs, 95th Cong. 132–52 (1977) (concluding that agency-set time limits are useful tools for reducing delay).

7. *See, e.g.*, Oil, Chem. & Atomic Workers Int'l Union v. Zegeer, 768 F.2d 1480 (D.C. Cir. 1985).

8. *See* Les Garner, *Management Control in Regulatory Agencies: A Modest Proposal for Reform*, 34 ADMIN. L. REV. 465, 475–79 (1982) (discussing NLRB and ICC); Richard B. Capalli, *Model for Case Management: The Grant Appeals Board*, 1986 ACUS 663 (discussing HHS Grant Appeals Board); Charles Pou, Jr. & Charlotte Jones, *Agency Time Limits as a Tool for Reducing Regulatory Delay*, 1986 ACUS 835 (discussing various agencies).

9. *See* GOV'T ACCOUNTABILITY OFFICE, FEDERAL RULEMAKING—IMPROVEMENTS NEEDED TO MONITORING AND EVALUATION OF RULES DEVELOPMENT AS WELL AS TO THE TRANSPARENCY OF OMB REGULATORY REVIEWS 14–17 (GAO-09-205, April 2009), *available at* http://www.gao.gov/new.items/d09205.pdf (identifying agencies that use milestones in their rulemaking process).

2. Interagency Coordination and Review

Often several agencies have jurisdiction over a particular issue or area or over different but related areas.[10] The Federal Trade Commission provides a good illustration of this phenomenon. It shares with the Antitrust Division of the Department of Justice the authority to prosecute certain antitrust violations.[11] In the food and drug area, the FTC polices unfair or deceptive product advertising by sellers, while the FDA prescribes labeling standards for the products.[12] A similar overlap of jurisdiction exists between FTC regulation of advertising and the FCC's regulation of the broadcast media.[13] Another example is the overlap of the jurisdiction of several federal agencies in the area of pesticides regulation.[14] EPA and the Department of Agriculture have jurisdiction over pesticide applications, and OSHA is authorized to regulate hazards involved in pesticide manufacture. Similarly, numerous agencies have authority to regulate asbestos hazards,[15] practices concerning the privacy protection of consumer financial information,[16] and federal acquisition regu-

---

10. For an in-depth look at interagency coordination, including joint rulemaking, see Jody Freeman & Jim Rossi, *Agency Coordination in Shared Regulatory Space,* 125 HARV. L. REV. 1131, 1166–73 (2012). ACUS is currently considering a proposed recommendation based on this work).
11. The FTC has concurrent jurisdiction with the Department of Justice in proceedings against price discrimination, exclusive dealing, acquisitions of stock or assets, and interlocking directorates that are prohibited by the Clayton Act. 2 Trade Reg. Rep. (CCH) ¶ 8550.
12. *See* Working Agreement Between FTC and FDA (June 9, 1954), 3 Trade Reg. Rep. (CCH) ¶ 9850.
13. *See* Liaison Agreement Between FCC and FTC (Apr. 27, 1972), 3 Trade Reg. Rep. (CCH) ¶ 9852.
14. Overlapping jurisdiction or the existence of "gray" areas of jurisdiction can sometimes lead to disputes and litigation. *See* Organized Migrants in Cmty. Action, Inc. v. Brennan, 520 F.2d 1161 (D.C. Cir. 1975) (discussing OSHA and EPA jurisdiction over pesticide application).
15. EPA has jurisdiction to control asbestos under the Toxic Substances Control Act, 15 U.S.C. §§ 2601–2692; Clean Water Act, 33 U.S.C. §§ 1251–1387; and Clean Air Act, 42 U.S.C. §§ 7401–7471q. OSHA has jurisdiction over workplace asbestos hazards, and the Consumer Product Safety Commission has responsibility for asbestos hazards in consumer products. *See, e.g.*, OSHA, Final Rules, Occupational Exposure to Asbestos, 51 Fed. Reg. 22,612, 22,613–14 (June 20, 1986).
16. *See, e.g.*, the Gramm-Leach-Bliley Act (GLBA), Pub. L. No. 106-102, 113 Stat. 1338 (1999) (codified at 15 U.S.C. §§ 6801 *et seq.*) (giving various agencies (federal banking agencies, the National Credit Union Administration, the Secretary of the Treasury, the SEC, and the FTC) broad rulemaking authority to "prescribe, after consultation as appropriate with representatives of State insurance authorities designated by the National Association of Insurance Commissioners, such regulations as may be necessary to carry out the [privacy protection] purposes of this subchapter with respect to the financial institutions subject to their jurisdiction"). In 2010, the Dodd-Frank Wall Street Reform and Consumer Protection Act added the Bureau of Consumer Financial Protection to the mix. Pub. L. 111-203, 123 Stat. 1376 (2010) (to be codified at 12 U.S.C. § 5301 note); *see also* Trans Union LLC v. FTC, 295 F.3d 42 (D.C. Cir. 2002) (upholding the FTC's rules).

lations.[17] EPA and DOT have recently issued a joint final rule on motor vehicle fuel economy labeling requirements.[18]

Where overlapping or related jurisdiction exists, it is clearly essential that the agencies involved consult with one another at the earliest possible stage in the rulemaking proceedings. In some cases, statutory provisions mandate such consultation. The Federal Insecticide, Fungicide, and Rodenticide Act, for example, requires that EPA submit its proposed rules to the Department of Agriculture for comment.[19] The Toxic Substances Control Act contains a detailed procedure under which EPA coordinates with the other federal agencies that have potential jurisdiction to regulate the substance in question.[20] In other cases, agencies have set up informal groups to coordinate implementation of their parallel, and often overlapping, regulatory responsibilities. An important example in the early 1980s was the Interagency Regulatory Liaison Group, formed by OSHA, EPA, CPSC, FDA, and the Department of Agriculture to coordinate their approaches to regulation of certain hazardous chemicals.[21] The Clinton Administration established the Regulatory Working Group, chaired by the Office of Information and Regulatory Affairs (OIRA) Administrator, to coordinate regulatory approaches and develop innovations.[22]

---

17. The Federal Acquisition Regulations (FAR) System, which comprehensively describes the federal government acquisition system, are codified at Title 48 of the *Code of Federal Regulations*. The government-wide acquisition regulations in Chapter 1 of Title 48 are jointly issued by the General Services Administration, the Department of Defense, and the National Aeronautics and Space Administration. For more information on the Defense FAR system, *see* http://www.acq.osd.mil/dpap/dars/index.html; for the Civilian FAR, *see* https://www.acquisition.gov/comp/caac/index.html.

18. Environmental Protection Agency & Department of Transportation, Final Rule, Revisions and Additions to Motor Vehicle Fuel Economy Label, 76 Fed. Reg. 39,478 (July 6, 2011). For a comprehensive account of this apparently successful joint rulemaking, see Jody Freeman, *The Obama Administration's National Auto Policy: Lessons from the "Car Deal,"* 35 HARV. ENVTL. L. REV. 343 (2011).

19. 7 U.S.C. §§ 136, 136w; *see also* EPA, Proposed Rule, Special Reviews of Pesticides; Criteria and Procedures, 50 Fed. Reg. 12,188, 12,200–03 (Mar. 27, 1985). In its proposal, EPA published the Department of Agriculture's comments on the proposal, as well as EPA's responses to the comments. *Id.*

20. 15 U.S.C. § 2608(d). The TSCA procedures EPA and OSHA followed in determining which agency would regulate methylenedianiline (MDA) are described in the preamble to OSHA's proposed standard on MDA. Proposed Rule, Occupational Exposure to MDA, 54 Fed. Reg. 20,672, 20,672–73 (May 12, 1989).

21. *See* Richard A. Merrill, *Federal Regulation of Cancer Causing Chemicals*, 1982 ACUS (vol. 2) 21, 176–78; *see also* Final Rule, Asbestos, *supra* note 15 (referring to Federal Asbestos Task Force established in June 1983 to coordinate federal regulatory actions with regard to asbestos). ACUS has recommended the increased use of interagency groups in the area of biotechnology regulation. ACUS Recommendation 89-7, *Federal Regulation of Biotechnology*, 54 Fed. Reg. 53,494 (Dec. 29, 1989); *see also* Sidney A. Shapiro, *Biotechnology and the Design of Regulation*, 17 ECOLOGY L.Q. 1 (1990).

22. Exec. Order 12,866 § 4(d), 58 Fed. Reg. 51,735 (2003). This was in response to a recommendation by the National Performance Review, *see* OFFICE OF THE VICE PRESIDENT, CREATING A GOVERNMENT

Agency officials should be attentive to statutory requirements for interagency coordination during rulemaking. Whether coordination is legally required or has been undertaken as a matter of agency discretion and good management, the agency's posture will be much better in relation to other agencies, the courts, and the public if interagency coordination and review begins early and continues throughout the rulemaking process.

3. *International Regulatory Cooperation*

In addition to the need for interagency coordination, agency rulemakers in some agencies must be concerned about the need to coordinate their regulatory activities, such as information gathering, rulemaking, and enforcement, with foreign (including regional and international) regulatory bodies.[23] As the Administrative Conference noted in 1991, "The substantive problems facing agencies have parallels, to a greater or lesser extent, in the problems facing those agencies' counterparts in foreign countries. The policies and procedures developed by governments abroad are likely to be of interest and benefit to American regulators, and those developed here may be of utility abroad."[24]

Not only can such international cooperation prove to be mutually beneficial, it may be necessary to have a coherent international regulatory program—in financial services,[25] aviation,[26] food and drug,[27] or pesticide[28] regulation, for example. More-

---

THAT WORKS BETTER AND COSTS LESS, NATIONAL PERFORMANCE REVIEW, IMPROVING REGULATORY SYSTEMS 17–22 (1993). The members of the Regulatory Working Group are listed in OFFICE OF MGMT. & BUDGET, REPORT ON EXECUTIVE ORDER NO. 12,866, 59 Fed. Reg. 24,293 (May 10, 1994). It was inactive in the Bush II Administration but has recently been reactivated by President Obama. *See* E.O. 13,609 § 2.

23. *See* ACUS Recommendation 91-1, *Federal Agency Cooperation with Foreign Government Regulators*, 56 Fed. Reg. 33,842 (July 24, 1991). ACUS updated this recommendation in 2011, *see* ACUS Recommendation 2011-6, *International Regulatory Cooperation* (Dec. 8, 2011), 77 Fed. Reg. 2259 (Jan. 17, 2012). *See also* the background report, Michael T. McCarthy, *International Regulatory Cooperation, 20 Years Later: Updating ACUS Recommendation 91-1*, *available at* http://www.acus.gov/wp-content/uploads/downloads/2011/10/COR-IRC-report-10-19-11.pdf.

24. ACUS Recommendation 91-1, *supra* note 23, at 33,843.

25. *See, e.g.*, the activities of the International Organization of Securities Commissions, http://www.iosco.org/about/index.cfm?section=categories, and the Financial Stability Board, http://www.financialstabilityboard.org.

26. *See, e.g.*, George A. Bermann, *Regulatory Cooperation with Counterpart Agencies Abroad: The FAA's Aircraft Certification Experience*, 24 LAW & POL'Y INT'L BUS. 669 (1993).

27. *See* FDA, Notice, International Conference on Harmonisation, 60 Fed. Reg. 43,910 (Aug. 23, 1993). *See generally* Joseph G. Contrera, Comment, *The Food and Drug Administration and the International Conference on Harmonization: How Harmonious Will International Pharmaceutical Regulations Become?*, 8 ADMIN. L.J. AM. U. 927 (1995).

28. *See* U.S. GEN. ACCOUNTING OFFICE, PESTICIDES—A COMPARATIVE STUDY OF INDUSTRIALIZED NATIONS' REGULATORY SYSTEMS: REPORT TO THE SEN. COMMITTEE ON AGRICULTURE, NUTRITION, AND FORESTRY (GAO-PEMD-93-17, July 1993), *available at* http://www.gao.gov/assets/160/153626.pdf.

over, the rise of international regulatory organizations like the European Union has made this cooperation more necessary and feasible.[29]

ACUS has recently updated its recommendation, but continues to suggest that agencies with counterpart international regulatory "cousins" should consider adopting various modes of cooperation with those agencies. These include:

3. When agencies conclude that they have legal authority and the interest in cooperation from foreign authorities, and that cooperation would further agencies' missions or promote trade and competitiveness without detracting from their missions, they should consider various modes of cooperation with those authorities, including but not limited to:

    (a) establishment of common regulatory agendas;

    (b) exchange of information about present and proposed foreign regulation;

    (c) concerted efforts to reduce differences between the agency's rules and those adopted by foreign government regulators where those differences are not justified;

    (d) holding periodic bilateral or multilateral meetings (either in person or by teleconference or videoconference) to assess the effectiveness of past cooperative efforts and to chart future ones; and

    (e) mutual recognition of tests, inspections, clinical trials, and certifications of foreign agencies.

4. To deploy limited resources more effectively, agencies should, where appropriate and practicable, identify foreign authorities that maintain high quality and effective standards and practices and identify areas in which the tests, inspections, or certifications by agencies and such foreign agencies overlap. Where appropriate and practicable, agencies should:

    (a) consider dividing responsibility for necessary tests, inspections, and certifications and mutually recognizing their results;

    (b) create joint technical or working groups to conduct joint research and development and to identify common solutions to regulatory problems (for example, through parallel notices of proposed rulemaking);

    (c) establish joint administrative teams to draft common procedures and enforcement and dispute resolution policies; and/or

---

29. For a report bearing on these trans-Atlantic ties, see John F. Morrall III, Determining Compatible Regulatory Regimes between the U.S. and the EU (U.S. Chamber of Commerce White Paper) (2011) at 23, *available at* http://www.uschamber.com/sites/default/files/grc/Determining%20Compatible%20Regulatory%20Regimes%20-%20Final_0.pdf; *see also* EU-US High-Level Regulatory Cooperation Forum, Report to the Transatlantic Economic Council, October 15, 2008, *available at* http://www.whitehouse.gov/sites/default/files/omb/oira/irc/hlrcf_summary_report_october_2008.pdf; George A. Bermann, *Regulatory Cooperation Between the European Commission and U.S. Administrative Agencies*, 9 ADMIN. L.J. AM. U. 933 (1996).

(d) document and publish cost savings and regulatory benefits from such mutual arrangements.

5. To assess whether foreign authorities maintain high quality and effective standards and practices, agencies should develop and maintain relationships with foreign counterparts by providing training and technical assistance to foreign authorities and developing employee exchange programs, as resources permit. Agencies should also, as resources permit, review whether foreign or international practices would be appropriate for adoption in the United States.

6. Agencies should engage in exchanges of information with foreign authorities to promote better, evidence-based decision-making. Types of information exchanges can range from formal agreements to share data to informal dialogues among agency staff. To the extent practicable, information exchange should be mutually beneficial and reciprocal. Prior to exchanging information, agencies must reach arrangements with foreign counterparts that will protect confidential information, trade secrets, or other sensitive information.

7. When engaging in regulatory dialogues with foreign authorities, agencies should seek input and participation from interested parties as appropriate, through either formal means such as Federal Register notices and requests for comments or informal means such as outreach to regulated industries, consumers, and other stakeholders. Agencies should, where consistent with their statutory authority, missions, and the public interest, consider petitions by private and public interest groups for proposed rulemakings that contemplate the reduction of differences between agency rules and the rules adopted by foreign authorities, where those differences are not justified. While international consultations of the sort described in this recommendation do not usually depart from an agency's standard practices in compliance with applicable procedural statutes, an agency engaged in such consultations should describe those consultations in its notices of proposed rulemaking, rulemaking records, and statements of basis and purpose under the Administrative Procedure Act. Where the objective of aligning American and foreign agency rules has had a significant influence on the shape of the rule, that fact also should be clearly acknowledged.

8. Agencies should promote to foreign authorities the principles that undergird the United States administrative and regulatory process, including, as appropriate:
(a) transparency, openness and public participation,
(b) evidence-based and risk-informed regulation,
(c) cost-benefit analysis,
(d) consensus-based standard setting,
(e) accountability under the law,
(f) clearly defined roles and lines of authority,
(g) fair and responsive dispute resolution procedures, and
(h) impartiality.

An agency engaging in international regulatory cooperation should also be alert to the possibility that foreign regulatory bodies may have different regulatory objectives, particularly where a government-owned or controlled enterprise is involved.[30]

These sorts of cooperative endeavors will not always produce identical regulations, of course. In its 1991 recommendation, ACUS urged that where an agency ultimately "proposes a rule that differs from the rule proposed by the foreign counterpart, it should specify the difference in its notice of proposed rulemaking and request that it be specified in any corresponding foreign notice."[31] This has now been implemented by a database, "Notify U.S.," established by the National Institute of Science and Technology (NIST) within the Department of Commerce.[32] As described in the ACUS study,

> It contains proposed mandatory product standards and conformity assessment procedures from other countries that may significantly affect trade. The Notify U.S. database compiles summary information on foreign measures, allows users to request complete texts, guides U.S. entities in preparing comments, and forwards these comments to foreign regulators. NIST is also responsible for notifying foreign countries of proposed U.S. federal and state measures that may have significant trade effects.[33]

On the other hand, sometimes international negotiations will produce an agreement that an agency wishes to implement through rulemaking. This, of course, cannot be done without going through the normal rulemaking process. ACUS has made clear that agencies should make sure that affected interests are informed of the international consultations that produced the rulemaking.

In this connection, it is interesting to note that the government's online system that provides information and status updates on the unified regulatory agenda and regulatory review process has added a data element on international impacts.[34] Proposed rules submitted to OIRA for review are categorized and searchable by whether they have international impact. Moreover, agencies should be aware that the U.S. Trade Representative in the White House has the statutory responsibility "for coordinating United States discussions and negotiations with foreign countries for the purpose of establishing mutual arrangements with respect to standards-related activities,"[35] and that a State Department regulation obliges agencies to consult with OIRA before entering into international agreements that require significant regulatory action.[36]

---

30. ACUS Recommendation 2011-6, *supra* note 23, at ¶¶ 3–8. On May 1, 2012, President Obama built on this recommendation in Executive Order 13,609, "Promoting Intenational Regulatory Cooperation," 77 Fed. Reg. 26,413 (May 4, 2012).
31. ACUS Recommendation 91-1, *supra* note 23, at ¶ 8 (c).
32. *See* Notify U.S., https://tsapps.nist.gov/notifyus/data/index/index.cfm.
33. *See* McCarthy, *supra* note 23, at 6.
34. *See id.* at 17. The website is www.reginfo.gov.
35. 19 U.S.C. § 2541.
36. *See* 22 C.F.R. § 181.4(e)(2).

Finally, it should be noted that the Trade Agreements Act prohibits agencies from setting standards that create "unnecessary obstacles to the foreign commerce of the United States" and also requires that in developing U.S. standards, agencies give consideration to international standards and, where appropriate, make them the basis for U.S. standards.[37]

4. The Final Regulatory Analysis and OMB Review

Under Executive Order 12,866, federal agencies conducting rulemakings must also report their planned issuance of a final rule to OIRA, and it may be subject to review and clearance if it is deemed to be "significant." A final regulatory analysis must also be submitted if the rule meets the order's criteria for economic or other special significance.[38] As with proposed rule submissions, OMB has 90 days to complete this review, with the possibility of one 30-day extension.[39] However, the review period is limited to 45 days if OIRA has previously reviewed the supporting information and there has been no change in the circumstances or facts pertaining to the rule.[40] An earlier chapter discusses the content of the regulatory analysis.[41] In the final regulatory analysis, the agency typically will incorporate the earlier analysis, making appropriate changes in response to information received in public proceedings after the initial analysis was prepared. Absent a controlling statutory deadline, an agency is required by E.O. 12,866 to refrain from publishing a final analysis or final rule until OIRA has completed or waived its review or until the time limit for review has expired.[42]

The rulemaking agency must also keep in mind its responsibility to obtain appropriate clearance for information-collection requirements from OMB under the Paperwork Reduction Act.[43] In particular, under the Act, the agency is required, in publishing its final rule, to respond to OMB's comments or explain why it rejected OMB's comments.[44] In addition, the agency must comply with legal requirements for preparing a final environmental impact analysis,[45] a final regulatory flexibility

---

37. 19 U.S.C. § 2532.
38. *See* Part III, ch. 2, for a description of these requirements, which are basically the same at the proposed rule stage.
39. *See supra* Part I(D)(2).
40. Exec. Order 12,866 § 6(b)(2)(B).
41. *See supra* Part III, ch. 2(A)(2), especially the discussion of OMB Circular A-4.
42. Exec. Order 12,866 § 8. The agency must refrain from publishing or otherwise issuing the final rule if OIRA returns it for further consideration under § 6(b)(3).
43. *See supra* Part II, ch. 3(D) and Part III, ch. 2(B) for a detailed discussion of these requirements.
44. 44 U.S.C. § 3507(d)(2). If the agency has substantially changed information collection requirements from the NPRM, it must submit the final rule to OMB for approval at least 60 days before *Federal Register* publication. 5 C.F.R. § 1320.13(g)(2).
45. *See supra* Part II, ch. 3(B).

analysis,[46] a final statement under the Unfunded Mandates Reform Act,[47] as well as analyses as required under executive orders on federalism, the Takings Clause of the Constitution, civil justice reform, and the protection of children from environmental health risks.[48]

In addition, before the rule may become effective, the agency must submit the final rule to each House of Congress and to the Comptroller General under the congressional review statute.[49]

5. *Legal and Jurisdictional Issues*

In some controversial rules, commenters will challenge one or more of the agency's statutory interpretations, or even its jurisdiction to issue the rule. Such challenges, of course, are often made in court after the rule is issued (see the discussion in Part IV, Chapter 2(A)(4)). Agencies thus may feel the need to defend their legal interpretations in their preamble, sometimes in a section denominated "legal authority."[50] There is little literature on how agencies actually engage in legal interpretations, but practices surely differ from agency to agency.[51]

---

46. *See supra* Part II, ch. 3(C); Part III, ch. 2(C); *see also* Associated Fisheries of Me., Inc. v. Daley, 127 F.3d 104, 116 (1st Cir. 1997) (finding that the agency complied with the Regulatory Flexibility Act when the analysis considered many alternatives, was "sensitiv[e]" to the burden on small businesses in the regulated industry, adopted measures to ease the burden, and explained why some alternatives were rejected). Because the plaintiff could not identify any "significant alternative" not included in the agency's notice, this spoke to the "thoroughness" of the agency's analysis. *Id.* at 117.
47. *See supra* Part II, ch. 3(G); Part III, ch. 2(D).
48. *See supra* Part III, ch. 2(H).
49. *See infra* Part III, ch. 7(A)(5)(b).
50. For an exceptionally lengthy example, see the FDA tobacco rule's preamble, Department of Health & Human Services, Food and Drug Administration, Final Rule, Regulations Restricting the Sale and Distribution of Cigarettes and Smokeless Tobacco to Protect Children and Adolescents, 61 Fed. Reg. 44,396, 44,000–17 (Aug. 28, 1996). The FDA's jurisdictional claim was later rejected by the Supreme Court in *FDA v. Brown & Williamson Tobacco Corp.*, discussed in Part IV, ch. 2 *infra* at notes 160–61.
51. For one of the few analyses of this, see Jerry Mashaw, *Agency Statutory Interpretations*, 57 ADMIN. L. REV. 501 (2005). He looked closely at the statutory interpretations made by EPA and Department of HHS in rulemaking preambles and found that the former was much more attuned to the principles of *Chevron* in its interpretations. *Id.* at 531–32. Professor Pierce has argued in response that when agencies select between permissible constructions of statute, they are not really engaging in interpretation. Richard J. Pierce, Jr., *How Agencies Should Give Meaning to the Statutes They Administer: A Response to Mashaw and Strauss*, 59 ADMIN. L. REV. 197, 200, 204–05 (2007).

6. Determining the Effective Date and Compliance Date for the Final Rule

In some situations, determining the effective date (and/or compliance date)[52] of a final rule may be important. Regulated persons or those relying on a rule may need to know exactly when it becomes enforceable. The APA's requirements in this regard are clear, but uncertainties have been created by OMB and congressional review.

a. APA requirements; OIRA review—With narrow but significant exceptions,[53] the APA provides that agency rules may not be made effective until 30 days after publication in the *Federal Register*.[54] The delayed effective date provision was included to give persons affected by the rule a reasonable time to comply with the rule or take other action.[55] Such action might include petitioning for exemption from rule requirements or pursuing judicial review of the rule. The delayed effective date provision also gives the agency an opportunity to modify the rule to avoid previously unforeseen and undesirable consequences of its rule.

While the APA sets a minimum delayed effective date for agency rules, an agency may, in its discretion, set a more delayed effective date for some or all of the requirements of a rule, and it may also provide for an even more delayed compliance date.[56] A longer period would normally be appropriate where, for example, the obligations imposed are onerous, would involve considerable expenditure of time and money, or for some other sound reason. In some cases, courts upholding the feasibility of a regulatory provision have relied on the fact that the agency has provided a lengthy delayed effective date, thus facilitating compliance.[57] An agency's discretion to extend the time for compliance would, of course, be constrained by public policy con-

---

52. The Office of the Federal Register maintains a distinction between the effective date (the date that the rule affects the current CFR) and the compliance date (the date by which regulated persons must comply). *See* DOCUMENT DRAFTING HANDBOOK, *infra* note 162, at 2-11, 2-12.
53. *See supra* Part II, ch. 1(D)(4)(d), for a discussion of these exceptions.
54. 5 U.S.C. § 553(d).
55. ATTORNEY GENERAL'S MANUAL ON THE ADMINISTRATIVE PROCEDURE ACT 36 (1947), *reprinted in* WILLIAM F. FUNK, JEFFREY S. LUBBERS & CHARLES POU, JR., FEDERAL ADMINISTRATIVE SOURCEBOOK 39, 73 (4th ed. 2008).
56. *See supra* note 52. Similarly, the agency may decide to set different compliance dates for various portions of a rule. Thus, for example, under the Federal Railroad Administration's rules on random drug testing published on November 21, 1988, the effective date was December 21, 1988, but staggered compliance dates were set as follows: railroad random testing program submission—June 19, 1989; Transportation Workplace Drug Testing Programs implementation and prohibition of nonmedical drug use programs—July 19, 1989; and implementation of random testing—November 20, 1989. Federal Railroad Administration, Final Rule, Random Drug Testing, 53 Fed. Reg. 47,102 (Nov. 21, 1988).
57. United Steelworkers of Am. v. Marshall, 647 F.2d 1189, 1278 (D.C. Cir. 1980) ("The extremely remote deadline at which the primary smelters are to meet the final [permissible exposure limit] is perhaps the single most important factor supporting the feasibility of the standard.").

siderations, for example, where the rule in question is intended to protect the public health.[58] Some enabling statutes limit agency discretion in delaying effective dates.[59]

Determining the effective date of rules, especially major rules, has also been complicated somewhat by requirements for OMB review. E.O. 12,866 does place a limit of 90 days (plus one 30-day extension) for OIRA review, so agencies obviously must await the completion of this period before determining an effective date.[60] In addition, the Paperwork Reduction Act gives OMB 60 days after publication of a final rule to disapprove any collection of information in the agency's rule.[61] Thus, it is possible that critical aspects of some proposed rules may not be made effective until at least 60 days following publication of the rule. Of course, if OMB's initial proposed objections are satisfied, this requirement will not delay the rule's taking effect.

b. Congressional review—special impact on major rules—The congressional review process added in 1996[62] adds quite a bit of uncertainty about the effective date of major rules. The details of the overall process are described in Part II,[63] but it is important to note that under this law, major rules[64] may not go into effect for at least 60 days to permit Congress to review them first. Under the Act, a non-major rule's effective date is not affected, but a major rule takes effect, unless disapproved, on the *latest* of three possible dates: (1) 60 calendar days after Congress receives the report or the rule is published in the *Federal Register*; (2) where Congress has passed a joint resolution of disapproval of the rule that is subsequently vetoed by the President, 30 session days after Congress receives the veto or, if earlier, the date on which either house of Congress votes and fails to override the veto; or (3) the date on which the

---

58. *See* Indus. Union Dep't v. Hodgson, 499 F.2d 467, 481 (D.C. Cir. 1974) (reversing OSHA's four-year delayed effective date for lower permissible exposure limit for asbestos).

59. *See, e.g.*, National Traffic & Vehicle Safety Act of 1966, 15 U.S.C. § 1392(c) (repealed) (requiring that rules be effective within one year of issuance). NHTSA, in issuing its Occupant Crash Protection Final Rule in 1984 on remand from the Supreme Court in *Motor Vehicle Mfrs. Ass'n v. State Farm Mutual Automobile Ins. Co.*, 463 U.S. 29 (1983), found "good cause" for delaying the compliance date for more than one year. Dep't of Transportation, National Highway Traffic Safety Administration, Final Rule, Occupant Crash Protection, 49 Fed. Reg. 28,962, 29,009 (July 14, 1984).

60. Exec. Order 12,866 § 6(b)(2). The order reduces the period to 45 days, if "OIRA has previously reviewed [the rule] and there has been no material change in the facts and circumstances." *Id.* § 6(b)(2)(B). There are also provisions for emergency situations. *Id.* § 6(a)(D).

61. 44 U.S.C. § 3507(d)(4).

62. Pub. L. No. 104-121, 110 Stat. 857, Title II, subtitle E, codified at 5 U.S.C. §§ 801–808. *See generally* Daniel Cohen & Peter L. Strauss, *Congressional Review of Agency Regulations*, 49 ADMIN. L. REV. 95 (1997).

63. *See supra* Part II, ch. 3(J).

64. Major rules are defined in a similar fashion to the operative definition of Exec. Order 12,866 and indeed make the determination of the OIRA Administrator controlling. *See* 5 U.S.C. § 804(2).

rule would otherwise go into effect if not for this review requirement.[65] If either House votes to reject a joint resolution of disapproval, the rule goes into effect at that time.[66]

It should be noted that the Court of Appeals for the Federal Circuit has held that the CRA does not *alter* major rules' effective dates, but simply suspends their operation pending the outcome of congressional review:

> [T]he CRA does not change the date on which the regulation becomes effective. It only affects the date when the rule becomes operative. In other words, the CRA merely provides for a 60-day waiting period before the agency may enforce the major rule so that Congress has the opportunity to review the regulation.[67]

The Act's review period is intended to give members of Congress the opportunity to introduce a joint resolution of disapproval—which, during the first 60 calendar days (not counting recesses of more than three days) after submission or publication of the rule, is subject to a fast-track (i.e., anti-filibuster) legislative procedure in the Senate. Even after that fast-track period has expired, Congress may still use its normal procedures to enact a resolution. Thus, an agency cannot be absolutely certain until the close of the legislative session that its rule will not be overturned.[68]

If Congress enacts a joint resolution of disapproval of a rule (which requires either a presidential signature or a veto override), the Act provides that the rule is immediately deprived of any effect. If it had already gone into effect, either because the deadline had expired for a major rule or because the rule was a non-major rule, it "shall be treated as though such rule had never taken effect."[69] This could obviously cause problems if interested persons had relied on the effectiveness of the rule. One way for agencies to avoid this uncertainty, where feasible, is to provide for a compliance date far into the future.

c. Retroactivity concerns—Another issue is the validity of an agency rule with a retroactive effective date. Under the APA, the term *rule* is defined as an agency statement of "general or particular applicability and *future effect*."[70] Where agency policy

---

65. 5 U.S.C. § 801(a)(3).

66. *Id.* § 801(a)(5). Note that supporters of a popular rule can engineer such a vote early in the 60-day period to hasten the rule's effective date. *See, e.g.*, S.J. Res. 60, 104th Cong. (1996) (rejecting resolution disapproving Medicare rule).

67. Liesegang v. Sec'y of Veterans Affairs, 312 F.3d 1368, 1375 (Fed. Cir. 2002), *as modified* 65 Fed. App. 717 (2003), *applied in* Nat. Res. Def. Council v. Abraham, 355 F.3d 179, 202 (2d Cir. 2004).

68. Further uncertainty is caused by the fact that the Act also provides that any rule submitted in the last 60 session/legislative days of the current session (a period that is almost impossible to forecast) is treated for review (though not effective-date) purposes as if it were submitted on the fifteenth session/legislative day of the next session. 5 U.S.C. § 801(d)(1).

69. 5 U.S.C. § 801(f).

70. *Id.* § 551(4) (emphasis added).

is enunciated in the course of adjudication, the courts have held that retroactive application is permitted "unless the inequities produced by retroactive application are not
counterbalanced by sufficiently significant statutory interests."[71] However, where the
policy is embodied in a legislative rule, different considerations apply. In *Bowen v.
Georgetown University Hospital*,[72] the Supreme Court held that an HHS rule on recovery of Medicare costs with a retroactive effective date was invalid. The majority
based its decision on the provisions of the Medicare statute, which it read to preclude
retroactive rulemaking in the context of the case.[73] The Court held that "statutory
grants of rulemaking authority will not be understood to encompass the power to
promulgate retroactive rules unless that power is conveyed by express terms."[74] The
majority opinion does, therefore, allow retroactive rulemaking when Congress expressly permits it—notwithstanding the APA's definitional section.[75]

In a concurring opinion, Justice Scalia went even further, stating that retroactive
application of a rule was contrary to the APA itself.[76] He distinguished retroactive
rules from those with "secondary retroactivity"—a rule with "exclusively future effect" that "affect[s] past transactions"[77]—a rule that, Justice Scalia stated, may be
valid under the APA if "reasonable."[78] His reliance on the APA definition has, how-

---

71. Georgetown Univ. Hosp. v. Bowen, 821 F.2d 750, 756 (D.C. Cir. 1987), *aff'd on other grounds*,
     488 U.S. 204 (1988). *See also* Beazer East, Inc. v. EPA, 963 F.2d 603, 609–10 (3d Cir. 1992)
     (quoting NLRB v. Bell Aerospace, 416 U.S. 267, 295 (1974)) ("[N]othing in the APA prohibits
     an agency from adopting or revising an interpretation of a regulation that has been properly
     promulgated in an adjudication and applying that interpretation retroactively. If the agency
     affords the party a 'full opportunity to be heard before the [agency] makes its determination,'
     we cannot second-guess the agency decision whether to interpret a standard by rulemaking or
     by adjudication."). *But see* the cases discussed *supra* in Part II, ch. 2(A)(3).
72. 488 U.S. 204 (1988).
73. *Id.* at 213–16.
74. *Id.* at 204.
75. For an example of an explicit statutory provision on retroactivity, see 42 U.S.C. § 1395hh(e)(1)
     (allowing the Secretary of HHS to permit retroactive application). *See also* Nat'l Petrochemi-
     cal & Refiners Ass'n v. EPA, 630 F.3d 145 (D.C. Cir. 2010), *reh'g en banc denied*, 643 F.3d
     958 (D.C. Cir. 2011) (finding that "any primary retroactive effects were implicitly authorized
     [by the statute] and EPA reasonably balanced any retroactive effects against the benefits of
     applying the . . . regulations to the full calendar year.").
76. *Id.* at 216 (Scalia, J., concurring). This was also the rationale employed by the D.C. Circuit in
     Bowen, 821 F.2d 750 (D.C. Cir. 1987).
77. *Id.* at 219.
78. For examples of "reasonable" "secondarily retroactive" rules, *see* Mobile Relay Assoc. v.
     FCC, 457 F.3d 1. 10 (D.C. Cir. 2006) (agency decision to reband segments of spectrum was
     not retroactive rulemaking as to licensee's prior purchase of eight licenses at auction since
     agency order was purely prospective in that it only altered future effect of licensee's action
     and upset its expectations based on prior law); *see also* U.S. AirWaves, Inc. v. FCC, 232 F.3d
     227, 233 (D.C. Cir. 2000).

ever, been strongly criticized by commentators,[79] and in a later opinion he may have moderated his views.[80]

But the blackletter principle of *Georgetown Hospital* is "easy to state, less easy to apply."[81] Applying it, the D.C. Circuit struck down the retroactivity of Department of Labor rules created under the Black Lung Benefits Act to pending claims, even though the Department did not maintain the regulations were retroactive, because some of the new rules created a change from the position of other courts of appeals and increased potential liability.[82]

However, in a case involving a rule issued by the State Department to bar the taxation of foreign mission property, the Second Circuit, while rejecting the Government's "contention that the antiretroactivity presumption is generally inapplicable to foreign affairs cases involving public rights,"[83] nevertheless allowed the ret-

---

79. *See* ERNEST GELLHORN & RONALD M. LEVIN, ADMINISTRATIVE LAW AND PROCESS IN A NUTSHELL 301 (4th ed. 1997) (arguing Scalia's reasoning is "flawed" because the APA language is "merely a definition, not an enabling provision . . . . [A] holding that a retroactive rule is not a 'rule' for APA purposes . . . would *permit* the agency to issue them *without the safeguards of APA rulemaking procedures*—surely an anomalous result . . . ."); William V. Luneburg, *Retroactivity and Administrative Rulemaking*, 1990 DUKE L.J. 106, 144 (arguing APA definition of rule "does not say 'only for the future,' but Justice Scalia's gloss added the crucial word").

80. Smiley v. Citibank, 517 U.S. 735, 744 n.3 (1996) (upholding agency regulation even though it would thereby have retroactive effect on transactions that "occurred at a time when there was no clear agency guidance").

81. Arkema Inc. v. EPA, 618 F.3d 1 (D.C. Cir. 2010). In this case, a divided D.C. Circuit panel struck down an EPA rule that altered an emission-trading allowance program in future years that the majority found "attache[d] new legal consequences to events completed before its enactment." *Id.* at 7. In dissent, Judge Randolph argued that the new rule did not alter the program in unexpected ways, and even if it did, it essentially amounted only to secondary retroactivity. *Id.* at 11.

82. Nat'l Mining Ass'n v. Dep't of Labor, 292 F.3d 849, 860 (D.C. Cir. 2002). *See also* Sierra Club v. Whitman, 285 F.3d 63 (D.C. Cir. 2002) (refusing to compel EPA to make nonattainment designation under the Clean Air Act retroactive); Univ. of Iowa Hosps. & Clinics v. Shalala, 180 F.3d 943, 951–52 (8th Cir. 1999) (invalidating a rule requiring hospitals to have undertaken time studies of office space usage during the base year—five years before the standard's enactment—as impermissible retroactive rule); Rock of Ages Corp. v. Sec'y of Labor, 170 F.3d 148, 158 (2d Cir.1999) (finding that Federal Mine Safety and Health Review Commission unreasonably gave retroactive effect to MSHA regulation); Cort v. Crabtree, 113 F.3d 1081, 1086–87 (9th Cir. 1997) (holding that the Bureau of Prisons could not retroactively apply a new definition of "nonviolent offense" to render certain prisoners ineligible for a sentence reduction program).

83. City of New York v. Permanent Mission of India to United Nations, 618 F.3d 172, 200 (2d Cir. 2010) (the argument was based on an analogy to *Republic of Austria v. Altmann,* 541 U.S. 677, 696–97 (2004), where the Supreme Court declined to apply an antiretroactivity presumption to the Foreign Sovereignty Immunity Act and held that its standards for sovereign immunity apply to claims based on conduct predating the Act's enactment). *See also* Empresa Cubana Exportadora de Alimentos y Productos Varios v. U.S. Dep't of the Treasury, 638 F.3d 794, 800 (D.C. Cir. 2011) ("presumption against retroactivity does not apply" where the purported retroactive rule did not disturb a "vested right").

roactive application of the bar, finding that "application of the antiretroactivity clear statement rule is misplaced because the values that underlie that rule are not sufficiently implicated" in this case.[84]

It should also be noted that the anti-retroactivity doctrine does not really apply to non-legislative rules. An interpretative rule or statement of policy will naturally be "in effect" before, during, and after the time of issuance.[85]

7. Disqualification of Decisionmakers

The acceptability of rules and, indeed, the repute of the administrative process may be seriously impaired if the judgment of agency officials who determine the content of rules is believed to have been tainted by conflicts of interest, inflexible prejudgment of pertinent facts, or manifestations of hostility toward particular interests. The propriety of certain agency officials' participation in rulemaking has been an issue in a few cases. In each case, there were allegations that the agency official was biased or had prejudged the issues in the proceeding, and the court was asked to disqualify the official from further participation or to invalidate the final agency rule. The decisions in these cases firmly establish that the disqualification standard applicable to adjudication is inappropriate for informal rulemaking; rather, those seeking disqualification in the rulemaking context must make a "clear and convincing showing . . . [of] an unalterably closed mind."[86]

This standard was first enunciated in *Ass'n of National Advertisers v. FTC*,[87] in which the D.C. Circuit considered whether certain statements of the FTC Chairman warranted his disqualification from participating in a rulemaking proceeding conducted under the Magnuson-Moss Warranty–Federal Trade Commission Improvements Act.[88] The court refused to disqualify the chairman for remarks made prior to the proceeding. After rejecting a characterization of Magnuson-Moss Act rulemaking as "quasi-adjudicative," the court concluded that the disqualification standard applicable to adjudication is not appropriate for rulemaking because of the different nature of the factual conclusions reached in each type of proceeding.[89]

---

84. *Id.* The court reasoned that, as with the statute in *Altmann*, retroactive application of the rule barring taxation would not affect private rights nor upset significant reliance interests. *See id.* at 196.

85. *See* Geoffrey C. Weien, Note, *Retroactive Rulemaking*, 30 HARV. J. L. & PUB. POL'Y 749, 754 (2007).

86. Ass'n of Nat'l Advertisers v. FTC, 627 F.2d 1151, 1170 (D.C. Cir. 1979), *cert. denied*, 447 U.S. 921 (1980).

87. *Id.*

88. 15 U.S.C. § 57a.

89. In so concluding, the court relied upon Professor Davis's distinction between "legislative" and "adjudicative" facts. The court stated:

> The factual predicate of a rulemaking decision substantially differs in nature and in use from the factual predicate of an adjudicatory decision. The factual predicate of adjudica-

The court also emphasized the differences in the roles of rulemakers and adjudicators. The majority opinion stated that the "view of a neutral and detached adjudicator is simply an inapposite role model for an administrator who must translate broad statutory commands into concrete social policies. If an agency official is to be effective, he must engage in debate and discussion about the policy matters before him."[90] The same standard was subsequently applied in *Lead Industries Ass'n v. EPA*[91] and *United Steelworkers of America v. Marshall.*[92] This standard obviously makes it difficult for challengers to seek to disqualify rulemaking officials, or even to obtain a court's permission to grant discovery to try to show such bias.[93] But it is not impossible—in one case the Secretary of HUD was disqualified from a remanded rulemaking based on his comments to the press that HUD would approve the rule regardless of negative comments received during the comment period.[94]

The Administrative Conference studied the issues raised by the *Association of National Advertisers* decision and recommended[95] that disqualification for bias in rulemaking be limited to prejudgments of particular "adjudicative" or "specific" facts, where it may be inferred from the particular statutory framework, agency procedural

---

tion depends on ascertainment of "facts concerning the immediate parties—who did what, where, when, how, and with what motive or intent." By contrast, the nature of legislative fact is ordinarily general, without reference to specific parties.

627 F.2d at 1161 (citation omitted).

90. *Id.* Judge Leventhal, in a concurring opinion, contrasted the roles of adjudicator and rulemaker as follows:

One can hypothesize beginning an adjudicatory proceeding with an open mind, indeed a blank mind, a tabula rasa devoid of any previous knowledge of the matter. In sharp contrast, one cannot even conceive of an agency conducting a rulemaking proceeding unless it had delved into the subject sufficiently to become concerned that there was an evil or abuse that required regulatory response. It would be the height of absurdity, even a kind of abuse of administrative process, for an agency to embroil interested parties in a rulemaking proceeding, without some initial concern that there was an abuse that needed remedying, a concern that would be set forth in the accompanying statement of the purpose of the proposed rule.

Id. at 1176.

91. 647 F.2d 1130, 1179 (D.C. Cir. 1980).
92. 647 F.2d 1189, 1208–10 (D.C. Cir. 1980).
93. *See* Judge Friedman's order denying a motion for such discovery in *Air Transport Ass'n of America v. National Mediation Board,* 719 F. Supp. 2d 26 (D.D.C. 2010) (Case 1:10-cv-00804-PLF, Document 44 Filed 06/04/10), *available at* http://www.airlines.org/Documents/ATA%20v.%20NMB%20Opening%20Brief%20-%20ECF%20Stamped.pdf. The D.C. Circuit affirmed this ruling, 663 F.3d 476, 487–88 (D.C. Cir. 2011).
94. Nehemiah Corp. of Am. v. Jackson, 546 F. Supp. 2d 830 (E.D. Cal. 2008). In another case involving the same HUD rulemaking, Judge Friedman of the D.C. District Court found these statements "distressing" but did not need to decide the prejudgment claim, remanding the rule for failure to disclose important data in the NPRM, Penobscot Indian Nation v. U.S. Dep't of Housing & Urban Development, 539 F. Supp. 2d 40, 46 n.5 (D.D.C. 2008).

choices, or other special circumstances that the agency's determination of those facts is to be based on an evidentiary record developed in the proceeding.

On the other hand, the Conference recognized that a rulemaking proceeding should be conducted with decorum and respect for the interests of all concerned, and agency officials should avoid intemperate expression or other behavior suggestive of an irrevocable commitment to a predetermined outcome of the proceeding. This does not mean, however, that agency officials may not express judgments on factual issues based on previous experience or on information received during a proceeding. Neither does it suggest that officials may not act upon nor voice opinions in interchanges with committees of Congress, other administrative bodies, the public, and regulated groups; such activity is desirable conduct for administrators, not an abnormality to be shunned.[96]

Perhaps of greater significance to agency rulemakers is disqualification sought on the basis of an alleged conflict of interests. Under Executive Order 12,674[97] and regulations of the Office of Government Ethics,[98] federal agencies are required to regulate employee conduct with respect to conflicts of interest. Moreover, it is a criminal offense for a government official to participate personally and substantially in a "particular matter in which, to his knowledge, he, his spouse, minor child, partner, organization in which he is serving . . . or any person or organization with whom he is negotiating or has any arrangement concerning prospective employment, has a financial interest."[99]

In general, the cited provisions and the requirements for employee reports deal with financial or associational interests of a commercial or financial character. Agency rules do not often deal with possible conflicts arising from either prior employment or activities on behalf of political, religious, civic, or other organizations. However, the Administrative Conference recommended that agency regulations provide for recusal (that is, withdrawal from participation) if a significant non-financial interest of the official is likely to be substantially affected by the outcome of the proceeding and for

95. ACUS Recommendation 80-4, *Decisional Officials' Participation in Rulemaking Proceedings*, 45 Fed. Reg. 46,776 (July 11, 1980). The recommendation is based on Peter L. Strauss, *Disqualification of Decisional Officials in Rulemaking*, 80 Colum. L. Rev. 990 (1980).
96. ACUS Recommendation 80-4, *supra* note 95. On the issue of contacts between agency rulemaking officials and Congress and members of the public, *see* Sierra Club v. Costle, 657 F.2d 298 (D.C. Cir. 1981), discussed in Part III, ch. 6.
97. 54 Fed. Reg. 15,159 (Apr. 12, 1989), as modified by Exec. Order 12,731, 55 Fed. Reg. 42,547 (Oct. 17, 1990), and as supplemented by the "ethics pledge" for political appointees established in Exec. Order 13,490, 74 Fed. Reg. 4673 (Jan. 26, 2009).
98. 5 C.F.R. pt. 2634 (financial disclosure), pt. 2635 (standards of ethical conduct), pt. 2636 (outside income), pts. 2637, 2641 (post-employment conflicts), pt. 2638 (agency ethics programs), pt. 2640 (waivers).
99. 18 U.S.C. § 208. The term "particular matter" has been interpreted by the Department of Justice to include rulemaking. *See* Memorandum Opinion for the Chief Counsel Food and Drug Administration, 2 Op. Off. Legal Counsel 151, 155 (1978).

"cooling-off" periods for new officials with respect to participation in proceedings affecting prior employers, clients, or other financial interests.[100] The agency should make clear that these regulations are aids to agency self-management and are not intended to expand the scope of judicial review of rulemaking proceedings. Thus, although the Administrative Conference took a narrow view of the circumstances in which an agency should be obliged to disqualify a rulemaking official, it believed agencies should consider formulating standards for officials' conduct that are more exacting than the minimum legal standards.

B. The Statement of Basis and Purpose

Section 553(c) of the APA provides that, after consideration of relevant material presented in the rulemaking, "the agency shall incorporate in the rules adopted a concise general statement of their basis and purpose."[101] A contemporaneous interpretation of the statement of basis and purpose requirement in the APA was that it was "not intended to require an elaborate analysis of rules or of the detailed considerations upon which they are based but [rather] is designed to enable the public to obtain a general idea of the purpose of, and a statement of the basic justification for, the rules."[102] Certainly a major purpose of the statement of basis and purpose, which constitutes most of what is commonly referred to as "the preamble"[103] to a rule, is to inform the public of the supporting reasons and purposes of the final rule. Agencies often use the statement to advise interested persons how the rule will be applied, to respond to questions raised by comments received during the rulemaking, and as a "legislative history" that can be referred to in future applications of the rule.

1. Impact of Judicial Review

Although the original purpose for including the statement of basis and purpose requirement in the APA may have been to inform the public, it has also become the primary document that judges turn to in deciding the validity of challenged rules. What reviewing courts expect of statements of basis and purpose was long ago stated in the following language from the D.C. Circuit's 1968 opinion in *Automotive Parts & Accessories Ass'n v. Boyd*:[104]

---

100. ACUS Recommendation 80-4, *supra* note 95.

101. 5 U.S.C. § 553(c).

102. ADMINISTRATIVE PROCEDURE ACT: LEGISLATIVE HISTORY 225, S. Doc. No. 248 79-258 (1946); *see also* ATTORNEY GENERAL'S MANUAL, *supra* note 55, at 32. In 1993 ACUS suggested that Congress "[r]estate the 'concise' statement of basis and purpose requirement by codifying existing doctrine that a rule must be supported by a 'reasoned statement,' and that such statement respond to the significant issues raised in public comments." ACUS Recommendation 93-4, *Improving the Environment for Agency Rulemaking*, ¶ IV(D), 59 Fed. Reg. 4670 (Feb. 1, 1994).

103. *See* 1 C.F.R. § 18.12.

104. 407 F.2d 330 (D.C. Cir. 1968).

[I]t is appropriate for us . . . to caution against an overly literal reading of the statutory terms "concise" and "general." These adjectives must be accommodated to the realities of judicial scrutiny, which do not contemplate that the court itself will, by a laborious examination of the record, formulate in the first instance the significant issues faced by the agency and articulate the rationale of their resolution. We do not expect the agency to discuss every item or opinion included in the submissions made to it in informal rulemaking. We do expect that, if the judicial review which Congress has thought it important to provide is to be meaningful, the "concise general statement of . . . basis and purpose" mandated by Section 4 [now 5 U.S.C. § 553] will enable us to see what major issues of policy were ventilated by the informal proceedings and why the agency reacted to them as it did.[105]

It has also been suggested that the statement of basis and purpose serves a critical self-education purpose for the agency.[106] Thus, in preparing the explanation for the rule, the agency has an opportunity to confront its planned action in detail, including all the steps in its reasoning process, and to judge whether the action embodied in the draft statement of basis and purpose is indeed one that it wishes to take.

The Supreme Court reinforced the importance of the statement of basis and purpose in 1983 in *Motor Vehicle Manufacturers Ass'n v. State Farm Mutual Automobile Insurance Co.*[107] There, the Court vacated the National Highway Traffic Safety Administration's rule rescinding its earlier rule requiring passive restraints in automobiles. While making it clear that it was judging the rule under an "arbitrary and capricious" standard of review, which does not permit the Court to substitute its judgment for that of the agency, the Supreme Court elaborated on the process an agency must follow to avoid a finding of arbitrariness or capriciousness.[108] "The Agency must examine the relevant data and articulate a satisfactory explanation for its action," the Court said, including "a 'rational connection between the facts found and the choice made.'"[109] An agency decision could be arbitrary or capricious if the agency relied on factors Congress did not intend to be considered, "entirely failed" to consider an important aspect of the problem, or offered an explanation for its decision that "runs counter to the evidence" or that was "so implausible" that it could not be ascribed to a difference of view or the product of agency expertise.[110] The Supreme Court overruled the agency rescission because it gave "no consideration whatever" to modify-

---

105. *Id.* at 338.
106. *See, e.g.*, Dry Color Mfrs. Ass'n v. Dep't of Labor, 486 F.2d 98, 105 (3d Cir. 1973) (stating that requirement for statement of basis and purpose "provides an internal check on arbitrary agency action by insuring that prior to taking action an agency can clearly articulate the reasons for its decision").
107. 463 U.S. 29 (1983).
108. *Id.* at 41–43.
109. *Id.* at 43 (quoting Burlington Truck Lines, Inc. v. United States, 371 U.S. 156 (1962)).
110. *Id.*

ing the standard to require air bags only.[111] "At the very least," the Supreme Court said, "this alternative way of achieving the objectives of the Act [the use of air bags] should have been addressed and adequate reasons given for its abandonment."[112]

The *State Farm* decision involved the rescission of a rule, but the Supreme Court held that the same standard of review would pertain to both rescission and promulgation of rules.[113] This decision has been followed by both the Supreme Court and the courts of appeals since 1983. Thus in 1986, the Supreme Court in *Bowen v. American Hospital Ass'n*[114] vacated HHS rules on emergency health care for handicapped infants, saying, "Agency deference has not come so far that we will uphold regulations whenever it is possible to 'conceive a basis' for administrative action."[115] "Our recognition of Congress's need to vest administrative agencies with ample power to assist in the difficult task of governing a vast and complex industrial nation," the Court said, "carries with it the correlative responsibility of the agency to explain the rationale and factual basis for its decision even though we show respect for the agency's judgment in both."[116]

Since *State Farm*, numerous courts of appeals have considered the adequacy of agencies' statements of basis and purpose for rules and in some cases have vacated agency rules because the statement was inadequate.

In *Independent U.S. Tanker Owners Committee v. Dole*,[117] for example, the D.C. Circuit vacated a DOT rule because the statement of reasons was inadequate.[118] Referring to the APA requirements, the court said that the statement "need not be an exhaustive, detailed account of every aspect of the rulemaking proceedings,"[119] but "such a statement should indicate the major issues of policy that were raised in the proceedings and explain why the agency decided to respond to these issues as it did, particularly in light of the statutory objectives that the rule must serve."[120] The court concluded that the Secretary of Transportation had failed to give an adequate account of how the rule served the statutory objectives and "why alternative measures were rejected in light of them."[121] The court said that while the secretary was free to consider non-statutory factors, "she is not free to substitute new goals in place of the statutory objectives without explaining how these actions are consistent with her authority under the statute."[122] The court concluded, "[I]n the absence of such discus-

---

111. *Id.* at 51.
112. *Id.* at 48.
113. *Id.* at 41–42; *see also* discussion *infra* at Part IV, ch. 2(A)(2).
114. 476 U.S. 610 (1986).
115. *Id.* at 626.
116. *Id.* at 627.
117. 809 F.2d 847 (D.C. Cir. 1987).
118. *Id.* at 852.
119. *Id.*
120. *Id.*
121. *Id.*
122. *Id.* at 854.

sion the court can only conclude that the action was arbitrary and capricious."[123]

In *Action on Smoking & Health v. CAB*,[124] the D.C. Circuit vacated an agency rule rescinding certain earlier regulations that afforded protections to nonsmokers against breathing tobacco smoke, finding the CAB's explanation for the action "palpably inadequate."[125] The agency's refusal to promulgate several other regulations that had been suggested by members of the public was also set aside because the CAB failed to provide an adequate explanation for their rejection.[126]

On the other hand, the Fourth Circuit has taken a more restrained view of the requirement:

> To satisfy the basis-and-purpose requirements of the APA, the agency need not provide an exhaustive explanation of an administrator's reasoning for adopting a rule. Required is a concise general statement of the regulation's basis and purpose. There is no obligation to make references in the agency explanation to all the specific issues raised in comments. The agency's explanation must simply enable a reviewing court to see what major issues of policy were ventilated by the informal proceedings and why the agency reacted to them the way it did.[127]

---

123. *Id.*
124. 699 F.2d 1209 (D.C. Cir. 1983).
125. *Id.* at 1217.
126. *Id.* at 1217–19. The court, referring to the APA's requirement that the public have an opportunity to comment on proposed rules, ruled that the opportunity to comment "is meaningless unless the agency responds to specific points raised by the public." *Id.* at 1217 (quoting Alabama Power Co. v. Costle, 636 F.2d 323, 384 (D.C. Cir. 1979)). Subsequently, the CAB reissued a part of the revised rule without notice and comment, accompanied by what the agency argued was an adequate statement of reasons. This second rule was also vacated. *See* Action on Smoking & Health v. CAB, 713 F.2d 795 (D.C. Cir. 1983). Rejecting the argument that notice and comment was unnecessary because the earlier remand required the agency only to provide an adequate explanation for the rule, the court held that the statement of basis and purpose must be "contemporaneous" with the rule issued; the CAB statement, issued two years later, did not "accompany" the rule and consequently was treated by the court as an invalid post hoc explanation of the rule. *Id.* at 799–801. Nor could the rule be upheld as a "new" rule, because the agency had not provided for notice and comment, and the APA's "good cause" exemption to the notice-and-comment requirements was inapplicable. *Id.* at 801; *see also* Action for Children's Television v. FCC, 821 F.2d 741, 745 (D.C. Cir. 1987) (invalidating FCC's withdrawal of children's television commercialization guidelines because of inability to "unearth" a reasoned basis for the agency's action); *accord* Lloyd Noland Hosp. & Clinic v. Heckler, 762 F.2d 1561, 1566–67 (11th Cir. 1985).
127. 1000 Friends of Maryland v. Browner, 265 F.3d 216, 238 (4th Cir. 2001) (quoting South Carolina *ex rel.* Tindal v. Block, 717 F.2d 874, 886 (4th Cir. 1983); *see also* Mortg. Investors Corp. of Ohio v. Gober, 220 F.3d 1375 (Fed. Cir. 2000) (upholding a final rule that was virtually unchanged from the proposed rule, because DVA considered, and responded to, proposals for alternative procedures from the public and Members of Congress).

Nevertheless, an agency must invest a great deal of time and effort in preparing the statement of basis and purpose if its rule is to withstand close judicial review. As the Supreme Court stated long ago, "[t]he courts may not accept appellate counsel's post hoc rationalizations for agency action."[128] Thus an inadequate statement may result in the rule's being remanded by the reviewing court, because an agency may normally not rely on briefs to the court as the vehicle for explanation of the basis for a rule. Such later justifications are highly vulnerable as post hoc rationalizations that will be ignored by the court.[129]

2. *Discussion of Alternatives*

It is also critical that the agency deal fully with major alternative resolutions for the issues in the proceeding, explaining clearly why they were rejected in favor of the option selected. This explanation is now required to be included in the various final regulatory analyses (which may be consolidated) for certain rules by Executive Order 12,866, the Regulatory Flexibility Act, and the Unfunded Mandates Reform Act.[130] Although obviously it would be difficult or impossible for the agency to discuss all possible alternatives, it must address significant ones.[131] The cases discussed above show that where the agency is rescinding or modifying a rule, it must also fully ex-

---

128. Burlington Truck Lines, Inc. v. United States, 371 U.S. 156, 168 (1962) (citing Securities & Exchange Comm'n v. Chenery Corp., 332 U.S. 194, 196 (1947)). *See also* Morgan Stanley Capital Grp. Inc. v. Public Util. Dist. No. 1 of Snohomish Cnty., Wash., 554 U.S. 527, 544 (2008) ("We will not uphold a discretionary agency decision where the agency has offered a justification in court different from what it provided in its opinion.") However, in this case the Court declined to remand the case because:

> FERC has lucked out: The *Chenery* doctrine has no application to [this] cases, because we conclude that the Commission was *required,* under our [previous decision] to apply the [presumption that it did apply] in [this case]. That it provided a different rationale for the necessary result is no cause for upsetting its ruling. To remand would be an idle and useless formality. *Chenery* does not require that we convert judicial review of agency action into a ping-pong game.

> *Id.* at 544–45 (citation and internal quotation marks omitted).

129. *See, e.g.,* Yale-New Haven Hosp. v. Leavitt, 470 F.3d 71, 82 (2d Cir. 2006) (holding that "to the extent that an agency may supplement the record on judicial review of the validity of a rule that is interpretive, it may do so only if the proffered evidence illuminates the original record and does not advance new rationalizations for the agency's action."). This also applies to agency interpretations of statutes. *See* City of Kansas City, Mo. v. Dep't of Hous. & Urban Dev., 923 F.2d 188, 192 (D.C. Cir. 1991) ("The agency construction for which HUD seeks deference was never promulgated by the Secretary, or his designee, nor by administrative regulations, nor by decisions in agency adjudications; rather, agency counsel contends that the 'permissible construction of the statute' for which it seeks approval as the agency's litigation posture in this case. For purposes of *Chevron,* this is patently insufficient.").

130. *See* discussion *supra* Part III, ch. 2(G).

131. *See supra* text accompanying notes 107–13 for a discussion of the Supreme Court's *State Farm* decision.

plain its reasons for doing so and for not adopting alternative ways of changing the existing regulations. Of particular importance is the agency's explanation of how the regulation furthers the policies of its enabling statute.[132] Where the final rule varies from the proposal, the preamble should explain in as much detail as possible why the final rule is a "logical outgrowth" of the proposal.[133]

3. *Response to Comments*

A key part of preambles to final rules is the agency's response to significant public comments. This is a requirement that has evolved over the years. As Robert Hamilton noted in a book review of the *Davis Treatise* in 1979:

> Before 1970 agencies often dismissed objections rather curtly. For example, in promulgating significant regulations relating to stationary sources of air pollution in 1971, EPA dismissed a large number of critical comments with these two sentences:
>
> > In the comments on the proposed standards, many questions were raised as to costs and demonstrated capability of control systems to meet the standards. These comments have been evaluated and investigated, and it is the Administrator's judgment that emission control systems capable of meeting the standards have been adequately demonstrated and that the standards promulgated herein are achievable at reasonable costs.[134]

This sort of response would not suffice today. The purpose of the preamble "is, at least in part, to respond in a reasoned manner to the comments received, to explain how the agency resolved any significant problems raised by the comments, and to show how that resolution led the agency to the ultimate rule."[135] "'Consideration of comments as a matter of grace is not enough.' It must be made with a mind that is open to persuasion."[136]

---

132. *See, e.g.*, Hazardous Waste Treatment Council v. EPA, 886 F.2d 355, 365 (D.C. Cir. 1989) (EPA statement of basis and purpose was inadequate where it adopted a particular approach in its NPRM and then in its final rule "proceed[ed] in a different direction simply on the basis of an unexplained and unelaborated statement that it might have been wrong when it earlier concluded otherwise"); Int'l Union, UAW v. Pendergrass, 878 F.2d 389, 399–400 (D.C. Cir. 1989).

133. *See supra* Part III, ch. 3(E).

134. Robert W. Hamilton, *Book Review, Administrative Law Treatise (Second Edition, Volume I),* 127 U. Pa. L. Rev. 855, 861 n.51 (1979), *citing* 36 Fed. Reg. 24,876–77 (Dec. 23, 1971). The Selective Service System's final rules governing alternatives to military service also provide an illustration of this kind of statement. The preamble stated, "All comments that were received timely have been carefully considered. The final rule is identical with the proposed rule." 48 Fed. Reg. 16,675, 16,676 (Apr. 19, 1983).

135. Indep. U.S. Tanker Owners Comm. v. Lewis, 690 F.2d 908, 919 (D.C. Cir. 1982) (invalidating an agency rule for inadequate response to comments).

136. Advocates for Hwy. & Auto Safety v. Fed. Hwy. Admin., 28 F.3d 1288, 1292 (D.C. Cir. 1994) (citing McLouth Steel Products Corp. v. Thomas, 838 F.2d 1317, 1323 (D.C. Cir. 1988)).

This does not mean that the agency must respond to each individually identified comment in the statement of basis and purpose. It is enough that the agency discuss the significant issues raised in the comments.[137] The Ninth Circuit has explained that "significant" comments are "limited to those which 'raise relevant points, and which, if adopted, would require a change in the agency's proposed rule.'"[138] Frequently, interested persons will make the same points, and responding to each comment would be unnecessarily repetitive. However, "boilerplate" statements that all comments were carefully considered, without further discussion, are not likely to receive a favorable reaction from reviewing courts. It should be noted, however, that the D.C. Circuit has "determined that '[a]gencies are free to ignore . . . late fil[ed comments].'"[139] On the other hand, courts may sometimes allow the supplementation of the record with a late-filed comment upon a challenger's request.[140]

Additional requirements for agency response to comments may apply to some rulemakings. The Regulatory Flexibility Act requires the final regulatory flexibility analysis to evaluate public comments on the initial analysis and to state any changes made in the rule in response to the comments.[141] Agencies preparing final environmental impact statements must respond to comments received on the initial EIS.[142] As

---

137. *See* Northside Sanitary Landfill, Inc. v. Thomas, 849 F.2d 1516 (D.C. Cir. 1988); *see also* Reytblatt v. U.S. Nuclear Regulatory Comm'n, 105 F.3d 715, 722 (D.C. Cir. 1997) (NRC's response to commenters' concerns, which were made "in general and highly abusive terms," was appropriate); Pub. Citizen, Inc. v. FAA, 988 F.2d 186 (D.C. Cir. 1993) ("Courts will uphold a decision of less than ideal clarity if the agency's path may reasonably be discerned.") (quoting Bowman Transp., Inc. v. Arkansas-Best Freight Sys., Inc., 419 U.S. 281, 286 (1974)). *But see* La. Fed. Land Bank Ass'n, FLCA v. Farm Credit Admin., 336 F.3d 1075, 1080–81, 1085 (D.C. Cir. 2003) (remanding—but not vacating—rule where proposed rule prompted over 270 comments, including the one submitted by the plaintiffs, and where preamble to the final rule said "almost nothing" about the comments).
138. Safari Aviation Inc. v. Garvey, 300 F.3d 1144, 1151 (9th Cir. 2002) (quoting Am. Mining Cong. v. EPA, 965 F.2d 759, 771 (9th Cir. 1992)), *accord* City of Portland, Ore. v. EPA, 507 F.3d 706, 715 (D.C. Cir. 2007) (citing Home Box Office, Inc. v. FCC, 567 F.2d 9, 35 n. 58 (D.C. Cir. 1977).
139. *Reytblatt*, 105 F.3d at 723 (quoting Personal Watercraft Indus. Ass'n v. Dep't of Commerce, 48 F.3d 540, 543 (D.C. Cir. 1995)). But note that agencies may, in their discretion, accept late comments. For example, the Department of Agriculture excludes any late comments from its rulemaking records, though they remain available under the Freedom of Information Act. 7 C.F.R. § 1.27.
140. *See* Ad Hoc Metals Coal. v. Whitman, 227 F. Supp. 2d 134, 140–42 (D.D.C. 2002) (supplementation of administrative record was appropriate in actions seeking judicial review of final EPA rule to include comments submitted by industry representatives at meeting with EPA officials critical of human health data relied upon by EPA in formulating rule, even though meeting took place eight months after close of comment period, where final rule was not issued until more than four months later and EPA considered comments prior to issuance of final rule, and where EPA did include comments from another group made at similar meeting).
141. 5 U.S.C. § 604(a)(2).
142. 40 C.F.R. § 1503.4.

discussed earlier,[143] under the Paperwork Reduction Act, OMB has the right to comment on an information collection requirement in a proposed rule,[144] and the agency's response to OMB's comments must accompany *Federal Register* publication of its final rule.[145] The Unfunded Mandates Reform Act requires agencies to summarize and evaluate comments and concerns presented by state, local, and tribal governments.[146] Finally, E.O. 12,866 requires an agency, after the rule "has been published in the Federal Register or otherwise issued to the public," to make available its submissions to OIRA and to identify the changes made to the draft submitted to OIRA,[147] and it may be efficient to include some of this information in the statement of basis and purpose.

Although in many cases a preamble may be very detailed,[148] the agency's statement of basis and purpose should be tailored to each record and each agency action.[149] Rules promulgated by health and safety regulatory agencies are often accompanied by preambles having a section-by-section analysis explaining the rationale for adoption of rule provisions and for rejecting alternatives.[150] Where the costs and technological aspects of a major regulation are particularly in issue, a more extensive summary of the regulatory impact analysis is normally included.[151]

C. Publication of the Final Rule

The APA requires agencies to publish in the *Federal Register* all "substantive rules of general applicability."[152] Failure to publish makes a final rule unenforceable against any person not having actual and timely notice of its terms.[153] The APA requires that the statement of basis and purpose be incorporated in the rule,[154] so the

---

143. *See supra* Part II, ch. 3(D); Part III, ch. 2(B).

144. 44 U.S.C. § 3507(d)(1).

145. *Id.* § 3507(d)(2).

146. 2 U.S.C. § 1532(a)(5)(A).

147. Exec. Order 12,866, § 6(a)(3)(E).

148. An example of a very detailed statement of basis and purpose is the NHTSA preamble to the final rule on Federal Motor Vehicle Safety Standard, Occupant Crash Protection, *supra* note 59.

149. Note that the FTC's staff manual provides that such statements "should not exceed 100 double-spaced pages, including footnotes, which may be single-spaced." *See* FTC ADMINISTRATIVE STAFF MANUAL: OPERATING MANUAL, Rulemaking ch. 7, § 3.24.2.1, *available at* http://www.ftc.gov/foia/ch07rulemaking.pdf.

150. *See, e.g.*, OSHA, Final Rule, Occupational Exposure to Formaldehyde, 52 Fed. Reg. 46,168 (Dec. 4, 1987).

151. *See* Summary of Regulation Impact and Regulatory Flexibility Analysis, *id.* at 46,237–42.

152. 5 U.S.C. § 552(a)(1)(D).

153. *See id.* § 552(a)(1). However, courts have held that publication of a rule in the *Federal Register* is not necessary where the action is only the direct implementation of the plain terms of the statute. *See* Kaspar Wire Works, Inc. v. Sec'y of Labor, 268 F.3d 1123, 1132 (D.C. Cir. 2001); Malkan FM Assoc. v. FCC, 935 F.2d 1313, 1318 (D.C. Cir. 1991).

154. *See* 5 U.S.C. § 553(c).

statement of basis and purpose is also subject to the publication requirement. The Regulatory Flexibility Act requires that the agency make copies of the final RFA available to the public and publish at least a summary of it in the *Federal Register.*[155] In addition, the congressional review process has led some agencies to wait until the rules have been dispatched to the required congressional offices before sending them to the *Federal Register.*[156]

1. Section 552 Requirements

Section 552 of the APA contains the general publication requirements for agency documents.[157] With respect to rules, subsection (a)(1) provides that agencies must publish in the *Federal Register*:

(C) rules of procedure . . . ;
(D) substantive rules of general applicability adopted as authorized by law, and statements of general policy or interpretations of general applicability formulated and adopted by the agency; and
(E) each amendment, revision, or repeal of the foregoing.

Except to the extent that a person has actual and timely notice of the terms thereof, a person may not in any manner be required to resort to, or be adversely affected by, a matter required to be published in the *Federal Register* and not so published.[158] This provision requires that final rules of general applicability be published in the *Federal Register*, at least in final form,[159] and that agencies may not apply improperly unpublished rules to a person unless that person has actual notice.[160] Note, however,

---

155. *Id.* § 604(b).
156. *Congressional Review Act, Hearings before the House Subcomm. on Commercial and Admin. Law of the Comm. on the Judiciary,* 104th Cong. 3 (1997) (testimony of Jon Cannon, General Counsel, EPA).
157. 5 U.S.C. § 552. This section derives from the original section 3 of the APA. It has been amended numerous times, most significantly by the addition of the Freedom of Information Act. This discussion relates only to the "affirmative obligations" of publication and disclosure of rules under subsection 552(a).
158. *Id.* The next sentence states: "For the purpose of this paragraph, matter reasonably available to the class of persons affected thereby is deemed published in the Federal Register when incorporated by reference therein with the approval of the Director of the Federal Register." *Id.* § 552 (a)(1)(e).
159. In one case, the First Circuit hinted that the military and foreign affairs exemption in section 553 might also apply to section 552(a). *See* United States v. Ventura-Melendez, 321 F.3d 230, 233 (1st Cir. 2003).
160. For a discussion of cases where courts have found actual notice of unpublished rules, see *United States v. Ventura-Melendez, id.* (conviction of trespassing in a security zone created by an unpublished rule upheld due to the defendants' actual notice of the rule; the court upheld the district court's finding that actual notice existed, despite defendants' claim to the contrary). *See generally* Colleen R. Courtade, Annotation, *What Rules, Statements, and Interpretations by Federal Agencies Must Be Published,* 77 A.L.R. Fed. 572 (1986 & Supp.1990).

that this "enforcement provision" would seemingly allow an agency to decide to opt, in some circumstances, to provide rules (e.g., procedural rules) directly to a party (in advance of a proceeding) instead of publishing them in the *Federal Register*.[161] The publication requirements of section 552 are also discussed in Part II, ch. 1(E).

2. Federal Register *Requirements*

Title 1 of the *Code of Federal Regulations* contains the rules of the Administrative Committee of the Federal Register governing the filing and publication of documents in the *Federal Register.* Agency rulemakers should also consult the very helpful *Document Drafting Handbook*, published by the Office of the Federal Register (OFR) (in an updated, online version), for a compilation of rules, form letters, frequently asked questions, and other hints.[162] An earlier chapter in this Part discussed the general format requirements that apply to documents submitted for publication in the *Federal Register* as well as the requirements governing incorporation by reference of material into rules.[163] However, other requirements and provisions are particularly relevant to publication of final rules.

First, agencies should not expect the OFR to publish a final rule that does not comply with the *Register*'s minimum requirements.[164] One requirement agencies should be especially aware of is that the OFR "will not accept a document for filing and publication if it combines material that must appear under more than one category in the *Federal Register*."[165] Thus, a single document containing both final rule text and proposed rule text will not be accepted for publication.[166] The reasons for this requirement are that proposed and final rules appear in different sections of the *Federal Register*, and certain categories of documents, such as final rules, are included in the *Code of Federal Regulations*, but other categories appear only in the daily *Federal Register.*

Ordinarily, agencies may not cross-reference the rules of another agency.[167] From a practical point of view, use of cross-referencing to replace regulatory text would make the *Federal Register* system difficult to use, because the reader would have to look outside an agency's regulations to ascertain the nature of the entire regulatory scheme.

---

161. E-mail comment to administrative law listserv by Professor Bill Funk (Dec. 5, 1995) (on file with the author).
162. National Archives of the United States, Office of the Federal Register, Document Drafting Handbook (October 1998 revision, with supplements) [hereinafter Document Drafting Handbook], *available at* http://www.archives.gov/federal-register/write/handbook/ddh.pdf.
163. *See supra* Part III, ch. 3(C).
164. The Director of the Federal Register is specifically authorized to return nonconforming documents to the issuing agency. 1 C.F.R. § 2.4(b).
165. *Id.* § 18.2(a).
166. *But see supra* Part II, ch. 1(D)(4)(d), for a discussion of "direct-final rules."
167. Section 552(a) of the APA states that each agency must separately state and currently publish its regulations. *See also* 1 C.F.R. § 21.21.

Agencies also must submit the full text of a final rule to the OFR for publication, unless the Director of the OFR approves incorporation by reference of material in the rule. This requirement is statutory,[168] and failure to comply with it can lead to invalidation of the rule.[169] To avoid the expense of publication, some agencies have attempted to incorporate agency-produced materials into final rules by reference. However, the rules of the *Federal Register* generally do not allow agencies to incorporate by reference documents of the agency or material previously published in the *Federal Register* or the *United States Code*.[170] An agency will have violated the Administrative Committee of the Federal Register's regulations if it publishes in the *Federal Register* a document that attempts to incorporate by reference the text of a proposed rule previously published in the *Federal Register*.[171] See the extensive discussion about restrictions on "incorporation by reference" in Chapter 3(C), most of which apply equally to preambles of final rules.

The Administrative Committee of the Federal Register has published detailed rules on "Preparation and Transmittal of Documents Generally."[172] In particular, these rules prescribe a format for preambles to *Federal Register* documents[173] and require that they contain the following information:

1. The name of the issuing agency.
2. Summary. This is a "brief statement," "in simple language," of the action taken, the reasons for the action, and its intended effect.
3. Relevant dates, such as effective date, hearing date, and so on.
4. Relevant addresses.
5. Names and addresses of agency persons to contact for further information.
6. Supplementary information. This is the main body of the preamble. The agency is required in this section to include a discussion of the background and major issues; in the case of a final rule, how the final rule is different from the proposal; "a response to substantive public comments received"; and any other appropriate information.[174]

---

168. Section 552(a)(1)(D) of the APA requires agencies to publish substantive rules of general applicability. Although agencies are not required to publish the text of a proposed rule, final rules must be published in their entirety. 5 U.S.C. § 553(b).

169. *See, e.g.*, Appalachian Power Co. v. Train, 566 F.2d 451, 455 (4th Cir. 1977).

170. 1 C.F.R. § 51.7(b)–(c).

171. *Id.* §§ 21.1, 21.21(c). When an agency publishes all applicable requirements in the text of the rule itself, this serves the interest of promoting compliance. *See, e.g.*, OSHA, Final Rule, Electrical Standards for Construction, 51 Fed. Reg. 25,294, 25,296 (July 11, 1986) (revising the construction safety standard and incorporating relevant National Electrical Code (NEC) requirements into text of the standard so that "employers will no longer have to refer to the NEC to determine their obligations under OSHA").

172. 1 C.F.R. pt. 18.

173. *Id.* § 18.12; *see also id.* pt. 22; DOCUMENT DRAFTING HANDBOOK, *supra* note 162.

174. 1 C.F.R. § 18.12.

Agencies also must observe the Administrative Committee of the Federal Register's filing rules. The Federal Register Act requires all documents, including rules, to be filed with the OFR for publication, and "[u]pon filing, at least one copy shall be immediately available for public inspection in the Office."[175] But the Administrative Committee does not consider delivery of a document to the *Register* to constitute a filing. Its regulations provide that:

> A document is considered filed with the Office of the Federal Register after it has been received and processed by the OFR and made available for public inspection . . . .[176]
>
> The OFR must file each document for public inspection on the working day before date of publication. The issuing agency may request in writing an earlier filing date.[177]
>
> The OFR will not release information concerning a document to the public before the document is filed for public inspection.[178]

The *Federal Register* filing requirements are especially important to agencies issuing emergency rules under the APA or some other statute. If given advance warning, the staff of the OFR will work with agencies to expedite the filing and publication of emergency rules.[179]

The "issuance" date can also be important if it initiates a deadline for filing a petition for judicial review.[180]

Besides establishing publication requirements,[181] the OFR provides valuable assistance and services to agencies publishing final rules. For example, the OFR will publish rules as a separate part of the *Register,* and agencies can request re-

---

175. 44 U.S.C. § 1503.

176. 1 C.F.R. §§ 1.1, 17.2.

177. *Id.* §§ 3.2(b), 17.2.

178. *Id.* § 17.1.

179. The Office of the Federal Register has special rules for publication and filing of emergency rules. 1 C.F.R. §§ 17.3–17.6. The *Document Drafting Handbook* contains instructions for seeking emergency filings and publications. *See* DOCUMENT DRAFTING HANDBOOK, *supra* note 162, at § 8.7 & App. A.

180. Pub. Citizen v. Mineta, 343 F.3d 1159 (9th Cir. 2003) (for purposes of the initiating period for filing a petition for judicial review, NHTSA regulation is "issued" on the date that regulation is made available for public inspection; in this case the best evidence was the filing date published in the *Federal Register*). *See also* Council Tree Commc'ns v. FCC, 503 F.3d 284 (3d Cir. 2007) (holding that a petition to review a rulemaking order of the FCC is incurably premature when it is filed before the rulemaking order is published in the *Federal Register*); Verizon v. FCC, Nos. 11-1014 & 11-1016, 2011 WL 1235523 (D.C. Cir. April 4, 2011) (dismissing premature challenge); W. Union Tel. Co. v. FCC, 773 F.2d 375, 378, 380 (D.C. Cir. 1985) (same).

181. It should be noted that the Administrative Committee's format requirements are not intended to affect the validity of any document that is "filed and published under law." 1 C.F.R. § 5.1(c).

prints of the separate part.[182] It should also be noted, however, that agencies must "pay" the OFR a fee, on a per-page basis, for publication of documents in the *Federal Register.*[183]

It is permissible in some circumstances for an agency to withdraw a rule submitted to the OFR prior to publication.[184] As described in Part II above,[185] the Card Memorandum, issued at the beginning of President Bush II's Administration, directed the heads of executive agencies to withdraw regulations sent to the OFR but not yet published. As one commentator wrote,

> Although the ostensible goal of the Card Memorandum was "to ensure that the President's appointees have the opportunity to review any new or pending regulations," it was undoubtedly designed to address the conspicuous increase in the number of regulations issued in the final months of the Clinton Administration. Agencies responded to the Card Memorandum's directives and withdrew 124 regulations from the OFR and postponed the effective dates of ninety regulations.[186]

Similar efforts were made by the Reagan Administration in 1981, which suspended numerous regulations in order to allow for reconsideration, and the Clinton Administration, which issued a directive to withdraw unpublished rules developed by agencies under the first Bush Administration.[187] The Obama Administration, followed this practice by directing agencies to withdraw all proposed or final regulations that have not been published in the *Federal Register*, consider delaying for 60 days (with a public comment period) all published rules that had not yet gone into effect, and to refrain from sending any additional rules (other than emergency rules,

---

182. *Id.* § 12.1.
183. The minimum per-page fee for FY 2011 is $477. *See* U.S. Gov't Printing Office, Circular Letter No. 777 (July 2, 2010), http://www.gpo.gov/customers/letters/777.htm.
184. *See* Office of the Federal Register's regulation on "withdrawal or correction of filed documents," 1 C.F.R. § 18.13.
185. Part II, ch. 1(D)(4)(f).
186. William M. Jack, *Taking Care That Presidential Oversight of the Regulatory Process Is Faithfully Executed: A Review of Rule Withdrawals and Rule Suspensions under the Bush Administration's Card Memorandum*, 54 ADMIN. L. REV. 1479, 1480–81 (2002). For a critical look at the Clinton "midnight rules" in the context of the mining industry, see Andrew P. Morriss, Roger E. Meiners & Andrew Dorchak, *Between a Hard Rock and a Hard Place: Politics, Midnight Regulations and Mining*, 55 ADMIN. L. REV. 551 (2003). Another commentary claims that the Bush II Administration deliberately scheduled publication of controversial rules during the holiday period to avoid public scrutiny. *See* Robin Kundis Craig, *The Bush Administration's Use and Abuse of Rulemaking. Part II: Manipulating the Federal Register*, 29 ADMIN. & REG. L. NEWS 5 (Fall 2003).
187. *See* Jack, *supra* note 186, at 1488, 1498.

or rules subject to legislative or judicial deadlines) to the *Federal Register* until they were reviewed by an agency head appointed by President Obama.[188]

In *Kennecott Utah Copper Corp. v. Department of Interior*,[189] the D.C. Circuit considered procedural challenges to the withdrawal of a rule that had been sent to the OFR on January 19, 1993, the final day of the Bush I Administration. On January 21, 1993, immediately after President Clinton took office, before the OFR filed the rule for public inspection, and prior to publication in the *Federal Register*, Clinton Administration officials ordered the withdrawal of the rule. Kennecott Copper and several other industry petitioners sued the DOI, alleging violations of both the Federal Register Act and APA.

The court rejected these challenges.[190] With respect to the Federal Register Act, the court concluded, "[A]llowing agencies to withdraw documents during the relatively brief processing period is consistent with the [Act's] purpose. . . ."[191] Moreover, because the DOI withdrawal occurred just two days after the OFR received the rule, the court found that "allow[ing] agencies to withdraw documents during the confidential processing period is reasonable."[192] The court also rejected Kennecott Copper's argument that reopening the comment period after the rule had been withdrawn amounted to a new regulation. It found that, because the OFR never "issued" the rule, its decision to withdraw the rule "did not alter substantive legal obligations under previously published regulations . . . ."[193] Specifically, the court found a withdrawal does not involve "formulating" a rule, but only the rejection of "a document that had not yet been published." Finally, the court refused to find that the agency was "amend[ing]" or "repeal[ing] a rule," "because the 1993 [rule] never became a rule subject to amendment or repeal."[194]

3. *Plain Language Requirements*

In drafting the final rule, the agency needs to be mindful not only of the style requirements of the *Document Drafting Handbook*, but also of the clarity of the rule.

---

188. Memorandum for the Heads of Executive Departments and Agencies from Rahm Emanuel, Assistant to the President and Chief of Staff (Jan. 20, 2009), 74 Fed. Reg. 4435 (Jan. 26, 2009). See also the supplemental memo from OMB Director Peter Orszag, http://www.whitehouse.gov/sites/default/files/omb/assets/agencyinformation_memoranda_2009_pdf/m09-08.pdf. For more discussion of the ramifications of the Emanuel Memorandum, see Part II, ch. 1(D)(4)(f).
189. 88 F.3d 1191 (D.C. Cir. 1996).
190. The following account is largely drawn from Jack, *supra* note 186, at 1488–92.
191. *Kennecott Copper*, 88 F.3d at 1206.
192. *Id.*
193. *Id.* at 1207.
194. *Id.* at 1209. *See also* Chen v. Immigration and Naturalization Serv., 95 F.3d 801 (9th Cir.) (asylum applicant could not rely on a rule that had been sent to the Office of Federal Register but was withdrawn before publication by incoming Clinton Administration because the rule had no legal effect).

In 1998, President Clinton issued a Memorandum for the Heads of Executive Departments and Agencies on "Plain Language in Government Writing" (June 1, 1998), requiring the use of plain language in all proposed and final rules.[195] This memo remains in effect, and guidance for complying with it has been incorporated into the *Document Drafting Handbook*.[196] President Obama's Executive Order 13,563 also states that "[our regulatory system] must ensure that regulations are accessible, consistent, written in plain language, and easy to understand."[197] In addition, the federal banking agencies are under a statutory obligation to use plain language in their proposed and final rules.[198]

The Plain Language Action & Information Network, a government-wide group of volunteers,[199] has produced a lengthy set of guidelines for preparing documents in plain English.[200] Note also the enactment of the Plain Writing Act of 2010,[201] a mostly hortatory law that requires agencies and OMB to take various steps and make various reports about their actions in ensuring the use of plain writing in agency documents. Notably, although the Act does not cover rulemaking documents, an implementing memo from OIRA Director Sunstein emphasized that "rulemaking preambles are not exempted, and

---

195. Memorandum for the Heads of Executive Departments and Agencies on "Plain Language in Government Writing" (June 1, 1998), 63 Fed. Reg. 31,884 (June 10, 1998).
196. *See* DOCUMENT DRAFTING HANDBOOK, *supra* note 162, at pt. II.
197. Exec. Order No. 13,563, Improving Regulation and Regulatory Review § 1, 76 Fed. Reg. 3821 (Jan 21, 2011).
198. *See* Section 722(a) of the Gramm-Leach-Bliley Act, Pub. L. 106-102, 113 Stat. 1338 (1999) (codified at 12 U.S.C. § 4809); *see, e.g.*, Office of Thrift Supervision, Department of the Treasury, Proposed Rule, Assessments and Fees, 69 Fed. Reg. 6201, 6208 (Feb. 10, 2004):

    OTS invites comments on how to make this proposed rule easier to understand. For example:

    (1) Have we organized the material to suit your needs? If not, how could the material be better organized?
    (2) Do we clearly state the requirements in the rule? If not, how could the rule be more clearly stated?
    (3) Does the rule contain technical language or jargon that is not clear? If so, what language requires clarification?
    (4) Would a different format (grouping and order of sections, use of headings, paragraphing) make the rule easier to understand? If so, what changes to the format would make the rule easier to understand?

199. For more information about PLAIN, see its website at http://www.plainlanguage.gov/site/about.cfm.
200. FEDERAL PLAIN LANGUAGE GUIDELINES (Mar. 2011, rev. May 2011), *available at* http://www.plainlanguage.gov/howto/guidelines/FederalPLGuidelines/FederalPLGuidelines.pdf. For useful commentary on writing regulations in plain language, see THOMAS A. MURAWSKI, WRITING READABLE REGULATIONS (Carolina Academic Press, 1999); Steven L. Schooner, *Communicating Governance: Will Plain English Drafting Improve Regulation?*, 70 GEO. WASH. L. REV. 163 (2002) (book review).
201. Pub. L No. 111-274, 124 Stat. 2861 (2010) (codified at 5 U.S.C. § 301 note).

long-standing policies currently in effect require regulations to be written in a manner that is 'simple and easy to understand.'"[202] Moreover, another Sunstein memo advised agencies that "regulatory preambles for lengthy or complex rules (both proposed and final) should include straightforward executive summaries. These summaries should separately describe major provisions and policy choices. Such executive summaries should generally be placed at the start of regulatory preambles."A suggested template was attached to this memo as an appendix.[203]

4. *"Issuance" and "Promulgation" of the Final Rule*

Under 28 U.S.C. § 2112, prior to its amendment in 1988, the precise date and time of issuance of a rule was critical for purposes of selection of venue for court review. Thus, under the original statute, review of the rule would take place in the circuit in which the proceeding "was first instituted." This gave rise to the much-criticized "race-to-the-courthouse" phenomenon, where each party sought to obtain review of the rule in a forum it thought favorable to its point of view. However, following a recommendation of the Administrative Conference,[204] Congress in 1988 amended 28 U.S.C. § 2112 to provide for random selection of a court of appeals for review purposes from among all courts in which multiple petitions for review were filed within 10 days of the issuance of the order by the agency.[205] Thus, the "race to the courthouse" was eliminated for all practical purposes, because all petitions filed within 10 days of the issuance of the order are now treated equally for venue pur-poses, and there is no incentive for a party to be the first to file.[206]

5. *Dissents*

As with proposed rules, members of agency boards or commissions may wish to dissent from the final rule. The APA is silent on this matter, so how the dissent is pub-

---

202. Memorandum for the Heads of Executive Departments and Agencies, and Independent Regulatory Agencies, from Cass R. Sunstein, OIRA Administrator, *Final Guidance on Implementing the Plain Writing Act of 2010*, at 5 (April 13, 2011), *available at* http://www.whitehouse.gov/sites/default/files/omb/memoranda/2011/m11-15.pdf.

203. Memorandum for the Heads of Executive Departments and Agencies from Cass R. Sunstein, OIRA Administrator, *Clarifying Regulatory Requirements: Executive Summaries* (Jan. 4, 2012), *available at* http://www.whitehouse.gov/sites/default/files/omb/inforeg/for-agencies/clarifying-regulatory-requirements_executive-summaries.pdf.

204. ACUS Recommendation 80-5, *Eliminating or Simplifying the 'Race to the Courthouse' in Appeals from Agency Action*, 45 Fed. Reg. 84,954 (Dec. 24, 1980).

205. Pub. L. No. 100-236, 101 Stat. 1731 (1988) (codified at 28 U.S.C. § 2112(a)).

206. *See also* discussion *infra* Part IV, ch. 1 (D). On the question of when a rule is "issued" or "promulgated" for purposes of determining the application of the 10-day rule, *see* United Technologies Corp. v. OSHA, 836 F.2d 52 (2d Cir. 1987); Nat'l Grain & Feed Ass'n v. OSHA, 845 F.2d 345 (D.C. Cir. 1988).

lished or otherwise publicized is a matter for the agency (majority) to decide. Agencies typically allow the dissenting member to publish his or her dissent in the final rule preamble, but occasionally the dissent is paraphrased or published elsewhere.[207]

---

207. *See, e.g.*, National Mediation Board, Final Rule, Representation Election Procedure, 75 Fed. Reg. 26,062, 26,083–88 (May 11, 2010) (dissenting statement); NLRB, Final Rule, Representation—Case Procedures, Notification of Employee Rights Under the National Labor Relations Act, 76 Fed. Reg. 54,006, 54,037–42 (Aug. 30, 2011) (dissenting statement); NLRB, Final Rule, Representation—Case Procedures, 76 Fed. Reg. 80,138, 80,146 (Dec. 22, 2011) (indicating that one member who had dissented from the proposed rule also had voted against the final rule, but had not yet supplied a dissent or similar statement in connection with the final rule itself). The majority authorized the publication of such a document in the *Federal Register*, together with any separate concurring opinion, when they are made available, and delayed the effective date of the final rule so that he would have over 90 days to write a dissent and have it published prior to the effective date of the rule. However, no such dissent was published in the *Federal Register*. *See also* Federal Energy Regulatory Commission, Final Rule, 72 Fed. Reg. 39,904, 40,046 (July 20, 2007) (containing "attachment to final rule" with statement of one Commissioner, dissenting in part); Consumer Product Safety Commission, Final Rule, 71 Fed. Reg. 42,028 (July 25, 2006) (indicating that the Commission voted 2-1 to issue the final interpretative rule, and that the majority members filed statements that are available from the Office of the Secretary or on the Commission's website).

Chapter 8

Review of Existing Rules

In recent years there has been an emphasis on agency review and reevaluation of *existing* regulations.[1] Complaints about "regulatory overload" have become common.[2] Scholars have commented that agencies have difficulty reviewing their existing regulations, given their responsibilities to develop new ones in this period of staffing and resource constraints. Professor Pierce has articulated this dilemma clearly:

> Conditions in all of these fields, and our understanding of the underlying science, change so rapidly that the average rule probably has a useful life of no longer than a decade. Agencies should be reviewing and revising their rules on a regular basis. Yet, agencies rarely amend rules because the amendment process is as daunting as the process of promulgating a rule.[3]

Others have pointed out that agencies fall into "regulatory ruts."[4] Most of the

---

1. *See generally* Sidney A. Shapiro, *Agency Review of Existing Regulations*, 1994–1995 ACUS 411 (1995), *available at* http://www.acus.gov/wp-content/plugins/download-monitor/download.php?id=98. This report was based on a report written for the ABA's Section of Administrative Law and Regulatory Practice. *See* Neil R. Eisner & Judy Kaleta, Federal Agency Reviews of Existing Regulations (1994).
2. *See, e.g.*, Mercatus Center, Do More Regulations Equal Less Safety?, *available at* http://mercatus.org/sites/default/files/publication/More-Regulations-Less-Safety.pdf (discussing regulatory overload). In the U.K. this sentiment has recently led to the adoption of a "one-in-one-out" program for regulations. *See One-in, One-out*, Dep't for Bus. Innovation & Skills, http://www.bis.gov.uk/policies/bre/better-regulation-framework/one-in-one-out (last visited Dec. 7, 2011). Proposals like this imply that an optimum regulatory equilibrium has been reached. In the U.S., of course, Office of Management and Budget (OMB) review helps police agency rulemakings to the point that OMB reports have regularly estimated high aggregate net benefits for the rules it reviews. *See* discussion *supra* Chapter 2(A)(2).
3. Richard J. Pierce, Jr., *Seven Ways to Deossify Agency Rulemaking*, 47 Admin. L. Rev. 59, 61 (1995). Indeed, Professors Blais and Wagner suggest that revising rules is more daunting. Lynn E. Blais & Wendy E. Wagner, *Emerging Science, Adaptive Regulation, and the Problem of Rulemaking Ruts*, 86 Tex. L. Rev. 1701, 1710 (2008) (arguing that "revision of existing rules may be even more likely to fall victim to the factors responsible for the ossification of initial rulemaking" because the revision process is subject to notice-and-comment procedures and, during judicial review, courts tend to provide more scrutiny to revisions).
4. Blais & Wagner, *supra* note 3, at 1704 ("While revisions may—and indeed do—sporadically and erratically emerge from these rulemaking ruts, it is much more likely that existing standards will stay deeply embedded in the ossification mud.").

complaints about this syndrome have come from the regulated business community, though it should be noted that health and safety advocates also become frustrated with outmoded standards.[5] The relative consensus on the need for "lookback" has led to a series of mandates coming out of the White House from the last four Presidents.

The Regulatory Flexibility Act is the only statute that requires agencies to undertake periodic reviews of regulations—for those that have "a significant economic impact upon a substantial number of small entities."[6] But President Bush I mandated a "top to bottom review" of existing regulations in 1992 when he ordered a 90-day moratorium on new regulations.[7] President Clinton institutionalized that mandate in Executive Order 12,866, which required agencies to review existing regulations to ensure that they are still timely, compatible, effective, and do not impose unnecessary burdens.[8] In the Bush II Administration, OIRA regularly solicited nominations of rules that should be reviewed for ineffectiveness or inefficiency.[9] President Obama has made this practice a centerpiece of his regulatory program.[10]

---

5. *See id.* ("Indeed, in such an environment, regulatory revisions may be as likely to regress in favor of regulated parties as they are to advance toward more stringent standards.").

6. 5 U.S.C. § 610. See *supra* Part II, ch. 3(C) for a discussion of the Act. *See also* OFFICE OF MGMT. & BUDGET, EXEC. OFFICE OF THE PRESIDENT, DRAFT REPORT TO CONGRESS ON THE COSTS AND BENEFITS OF FEDERAL REGULATIONS, 67 Fed. Reg. 15,014, 15,033 (Mar. 28, 2002) (requesting comments on "needed reforms of regulations unnecessarily impacting small businesses and identification of specific regulations and paperwork requirements that impose especially large burdens on small businesses and other small entities without an adequate benefit justification"). Of course, the APA also requires agencies to respond to petitions for rulemaking, which include petitions for the "issuance, amendment, or repeal of a rule." *Id.* § 553(e). *See* discussion *supra* ch. 1(A)(2).

7. State of the Union Address, 1 PUB. PAPERS 156, 159 (Jan. 28, 1992); *see also* Letter to Congressional Leaders Transmitting a Report on Federal Regulatory Policy, 1 PUB. PAPERS 2258 (Jan. 15, 1993); Shapiro, *supra* note 1, at 411.

8. *See* Exec. Order 12,866, § 5, 3 C.F.R. 638, 644 (1994). The order requires agencies to "submit to OIRA a program" to undertake such a review. *Id.* Agencies are also directed to "identify any legislative mandates that require the agency to promulgate or continue to impose regulations that the agency believes are unnecessary or outdated by reason of changed circumstances." *Id.*

9. *See* OFFICE OF MGMT. & BUDGET, DRAFT 2004 REPORT TO CONGRESS ON THE COSTS AND BENEFITS OF FEDERAL REGULATIONS, Notice of availability and request for comments, 69 Fed. Reg. 7987 (Feb. 20, 2004); *see also* Cindy Skrzycki, *Charting Progress of Rule Reviews Proves Difficult*, WASH. POST, Dec. 7, 2004, at E-1 (reporting that OIRA received 71 nominations in 2001, 316 in 2002, and 189 in 2004; it did not solicit in 2003); OIRA, REGULATORY REFORM OF THE U.S. MANUFACTURING SECTOR: A SUMMARY OF AGENCY RESPONSES TO PUBLIC REFORM NOMINATIONS (Mar. 9, 2005), *available at* http://www.whitehouse.gov/sites/default/files/omb/assets/omb/inforeg/reports/manufacturing_initiative.pdf; *Regulatory Reform, Hearing before the House Subcommittee on Energy Policy, Natural Resources and Regulatory Affairs of the Committee on Government Reform*, 108th Cong. (Nov. 17, 2004) (statement of John D. Graham, Administrator of OIRA), *available at* http://www.whitehouse.gov/omb/legislative/testimony/graham/111704_graham_reg_reform.html.

10. *See* Exec. Order 13,563 § 6, issued Jan. 18, 2011, 76 Fed. Reg. 3821 (Jan. 21, 2011), and ensuing memoranda, discussed below.

President Clinton asked agencies to review, page by page, their existing regulations to eliminate those that are unduly burdensome, outdated, or in need of revision.[11] The review was to consist of five criteria: (1) Is a regulation obsolete? (2) Could its intended goal be achieved in more efficient, less intrusive ways? (3) Are there better private-sector alternatives, such as market mechanisms, that can better achieve the public good envisioned by the regulation? (4) Could private business, setting its own standards and being subject to public accountability, do the job as well? (5) Could the states or local governments do the job, making federal regulation unnecessary?[12]

In June 1995, President Clinton announced that as a result of this effort, 16,000 pages of the *Code of Federal Regulations* were to be eliminated and another 31,000 were to be "reinvented."[13] In September 1995, OIRA reported that about 75 percent of those pages had actually been eliminated and about 50 percent had been reinvented.[14] In addition, agency-specific and program-specific reforms were undertaken, resulting in a series of success stories trumpeted by the Clinton Administration.[15]

Nevertheless, the Bush II Administration did not find past efforts very successful and instead sought public comment on specific rules that needed reform. In arguing that "[p]ast efforts at broad reviews of existing regulations . . . were largely unsuccessful,"[16] it quoted Sally Katzen, OIRA Administrator in the Clinton Administration as noting

---

11. Memorandum for Heads of Departments and Agencies From William J. Clinton on Regulatory Reinvention Initiative, 1 PUB. PAPERS 304 (Mar. 4, 1995).

12. *Id.*

13. Remarks by the President to the White House Conference on Small Business, 1 PUB. PAPERS 865, 868–69 (June 12, 1995).

14. *See* OFFICE OF MGMT. & BUDGET, OFFICE OF INFORMATION AND REGULATORY AFFAIRS, MORE BENEFITS, FEWER BURDENS: CREATING A REGULATORY SYSTEM THAT WORKS FOR THE AMERICAN PEOPLE, A REPORT TO THE PRESIDENT ON THE THIRD ANNIVERSARY OF EXECUTIVE ORDER 12,866 39–40 (1996). *But see* U.S. GEN. ACCOUNTING OFFICE, REGULATORY REFORM: AGENCIES' EFFORTS TO ELIMINATE AND REVISE RULES YIELD MIXED RESULTS 8 (GAO/GGD-98-3) (Oct. 1997) (reporting that four agencies (DOT, EPA, HUD, OSHA) reported a reduction of 5,500 pages during this initiative when the *net* reduction was only 900 pages).

15. MORE BENEFITS, FEWER BURDENS, *supra* note 14, at 40–50; *see also* THE NEW OSHA: REINVENTING WORKER SAFETY AND HEALTH (1995); THE NEW SBA: REINVENTING SERVICE TO THE SMALL BUSINESS COMMUNITY (1995); REINVENTING HEALTH CARE REGULATIONS (1995); REINVENTING FOOD REGULATIONS: NATIONAL PERFORMANCE REVIEW (1996). Because of these activities (or perhaps *in spite of* them), many of the regulatory reform bills introduced in the 104th and 105th Congresses included elaborate new procedures for the agency review of existing regulations along with more rigorous provisions on outside petitions to trigger the process. OSHA has continued its long-running standards improvement project. *See* Department of Labor, Occupational Safety and Health Administration, Final Rule, *Standards Improvement Project—Phase III*, 76 Fed. Reg. 33,590 (June 8, 2011) (issuing revised standards and detailing history of the project since 1996).

16. DRAFT REPORT TO CONGRESS ON THE COSTS AND BENEFITS OF FEDERAL REGULATIONS, *supra* note 6, at 15,033–34.

that bureaucratic incentives make such review a difficult undertaking. While the "lookback" process had begun under E.O. 12866, she said, "it had proven more difficult to institute than we had anticipated. * * * [A]gencies are focused on meeting obligations for new rules, often under statutory or court deadlines, at a time when staff and budgets are being reduced; under these circumstances, it is hard to muster resources for the generally thankless task of rethinking and rewriting current regulatory programs" . . . . [17]

Accordingly, OMB "established a modest process to review and improve old rules based on a public comment process."[18]

In January 2011, President Obama mandated, in Executive Order 13,563, that:

To facilitate the periodic review of existing significant regulations, agencies shall consider how best to promote retrospective analysis of rules that may be outmoded, ineffective, insufficient, or excessively burdensome, and to modify, streamline, expand, or repeal them in accordance with what has been learned. Such retrospective analyses, including supporting data, should be released online whenever possible.[19]

The Order went on to require agencies to develop a preliminary plan "consistent with law and its resources and regulatory priorities, under which the agency will periodically review its existing significant regulations to determine whether any such regulations should be modified, streamlined, expanded, or repealed."[20] In October 2011, OIRA expanded the requirement by requiring regular reports, and providing a template for such reports:

Agency reports should describe past progress, anticipated accomplishments, and proposed timelines for relevant actions, with an emphasis on high-priority reforms. Agencies shall submit such reports to OIRA on the second Mon-

---

17. *Id.*
18. *Id.* For a review of the results of OMB's 2001 review effort, see U.S. GEN. ACCOUNTING OFFICE, RULEMAKING: OMB'S ROLE IN REVIEWS OF AGENCIES' DRAFT RULES AND THE TRANSPARENCY OF THOSE REVIEWS 103–09 (GAO-03-929) (Sept. 2003), www.gao.gov/new.items/d03929.pdf (documenting influence of the Mercatus Center at George Mason University).
19. Exec. Order 13,563 § 6(a), issued Jan. 18, 2011, 76 Fed. Reg. 3821, 3822 (Jan. 21, 2011). *See also* Memorandum from Cass R. Sunstein, Administrator, Office of Info. & Regulatory Affairs, Office of Mgmt. & Budget, to the Heads of Executive Departments and Agencies, "Retrospective Analysis of Existing Significant Regulations," M-11-19 (Apr. 25, 2011) *available at* http://www.whitehouse.gov/sites/default/files/omb/memoranda/2011/m11-19.pdf. The memo references "An emerging literature [that] explores potential methods of evaluation, including randomized trials and quasi-experimental methods" (citing Michael Greenstone, *Toward a Culture of Persistent Regulatory Experimentation and Evaluation*, in NEW PERSPECTIVES ON REGULATION (David Moss & John Cistemino eds., Cambridge, Mass.: The Tobin Project, Inc., 2009).
20. *Id.* at § 6(b). As of March 17, 2012, 30 final agency plans were catalogued at http://www.whitehouse.gov/21stcenturygov/actions/21st-century-regulatory-system.

day of January, May, and September for the period of a year from the date of this memorandum, and semi-annually on the second Monday of January and July for each year thereafter. Agencies shall make these reports available to the public within a reasonable period (not to exceed two weeks from submission). It is recommended that agencies publish their reports online on the agency's Open Government Webpage (www.agency.gov/open).[21]

As this Guide went to press, President Obama issued a new Executive Order13,610, Identifying and Reducing Regulatory Burdens (May 10, 2012),[22] which builds on E.O. 13,563 and requires executive agencies to seek public suggestions on such reviews, release retrospective analyses to the public whenever practicable, give priority to initiatives that will produce monetary or paperwork savings or reduce burdens on small businesses, and consider cumulative burdens of regulation. Section 4 of the Order requires that draft reports be submitted to OIRA on the second Monday of January and July (unless directed otherwise through subsequent guidance from OIRA) with final reports available to the public within at least three weeks later.

The Administrative Conference has supported the idea that "agencies have an obligation to develop systematic processes for reviewing existing rules, regulations and regulatory programs on an ongoing basis."[23] It did, however, issue some cautionary advice for proponents of such mandates:

> Given the difference among agencies, however, processes for review of existing regulations should not be a "one-size-fits-all," but should be tailored to meet agencies' individualized needs. Thus the President, as well as Congress, should avoid mandating standardized or detailed requirements. Moreover, the review should focus on the most important regulations, and offer sufficient time and resources to ensure meaningful analysis. Tight time frames or review requirements applicable to *all* regulations, regardless of their narrow or limited impact, may prevent agencies from being able to engage in a meaningful effort. It is important that priority-setting processes be developed that allow agencies, in consultation with the Office of Management and Budget and the public (including but not limited to the regulated communities), to determine where their efforts should be directed.[24]

---

21. Memorandum from Cass R. Sunstein, Administrator, Office of Info. & Regulatory Affairs, Office of Mgmt. & Budget, to the Heads of Executive Departments and Agencies, "Retrospective Analysis of Existing Significant Regulations" (Oct 26, 2011), *available at* http://www.whitehouse.gov/sites/default/files/omb/assets/inforeg/implementation-of-retrospective-review-plans.pdf.

22. 77 Fed. Reg. 28,469 (May 14, 2012).

23. ACUS Recommendation 95-3, *Review of Existing Agency Regulations*, 60 Fed. Reg. 43,109 (Aug. 18, 1995). The ABA also supported such reviews. *See* House of Delegates Resolution (August 1995), Summary of Actions of the House of Delegates (1995 Annual Meeting) at 48, based on a report and recommendation of the Section of Administrative Law and Regulatory Practice. *Id.* at 341.

24. ACUS Recommendation 95-3, *supra* note 23, at 43,109.

The Conference also suggested that in undertaking the look-back processes:

A. Agencies should provide adequate resources to ensure senior-level management participation in the review of existing regulations.
B. As part of the review process, agencies should review information in their files as well as other available information on the impact and the effectiveness of regulations, and where appropriate, should engage in risk assessment and cost-benefit analysis of specific regulations.

Of course, it would assist in the review of existing regulations (and also help in the development of new regulations) if good ex post evaluations could be conducted to validate pre-regulation estimates of benefit and cost. OMB discussed this growing body of literature in its 2005 Report to Congress.[25]

---

25. OFFICE OF MGMT. & BUDGET, EXECUTIVE OFFICE OF THE PRESIDENT, DRAFT 2005 REPORT TO CONGRESS ON THE COSTS AND BENEFITS OF FEDERAL REGULATIONS 39–44 (2005), *available at* http://www.whitehouse.gov/sites/default/files/omb/assets/omb/inforeg/2005_cb/draft_2005_cb_report.pdf. *See also* Larry McCray, *Planned Adaptation in Federal Regulation: An Initial Assessment of Adaptability in US Health and Safety Regulation* (MIT Political Econ. and Tech. Policy Program, Version 3.3, Aug. 27, 2005), *available at* http://web.mit.edu/cis/PETP%20-%20McCray%20Working%20Paper.doc (examining various cases of retrospective analyses of existing rules); comments of former OIRA Administrator Sally Katzen, transcript of American University's Center for Rulemaking, E-rulemaking Conference at 92 (Jan. 2004), *available at* http://www.american.edu/academic.depts/provost/rulemaking/transcripts.pdf:

> I'd rather do . . . some serious retrospective analyses of actual rulemaking proceedings. Take a significant rule, and five years after it goes into effect, go back and look at the estimates of costs when the rule was being developed. Were they overstated or, conceivably, understated? Look at the benefits. Were they overstated or understated? This will tell you something about the quality of the process that produces the rule. That, I believe, would be informative and constructive. That, I think, is money [well] spent.

See also U.S. GOV'T ACCOUNTABILITY OFFICE, REGULATORY REFORM: PRIOR REVIEWS OF FEDERAL REGULATORY PROCESS INITIATIVES REVEAL OPPORTUNITIES FOR IMPROVEMENT 10 (GAO-05-939T) (July 27, 2005) (testimony of J. Christopher Mihm before the House Subcomm. on Regulatory Affairs, Comm. on Govt. Reform) (suggesting the need for more retrospective analysis); John D. Graham, *Saving Lives Through Administrative Law and Economics*, 157 U. PA. L. REV. 395, 527 (2008) (citing sources in notes 563–65):

> A more robust validation literature is urgently needed. If lifesaving rules are to be modernized periodically based on real-world implementation, accurate information will be needed on how many lives were saved, what the overall benefits were, and how much the rules cost society. Moreover, any systematic biases of [cost-benefit analysis] will be disclosed in a persuasive way only with a more comprehensive program of validation research. Without validation, proregulation activists will continue to assert that [cost-benefit analysis] is biased against lifesaving rules, while antiregulation activists will continue to assert that regulators "cook the numbers" to justify more regulation.

As a legal matter, it should also be noted that, as the Supreme Court stated in *United States v. Nixon*,[26] extant regulations have the force of law until they are revoked—even, as in that case, when it was a rule issued without notice and comment.[27] Under the APA, repealing or amending existing rules constitutes "rulemaking"[28] and therefore would likely require notice and comment, especially if the existing rule was so promulgated.[29] Moreover, although agencies have wide discretion in amending or revoking their regulations, such actions are still subject to "arbitrary and capricious" review.[30] And revoking a rule that made an agency's prior conduct illegal does not retroactively cure the illegal conduct.[31]

Finally, it would be salutary if agencies would also periodically review their *proposed* rules that have been pending for a long time without action and, where necessary, publicly withdraw them.[32]

---

26. 418 U.S. 683 (1974).
27. The rule at issue in that case was a delegation of authority from the Attorney General to the Special Prosecutor, 418 U.S. at 694–96 (citing United States *ex rel.* Accardi v. Shaughnessy, 347 U.S. 260 (1954)).
28. 5 U.S.C. § 551(5); *see also* Motor Vehicle Mfrs. Ass'n v. State Farm Mut. Auto. Ins. Co., 463 U.S. 29 (1983).
29. And perhaps even if it were originally issued without notice and comment.
30. *See, e.g.*, Fox Television Stations, Inc. v. FCC, 280 F.3d 1027, 1052–53 (D.C. Cir. 2002) (vacating a rule after finding that FCC had improperly failed to initiate a proceeding to repeal it).
31. *See, e.g.*, Nader v. Bork, 366 F. Supp. 104 (D.D.C. 1973) (revocation of rules concerning dismissal of special prosecutor did not make the firing of Archibald Cox legal).
32. *See, e.g.*, 56 Fed. Reg. 67,440 (Dec. 30, 1991) (withdrawing 89 FDA proposals, most of which had been pending for more than 10 years). Note that an agency notice of proposed rulemaking may become "too old" at some point anyway, at least without an additional opportunity to comment. *See* Idaho Farm Bureau Fed'n v. Babbitt, 58 F.3d 1392, 1404 (9th Cir 1995) (upholding a Fish and Wildlife rule originally proposed in 1985 and issued in 1992, but only because FWS allowed a second round of comments on new studies in 1992).

PART IV

JUDICIAL REVIEW OF AGENCY RULEMAKING

The three chapters in this part offer a general summary of the law on judicial review of agency rulemaking action.* Chapter 1 considers the *availability* of review, including such topics as reviewability, standing, venue, and timeliness (finality, exhaustion, and ripeness). Chapter 2 deals with the *scope* of judicial review and discusses the relationships, and the differences, between the various standards of review applied by the courts when reviewing agency rules. This includes the expanding jurisprudence on the meaning of "arbitrary and capricious" and on the *Chevron* case and its progeny. Chapter 3 deals with an increasingly important area of the law: court review of agency inaction. In the rulemaking context, this includes suits where the agency has refused to initiate rulemaking, suits alleging that an agency has unreasonably delayed the completion of rulemaking, and suits where an agency refused to issue a rule after the rulemaking has been completed.

---

* For a more detailed discussion of the principles of judicial review of federal administrative agency action, see the companion book published by the ABA Section on Administrative Law and Regulatory Practice, A GUIDE TO JUDICIAL AND POLITICAL REVIEW OF FEDERAL AGENCIES 1-209, 251-74 (John F. Duffy & Michael Herz eds., 2005) [hereinafter ABA GUIDE TO JUDICIAL REVIEW]. A new edition of this book is forthcoming in 2012.

Chapter 1

Availability of Judicial Review

This chapter considers a variety of topics related to the availability of judicial review of agency action. Unlike most topics included in this *Guide*, which relate specifically to rulemaking, the topics in this chapter cut across much of the field of administrative law.

Reviewability—whether the action in question is reviewable at all—will be discussed first. Then the issue of who has standing to challenge a rule will be considered. Next is a discussion of the proper forum for review—the court of appeals or the district court—and the proper venue for the proceeding. Finally, several issues relating to timeliness of a petition for review will be discussed: whether the petitioner is required to exhaust administrative remedies before obtaining review and whether the challenged agency action is deemed to be "final" and "ripe" for purposes of review. The finality and ripeness doctrines also raise issues of whether review may be obtained prior to enforcement against a violation of the rule and whether review must be sought within the time prescribed by a statute.

A. Is the Agency Action Reviewable?

In *Citizens to Protect Overton Park v. Volpe*,[1] the Supreme Court addressed the threshold question of whether petitioners were entitled to "any judicial review" of the Secretary of Transportation's action approving the building of a highway through a park in Memphis. The Supreme Court applied the presumption of reviewability that is embodied in section 701 of the Administrative Procedure Act (APA). Section 701 provides that the action of "each authority of the Government of the United States" is subject to judicial review, except where "statutes preclude judicial review"[2] or "where agency action is committed to agency discretion by law."[3] The Court found no indication in the applicable statute that Congress sought to limit judicial review and no "showing of 'clear and convincing' evidence of a . . . legislative intent to restrict access to judicial review," as required by the Court's earlier decision in *Abbott Labo-*

---

1. 401 U.S. 402 (1971).
2. 5 U.S.C. § 701(a)(1).
3. 5 U.S.C. § 701(a)(2).

ratories v. Gardner.[4] Further, the Court said, the exception from review for actions "committed to agency discretion" in the APA is narrow and is applicable only in "rare instances where 'statutes are drawn in such broad terms that in a given case there is no law to apply.'"[5] This, the Court held, was not the situation in *Overton Park*.

This presumption of reviewability of agency action, articulated by the Supreme Court in the *Abbott Laboratories* and *Overton Park* decisions, has been consistently applied over the years by the courts except in the context of challenges to agency refusals to enforce a statute.[6] Moreover, enabling statutes for regulatory and benefit programs typically provide for judicial review, and where none is expressly provided, the APA has been the basis for review except in the rare case where one of the APA exceptions is applicable.[7]

The issue of reviewability usually reaches the courts when there is some indication that Congress may have intended to preclude judicial review. Two leading cases in which the Supreme Court considered reviewability involved determinations by the Secretary of Agriculture and the Secretary of Health and Human Services (HHS). *Block v. Community Nutrition Institute*[8] involved the reviewability of milk market orders issued by the Secretary of Agriculture under the Agricultural Marketing Agreement Act. The Supreme Court held that the presumption favoring judicial review would be overcome when a contrary congressional intent was "fairly discernible in the statutory scheme."[9] The Court said that *Abbott Laboratories'* "clear and convincing" test was not a "rigid evidentiary test but a useful reminder to courts that, where substantial doubt about congressional intent exists [on the review issue], the presumption favor-

---

4. Citizens to Protect Overton Park, 401 U.S. at 410 (citing Abbott Labs. v. Gardner, 387 U.S. 136, 141 (1967)). *Abbott Labs.* permitted judicial review of a rule at the pre-enforcement stage and is discussed *infra* sec. (E). For an example of a statute that was read to preclude judicial review, *see* Carolina Medical Sales, Inc. v. Leavitt, 559 F. Supp. 2d 69 (D.D.C. 2008) (holding that the Medicare Prescription Drug Improvement and Modernization Act precluded judicial review of HHS's decision to single out mail order, and not store-front, diabetic supplies as an item and service for competitive bidding). For an interesting political science thesis surveying federal laws curtailing court jurisdiction, see Benjamin J. Keele, *Ganging Up Against the Courts: Congressional Curtailment of Judicial Review, 1988–2004*, 7 PI SIGMA ALPHA UNDERGRADUATE J. POL. 174 (2007), *available at* http://digitalcommons.unl.edu/poliscitheses/2/.

5. 401 U.S. at 410 (quoting LEGISLATIVE HISTORY OF THE APA, S. REP. No. 752, 26 (1945)).

6. This exception, developed by the Supreme Court in *Heckler v. Chaney*, 470 U.S. 821 (1985), is discussed *infra* Part IV, ch. 3. In recent years, the Courts has expanded the exception to encompass suits challenging the government's failure to implement programmatic statutes. *See* Norton v. S. Utah Wilderness Soc., 542 U.S. 55 (2004), discussed *infra* at E(3)(d).

7. It should be noted, however, that § 704 of the APA provides also that an action may not be reviewable if there is an "adequate remedy in a court." This can have some application if there is a dispute about in which court a party can bring the case—especially an unreasonable delay claim. *See* Vietnam Veterans of Am. v. Shinseki, 599 F.3d 654, 658, 659–61 (D.C. Cir. 2010).

8. 467 U.S. 340 (1984).

9. *Id.* at 351 (quoting Ass'n of Data Processing Serv. Orgs., Inc. v. Camp, 397 U.S. 150, 157 (1970)).

ing review of administrative action is controlling."[10] However, because it was "fairly discernible" from the legislative scheme that Congress did not intend to grant to consumers the right to review milk market orders, the Court would carry out that intent.[11]

The *Community Nutrition* decision seemed to have backed away somewhat from the strongly stated presumption of review in *Abbott Laboratories* and *Overton Park*. Whatever the proper understanding of that decision, in 1986 the Supreme Court returned to a more literal application of the "clear and convincing" test. In *Bowen v. Michigan Academy of Family Physicians*,[12] involving review of HHS Medicare regulations, the Supreme Court found that the presumption favoring judicial review had not been overcome, despite statutory language expressly limiting judicial review of certain types of issues. The Court stated: "We ordinarily presume that Congress intends the executive to obey its statutory commands" and therefore that the Congress "expects the courts to grant relief when an executive agency violates such command."[13] This remains the basic rule, although in several cases decided after *Michigan Academy*, the courts have found certain actions by executive officers to be so discretionary as to be unreviewable.

In *Webster v. Doe*,[14] for example, the Supreme Court held that a decision by the Director of the Central Intelligence Agency (CIA) to terminate an employee because of alleged homosexuality was not reviewable under the APA. The pertinent statute authorized the Director to terminate officers or employees of the agency "whenever

---

10. *Id.*
11. *Id.* The Supreme Court acknowledged that milk handlers were afforded the right to review under the statute. *Id.* at 346. Looking at the entire "statutory scheme," the Court discovered a "clear" congressional intent "to limit the classes" entitled to participate in the development of milk market orders and "to foreclose consumer participation in the regulatory process." *Id.* at 346–47.
12. 476 U.S. 667 (1986).
13. *Id.* at 681. *But see Thunder Basin Coal Co. v. Reich*, 510 U.S. 200 (1994), where the Court was unwilling to imply a right to challenge a mine safety regulation in district court in advance of an administrative enforcement action brought by the Labor Department. The Court ruled that the comprehensive statutory enforcement scheme prevented the district court from exercising subject-matter jurisdiction over the challenge. However, in this case, Justice Scalia, for the Court, took pains to distinguish *Abbott Labs.*, 510 U.S. 200, 212 (1994). Similarly, in *Shalala v. Ill. Council on Long-Term Care*, 529 U.S. 1 (2000), the Court, in a 5-4 decision, distinguished *Michigan Academy*. This case involved an attempt to seek pre-enforcement review of HHS regulations issued under Part A of Medicare. The Court held that the Council first had to exhaust its available administrative remedies within the Part A formal agency adjudication process before seeking review. *Michigan Academy* was distinguished because, under Part B of Medicare at issue in that case, without allowing judicial review of the regulations, challengers to the regulations would have been denied *any* opportunity to raise legal questions, since Part B adjudication was performed by non-government intermediaries that could not rule on legal questions.
14. 486 U.S. 592 (1988).

he shall deem such termination necessary or advisable in the interests of the United States."[15] The Court construed section 701(a)(1) as precluding review where Congress expressed an intent to prohibit judicial review and section 701(a)(2) as precluding review in the rare instances where the statute is drawn in such broad terms that in a given case there is no law to apply.[16] Construing the CIA statute, the Court concluded that because the CIA Director may dismiss an employee whenever he or she "deems" it necessary, this standard "fairly exudes deference to the Director" and "forecloses the application of any meaningful judicial standard of review."[17]

The *Webster* Court, however, also held that *constitutional* claims against the director were not barred and stated that where Congress intends to preclude judicial review of constitutional claims, its intent to do so must be clear to avoid the "serious constitutional question" that would arise "if a federal statute were construed to deny any judicial forum for a colorable constitutional claim."[18]

In another prominent case, the Third Circuit dismissed Senator Arlen Specter's claim under the APA that the Defense Secretary and the Defense Base Closure and Realignment Commission violated both procedural and substantive requirements of the Defense Base Closure and Realignment Act of 1990 but said the President's actions could be reviewed for unconstitutionality.[19] Senator Specter's challenge was based on the Secretary of Defense's recommendation to close a Philadelphia naval shipyard pursuant to the Act. The Act's procedure required the Defense Secretary to make recommendations to the independent Commission, which then made its own report to the President, who could reject or accept the Commission's recommendation in whole. The President's recommendation was then subject to congressional approval through joint resolution within 45 days. Absent congressional action, the Secretary of Defense was to implement the President's recommendations. In a unanimous opinion, the Supreme Court reversed the Third Circuit's decision, and held that the President's decision was unreviewable because the Base Closure Act allowed the President ultimate discretionary authority to approve or disapprove the recommendations of the Commission.[20]

---

15. 50 U.S.C. § 403(c).
16. 486 U.S. at 592.
17. *Id.* at 600. *See also* Dep't of Navy v. Egan, 484 U.S. 518 (1988) (denial of security clearance not reviewable).
18. 486 U.S. at 603 (quoting Bowen v. Mich. Acad. of Physicians, 476 U.S. 667, 681 n.12 (1986)). Justices O'Connor and Scalia dissented in *Webster v. Doe* on the availability of review of constitutional issues. *Id.* at 604.
19. Dalton v. Specter, 511 U.S. 462 (1994).
20. *Id.*; *cf.* Franklin v. Massachusetts, 505 U.S. 788 (1992) (holding the President is not an "agency" under the APA, and the agency's recommendations to the President are not "final agency action" for purposes of the judicial review provisions of the APA); *see also* Nat'l Fed'n of Fed. Emps. v. United States, 905 F.2d 400, 405 (D.C. Cir. 1990) (rejecting a federal employee challenge to base closing decisions: "[T]he problem is not that the Act is devoid of criteria; . . . the Act (through the Charter) sets forth nine specific criteria to be considered in making base closing decisions. Rather the rub is that the subject matter of those criteria is not 'judicially manage-

Nevertheless, these cases should be seen as exceptions to the presumption of reviewability.

B. Who Has Standing to Obtain Judicial Review?

1. *Under the APA*

Standing refers to the question whether the person or entity challenging an agency action has the right to secure judicial review. The APA's standing section, 5 U.S.C. § 702, provides, in pertinent part, that "[a] person suffering legal wrong because of agency action, or adversely affected or aggrieved by agency action within the meaning of a relevant statute, is entitled to judicial review thereof." Thus, section 702 states a presumption of standing to seek judicial review of agency action if a challenge is brought by a person who is "adversely affected or aggrieved" by the action "within the meaning of a relevant statute."

However, courts deciding the standing of a person[21] challenging a rule also must heed limitations on federal court jurisdiction imposed by the "case or controversy" requirement of Article III of the Constitution.[22] Article III's "case or controversy"

---

able.'" (quoting *Heckler v. Chaney*, 470 U.S. 821, 830 (1985))); *cf.* Dist., No. 1, Pac. Coast Dist., Marine Eng'rs's Beneficial Ass'n v. Maritime Admin., 215 F.3d 37, 41–42 (D.C. Cir. 2000) (finding an order granting applications to transfer the registry of eight vessels from the United States was "committed to agency discretion by law"). Although the agency regulations provided specific criteria to govern its decisions regarding transfers of registry, "the subject matter of the agency's decision does not admit of judicially manageable standards." Nor was there a different standard under the Hobbs Act. *Id.* at 42.

21. It is clear that animals can be denied standing. *See* Cetacean Cmty. v. Bush, 386 F.3d 1169, 1179 (9th Cir. 2004) (ruling that if "Congress and the President intended to take the extraordinary step of authorizing animals as well as people and legal entities to sue, they could, and should, have said so plainly. In the absence of any such statement in the ESA, the MMPA, or NEPA, or the APA, we conclude that the Cetaceans do not have statutory standing to sue" (citation and internal quotation mark omitted)); *see also* Cass R. Sunstein, *Standing for Animals (With Notes on Animal Rights)*, 47 UCLA L. REV. 1333 (2000) (arguing that Congress could grant standing to animals, but has not); Katherine A. Burke, *Can We Stand for It? Amending the Endangered Species Act with an Animal-Suit Provision*, 75 U. COLO. L. REV. 633 (2004) (same). In a few cases, animals have been listed as the named plaintiff because defendants did not object and because there were other human plaintiffs.

22. The Supreme Court explained Article III's "case-or-controversy" limitation in 1968 as follows:

> As is so often the situation in constitutional adjudication, those two words [*case* and *controversy*] have an iceberg quality, containing beneath their surface simplicity submerged complexities which go to the very heart of our constitutional form of government. Embodied in the words . . . are two complementary but somewhat different limitations. In part those words limit the business of federal courts to questions presented in an adversary context and in a form historically viewed as capable of resolution through the judicial

limitation was summarized by the Supreme Court in *Lujan v. Defenders of Wildlife*[23] as follows:

> Over the years, our cases have established that the irreducible constitutional minimum of standing contains three elements. First, the plaintiff must have suffered an "injury in fact"—an invasion of a legally protected interest which is (a) concrete and particularized, and (b) "actual or imminent, not 'conjectural' or 'hypothetical.'" Second, there must be a causal connection between the injury and the conduct complained of—the injury has to be "fairly . . . trace[able] to the challenged action of the defendant, and not . . . the result [of] the independent action of some third party not before the court." Third, it must be "likely," as opposed to merely "speculative," that the injury will be "redressed by a favorable decision."[24]

The *Lujan II* decision added the "causation" (sometimes called "traceability") and "redressability" (sometimes called "remediability") portions of the test, which are now recognized as part of the Article III case-or-controversy requirement.[25]

Participants in agency rulemaking proceedings usually are members of a class that stands to benefit or lose by the final agency rule, and standing is not normally an obstacle to review. However, some rulemaking participants—typically organizations—who have sought to challenge a rule have been denied standing because they failed to show that they would be adversely affected or injured by the rule. This was *not* the case, even though the applicability of the *Lujan II* test was reaffirmed, in the contentious and highly publicized global-warming case of *Massachusetts v. EPA* in 2007.[26]

---

process. And in part those words define the role assigned to the judiciary in a tripartite allocation of power to assure that the federal courts will not intrude into areas committed to the other branches of government. Justiciability is the term of art employed to give expression to this dual limitation placed upon federal courts by the case-and-controversy doctrine.

Flast v. Cohen, 392 U.S. 83, 94–95 (1968). The Court further remarked that "the emphasis in standing problems is on whether the party invoking federal court jurisdiction has 'a personal stake in the outcome of the controversy.'" *Id.* at 101 (citing Baker v. Carr, 369 U.S. 186, 204 (1962)). *Flast* remains the only Supreme Court case to allow taxpayer's standing—to challenge a congressional spending action as a violation of the Establishment Clause. *See* Hein v. Freedom From Religion Found., Inc., 551 U.S. 587 (2007) (declining to extend *Hein* to allow taxpayer challenges to executive expenditures).

23. 504 U.S. 555 (1992) [hereinafter *Lujan II*].
24. *Id.* at 560–61 (footnotes omitted). *See also* the summary by the D.C. Circuit in *Am. Library Ass'n v. FCC*, 401 F.3d 489, 492–93 (D.C. Cir. 2005).
25. See Cynthia Farina's lucid discussion of standing, and especially traceability and redressability, in chapter 2 of the ABA Guide to Judicial Review at 19, 43–49. (This Guide uses the word "redressability" instead of "redressibility" because the Supreme Court has used that spelling the majority of times.)
26. 549 U.S. 497 (2007).

But it *was* the case two years later in the less publicized decision in *Summers v. Earth Island Institute*.[27] Each of these two decisions were 5-4.

In short, standing law often resembles a pendulum, with swings from liberality to strictness on the part of the Supreme Court, and it is plagued by assertions that it is results-oriented.[28]

2. *Organizational Standing*

The standing of organizations to challenge agency action is particularly important with regard to review of agency rules. Organizations may sue in their own capacities or on behalf of their members.[29] The principal guidance on the standing of an organization to challenge action affecting its members was provided by the Supreme Court in 1977 in *Hunt v. Washington State Apple Advertising Commission*.[30] The Court there sensibly held that an association has standing to bring a suit on behalf of its members if one or more members would otherwise have standing to sue in their own right, the interests the association seeks to protect are germane to the association's purpose, and the litigation does not require the participation of individual members.[31]

In *Sierra Club v. Morton*,[32] the Supreme Court affirmed that standing may be obtained by those seeking to redress injury to aesthetic and environmental interests even though their injury is shared by a large number of people. However, the Court held that not only must there be an injury to a cognizable interest, but the standing test

---

27. 555 U.S. 488 (2009).
28. *See, e.g.*, Richard J. Pierce, *Is Standing Law or Politics?*, 77 N.C. L. REV. 1741, 1759–60 (1999) (finding that on the D.C. Circuit, from 1993 to 1998, Republican judges voted to deny standing to environmental plaintiffs in 79.2% of cases, while Democratic judges voted to deny standing to environmental plaintiffs in only 18.2% of cases). More fundamentally, Judge Posner has declared that "[s]ome of the most frequently mentioned grounds for the constitutional doctrine of standing are tenuous." Am. Bottom Conservancy v. U.S. Army Corps of Engrs., 650 F.3d 652, 655 (7th Cir. 2011) (Posner, J.).
29. *See* Am. Legal Found. v. FCC, 808 F.2d 84, 89 (D.C. Cir. 1987) ("When an organization seeks standing to litigate, it may do so in two capacities. First, and most obviously, it may sue on its own behalf. In this institutional capacity, the organization's pleadings must survive the same standing analysis as that applied to individuals. Second, even if an organization itself has suffered no 'injury in fact,' the organization may nonetheless sue in certain circumstances on behalf of its members."(citations omitted)).
30. 432 U.S. 333 (1977).
31. *Id.* at 343. It is noteworthy that the Apple Advertising Commission was found to have standing even though it was not technically a membership organization. The Court reaffirmed these organizational standing requirements in *Int'l Union UAW v. Brock,* 477 U.S. 274, 288–90 (1986); *see also* Grassroots Recycling Network, Inc. v. EPA, 429 F.3d 1109, 1111 (D.C. Cir. 2005) (denying organization standing because none of the members had standing to sue as individuals); Pub. Citizen v. FTC, 869 F.2d 1541, 1545, 1551 (D.C. Cir. 1989); Ctr. for Auto Safety v. Nat'l Highway Safety Admin., 793 F.2d 1322, 1328–29 (D.C. Cir. 1986).
32. 405 U.S. 727, 734 (1972).

also requires that "the party seeking review be himself among the injured."[33] Because the Sierra Club had not alleged injury to any individual members of the organization, but only to its own long-standing commitment to protecting the environment, the Court denied standing.[34] Thus the organizational standing test must be considered together with cases addressing the requirement that organizations allege injury to their specific activities or to their members' activities. The case law on this injury showing has been evolving.

3. The Injury-in-Fact Test

a. Origins—The case that first equated the case-and-controversy requirement with an injury-in-fact test, *Ass'n of Data Processing Service Organizations, Inc. v. Camp*,[35] explicitly recognized "that interest, at times, may reflect 'aesthetic, conservational, and recreational' as well as economic values."[36] This view was approved in *Sierra Club*,[37] and shortly thereafter the Court decided a case that may be the "high-water mark" of liberal standing. In *United States v. Students Challenging Regulatory Agency Procedures (SCRAP)*,[38] an association of five law students was found to have standing to challenge a general surcharge on freight shipped by rail on the ground that the rate increase would discourage the use of recyclable materials. SCRAP alleged that each of its members

> was caused to pay more for finished products, that each of its members [uses the Washington, D.C., area for recreation and aesthetic purposes] and that these uses have been adversely affected by the increased freight rates, that each of its members breathes the air within the Washington metropolitan area . . . and that this air has suffered increased pollution caused by the modified rate structure, and that each member has been forced to pay increased taxes because of the sums which must be expended to dispose of otherwise reusable waste materials.[39]

The Court granted standing on the basis of these allegations, stating, "To deny

---

33. *Id.* at 734–35.
34. *Id.* at 739–40. But the Court virtually invited the Sierra Club to move to amend its complaint to add such an allegation. *Id.* at 735 n.8; *see also* Int'l Primate Prot. League v. Adm'rs of the Tulane Educ. Fund, 895 F.2d 1056 (5th Cir. 1990) (applying the individual injury requirement to deny standing).
35. 397 U.S. 150 (1970).
36. *Id.* at 154.
37. *See id.* at 734 ("Aesthetic and environmental well-being, like economic well-being, are important ingredients of the quality of life in our society, and the fact that particular environmental interests are shared by the many rather than the few does not make them less deserving of legal protection through the judicial process.").
38. 412 U.S. 669 (1973).
39. *Id.* at 678.

standing to persons who are in fact injured simply because many others are also injured, would mean that the most injurious and widespread Government actions could be questioned by nobody. We cannot accept that conclusion."[40] This was followed in 1986 by *Japan Whaling Ass'n v. American Cetacean Society*,[41] where the Court found that the plaintiffs had "undoubtedly . . . alleged a sufficient 'injury in fact' in that the whale watching and studying of their members will be adversely affected by continued whale harvesting."[42]

b. The Lujan *cases*—But in 1990 the Supreme Court took a decidedly different approach in *Lujan v. National Wildlife Federation (Lujan I)*,[43] in which the Court denied the National Wildlife Federation standing to obtain review of the Bureau of Land Management's land-withdrawal program. The Federation alleged that the Bureau had failed to properly fulfill numerous duties under various authorities, with the result that previously withdrawn lands would be returned to the public domain and opened up to mining activities that would destroy the lands' natural beauty, thus interfering with the Federation's aesthetic and environmental interests. Unlike the situation in *Sierra Club v. Morton*,[44] the Federation had submitted affidavits by individual members who alleged their interests would be injured by a continuation of the Bureau's actions.[45] The government nevertheless sought dismissal of the case for lack of standing.

Justice Scalia, writing for the Court, found that the Federation was a proper representative of the individual members' interests[46] and that the interests raised were within the zone of interests of the statute.[47] The Court nevertheless held that the Federation lacked standing under 5 U.S.C. § 702 to bring the action in federal court, concluding that the facts alleged in the affidavits of individual organization members did not establish that those particular members' interests would be affected by the government's actions.[48] The land in dispute covered millions of acres, and the Court reasoned that the affidavits failed to show use of specific portions of that land. The Court also ruled

40. *Id.* at 688.
41. 478 U.S. 221 (1986).
42. *Id.* at 231 n.4 (citing *Sierra Club* and *SCRAP*).
43. 497 U.S. 871 (1990).
44. 405 U.S. at 727.
45. 497 U.S. at 880.
46. The Court found that the allegedly affected interests set forth in the individuals' affidavits were sufficiently related to the purposes of the organization so that "respondent [National Wildlife Federation] meets the requirements of § 702 if any of its members do." *Id.* at 885 (citing Hunt v. Wash. State Apple Advertising Comm'n, 432 U.S. 333 (1977)).
47. *Id.* at 883 ("We also think that whatever 'adverse effect' or 'aggrievement' is established by the affidavits was 'within the meaning of the relevant statute'—i.e., met the 'zone of interests' test."). See the next section for a discussion of the zone-of-interests test.
48. *Id.* at 890. Justice Scalia characterized the *SCRAP* case as an "expansive expression of what would suffice for § 702 review" that "has never since been emulated by this Court." *Id.* at 889.
49. *Id.* at 889. The Court also found a lack of finality and ripeness for review. This case was a precursor to *Norton v. Southern Utah Wilderness Alliance* and *Summers v. Earth Island Institute*, discussed below.

out the possibility that any such affidavits could form the basis for challenging the entire plan—which was held not to constitute "agency action."[49]

Two years later in *Lujan v. Defenders of Wildlife (Lujan II)*,[50] the Court, again in an opinion by Justice Scalia, similarly ruled against standing by members of a public interest group who sought to appeal a ruling that a requirement in the Endangered Species Act (that a federal agency must consult with the Secretary of the Interior before taking action that might jeopardize an endangered species) was inapplicable to projects in foreign countries. The plaintiffs filed affidavits stating that they had personally traveled to such sites to study the threatened species and planned to do so again, but the Court held these to be insufficient: "such 'some day' intentions—without any description of concrete plans, or indeed even any specification of when the some day will be—do not support a finding of the 'actual or imminent' injury that our cases require."[51]

c. The pendulum swings back in Akins *and* Laidlaw—Although *Lujan II* remains a leading case with respect to traceability and redressability (discussed below), its constrained application of the injury-in-fact doctrine has lost some steam. For example, in 1998, in *FEC v. Akins*,[52] the Court held that a group of voters had standing to complain that the Federal Election Commission's action deprived them of information—specifically, lists of donors to an organization and campaign-related contributions and expenditures that the Federal Election Campaign Act allegedly required the organization to make public. The Court held that this satisfied the "injury in fact" requirement for Article III standing, despite a government claim that the action involved only a "generalized grievance." Justice Breyer's opinion for a six-Justice majority said, "Often the fact that an interest is abstract and the fact that it is widely shared go hand in hand. But their association is not invariable, and . . . [s]uch an interest, where sufficiently concrete, may count as an 'injury in fact' . . . . We conclude that, similarly, the informational injury at issue here, directly related to voting, the most basic of political rights, is sufficiently concrete and specific . . . ."[53] Thus, as Professor Funk noted, the majority separated "generalized grievances" into two subsets:

---

50. 504 U.S. 555 (1992). Chief Justice Roberts argued this case for the government when he was Deputy Solicitor General. Shortly thereafter, while in private practice, he defended the decision at a symposium concerning the case, John G. Roberts, Jr., *Article III Limits on Statutory Standing*, 42 Duke L.J. 1219 (1993).

51. 504 U.S. at 564. A plurality of the Court also found a lack of redressability. *Id.* at 567. In addition, Justice Scalia rejected the Eighth Circuit's holding "that the injury-in-fact requirement had been satisfied by congressional conferral upon *all* persons of an abstract, self-contained, noninstrumental 'right' to have the Executive observe the procedures required by law." *Id.* at 573. But he also agreed in a footnote that "procedural rights" are "special." *Id.* at 572 n.7. The concept of "procedural injury" for standing purposes has been cut back in later cases. See below.

52. 524 U.S. 11 (1998). *Akins'* concept of an informational injury has been trimmed in later cases. *See infra* subsec. (f).

53. *Id.* at 24–25.

Where the injury is abstract and indefinite, the Court suggests that there simply is no constitutionally cognizable injury, and hence Congress could not grant judicial review of such an injury. However, where the injury is concrete, but widely shared, even shared by all people, only the prudential limitation would apply, and where, as here, Congress explicitly provides for review, that provision resolves the prudential question.[54]

In the same year, the D.C. Circuit's en banc decision in *Animal Legal Defense Fund v. Glickman*[55] upheld the standing of a plaintiff who challenged the adequacy of regulations issued by the Secretary of Agriculture under the Animal Welfare Act[56] concerning the handling, care, and transportation of animals. The original panel had held, 2-1, that none of the plaintiffs had standing.[57] The en banc court reversed, 7-4, holding that at least one of the plaintiffs, an individual who made frequent visits to a game farm where he observed primates housed in allegedly inhumane conditions, did have standing. The majority referred to "myriad cases recognizing individual plaintiffs' injury in fact based on affronts to their aesthetic interests in observing animals living in humane habitats, or in using pristine environmental areas that have not been despoiled."[58]

The trend continued the next year when the Supreme Court decided *Friends of the Earth, Inc. v. Laidlaw*,[59] involving a citizen suit under the Clean Water Act by an environmental group against a company whose pollution discharges into a river exceeded the amounts allowed by the company's discharge permit. The case also dealt with special concerns involving standing and mootness in the context of citizen suits when the cited violations of the statute had ceased, but the Court's analysis of whether the environmental group had standing even before the violations had ceased was significant in its acceptance of plaintiff's claims of environmental and recreational injury.

The 7-2 decision first held that "[t]he relevant showing for purposes of Article III standing, however, is not injury to the environment but injury to the plaintiff."[60] It then went on to conclude that various sworn statements of association members "adequately documented injury in fact."[61] The Court specifically stated that *Lujan II* "is not to the contrary,"[62] characterizing the affidavits and testimony presented by the environmental group in this case as asserting that the effects of the discharges "di-

---

54. William Funk, *Supreme Court News*, 24 ADMIN. & REG. L. NEWS 13, 15 (Fall 1998).
55. 154 F.3d 426 (D.C. Cir. 1998) (en banc).
56. *See* 7 U.S.C. § 2143(a).
57. 130 F.3d 464 (D.C. Cir. 1997).
58. *Id.* at 437. The majority also found that the plaintiff met the requisite causation, redressability, and zone-of-interests requirements.
59. 528 U.S. 167 (2000).
60. *Id.* at 181.
61. *Id.* at 183.
62. *Id.*

rectly affected those affiants' recreational, aesthetic, and economic interests."[63] And that "[t]hese submissions present dispositively more than the mere 'general averments' and 'conclusory allegations' found inadequate in [*Lujan II*]."[64] Justices Scalia and Thomas dissented vociferously.

Just how far the injury-in-fact pendulum has swung is shown by the D.C. Circuit's decision in *American Society for Prevention of Cruelty to Animals v. Ringling Bros. and Barnum & Bailey Circus*,[65] where Judge Randolph stated: "To generalize from *Glickman* and *Laidlaw*, an injury in fact can be found when a defendant adversely affects a plaintiff's enjoyment of flora or fauna, which the plaintiff wishes to enjoy again upon the cessation of the defendant's actions." The court upheld the standing of a former elephant trainer to challenge the circus's treatment of animals under the Endangered Species Act.[66]

It can also help plaintiffs to achieve standing where Congress has made findings that indicate that an injury might flow from a statutory violation.[67]

d. Massachusetts v. EPA—The pendulum swing became even more evident in *Massachusetts v. EPA*.[68] In this well-known case, the Supreme Court upheld a challenge brought by environmental and state petitioners to EPA's denial of a petition for a rulemaking to limit greenhouse gas emissions from motor vehicles. In so doing, the Court split sharply 5-4 on standing. In applying *Lujan II*, the majority found that, at

---

63. *Id.* at 184. *See also* William W. Buzbee, *The Story of* Laidlaw: *Standing and Citizen Enforcement*, in ENVIRONMENTAL LAW STORIES 201, 230 (Richard J. Lazarus & Oliver A. Houck eds., 2005) ("[I]t is difficult to overstate how completely *Laidlaw* revived citizen suits for environmental plaintiffs.").

64. *Id.*; *see also* Am. Bottom Conservancy v. U.S. Army Corp of Eng'rs, 650 F.3d 652, 657 (7th Cir. 2011) (Posner J.) (finding constitutional standing based on environmental group members' affidavits that granting permit to waste disposal company for planned landfill would "diminish the wildlife population visible to them and therefore their enjoyment of wildlife"); Am. Canoe Ass'n, Inc. v. Murphy Farms, Inc., 326 F.3d 505, 517–20 (4th Cir. 2003) (applying *Laidlaw* and finding that plaintiffs bringing a citizen suit under the Clean Water Act satisfied the injury-in-fact and traceability requirements for Article III standing).

65. 317 F.3d 334, 337 (D.C. Cir. 2003).

66. The court found that it was enough that the trainer had "stated a desire to visit the elephants." *Id.* at 338 (marking quite a difference from the Scalia analysis of the petitioners in *Lujan II*). *But see* Am. Soc. for Prevention of Cruelty to Animals v. Feld Entm't, Inc., 659 F.3d 13, 20–22 (D.C. Cir. 2011) (holding that a former circus barn helper, claiming that two techniques used to control circus elephants harmed the elephants in violation of the Endangered Species Act, was properly denied standing because he had failed to credibly prove a "personal attachment" to the elephants causing an aesthetic injury from seeing them mistreated).

67. *See, e.g.*, Renee v. Duncan, 623 F.3d 787 (9th Cir. 2010) (ruling that a challenge by parents to Department of Education regulation concerning teacher certification was allowed where congressional findings had concluded that properly certified teachers produced a better education).

68. 549 U.S. 497 (2007).

least as to petitioner Massachusetts,[69] a sufficient showing was made that EPA's failure to regulate tailpipe emissions of greenhouse gases would cause a redressable injury in fact—a loss of coastal land due to rising sea levels tied to global warming. The majority also found that the harm met the test for concreteness and particularity despite its generalized nature,[70] and that "EPA's steadfast refusal to regulate greenhouse gas emissions presents a risk of harm to Massachusetts that is both 'actual' and 'imminent.'"[71]

Chief Justice Roberts's dissent disputed each of these conclusions. He especially chided the majority for its finding that any harm caused by global warming was particularized enough for standing purposes.

Whether this headline-producing decision will have legs beyond the global-warming context is unclear. Other similar decisions issued in recent years by lower courts have been more strict in their injury-in-fact determinations.[72] And the majority's special solicitude for the state plaintiff has already led the D.C. Circuit to limit the scope of its injury-in-fact findings in global-warming cases to those cases involving state petitioners.[73]

e. Cutting back on "probabilistic injury"—Moreover, the majority's willingness to consider a risk of harm as an injury in *Massachusetts v. EPA* has already been decidedly

---

69. The majority found that states have a special claim to standing in the federal courts to protect their "quasi-sovereign" interests, *citing* Georgia v. Tennessee Copper Co., 206 U.S. 230, 237 (1907). *Id.* at 519.

70. *Massachusetts,* 549 U.S. at 522 ("That these climate-change risks are 'widely shared' does not minimize Massachusetts' interest in the outcome of this litigation." (citing Federal Election Comm'n v. Akins, 524 U.S. 11, 24 (1998))).

71. *Id.* at 521.

72. *See* Summers v. Earth Island Inst., 555 U.S. 488 (2009), discussed below.

73. *See* Center for Biological Diversity v. United States Dept. of Interior, 563 F.3d 466 (D.C. Cir. 2009), where Judge Sentelle, who had been reversed by the Supreme Court in *Massachusetts v. EPA*, held that the case stood "only for the limited proposition that, where a harm is widely shared, a sovereign, suing in its individual interest, has standing to sue where that sovereign's individual interests are harmed, wholly apart from the alleged general harm." *Id.* at 476–77. The court found environmental plaintiffs lacked standing to challenge an offshore oil-leasing program as causing global warming because the harm was too speculative. The court also denied standing to a plaintiff Indian tribe, which it did recognize as a sovereign, because the tribe failed to allege that it would suffer "its own individual harm apart from the general harm caused by climate change." *Id.* at 477. *But see* Connecticut v. Am. Elec. Power Co., Inc., 582 F.3d 309 (2d Cir. 2009), *aff'd on standing by an equally divided Court, but rev'd on other grounds,* Am. Elec. Power Co, Inc., v. Connecticut, 131 S. Ct. 2527 (2011) (taking a broader view of states' power to assert standing). For detailed analysis of doctrines governing standing for states in federal courts, *see generally* Kathryn A. Watts & Amy J. Wildermuth, Massachusetts v. EPA: *Breaking New Ground on Issues Other Than Global Warming*, 102 Nw. U. L. Rev. 1029 (2007) (discussing how the Court in *Massachusetts* essentially adopted the D.C. Circuit's well-settled views on the subject); Amy J. Wildermuth, *Why State Standing in* Massachusetts v. EPA *Matters*, 27 J. Land, Resources, & Envtl. L. 273 (2007).

cut back. Indeed, it has become more clear since that petitioners claiming a only *probability* of harm caused by the government's action may not satisfy the injury-in-fact test.[74] In *Mountain States Legal Foundation v. Glickman*,[75] the D.C. Circuit had held in 1996 that standing would be allowed if petitioners could show "at least *both* (i) a *substantially* increased risk of harm and (ii) a *substantial* probability of harm with that increase taken into account."[76] But in 2007, in *Public Citizen, Inc. v. National Highway Traffic Safety Administration*,[77] the court denied standing to a public interest group who claimed that deficiencies in an agency safety standard increased the risk to its members of suffering harm in auto accidents.[78] As Professors Watts and Murphy have commented, "One might think that an increased risk of injury in the *future* causes an actual injury in the *present*—if only because it is unpleasant in the present to contemplate running an elevated risk in the future."[79] However, according to Judge Kavanaugh, "this injury could not suffice for standing, however, because it was too abstract (rather than concrete) and generalized (rather than particularized or differentiated)."[80] Moreover, an alternative argument—that "ultimate harms that will be suffered by individuals in car accidents" due to the standard's flaws did not suffice because the risk that any given individual will suffer such harm due to the standard was "remote and speculative."[81] The court did allow a remand to permit Public Citizen to show that it met the test of *Mountain States*, but the court rejected that showing in an ensuing opinion.[82]

Two year later, in *Summers v. Earth Island Institute*,[83] the Supreme Court signaled its agreement with the D.C. Circuit's more restrictive approach in *Public Citizen*. In *Summers*, a broad procedural challenge to a Forest Service approval of a salvage sale in a particular tract of national forest land, bolstered by affidavits of members' visits to that tract, was settled, leaving challenges to several other tracts unresolved. But the challenges to those tracts lacked any particularized affidavits, other than an affidavit supplied by one member (Mr. Bensman) who alleged he "has visited many National

---

74. For a case finding the plaintiff's affidavits averring injury to be too speculative, *see* Grassroots Recycling Network, Inc. v. EPA, 429 F.3d 1109, 1112–13 (D.C. Cir. 2005). *But see* Sabre, Inc. v. Dep't of Transp., 429 F.3d 1113, 1117–19 (D.C. Cir. 2005) (finding standing to challenge agency's assertion of enforcement jurisdiction over practices that petitioner plans to take based on sealed supplemental declaration confirming present existence of such marketing plans).

75. 92 F.3d 1228, 1234–35 (D.C. Cir. 1996).

76. Public Citizen, Inc. v. Nat'l Highway Traffic Safety Admin., 489 F.3d 1279, 1295 (D.C. Cir. 2007) (citing *Mountain States Legal Found.*, 92 F.3d at 1234–35).

77. 489 F.3d 1279 (D.C. Cir. 2007).

78. *Id.* at 1291.

79. Kathryn Watts & Richard Murphy, *Judicial Review* chapter, *in* DEVELOPMENTS IN ADMINISTRATIVE LAW AND REGULATORY PRACTICE 2007-2008, at 107 (Jeffrey S. Lubbers ed., 2009).

80. *Id.* at 108 (citing *Public Citizen*, 489 F.3d at 1297–98).

81. *Id.* (quoting *Public Citizen*, 489 F.3d at 1293).

82. Public Citizen, Inc. v. Nat'l Highway Traffic Safety Admin., 513 F.3d 234, 238–41 (D.C. Cir. 2008).

83. 555 U.S. 488 (2009).

Forests and plans to visit several unnamed National Forests in the future."[84] Justice Scalia, writing for the majority of five Justices, found that this affidavit was not sufficient to allow the suit to continue.

> There may be a chance, but is hardly a likelihood, that Bensman's wanderings will bring him to a parcel about to be affected by a project unlawfully subject to the regulations. Indeed, without further specification, it is impossible to tell *which* projects are (in respondents' view) unlawfully subject to the regulations. . . . Here we are asked to assume not only that Bensman will stumble across a project tract unlawfully subject to the regulations, but also that the tract is about to be developed by the Forest Service in a way that harms his recreational interests, and that he would have commented on the project but for the regulation. Accepting an intention to visit the National Forests as adequate to confer standing to challenge any Government action affecting any portion of those forests would be tantamount to eliminating the requirement of concrete, particularized injury in fact.[85]

While perhaps in line with *Lujan II*'s rejection of general affidavits of plans to travel to view animals overseas, and perhaps a result of a pleading failure (in that one of the plaintiff organizations should have located a member who had specific plans to visit the remaining tracts), the case illustrates the technical nature of the standing test.

Justice Breyer, for the dissenters, argued for a more practical approach. "A threat of future harm may be realistic even where the plaintiff cannot specify precise times, dates, and GPS coordinates" for the expected injury.[86] Not surprisingly, he invoked *Massachusetts v. EPA* in support of his argument.

Professors Watts and Murphy lamented that "[h]ad Justice Breyer found one more justice to join him, the law of associational standing would have shifted to a more, dare one say, realistic and probabilistic understanding of the concept of injury as applied to large voluntary organizations. This would have reduced the need for massive organizations such as Sierra Club to play the game of finding just the right member who can allege just the right assertions for standing."[87]

In 2010, the Supreme Court, in *Monsanto Co. v. Geertson Seed Farms*,[88] without even citing *Summers*, reopened the door to at least some forms of probabilistic injury claims. It upheld the standing of alfalfa farmers who were seeking an injunction against the deregulation of genetically modified alfalfa plants even though their injuries were characterized by the marketers as alleged risks of future contamination. In so doing, the unanimous Court agreed that the farmers had established a "reasonable probabil-

---

84. *Id.* at 495.
85. *Id.* at 495–96 (emphasis in original).
86. *Id.* at 506.
87. Kathryn Watts & Richard Murphy, *Judicial Review Chapter, in* Developments in Administrative Law and Regulatory Practice 2008-2009, at 101 (Jeffrey S. Lubbers ed., 2010).
88. 130 S. Ct. 2743 (2010).

ity" that their crops would be contaminated by the deregulation, and, perhaps more importantly, that that probability had led to immediate testing and prevention costs that were clearly concrete injuries in fact.[89]

This brings us back full circle to the D.C. Circuit's *Mountain States Legal* test for "probabilistic standing"[90] which seems to remain a good guide to this corner of the standing law.[91]

f. Special rules for "procedural injuries" or "informational injuries"?—In *Lujan II,* Justice Scalia wrote in a footnote that "procedural rights" are "special."[92] Professor Farina concluded that, properly interpreted, *Lujan II* "does not disturb existing understandings that a justiciable claim may be presented by the agency's failure to comply with statutory mandates (1) that certain factors be analyzed or considered, or (2) that certain forms of participation be allowed *even though* these mandates be deemed 'merely' procedural."[93] However, in *Town of Castle Rock, Colorado v. Gonzales,* the Supreme Court began to signal that this was a limited exception. The Court, in dicta, suggested that an entitlement to "nothing but procedure" is "inadequate even to sup-

---

89. *Id.* at 2754–55. A similar case is *Sherley v. Sibelius,* 610 F.3d 69 (D.C. Cir. 2010) (allowing doctors who conducted research with adult stem cells to challenge proposed expansion of federal funding to embryonic stem cell research, because of immediate costs of time spent on preparing competitive grant applications). *See also* Amnesty Int'l USA v. Clapper, 638 F.3d 118 (2d Cir. 2011), *reh'g en banc denied,* 667 F.3d 163 (2011) (holding that the plaintiffs challenging the constitutionality of a statute allowing interception of communications from overseas U.S. citizens have standing based on the present injury caused by their reasonable fear that avoiding future injury requires them to take costly steps to avoid future interceptions); Am. Bottom Conservancy v. U.S. Army Corp of Eng'rs, 650 F.3d 652, 658 (7th Cir. 2011) (Posner, J.) (finding that the injury to environmental group members from granting federal permit to a waste disposal company for a planned landfill was not conjectural because it was "likely" that the company would be able to navigate the supplementary state permitting process).

90. *Supra* note 75.

91. *See also* Bradford C. Mank, Summers v. Earth Island Institute: *Its Implications for Future Standing Decisions,* 40 ENVTL. L. REP. NEWS & ANALYSIS 10,958 (2010); Michelle Fon Anne Lee, *Surviving* Summers, 37 ECOLOGY L.Q. 381 (2010); Bradford Mank, *Revisiting the* Lyons *Den:* Summers v. Earth Island Institute's *Misuse of* Lyons's *"Realistic Threat" of Harm Standing Test,* 42 ARIZ. ST. L.J. 837 (2010); Robin Kundis Craig, *Removing "The Cloak of a Standing Inquiry": Pollution Regulation, Public Health, and Private Risk in the Injury-in-Fact Analysis,* 29 CARDOZO L. REV. 149 (2007); Daniel A. Farber, *Uncertainty as a Basis for Standing,* 33 HOFSTRA L. REV. 1123 (2005).

92. *Lujan II,* 504 U.S. 555, 572 n.7 (1992).

93. Farina, ABA GUIDE TO JUDICIAL REVIEW, *supra* note 25, at 35. For a case upholding standing on this ground, *see* Elec. Power Supply Ass'n v. FERC, 391 F.3d 1255, 1262 (D.C. Cir. 2004) (holding the Commission's rule providing for an exemption from the APA ex parte communications ban in formal proceedings could adversely affect members' "particularized interests in fair decision making").

port standing."[94] And, in *Summers v. Earth Island Institute*,[95] the Court, through Justice Scalia, made clear that although a congressionally granted procedural right could obviate the need to meet the redressability prong of the standing test, its asserted violation would not, in and of itself, suffice for injury in fact.

In *Summers*, as the majority characterized it, the environmental challengers argued they had standing because:

> [T]hey have suffered procedural injury, namely that they have been denied the ability to file comments on some Forest Service actions and will continue to be so denied. But deprivation of a procedural right without some concrete interest that is affected by the deprivation—a procedural right *in vacuo*—is insufficient to create Article III standing. Only a "person who has been accorded a procedural right to protect *his concrete interests* can assert that right without meeting all the normal standards for redressability and immediacy." . . . It makes no difference that the procedural right has been accorded by Congress. That can loosen the strictures of the redressability prong of our standing inquiry—so that standing existed with regard to the Burnt Ridge Project, for example, despite the possibility that Earth Island's allegedly guaranteed right to comment would not be successful in persuading the Forest Service to avoid impairment of Earth Island's concrete interests. Unlike redressability, however, the requirement of injury in fact is a hard floor of Article III jurisdiction that cannot be removed by statute.[96]

As Professor Jordan has explained, in *Summers* the Court "emphasized that a denial of an alleged right to file comments is not by itself sufficient to support a claim of 'procedural standing.' Instead the denial of the procedural right must affect 'some concrete interest,' such as an environmental harm as to which the plaintiff would have standing."[97] Nor does the denial of a petition for rulemaking guarantee petitioners' standing.[98]

---

94. 545 U.S. 748, 764 (2005). *See also* Ctr. for Law & Educ. v. Dep't of Educ., 396 F.3d 1152, 1159–60 (D.C. Cir. 2005) (denying an advocacy group standing to challenge final rule on the basis of an alleged defect in the composition of a negotiated rulemaking committee, due to a lack of particularized harm).

95. 555 U.S. 488 (2009).

96. *Id.* at 496–97 (citation omitted).

97. William S. Jordan III, *News from the Circuits*, 36 ADMIN. & REG. L. NEWS 21 (Winter 2011). *But see* Ctr. for Biological Diversity v. U.S. Dep't of Interior, 563 F.3d 466, 479 (D.C. Cir. 2009) (finding environmental plaintiffs did show a concrete procedural injury in that Interior's alleged violation of the National Environmental Policy Act (NEPA) and the Outer Continental Shelf Lands Act in failing to give proper consideration to the costs of greenhouse gas emissions and the effects of global warming "could cause a substantial increase in the risk to their enjoyment of the animals affected by offshore drilling, and that our setting aside and remanding of the Leasing Program would redress their harm").

98. *See* Illinois Mun. Gas Agency v. FERC, 258 Fed. App'x 336, 337 (D.C. Cir. 2007) (Denial of a petition for rulemaking does create a cause of action, but does not necessarily confer standing.).

The same fate seems to be befalling the concept of "informational injury" recognized in *FEC v. Akins*, discussed above.[99] After *Akins*, lower courts were divided in their interpretation of this concept.[100] *Summers'* treatment of procedural injury has seemed to affect courts' treatment of informational injury as well. For instance, in *The Wilderness Society, Inc. v. Rey*,[101] the Ninth Circuit reversed a district court's grant of standing to environmental plaintiffs who claimed an informational injury from a Forest Service regulation restricting notice of proposed actions "concerning projects and activities implementing land and resource management plans for the National Forest System."[102] The plaintiffs contended that the information would have assisted them in "furthering [its] goals of forest conservation, and in educating [its] members and the public in general about environmentally harmful Forest Service projects."[103] The appeals court, citing *Summers*, determined that this argument "simply reframes every procedural deprivation in terms of informational loss. This approach would allow an end run around the Supreme Court's procedural injury doctrine and render its direction in *Summers* meaningless."[104] It distinguished *Akins* and cases involving the Federal Advisory Committee Act as situations where the deprivation of statutorily required information was the injury itself. On the other hand, the Forest Service law's notice requirements were intended not to provide a right to information but instead "as a predicate to public comment."[105]

g. Proof of injury—Of course, it is necessary for petitioners to make sure that evidence of such injury appears in the rulemaking record. As the Tenth Circuit stated:

---

99. 524 U.S. 11 (1998). *See* text accompanying note 52.
100. *Compare* Pub. Citizen v. DOJ, 491 U.S. 440, 449 (1989) (holding an alleged informational injury from a violation of the Federal Advisory Committee Act was enough to confer standing), Am. Canoe Ass'n, Inc. v. City of Louisa Water & Sewer Comm'n, 389 F.3d 536, 546 (6th Cir. 2004) (finding that Clean Water Act violations affected the plaintiffs' "monitoring and reporting obligations to their members"), *with* Heartwood Inc. v. U.S. Forest Serv., 230 F.3d 947 (7th Cir. 2000) (ruling that the deprivation of information required by NEPA constitutes cognizable injury), *with* Judicial Watch v. FEC, 180 F.3d 277 (D.C. Cir. 1999) (denying informational standing to plaintiffs who complained they were deprived of information when FEC failed to act on their complaints of alleged FECA violations). *See also* Farina, ABA GUIDE TO JUDICIAL REVIEW, *supra* note 25, at 31–33; Salt Inst. v. Leavitt, 440 F.3d 156 (4th Cir. 2006) (distinguishing *Akins* and rejecting standing based on informational injury where Information Quality Act did not create any right to information).
101. 622 F.3d 1251 (9th Cir. 2010).
102. *Id.* at 1258–59.
103. *Id.* at 1259 (alterations in original).
104. *Id.* at 1260.
105. *Id.* at 1259. The court added: "To ground a claim to standing on an informational injury, the [statute in question] must grant a right to information capable of supporting a lawsuit." In support of this, it cited Cass R. Sunstein, *Informational Regulation and Informational Standing:* Akins *and Beyond*, 147 U. PA. L. REV. 613, 642–43 (1999) (concluding that the "principal question after *Akins*, for purposes of 'injury in fact,' is whether Congress or any other source of law gives the litigant a right to bring suit").

[S]tanding cannot be inferred argumentatively from [the party's] averments . . . but rather must affirmatively appear in the record." Such affidavits must "allege concrete injuries or threats of injuries."[106] And in *Sierra Club v. EPA*,[107] the D.C. Circuit indicated that "a petitioner whose standing is not self[-]evident should establish its standing by the submission of its arguments and any affidavits or other evidence appurtenant thereto at the first appropriate point in the review proceeding." As the court later expanded, "In other words, *Sierra Club* makes it clear that a party who knows or should know that there are doubts about its standing should address those doubts before oral argument."[108] Because standing is jurisdictional, even if both petitioners and the government assume that the petitioners' standing was self-evident, the court may raise the standing issue *sua sponte*. But the D.C. Circuit later made clear that "[n]othing in *Sierra Club* suggests that it is intended to create a 'gotcha' trap whereby parties who reasonably think their standing is self-evident nonetheless may have their cases summarily dismissed if they fail to document fully their standing at the earliest possible stage in the litigation."[109] Thus, in that case the court allowed the association petitioner to submit additional affidavits to establish injury-in-fact to one or more of its members.[110] The association did so and the court later granted standing to it.[111]

The courts have also made clear that although participation in rulemaking at the agency level "does not, in and of itself, satisfy *judicial* standing requirements,"[112] it may in some situations be a prerequisite.[113]

---

106. *See, e.g.*, Heartwood Inc., v. Agpaoa, 628 F.3d 261 (6th Cir. 2010) (denying standing because plaintiffs' affidavits were not sufficiently particularized concerning the large area affected by the allegedly illegal logging plan); Cent. & S.W. Servs., Inc. v. EPA, 220 F.3d 683, 702 (5th Cir. 2000) (denying standing because the environmental organization's affidavits "do not demonstrate that [the two members] are threatened with injury from PCBs to any greater extent than any other person in the United States who drives on the country's roadways and drinks water in a town that has landfills").

107. 292 F.3d 895, 900 (D.C. Cir. 2002). On the issue of affidavits, *see generally* Amy J. Wildermuth & Lincoln L. Davies, *Standing, on Appeal*, 2010 U. ILL. L. REV. 957. *Sierra Club* is discussed at 986–91.

108. Am. Library Ass'n v. FCC, 401 F.3d 489, 493 (D.C. Cir. 2005).

109. *Id.*

110. *Id.* at 495–96.

111. *See* Am. Library Ass'n. v. FCC, 406 F.3d 689 (D.C. Cir. 2005). *But see* Int'l Bhd. of Teamsters v. Transp. Sec. Admin., 429 F.3d 1130, 1136 n.4 (D.C. Cir. 2005) (plaintiff union denied organizational standing to challenge agency guidance because its "post-argument proffer does not clear up the standing issue").

112. Ctr. for Auto Safety v. Nat'l Highway Safety Admin., 793 F.2d 1322, 1329 n.41 (D.C. Cir. 1986), *accord* Competitive Enter. Inst. v. Dep't of Transp., 856 F.2d 1563, 1565 (D.C. Cir. 1988) ("Petitioners do not have a right to seek court review of administrative proceedings merely because they participated in them.").

113. *See* discussion *infra* section E(1).

4. Causation (Traceability and Redressability)

Although *Lujan II* treated traceability and redressability as two separate strands of the standing analysis,[114] the "elements are typically treated in tandem" as part of the "causation" analysis.[115] As *Lujan II* described it in simple terms, causation means that "the action or inaction has caused [the plaintiff's] injury," and redressability means that "a judgment preventing or requiring the action will redress it."[116] In challenges to rulemaking, these issues normally arise where "the purported cause of injury (i.e., promulgation of final rules) and the injury itself is [sic] separated by intervening actors and events."[117] In those situations, the D.C. Circuit has observed that "the causation and redressability inquiries may appear to merge":[118]

> In such cases, both prongs of standing analysis can be said to focus on principles of causation: fair traceability turns on the causal nexus between the agency action and the asserted injury, while redressability centers on the causal connection between the asserted injury and judicial relief. *Despite these similarities, however, each inquiry has its own emphasis.* Causation remains inherently historical; redressability quintessentially predictive.[119]

Lujan II was also noteworthy for another observation—to the effect that regulated parties can more easily demonstrate causation than beneficiaries of regulation, including in the latter group individuals and organizations who challenge agency rules as being too weak:

> When the suit is one challenging the legality of government action or inaction, the nature and extent of facts that must be averred (at the summary judgment stage) or proved (at the trial stage) in order to establish standing depends con-

---

114. *See* quotation *supra* text accompanying note 23.
115. *See* Farina, ABA GUIDE TO JUDICIAL REVIEW, *supra* note 25, at 43 (citing 3 KENNETH CULP DAVIS & RICHARD J. PIERCE, JR., ADMINISTRATIVE LAW TREATISE § 16.8, at 29 (3d ed. 1994) ("If there are cases in which redressability differs from [traceability], they are rare.")).
116. *Lujan II*, 504 U.S. 555, 562 (1992). *See also* the passage from *Summers*, text at note 96, *supra*.
117. Ctr. for Law & Educ. v. Dep't of Educ., 396 F.3d 1152, 1160 n.2 (D.C. Cir. 2005).
118. *Id.* (citing Freedom Republicans v. FEC, 13 F.3d 412, 418 (D.C. Cir. 1994). Indeed, the D.C. Circuit has pointed out that redressability is "the element of standing that is virtually always merely the reciprocal of causation. As a separate element, it is implicated only when the court's power to redress an injury caused by an illegal act is independently impaired." Vietnam Veterans of Am. v. Shinseki, 599 F.3d 654, 658 (D.C. Cir. 2010) (citations omitted).
119. *Id.* (citing Freedom Republicans v. FEC, 13 F.3d 412, 418 (D.C. Cir. 1994)) (emphasis added by citing court). In *Center for Law & Education*, the court denied standing to a parent seeking to challenge the result of a negotiated rulemaking conducted by the Department of Education because "the connection between the beginning and end of the purported chain [of causation] remains so attenuated that we cannot hold the alleged injury to be 'fairly traceable to' the final agency rules 'and not the result of the independent action' of the State of Illinois." *Id.* at 1161 (quoting *Lujan II*, 504 U.S. at 562).

siderably upon whether the plaintiff is himself an object of the action (or for-gone action) at issue. If he is, there is ordinarily little question that the action or inaction has caused him injury, and that a judgment preventing or requiring the action will redress it. When, however, as in this case, a plaintiff's asserted injury arises from the government's allegedly unlawful regulation (or lack of regula-tion) of *someone else*, much more is needed. In that circumstance, causation and redressability ordinarily hinge on the response of the regulated (or regu-lable) third party to the government action or inaction—and perhaps on the response of others as well. . . . Thus, when the plaintiff is not himself the object of the government action or inaction he challenges, standing is not precluded, but it is ordinarily "substantially more difficult" to establish.[120]

This passage has been has been characterized as creating "potential causation hurdles that asymmetrically burden beneficiary standing."[121] These problems have generally not been too severe, because courts have allowed challengers to argue that for standing purposes, "[t]he proper comparison for determining causation is not be-tween what the agency did and the status quo before the agency acted. Rather, the proper comparison is between what the agency did and what the plaintiffs allege the agency should have done under the statute."[122] Nor is a causation problem posed simply because the agency continues to maintain enforcement discretion.[123] And some agency failures to provide legally required information[124] or follow procedural or analytical requirements have, without further showings, been held to present a justi-ciable claim.[125] Finally, Congress retains the power to "articulate chains of causation that will give rise to a case or controversy where none existed before."[126]

Nevertheless, the potential asymmetric burdens to beneficiary standing remain problematic.

---

120. *Lujan II*, 504 U.S. 555, 562 (1992). Note, however, that only a plurality of the Court joined part III(B) of the opinion that applied the redressability prong to this case. Justice Kennedy, joined by Justice Souter, explained: "In light of the conclusion that respondents have not demonstrated a concrete injury here sufficient to support standing under our precedents, I would not reach the issue of redressability that is discussed by the plurality in Part III-B." *Id.* at 580 (Kennedy, J. concurring).
121. Farina, ABA GUIDE TO JUDICIAL REVIEW, *supra* note 23, at 44.
122. Animal Legal Def. Fund v. Glickman, 154 F.3d 426, 441 (D.C. Cir. 1998) (en banc).
123. *See* FEC v. Akins, 524 U.S. 11, 25 (1998) (finding "respondents' 'injury in fact' is 'fairly traceable' to the FEC's decision not to issue its complaint, even though the FEC might reach the same result exercising its discretionary powers lawfully").
124. *Id.*
125. *See* note 100 *supra. But see generally supra* subpart (B)(3)(f).
126. *Lujan II*, 504 U.S. 555, 580 (1992) (Kennedy, J. concurring). The *Laidlaw* case provides an example of court deference to congressional findings about the effects of the statutory rem-edy on private behavior.

5. *Prudential Principles Governing Standing*

In addition to the Constitution's "case or controversy" requirement, interpreted to mandate "injury-in-fact," federal courts apply certain "prudential principles" to decide whether to grant standing to parties challenging agency action. The Supreme Court explained:

> Although we have not exhaustively defined the prudential dimensions of the standing doctrine, we have explained that prudential standing encompasses "the general prohibition on a litigant's raising another person's legal rights, the rule barring adjudication of generalized grievances more appropriately addressed in the representative branches, and the requirement that a plaintiff's complaint fall within the zone of interests protected by the law invoked."[127]

Unlike the constitutional requirements, Congress may by statute eliminate prudential standing concerns by expanding standing to the full limit allowed by the Constitution.[128]

    a. Avoiding abstract and generalized questions. Among other things, these prudential standing principles are designed to avoid having courts decide abstract questions of wide public significance that other governmental institutions may be more competent to address.[129] Thus, courts may decline to accept jurisdiction where the plaintiff, rather than asserting his or her own legal rights and interests, rests his or her claim on the rights or interests of third parties.[130] Courts will refrain from deciding "'abstract questions of wide public significance' which amount to 'generalized grievances,' pervasively shared and most appropriately addressed in the representative branches."[131] This principle has been applied to deny standing to Members of Congress who sought to overturn the line item veto legislation where the Court held that the Members "alleged no injury to themselves as individuals . . . [and] the institutional injury they allege is wholly abstract and widely dispersed."[132]

---

127. Elk Grove Unified Sch. Dist. v. Newdow, 542 U.S. 1 (2004) (quoting Allen v. Wright, 468 U.S. 737, 751 (1984)).
128. Ctr. for Auto Safety v. Nat'l Highway Safety Admin., 793 F.2d 1322, 1335 (D.C. Cir. 1986) (citing Warth v. Seldin, 422 U.S. 490, 501 (1974)). The D.C. Circuit concluded that "[t]he broad standing to challenge [fuel economy] standards established by [the statute] removes any necessity to limit judicial review for prudential reasons." *Id.* at 1336.
129. Warth v. Seldin, 422 U.S. 490, 499 (1974). *But see* the discussion of *FEC v. Akins*, text at notes 52–54.
130. Americans United for Separation of Church and State, Inc. v. Valley Forge Christian Coll., 454 U.S. 464, 474 & n.10 (1982).
131. *Id.* at 475 (citing Warth v. Seldin, 422 U.S. 490, 499–500 (1974)); *see also* Allen v. Wright, 468 U.S. 737, 754–55 (1984); Int'l Primate Prot. League v. Adm'rs of the Tulane Educ. Fund, 895 F.2d 1056, 1060 (5th Cir. 1990).
132. Raines v. Byrd, 521 U.S. 811 (1997). *But see* U.S. House of Representatives v. U.S. Dep't of Commerce, 11 F. Supp. 2d 76, 83–90 (D.D.C. 1998) (three-judge court) (holding that the House

b. The "zone-of-interests" test. The zone-of-interests test, first enunciated by the Supreme Court in 1970, is often included among the prudential standing principles, but it may also be viewed as an interpretation of 5 U.S.C. § 702. Because agency rules are based on statutes and review typically is governed by section 702, the zone-of-interests test is particularly important in the rulemaking context.

This test also originated with *Ass'n of Data Processing Service Organizations, Inc. v. Camp*,[133] in which Justice Douglas, writing the majority opinion, first addressed the injury requirement for constitutional standing and then added "apart from the 'case' or 'controversy' test," standing concerns "the question whether the interest sought to be protected by the complainant is arguably within the zone of interests to be protected or regulated by the statute or constitutional guarantee in question."[134] The Court went on to hold that the plaintiffs, who were in the business of supplying data-processing services, had standing to challenge a Comptroller of the Currency ruling allowing national banks to provide data-processing services to other banks and their customers.[135] The Court held that data processors were within the zone of interests established by the Bank Service Corporation Act.[136]

Two partially dissenting Justices in *Ass'n of Data Processing Service Organizations* criticized the zone-of-interests test as a "wholly unnecessary and inappropriate second step upon the constitutional requirement for standing."[137] The test subsequently generated much confusion among the lower courts as well as criticism in legal literature.[138]

---

had standing to challenge the methodology for conducting the census), *aff'd on other grounds*, Dep't of Commerce v. U.S. House of Representatives, 525 U.S. 316 (1999). The Supreme Court did not reach the question of the House's standing, since it found other parties had standing. Justices Stevens and Breyer, who dissented on the merits, would have also ruled that the House had standing because it has a concrete and particularized "institutional interest in preventing its unlawful composition." 525 U.S. at 365 (Stevens, J., dissenting).

133. *Supra* note 35.

134. Ass'n of Data Processing Serv. Org., Inc. v. Camp, 397 U.S. 150, 153 (1970).

135. The Court concluded as follows:

The [Bank Service Corporation Act and the National Bank Act] are clearly "relevant" statutes within the meaning of § 702. The Acts do not in their terms protect a specified group. But their general policy is apparent; and those whose interests are directly affected by a broad or narrow interpretation of the Acts are easily identifiable. It is clear that petitioners, as competitors of national banks which are engaging in data processing services, are within that class of "aggrieved" persons who, under § 702, are entitled to judicial review of "agency action."

Id. at 157.

136. *Id.* at 155.

137. *Id.* at 169 (Brennan, J., concurring and dissenting).

138. Writing in 1982, Professor Davis wrote that "the 'zone' test is sometimes used, but most of the time it is not, and no guides exist as to whether or when it is used." KENNETH CULP DAVIS, ADMINISTRATIVE LAW TREATISE § 24:17 (2d ed. 1982); *see also* Clarke v. Securities Indus. Ass'n, 479 U.S. 388, 396 n.11 (1987) (citing scholarly criticism of the test).

In *Clarke v. Securities Industry Association*,[139] the Supreme Court seemed to loosen the test. *Clarke* also involved another challenge to a Comptroller of the Currency decision brought by competitors of national banks. The Comptroller had approved the applications of two national banks to establish offices offering discount brokerage services at various locations, and an association of securities brokers and investment bankers sought review on the ground that this action violated the National Bank Act's branching restrictions. The Court reviewed the legislative history of the McFadden Act (which had amended the National Bank Act) and concluded that the association asserted "a plausible relationship to the policies underlying §§ 36 and 81 of the National Bank Act," and, therefore, had standing to bring the lawsuit.[140]

The Court, however, applied a more demanding zone-of-interests test in *Air Courier Conference v. American Postal Workers Union*.[141] The Postal Service had issued a regulation loosening its statutory monopoly on mail delivery, allowing private companies to provide overnight service to foreign countries. Two postal worker unions challenged the regulation, but the Court denied standing because the unions were not within the relevant zone of interests. The Court said that the relevant statute "exists to ensure that postal service will be provided to the citizenry at large, and not to secure employment for postal workers."[142] The unions argued that the statutes governing labor-management relations provided the necessary nexus, but the Court refused to permit this "leapfrog."[143]

A lower court case decided between *Clarke* and *Air Courier Conference* that provides a good illustration of the application of the zone-of-interests test to decide standing in a rulemaking case is *Hazardous Waste Treatment Council v. EPA*.[144] The D.C.

---

139. 479 U.S. 388 (1987).
140. *Id.* at 403. In deciding the standing question, the *Clarke* majority expounded at length on the meaning of the zone-of-interests test and sought to explain it as "a gloss on the meaning" of 5 U.S.C. § 702 intended to place some limit on the broad "adversely affected" language of that provision. *Id.* The Court explained the test as follows:

> The "zone of interest" test is a guide for deciding whether, in view of Congress' evident intent to make agency action presumptively reviewable, a particular plaintiff should be heard to complain of a particular agency decision. In cases where the plaintiff is not itself the subject of the contested regulatory action, the test denies a right of review if the plaintiff's interests are so marginally related to or inconsistent with the purposes implicit in the statute that it cannot reasonably be assumed that Congress intended to permit the suit. The test is not meant to be especially demanding; in particular, there need be no indication of congressional purpose to benefit the would-be plaintiff.

> *Id.* at 399–400 (footnote and citation omitted).
141. 498 U.S. 517 (1991).
142. *Id.* at 528.
143. *Id.* at 530.
144. 861 F.2d 277 (D.C. Cir. 1988); *see also* Pub. Citizen v. FTC, 869 F.2d 1541, 1547 n.8 (D.C. Cir. 1989) (stating the zone-of-interests test only "requires some indicia—however slight—that the litigant before the court was intended to be protected, benefited or regulated by the statute under which suit is brought" (citations omitted)).

Circuit was petitioned by a trade association of firms engaged in the treatment of hazardous waste and the manufacture of waste treatment equipment to review an EPA rule under the Resource Conservation and Recovery Act of 1976. The gist of the complaint was that EPA's rule was not as comprehensive or as strict as the statute required, thus causing injury to the environment and a diminished market for their services and equipment.

The court concluded that association members whose waste treatment facilities would be adversely affected by contaminated waste clearly had standing to challenge the rule.[145] However, the majority held that association members who complained of business loss did not have standing under the zone-of-interests test because their interest was only "marginally related" to the Act's environmental purposes.[146] The court said, "When we grant standing to a party with only an oblique relation to the statutory goal, we run the risk that the outcome could, even assuming technical fidelity to law, in fact thwart the congressional goal."[147] The association, therefore, was found to have standing to challenge only those aspects of EPA's rules that affected user or "consumer" interests and not those aspects that related to business or competitor interests.[148]

The pendulum swung back again in another banking case decided by the Supreme Court in 1998. The issue was whether banks challenging the regulatory practices of the National Credit Union Administration were within the zone of interests sought to be protected by the Federal Credit Union Act. In *National Credit Union Admin. v. First City Bank*, the Supreme Court, by a 5-4 vote, affirmed the D.C. Circuit's decision that the bank plaintiffs had standing, holding that the banks were within the zone of interests protected by the membership limitations in the Federal Credit Union Act.[149] The majority found this case to be analogous to the competitors' standing allowed in *Data Processing*, *Clarke*, and other financial services cases. *Air Courier* was distinguished on the grounds that in enacting the postal monopoly law at issue in that case, Congress had not intended to protect the interests of the postal union. What was most striking in this case was that the most conservative Justices (Rehnquist, Thomas, and Scalia) all voted to grant standing, while the most liberal Justices (Breyer, Souter, and Stevens) voted to deny standing.[150]

---

145. 861 F.2d at 282.
146. *Id.* at 283. In earlier cases applying the zone-of-interests test, courts found that entrepreneurs seeking to protect their competitive advantage had no standing to challenge Occupational Safety and Health Administration standards, which were issued under a statute whose purpose was worker safety, not business advantage. *See* Fire Equip. Mfrs. Ass'n, Inc. v. Marshall, 679 F.2d 679, 682 (7th Cir. 1982); Calumet Indus. v. Brock, 807 F.2d 225 (D.C. Cir. 1986).
147. 861 F.2d at 283–84.
148. *Id.* at 285–87.
149. 522 U.S. 479 (1998). The D.C. Circuit decisions are First Nat'l Bank & Trust Co. v. Nat'l Credit Union Admin., 988 F.2d 1272 (D.C. Cir. 1993) (finding standing); 90 F.3d 525 (D.C. Cir. 1996) (deciding case on merits against the agency).
150. On the merits, the majority went on to overturn the agency's interpretation of the Act, applying step one of *Chevron. See* discussion *infra* Part IV, ch. 2 n.164.

Justice Thomas for the majority restated the test as follows: "[I]n applying the 'zone of interests' test . . . we first discern the interests arguably . . . to be protected by the statutory provision at issue; we then inquire whether the plaintiff's interests affected by the agency action in question are among them."[151] He then added a footnote defending this test:

> Contrary to the dissent's contentions, our formulation does not "eviscerat[e]" or "abolis[h]" the zone of interests requirement. Nor can it be read to imply that, in order to have standing under the APA, a plaintiff must merely have an interest in enforcing the statute in question. The test we have articulated . . . differs only as a matter of semantics from the formulation that the dissent has accused us of "eviscerating" or "abolishing" . . . .[152]

Nevertheless, the Supreme Court seemed to be sending a message to loosen the zone-of-interests test, and most lower courts have now accepted the language from *Clarke* that the zone-of-interests test excludes only those whose interests are "so marginally related to or inconsistent with the purposes implicit in the statute that it cannot reasonably be assumed that Congress intended to permit the suit."[153] One exception is the D.C. Circuit panel in *American Federation of Government Employees, AFL-CIO v. Rumsfeld*,[154] which found that employees of a military base and their union failed the zone-of-interests test in their challenge to a lack of safety and health programs at the base, because the OSHA Act did not authorize private rights of action. This decision is a potentially broad reading of the zone-of-interests test.

The Supreme Court also made clear that the zone-of-interests test is a prudential limitation on standing and that Congress can modify it. In *Bennett v. Spear*,[155] the

---

151. 522 U.S. at 935 (internal quotation marks omitted).
152. *Id.* at 936 n.7 (alteration in original) (citation omitted).
153. *See* Thompson v. N. Am. Stainless, LP, 131 S. Ct. 863, 870 (2011) (citing *Clarke* and restating the test). *See also* Harvey v. Veneman, 396 F.3d 28, 34–35 (1st Cir. 2005) (citing *Clarke*); PDK Labs. Inc. v. DEA, 362 F.3d 786, 791 (D.C. Cir. 2004) (finding customer of importer challenging agency suspension of importation to be within the zone, citing *Clarke* and *National Credit Union Administration*).
154. 321 F.3d 139 (D.C. Cir. 2003); *see also* Nat'l Ass'n of Home Builders v. U.S. Army Corps of Eng'rs, 417 F.3d 1272, 1287–88 (D.C. Cir. 2005) (association of local government public works agencies failed to show it was within NEPA's zone of interests in challenging the Corps' rulemaking for the failure to do a programmatic environmental impact statement); Rosebud Sioux Tribe v. McDivitt, 286 F.3d 1031 (8th Cir. 2002) (interests of lessee of land from Indian Tribe was not within the zone of interests to be protected or regulated by statutes enacted to protect Indian interests); TAP Pharms. v. Dep't of Health & Human Servs., 163 F.3d 199, 202–08 (4th Cir. 1998) (drug manufacturer's interest in selling its drug was not within the zone of interests protected by Medicare Part B, and such interest thus did not provide the manufacturer with prudential standing to challenge the benefits administrator's Medicare Part B reimbursement policy). *But see* Amgen, Inc. v. Scully, 357 F.3d 103, 110 (D.C. Cir. 2004) (declining to follow *TAP Pharmaceuticals*).
155. 520 U.S. 154 (1997).

Court addressed the citizen suit provision of the Endangered Species Act that authorizes "any person" to sue to challenge certain violations of the Act. The challengers sought to overturn an agency biological opinion and a related jeopardy determination issued under the Act, which would have required modification in a water project to protect two species of fish. The plaintiff ranchers who challenged the modification alleged that the government had violated a directive to "take into consideration the economic impact" and to use "the best scientific data available." The Court, per Justice Scalia, permitted this aspect of the lawsuit to proceed as a citizen suit because it deemed this directive to state a nondiscretionary duty on the part of the government official. The Court further held that the "any person" language "negates the zone-of-interests test (or, perhaps more accurately, expands the zone of interests)."[156] The Court also addressed other claims made by plaintiffs alleging that the agency's ultimate actions were arbitrary and capricious. These APA claims were not encompassed by the citizen suit provision, so it was necessary for the Court to decide whether plaintiffs' economic interests fell within the zone of interests to be protected or regulated by the Act. The government maintained that only those seeking to expand species protections should fall within that zone, but the Court disagreed.[157]

C. The Proper Forum for Review: Court of Appeals or District Court?

The forum for judicial review of agency rules, as for review of other agency action, is determined by statute. The APA contains only a general directive providing that review may be governed by a particular statute, such as the one authorizing the rule, or by a statute governing the review of orders of particular agencies.[158] If not, review would be predicated on the more general jurisdictional statutes and would be sought in the district court; the latter is normally called, somewhat misleadingly, "nonstatutory review."

1. Statutory Review

Statutes containing judicial review provisions applicable to rulemaking generally call for direct, pre-enforcement review in the courts of appeals.[159] Most of the

---

156. *Id.* at 164.
157. Significantly, the Court looked to the specific language of the provision in question, not the overall Act. It stated, "While this [provision] no doubt serves to advance the ESA's overall goal of species preservation, we think it readily apparent that another objective (if not indeed the primary one) is to avoid needless economic dislocation produced by agency officials zealously but unintelligently pursuing their environmental objectives." *Id.* at 176–77. The Court also found that plaintiffs had suffered injury in fact, and that the agency's action was "final." *Id.* at 178.
158. 5 U.S.C. § 703.
159. A significant exception is the National Labor Relations Act, which is silent on the subject, thereby allowing challengers of Board rules to file in district courts.

major rulemaking programs are covered by such a provision, and statutes establishing the programs normally contain requirements as to venue, timing of review, and scope of review.

One special judicial review statute, the Administrative Orders Review Act (colloquially known as the Hobbs Act),[160] governs the review of "orders" of several important agencies.[161] Court decisions have established that such orders issued by these agencies include "rules" for the purpose of judicial review.[162] The Act provides for review in the courts of appeals.[163]

The Administrative Conference recommended placing direct review of rules in the courts of appeals in instances where (1) the rule is so significant that a district court decision would likely be appealed, and (2) where other "orders" of agencies are already reviewed that way. The complete Conference statement on the subject is as follows:

The appropriate forum for the review of rules promulgated pursuant to the notice-and-comment procedures of 5 U.S.C. 553 should be determined in the light of the following considerations:

(a) Absence of a formal administrative record based on a trial-type hearing does not preclude direct review of rules by courts of appeals because: (i) Compliance with procedural requirements of 5 U.S.C. 553, including the requirement of a statement of reasons for the rule, will ordinarily produce a record adequate to the purpose of judicial review, and (ii) the administrative record can usually be supplemented, if necessary, by means other than an evidentiary trial in a district court.

(b) Direct review by a court of appeals is appropriate whenever: (i) An initial district court decision respecting the validity of a rule will ordinarily be appealed or (ii) the public interest requires prompt, authoritative determination of the validity of the rule.

(c) Rules issued by agencies that regularly engage in formal adjudication and whose "orders" are subject by statute to direct review by the courts of appeals will normally satisfy the criteria of (b) above and in any event should be reviewable directly by the court of appeals.

(d) Rules of other agencies that do not satisfy the criteria of (b) above should generally be reviewable in the first instance by the district courts.[164]

---

160. 28 U.S.C. §§ 2341–2351.
161. The Act applies, for example, to certain orders of the Departments of Agriculture and Transportation, Federal Communications Commission, Federal Maritime Commission, Nuclear Regulatory Commission, Merit Systems Protection Board, and Surface Transportation Board.
162. *See* David P. Currie & Frank I. Goodman, *Judicial Review of Federal Administrative Action: Quest for the Optimum Forum*, 75 COLUM. L. REV. 1, 39–40 (1975).
163. 28 U.S.C. § 2342.
164. ACUS Recommendation 75-3, *The Choice of Forum for Judicial Review of Administrative Action*, 40 Fed. Reg. 27,926 (July 2, 1975); *see also* Fla. Power & Light v. Lorian, 470 U.S. 729, 744 (1985) (noting that "factfinding capacity of the district court is . . . typically unnecessary to judicial review of agency decisionmaking").

In October 1984, the D.C. Circuit, in *Telecommunications Research and Action Center (TRAC) v. FCC*,[165] decided that where a statute places review of agency action in the court of appeals, a suit seeking relief that might affect the court of appeals' *future* jurisdiction is also subject to the exclusive jurisdiction of the court of appeals. *TRAC* involved a suit by public interest groups and nonprofit corporations for a writ of mandamus to compel the FCC to decide certain unresolved proceedings that had been pending for some time. Recognizing that the law of the circuit was in "disarray" on the issue of the proper forum for claims of agency unreasonable delay, the court attempted to resolve the jurisdictional question.[166] The court first noted that there was no dispute that the court of appeals, which was assigned jurisdiction by statute over final FCC actions, also had jurisdiction over claims of unreasonable delay.[167] It then reached the further conclusion, based on an analysis of the relevant statutes and "compelling policy reasons," that the court of appeals' jurisdiction was exclusive.[168] Noting that appellate courts "develop an expertise concerning the agencies assigned them for review," the court concluded that exclusive court of appeals jurisdiction "promotes judicial economy and fairness to the litigants by taking advantage of that expertise" and "eliminates duplicative and potentially conflicting review and the delay and expense incidental thereto."[169]

The language of the *TRAC* decision is broad, and its holding has been applied to agencies other than the FCC and to rulemaking proceedings as well as to adjudication. For example, in *International Union, U.A.W. v. Donovan*,[170] the D.C. Circuit, noting that the OSHA statute vested exclusive review of OSHA standards in the court of appeals,[171] held that the court of appeals had exclusive jurisdiction in the case[172] and that the district court properly transferred the case to the court of appeals.[173] The Seventh Circuit has also held that "[i]f a decision of an administrative agency is based, in substantial part, on a statutory provision providing for exclusive review by a court of appeals, then the entire proceeding must be reviewed by a court of appeals."[174] In

---

165. 750 F.2d 70 (D.C. Cir. 1984).
166. *Id.* at 75. The court also considered the merits of the question when agency delay was "unreasonable." *Id.* at 79–81. *See* discussion *infra* Part IV, ch. 3(B)(2).
167. This conclusion was based on the All Writs Act, 28 U.S.C § 1651(a), the APA, 5 U.S.C. §§ 555(b), 706(1), and statutes referring expressly to FCC orders, 28 U.S.C. § 2342(i) and 47 U.S.C. § 402(a).
168. 750 F.2d at 78.
169. *Id.* The court indicated, however, that there might be a "small category of cases" not subject to court of appeals review in which denial of review in the district court "will truly foreclose all judicial review." *Id.*
170. 756 F.2d 162 (D.C. Cir. 1985).
171. 29 U.S.C. § 655(f).
172. 756 F.2d at 165. The case involved a suit to force OSHA to issue a formaldehyde standard.
173. *Id.*; *see also* Ukiah Adventist Hosp. v. FTC, 981 F.2d 543 (D.C. Cir. 1992).
174. *See* Suburban O'Hare Comm'n v. Dole, 787 F.2d 186, 192–93 (7th Cir. 1986); *see also* Alliance for Legal Action v. FAA, 69 F. App'x 617, 620–21, 2003 WL 21546006 (4th Cir.) (table case) (holding that as long as part of an FAA order is issued pursuant to Part A authority, review of the order is within the exclusive jurisdiction of the courts of appeals under § 46110(a)).

general, cases decided after *TRAC* have utilized a two-part test to determine whether jurisdiction to review agency action lies in the district court or in the court of appeals: (1) does the statute commit review of agency action to the court of appeals, and (2) does the action seek relief that might affect the circuit court's jurisdiction?[175]

The Administrative Conference recommended that, as a general rule, the *TRAC* principles should be followed.[176] It also recommended that where jurisdiction of delay cases lies in the court of appeals, procedures be developed to ensure prompt and efficient disposition of the claims.[177]

2. Non-statutory Review

If there is no specifically applicable judicial review provision governing the agency's rule, the challenger will normally attempt to seek review through an action for an injunction or declaratory relief in the district court. Jurisdiction must be obtained through one of the general jurisdictional statutes. The most frequently asserted provision is 28 U.S.C. § 1331, the so-called federal question provision, which gives the district courts "original jurisdiction of all civil actions wherein the matter in controversy . . . arises under the Constitution, laws, or treaties of the United States . . . ." Until 1976, this section also contained a $10,000 jurisdictional amount requirement, but following the recommendation of the Administrative Conference,[178] this provision was eliminated for suits against the United States, a federal agency, or federal officer or employee acting in his or her official capacity.[179] Other jurisdictional bases have been less often invoked since this 1976 amendment, but possibilities include 28 U.S.C. § 1337 (actions arising under commerce-related statutes) and 28 U.S.C. § 1361 (mandamus jurisdiction). The APA was held not to be an independent basis for jurisdic-

---

175. *See, e.g.*, Natural Res. Def. Council v. Abraham, 355 F.3d 179, 194 (2d Cir. 2004) ("bifurcated and piecemeal review is disfavored," thus the court of appeals has jurisdiction to review challenge to DOE's delay of effective date of energy-efficiency rules where it would have jurisdiction to review merits of rules). *But see* Am. Farm Bureau v. EPA, 121 F. Supp. 2d 84 (D.D.C. 2000) (finding that challenges to agency inaction under provisions of the Act in question should be heard by the district court).

176. ACUS Recommendation 88-6, *Judicial Review of Preliminary Challenges to Agency Action*, 53 Fed. Reg. 39,585 (Oct. 11, 1988). The recommendation is based on Thomas O. Sargentich, *Jurisdictional Debate in Administrative Law: A Comment on* Telecommunications Research and Action Center v. FCC, 1988 ACUS 281; *see also* Thomas O. Sargentich, *The Jurisdiction of Federal Courts in Administrative Cases: Developments*, 41 ADMIN. L. REV. 201 (1989).

177. Recommendation 88-6, *supra* note 176.

178. ACUS Recommendation 68-7, *Elimination of Jurisdictional Amount Requirement in Judicial Review*, 1968 ACUS 170.

179. Pub. L. No. 94-574, 90 Stat. 2721 (1976) (codified at 28 U.S.C. § 1331). In 1980, Congress eliminated the jurisdictional amount for all federal question cases. Pub. L. No. 96-486, 94 Stat. 2369 (1980).

tion in 1977 but only after the question was rendered largely moot by the amendment to section 1331.[180]

Non-statutory review is conducted by a district court, but such review is also on the administrative record and is normally subject to the "arbitrary or capricious" review provisions. District courts usually rely on the rulemaking record assembled by the agency, and if that record is inadequate, a remand to the agency is the remedy.[181] Also, the D.C. Circuit has held that when the district court has first reviewed an agency action under the APA, on appeal, the appeals court will review the administrative action "directly," under the arbitrary-and-capricious standard, without according any "particular deference to the judgment of the district court."[182]

D. The Venue (Location) of Review

There is no single provision governing venue for petitions for review of rules in the courts of appeals. The Administrative Orders Review Act, for example, provides for the filing of petitions in the circuit where "the petitioner resides or has its principal office, or in the [D.C. Circuit]."[183] Certain other specific statutes providing for review in the courts of appeals, such as the OSHA Act, contain similar venue language.[184] Other statutes provide for *exclusive* review of certain types of rules in the D.C. Circuit. The Clean Air Act, for example, provides for exclusive review of certain "nationally applicable" regulations in the D.C. Circuit, with "locally or regionally applicable" rules reviewable in "the appropriate circuit."[185] The Clean Water Act, on the other hand, places review of all rules under the Act in the circuit where the objecting party "resides or transacts such business."[186]

In the 1980s, critics of provisions permitting or requiring review in the D.C. Circuit proposed changes in the venue laws in an attempt to have more cases filed in the "local" districts and circuits.[187] The Administrative Conference recommended *against*

---

180. Califano v. Sanders, 430 U.S. 99 (1977).

181. Camp v. Pitts, 411 U.S. 138, 142–43 (1973); *cf.* Nat'l Nutritional Foods v. Weinberger, 512 F.2d 688 (2d Cir. 1975). District courts sometimes do hold evidentiary hearings on review of agency action, as where de novo review is required by statute. *See, e.g.*, 8 U.S.C. § 1105(a)(5).

182. Natural Res. Def. Council, Inc. v. Daley, 209 F.3d 747, 752 (D.C. Cir. 2000) (citing Associated Builders & Contractors, Inc. v. Herman, 166 F.3d 1248 (D.C. Cir. 1999)), *accord* Oceana, Inc. v. Locke, No. 10-5299, 2011 WL 2802989 (D.C. Cir. May 13, 2011). *See also* Am. Bioscience, Inc. v. Thompson, 269 F.3d 1077, 1083 (D.C. Cir. 2000) ("[W]hen a party seeks review of agency action under the APA, the district judge sits as an appellate tribunal. The entire case on review is a question of law.") (footnote omitted) (internal quotation marks omitted).

183. 28 U.S.C. § 2343.

184. 29 U.S.C. § 655(f).

185. 42 U.S.C. § 7607(b)(i).

186. 33 U.S.C. § 1369(b)(i); *see* ACUS Recommendation 76-4, *Judicial Review Under the Clean Air Act and Federal Water Pollution Control Act*, 41 Fed. Reg. 56,767 (1976); David Currie, *Judicial Review Under Federal Pollution Laws*, 62 Iowa L. Rev. 1221 (1977).

187. *See, e.g.*, National Legal Center for the Public Interest, Venue at the Crossroads (1982).

any fundamental changes in the venue laws governing suits against the government, although it did urge enactment of a provision that would require notification of state attorneys general of certain suits filed in the District Court for the District of Columbia and a modification of the venue transfer provision, 28 U.S.C. § 1404, to explicitly provide that intervenors may seek transfer.[188]

Because the venue provisions in many of the individual statutes governing direct review of rules in the courts of appeals allow for review in several possible circuits, and because there are perceived differences in the various circuits' approach to judicial review, "forum shopping" opportunities abound. Consequently, multiple appeals are filed in different circuits as parties seek to bring lawsuits in the forum thought to be most favorable to them. Prior to 1988, under 28 U.S.C. § 2112(a), the agency was required to file the record of the proceedings in the circuit in which the *first* petition was filed. Because filing rules in the circuits normally permit cursory petitions for review, the "first to file" rule of section 2112(a) and modern communications technology combined to precipitate "races to the courthouse," which became subject to bitter litigation[189] and widespread criticism.[190]

To reduce forum-shopping litigation, the Administrative Conference in 1980 recommended legislation to authorize the Administrative Office of the U.S. Courts to oversee a random selection procedure for choosing the court with initial jurisdiction to conduct the review proceeding when multiple petitions have been filed.[191] This approach, designed to eliminate races to the courthouse by eliminating any advantage for "first filed" petitions, was adopted by Congress in 1988.[192] Under this amendment to section 2112(a), if within 10 (calendar) days of the issuance of the agency order the agency receives petitions for review in two or more courts of appeals, the agency notifies the Judicial Panel on Multidistrict Litigation. The panel then designates "by means of random selection" a single court of appeals from among those in which petitions were filed and consolidates the petitions for review in that court of appeals. If only one petition for review is filed within the 10-day period, that court of appeals hears the appeal. The amendment provides that a stay may be issued by any court of appeals in which proceedings related to an agency order have been filed, but the stay may be modified or revoked by any court of appeals to which the proceeding is transferred. Finally, the amendment, like the original section 2112, provides: "For

---

188. ACUS Recommendation 82-3, *Federal Venue Provisions Applicable to Suits Against the Government*, 47 Fed. Reg. 30,706 (July 15, 1982).

189. *See, e.g.*, Indus. Union Dep't v. Bingham, 570 F.2d 965 (D.C. Cir. 1977).

190. *See, e.g.*, Thomas O. McGarity, *Multi-Party Forum Shopping for Appellate Review of Administrative Action*, 129 U. PA. L. REV. 302 (1980).

191. ACUS Recommendation 80-5, *Eliminating or Simplifying the 'Race to the Courthouse' in Appeals from Agency Action*, 45 Fed. Reg. 84,954 (Dec. 24, 1980).

192. Pub. L. No. 100-236, 101 Stat. 1731 (1988) (codified as amended at 28 U.S.C. § 2112(a)).

the convenience of the parties in the interest of justice, the court in which the record is filed may thereafter transfer all the proceedings with respect to that order to any other court of appeals."[193]

In 2011, the Judicial Panel on Multidistrict Litigation revised its implementing rules, which contain more detailed procedures for carrying out the amendment.[194] The selection process operates by having the clerk of the panel or its representative "randomly select a circuit court of appeals from a drum containing an entry for each circuit wherein a constituent petition for review is pending."[195] The rules expressly provide that multiple petitions in a single circuit "shall be allotted only a single entry in the drum."[196]

The venue of review of non-statutory review actions against the federal government brought in district court is governed by 28 U.S.C. § 1391(e)(1), which allows suit "in any judicial district in which (A) a defendant in the action resides; (B) a substantial part of the events or omissions giving rise to the claim occurred, or a substantial part of property that is the subject of the action is situated, or (C) the plaintiff resides if no real property is involved in the action."[197] This obviously gives the plaintiff wide latitude in choosing the forum.

E. The Appropriate Timing for Judicial Review

The courts have developed a number of concepts to determine whether a case should be judicially reviewable at a particular time. These concepts, which include the notions of finality, exhaustion of remedies, and ripeness, are attempts to balance the efficient use of judicial and agency resources and interests of parties challenging agency action. The concepts are sometimes difficult to distinguish, and they overlap and interrelate in a number of ways.[198] In one recent simplifying decision, however, involving a pre-enforcement challenge to an agency policy, the D.C. Circuit has stated that *standing* and *ripeness* are not separate requirements. Standing's requirement of injury-in-fact does not present "an independent jurisdictional barrier" when a petitioner demonstrates hardship for ripeness purposes. "[W]e need not analyze standing separately because 'it is clear that [any challenge to petitioner's standing] is not an independent issue from ripeness.'"[199]

---

193. 28 U.S.C. § 2112(a)(3).
194. Rules of Procedure of the U.S. Judicial Panel on Multidistrict Litigation, rules 25.1–25.6 (filed July 6, 2011), *available at* http://www.jpml.uscourts.gov/Rules___Procedures/Panel_Rules-Amended-7-6-2011.pdf.
195. *Id.* rule 25.5.
196. *Id.* This provision would negate any advantage derived from "stuffing the ballot box."
197. 28 U.S.C.A. § 1391(e)(1), as amended by Pub. L. No. 112-63, 125 Stat 758, 764 (Dec. 7, 2011).
198. *See* Ticor Title Ins. Co. v. FTC, 814 F.2d 731 (D.C. Cir. 1987) (dismissing a facial constitutional challenge to FTC's prosecutorial authority, but splitting three ways on whether dismissal was properly based on exhaustion, ripeness, or finality).
199. Venetian Casino Resort LLC v. Equal Emp't Opportunity Comm'n, 409 F.3d 359, 366–67 (D.C. Cir. 2005).

1. Finality

The "finality" requirement derives from the APA, which provides for judicial review of "final agency action."[200] It has been held not to be a jurisdictional requirement;[201] instead it is primarily concerned with protecting the integrity of the administrative process and preventing waste of judicial resources on an agency position that may be changed.[202]

The Supreme Court's summary of the law of finality in *Bennett v. Spear*[203] is now the widely cited test:

> As a general matter, two conditions must be satisfied for agency action to be "final": First, the action must mark the "consummation" of the agency's decisionmaking process—it must not be of a merely tentative or interlocutory nature. And second, the action must be one by which "rights or obligations have been determined," or from which "legal consequences will flow."[204]

In the context of challenges to rulemaking, finality is generally not a major issue if the rule being challenged is a final legislative rule. Serious finality issues can, however, arise when the agency action is a non-legislative rule such as a policy statement. Pre-enforcement challenges to such guidance face an uphill battle in meeting the "consummation" and "legal consequences" prongs of the *Bennett* test for finality, even if the guidance has been subjected to notice and comment.[205]

In some cases, however, challengers might argue the guidance is a de facto rule or binding norm. For example, see *Barrick Goldstrike Mines Inc. v. Browner*,[206] where

---

200. 5 U.S.C. § 704.
201. Trudeau v. FTC, 456 F.3d 178, 183–84 & nn. 6–7 (D.C. Cir. 2006); *accord* Nulankeyutmonen Nkihtaqmikon v. Impson, 503 F.3d 18, 33 (1st Cir. 2007); Long Term Care Partners, LLC v. United States, 516 F.3d 225 (4th Cir. 2008) (citing Arbaugh v. Y & H Corp., 546 U.S. 500 (2006)).
202. *See generally* FTC v. Standard Oil Co., 449 U.S. 232 (1980). For a modern version of that case, *see* Reliable Automatic Sprinkler Co., Inc. v. Consumer Product Safety Comm'n, 324 F.3d 726, 730 (D.C. Cir. 2003).
203. 520 U.S. 154 (1997).
204. *Id.* at 177–78 (citation omitted); *see also* Nat'l Ass'n of Home Builders v. Norton, 415 F.3d 8 (D.C. Cir. 2005) (finding that a "recommended survey protocol" for endangered butterfly issued by Fish and Wildlife Survey was not final for the purposes of judicial review because they are not "documents 'by which rights or obligations have been determined, or from which legal consequences will flow'" (quoting *Bennett*, 520 U.S. at 178)).
205. New Jersey v. U.S. Nuclear Regulatory Comm'n, 526 F.3d 98, 103 (3d Cir. 2008) (guidance document concerning proposed long-term control license for certain facilities was not final order of NRC even though although it had been subjected to public notice and comment).
206. 215 F.3d 45 (D.C. Cir. 2000) (finding EPA guideline final and ripe for review). The classic case is *National Automatic Laundry & Cleaning Council v. Schultz*, 443 F.2d 689, 702 (D.C. Cir. 1971) (Leventhal, J.) (holding that a letter ruling signed by the agency head "following reflective examination" was final and ripe for review). *See also* Oregon v. Ashcroft, 368 F.3d 1118 (9th Cir. 2004), *aff'd*, Gonzales v. Oregon, 546 U.S. 243 (2006)) (enjoining an interpretive rule

Judge Randolph made clear that policy statements can, in some circumstances, be considered "final" for the purposes of judicial review.

That the issuance of a guideline or guidance may constitute final agency action has been settled in this circuit for many years. In *Better Government,* we rejected the proposition that if an agency labels its action an "informal" guideline, it may thereby escape judicial review under the APA. In *Ciba-Geigy,* we held that a letter from an agency official stating the agency's position and threatening enforcement action unless the company complied constituted final agency action. In *Appalachian Power Co. v. EPA,* we held again that a guidance document reflecting a settled agency position and having legal consequences for those subject to regulation may constitute "final agency action" for the purpose of judicial review.[207]

In a procedural challenge to a guidance document (issued without notice and comment), the D.C. Circuit explained:

> Under our precedents, the question of whether an agency document is a final "regulation . . . or requirement" [under the RCRA statute] is substantially similar to the question of whether it is a legislative rule under the APA. Thus, . . . because there is no dispute that the . . . guidance document was not issued pursuant to APA rulemaking procedures, there are only two options: "Either the petition [for review] must be dismissed for lack of jurisdiction" because the guidance *is not* a final regulation . . . "or the . . . [g]uidance should be vacated" on the merits because it *is* a final regulation but was promulgated in violation of the APA.[208]

The court, in a later case, seemed to say that the logical conclusion of this reasoning was that a valid (non-binding) policy statement cannot meet the second prong of the *Bennett v. Spear* finality test precisely because it lacks the sort of

---

issued by the Attorney General which declares that physician-assisted suicide serves no "legitimate medical purpose" as required for legal prescription of a controlled substance after finding it final and ripe for review). In *Oregon v. Ashcroft,* the majority's justiciability discussion, *id.* at 1120–21, is brief, but Judge Wallace's dissent on the merits contains a thoughtful discussion of finality, *id.* at 1146–48, in which he agrees that the directive is "final" because it "clearly marks the consummation of the Attorney General's decision making process" and "created direct and immediate consequences for physicians who wish to prescribe controlled substances for assisted suicide." Neither the Supreme Court majority nor the dissenters addressed finality.

207. *Id.*, 215 F.3d at 48 (citing Better Gov't Ass'n v. Dep't of State, 780 F.2d 86, 93 (D.C. Cir. 1986); Ciba-Geigy Corp. v. EPA, 801 F.2d 430, 436–39 n.9 (D.C. Cir. 1986); Appalachian Power Co. v. EPA, 208 F.3d 1015, 1020–23 (D.C. Cir. 2000); Bennett v. Spear, 520 U.S. 154, 177–78 (1997)) (some citations and internal quotations omitted).

208. Cement Kiln Recycling Coal. v. EPA, 493 F.3d 207, 226 (D.C. Cir. 2007) (citations omitted). While the case was interpreting the finality provision of the RCRA statute, it seems applicable to an APA finality defense as well.

binding legal force that could determine "rights or obligations" or lead to "legal consequences."[209]

These kinds of decisions have led commentators to wonder whether this type of "mechanical" approach might lead to "the counter-intuitive conclusion that an agency legal interpretation cannot have 'legal consequences' for a party for the sake of finality unless the interpretation is either embodied in a legislative rule or in a final order directed at the party itself."[210] This seems too mechanical because "[o]ther agency legal interpretations can obviously . . . have grave consequences for regulated entities."[211] And contrary to the above language, the D.C. Circuit has been open to challenges to policies issued in ways other than through legislative rules or final orders directed at the party itself.[212]

The issue arises in various contexts. For example, courts have normally but not always refused to directly review agency statements made in the preamble to a proposed or final rule.[213] In two cases involving agency notices that have had economic

---

209. Cohen v. United States, 578 F.3d 1, 6 (D.C. Cir. 2009) (finding an IRS "notice" to be reviewable because it was not a valid policy statement, using the same test for procedural validity and reviewability). This decision was partially vacated and then partially affirmed and partially reversed en banc, but the finality aspect of the panel decision was not revisited. Cohen v. United States, 650 F.3d 717, 723 (D.C. Cir. 2011) (en banc). *See also* Ctr. for Auto Safety, Inc. v. Nat'l Hwy. Traffic Safety Admin., 452 F. 3d 798 (D.C. Cir. 2006) (letters concerning automakers' regional recalls amounted to a general statement of policy rather than a binding rule, and therefore were not subject to review); New Jersey v. U.S. Nuclear Regulatory Comm'n, 526 F.3d 98, 102–03 (3d Cir. 2008) (NRC guidance document not final agency action). For a thoughtful treatment of these issues, see Gwendolyn McKee, *Judicial Review of Agency Guidance Documents: Rethinking the Finality Doctrine*, 60 Admin. L. Rev. 371 (2008).

210. Kathryn A. Watts & Richard Murphy, *Judicial Review* chapter, Developments in Administrative Law and Regulatory Practice 2009-2010, at 74 (Jeffrey S. Lubbers ed., 2011).

211. *Id.*

212. *See* Teva Pharms. USA, Inc. v. Sebelius, 595 F.3d 1303 (D.C. Cir. 2010) (FDA statutory interpretation adopted in informal adjudications that, if applied to the plaintiff drug manufacturer, would have deprived it of the right to be the exclusive generic marketer of a drug for a period of six months ruled sufficiently final, as part of ripeness analysis, because agency had taken the position that its interpretation was compelled by the statutory text and therefore was unlikely to change it, and that it would have a clear legal consequence on the plaintiff); Reckitt Benckiser Inc. v. EPA, 613 F.3d 1131, 1138 (D.C. Cir. 2010) (EPA policy regarding re-registration of rodenticides was definitive and unequivocal and "has practical and significant legal effects"). See Watts & Murphy, *supra* note 210, at 73–76 for some helpful commentary on these two cases.

213. *See* Natural Resources Def. Council v. EPA, 559 F.3d 561, 564–65 (D.C. Cir. 2009) ("While preamble statements may in some unique cases constitute binding, final agency action susceptible to judicial review, this is not the norm."); New York v. EPA, 413 F.3d 3, 20–21 (D.C. Cir. 2005) (finding that a challenge to an allegedly new interpretation of an existing rule contained in the preamble to a new rule was not ripe); Ariz. Pub. Serv. Co. v. EPA, 211 F.3d 1280, 1296 (D.C. Cir. 2000) (challenge to conclusion in preamble to a final rule not ripe, particularly where agency subsequently published a notice suggesting it had not made up its mind on the issue); Fla. Power & Light Co. v. EPA, 145 F.3d 1414 (D.C. Cir. 1998) (where applicable statute allowed

impact on regulated parties, the Third Circuit denied review because they were only advisory warnings.[214] There has also been a recent flurry of cases, with different results, concerning the finality of agency letters.[215]

---

for review of "final rules," court finds statement made in proposed rule preamble to not be final because the statements had not been published in the CFR and did not have binding effect on private parties or the agency); Envtl. Prot. Info. Ctr. v. Pac. Lumber Co., 266 F. Supp. 2d 1101, 1123 n.17 (N.D. Cal. 2003 (preamble statement not binding).

But see Whitman v. Am. Trucking Ass'ns, Inc., 531 U.S. 457, 477–79 (2001) (finding EPA implementation policy to be reviewable based on materials published in the explanatory preamble to EPA's final ozone standard in which EPA announced that it had reconsidered aspects of its implementation policy); Sabre, Inc. v. Dep't of Transp., 429 F.3d 1113, 1116 (D.C. Cir. 2005) (finding a jurisdictional claim made by the agency in the preamble to a final rule to be reviewable); La. Envtl. Action Network v. EPA, 172 F.3d 65, 69 (D.C. Cir. 1999) (reviewing a preamble where EPA agreed that the preamble was a "regulation"); Kennecott Utah Copper Corp. v. DOI, 88 F.3d 1191, 1222 (D.C. Cir. 1996) (holding that "a preamble may under some circumstances be reviewable" but only where the petitioners "have . . . demonstrated that the [challenged] preamble has a direct and immediate rather than a distant and speculative impact upon them").

214. *See* Aerosource Inc. v. Slater, 142 F.3d 572, 581 (3d Cir. 1998) (holding the FAA's refusal to withdraw alert concerning company's service work was not a "final order" under the Act, notwithstanding its "severe adverse impact on the company); Hindes v. FDIC, 137 F.3d 148, 162 (3d Cir. 1998) (holding the FDIC's notification to bank of the need to increase capitalization or risk cancellation of deposit insurance was "merely the first step of multi-step" process and was not a final order).

215. *See* Holistic Candlers and Consumers Ass'n v. Food & Drug Admin., 664 F.3d 940, 943–44 (D.C. Cir. 2012) (finding warning letters to fail both prongs of *Bennett v. Spear*'s finality test because the letters stated that the violations discussed in the letters "may" lead to enforcement action, and allowed recipients to respond with information that "FDA will evaluate"). Because the court found the letters to not constitute final agency action, it concluded it did not need to address ripeness issues. *Id.* at 943 n.4. *See also* Indep. Equip. Dealers Ass'n v. EPA, 372 F.3d 420 (D.C. Cir. 2004) (rejecting a challenge to a series of EPA letters concerning importation requirements for selling or importing off-road engines; they were held to be non-final because they had no "concrete impact" on the association or its members); Air Brake Sys., Inc. v. Mineta, 357 F.3d 632 (6th Cir. 2004) (finding that the NHTSA Chief Counsel's opinion letters do not "directly bind" petitioner; they "are simply advisory opinions about a set of facts presented to the Chief Counsel. In the final analysis, these letters do not constitute 'final' agency action subject to review under the APA"); Reliable Automatic Sprinkler Co., Inc. v. Consumer Prod. Safety Comm'n, 324 F.3d 726, 730 (D.C. Cir. 2003) (holding that a letter from agency compliance officials informing the company that agency intended to make the preliminary determination that the product presented a substantial product hazard, as defined by the Consumer Product Safety Act, and requesting company to take "voluntary corrective action," was not final agency action); Colo. Farm Bureau Fed'n v. U.S. Forest Serv., 220 F.3d 1171, 1174 (10th Cir. 2000) (holding that neither an agreement between the U.S. Department of the Interior and the state of Colorado concerning programs to manage Colorado's declining native species nor a letter written from the regional forester pledging the Forest Service's readiness to aid Colorado in implementing a lynx recovery plan is final agency action); Ass'n of Int'l Auto. Mfrs., Inc. v. Comm'r, Mass. Dep't of Envtl. Prot., 208 F.3d 1, 4–5 (1st Cir. 2000) (holding an EPA opinion letter regarding questions that the court had referred to the agency under the doctrine of primary jurisdiction was not final

And in *Flue-Cured Tobacco Cooperative Stabilization Corp. v. EPA*,[216] the Fourth Circuit declined to review an EPA statutorily required report regarding the health hazards of secondhand smoke. The court conceded that the report was the consummation of the agency decision-making process, but concluded that it was not final action because it had no direct legal effects.[217] Professor Seidenfeld has argued that "a more straightforward analysis leading to the same conclusion as that reached by the Fourth Circuit panel is that the Report simply is not agency action (final or otherwise) as that term is defined by the APA."[218]

Another area where the issue of finality (and of ripeness)[219] has particular bite is when the action challenged is part of a planning process. Since *Lujan I*, there have been numerous cases concerning the finality of the Forest Service's actions regarding forest plans.[220] In *Sierra Club v. Peterson*,[221] the Fifth Circuit ruled that a challenge to the Service's timber management practices as not complying with a forest management plan and accompanying regulations was "precisely the type of programmatic challenge that the Supreme Court disallowed in *Lujan*."[222] The court characterized the challenge as seeking "'wholesale improvement' of the Forest Service's 'program' of timber management in the Texas forests, objecting to Forest Service practices throughout the four national forests in Texas and covering harvesting from the 1970s to

---

agency action because the agency refused to state that the letter reflected its definitive position on the issues, and because the letter's only effect would be via its influence on the court's decision in this case); Mobile Exploration & Producing U.S., Inc. v. Dep't of the Interior, 180 F.3d 1192, 1197–99 (9th Cir. 1999) (agency audit engagement letter initiating a proceeding not a final agency action). *But see* Ciba-Geigy Corp. v. EPA, 801 F.2d 430, 436 (D.C. Cir. 1986) (holding a letter in which the Director of Pesticide Programs "unequivocally" stated the agency's relevant position was sufficiently final for purposes of judicial review). *See also* Kevin M. McDonald, *Are Agency Advisory Opinions Worth Anything More Than the Government Paper They're Printed On?*, 37 Tex. Tech L. Rev. 99 (2004) (comparing the courts' analyses in *Ciba Geigy* and *Air Brake Systems*; preferring the former); Randolph J. May, *Ruling Without Real Rules—Or How to Influence Private Conduct Without Really Binding*, 53 Admin. L. Rev. 13 (2001) (discussing the effect of posting and subsequent withdrawal of controversial OSHA compliance letter from agency website).

216. 313 F.3d 852 (4th Cir. 2002).
217. *Id.* at 858–59.
218. Mark Seidenfeld, *Judicial Review Chapter*, Developments in Administrative Law and Regulatory Practice 2002-2003, at 100 (Jeffrey S. Lubbers ed., 2004). For a somewhat similar case, *see* Invention Submission Corp. v. Rogan, 357 F.3d 452 (4th Cir. 2004) (holding the PTO's conduct in engaging in advertising campaign to warn the public about invention promotion scams was not final agency action subject to judicial review under the APA).
219. For a consideration of ripeness of non-legislative rules, see subsec. E(3), *infra*.
220. *See* text at notes 43–49 for a discussion of *Lujan I*.
221. 228 F.3d 559 (5th Cir. 2000) (en banc).
222. *Id.* at 566.
223. *Id.* (citing *Lujan I*).

timber sales which have not yet occurred."[223] The court emphasized that the environmental groups may not "challenge an entire program by simply identifying specific allegedly improper final agency actions within that program, which is precisely what they did here."[224] Similarly, in *Ecology Center, Inc. v. United States Forest Service*,[225] the Ninth Circuit rejected a challenge to the Service's failure to monitor the land uses in the Kootenai National Forest. The court found that the alleged failure to monitor was not the "culmination of a decision making process," but rather was "several steps removed from final agency action."[226]

In addition, as discussed below, if an agency's *failure to act* in a rulemaking context is being challenged, there may be a question whether the "action" (that is, the failure to act) is a final agency position.[227]

And finally, one case raised the issue of finality of a district court remand order for the purposes of review.[228] The case arose when the district court remanded an Endangered Species Act listing to the Commerce Department, which decided (after a change in administrations) not to appeal, and an intervener environmental group sought to do so. The Ninth Circuit ruled that the action was final *vís a vis* the agency but not to other parties, limiting them to the option of participating in the reopened rulemaking and then appealing that result if they wished.

2. Exhaustion

Exhaustion of administrative remedies is a prudential judicial construct that generally requires a party to go through all the stages of an administrative proceeding before going to court. The "exhaustion" requirement ensures that the agency action

224. *Id.* at 567. *But see* Wilderness Soc'y v. Thomas, 188 F.3d 1130 (9th Cir. 1999) (allowing plaintiffs to challenge site-specific decisions to allow grazing on forest lands, and while doing so, to also seek review of the plan where the plan was a factor leading to a site-specific action).
225. 192 F.3d 922 (9th Cir. 1999).
226. *Id.* at 925; *see also* Nat'l Parks Conservation Ass'n v. Norton, 324 F.3d 1229, 1238 (11th Cir. 2003) (holding the Park Service was actively planning the prospective management of park area under dispute by crafting four management alternatives and a draft EIS that evaluates each of these options; under these circumstances, the court cannot conclude that the agency has taken any final action or engaged in a pattern of reviewable inaction). *But see* Nat'l Ass'n of Home Builders v. U.S. Army Corps of Eng'rs, 417 F.3d 1272, 1280–81 (D.C. Cir. 2005) (allowing homebuilders to challenge the Corps' promulgation of nationwide permits and attendant conditions over environmental groups' objection that action was not final as to homebuilders).
227. *See infra* subsec. (E)(3)(d); *infra* Part IV, ch. 3. In this connection, *see* Norton v. Southern Utah Wilderness Alliance, 542 U.S. 55 (2004) (rejecting a challenge to the Interior Department's alleged failure to implement its statutory duty to protect Wilderness Study Areas in Utah from increased use of off-road vehicles). The Court ruled that an agency failure to act is only reviewable where: (a) the action the agency purportedly should have taken was "discrete," and (b) that action was "required" by law. *Id.* at 2379.
228. *See* Alsea Valley Alliance v. Dep't of Commerce, 358 F.3d 1181 (9th Cir. 2004).

being challenged is the final agency position and that the agency has had the opportunity to bring its expertise to bear and to correct any errors it may have made at an earlier stage, thus potentially resolving disputes before they come to court.[229] This classic exhaustion issue, while important in many areas of administrative law, is not often an issue in judicial review of rules, because rulemaking procedures are generally complete before there is a rule to challenge.

However, a new form of exhaustion requirement (closely related to standing) is taking on increasing importance in the rulemaking context. Some statutes specifically require persons to raise issues in the agency rulemaking before they can seek judicial review of those issues,[230] and there is an emerging trend among the circuits that petitioners have essentially waived their right to raise issues in challenging agency rules if they had not raised them during the notice-and-comment period.[231] The D.C. Circuit has followed this principle in numerous rulemaking cases.[232] The Fifth and Sixth Circuits have now joined the D.C. Circuit.[233]

---

229. *See generally* McGee v. United States, 402 U.S. 479 (1971).

230. *See, e.g.*, 47 U.S.C. § 405 (challengers may not rely "on questions of fact or law upon which the [FCC] has been afforded no opportunity to pass"). For an early case applying exhaustion analysis to a challenge to an FCC rulemaking, *see* Washington Ass'n for Television and Children v. FCC, 712 F.2d 177 (D.C. Cir. 1983). *See also* Clean Air Act, 42 U.S.C. § 7607(d)(7)(B) ("Only an objection to a rule or procedure which was raised with reasonable specificity during the period for public comment (including any public hearing) may be raised during judicial review.").

231. There may be situations in the context of challenges to agency delay or inaction where the failure to file a petition for rulemaking may prevent consideration of the challenge on the basis of failure to exhaust administrative remedies. *But see* Pub. Citizen v. NRC, 901 F.2d 147 (D.C. Cir. 1990).

232. *See* City of Portland, Or. v. EPA, 507 F.3d 706, 710 (D.C. Cir. 2007) ("Because neither Walla Walla nor any other party raised this argument before the Agency during the rulemaking process, however, it is waived, and we will not consider it.'); Small Bus. in Telecomms. v. FCC, 251 F.3d 1015, 1026 (D.C. Cir. 2001) (failure to raise issue regarding regulatory flexibility analysis during rulemaking precluded judicial review of the issue); Military Toxics Project v. EPA, 146 F.3d 948, 956–57 (D.C. Cir. 1998) ("We need not reach this challenge on the merits, however, because as the EPA also points out, neither the MTP nor anyone else commented during the rulemaking process that the Rule as drafted would permit the DOD unilaterally to free itself from the strictures imposed by the RCRA. The MTP has thus waived the argument and may not raise it for the first time upon appeal."); Nat'l Ass'n of Mfrs. v. U.S. Dep't of the Interior, 134 F.3d 1095, 1111 (D.C. Cir. 1998) ("NAM failed to raise this argument in the rulemaking proceedings below, and we find no reason to excuse NAM's failure to exhaust its administrative remedies."); Natural Res. Def. Council, Inc. v. EPA, 25 F.3d 1063, 1073 (D.C. Cir. 1994) (similar).

233. *See* BCCA Appeal Group v. EPA, 355 F.3d 817, 829 n.10 (5th Cir 2003) (rejecting its earlier contrary view in Am. Forest & Paper Ass'n v. EPA, 137 F.3d 291, 295 (5th Cir. 1998)); Mich. Dept. of Envtl. Quality v. Browner, 230 F.3d 181, 183 n.1 (6th Cir. 2000). *See also* 1000 Friends of Md. v. Browner, 265 F.3d 228 (4th Cir. 2001) (even if the "waiver rule" applies, petitioner's comments sufficiently raised the issue now being raised on judicial review); Indus. Envtl. Ass'n v. Browner, 225 F.3d 662, 663 n.4 (9th Cir. 2000) (table case) ("The claim of participation rights

In part, this trend is to spare the agency from the burden of having to respond to vague comments. As Judge Randolph wrote in a recent case:

> We have held that Section 307 of the Clean Air Act bars litigants from arguing against a particular section of a rule on judicial review if they failed to identify the particular section in their comments during the rulemaking. . . . A citation to the section of the rule or a description of it may be all that is needed. If a comment lacking even that low level of specificity sufficed, the agency would be subjected to verbal traps. Whenever the agency failed to detect an obscure criticism of one aspect of its proposal, the petitioner could claim not only that it had complied with Section 307 but also that the agency acted arbitrarily because it never responded to the comment. Rulemaking proceedings and the legal doctrines that have grown up around them are intricate and cumbersome enough. Agency officials should not have to wade through reams of documents searching for "'implied' challenges."[234]

However, challenges to the *application* of a rule are treated differently in this regard.[235] Moreover, the D.C. Circuit has allowed challenges by non-commenters when the application of the rule to the challengers was not clear and the agency denied a petition for reconsideration.[236]

It should also be noted that in several cases, the Supreme Court has interpreted certain statutes to require challengers to agency regulations to first bring those challenges in the agency adjudication process created by such statute. The Court has used the language of exhaustion of remedies in such cases.[237]

3. Ripeness

The concept of "ripeness" is the one most likely to surface in a pre-enforcement challenge to a legislative rule. Ripeness addresses the appropriateness of judicial re-

---

is particularly weak coming from a group of regulated entities who failed to even comment on EPA's proposed rule during the applicable comment period."). The "exhaustion" requirement may also be subject to a "futility" exception, *see* Comite De Apoyo A Los Trabajadores Agricolas v. Solis, 2010 WL 3431761 *18 (E.D. Pa. Aug. 30, 2010) (agency cannot complain that challenger had failed to comment on an issue when the agency rejected similar comments from others as outside the scope of the rulemaking).

234. Natural Res. Def. Council v. EPA, 559 F.3d 561, 564 (D.C. Cir. 2009).
235. *See* Murphy Exploration & Prod. Co. v. U.S. Dep't of Interior, 270 F.3d 957 (D.C. Cir. 2001) (distinguishing earlier cases and holding that the producer's failure to challenge the rule while participating in rulemaking proceedings did not estop it from challenging rule in separate proceeding in which rule was being applied).
236. Portland Cement Ass'n v. EPA, 665 F.3d 177,186 (D.C. Cir. 2011) ("While we certainly require some degree of foresight on the part of commenters, we do not require telepathy.").
237. *See* Thunder Basin Coal Co. v. Reich, 510 U.S. 200 (1994) and Shalala v. Ill. Council on Long Term Care, 529 U.S. 1 (2000), discussed *supra* note 13.

view at a particular time and is primarily concerned with ensuring that issues are in a posture fit for judicial review. As the Supreme Court said in *Abbott Laboratories v. Gardner*,[238] ripeness's "basic rationale is to prevent the courts, through avoidance of premature adjudication, from entangling themselves in abstract disagreements over administrative policies, and also to protect the agencies from judicial interference until an administrative decision has been formalized and its effects felt in a concrete way by the challenging parties."[239]

Ripeness is a two-pronged concept: the issues must be "fit[ ] . . . for judicial decision," and delaying review must cause hardship for the challenging party.[240] As the D.C. Circuit has put it recently, "The 'fitness' prong of the analysis generally addresses 'whether the issue is purely legal, whether consideration of the issue would benefit from a more concrete setting, and whether the agency's action is sufficiently final.'"[241] This fitness test obviously overlaps somewhat with the test for finality under the APA, discussed above.

In the context of a *procedural* challenge to a guidance document, the D.C. Circuit has stated:

> We have held that when a challenge to an agency document as a "legislative rule is largely a legal, not a factual, question"—that is, when it turns only on whether the document "on its face . . . purports to bind both applicants and the Agency with the force of law"—the claim is fit for review. However, "[w]here we believed the agency's practical application of a statement would be important, we have found the issue not" fit for judicial determination.[242]

Thus, more generally, whether a challenge to a guidance document "is fit for review turns in significant part on whether that challenge can be resolved on the face of the document, or whether it depends as well on the way in which the document will be applied."[243]

As for the challenger's hardship, which must outweigh any interests in deferring review, it must be more than speculative and involve more than just additional litigation costs.[244] This too leads to an obvious overlap between the hardship prong and the injury-in-fact test for standing, discussed above.[245]

---

238. *Supra* note 4.

239. 387 U.S. 136, 148–49 (1967).

240. *Id.*

241. Teva Pharms. USA, Inc. v. Sebelius, 595 F.3d 1303, 1308 (D.C. Cir. 2010) (quoting Nat'l Ass'n of Home Builders v. U.S. Army Corps of Eng'rs, 440 F.3d 459, 463 (D.C. Cir. 2006)).

242. Cement Kiln Recycling Coal. v. EPA, 493 F.3d 207, 216 (D.C. Cir. 2007) (quoting General Elec. Co. v. EPA, 290 F.3d 377, 380 (D.C. Cir. 2002) and Pub. Citizen, Inc. v. Nuclear Regulatory Comm'n, 940 F.2d 679, 683 (D.C. Cir. 1991)).

243. *Id.*

244. Abbott Labs. v. Gardner, 387 U.S. 136, 153 (1967).

245. *See* Sabre, Inc. v. Dep't of Transp., 429 F.3d 1113, 1120 (D.C. Cir. 2005) (recognizing this overlap and putting burden on the agency to offer plausible institutional reasons for delaying

a. Ripeness and pre-enforcement review—Ripeness issues arise most often in the context of pre-enforcement review of rules. Prior to 1967, agency rules were normally challenged at the time the agency sought to enforce its rule against a particular party. In *Abbott Laboratories*, however, the Supreme Court held that a rule could be challenged before it was enforced, if the case was ripe for review. Such pre-enforcement review is quite common now. In an early study for the Administrative Conference, Frederick Davis found five patterns of judicial review statutes:[246]

1. Legislation that confers rulemaking power on the agency but makes no provision for or reference to judicial review;
2. Legislation that provides for judicial review in federal district court but establishes no time limit within which review must be sought;
3. Legislation that provides for direct pre-enforcement review within a prescribed time period after promulgation and explicitly preserves the jurisdiction of the appropriate court to review the validity of regulations after the prescribed period in enforcement proceedings;
4. Legislation that provides for direct pre-enforcement review within a prescribed time period following promulgation but is silent about the availability of review in enforcement proceedings or otherwise; and
5. Legislation that provides for direct pre-enforcement review within a prescribed time period and prohibits, except under limited conditions, review of the rule in an enforcement proceeding.

The following discussion covers the categories 1, 2, 4, and 5.

(1) No pre-enforcement review statute. Abbott Laboratories involved a challenge to rules in a context where no statute other than the APA affected the appropriate timing for judicial review. The case dealt with an industry challenge to final rules of the Food and Drug Administration (FDA) requiring that a drug's generic name appear on all labels and other printed material.[247] The Court held that drug manufacturers could challenge the rules immediately, because the rules would have an immediate and direct impact. The decision meant that the industry would not be required to violate the rules and wait until enforcement proceedings were instituted before they could challenge rules they believed were invalid. The rules were "fit for judicial decision," because the merits of the case involved a pure legal question—whether the

---

review when plaintiffs have met the fitness-for-review prong and also shown injury in fact). *See also* Venetian Casino Resort LLC v. Equal Emp't Opportunity Comm'n, 409 F.3d 359 (D.C. Cir. 2005) (in the context of pre-enforcement review, standing and ripeness are not separate requirements).

246. Frederick Davis, *Judicial Review of Rulemaking: New Patterns and New Problems*, 1981 Duke L. J. 279, 280–81.

247. *Abbott Labs.*, 387 U.S. at 138–39.

Food, Drug, and Cosmetic Act authorized such rules[248]—and there were no other factors raised by the agency that would justify deferring review.[249]

In a case decided the same day, the Court held that immediate review of another FDA final rule was not appropriate. In *Toilet Goods Association v. Gardner*,[250] the Court held that an FDA rule allowing the Commissioner to suspend certification of additives when manufacturers refuse access to agency inspectors was not ripe for review. Although agreeing that the rule was final and that the issue of whether the rule was within the agency's power was a legal one, the Court found that these considerations were outweighed by others. The rule had no clear immediate or irreparable impact; it would come into play only if access was refused, and even then no action was mandated. Moreover, the validity of any action on the part of the Commissioner would depend on the particular situation where certification was denied.[251]

In an important 1990 decision, the Supreme Court reiterated that for a challenge to agency action to be ripe for review, there must be either a substantive rule—which, as a practical matter, requires the plaintiff to adjust his or her conduct immediately—or some concrete action applying the regulation to the claimant in a fashion that harms or threatens to harm him or her. In *Lujan v. National Wildlife Federation (Lujan I)*,[252] the Court declined to hear a challenge to the Department of the Interior's land-withdrawal program that was not directed to explicit regulations, but instead challenged some changing policies for reviewing classifications of public lands. The Court noted that there was no other statutory source of review authority, and the "concrete effects normally required for APA review" had not been alleged.[253]

---

248. *Id.* at 149.

249. *Id.* at 148–56

250. 387 U.S. 158 (1967).

251. In a third case decided that day, the Court held several other FDA regulations ripe for review where they had immediate and substantial impacts and consideration of the legal issues would not be facilitated if raised in specific factual situations. Toilet Goods Ass'n v. Gardner, 387 U.S. 167 (1967); *see also* Ronald M. Levin, *The Story of the* Abbott Labs *Trilogy: The Seeds of the Ripeness Doctrine, in* ADMINISTRATIVE LAW STORIES 430 (Peter L. Strauss ed., 2006) (showing how divided the Supreme Court was during its deliberation of *Abbott Labs* and its companion cases).

252. 497 U.S. 871 (1990); *see also supra* discussion in subsec. B(2) (regarding the standing aspect of this case).

253. *Id.* at 891. The Court also noted that there was neither "agency action" within the meaning of § 702 of the APA nor "final agency action" within the meaning of § 704. *See also* Wilderness Soc'y v. Alcock, 83 F.3d 386, 390 (11th Cir. 1996) (citing *Lujan I* and dismissing appeal brought by environmental groups challenging Secretary of Agriculture's plan for managing the Cherokee National Forest on grounds that the claim was not ripe for review because only later decisions under plan would determine what specific actions the Department would take pursuant to the plan). *But see* Nat'l Ass'n of Home Builders v. U.S. Army Corps of Eng'rs, 417 F.3d 1272, 1282–83 (D.C. Cir. 2005) (allowing homebuilders to challenge the Corps' promulgation of nationwide permits and attendant conditions over environmental groups' objection that the challenge was not ripe, and distinguishing *Lujan I*).

This trend continued in *Reno v. Catholic Social Services*,[254] which held as unripe a challenge by immigrants to INS regulations that tightened the criteria for applying for permanent residence because the respondents had not actually filed an application that had been rejected.[255] The opinion rejected the dissenters' arguments that the situation squarely fit within *Abbott Laboratories* because the regulations placed the immigrants in a legal limbo and increased the risk that application periods would expire.

In *Ohio Forestry v. Sierra Club*,[256] the Supreme Court elaborated on the *Abbott Laboratories* test, but its result made it difficult to challenge the sort of agency planning documents that are required under many natural resources statutes.[257] The case concerned the ripeness for immediate review of a forest plan adopted by the Forest Service authorizing the cutting of timber in a national forest in Ohio. The regional forester adopted a 10-year plan for Wayne National Forest, which designated 126,107 acres from which timber could be removed or cut. During the 19-year life of the plan, 7.5 million board feet of timber could be cut per year. The plan designated that 80 percent of all timbering techniques would be "even-aged" management (a technique that allows "clearcutting").[258] The court of appeals ruled that the resulting plan was arbitrary and capricious because it was based upon an artificial narrowing of options.[259]

But the unanimous Supreme Court reversed on ripeness grounds, saying that many steps had to take place under the plan before trees would actually be cut, including the approval by the Forest Service of permits for particular logging projects. In his ripeness analysis, Justice Breyer, for the Court, noted that the National Forest Man-

---

254. 509 U.S. 43 (1993).

255. This decision has been strongly criticized by commentators. Even the "Nutshell" on administrative law, which tends to avoid editorializing, labeled this decision "dubious" because "the issues facing the Court were as fully developed as they would ever be." ERNEST GELLHORN & RONALD M. LEVIN, ADMINISTRATIVE PROCESS IN A NUTSHELL 382 (4th ed. 1997).

256. 523 U.S. 726 (1998).

257. The statute involved in this case, the National Forest Management Act of 1976, requires the Secretary of Agriculture to "develop, maintain, and, as appropriate, revise land and resource management plans for units of the National Forest System." 90 Stat. 2949, *as renumbered and amended*, 16 U.S.C. § 1604(a). *See also* 16 U.S.C. § 1539(a)(2) ("habitat conservation plans" approved by the Secretary of the Interior under the Endangered Species Act, § 10); 16 U.S.C. § 1455(d) (state "coastal zone management programs" subject to the approval of the Secretary of Commerce under the Coastal Zone Management Act, § 306).

258. *See* 523 U.S. at 729.

259. 105 F.3d. 248 (6th Cir. 1997). The Forest Service argued that its even-aged management plan was based on evidence that timbering would provide new opportunities for recreation that would, in turn, preserve and enhance the diversity of plant and animal communities in the Wayne National Forest. But the court pointed out that the Forest Service's own records reflected that this forest is surrounded by and intermingled with privately held land that already contains an abundance of diverse plant and animal life. Finally, the court concluded that the kind of recreational activities that are in demand in this forest, like fishing and hiking, are harmed by clearcutting. *Id.*

agement Act does not specifically provide for immediate judicial review of such plans, and then he set forth a three-part ripeness test:[260]

1. Would delayed review cause legal or practical hardship to plaintiffs? (The Court answers "no," because Sierra Club can challenge individual projects. Nor does Sierra Club have to modify behavior, like Abbott did. Increased litigating costs are not enough.)
2. Would judicial intervention inappropriately interfere with further administrative action? (The Court says "yes," it might hinder the Forest Service's refinement of its policies.)
3. Would courts benefit from further factual development? (The Court says "yes," immediate review would be time-consuming and require predictions of changing technical issues.)

The decision does not completely foreclose review of forest plans. Justice Breyer did say that if Sierra Club had been able to show some immediate environmental harm from the plans—such as approval of motorcycles into a bird-watching area—that would have been a ripe claim, but the club complained only about the plan's impact on timber harvesting.[261] However, the upshot of this decision is that the Forest Service can insulate itself from judicial review of its plans by keeping them as general as possible—a tack that certainly undercuts the value of the planning process. After this decision, the Bush Administration took advantage of it by crafting a forest-planning process that was designed to produce the most general of plans, exempted from NEPA,[262] and with the important decisions made at the site-specific level by the Forest Supervisor.[263]

---

260. *See* 523 U.S. at 733–37.
261. *Id.* at 739. *See also* Laub v. U.S. Dep't of Interior, 342 F.3d 1080, 1087–91 (9th Cir. 2003) (concluding that a "procedural" challenge under NEPA to a "programmatic" environmental impact statement that did not include site-specific plans was ripe for review, and distinguishing *Ohio Forestry Ass'n*).
262. This exemption is important because the courts have held that NEPA challenges and Regulatory Flexibility challenges are ripe for review immediately. *See* Nat'l Ass'n of Home Builders v. U.S. Army Corps of Eng'rs, 417 F.3d 1272, 1286 (D.C. Cir. 2005) (finding the homebuilders' claim that the Corps violated the Regulatory Flexibility Act was ripe: "[A]s with a NEPA challenge, the appellants may complain of the Corps' alleged failure to comply with the procedures set forth in sections 604 and 605 of the RFA at the time the alleged failure occurred, *i.e.*, when the Corps issued the [rules] without complying with those procedures. In sum, the appellants' RFA challenge 'can never get riper.'" (citing *Ohio Forestry Ass'n*, 523 U.S. at 737)).
263. *See* Department of Agriculture, Forest Service, Final Rule, National Forest System Land Management Planning, 70 Fed. Reg. 1023, 1024 (Jan. 5, 2005), codified at 36 C.F.R. pt. 219 (describing, in the preamble, the final rule as "a paradigm shift," designed to make forest planning "more strategic and less prescriptive in nature"). *See also* Robert B. Keiter, *Ecological Concepts, Legal Standards, and Public Land Law: An Analysis and Assessment*, 44 Nat. Res. J. 943,

Thus, it seems clear that the Supreme Court has placed greater "ripeness" barriers in front of challengers to agency action, especially where nonregulated parties are challenging agency rulemakings that are not covered by pre-enforcement review statutes.[264] This asymmetry has also been noted with respect to the causation prong of the standing test (see section (B)(4) above).[265]

(2) Pre-enforcement review statutes. Because ripeness is primarily a prudential concept, and thus subject to congressional direction, Congress has, since *Abbott Laboratories*, provided explicitly for pre-enforcement review in many regulatory statutes.[266]

---

951 (2004) ("Overall, the Bush administration's 2005 planning regulations represent a determined effort to minimize the Forest Service's legal obligations and hence the opportunity to challenge agency planning decisions."). However, this plan was enjoined for violations of the APA, NEPA, and the ESA in *Citizens for Better Forestry v. U.S. Dep't of Agriculture* (*Citizens II*), 481 F. Supp. 2d 1059 (N.D. Cal. 2007). The agency republished it with a final EIS in 2008, National Forest System Land Management Planning, 73 Fed. Reg. 21,468 (Apr. 21, 2008), but this was also enjoined in *Citizens for Better Forestry v. U.S. Dep't of Agriculture*, 632 F. Supp. 2d 968 (N.D. Cal. 2009), because the court found the agency had relied on the same NEPA and ESA arguments. In 2011, the Obama Administration proposed a revised plan, 76 Fed. Reg. 8480 (Feb. 14, 2011).

264. A series of environmental cases had challenges that failed on ripeness grounds. *See, e.g.*, Am. Canoe Ass'n v. U.S. Envtl. Prot. Agency, 289 F.3d 509 (8th Cir. 2002) (holding EPA's approval of a state's list of polluted waters was not ripe for judicial review despite the agricultural organization's argument that the listing would lead to tighter controls on farming activities and this would depress the value of affected agricultural properties); Coal. for Sustainable Res., Inc. v. U.S. Forest Serv., 259 F.3d 1244 (10th Cir. 2001) (holding the agency's failure to adopt an environmental group's preferred forest-management practices, including increased timber harvesting and greater tolerance of forest fires and insect infestations, was not ripe for review); Natural Res. Def. Council v. FAA, 292 F.3d 875 (D.C. Cir. 2002) (holding FAA letters containing suggestions that airborne sightseeing tours out of the Jackson Hole Airport were lawful, tentative, and not ripe for review); Cent. & S. W. Servs., Inc. v. EPA, 220 F.3d 683, 690 (5th Cir. 2000) (holding a challenge to EPA's failure to preempt state and local rules for disposal rules was not ripe). For a fuller discussion of some of these cases, see Jonathan Entin, *Environmental and Natural Resources Protection Chapter*, Developments in Administrative Law and Regulatory Practice 2001-2002, at 311–14 (Jeffrey S. Lubbers ed., 2003).

265. Some commentators have urged a cutback on pre-enforcement review of rules as a way of ameliorating the problem of "ossification" of rulemaking. *See* Jerry L. Mashaw, *Improving the Environment of Agency Rulemaking: An Essay on Management, Games, and Accountability*, 57 Law & Contemp. Probs. 185 (1994). *But see* Mark Seidenfeld, *Playing Games with the Timing of Judicial Review: An Evaluation of Proposals to Restrict Pre-Enforcement Review of Agency Rules*, 58 Ohio St. L.J. 85 (1997).

266. *See, e.g.*, FTC Act, 15 U.S.C. § 57a(e); Hobbs Act, 28 U.S.C. § 2342; OSHA Act, 29 U.S.C. § 655(f); Clean Air Act, 42 U.S.C. § 7607(b). The Court in *Lujan I* expressly recognized that "[s]ome statutes permit broad regulations to serve as the 'agency action,' and thus to be the object of judicial review directly, even before the concrete effects normally required for APA review are felt." 497 U.S. at 891. Normally, absent a more specific deadline, challenges to agency rules must be brought within the usual six-year statute of limitations. *See* Solid Waste Agency of N. Cook Cnty. v. U.S. Army Corps of Eng'rs, 191 F.3d 845, 853 (7th Cir. 1999), *rev'd on other*

Under these statutes, petitions for court review of rules may, and often must, be filed within a short, specified time after the rule is promulgated.

The courts generally have treated these time limits as jurisdictional; that is, they have dismissed petitions for review not brought within the specified time limit,[267] because limits serve "the important purpose of imparting finality into the administrative process, thereby conserving administrative resources."[268] Courts may entertain untimely review petitions in exceptional circumstances, but any exceptions are "carefully scrutinized" to ensure that the important policies underlying finality will not be undermined.[269] Note, however, that in some circumstances the presence of a time limit for review may not forestall a reviewing court from finding a timely petition for review unripe. For example, in *Atlantic States Legal Foundation v. EPA*,[270] petitioners challenged an EPA rule issued under its Project XL Program authorizing a pilot program in New York that would allow utilities to store hazardous waste without obtaining a permit. The D.C. Circuit, sua sponte, dismissed the petition on ripeness grounds because of the many steps that the state of New York would have to take to effectuate the pilot program. The court made that disposition notwithstanding that the Solid Waste Disposal Act[271] requires a petition for review to be filed within 90 days of the promulgation of a final regulation by EPA.

The court first reiterated that "even purely legal issues may be unfit for review."[272]

> So here. No one can say with certainty that the New York authorities will adopt the Project XL regulations as they are now written or will modify them. Even if New York does adopt the regulations *en masse*, we still would not know which utilities will opt into the program or where they will locate their central collection facilities. Yet a "claim is not ripe for adjudication if it rests upon contingent future events that may not occur as anticipated, or indeed may not occur at all."[273]

---

grounds, 531 U.S. 159 (2001) (recognizing that "[t]here is a general six-year statute of limitations for civil actions against the United States found in 28 U.S.C. § 2401(a), which applies to lawsuits brought pursuant to the APA," but expressing "doubt that a party must (or even may) bring an action under the APA before it knows that a regulation may injure it or even be applied to it"). *See also* P & V Enters. v. U.S. Army Corps of Eng'rs, 516 F.3d 1021, 1023 (D.C. Cir. 2008) (referencing § 2401(a)).

267. Eagle-Picher Indus. v. EPA, 759 F.2d 905, 911 (D.C. Cir. 1985).
268. Natural Res. Def. Council v. NRC, 666 F.2d 595 (D.C. Cir. 1981).
269. *Eagle-Picher Indus.*, 759 F.2d at 909–12. Among the exceptions mentioned by the court are inadequate notice, confusion on the law of proper forum, and lack of ripeness. *Id.*
270. 325 F.3d 281 (D.C. Cir. 2003).
271. 42 U.S.C. § 6976(a)(1).
272. 325 F.3d at 284 (citing Aulenback, Inc. v. Fed. Hwy. Admin., 103 F.3d 156, 167 (D.C. Cir. 1997)).
273. *Id.* (citing Texas v. United States, 523 U.S. 296, 300 (1998)).
274. *Id.* at 285 (citing La. Envtl. Action Network v. Browner, 87 F.3d 1379, 1385 (D.C. Cir. 1996) and Baltimore Gas & Elec. Co. v. ICC, 672 F.2d 146, 149 (D.C. Cir. 1982)).

As for the time limit, the court said that the "time limit does not begin to run until the claim ripens."[274] Therefore, "as long as petitioners bring another petition for review within ninety days of the time a utility provides notice of a site it intends to use as a central collection facility under these rules, the petition will be timely."[275]

Because statutory pre-enforcement review provisions generally provide explicitly for review immediately after a rule is promulgated, the question arises whether the validity of a rule may also be challenged in the context of a later enforcement or other proceeding and, if so, which issues are reviewable. In some statutes, Congress expressly prohibited review in enforcement proceedings or at least seemed to do so,[276] but such provisions have been very narrowly interpreted.[277]

In 1982, the Administrative Conference recommended that "in drafting a statute that provides for adequate preenforcement judicial review of rules, Congress should consider whether to limit the availability of review at the enforcement stage."[278] Four factors were identified as favoring such a limitation: (1) the likelihood that the rulemaking will attract widespread participation; (2) the likelihood that it will involve "complex procedures" or "intensive exploration of the issues"; (3) the likelihood that affected parties will incur substantial and immediate costs in complying; and (4) the need for prompt compliance with the rule on a national or industry-wide basis.[279] The recommendation urged that

> [w]hen Congress decides to limit the availability of judicial review of rules at the enforcement stage, it should ordinarily preclude review only of issues relating to procedures employed in the rulemaking or the adequacy of factual support for the rule in the administrative record. Judicial review of issues relating to the constitutional basis for the rule or the application of the rule to a particular respondent or defendant should be permitted when these issues are raised in subsequent suits or as defenses to subsequent enforcement actions (subject to the principles of collateral estoppel and stare decisis). Judi-

---

275. *Id.* at 285–86.
276. *See, e.g.*, Clean Air Act, 42 U.S.C. § 7607(b)(1)–(2). Under subsection (1), petitions for review "shall be filed" within 60 days of promulgation of a rule; if the petition is based "solely on grounds" arising after the 60th day, however, the petition "shall be filed" within 60 days after such grounds arise. *Id.* § 7607(b)(1). Under subsection (2), action of EPA "with respect to which review could have been obtained" under subsection (1) "shall not be subject to judicial review in civil or criminal proceedings for enforcement." *Id.* § 7607(b)(2). *See also* CERCLA, 42 U.S.C. § 9613(a).
277. Adamo Wrecking Co. v. United States, 434 U.S. 275 (1978) (narrowly construing 42 U.S.C. § 7607(b)(2) of the Clean Air Act).
278. ACUS Recommendation 82-7, *Judicial Review of Rules in Enforcement Proceedings*, 47 Fed. Reg. 58,208 (1982). This recommendation was based on Paul R. Verkuil, *Congressional Limitations on Judicial Review of Rules: The Jurisprudential Implications*, 1982 ACUS 443, *reprinted as Congressional Limitations on Judicial Review of Rules*, 57 TUL. L. REV. 733 (1983); *see also* Frederick Davis, *supra* note 246.
279. ACUS Recommendation 82-7, *supra* note 278.

cial review of issues relating to the statutory authority for the rule should be precluded at the enforcement stage only where Congress has concluded that there is a compelling need to achieve prompt compliance with the rule on a national or industry-wide basis.[280]

The courts have followed many of these principles. For example, the D.C. Circuit has made clear that if a party does miss the pre-enforcement review time deadline, where the statute does not explicitly provide otherwise, this does not foreclose a *substantive* challenge to the rule at the time of enforcement. In an early case[281] the court set out the following guidelines, which are still valid today: (1) procedural challenges must generally be brought within the statutory review period if one exists; (2) where a litigant is challenging a lack of statutory authority for the rule, such challenge may be brought in an enforcement proceeding; and (3) if the substantive challenge involves an argument other than a lack of statutory authority, it may be raised in an enforcement proceeding or on review of a subsequent petition for rulemaking that addresses the particular issues.[282]

In *Independent Community Bankers of America v. Board of Governors of Federal Reserve System*,[283] the D.C. Circuit stated with respect to challenges brought outside a statutory time limit:

> We have frequently said that a party against whom a rule is applied may, at the time of application, pursue substantive objections to the rule, including claims that an agency lacked the statutory authority to adopt the rule, even where the petitioner had notice and opportunity to bring a direct challenge within statu-

---

280. *Id.* In *Independent Community Bankers of America*, 195 F.3d 28, 35 (D.C. Cir. 1999), the court cited this recommendation:

> The Administrative Conference of the United States in 1982 urged Congress not to prohibit challenges to the statutory authority for a rule unless there were a compelling need for prompt compliance on a national or industry wide basis, . . . and the dearth of statutes that prohibit review after the statutory period has run suggests that Congress has generally agreed [citing Davis, *supra* note 246]. The statute at issue here, 12 U.S.C. § 1848 (1994), contains no such explicit bar.

281. Nat'l Labor Relations Bd. Union v. Fed. Labor Relations Auth., 834 F.2d 191, 195–97 (D.C. Cir. 1987).

282. *Id.* at 195; *see also* Graceba Total Commc'ns, Inc. v. FCC, 115 F.3d 1038, 1040 (D.C. Cir. 1997):

> Because "administrative rules and regulations are capable of continuing application," limiting review of a rule to the period immediately following rulemaking "would effectively deny many parties ultimately affected by a rule an opportunity to question its validity." *Functional Music, Inc. v. FCC*, 274 F.2d 543, 546 (D.C. Cir. 1958). For this reason, we permit both constitutional and statutory challenges to an agency's application or reconsideration of a previously promulgated rule, even if the period for review of the initial rulemaking has expired.

283. 195 F.3d 28 (D.C. Cir. 1999).

tory time limits. . . . By contrast, we have said that procedural attacks on a rule's adoption are barred even when it is applied.[284]

The D.C. Circuit has since cited this case as authoritative:

Although one court has held that the Clean Air Act, 42 U.S.C. § 7607(b), deprived it of jurisdiction to review EPA regulations when they are applied, *see Potomac Elec. Power Co. v. EPA*, 650 F.2d 509, 513 (4th Cir. 1981), we have ruled that preclusion must be explicit for review to be barred in an enforcement action, *see Indep. Cmty. Bankers of Am. v. Bd. of Governors of Fed. Reserve Sys.*, 195 F.3d 28, 34 (D.C. Cir. 1999), and that even express preclusion may not operate when the issue would have been unripe during the period of statutory review. *See Clean Air Implementation Project v. EPA*, 150 F.3d 1200, 1204 (D.C. Cir. 1998).[285]

The requirement for the timely filing of review petitions must be distinguished from the issue of ripeness. There may be cases that would not yet be ripe within the statutory review period,[286] or that remain ripe after the period expires,[287] but in general, challenges must be brought within relevant statutory time limits.[288]

Note, however, that the presence of a statutory time limit for review may also make it unnecessary for the challenger of a rule to satisfy the "hardship" prong of the ripeness test. The D.C. Circuit has declared that "[w]here the first prong of the . . . ripeness test is met and Congress has emphatically declared a preference for

---

284. *Id.* at 34. *But see* Deering Milliken, Inc. v. Occupational Safety & Health Review Comm'n, 630 F.2d 1094 (5th Cir. 1980) (holding that procedural challenge was not precluded after expiration of statutory review period).

285. Amfac Resorts, LLC v. U.S. Dep't of the Interior, 282 F.3d 818, 827 (D.C. Cir 2002) (Randolph, J.), *vacated in part on other grounds*, Nat'l Park Hospitality Ass'n v. Dep't of Interior, 538 U.S. 803 (2003). In *Clean Air Implementation Project v. EPA*, Judge Randolph had said:

We have not considered [express preclusion] statutes as requiring the court to adjudicate issues raised in a preenforcement challenge to a rule unless those issues are suitable for decision. If the issues are not of that nature, we will dismiss the petition as unripe. A necessary corollary is that if the issues later become justiciable, as a result for instance of an enforcement action, the petitioner may then raise those issues . . . .

150 F.3d 1200, 1204 (D.C. Cir. 1998) (citations and footnote omitted). *But see* Nat'l Mining Ass'n v. Fowler, 324 F.3d 752, 758 (D.C. Cir. 2003) (distinguishing *Clean Air Implementation Project*).

286. *See supra* text accompanying notes 267–73.

287. *See* the discussion *infra* subsec. (d).

288. *See* AFL-CIO v. OSHA, 905 F.2d 1568 (D.C. Cir. 1990) (holding that the statutory phrase "prior to the sixtieth day" means that a petition filed *on* the sixtieth day was too late); *see also* Simmons v. ICC, 716 F.2d 40 (D.C. Cir. 1983) (holding that an intervenor, in an action for review of a rule issued by the ICC, could not continue the lawsuit on its own where the petitioner was dismissed on jurisdictional grounds, and where the petition to intervene was not filed within the 60-day statutory time limit).

immediate review[,] . . . no purpose is served by proceeding to the [hardship] prong."[289]

Another issue raised by statutory time limits is the effect an agency's reconsideration of a rule may have on interested persons' rights to petition for court review. Courts have held that even if the original period for seeking review of a rule has expired, a new period for seeking review may begin if the agency later reopens issues. In determining whether issues have been reopened, courts look to "the entire context of the rulemaking."[290] In *Public Citizen v. Nuclear Regulatory Commission*,[291] the agency had republished an existing temporary policy statement on nuclear power plant personnel training. Plaintiffs challenged the validity of the action as contrary to the statute. The court held that the NRC had reconsidered the underlying issues in republishing the rule and that a challenge filed within the newly started time period could be heard.[292]

The court has since made clear that the "reopening doctrine" "only applies . . . where the entire context demonstrates that the agency ha[s] undertaken a serious, substantive reconsideration of the [existing] rule. It is designed to ensure that when the agency . . . by some new promulgation creates the opportunity for renewed comment and objection, affected parties may seek judicial review, even when the agency

---

289. Cement Kiln Recycling Coalition v. EPA, 493 F.3d 207, 215 (D.C. Cir. 2007) (alterations in original) (citing General Elec. Co. v. EPA, 290 F.3d 377, 381 (D.C. Cir. 2002).

290. Pub. Citizen v. NRC, 901 F.2d 147, 150 (D.C. Cir. 1990) ("If in proposing a rule the agency uses language that can reasonably be read as an invitation to comment on portions the agency does not explicitly propose to change, or if in responding to comments the agency uses language that shows that it did in fact reconsider an issue, a renewed challenge to the underlying rule or policy will be allowed."). *But see* United Transp. Union–Ill. Legislative Bd. v. Surface Transp. Bd., 132 F.3d 71, 76 (D.C. Cir. 1998) ("An agency does not 'reopen' an issue, however, when in response to comments that are beyond the scope of the rulemaking it merely reaffirms its prior position. 'The "reopening" rule is not a license for bootstrap procedures by which petitioners can comment on matters other than those actually at issue, goad an agency into a reply, and then sue on the grounds that the agency had reopened the issue.'" (citation and internal quotation mark omitted) (quoting Massachusetts v. ICC, 893 F.2d 1368, 1372 (D.C. Cir. 1990))).

291. 901 F.2d 147 (D.C. Cir. 1990).

292. *Id.* at 152–53 & n.1 (D.C. Cir. 1990) (citing "this circuit's long-standing rule that although a statutory review period permanently limits the time within which a petitioner may claim that an agency action was procedurally defective, a claim that agency action was violative of statute may be raised outside a statutory limitations period, by filing a petition for amendment or rescission of the agency's regulations, and challenging the denial of that petition"). The court also held that the statute required mandatory standards rather than the voluntary policy statement the agency had promulgated. *Id.* at 155–56. *But see* Natural Res. Def. Council v. Nuclear Regulatory Comm'n, 666 F.2d 595, 601–02 (1981) (stating that in the *Hobbs Act* case involving an order, not a rule, filing a petition for reconsideration would toll the time limit, but that petitioning to *reopen* the issue years later and then challenging the underlying order would not suffice).

decides not to amend the long-standing rule at issue."[293] Applying this rule, the court held it is not enough for reopening purposes for an agency to publish an ANPRM on a rule that is no longer subject to review and then announce via a press release that it is suspending the rulemaking.[294]

When an agency amends a rule for which the time for appeal has passed, it may risk reopening the original rule for challenge as well, if the court finds that the amendments have revised the rule in a way that "alters the stakes for judicial review of the original rule."[295]

b. When is the rule "issued" for time-limits purposes? Cases involving agency rulemaking have raised the issue of the proper manner for calculating the limitations period for filing petitions for judicial review. In *Public Citizen v. NRC*, the D.C. Circuit rebuffed an attempt by the NRC to argue that placing a rule in its own public document room served as the "starting gun" for the applicable statutory time limit on challenging agency action:

> Although an agency has "considerable latitude in determining the event that triggers commencement of the judicial review period," it must do so reasonably, bearing in mind that "[b]efore any litigant reasonably can be expected to present a petition for review of an agency rule, he first must be put on fair notice that the rule in question is applicable to him." We do not see how the mere placement of a decision in an agency's public files, without any other announcement, can start the clock running for review. . . . Potential petitioners cannot be expected to squirrel through the Commission's public document room in search of papers that might reflect final agency action.[296]

In two OSHA cases, the D.C. Circuit held that the 60-day period for filing challenges after OSHA standards have been "promulgated" begins to run when the stan-

---

293. P & V Enters. v. U.S. Army Corps of Eng'rs, 516 F.3d 1021, 1024 (D.C. Cir. 2008) (alterations in original) (citations and internal quotation marks omitted).

294. *See id.* In this case the old rule had been promulgated in 1986 and direct challenges were barred by the general six-year statute of limitations against civil actions brought against the United States, 28 U.S.C. § 2401(a).

295. *See* Kennecott Utah Copper Corp. v. U.S. Dept. of Interior, 88 F.3d 1191, 1226–27 (D.C. Cir. 1996) (industry petitioners allowed to challenge 1986 rule amended by 1994 rule because "the revision of those underlying regulations significantly alters the stakes of judicial review." *See also* Sierra Club v. EPA, 551 F.3d 1019, 1026 (D.C. Cir. 2008) ("Just as the court in *Kennecott* agreed with industry that the agency had constructively reopened a regulation when it incorporated amended regulations that expanded available remedies and thus altered its financial incentives for challenging the regulation, so too here from the perspective of environmental petitioners' interests and allocation of resources the general duty may not have been worth challenging in [1994], but the [revised] regulations gave [that duty] a new significance").

296. *Pub. Citizen*, 901 F.2d at 153 (citations omitted).

dard is *published* in the *Federal Register* rather than from the date the document is *filed* in the Office of the Federal Register.[297]

Later decisions under other statutes have tried to sort out the difference between the "issuance," "filing," and "publication" date. Several decisions of the D.C. Circuit have settled on the *Federal Register* publication date, though not always accurately.[298] But the Ninth Circuit has held that the date the rule was "filed" with the Office of the Federal Register was the key date for starting the time period for bringing a court challenge.

In *Coalition for Noncommercial Media v. FCC,*[299] the D.C. Circuit focused on the publication date in the *Federal Register.* The Sixth Circuit agreed with this approach in *Arctic Express, Inc. v. U.S. Department of Transportation,*[300] where a guidance document was challenged after the expiration of a 60-day statutory time limit. Here the court also focused on the date the guidance document was published in the *Federal Register.* On the other hand, in the most recent case, in *Public Citizen v. Mineta,*[301] the Ninth Circuit refused to defer to NHTSA's interpretation as to when the rule was "issued," and instead ruled that the key date was when it was filed with the Office of the Federal Register.[302]

A petition for judicial review can also be challenged on the basis that it was filed too early. In *Small Business in Telecommunications v. FCC,*[303] the court ruled that the petition for review of an FCC order was "incurably premature" because the FCC had not yet made "entry of the agency order," or in other words, there was no public notice, as the order was not yet published in the *Federal Register* as required under FCC rules.

---

297. Nat'l Grain & Feed Ass'n v. OSHA, 845 F.2d 345 (D.C. Cir. 1988); *accord* Technologies Corp. v. OSHA, 836 F.2d 52 (2d Cir. 1987).

298. In *National Air Transportation Ass'n v. McArtor,* 866 F.2d 483, 486 (D.C. Cir. 1989), the court found the petition for review timely because the FAA rule was "issued" on November 26, 1987, and the petition for review was filed on January 22, 1988. Confusingly, however, the Westlaw version of the rule listed its publication in the *Federal Register* as December 2, the rule itself says it was "issued" on November 25, and the "filing" date was stated to be November 27.

299. 249 F.3d 1005, 1007 (D.C. Cir. 2001) (finding petition timely under a 60-day deadline, but not a 30-day deadline). In that case, May 4 was the *Federal Register* publication date even though the "filing" date in the Office of the Federal Register was stated to be May 3. *See* 65 Fed. Reg. 25,865 (May 4, 2000).

300. 194 F.3d 767, 770–71 (6th Cir. 1999) (citations omitted).

301. 343 F.3d 1159, 1164–65 (9th Cir. 2003).

302. Thus the petition was timely. In this case, NHTSA claimed that the rule was actually issued 11 days before the filing date, but "it failed to document or explain this filing." *Id.* at 1167.

303. 251 F.3d 1015, 1023–24 (D.C. Cir. 2001). *See also* Council Tree Commc'ns, Inc. v. FCC, 503 F.3d 284 (3d Cir. 2007) (entities' petition for review of FCC's new spectrum licensing rules was incurably premature because one order at issue was non-final, and the reconsideration order had not been published in the *Federal Register* at the time the petition was filed; in addition, the All Writs Act did not permit the court to excuse the prematurity); Verizon v. FCC, Nos. 11-1014 & 11-1016, 2011 WL 1235523 (D.C. Cir. April 4, 2011) (dismissing premature challenge); W. Union Tel. Co. v. FCC, 773 F.2d 375, 378, 380 (D.C. Cir. 1985) (same).

Interesting finality and deadline issues can also be raised by interim final rules. In *Beverly Enterprises, Inc. v. Herman*,[304] the Department of Labor's interim final rule was published in December 1990. The agency, as is usual, pledged to review all comments and to publish a final rule later. This did not occur until 1994. When the plaintiff challenged the rule in 1999, the government moved to dismiss under the federal six-year statute of limitations. The district court agreed with the defendants that the 1990 interim final rule was "final" agency action that could have been challenged under the APA. Thus the petitioner's challenge to the interim final rule was time-barred. However, the court then decided that "[t]o the extent that Beverly's claim is a pre-enforcement challenge to the codification of the January 1994 final rule, however, that claim is timely."[305]

   c. Time limits and challenges to non-legislative rules. When a statutory time limit applies to challenges to an agency's rules or regulations, potential challengers to agency non-legislative rules may face a quandary. Is the agency action reviewable, and if so, is it subject to the time limit? Failure to bring a challenge within the time limits may lead to preclusion later if the court finds that the action had been ripe for review during that period. While most agency non-legislative rules are not ripe (or final)[306] for judicial review,[307] some agency policy statements, guidance, and even letters announcing agency enforcement programs have been held reviewable even though direct injury or hardship will be incurred only in an (uncertain) enforcement action.[308]

---

304. 50 F. Supp. 2d 7 (D.D.C. 1999).

305. *Id.* at 16–17.

306. *See supra* section E(1).

307. *See, e.g.*, Nat'l Park Hospitality Ass'n v. Dep't of Interior, 538 U.S. 803 (2003) (finding the Park Service policy statement unreviewable); *see also* Am. Trucking Ass'ns, Inc. v. ICC, 747 F.2d 787 (D.C. Cir. 1984) (Scalia, J.) (finding the policy statement unripe because "[a]t most the policy statement means that future actions of the Commission (its licensing of contract carriers) may be damaging to the petitioners—but that prospect in no way affects any action they must take or should take at the present time").

308. *See* Sabre, Inc. v. Dep't of Transp., 429 F.3d 1113, 1120–21 (D.C. Cir. 2005) (finding assertion of enforcement jurisdiction over petitioner's planned activity ripe, and distinguishing *Nat'l Park Hospitality Ass'n*); Venetian Casino Resort LLC v. Equal Emp't Opportunity Comm'n, 409 F.3d 359, 364 (D.C. Cir. 2005) (finding a challenge to an agency policy of disclosing trade secrets "fit for review because it presents a clear-cut legal question"); Barrick Goldstrike Mines Inc. v. Browner, 215 F.3d 45, 48 (D.C. Cir. 2000) (finding an EPA guidance final and ripe for review); Appalachian Power Co. v. EPA, 208 F.3d 1015, 1023 (D.C. Cir. 2000) (holding a guidance stating an agency's settled position to be reviewable); Ciba-Geigy Corp. v. U.S. EPA, 801 F.2d 430, 436 (D.C. Cir. 1986) (holding a letter in which Director of Pesticide Programs "unequivocally" stated agency's relevant position to be sufficiently final for purposes of judicial review); Better Gov't Ass'n v. Dep't of State, 780 F.2d 86, 93 (D.C. Cir. 1986) (finding an interpretation of administrative guidelines fit for review where the agencies had said nothing to suggest that "further procedural or substantive evolution is expected"); Nat'l Automatic Laundry & Cleaning Council v. Shultz, 443 F.2d 689, 702 (D.C. Cir. 1971) (holding an advice letter signed by the agency head "following reflective examination" was final and ripe for review).

This last statement may need to be qualified after the 2003 Supreme Court decision in *National Park Hospitality Ass'n v. Department of the Interior (NPHA)*,[309] where the Court addressed the issue or ripeness of non-legislative rules in a somewhat unusual context. The National Park Service (NPS) had issued regulations that included a provision stating that concession contracts are not contracts within the meaning of the Contract Disputes Act.[310] Because the NPS had no authority to administer that Act, this provision had no legal force, but the Service contended that its regulation nonetheless constituted an interpretive rule that warranted deference. The majority of the Court rejected this argument because the NPS did not administer the Contracts Disputes Act. Rather, the Court concluded that the provision was "nothing more than a 'general statemen[t] of policy,'"[311] and that because the statement had no legal effect and imposed no hardship on potential concessionaires, it was not ripe for judicial review even though the issue was strictly a legal one. Several dissenting Justices pointed out that the concessionaires would indeed face higher dispute resolution costs because of the NPS's position, but this view did not prevail. As Professor Seidenfeld has commented, "The *NPHA* majority, however, seems to imply that agency interpretative rules have legal significance that might make them ripe for review, while statements of policy have no legal force and hence will not be ripe for review."[312] This would amount to significant change in doctrine, were it to survive as a bright line.

Nevertheless, given the possibility of reviewability of non-legislative rules, where there is a statutory filing deadline, a challenger is well advised to make a "protective" filing within the statutory time period, even if there is a chance that the challenged agency action will be found to be not yet ripe for review,[313] especially since a finding of lack of ripeness should not foreclose an as-applied challenge later on.[314]

d. Ripeness (and finality) issues in challenges to agency inaction or delay in rulemaking. Ripeness and finality are often issues in suits challenging agency inac-

---

309. 538 U.S. 803 (2003).

310. 36 C.F.R. § 51.3 (2003).

311. 538 U.S. at 809.

312. Mark Seidenfeld, *Judicial Review* chapter, DEVELOPMENTS IN ADMINISTRATIVE LAW AND REGULATORY PRACTICE 2002-2003, at 95 (Jeffrey S. Lubbers ed., 2004).

313. *See* Eagle-Picher Indus. v. EPA, 759 F.2d 905, 905 (D.C. Cir. 1985). In that case, petitioners challenged EPA's Hazardous Ranking System under CERCLA, 42 U.S.C. § 9601 *et seq.*, after the 90-day statutory review period had expired, arguing that they were not time-barred because they believed their challenge to the validity of the regulation would not have been ripe during the 90-day period. The court held that, generally, "[i]f there is *any* doubt about the ripeness of a claim, petitioners must bring their challenge in a timely fashion or risk being barred." *Id.* at 914. Although the court found that the case would have been ripe during the 90-day period, and was thus untimely, it heard the case on the merits because the relationship between ripeness and statutory review provisions had previously been "largely uncharted." *Id.* at 919.

314. *See* Clean Air Implementation Project v. EPA, 150 F.3d 1200, 1204 (D.C. Cir. 1998).

tion or delay.[315] In these cases, there is usually no clear action by an agency that is definitely final, yet that inaction is itself often the gravamen of the complaint.[316] Courts have used ripeness and finality analysis in these cases and have been willing in some situations to hear the case on its merits, although the standard of review is narrow and the relief granted is usually very limited.[317]

Moreover, the recent unanimous decision by the Supreme Court in *Norton v. Southern Utah Wilderness Alliance*,[318] rejecting a challenge to the Interior Department's alleged failure to implement its statutory duty to protect Wilderness Study Areas in Utah from increased use of off-road vehicles, casts doubt on the possibility of "failure to act" suits unless the action the agency purportedly should have taken was "discrete" and "required" by law.[319]

In cases alleging agency delay in acting on petitions for rulemaking or in completing rulemaking proceedings,[320] the issue also can arise as to whether the agency action is sufficiently final to be fit for judicial review. The agency often argues that until it decides on a final course of action, judicial review is not appropriate. Courts have observed, however, that sometimes "administrative inaction has precisely the same impact on the rights of the parties as denial of relief," and where this is so, "an agency cannot preclude judicial review by casting its decision in the form of inaction rather than in the form of an order denying relief."[321] They have then gone on to consider whether the particular case is ripe for review.[322]

In *Environmental Defense Fund v. Hardin*,[323] the D.C. Circuit held that EPA's failure to act on a request for interim suspension of DDT was "tantamount to an order denying suspension."[324] Such action was sufficiently final and resulted in sufficient hazard to the public to make the challenge ripe for judicial resolution.[325]

---

315. *See infra* Part IV, ch. 3, for a discussion of review of such cases on the merits.

316. *See* Telecomms. Research & Action Ctr. v. FCC, 750 F.2d 70, 75 (D.C. Cir. 1984). *See also* the forest-planning cases discussed *supra* text at notes 219–27, 261–63.

317. *See infra* Part IV, ch. 3.

318. 542 U.S. 55 (2004). This case is also discussed *infra* in ch. 3(A).

319. Id. at 62–63. The Court found the "discreteness" requirement in the list of items in the APA's definition of "agency action," and the "legally required" requirement by finding that the APA carried forward traditional concepts of mandamus. For a fuller discussion of this case, see Richard Murphy, *Judicial Review* chapter, DEVELOPMENTS IN ADMINISTRATIVE LAW AND REGULATORY PRACTICE 2003-2004, at 84–88 (Jeffrey S. Lubbers ed., 2004).

320. If the agency has taken action in rejecting the request for rulemaking or in deciding not to issue a standard, finality questions would not ordinarily arise, but issues of reviewability are present. *See* discussion *infra* Part IV, ch. 3(B)(1).

321. Envtl. Def. Fund v. Hardin, 428 F.2d 1093, 1099 (D.C. Cir. 1970).

322. *Id.*; *see also* Pub. Citizen Health Res. Grp. v. FDA, 740 F.2d 21 (D.C. Cir. 1984).

323. 428 F.2d 1093 (D.C. Cir. 1970).

324. *Id.* at 1099.

325. Although the court found the case ripe for review, it concluded that "meaningful review" was impossible because of the absence of any record of agency action; it therefore remanded to the agency for a "statement of reasons for [its] silent but effective refusal to suspend." *Id.* at 1099–1100.

A similar analysis has been used in cases challenging an agency's delay in issuing a rule. *Public Citizen Health Research Group v. FDA*[326] involved alleged FDA delay in requiring aspirin products to carry a warning about Reye's syndrome. Because FDA had not yet decided the labeling issue,[327] the court considered whether the issue was "sufficiently final to be fit for review."[328] Although the court refused to treat the agency's tentative conclusions as final action, it noted that "at some point administrative delay amounts to a refusal to act with sufficient finality and ripeness to permit judicial review."[329] While not finding that to be the case in this instance, the court did remand the case to the district court for determination whether the agency's delay was "unreasonable."[330]

---

326. 740 F.2d 21 (D.C. Cir. 1984).
327. FDA had earlier concluded that aspirin products should be labeled, reversed itself and not published a draft proposed rule on the issue, and then published an advanced notice of proposed rulemaking saying that it was "considering proposing" a rule. No further action was taken. 740 F.2d at 24–27.
328. *Id.* at 30.
329. *Id.* at 32. *But see* Envtl. Prot. Info. Ctr. v. Pac. Lumber Co., 266 F. Supp. 2d 1101, 1122 (N.D. Cal. 2003) ("This court finds that EPA's decision not to amend the regulation marked the consummation of its decisionmaking process, despite its generalized statement to continue studying the problem.").
330. 740 F.2d at 35; *see also infra* Part IV, ch. 3, for a discussion of this case.

Chapter 2

The Scope of Judicial Review

Rulemaking is conducted within a legal framework that rests on statutes and presidential directives, but rulemaking procedure has also been significantly influenced by court-made law. This chapter examines perhaps the most important court-made law on rulemaking—that interpreting the scope of judicial review of agency rules.

A. Scope of Review—General Provisions

The scope of judicial review is the standard by which a court will judge the validity of the agency action in review proceedings. Unless the enabling statute for a particular regulatory program specifies a different standard, the provisions of the Administrative Procedure Act govern. Although enabling statutes occasionally provide for a "substantial evidence" test or some other standard in court review of agency rules,[1] more often the enabling statute either contains no specific provision on scope of review or it expressly incorporates the APA provisions. The relevant section of the APA is 5 U.S.C. § 706, which provides as follows:

Scope of review

To the extent necessary to decision and when presented, the reviewing court shall decide all relevant questions of law, interpret constitutional and statutory provisions, and determine the meaning or applicability of the terms of an agency action. The reviewing court shall—

(1) compel agency action unlawfully withheld or unreasonably delayed; and

(2) hold unlawful and set aside[2] agency action, findings, and conclusions found to be—

---

1. *See, e.g.*, Medical Device Amendments, 21 U.S.C. § 360g(c); OSH Act, 29 U.S.C. § 655(f).

2. A threshold question is presented by the opening clause in section 706(2) as to whether this compels a court to "vacate" or completely invalidate an improperly issued rule or whether the court may simply remand the rule case back to the agency for additional proceedings without vacating it. *See, e.g.*, Am. Mining Cong. v. U.S. Army Corps of Eng'rs, 962 F. Supp. 2, 4 (D.D.C. 1997) ("the ordinary result" when a court finds an agency's rule unlawful is that the rule is "vacated," not just with respect to the plaintiffs who brought the action but with respect to all parties, citing numerous cases). This issue is treated more fully in section C, *infra*. *See* Checkosky

(A) arbitrary, capricious, an abuse of discretion, or otherwise not in accordance with law;

(B) contrary to constitutional right, power, privilege, or immunity;

(C) in excess of statutory jurisdiction, authority, or limitations, or short of statutory right;

(D) without observance of procedure required by law;

(E) unsupported by substantial evidence in a case subject to sections 556 and 557 of this title or otherwise reviewed on the record of an agency hearing provided by statute; or

(F) unwarranted by the facts to the extent that the facts are subject to trial de novo by the reviewing court.

In making the foregoing determinations, the court shall review the whole record or those parts of it cited by a party, and due account shall be taken of the rule of prejudicial error.

In the review of informal rulemaking, sections 706(1) and 706(2)(A), (B), (C), and (D) are applied most often. Subsections 706(2)(E) and (F), providing for "substantial evidence" and de novo review, are not applicable to informal rulemaking unless they are expressly adopted in an agency-enabling statute. Each of the relevant subsections of section 706 will be treated separately in this chapter.

1. APA Section 706(1): "agency action unlawfully withheld or unreasonably delayed"

This subsection, authorizing a court to "compel agency action unlawfully withheld or unreasonably delayed," is increasingly being invoked in suits challenging agency inaction in rulemaking, often in conjunction with other statutory provisions.[3] These suits typically allege unreasonable agency delay in completing rulemaking, agency refusal to initiate rulemaking, or agency refusal to issue a rule, in whole or in part, when rulemaking is completed.

In 1985 the Supreme Court held, in *Heckler v. Chaney*,[4] that court review is presumptively unavailable where an agency refuses to undertake an *enforcement* action. Although the reach of *Chaney* was initially uncertain, the Supreme Court, in *Massa-*

---

v. SEC, 23 F.3d 452 (D.C. Cir. 1994) (discussing the intracircuit debate on this point); *see also* Ronald M. Levin, *"Vacation" at Sea: Judicial Remedies and Equitable Discretion in Administrative Law*, 53 DUKE L.J. 291 (2003) [hereinafter Levin, *Vacation at Sea*]; Peter L. Strauss, *The Rulemaking Continuum*, 41 DUKE L.J. 1463, 1471 n.30 (1992) (speculating that the remand stratagem may be a way of "limit[ing] the ossification effect").

3. *See, e.g.*, 5 U.S.C. § 555(b) ("[W]ithin a reasonable time, each agency shall proceed to conclude a matter presented to it."). Some enabling statutes expressly provide for court review of agency inaction in certain circumstances. *See, e.g.*, 49 U.S.C. § 10,326(b)(2), *applied in* Western Fuels-Illinois, Inc. v. ICC, 878 F.2d 1025 (7th Cir. 1989).

4. 470 U.S. 821 (1985).

chusetts v. EPA,[5] made clear that courts should not apply that decision to agency inaction in rulemaking. They typically do, however, apply a highly deferential standard in reviewing challenges alleging that agency rulemaking action is being "unlawfully withheld or unreasonably delayed."

The Supreme Court's 2004 decision in *Norton v. Southern Utah Wilderness Alliance*[6] has also made some types of challenges to agency inaction highly problematic. The Tenth Circuit reversed the district court's dismissal of the suit, but the Supreme Court unanimously reversed. The Court held that a § 706(1) claim can proceed only where a plaintiff asserts that an agency failed to take a "discrete agency action that it is required to take" and that the required-action limitation rules out judicial direction of even discrete agency action that is not demanded by law.[7]

This case, along with the reasons for the courts' deferential approach and the developing case law on judicial review of challenges to agency inaction, are discussed more fully in Part IV, Chapter 3.

2. APA Section 706(2)(A): "arbitrary, capricious, an abuse of discretion, or otherwise not in accordance with law"

This standard of review, commonly referred to as the "arbitrary and capricious" test,[8] is the traditional standard applied by courts in reviewing agency rules promulgated after informal rulemaking. While the substantive rationality of an agency rule has been the main locus of review under the arbitrary and capricious test, the test also has become a "catch-all" provision, "picking up . . . administrative misconduct not covered by the other more specific paragraphs [of section 706]."[9] Courts applying the test usually focus on the following three components of review under this standard: (1) whether the rulemaking record supports the factual conclusions upon which the rule is based, (2) the "rationality" or "reasonableness" of the policy conclusions underlying the rule, and (3) the extent to which the agency has adequately articulated the basis for its conclusions.[10] Although courts often discuss procedural issues and the

---

5. 549 U.S. 497 (2007).
6. 542 U.S. 55 (2004).
7. 542 U.S. at 64.
8. Sometimes referred to as the "arbitrary or capricious" test or the "abuse of discretion" test. *See* Ronald M. Levin, *Scope of Review Legislation: The Lessons of 1995*, 31 WAKE FOREST L. REV. 647, 649 n.13 (1996) [hereinafter Levin, *Scope of Review Legislation*]. Note, however, that a Westlaw search of federal cases conducted December 31, 2011, turned up 270 cases using "and" and only 36 using "or."
9. Ass'n of Data Processing Serv. Orgs., Inc. v. Bd. of Governors (*Data Processing*), 745 F.2d 677, 683 (D.C. Cir. 1984).
10. As Professor Levin points out, "The courts' use of [§ 706(2)(A)] for the purpose of reviewing factual judgments has always seemed a bit awkward, because the notion of 'abuse of discretion' is most naturally understood as denoting a mistake that an agency makes while exercising policy judgment, not while finding facts." Levin, *Scope of Review Legislation, supra* note 8, at 649.

validity of the agency's statutory interpretation as part of arbitrary and capricious review, these issues will be discussed below with respect to separate subsections of section 706 of the APA.[11]

The meaning of the terms "arbitrary," "capricious," "abuse of discretion," and "not in accordance with law" is by no means self-evident,[12] and reviewing courts' interpretations of this subsection have changed over time.

The *Blackletter Statement of Federal Administrative Law*,[13] published by the ABA Section of Administrative Law and Regulatory Practice, summarizes the judicial interpretations of the arbitrary and capricious test as follows:

> The court may set aside an agency action as an abuse of discretion (alternatively known in APA parlance as the "arbitrary and capricious" test), *see* APA § 706(2)(A), on any of several grounds. In practice, application of these grounds varies according to the nature and magnitude of the agency action. Thus, a court will typically apply the criteria rigorously during judicial review of high-stakes rulemaking proceedings (a practice commonly termed "hard look" review), but much more leniently when reviewing a routine, uncomplicated action. A court may not impose its own policy preferences on the agency. Commonly applied bases for reversal include the following:
>
> A. The agency relied on factors that may not be taken into account under, or ignored factors that must be taken into account under, any authoritative source of law. (The caselaw often describes this ground as an element of the arbitrary and capricious test, although it seems more properly understood as a component of the court's legal analysis.)
> B. The action does not bear a reasonable relationship to statutory purposes or requirements.
> C. The asserted or necessary factual premises of the action do not withstand scrutiny under the relevant standard of review
> D. The action is unsupported by any explanation or rests upon reasoning that is seriously flawed.
> E. The agency failed, without adequate justification, to give reasonable consideration to an important aspect of the problems presented by the action, such as the effects or costs of the policy choice involved, or the factual circumstances bearing on that choice.

11. *See* discussion *infra* subsecs. (A)(4) & (5).
12. *See* Weyerhaeuser Co. v. Costle, 590 F.2d 1011, 1024 (D.C. Cir. 1978) (discussing vagueness of formulations in various clauses in § 706(2) but especially § 706(2)(A)).
13. 54 ADMIN. L. REV. 1, 42–43 (2002) (cross-references omitted) as revised by action of the Council of the Section at its spring meeting in April 2012, attached to e-mail to author from Ron Levin (Apr. 25, 2012). For a thorough discussion of cases under these rubrics, see Lisa Schultz Bressman, chapter 8, *in* A GUIDE TO JUDICIAL AND POLITICAL REVIEW OF FEDERAL AGENCIES, at 177–95 (John F. Duffy & Michael Herz eds., 2005) [hereinafter ABA GUIDE TO JUDICIAL REVIEW]. An update of both the *Blackletter* and the GUIDE is pending.

F. The action, where inconsistent with prior agency policies or precedents, fails to display an awareness of the change in position, fails to explain a changed view of the facts, or fails to consider serious reliance interests that its prior policy engendered.

G. The agency failed, without an adequate justification, to consider or adopt an important alternative solution to the problem addressed in the action.

H. The agency failed to consider substantial arguments, or respond to relevant and significant comments, made by the participants in the proceeding that gave rise to the agency action.

I. The agency has imposed a sanction that is greatly out of proportion to the magnitude of the violation.

J. The action fails in other respects to rest upon reasoned decisionmaking.

Until the 1970s, the prevailing standard was that stated by the Supreme Court in the pre-APA case of *Pacific States Box & Basket Co. v. White*,[14] as follows: "[W]here the regulation is within the scope of authority legally delegated, the presumption of the existence of facts justifying its specific exercise attaches . . . ."[15] However, in 1971, the Supreme Court ushered in a new era of closer court scrutiny of agency rules in the landmark decision *Citizens to Preserve Overton Park v. Volpe*.[16]

In *Overton Park*, the Secretary of Transportation, after a "quasi-legislative" hearing, had approved federal funds for construction of a highway through a city park.[17] The Court found that section 706(2)(A) (that is, the arbitrary and capricious test) was the applicable test for review, and it construed the test as follows:

> To make this finding [whether the decision was arbitrary and capricious], the court must consider whether the decision was based on a consideration of the relevant factors and whether there had been a clear error of judgment. . . . Although this inquiry into the facts is to be searching and careful, the ultimate standard of review is a narrow one. The court is not empowered to substitute its judgment for that of the agency.[18]

At first, after *Overton Park*, the Supreme Court seemed to be unsure about whether the arbitrary and capricious test should apply to review of informal rulemaking. In *Overton Park*, the Court included what Paul Verkuil called at the time an "unfortunate dictum suggesting that the substantial evidence test should apply to informal rulemaking,"[19] a dictum that was seemingly applied a year later in another rulemaking

---

14. 296 U.S. 176 (1935).

15. *Id.* at 186.

16. 401 U.S. 402 (1971).

17. *See* Peter L. Strauss, Citizens to Preserve Overton Park v. Volpe—*of Politics and Law, Young Lawyers and the Highway Goliath, in* ADMINISTRATIVE LAW STORIES 258 (Peter L. Strauss ed., 2006) (providing a historical account of case).

18. *Overton Park*, 401 U.S. at 416 (citations omitted).

19. Paul R. Verkuil, *Judicial Review of Informal Rulemaking*, 60 VA. L. REV. 185, 212 (1974).

case in *United States v. Midwest Video*.[20] A year after that, in another informal adjudication case that had just come down, *Camp v. Pitts*,[21] the Court, in explaining why the arbitrary and capricious test was applicable, used language that seemed to require its application to informal rulemaking too:

> [I]t is also clear that neither the National Bank Act nor the APA requires the Comptroller to hold a hearing or to make formal findings on the hearing record when passing on applications for new banking authorities. Accordingly, the proper standard for judicial review of the Comptroller's adjudications is not the "substantial evidence" test which is appropriate when reviewing findings made on a hearing record.[22]

This was already the law in the D.C. Circuit, where since 1968 the court had been applying the arbitrary and capricious test to informal rulemaking, and this eventually was clearly accepted by the Supreme Court in the 1983 *State Farm* case.[23]

Overton Park's application of the arbitrary and capricious test was not without ambiguity. It seemed simultaneously to reflect both an intrusive and a deferential attitude. Moreover, there has subsequently been extensive discussion in cases and commentary about the differences between the arbitrary and capricious test, as described in *Overton Park*, and the "substantial evidence" test normally applied to adjudicatory decisions, formal rulemakings, and sometimes to rulemaking under particular enabling statutes.[24] Some courts and commentators have concluded that, at least when applied to court review of factual conclusions by agencies, the distinction between the substantial evidence and the arbitrary and capricious tests is "largely semantic."[25]

---

20. 406 U.S. 649, 671 (1972) ("The question remains whether the regulation is supported by substantial evidence that it will promote the public interest.").

21. 411 U.S. 138 (1973).

22. *Id.* at 140–41.

23. Motor Vehicle Mfrs. Ass'n of U.S., Inc. v. State Farm Mut. Auto. Ins. Co., 463 U.S. 29, 40–41 (1983) ("[W]e do not find the appropriate scope of judicial review to be the 'most troublesome question' in the case. . . . [M]otor vehicle safety standards are to be promulgated under the informal rulemaking procedures of § 553 of the Administrative Procedure Act. The agency's action in promulgating such standards therefore may be set aside if found to be 'arbitrary, capricious, an abuse of discretion, or otherwise not in accordance with law.'" (citing APA, 5 U.S.C. § 706(2)(A); *Overton Park* 401 U.S. at 414)).

24. *See* discussion *infra* subsec. 6.

25. *Data Processing, supra* note 9, at 684; *see also* Wileman Bros. & Elliott, Inc. v. Espy, 58 F.3d 1367 (9th Cir. 1995); Matthew J. McGrath, Note, *Convergence of the Substantial Evidence and Arbitrary and Capricious Standards of Review During Informal Rulemaking*, 54 Geo. Wash. L. Rev. 541 (1986). McGrath's view seems to have been first stated in Antonin Scalia & Frank Goodman, *Procedural Aspects of the Consumer Product Safety Act*, 20 UCLA L. Rev. 899, 935 n.138 (1973). *But see* AFL-CIO v. OSHA, 965 F.2d 962 (11th Cir. 1990) (discussing the contrary view that the substantial evidence test requires a more rigorous level of judicial scrutiny—even in the rulemaking context). In the oral argument in *Dickinson v. Zurko*, 527 U.S. 150 (1999), there was an extended discussion of the APA scope-of-review requirements, and one Justice stated: "I agree that clearly erroneous is higher than both arbitrary and capri-

Thus, in *Consumers Union of United States, Inc. v. FTC*,[26] involving review of a Federal Trade Commission rule relating to the sale of used cars, the D.C. Circuit concluded that "in the context of the APA, the substantial evidence test (which is applied only to formal adjudication and formal rulemaking . . .) and the arbitrary and capricious test (which governs review of *all* proceedings . . .) 'are one and the same' insofar as the requisite degree of evidentiary support is concerned."[27] The court held that the standard, as applied to the FTC rulemaking, demanded "such relevant evidence as a reasonable mind might accept as adequate to support a conclusion,"[28] and it went on to uphold the rule. Indeed, there is much truth in Professor David Zaring's insight that courts basically use a "reasonableness" test in applying each of the standards and that the complexity of the existing doctrine could be swept aside by substituting this one-word test.[29] Professor Pierce has signed onto this view, adding that "[a]n agency action is reasonable if it is consistent with the relevant statute and the available evidence, and if the agency has provided an adequate explanation of how it reasoned from the relevant statute and available evidence to reach its conclusions."[30]

a. Significant Supreme Court decisions applying the arbitrary and capricious test. In the early 1980s, the Supreme Court revisited the question of the scope of arbitrary and capricious review in two rulemaking cases. *Baltimore Gas & Electric Co. v. Natural Resources Defense Council, Inc.*[31] involved review of a series of generic rules issued by the Nuclear Regulatory Commission (NRC) to evaluate the environmental effects of a nuclear power plant's fuel cycle.[32] The D.C. Circuit had held the NRC rules to be arbitrary and capricious, finding that the agency made certain unsupported assumptions in issuing the rules and failed to factor into its decisional process certain factual uncertainties.[33] The Supreme Court reversed, noting that the NRC was making "predictions, within its area of special expertise, at the frontiers of science" and stating that the reviewing court "must generally be at its most deferen-

---

cious and substantial evidence. I tend to think that arbitrary and capricious and substantial evidence, however, are identical, and that the point of [706](E) is simply that the—that the substantial evidence has to be in the record." 1999 WL 190969, at *34.

26. 801 F.2d 417 (D.C. Cir. 1986).
27. *Id.* at 422 (quoting *Data Processing, supra* note 9).
28. *Id.* The relevant statutory provision is 15 U.S.C. § 57a(e)(3)(A), which also authorizes a "hybrid" form of rulemaking procedure.
29. *See generally* David Zaring, *Reasonable Agencies*, 96 VA. L. REV. 135 (2010). He goes so far as to suggest that this behavior extends to all types of judicial review of agency action, whether the case involves questions of law or fact, involves formal or informal procedures, the arbitrary and capricious test, or the *Chevron* analysis, discussed below.
30. Richard J. Pierce, Jr., *What Do the Studies of Judicial Review of Agency Actions Mean?*, 63 ADMIN. L. REV. 77, 96 (2011).
31. 462 U.S. 87 (1983).
32. This case was a later stage of the proceeding that first reached the Supreme Court in *Vermont Yankee Nuclear Power Corp. v. Natural Resources Defense Counsel*, 435 U.S. 519 (1978).
33. *See* Natural Res. Def. Council, Inc. v. NRC, 685 F.2d 459 (D.C. Cir. 1982).

tial" when examining this kind of scientific determination.[34] The Court further concluded that NRC's assumptions were "within the bounds of reasoned decisionmaking" and that the agency had "considered the relevant factors and articulated a rational connection between the facts found and the choice made."[35] "If the agency meets these requirements," the Court admonished, "it is not our task to determine what decision we, as Commissioners, would have reached."[36]

This sort of "soft look" seems antithetical to the "hard look" embraced by the Supreme Court in that very same term in *Motor Vehicle Manufacturers Association v. State Farm Mutual Automobile Insurance Co. (State Farm)*.[37] This time, however, it reversed the agency's rulemaking decision. At issue in *State Farm* was the National Highway Traffic Safety Administration's (NHTSA's) rescission of a rule, issued by a prior administration, requiring passive restraints (such as automatic seatbelts and air bags) in new cars. The Supreme Court first addressed the appropriate scope of judicial review of the rule rescission and concluded that the agency's enabling statute contemplated review under the APA's arbitrary and capricious standard.[38] The Court rejected appellant's argument that the rescission of a rule should be judged by the same deferential standard as review of an agency's refusal to promulgate a rule in the first place.[39]

---

34. Baltimore Gas & Electric Co., 462 U.S. at 103; *see also* Ethyl Corp. v. EPA, 541 F.2d 1 (D.C. Cir. 1976) (en banc). *See also In re* Polar Bear Endangered Species Act Listing and § 4(d) Rule Litigation, 794 F. Supp. 2d 65, 69 (D.D.C. 2011) (upholding listing of polar bears as "threatened" under the Endangered Species Act, because "the agency is operating at the frontiers of science." Another court has noted that particular deference may be given to "transitional" rules as well. *See* Tex. Office of Pub. Util. Counsel v. FCC, 265 F.3d 313, 325 (5th Cir. 2001).

35. 462 U.S. at 104–05.

36. *Id.* at 105; *see also* Marsh v. Ore. Natural Res. Council, 490 U.S. 360, 378 (1989) (holding an agency must have "discretion to rely on the reasonable opinions of its own qualified experts even if, as an original matter, a court might find the contrary views more persuasive"); FCC v. WNCN Listeners Guild, 450 U.S. 582, 595–96 (1981) (quoting FCC v. Nat'l Citizens Comm. for Broadcasting, 436 U.S. 775, 814 (1978)) (granting deference to the agency's "forecast of the direction in which future public interest lies"). Another way of putting this is, "Where issues involve elusive and not easily defined areas . . . , our review is considerably more deferential, according broad leeway to the [agency's] line-drawing determinations." Nuclear Energy Inst., Inc. v. EPA, 373 F.3d 1251, 1276 (D.C. Cir. 2004) (citation omitted) (approving the groundwater testing location for the Yucca Mountain nuclear waste repository).

37. 463 U.S. 29 (1983). *See* Andrew D. Siegel, *The Aftermath of* Baltimore Gas & Electric Co. v. NRDC: *A Broader Notion of Judicial Deference to Agency Expertise*, 11 Harv. Envt'l L. Rev. 331, 373 (1987) (noting and attempting to rationalize the divergence between the two lines of cases represented by *Baltimore Gas* and *State Farm*); *see also* Jerry L. Mashaw, *The Story of Motor Vehicle Mfrs. Ass'n of the U.S. v. State Farm Mutual Automobile Ins. Co.: Law, Science and Politics in the Administrative State, in* Administrative Law Stories 334 (Peter L. Strauss ed., 2006) (providing a historical account of the *State Farm* case).

38. *State Farm*, 463 U.S. at 41.

39. *Id.* "[T]he revocation of an extant regulation is substantially different than a failure to act," the Court said, in that the revocation "constitutes a reversal of the agency's former views as to the proper course [of regulation]." *Id.* at 42. The Court accordingly held that an agency "changing its course by rescinding a rule is obligated to supply a reasoned analysis for the change beyond that which may be required when the agency does not act in the first instance." *Id.*

The Supreme Court then considered the meaning of the arbitrary and capricious standard as applied to a rule rescission. Rejecting the government's argument that this requires "no more than the minimum rationality" needed for a statute to withstand a due process challenge, the Court held that the presumption of regularity afforded an agency in its regulatory activities was not equivalent to the "presumption of constitutionality" afforded legislation enacted by Congress.[40] The Court said that the scope of review under the arbitrary and capricious standard is "narrow and a court is not to substitute its judgment for that of the agency,"[41] but it then elaborated as follows:

> Normally, an agency rule would be arbitrary and capricious if the agency has relied on factors which Congress has not intended it to consider, entirely failed to consider an important aspect of the problem, offered an explanation for its decision that runs counter to the evidence before the agency, or is so implausible that it could not be ascribed to a difference in view or the product of agency expertise.[42]

Applying this standard, the Court unanimously decided that NHTSA had acted arbitrarily in rescinding the earlier rule without any consideration of the mandatory air bag option.[43] A majority further held that the record was not sufficient to enable it to conclude that the rescission of the passive restraint requirement was the product of reasoned decisionmaking.[44] While the Court conceded that "an agency's view of what is in the public interest" might change, "either with or without a change in circumstances," it insisted that an agency changing its course "must supply a reasoned analysis."[45] The Court remanded the matter to NHTSA for further consideration.[46]

The D.C. Circuit quickly followed *State Farm* in a similar decision involving a rescission of a rule in *International Ladies' Garment Workers' Union v. Donovan*,[47] which involved a challenge to the Department of Labor's rescission of restrictions on "homework" in certain industries under the Fair Labor Standards Act.[48] The D.C.

---

40. *Id.* at 44 n.9.
41. 463 U.S. at 43 (quoting *Overton Park*, 401 U.S. at 41).
42. *Id.* (citing SEC v. Chenery Corp., 332 U.S. 194 (1974), for the proposition that the reviewing court "should not attempt itself to make up for such deficiencies [in the agency explanation]"). It should also be noted that the Court also stated: "We will, however, 'uphold a decision of less than ideal clarity if the agency's path may reasonably be discerned.'" *Id.* at 43 (quoting Bowman Transp., Inc. v. Arkansas–Best Freight System, Inc., 419 U.S. 281, 286 (1974)).
43. *Id.* at 46–48.
44. *Id.* at 51–56.
45. *Id.* at 57. The Court's alternative rationale for the remand was the agency's complete failure to justify the promulgation of the "airbags only" rule. *Id.*
46. *Id.* For a comprehensive look at the impact of existing rules on agency discretion, see Harold J. Krent, *Reviewing Agency Action for Inconsistency with Prior Rules and Regulations*, 72 Chi.-Kent L. Rev. 1187 (1997).
47. 722 F.2d 795 (D.C. Cir. 1983).
48. Acting under the Fair Labor Standards Act, 29 U.S.C. §§ 201–219, the Department of Labor had issued long-standing regulations restricting the employment of workers in their homes. In

Circuit applied the arbitrary and capricious standard of review to the rescission, characterizing the agency's action as "a classic example of an agency attempt to modify a long-standing policy by rescinding regulations embodying that policy."[49] The court stated: "We cannot discern any rational basis for being less circumspect in reviewing the rescission of a regulation that has been uniformly supported since its adoption forty years ago, than the Supreme Court was in reviewing rescission of a highly controversial regulation [the NHTSA passive restraint rule]."[50] The court of appeals then examined the Secretary of Labor's rationale for rescinding the homework rule and concluded that the Secretary had failed to address known or reasonable options and to explain why such options were rejected.[51] This constituted a complete failure to satisfy the "quintessential aspects of reasoned decisionmaking," the court said, and was the "primary basis" for its decision to vacate the agency action.[52]

Nor was *State Farm*'s impact limited to rescission cases. The Supreme Court in 1986, in *Bowen v. American Hospital Association*,[53] reaffirmed its basic conclusion in *State Farm* that an agency regulation is not entitled to the same presumption of regularity as is a statute challenged under the Due Process Clause.[54] The Supreme Court vacated a rule issued by the Department of Health and Human Services dealing with health care for handicapped infants, stating that deference to agencies' decisions had "not come so far" that a regulation would be upheld whenever it is possible to "conceive a basis" for administrative action.[55] The Court asserted:

> Our recognition of Congress' need to vest administrative agencies with ample power to assist in the difficult task of governing a vast complex industrial Nation carries with it the correlative responsibility of the agency to explain the rationale and factual basis for its decision, even though we show respect for the agency's judgment in both.[56]

1981, the Secretary rescinded the homeworker regulations in the knitted outerwear industry. This decision was challenged by certain employers and associations, unions, and state labor enforcement officials. *See* Int'l Ladies' Garment Workers Union v. Donovan, 722 F.2d 795, 799 (D.C. Cir. 1983).

49. *Id.* at 812.
50. *Id.* at 814.
51. *Id.* at 818.
52. *Id.*; *see also* AFL-CIO v. Brock, 835 F.2d 912 (D.C. Cir. 1987) (reversing Department of Labor's action altering prior policy regarding minimum wage for foreign agricultural workers for lack of a reasoned explanation).
53. 476 U.S. 610 (1986) (plurality opinion).
54. *Id.* at 627. The main issue in the case was whether the regulation was authorized by section 504 of the Rehabilitation Act of 1973, 29 U.S.C. § 794; the Court, with four Justices dissenting, held that the regulation was not authorized. *Id.*
55. *Id.* at 626 (citing *State Farm*, 463 U.S. at 43).
56. *Id.* at 627.

The Supreme Court has reiterated the basic tenets of *State Farm* in several cases,[57] but it did not really re-examine it until 2009 in the important, but still a bit undefined, decision of *FCC v. Fox Television Stations, Inc.*[58] This decision is discussed below in the section concerning the scope of review of agency policy changes.

b. The "hard look" doctrine. Although the Supreme Court did not use the term "hard look" in *State Farm* (nor has it ever used the term to describe the review of agency action outside of the NEPA context),[59] commentators have noted that the *State Farm* decision "expressly endorses the primary elements, both substantive and procedural, of the hard-look doctrine."[60] As summarized by Professor McGarity,[61] under the hard-look approach, originally developed by the D.C. Circuit in the 1970s:[62]

> [T]he courts must take a hard look at the administrative record and the agency's explanatory material to determine whether the agency used the correct analytical methodology, applied the proper criteria, considered the relevant factors, chose from among the available range of regulatory options, relied upon appropriate policies, and pointed to adequate support in the record for material empirical propositions.[63]

Another well-known description of hard-look review in the context of a review sustaining a major EPA rule came at the end of Judge Wald's opinion in *Sierra Club v. Costle*:[64]

---

57. *See, e.g.*, Nat'l Ass'n of Home Builders v. Defenders of Wildlife, 551 U.S. 644, 658 (2007); Verizon Commc'ns v. FCC, 535 U.S. 467, 503 n.20 (2002).
58. 556 U.S. 502 (2009).
59. Search of "hard look" in the Westlaw Supreme Court database (March 30, 2012).
60. Cass R. Sunstein, *Deregulation and the Hard-Look Doctrine*, 1983 SUP. CT. REV. 177, 210. For an interesting essay on the history of the development of hard-look review, see Daniel B. Rodriguez, *Jaffe's Law: An Essay on the Intellectual Underpinnings of Modern Administrative Law Theory*, 72 CHI.-KENT L. REV. 1159, 1160 (1997) (describing Prof. Jaffe as "the intellectual architect of hard look review").
61. Thomas O. McGarity, *The Courts and the Ossification of Rulemaking: A Response to Professor Seidenfeld*, 75 TEX. L. REV. 525 (1997) [hereinafter McGarity, *Response to Professor Seidenfeld*].
62. According to McGarity:

    > Judge Leventhal originally coined the term in *Pikes Peak Broadcasting Co. v. FCC*, 422 F.2d 671, 682 (D.C. Cir. 1969), to characterize the attention that an agency was expected to give to the contentions of the parties under the Administrative Procedure Act, and later used the term to define the attention an agency was expected to give to the environmental effects of their activities under the National Environmental Policy Act.

    Id. at 527 n.5.
63. *Id.* at 527; *see also* Mark Seidenfeld, *Demystifying Deossification: Rethinking Recent Proposals to Modify Judicial Review of Notice and Comment Rulemaking*, 75 TEX. L. REV. 483 (1997) [hereinafter Seidenfeld, *Demystifying Deossification*].
64. 657 F.2d 298 (D.C. Cir. 1981).

We reach our decision after interminable record searching (and considerable soul searching). We have read the record with as *hard a look* as mortal judges can probably give its thousands of pages. We have adopted a simple and straight-forward standard of review, probed the agency's rationale, studied its references (and those of appellants), endeavored to understand them where they were intelligible (parts were simply impenetrable), and on close questions given the agency the benefit of the doubt out of deference for the terrible complexity of its job. We are not engineers, computer modelers, economists or statisticians, although many of the documents in this record require such expertise and more.[65]

More recent cases reviewing agency rulemaking do not often use the term "hard look," but they still regularly cite *State Farm*. Examples of cases remanding agency rules for violation of the arbitrary and capricious test have found that the agency failed to consider an issue that it was statutorily required to address;[66] failed adequately to explain why an annual standard could be appropriately evaluated based solely upon long-term studies;[67] failed either to interpret "(B)(iii) in harmony with (B)(i) and (B)(ii) or to explain why it need not do so";[68] failed adequately to consider costs imposed on the challengers and available alternatives to a regulatory requirement;[69] "neglected to consider a statutorily mandated factor";[70] failed to provide any explanation for its decision to establish subcategories;[71] failed to make a "rational connection between the facts found and the choice made";[72] issued a "rule [that] was a product of

---

65. *Id.* at 410 (footnote omitted) (emphasis added).
66. Owner-Operator Indep. Drivers Ass'n, Inc. v. Fed. Motor Carrier Safety Admin., 656 F.3d 580, 582 (7th Cir. 2011) ("Specifically, the Agency said nothing about the requirement that any regulation about the use of monitoring devices in commercial vehicles must 'ensure that the devices are not used to harass vehicle operators.'" (quoting 49 U.S.C. § 31137(a))).
67. Am. Farm Bureau Fed'n v. EPA, 559 F.3d 512, 522 (D.C. Cir. 2009).
68. Env'tl Defense, Inc., v. EPA, 509 F.3d 553, 561 (D.C. Cir. 2007).
69. Chamber of Commerce v. SEC, 412 F.3d 133, 144–45 (D.C. Cir. 2005).
70. Pub. Citizen v. Fed. Motor Carrier Safety Admin., 374 F.3d 1209, 1216 (D.C. Cir. 2004) (holding a rule arbitrary and capricious "because the agency neglected to consider a statutorily mandated factor—the impact of the rule on the health of drivers").
71. Ne. Md. Waste Disposal Auth. v. EPA, 358 F.3d 936, 948 (D.C. Cir. 2004) (per curiam) ("Did EPA explain its decision to establish subcategories based on aggregate plant capacity? We are, frankly, stunned to find that it did not. As the Agency concedes, there is *not one word* in the proposed or final rule that explains [this].") (emphasis in original).
72. Pub. Citizen, Inc. v. Mineta, 340 F.3d 39, 56 (2d Cir. 2003) (holding a DOT rule requiring the use of tire pressure–monitoring systems (TPMS) in new motor vehicles was arbitrary and capricious to the extent it adopted a one-tire, 30% TPMS standard because the rulemaking record lacks a satisfactory explanation that includes a "rational connection between the facts found and the choice made"; but holding the three-year phase-in period for installation of TPMS in new vehicles and allowance of four-tire, 25% TPMS standard, rather than four-tire, 20% standard, was not arbitrary and capricious).

pure political compromise, not reasoned scientific endeavor"[73]; offered neither support that the rule was "necessary to the public interest" nor an "adequate basis" that the purpose "would be accomplished";[74] did not "exercise sufficiently independent judgment";[75] provided projections that appear arbitrary, without record support;[76] offered no "affirmative justification" to support the elimination of a regulatory exemption;[77] established a presumption that was "irrationally broad" considering the agency changed its interpretation;[78] failed to adequately explain technical aspects of its rule;[79] used a model that improperly minimized crash risk, inconsistent with study of actual crash data underlying model;[80] "base[ed] its decision on a premise the agency itself has already planned to disrupt,"[81] and provided an explanation that was "too conclusory to permit this Court to evaluate its rationality."[82]

---

73. Midwater Trawlers Coop. v. Dep't of Commerce, 282 F.3d 710, 720 (9th Cir. 2002).
74. Fox Television Stations, Inc. v. FCC, 280 F.3d 1027, 1043–44 (D.C. Cir. 2002) (holding the FCC's 1998 decision to retain the national television station ownership rule was arbitrary and capricious because the FCC offered neither support that the rule was necessary to the public interest nor an "adequate basis" that limiting ownership (and thereby protecting diversity) would be accomplished by this rule).
75. Tex. Office of Pub. Util. Counsel v. FCC, 265 F.3d 313, 327–28 (5th Cir. 2001) (holding the FCC acted arbitrarily and capriciously when it did not "exercise sufficiently independent judgment" to determine the amount of a fund used to subsidize poor and rural telephone customers, instead relying almost entirely on private-party estimates, and failed to explain the process it used to create the amount). The FCC based its final figure on the fact that it fell within the range of estimates and it was agreed to by two parties, "which traditionally have had opposing interests." *Id.* at 328.
76. Appalachian Power Co. v. EPA, 249 F.3d 1032, 1053 (D.C. Cir. 2001) ("Future growth projections that implicitly assume a baseline of negative growth in electricity generation over the course of a decade appear arbitrary, and the EPA can point to nothing in the record to dispel this appearance."). After remand the court upheld the EPA's new explanation in *West Virginia v. EPA*, 362 F.3d 861, 870 (D.C. Cir. 2004).
77. Time Warner Entm't Co. v. FCC, 240 F.3d 1126, 1142–43 (D.C. Cir. 2001) (holding the FCC acted arbitrarily and capriciously when it eliminated a regulatory exemption because it offered no "affirmative justification" to support the elimination).
78. Nat'l Mining Ass'n v. Babbitt, 172 F.3d 906, 909–11 (D.C. Cir. 1999) (holding the Mining Act regulation creating a rebuttable presumption of causation of damage in a geographical area after earth movement was arbitrary and capricious for being "irrationally broad" in terms of the geographical area and considering the agency changed its interpretation of the regulation during the case).
79. Sierra Club v. EPA, 167 F.3d 658, 663–65 (D.C. Cir. 1999) (holding EPA's failure to adequately explain technical aspects of its rule-setting standards for medical waste incinerators requires remand).
80. Owner-Operator Indep. Drivers Ass'n v. Fed. Motor Carrier Safety Admin., 494 F.3d 188, 203 (D.C. Cir. 2007).
81. Portland Cement Ass'n v. EPA, 665 F.3d 177, 187 (D.C. Cir. 2011).
82. Am. Petroleum Inst. v. Johnson, 541 F. Supp. 2d 165, 184 (D.D.C. 2008). The court prefaced its holding by saying that it was "not suggesting that agencies are required to write law review articles (or judicial opinions) justifying their authority each time they promulgate a rule . . . [b]ut the circumstances here were peculiar."

For a particularly careful application of the arbitrary and capricious test to multiple challenges to an EPA Clean Water Act rule regulating pollution generated by concentrated animal-feeding operations, see Judge Katzmann's opinion in *Waterkeeper Alliance, Inc. v. U.S. EPA.*[83] In another representative case concerning a review of an agency *technical* regulation—in this case an EPA rule that prescribed a toxicity testing regime for effluents under the Clean Water Act—Judge Randolph's opinion discusses the scientific issues quite thoroughly, and in the end defers to EPA's evaluation of "scientific data within its technical expertise":[84]

> The ratified [toxicity] tests are not without their flaws. But perfection is not the standard against which we judge agency action. EPA's decision was informed by years of scientific studies, negotiation, and public notice-and-comment, and it represents the agency's expert judgment regarding the implementation of the aims of the Clean Water Act. Petitioners have not demonstrated that EPA ignored relevant record evidence, contradicted its own policies without explanation, or otherwise acted arbitrarily and capriciously.[85]

Other decisions affirming agency "technical" rules seem to hearken back to the "soft look" used by the Court in *Baltimore Gas and Electric* for rules "at the frontiers of science."[86]

Because of the seeming unpredictability of these decisions, some have argued that the hard-look doctrine is at least partially responsible for the "ossification" of

---

83. 399 F.3d 486 (2d Cir. 2005); *see also* Prometheus Radio Project v. FCC, 373 F.3d 372 (3d Cir. 2004) (exhaustively reviewing and partially remanding an FCC rule revising its regulations governing broadcast media ownership).

84. Edison Elec. Inst. v. EPA, 391 F.3d 1267, 1270 (D.C. Cir. 2004). The court also rejected the petitioners' contention that, because the test results will ultimately be used in enforcement proceedings, EPA's rulemaking had to conform to *Daubert* evidentiary standards. *Id.* at 1269 n.2.

85. *Id.* at 1274.

86. *See* discussion, *supra,* text at notes 31–36. *See also, e.g.,* Mobile Relay Assocs. v. FCC, 457 F.3d 1,8 (2006) ("We uphold the Commission if it makes a 'technical judgment' that is supported 'with even a modicum of reasoned analysis,' 'absent highly persuasive evidence to the contrary.'") (citing Hispanic Info. & Telecomm. Network v. FCC, 865 F.2d 1289, 1297–98 (D.C. Cir. 1989)). See also this Ninth Circuit rejection of a challenge to a Forest Service forest-thinning project by an environmental group:

> In essence, Lands Council asks this court to act as a panel of scientists that instructs the Forest Service how to validate its hypotheses regarding wildlife viability, chooses among scientific studies in determining whether the Forest Service has complied with the underlying Forest Plan, and orders the agency to explain every possible scientific uncertainty. As we will explain, this is not a proper role for a federal appellate court. But Lands Council's arguments illustrate how, in recent years, our environmental jurisprudence has, at times, shifted away from the appropriate standard of review and could be read to suggest that this court should play such a role.

The Lands Council v. McNair, 537 F.3d 981, 988 (9th Cir. 2008).

agency rulemaking.[87] Others have defended the doctrine as essential to ensure the appropriate level of judicial scrutiny of agency exercise of power.[88] Moreover, an empirical study of D.C. Circuit remands of rules under the hard-look test seems to indicate that in almost all of such cases the agency was able to recover and accomplish its regulatory goals despite or after the remand.[89]

To be sure, some courts have downplayed the hard-look aspect of *State Farm* and instead highlighted the Court's statement that "the court is not empowered to substi-

---

87. *See, e.g.,* Richard J. Pierce, Jr., *Waiting for* Vermont Yankee III, IV, *and* V? *A Response to Beermann and Lawson,* 75 GEO. WASH. L. REV. 902, 908–09 (2007); Richard J. Pierce, Jr., *Judicial Review of Agency Action in a Period of Diminishing Agency Resources,* 49 ADMIN. L. REV. 61 (1997); Richard J. Pierce, Jr., *Seven Ways to Deossify Agency Rulemaking,* 47 ADMIN. L. REV. 59 (1995); Jerry L. Mashaw, *Improving the Environment of Agency Rulemaking: An Essay on Management, Games, and Accountability,* 57 LAW & CONTEMP. PROBS. 185 (1994); Thomas O. McGarity, *Some Thoughts on "Deossifying" the Rulemaking Process,* 41 DUKE L.J. 1385 (1992); R. Shep Melnick, *Administrative Law and Bureaucratic Reality,* 44 ADMIN. L. REV. 245, 247 (1992); Richard J. Pierce, Jr., *The Unintended Effects of Judicial Review of Agency Rules: How Federal Courts Have Contributed to the Electricity Crisis of the 1990s,* 43 ADMIN. L. REV. 7 (1991); JERRY L. MASHAW & DAVID L. HARFST, THE STRUGGLE FOR AUTO SAFETY 225–54 (1990); Paul R. Verkuil, *Judicial Review of Informal Rulemaking: Waiting for* Vermont Yankee II, 55 TUL. L. REV. 418 (1981); *see also* Am. Radio Relay League v. FCC, 524 F.3d 227, 248 (D.C. Cir. 2008) (Kavanaugh, J. concurring in part, concurring in the judgment in part, and dissenting in part) ("[C]ourts . . . have grown *State Farm*'s 'narrow' § 706 arbitrary-and-capricious review into a far more demanding test. Application of the beefed-up arbitrary-and-capricious test has . . . [along with decisions expanding § 553 procedural requirements] gradually transformed rulemaking—whether regulatory or deregulatory rulemaking—from the simple and speedy practice contemplated by the APA into a laborious, seemingly never-ending process.").

88. Professor Seidenfeld defends the doctrine:

> The doctrine helps to ensure that agency decisions are determined neither by accommodation of purely private interests nor by surreptitious commandeering of the decisionmaking apparatus to serve an agency's idiosyncratic view of the public interest. Instead of merely looking at whether a regulation is within bounds acceptable under the statutory prescriptions governing agency discretion, the courts focus on the agency decisionmaking process. Essentially, under the hard look test, the reviewing court scrutinizes the agency's reasoning to make certain that the agency carefully deliberated about the issues raised by its decision.

Seidenfeld, *Demystifying Deossification, supra* note 63, at 491; *see also* Patricia M. Wald, *Judicial Review in the Time of Cholera,* 49 ADMIN. L. REV. 659 (1997); Thomas O. Sargentich, *The Critique of Active Judicial Review of Administrative Agencies: A Reevaluation,* 49 ADMIN. L. REV. 599 (1997); Robert A. Anthony, *Pro-Ossification: A Harder Look at Agency Policy Statements,* 31 WAKE FOREST L. REV. 667 (1996); Sidney A. Shapiro & Richard E. Levy, *Heightened Scrutiny of the Fourth Branch: Separation of Powers and the Requirement of Adequate Reasons for Agency Decisions,* 1987 DUKE L.J. 387; Sunstein, *supra* note 60.

89. *See* William S. Jordan, *Ossification Revisited: Does Arbitrary and Capricious Review Significantly Interfere With Agency Ability to Achieve Regulatory Goals Through Informal Rulemaking?,* 94 NW. U. L. REV. 393 (2000).

tute its judgment for that of the agency."[90] For example, in a case involving another NHTSA highway safety rule, *Center for Auto Safety v. Peck*,[91] the D.C. Circuit upheld a rule that modified past policy by reducing minimum performance standards for automobile bumpers.[92] In discussing the standard of review to be applied, the court emphasized that it would not substitute its judgment for that of the agency, particularly where the agency is called on to weigh the costs and benefits of alternative policies, because these decisions "epitomize the types of decisions that are most appropriately entrusted to the expertise of an agency."[93] The court rejected the argument that a reversal of long-standing agency policy requires heightened judicial scrutiny.[94] The court, citing *State Farm*, ruled that the same test on review applies "to the rescission or modification of a rule as to its initial promulgation"[95] and that an agency action is arbitrary and capricious only when there is an absence of "overall rational support," even if there are "uncertainties, analytic imperfections, or even mistakes."[96] Because NHTSA's conclusions were "within the range of those that a reasonable person could derive from the evidence presented," the court of appeals affirmed the agency action.[97] A decade later, the D.C. Circuit stated the *State Farm* test in more permissive terms: "Under the arbitrary and capricious standard (citing *State Farm*), this court does not substitute its judgment for that of the administrative agency. A regulatory decision in which the Commission must balance competing goals is therefore valid if the agency can show that its resolution "reasonably advances at least one of those objectives and [that] its decisionmaking process was regular."[98] Other decisions are similarly deferential to agency explanations and policy choices.[99]

---

90. *See* note 41, *supra.*
91. 751 F.2d 1336 (D.C. Cir. 1985).
92. NHTSA modified its rule, issued under the National Traffic and Motor Vehicle Safety Act, 15 U.S.C. §§ 1381–1431, and the Motor Vehicle Information and Cost Savings Act, 15 U.S.C. §§ 1901–1991, so that "lighter, less protective, and less costly bumpers" would satisfy the safety standard. *Id.* at 1338.
93. *Id.* at 1342.
94. *Id.* at 1342–43.
95. *Id.* at 1343.
96. *Id.* at 1370.
97. 751 F.2d at 1370. The court, in support of its conclusion that NHTSA's action was not arbitrary and capricious, described the rulemaking as being an "enterprise of much difficulty and scope" that was pursued "through a methodology that was sensible" and during which NHTSA "responded to, and often accommodated, every major criticism and suggestion." *Id.* Professor Seidenfeld notes other "decisions in which even the most free-market jurists have upheld government regulations under hard look review." Mark Seidenfeld, *Hard Look Review in a World of TechnoBureaucratic Decisionmaking—A Reply to Professor McGarity*, 75 TEX. L. REV. 558, 567–68 (1997).
98. U.S. AirWaves, Inc. v. FCC, 232 F.3d 227, 233 (D.C. Cir. 2000) (other citations omitted).
99. *See, e.g.,* Rural Cellular Ass'n v. FCC, 588 F.3d 1095, 1105 (D.C. Cir. 2009) ("[W]hen an agency's decision is primarily predictive, our role is limited; we require only that the agency acknowledge factual uncertainties and identify the considerations it found persuasive. . . . [Moreover] the FCC should be given "substantial deference" when acting to impose interim

In one opinion, however, the Fourth Circuit surely overstated the permissive view when it said, "[G]iven that Congress has the ability to enact a broad scheme for the conservation of endangered species, it is not for the courts to invalidate individual regulations."[100]

On the other hand, critics of the hard-look test argue that it allows so much judicial discretion "that a single unsympathetic or confused reviewing court can bring about a dramatic shift in focus or even the complete destruction of an entire regulatory program."[101] A favorite target is the Fifth Circuit's decision in *Corrosion Proof*

---

regulations."); SoundExchange Inc. v. Librarian of Congress, 571 F.3d 1220, 1225 (D.C. Cir. 2009) ("[W]e owe substantial deference to the agency's [ratemaking] decisions . . . because the four [statutory] objectives it must pursue point in different directions, requiring the agency first to predict the future course of the music industry and then to work an equitable division of projected music industry profits."); Stilwell v. Office of Thrift Supervision, 569 F.3d 514, 519, (D.C. Cir. 2009) ("Although [petitioner] has made a forceful submission, this claim is ultimately resolved by the deferential nature of arbitrary and capricious review of agency rules. The APA imposes no general obligation on agencies to produce empirical evidence. Rather, an agency has to justify its rule with a reasoned explanation. Moreover, agencies can, of course, adopt prophylactic rules to prevent potential problems before they arise. An agency need not suffer the flood before building the levee.") (citation omitted); BNSF Ry. Co. v. Surface Transp. Bd., 526 F.3d 770, 781 (D.C. Cir 2008) (upholding agency rule that changed methodology of its ratemaking, saying, "We decline to enter this hyper-technical fray. It is well established that an agency's predictive judgments about areas that are within the agency's field of discretion and expertise are entitled to particularly deferential review, so long as they are reasonable."); Marsh v. Ore. Nat. Res. Council, 490 U.S. 360, 377 n.23 (1989) ("[T]he difference between the 'arbitrary and capricious' and 'reasonableness' standards is not of great pragmatic consequence."); Sierra Club v. EPA, 356 F.3d 296, 306–07 (D.C. Cir. 2004) (holding EPA's adjustment of a model used to project ozone levels, after it showed too many exceedences in the Washington, D.C. area, was properly explained and not arbitrary and capricious); Sierra Club v. EPA, 353 F.3d 976, 986 (D.C. Cir. 2004) (Roberts, J.) (upholding EPA's hazardous air pollution standard for copper smelters over environmental group's challenge that agency did not adequately justify departure from past approaches: "This court has adopted an 'every tub on its own bottom' approach to EPA's setting of standards pursuant to the CAA, under which the adequacy of the underlying justification offered by the agency is the pertinent factor—not what the agency did on a different record concerning a different industry."); Tex. Office of Pub. Util. Counsel v. FCC, 265 F.3d 313, 322 (5th Cir. 2001) (discussing how the FCC "articulated rational reasons to the degree that it has changed prior policies" in view of fact that "the telecommunications market has undergone dramatic changes in the past few years"); Cellular Phone Taskforce v. FCC, 205 F.3d 82, 90–93 (2d Cir. 2000) (holding the FCC did not act arbitrarily and capriciously when it created guidelines for radio frequency radiation even though it (1) did not take "non-thermal" radiation effects into account, (2) did not consult with other "expert agencies" on scientific evidence, (3) rejected the recommendations of the National Council on Radiation Protection and Measurements, (4) concluded as a policy issue that it should not have "greater safety margins" in its guidelines, (5) did not adhere to the recommendations of experts, and (6) concluded its past rules were "adequate[]" and should not be changed).

100. Gibbs v. Babbitt, 214 F.3d 483, 498 (4th Cir. 2000).

101. McGarity, *Response to Professor Seidenfeld*, *supra* note 61, at 541 (discussing Corrosion Proof Fittings v. EPA, 947 F.2d 1201 (5th Cir. 1991)).

Fittings v. EPA,[102] in which the court overturned an EPA rule pertaining to human exposure to asbestos. The rulemaking had involved numerous scientific studies, consideration of various regulatory options, and receipt of more than 200 comments, yet the court "set aside the rule because of the agency's failure to calculate the 'costs and benefits' of each of the possible intermediate levels of regulation."[103]

More recently, the SEC suffered a similarly devastating defeat when the D.C. Circuit found its proxy access rule to be arbitrary and capricious for five separate reasons.[104] The SEC's rule, which would have allowed qualified shareholders, for the first time, to have their director nominees included in corporate proxy solicitation materials, was overturned because the agency:

1. neglected its statutory obligation to assess economic consequences of rule by not making tough choices about which of competing estimates regarding proxy contests was most plausible or to hazard a guess as to which was correct;
2. relied upon insufficient empirical data when it concluded that rule would improve board performance and increase shareholder value by facilitating election of dissident shareholder nominees;
3. failed to conduct serious evaluation of costs that could be imposed upon companies from use of rule by shareholders representing special interests, particularly union and government pension funds;
4. ignored the effect of the final rule upon total number of election contests; and
5. discussed the estimated frequency of nominations under the rule in an internally inconsistent manner.[105]

Of course, public interest groups can also employ this type of argument. For example, in *Center for Biological Diversity v. NHTSA*,[106] the court found that the agency had arbitrarily failed (1) to monetize benefits of greenhouse gas emissions reduction in setting of corporate average fuel economy (CAFE) standards for light trucks, and (2) to set overall fleet-wide average in setting CAFE standards, since it impermissibly relied on consumer demand to such an extent that it ignored the overarching goal of fuel conservation.

---

102. 947 F.2d 1201 (5th Cir. 1991).
103. McGarity, *Response to Professor Seidenfeld, supra* note 61, at 547 (citing Corrosion Proof Fittings v. EPA, 947 F.2d at 1217). Professor McGarity devotes extensive scathing commentary to this case. *Id.* at 541–49. Other cases he criticizes include *AFL-CIO v. OSHA*, 965 F.2d 962 (11th Cir. 1992), *Gulf South Insulation v. U.S. Consumer Product Safety Comm'n*, 701 F.2d 1137 (5th Cir. 1983), and *Leather Indus. v. EPA*, 40 F.3d 392 (D.C. Cir. 1994). *Id.* at 550–55.
104. Business Roundtable v. SEC, 647 F.3d 1144 (D.C. Cir. 2011).
105. Westlaw summary of holdings. The court chided the agency for "having failed once again—as it did most recently in *American Equity Investment Life Insurance Company v. SEC*, 613 F.3d 166, 167–68 (D.C. Cir. 2010), and before that in *Chamber of Commerce*, 412 F.3d [133, 136 (D.C. Cir (2005)]—adequately to assess the economic effects of a new rule." *Id.* at 1148.
106. 538 F.3d 1172 (9th Cir. 2008).

c. Scope of review of agency policy changes. The Supreme Court and lower courts have applied *State Farm* to numerous challenges to agency rules—some involving new policies and some involving changes in policy. Indeed, the Court itself recognized that "*State Farm* involved review of an agency's 'changing its course' as to the interpretation of a statute."[107] Other cases had made clear that unexplained inconsistency can be arbitrary and capricious.[108]

So, when the FCC announced a change in its long-standing policy regarding enforcement of its so-called indecency ban, under which non-repetitive, "fleeting" use of expletives on broadcast television was permitted, replacing it with a context-based approach that allowed such statements to be penalized, the broadcasters challenged it as both unconstitutional and arbitrary and capricious. The Second Circuit avoided the constitutional issue by finding the policy arbitrary and capricious because the FCC "fail[ed] to provide a reasoned analysis justifying its departure from the agency's established practice."[109] In so doing the court quoted from one of its earlier decisions, saying, 'Such a flip-flop must be accompanied by a reasoned explanation of why the new rule effectuates the statute *as well as or better than the old rule.*"[110]

The Supreme Court reversed 5-4.[111] Justice Scalia, writing for a plurality (Justice Kennedy concurring in part), recognized at the outset that the Second Circuit had "relied in part on Circuit precedent requiring a more substantial explanation for agency action that changes prior policy."[112] But he said he could find nothing in either the APA or *State Farm* "for a requirement that all agency change be subjected to more searching review."[113]

The key passage from his opinion is worth quoting in full:

To be sure, the requirement that an agency provide reasoned explanation for its action would ordinarily demand that it display awareness that it *is* changing position. An agency may not, for example, depart from a prior policy *sub silentio* or simply disregard rules that are still on the books. And of course the agency must show that there are good reasons for the new policy. But it need not demonstrate to a court's satisfaction that the reasons for the new policy are *better* than the reasons for the old one; it suffices that the new policy is permissible under the statute, that there are good reasons for it, and that the agency *believes* it to be better, which the conscious change of course adequately indicates. This means that the agency need not always provide a more detailed

107. Nat'l Ass'n of Home Builders v. Defenders of Wildlife, 551 U.S. 644, 659–60 (2007) (quoting PDK Labs. Inc. v. U.S. Drug Enforcement Admin., 362 F.3d 786, 799 (D.C. Cir 2004).
108. *See* Nat'l Cable & Telecomms. Ass'n v. Brand X Internet Servs., 545 U.S. 967, 981 (2005).
109. Fox Television Stations, Inc. v. FCC, 489 F.3d 444, 462 (2d Cir. 2007).
110. *Id.* at 457 (quoting N.Y. Council, Ass'n of Civilian Technicians v. Fed. Labor Relations Auth., 757 F.2d 502, 508 (2d Cir. 1985) (emphasis in original).
111. FCC v. Fox Television Stations, Inc., 556 U.S. 502, 129 S. Ct. 1800 (2009).
112. *Id.* at 129 S. Ct. 1810.
113. *Id.*

justification than what would suffice for a new policy created on a blank slate. Sometimes it must—when, for example, its new policy rests upon factual findings that contradict those which underlay its prior policy; or when its prior policy has engendered serious reliance interests that must be taken into account. It would be arbitrary or capricious to ignore such matters. In such cases it is not that further justification is demanded by the mere fact of policy change; but that a reasoned explanation is needed for disregarding facts and circumstances that underlay or were engendered by the prior policy.[114]

Thus, according to the Scalia opinion, there is normally no need for heightened scrutiny when an agency changes its policy position. In applying *State Farm*, he went on to find the FCC's new policy to be reasonable. To the court of appeals' finding that the FCC had produced no "evidence that suggests a fleeting expletive is harmful [and] . . . serious enough to warrant government regulation,"[115] he replied:

There are some propositions for which scant empirical evidence can be marshaled, and the harmful effect of broadcast profanity on children is one of them. One cannot demand a multiyear controlled study, in which some children are intentionally exposed to indecent broadcasts (and insulated from all other indecency), and others are shielded from all indecency. It is one thing to set aside agency action under the Administrative Procedure Act because of failure to adduce empirical data that can readily be obtained. See, *e.g., State Farm*, 463 U.S., at 46-56 (addressing the costs and benefits of mandatory passive restraints for automobiles). It is something else to insist upon obtaining the unobtainable.[116]

Justice Breyer, writing for the four dissenters, began by saying that the FCC had "failed adequately to explain *why* it *changed* its indecency policy." He agreed that a "heightened standard" was not required, but argued that:

[r]ather, the law requires application of the *same standard* of review to different circumstances, namely circumstances characterized by the fact that *change* is at issue. It requires the agency to focus upon the fact of change where change is relevant, just as it must focus upon any other relevant circumstance. It requires the agency here to focus upon the reasons that led the agency to adopt the initial policy, and to explain why it now comes to a new judgment.[117]

He also found that the FCC failed to adequately address two other critical aspects of the change in policy and then adds: "Had the FCC used traditional administrative notice-and-comment procedures, 5 U.S.C. § 553, the two failures I have just dis-

---

114. *Id.* at 1811 (citations omitted) (emphasis in original).
115. *Id.* at 1813 (quoting 489 F.3d at 461).
116. *Id.* at 1829 (Breyer, J. dissenting) (emphasis in original).
117. *Id.* at 1831 (Breyer, J. dissenting) (emphasis in original).

cussed would clearly require a court to vacate the resulting agency decision."[118]

Justice Kennedy's concurrence with all but one subpart of Justice Scalia's opinion complicates the take-away from this case, however. The one part of the opinion he does not concur with is part III(E), in which Justice Scalia addresses "The Dissent's Arguments."[119] And Justice Kennedy begins his opinion by saying that in the circumstances in which "the agency sets a new course that reverses an earlier determination but does not provide a reasoned explanation for doing so . . . I agree with the dissenting opinion of Justice Breyer that the agency must explain why 'it now reject[s] the considerations that led it to adopt that initial policy.'"[120] But in a rather tepid endorsement of the FCC's reasons for the change, he concludes: "The reasons the agency announces for this change are not so precise, detailed, or elaborate as to be a model for agency explanation. But, as the opinion for the Court well explains, the FCC's reasons for its action were the sort of reasons an agency may consider and act upon."[121]

Justice Kennedy's swing opinion thus leaves some doubt as to the force of the plurality's opinion. Professors Watts and Murphy explain the middle ground as follows: "Justice Kennedy therefore apparently agreed with the four dissenters that the question should be whether the *change* in policy is rational, *not* (as Justice Scalia and three other justices suggested) simply whether the new policy is rational."[122] Nevertheless, several lower courts have prominently cited *Fox TV Stations* in upholding contested policy changes.[123]

The case has reopened discussion among commentators about the proper place for political considerations both in agency policy change and in courts' assessments of it. In *Fox TV Stations*, Justice Kennedy and the four dissenters seemed to agree

---

118. *Id.* at 1837. While the FCC's original and changed policies had both been enunciated in adjudicative orders, for the purpose of the arbitrary and capricious analysis, that should be of little moment.

119. *Id.* at 1822 (Kennedy, J. concurring in part and concurring in the judgment).

120. *Id.*

121. *Id.* at 1824.

122. Kathryn Watts & Richard Murphy, *Judicial Review* chapter, DEVELOPMENTS IN ADMINISTRATIVE LAW AND REGULATORY PRACTICE 2008-2009, at 81 (Jeffrey S. Lubbers ed., 2010). For more commentary, *see* Ronald M. Levin, *Hard Look Review, Policy Change, and* Fox Television, 65 U. MIAMI L. REV. 555 (2011); Randy J. Kozel & Jeffrey A. Pojanowski, *Administrative Change*, 59 UCLA L. REV. 112 (2011).

123. *See, e.g.*, Air Transport Ass'n of Am., Inc. v. Nat'l Mediation Bd., 663 F.3d 476 (D.C. Cir. 2011) (National Mediation Board's change of long-standing union election ballot counting rules); Handley v. Chapman, 587 F.3d 273, 282 (5th Cir. 2009) (Bureau of Prisons change in its early release policy); Ad Hoc Shrimp Trade Action Comm. v. United States, 596 F.3d 1365, 1372 (Fed. Cir. 2010) (Department of Commerce's change in interpretation of rule for calculation of normal value for goods produced by multinational corporations). *But see* CBS Corp. v. FCC, 663 F.3d 122 (3d Cir. 2011), in which, after remand on the basis of *Fox TV Stations*, the Third Circuit reiterated its decision in a related case that the FCC's unexplained change in policy that led to a penalty based on Janet Jackson's Superbowl "wardrobe malfunction" (a "fleeting image" rather than a fleeting expletive) was arbitrary and capricious.

(perhaps making them the majority on this point) that agency policy changes should not be based on political factors.[124] On the other hand, there is an ongoing debate about the role of politics in arbitrary and capricious review more generally.

Professor Watts has argued that courts should give more deference to agencies under the arbitrary and capricious standard when agency decisions are influenced by political factors.[125] She concedes that "drawing a precise line between permissible and impermissible political influences is difficult," but argues that "legitimate political influences can roughly be thought of as those influences that seek to further policy considerations or public values, whereas illegitimate political influences can be thought of as those that seek to implement raw politics or partisan politics unconnected in any way to the statutory scheme being implemented."[126] Professor Mendelson has suggested that transparency and accountability could be enhanced if agencies publicly disclose presidential or executive influences on their rulemaking decisions.[127]

But other commentators have suggested that there are potential problems with overt politicization of agency policymaking or with allowing courts to overtly take politics into account in their review of policymaking changes.[128] Finally, Professor Seidenfeld has staked out a middle ground, contending that although the reasoned decisionmaking standard of judicial review should preclude a court from consider-

---

124. Stephen M. Johnson, *Disclosing the President's Role in Rulemaking: A Critique of the Reform Proposals*, 60 CATH. U. L. REV. 1003, 1030 (2011) (suggesting that "five Justices appeared to oppose the agency's decision to justify a change in position based on political factors."

125. Kathryn A. Watts, *Proposing a Place for Politics in Arbitrary and Capricious Review*, 119 YALE L.J. 2 (2009); *see also* Joshua McKarcher, *Restoring Reason: Reformulating the Swerve Doctrine of* Motor Vehicle Manufacturers v. State Farm, 76 GEO. WASH. L. REV. 1342 (2008).

126. Watts, *supra* note 125, at 9.

127. Nina A. Mendelson, *Disclosing 'Political' Oversight of Agency Decision-Making*, 108 MICH. L. REV. 1127, 1130 (2010).

128. Stephen M. Johnson, *Disclosing the President's Role in Rulemaking: A Critique of the Reform Proposals*, 60 CATH. U. L. REV. 1003, 1044 (2011) (suggesting that the possible unintended costs of the Watts and Mendelson proposals in terms of increased ossification of rulemaking, facilitation of partisan judging, and erosion of consistency and certainty might outweigh the accountability and transparency benefits of the proposals); Enrique Armijo, *Politics, Rulemaking, and Judicial Review: A Response to Professor Watts*, 62 ADMIN. L. REV. 573 (2010); *see also* Scott Keller, *Depoliticizing Judicial Review of Agency Rulemaking*, 84 WASH. L. REV. 419, 422 (2009) (suggesting that judicial review of agency rulemaking gives judges too much leeway to decide based on their political predilections); Richard J. Pierce, Jr., *Waiting for* Vermont Yankee III, IV, *and* V? *A Response to Beermann and Lawson*, 75 GEO. WASH. L. REV. 902, 908–09 (2007) ("[T]he results of hard-look review are easy to predict if you know the politics of the judges who apply the doctrine. Numerous studies have found that the results of hard-look review depend primarily on the political and ideological beliefs of the judges who apply the doctrine.") (citing studies); Patrick Garry, *Judicial Review and the Hard Look Doctrine*, 7 NEV. L. J. 151, 170 (2006) (arguing that the hard-look test is best seen as "inherent in the very process of judicial review").

ing politics in judicial review, it should be permissible for an agency to consider it in rulemaking.[129]

In summary, the Supreme Court's *State Farm* decision not only had a major impact on judicial review of deregulation during the Reagan years, it continues to have a significant, though still controversial, impact on the intensity of judicial review.

Notwithstanding the debate over how hard the hard-look test should be (especially when coupled with the apparent deference shown toward agency interpretations of statutes under the *Chevron* case—to be discussed below), it is still possible to offer the following reassurance to agency rulemakers:

1. A reviewing court normally will not substitute its judgment for that of the agency in making factual conclusions, as long as the agency's conclusions have a substantial basis in the record; this is particularly true where the subject matter is technical, on the frontiers of science, or involves a considerable exercise of agency expertise.

2. A reviewing court generally will defer to agency policy judgments, as long as they are "rational" or "reasonable"—concededly vague terms—and they are the product of what has traditionally been called "reasoned decisionmaking." To demonstrate that reasoned decisionmaking has taken place, an agency must explain in its statement of basis and purpose why it has rejected significant alternative options, why it has departed from past policies, and how its conclusions are derived from the facts in the record.

3. A reviewing court will apply these same principles to agency deregulation or other policy changes, with emphasis placed on the need for the agency to fully explain why the new action is being taken and why prior policy is being revised, but not necessarily why the reasons for the new policy are *better* than the reasons for the old one.

If agency rulemakers give careful attention to the factual underpinnings of the rule and reach their conclusions by means of "reasoned decisionmaking," this should ordinarily be enough to withstand claims that the agency was arbitrary and capricious in making its determination of fact, discretion, or policy. However agencies are cautioned that pleas to rely on the agency's "knowledge and expertise," without more, are likely to be rejected.[130]

---

129. Mark Seidenfeld, *The Irrelevance of Politics for Arbitrary and Capricious Review*, FSU COL-LEGE OF LAW, PUBLIC LAW RESEARCH PAPER NO. 565 (2011), *available at* http://papers.ssrn.com/sol3/papers.cfm?abstract_id=1961753.

130. *See* Int'l Union, United Mine Workers of Am. v. Mine Safety & Health Admin., 626 F.3d 84, 94 (D.C. Cir. 2010) (MSHA training provision held to be arbitrary and capricious because the agency identified no basis for it other than its "knowledge and expertise." "It does not identify what this knowledge and expertise is, nor point to a study or comparison of non-hands-on training. Its conclusory statement is unsupported by the rulemaking record."); *see also* Tripoli Rocketry Ass'n, Inc. v. Bureau of Alcohol, Tobacco, Firearms, & Explosives, 437 F.3d 75, 83 (D.C. Cir. 2006) ("the agency seeks to invoke its institutional expertise as a license for making unarticulated findings").

3. APA Section 706(2)(B): "contrary to constitutional right, power, privilege, or immunity"

This clause states the self-evident proposition that when reviewing agency action, including agency rules, the courts must decide any properly brought constitutional challenges. While the Due Process Clause of the Fifth Amendment theoretically applies to federal government rulemaking, in practice it plays little direct role in judicial review of rulemaking procedures. The reason for this is that the APA and many enabling statutes prescribe relatively detailed public participation procedures for rulemaking, and agency rulemaking that conforms to those procedures will almost always meet constitutional mandates as well.[131] It should be emphasized, however, that constitutional objections may be raised to the agency's status or structure, or to provisions in the underlying statute that may have significant impact on rulemaking under that statute. For example, where the underlying statute contains an unconstitutional legislative veto, the agency's authority to issue rules would be eliminated if the veto were held nonseverable.[132] Another example is where an agency head is challenged under Appointment Clause grounds.[133] Moreover, the rule itself may, of course, be challenged on a variety of constitutional grounds.[134] In cases raising the constitutionality of agency actions, the courts typically decide such questions de novo.

4. APA Section 706(2)(C): "in excess of statutory jurisdiction, authority, or limitations, or short of statutory right"

This clause expresses the familiar proposition that an agency's action must be within the authority delegated to it by the legislature. Reviewing courts are often faced with contentions that agency rules are beyond the agency's legal authority or that the agency incorrectly interpreted a statutory provision in issuing a rule.[135] In

---

131. *See* Vt. Yankee Nuclear Power Corp. v. Nat. Res. Def. Council, 435 U.S. 519, 542 n.16 (1978). *See also* Ernest Gellhorn & Glen O. Robinson, *Rulemaking "Due Process": An Inconclusive Dialogue*, 48 U. Chi. L. Rev. 201 (1981).

132. *See* Alaska Airlines, Inc. v. Brock, 480 U.S. 678 (1987) (upholding rulemaking authority under Airline Deregulation Act as severable from unconstitutional legislative veto); *see also* discussion *supra* Part I(C).

133. *See, e.g.,* SoundExchange, Inc. v. Librarian of Congress, 571 F.3d 1220, 1226 (D.C. Cir. 2009) (Kavanaugh, J., concurring) (suggesting that Copyright Royalty Board members were improperly appointed because they are "principal officers" of the United States).

134. *See, e.g.*, Initiative & Referendum Inst. v. USPS, 417 F.3d 1299 (D.C. Cir. 2005) (holding a USPS regulation that prohibited solicitation of signatures on petitions, polls, or surveys on Postal Service property violated Free Speech Clause of First Amendment).

135. The question of the scope of agency authority also is relevant to other rulemaking issues, such as whether the rule in question is a "legislative" or "non-legislative" rule. *See* discussion *supra* Part II, ch. 1(D).

dealing with these issues, courts are required to determine how much deference they will give to an agency's interpretation of its governing statutes.[136]

The Supreme Court long ago, in reviewing an action of state land commissioners, said, "In the construction of a doubtful and ambiguous law, the contemporaneous construction of those who were called upon to act under the law, and were appointed to carry its provisions into effect, is entitled to very great respect."[137] In the modern administrative state, this concept of deference has evolved into a complicated body of law.

In reviewing agency regulations, courts must often disentangle the legal, factual, and policy issues involved in an agency's promulgation of a rule. The difficulty of this task is illustrated by the Supreme Court's 1980 review of OSHA's "benzene" rule.[138] OSHA had issued a rule regulating the carcinogen benzene to a permissible level of one part benzene per million parts of air on the basis of what the agency termed a "policy" judgment—that in regulating carcinogens, no exposure level could be considered safe. Accordingly, OSHA set its standard at the lowest technologically feasible level that would not impair the viability of the regulated industries.[139] The Supreme Court vacated OSHA's standard, concluding that OSHA failed to show by substantial evidence that benzene constituted a "significant risk" at the current level of exposure.[140] The plurality opinion by Justice Stevens relied particularly on the statutory definition of "occupational safety and health standard" as one that was "reasonably necessary or appropriate to provide safe or healthful employment"[141] and interpreted this provision as requiring a finding of "significant health risk" before OSHA was authorized to regulate.[142] The Supreme Court, in effect overruling the agency's *policy* basis for its rule, viewed the issue as a *legal* question and reversed the agency's interpretation of its enabling statute. The Supreme Court refused to defer to the agency's interpretation of its enabling statute in light of the inconsistencies in OSHA's position and the statute's legislative history.[143]

---

136. The Administrative Conference addressed the issue of court review of agency statutory interpretations several times. *See* ACUS Recommendation 89-5, *Achieving Judicial Acceptance of Agency Statutory Interpretations*, 54 Fed. Reg. 28,973 (1989); *see also* ACUS Recommendation 79-6, *Elimination of the Presumption of Validity of Agency Rules and Regulations in Judicial Review, as Exemplified by the Bumpers Amendment*, 45 Fed. Reg. 2308 (1980); ACUS Recommendation 81-2, *Current Versions of the Bumpers Amendment*, 46 Fed. Reg. 62,806 (1981). The Bumpers Amendment, which was never enacted, would have modified the standard for court review of agency interpretations by reducing or eliminating judicial deference to such interpretations.

137. Edwards' Lessee v. Darby, 25 U.S. 206, 210 (1827).

138. Indus. Union Dep't, AFL-CIO v. Am. Petroleum Inst., 448 U.S. 607 (1980).

139. *Id.* at 613.

140. *Id.* at 653.

141. *Id.* at 639–46.

142. *Id.* at 614–15.

143. For a conspicuous non-deferential decision issued just after *Chevron*, see then-Judge Breyer's opinion in *Mayburg v. Sec'y of Health and Human Servs.*, 740 F.2d 100, 107 (1st Cir. 1984) ("In sum, we have paid particular attention to HHS's arguments; we have taken note of its experience

a. The Chevron *decision.* In 1984, the Supreme Court addressed more generally the scope of court review of agency legal determinations in the landmark case of *Chevron U.S.A. Inc. v. Natural Resources Defense Council.*[144] This case involved an EPA legislative rulemaking regulating emissions under the Clean Air Act. The Court, again in an opinion by Justice Stevens, upheld EPA's interpretation of the term "stationary source," as used in the Act, to allow plant-wide regulation of emission sources as one single source. In agreeing with EPA's construction of the statute, the Court set forth a two-part test for review of agency statutory interpretations:

(1) Has Congress "directly" spoken to the "precise" question at issue? "If the intent of Congress is clear, that is the end of the matter; for the court, as well as the agency, must give effect to the unambiguously expressed intent of Congress";[145] and

(2) If Congress has not done so, and the statute is "silent or ambiguous with respect to the specific issue," then the question for the court is whether "the agency's answer is based on a permissible construction of the statute."[146]

The Court said further that:

---

administering the statute and of its administrative needs; we have reached our decision with all those factors in mind. Having done so, we nonetheless believe, for the reasons stated [above], that the agency's interpretation of the statute is incorrect.").

144. 467 U.S. 837 (1984); *see also, e.g.*, Cass R. Sunstein, *Law and Administration After* Chevron, 90 COLUM. L. REV. 2071, 2075 (1990) ("[*Chevron*] has become a kind of *Marbury*, or counter-*Marbury*, for the administrative state. . . . [T]he decision has established itself as one of the very few defining cases in the last twenty years of American public law."); *see also* Thomas W. Merrill, *The Story of* Chevron: *The Making of an Accidental Landmark, in* ADMINISTRATIVE LAW STORIES 398, 427 (Peter L. Strauss ed., 2006) (opining that *Chevron* "is a striking instance of a case that became great not because of the inherent importance of the issue presented, but because the opinion happened to be written in a way that key actors in the legal system later decided to make it a great case"); Jody Freeman, *The Story of* Chevron: *Environmental Law and Administrative Discretion, in* ENVIRONMENTAL LAW STORIES 171, 172 n.10 (Richard J. Lazarus & Oliver A. Houck eds., 2005) (pointing out that "[i]n adopting this new rule of deference, the Supreme Court dismissed, with almost no serious discussion, a complex body of law aimed at calibrating judicial deference on matters of law to a number of relevant considerations (including agency expertise, the timing of the legal interpretation, and the relative consistency of the agency's position over time)"); *see also supra* Part I(B).

145. 467 U.S. at 842–43. On this point, the Court stated that the "judiciary is the final authority on issues of statutory construction and must reject administrative constructions which are contrary to clear congressional intent." *Id.* at 843 n.9. It also indicated that the courts "employ[] traditional tools of statutory construction" in doing this. *Id.* This statement obviously has a bearing on the issue of whether the courts should use legislative history, but it also raises the interesting issue of how much "respect" should be given to the agency's views on this issue. Prof. Herz refers to this as the "*Skidmore* within *Chevron* issue." *See* Michael Herz, ch. 5.05, ABA GUIDE TO JUDICIAL REVIEW, *supra* note 13, at 142–46.

146. *Id.* at 843.

> If Congress has explicitly left a gap for the agency to fill, there is an express delegation of authority to the agency to elucidate a specific provision of the statute by regulation . . . . Sometimes the legislative delegation to an agency on a particular question is implicit rather than explicit. In such a case, a court may not substitute its own construction of a statutory provision for a reasonable interpretation made by the administrator of an agency.[147]

The Court elaborated, stating that "[j]udges are not experts in the [technical] field, and are not part of either political branch of the Government."[148] By contrast, agencies are part of the executive branch of the government, which appropriately makes "policy choices—resolving the competing interests which Congress itself either inadvertently did not resolve, or intentionally left to be resolved by the agency charged with the administration of the statute in light of everyday realities."[149]

The first question asked by the reviewing court under *Chevron* is whether "Congress has directly addressed the precise question at issue." If so, the court is to "give effect to the unambiguously expressed intent of Congress." On the other hand, if the statute were found to be "silent or ambiguous with respect to the specific issue," the second question must then be asked: was the agency's interpretation "permissible" or "reasonable"? Thus, *Chevron* creates a presumption of deference to agency interpretations of ambiguous or silent statutes. This formula is, however, deceptively simple— and there is room for many arguments within the two steps.[150]

b. Step One of Chevron. Because step two provides a large degree of deference to an agency interpretation, most successful challenges succeed at step one, and it is not uncommon for reviewing judges to differ as to whether the statutory language at issue meets the threshold test of ambiguity. These differences began to occur within the Supreme Court soon after the *Chevron* decision. In *Chemical Manufacturers Association v. Natural Resources Defense Council*,[151] a 1985 case involving EPA policy on variances from toxic pollutant effluent limitations under the Clean Water Act, a majority of the Supreme Court followed the *Chevron* analysis and upheld the agency's interpretation of the Act. However, four Justices dissented, refusing to defer to EPA's

---

147. *Id.* at 843–44. This language has led some commentators to describe the *Chevron* test in terms of three steps, adding as an issue whether the statute delegates authority to the agency to fill in the gaps Congress left in the statute. *See* Homemakers N. Shore, Inc. v. Bowen, 832 F.2d 408, 412 (7th Cir. 1987) ("Different statutes transfer different sorts of implementing authority to agencies, and therefore there is not one but many standards of deference when agencies interpret statutory language.").

148. 467 U.S. at 865.

149. *Id.* at 865–66.

150. *See, e.g.,* Robin Kundis Craig, *Agencies Interpreting Courts Interpreting Statutes: The Deference Conundrum of a Divided Supreme Court*, 61 EMORY L. J. 1 (2011).

151. 470 U.S. 116 (1985).

interpretation, which they believed to be inconsistent with the clear intent of Congress.[152]

In 1990, the Court's majority refused to defer to the agency in *Dole v. United Steelworkers of America*,[153] where the Court reversed the Office of Management and Budget's interpretation of the Paperwork Reduction Act.[154] Relying on the language of the Act, the object and structure of the Act as a whole, and "traditional canons of construction,"[155] the majority declined to defer to OMB's interpretation of the Act's term *information collection request* to include third-party disclosure requirements, finding a clear congressional intent to the contrary.[156] Dissenting Justices questioned the majority's failure to adhere strictly to the *Chevron* doctrine.[157]

Four years later, in *MCI Telecommunications Corp. v. AT&T*,[158] the Supreme Court engaged in an exhaustive linguistic analysis. The Court refused to defer to the FCC's interpretation of its authority under the Communications Act of 1934 to "modify" any of the Act's requirements. The FCC's decision to use that authority to instill a more competitive climate in long-distance telephony had the effect of substantially deregulating the market. Justice Scalia, writing for the majority, held that the singular term *modify* could not be relied upon by the Commission to effect such sweeping changes in the regulatory framework governing the telecommunications industry. Commentators criticized the Court's examination of several different dictionaries to determine the meaning of the word *modify* in the statute.[159]

In an even more high-profile rejection of the agency's interpretation under step one, the Court in *FDA v. Brown & Williamson Tobacco Corp.*[160] split 5-4, with the majority rejecting the agency's interpretation of its jurisdictional statute at step one.

Brown & Williamson illustrates the potential breadth of the analysis at step one. The Court was reviewing the FDA's revised position that it did in fact have the authority to regulate the sale of cigarettes because nicotine is a "drug" and cigarettes were "drug delivery devices" within the meaning of the FDA's organic statute. As Professor Garrett recounts:

> The Court looked beyond the specific terms, which tended to support the
> FDA's assertion of jurisdiction, to observe that regulation of tobacco did not
> fit well within the Act's overall regulatory scheme. But it did not stop there;

---

152. *Id.* at 152–65.
153. 494 U.S. 26 (1990).
154. 44 U.S.C. §§ 3501–3520. Congress subsequently reinstated OMB's interpretation in the 1995 Amendments to the Act. *See supra* Part II, ch. 3(D).
155. 494 U.S. at 35.
156. *Id.* at 42–43.
157. *Id.* at 43–46.
158. 512 U.S. 218 (1994).
159. *See* Peter L. Strauss, *The Supreme Court, Textualism, and Administered Law*, 20 Admin. & Reg. L. News at 1, 13 (Fall 1994) (analyzing use of textualism in statutory interpretation by Supreme Court Justices).
160. 529 U.S. 120 (2000).

instead, the Court also observed that "the meaning of one statute may be affected by other Acts, particularly where Congress has spoken subsequently and more specifically to the topic at hand." Analyzing various tobacco-related laws passed after the [food and drug statute] over the last 35 years, the Court concluded that Congress had clearly excluded the regulation of tobacco products from the jurisdiction of the FDA.[161]

In another example of a dispute over whether a statutory term was unambiguous, in *Carcieri v. Salazar*,[162] the Court rejected the Department of the Interior's interpretation of the word "now" in a 1934 statute that allowed the Department to acquire land and hold it in trust for "Indians" defined as members of recognized tribes "now under Federal jurisdiction." In 1998, the Department had taken land in Rhode Island into trust for a tribe recognized in 1983, and the local authorities objected. Using a 1934 Webster's dictionary, a 6-3 majority held that the word was unambiguous in the statutory context and the Secretary's interpretation was therefore foreclosed.

May an agency attempt by regulation to alter the plain language of a statute in order to "cure a perceived ambiguity or change in the statute's reach that was created" by a judicial decision? One court has answered "no," finding that step one of *Chevron* does not permit such a result where the statutory language itself was unambiguous.[163]

There are, of course, many cases where courts have, under step one, rejected challengers' contentions that the agency action is clearly foreclosed by statute. But if judges wishes to invalidate an agency interpretation, it is much easier for them to do so under the first step. One reason is that courts are supposed to use the ordinary canons of construction of statutes in determining whether the statute is clear under step one.[164] In effect, then a canon of construction can effectively "trump" an agency's interpretation.[165]

---

161. Elizabeth Garrett, ch. 3.02, ABA GUIDE TO JUDICIAL REVIEW, *supra* note 13, at 60; *see also* Note, *"How Clear Is Clear" in* Chevron's *Step One?*, 118 HARV. L. REV. 1687 (2005).

162. 555 U.S. 379 (2009).

163. Van Hollen v. Federal Election Comm'n, — F. Supp. 2d ——, 2012 WL 1066717 (D.D.C., Mar. 30, 2012).

164. *See* note 145, *supra*; *see also* Nat'l Credit Union Admin. v. First Nat'l Bank & Trust Co., 522 U.S. 479, 501 (1998) ("finding the NCUA's interpretation violates the established canon of construction that similar language contained within the same section of a statute must be accorded a consistent meaning"); ArQule, Inc. v. Kappos, 793 F. Supp. 2d 214, 220 (D.D.C. 2011), *citing* Eagle Broadcasting Grp., Ltd. v. FCC, 563 F.3d 543, 552 (D.C. Cir. 2009). *See also* Elizabeth Garrett, *supra* note 161, at 68–81 (detailing all the ins and outs of actually applying various canons in the step one analysis. *Also see generally* Garrett's discussion at 55–84 of "Step One of *Chevron*."

165. *See* Kenneth A. Bamberger, *Normative Canons in the Review of Administrative Policymaking*, 118 YALE L.J. 64, 64 (2008) (making this point, but also suggesting a less rigid approach in which "the question of whether an agency policy comports with background norms should be considered as part of *Chevron's* case-by-case, step-two inquiry into whether the policy is reasonable").

More controversial, however, is whether it is appropriate to consult the legislative history in construing the statute under step one. The *Chevron* case itself strongly implied that legislative history is relevant under step one.[166] However, in a later restatement of *Chevron*, the Supreme Court omitted reference to legislative history with respect to step one: "If the agency interpretation is not in conflict with the plain language of the statute, deference is due."[167] Justice Scalia has been in the forefront of those bearing the "textualist" banner, arguing strenuously that it is improper to consult the legislative history.[168] Justice Breyer has taken the more pragmatic (and still generally prevailing)[169] position that examining the legislative debate is appropriate and can sometimes be helpful to reviewing judges.[170]

The *ABA Blackletter Statement* leans toward the Breyer position:

Under step one of the *Chevron* test, the reviewing court determines whether the statutory meaning with respect to the precise issue before it is "clear" (and

---

166. 467 U.S. at 843 ("If a court, employing traditional tools of statutory construction, ascertains that Congress had an intention on the precise question at issue, that intention is the law and must be given effect.").

167. Nat'l Ry. Passenger Corp. v. Boston & Maine Corp., 503 U.S. 407, 417 (1992).

168. *See, e.g.*, Green v. Bock Laundry Machine Co., 490 U.S. 504, 528 (1989); *see also* ANTONIN SCALIA, A MATTER OF INTERPRETATION: FEDERAL COURTS AND THE LAW 23–47 (1997). Also, Justice Scalia is the foremost user of dictionaries in statutory interpretation. *See, e.g.*, MCI Telecomms. Corp. v. AT&T, 512 U.S. 218, 225–26 (1994).

169. *See, e.g.*, Dunn v. CFTC, 519 U.S. 465 (1997) (consulting legislative history, treatises, and *Black's Law Dictionary* in interpreting commodities statute); Estate of Cowart v. Nicklos Drilling Co., 505 U.S. 469, 478 (1992) (examining legislative history of longshore statute and employing canons of statutory construction); Bell Atl. Tel. Cos. v. FCC, 131 F.3d 1044, 1047 (D.C. Cir 1997) ("The traditional tools include examination of the statute's text, legislative history, and structure, as well as its purpose.") (citations omitted). For a case where the Supreme Court used legislative history to find the agency's interpretation permissible under step two of *Chevron*, see *Babbitt v. Sweet Home Chapter of Cmties. for a Great Oregon*, 515 U.S. 687 (1995). But see then-D.C. Circuit Chief Judge Roberts' view that it is a "very rare situation where the legislative history of a statute is more probative of congressional intent than the plain text." Consumer Elecs. Ass'n v. FCC, 347 F.3d 291, 298 (D.C. Cir. 2003).

170. *See* STEPHEN BREYER, ACTIVE LIBERTY 85–101 (2005); Stephen Breyer, *On the Uses of Legislative History in Interpreting Statutes*, 65 S. CAL. L. REV. 845 (1992); *see also, e.g.*, Peter Strauss, *The Courts and the Congress: Should Judges Disdain Political History?*, 98 COLUM. L. REV. 242 (1998); Thomas W. Merrill, *Textualism and the Future of the* Chevron *Doctrine*, 72 WASH. U. L.Q. 351 (1994); Patricia Wald, *The Sizzling Sleeper: The Use of Legislative History in Construing Statutes in the 1988-89 Term of the United States Supreme Court*, 39 AM. U. L. REV. 277 (1990); William Eskridge, Jr., *The New Textualism*, 37 UCLA L. REV. 621 (1990). In one decision authored by Justice Breyer, the Court "invert[ed] the traditional *Chevron* analysis" by "look[ing] first to congressional intent and the policies embedded in the statute, and only second to the existence of textual ambiguity." *The Supreme Court, 2006 Term—Leading Cases*, 121 HARV. L. REV. 185, 395 (discussing *Zuni Public School District No. 89 v. Department of Education*, 550, U.S. 81 (2007)). Justice Kennedy agreed that the statute was ambiguous and therefore joined the result, but he criticized the way Justice Breyer's opinion "inverts *Chevron's* logical progression." Justice Scalia (joined by Chief Justice Roberts and Justice Thomas) strongly dissented.

thus, not "ambiguous"). Step one of *Chevron* does not dictate that courts use any particular method of statutory interpretation. However, the court should use "the traditional tools of statutory construction" to determine whether the meaning of the statute is clear with respect to the precise issue before it. For most judges, these tools include examination of the text of the statute, dictionary definitions, canons of construction, statutory structure, legislative purpose, and legislative history.[171]

c. Step Two of Chevron. Under step two of *Chevron*, if the statutory meaning on the precise issue before the court is not clear, or if the statute is silent on that issue, the court is required to defer to the agency's interpretation of the statute if that interpretation is "permissible." The *Blackletter Statement* provides two alternative approaches to this step:

> While there is no single, established method of conducting the step two analysis, two interrelated approaches are most prominent. First, courts regularly examine the same statutory materials relied on in step one, seeking to determine whether the statute, even if subject to more than one interpretation, can support the particular interpretation adopted by the agency. For example, the court might find that the statutory context, viewed as a whole, clearly rules out the option the agency selected, or a premise on which it relied. (Some courts, however, make essentially the same inquiry within step one when they determine whether the agency interpretation violates the clear meaning of the statute. As a practical matter, the court's review of these legal issues is not affected by which "step" is deemed to be involved. In either case, the court is measuring the interpretation against congressionally established limitations.)
>
> Second, in addition to engaging in conventional statutory construction, or in some cases instead of engaging in it, courts at step two of *Chevron* evaluate whether the agency, in reaching its interpretation, reasoned from statutory premises in a well-considered fashion. Courts may look, for example, to whether the interpretation is supported by a reasonable explanation and is logically coherent. In this regard, the step two inquiry tends to merge with review under the arbitrary and capricious standard.[172]

The Supreme Court has only rarely set aside an agency action under step two.[173]

---

171. 54 ADMIN. L. REV. 1, 37 (2002) (unchanged in 2012 revision, see note 13, *supra); see also* Garrett, *supra* note 161, at 63–68.

172. 54 ADMIN. L. REV. 1, 38 (2002) *(supra); see also* M. Elizabeth Magill, ch. 3.03, ABA GUIDE TO JUDICIAL REVIEW, *supra* note 13, at 85–102 (discussing "Step Two of *Chevron*").

173. Professor Magill identifies *AT&T Corp. v. Iowa Utils. Bd.*, 525 U.S. 366, 387–92 (1999), as the only instance, *supra* note 172, at 86. *Whitman v. Am. Trucking Ass'ns*, 531 U.S. 457 (2001), may be another one. Without specifying the step, the Court struck down the agency's interpretation, saying, "We find the statute to some extent ambiguous. We conclude, however, that the agency's interpretation goes beyond the limits of what is ambiguous and contradicts what in our view is

Chevron itself emphasized that "[t]he court need not conclude that the agency construction was the only one it permissibly could have adopted to uphold the construction, or even the reading the court would have reached if the question initially had arisen in a judicial proceeding."[174] In *Chevron*, the Court explained that a court must defer to the agency's interpretation of the ambiguous statutory term if it "represents a reasonable accommodation of conflicting policies that were committed to the agency's care by the statute."[175] In particular, the Court held that the agency's interpretation is entitled to deference when "the regulatory scheme is technical and complex, the agency considered the matter in a detailed and reasoned fashion, and the decision involves reconciling conflicting policies."[176] And it is also clear that normally an agency may change its interpretation and still claim *Chevron* deference.[177]

Other than that, however, it is not so clear how courts should proceed in step two. Theoretically, once the court has found the requisite ambiguity or silence in the statute under step one, the agency has a range of potential interpretations, some of which may be permissible and some not. Thus, under this theory, the court must decide whether the choice the agency made is permissible (or "reasonable"). As Professor

---

quite clear. We therefore hold the implementation policy unlawful." *Id.* at 481. For a more typical application of deference under step two, *see* Sherley v. Sebelius, 644 F.3d 388 (D.C. Cir. 2011) (NIH determination that ambiguous text of statute, which prohibited funding for "research in which a human embryo or embryos are destroyed," did not bar its funding a project using an embryonic stem cell that was previously derived because a stem cell was not an "embryo" and could not develop into a human being, was reasonable, and thus entitled to *Chevron* deference).

174. 467 U.S. at 843 n.11.
175. *Chevron*, 467 U.S. at 845 (quoting United States v. Shimer, 367 U.S. 374, 383 (1961)).
176. *Id.* at 865. The D.C. Circuit cited this statement approvingly in upholding EPA's interpretation of the word "modification" as it pertains to power plants under the Clean Air Act in *New York v. EPA*, 413 F.3d 3, 23 (D.C. Cir. 2005) (per curiam).
177. *See* Nat'l Cable & Telecomms. Ass'n v. Brand X Internet Servs., 545 U.S. 967, 980–82 (2005) (quoting Smiley v. Citibank (South Dakota), N. A., 517 U.S. 735, 742 (1996)) ("[I]f the agency adequately explains the reasons for a reversal of policy, 'change is not invalidating, since the whole point of *Chevron* is to leave the discretion provided by the ambiguities of a statute with the implementing agency.'"). The *Brand X* case is discussed *infra* text accompanying notes 247–51. For another example, see *Lawrence v. Chater*, where the Supreme Court addressed a situation in which the Social Security Administrator changed her interpretation of the Social Security Act during the course of litigation. 516 U.S. 163, 165 (1996) (per curiam). The Supreme Court determined that under the circumstances, a GVR (grant certiorari, vacate the judgment below, and remand the case) order was appropriate. *Id.* at 166. The Court cited the "principle that a new interpretation of a statute adopted by the agency charged with implementing it may be entitled to deference in the context of litigation to which the Government is a party." *Id.* Justices Scalia and Thomas dissented, partly on the grounds that the SSA Administrator changed her position too late to warrant *Chevron* deference (at the petition for certiorari stage). *Id.* at 187. But, at any rate, the case seems clearly to stand for the proposition that an agency may change its position and still receive *Chevron* deference. *Noted approvingly in* SKF USA Inc. v. United States, 254 F.3d 1022, 1030 (Fed. Cir. 2001).

Magill notes, "Many cases take this statutory approach to *Chevron* step two. But because *Chevron* and its progeny do not require that courts consult any particular set of statutory materials at step two, in fact the materials that courts examine are those that the courts might also examine at step one."[178] The difficulty with this is that courts at step one do not decide the issue of ambiguity of the statutory terms in the abstract; they tend to ask "whether the statute *forecloses*—through its clarity—the agency's interpretation."[179] Once the court answers this issue in favor of the agency, step two is, for all intents and purposes, satisfied as well. This is why Professor Levin has argued that "[s]tep one should be defined to encompass all contentions that a court seeks to resolve using the 'traditional tools of statutory construction,'"[180] and that "step two should be regarded as equivalent to arbitrar[y and capricious] review."[181] The *Blackletter* recognizes that only some reviewing courts have used this approach, but Professor Magill, writing in the *ABA Guide to Judicial and Political Review*, endorses the Levin approach:

> This analysis suggests that the statutory analysis that sometimes occurs at step two should be abandoned. Step one should be explicitly understood to operate in a way that it actually does: a determination whether the statute is ambiguous enough to permit the agency's interpretation. So framed, this inquiry permits the court to look at whatever statutory materials it chooses. If those materials *foreclose* the agency's interpretation, then the interpretation should be rejected at step one. If they *require* the agency's interpretation, then it should be upheld at step one. If the statutory materials *permit* the agency's interpretation, however, that should be the end of the examination of such materials. Step two . . . should consist of an examination of the reasonableness—as that term is understood in arbitrary and capricious caselaw—of the agency's interpretation.[182]

---

178. Magill, *supra* note 172, at 88.
179. *Id.* at 92 (citing cases) (emphasis in original).
180. Ronald M. Levin, *The Anatomy of* Chevron: *Step Two Reconsidered*, 72 Chi.-Kent L. Rev. 1253, 1283 (1997).
181. *Id.* at 1285.
182. Magill, *supra* note 172, at 93. She notes that commentators other than Professor Levin have agreed that "such an understanding can be squared with *Chevron* itself and with Supreme Court applications of *Chevron*, is consistent with if not required by general principles of administrative law, and is normatively attractive." *Id.* at 97 & n.167 (citing 1 Kenneth Culp Davis & Richard Pierce, Jr., Administrative Law Treatise § 7.4 at 263–67 (3d ed. 2000); Mark Seidenfeld, *A Syncopated* Chevron: *Emphasizing Reasoned Decisionmaking in Reviewing Agency Interpretations of Statutes*, 73 Tex. L. Rev. 83, 129–30 (1994)); *accord* Matthew C. Stephenson & Adrian Vermeule, Chevron *Has Only One Step*, 95 Va. L. Rev. 597 (2009); Gary S. Lawson, Commentary, *Reconceptualizing* Chevron *and Discretion: A Comment on Levin and Rubin*, 72 Chi.-Kent L. Rev. 1377 (1997). *See also* David Zaring, *Reasonable Agencies*, *supra* note 29.

Professor Levin noted in 1997 that the D.C. Circuit, "which uses *Chevron* as the basis for analysis of administrative interpretations more consistently than any other court, has been troubled by the jurisprudence of step two. It has been especially puzzled about the relationship between step two and the traditional 'arbitrary and capricious' test . . . ."[183] And Professor Pierce has echoed this view, stating that reversals by lower courts at step two "often are functionally indistinguishable from reversals predicated on an agency's failure to engage in reasoned decisionmaking."[184]

It now appears that the Supreme Court may be moving toward the Levin position. In a recent appeal from a deportation order, which turned on whether the agency applied the correct statutory provision for allowing relief, Justice Kagan, writing for a unanimous Court, stated in a footnote:

> The Government urges us instead to analyze this case under the second step of the test we announced in *Chevron* . . . to govern judicial review of an agency's statutory interpretations. Were we to do so, our analysis would be the same, because under *Chevron* step two, we ask whether an agency interpretation is "arbitrary or capricious in substance." But we think the more apt

---

183. Levin, *Anatomy of* Chevron, *supra* note 180, at 1254; *see also* Arent v. Shalala, 70 F.3d 610, 614–16, 619–21 (D.C. Cir. 1995) (upholding an FDA determination under the Nutritional Labeling and Education Act that substantial compliance with the mandatory food-labeling regulations was reached because 60 percent of surveyed food retailers complied by providing nutritional information for 90 percent of relevant fish and produce). Judge Edwards, applying *State Farm*, found parties' references to *Chevron* misplaced, because the agency clearly acted within its statutory authority in defining "substantial compliance." *Arent*, 70 F.3d at 614–16. Judge Wald, however, maintained that *Chevron* was the proper analysis, because, in her view, the question was whether the agency's interpretation was a permissible construction of the statute. *Id.* at 619–21.

184. DAVIS & PIERCE TREATISE, *supra* note 182, § 3.6 at 118. Professor Magill cites the following cases as good examples: Nat. Res. Def. Council v. Daley, 209 F.3d 747, 755–56 (D.C. Cir. 2000); Kennecott Utah Copper Corp. v. U.S. Dep't of Interior, 88 F.3d 1191, 1206 (D.C. Cir. 1996); Consumer Fed'n of Am. v. Dep't of Health & Human Servs., 83 F.3d 1497, 1504–05 (D.C. Cir. 1996); Envtl. Def. Fund v. EPA, 82 F.3d 451, 467 (D.C. Cir. 1996). *See* Magill, *supra* note 172, at 95 n.154. Others are Shays v. FEC, 414 F.3d 76, 96–97 (D.C. Cir. 2005) (finding two of five challenged FEC rules invalid under step one of *Chevron*, but not reaching whether the other three were "permissible" under *Chevron* step two because they were arbitrary and capricious due to the FEC's failure to provide a rational justification for them); Nat'l Org. of Veterans' Advocates, Inc. v. Sec'y of Veterans Affairs, 669 F.3d 1340 (Fed. Cir. 2012) (citations omitted) ("Although courts sometimes analyze a regulation under both the second step of *Chevron* and the APA independently, the issues raised will often overlap. Where, as here, a regulation will equally stand or fall under either review, a single analysis is appropriate."); Northpoint Tech., Ltd. v. FCC, 412 F.3d 145, 151 (D.C. Cir. 2005) (noting that the two tests overlapped); Nuclear Energy Inst., Inc. v. EPA, 373 F.3d 1251, 1268–73 (D.C. Cir. 2004), and Sierra Club v. Leavitt, 368 F.3d 1300, 1304 (11th Cir. 2004). *But see* New York v. EPA, 413 F.3d 3, 30–31 (D.C. Cir. 2005) (engaging in a separate arbitrary and capricious analysis).

analytic framework in this case is standard "arbitrary [or] capricious" review under the APA.[185]

This statement obviously seems to equate *Chevron* step two with an arbitrary and capricious analysis. However, the last comment that the Court is using a "standard" arbitrary and capricious analysis still implies that the *Chevron* step two version or "reasonableness" review is somehow different. Moreover, she also pointed out that agency's policy did not rest on "an interpretation of any statutory language," unlike the typical *Chevron* case.[186]

d. When does Chevron *apply?* Although *Chevron* is generally accepted as the leading case on judicial review of agency interpretations of statutes, a large body of law and commentary has developed as to when the *Chevron* doctrine is applicable.[187] This is now often referred to as "*Chevron* step zero."[188]

In a Supreme Court decision handed down in 1987, not long after *Chevron*, *Immigration and Naturalization Service v. Cardoza-Fonseca*,[189] the Court's majority refused to defer to an INS statutory interpretation, saying that *Cardoza-Fonseca* involved "a pure question of statutory construction [which is] for the courts to decide."[190] But "[i]t soon became clear that *Cardoza-Fonseca*'s dicta did not mean that *Chevron* applies only to interpretive questions that are mixed questions of law and fact and not to pure questions of law. *Cardoza-Fonseca* was merely a case decided at step one of *Chevron*."[191] More recently, the Court explicitly held that, despite some precedent to the contrary, "[w]e see no reason why our review of tax regulations should not be guided by agency expertise pursuant to *Chevron* to the same extent as our review of other regulations."[192]

However, if the statutory issue presented also raises serious constitutional questions, the Court has refrained from granting deference and has decided the issue de

---

185. Judulang v. Holder, 132 S. Ct. 476, 484 n.7 (2011). The Court held that the action of the agency in enforcing a test for deportation that was borrowed from a statute that applied to exclusions was arbitrary and capricious.

186. *Id.*

187. *See, e.g.*, Steven Croley, ch. 4 in ABA GUIDE TO JUDICIAL REVIEW, *supra* note 13, at 103–23 (discussing "The Applicability of the *Chevron* Doctrine").

188. The first use of this term was in Thomas W. Merrill & Kristin E. Hickman, Chevron's *Domain*, 89 GEO. L.J. 833, 836 (2000). For an authoritative analysis, see Cass R. Sunstein, Chevron *Step Zero*, 92 VA. L. REV. 187 (2006).

189. 480 U.S. 421 (1987). The case involved the validity of an INS interpretation of the Immigration and Nationality Act relating to the grant of asylum to refugees.

190. *Id.* at 446, 448. Justice Scalia, although concurring in the result, stated that the majority "badly misinterpreted" *Chevron* by implying that courts may substitute their interpretation of a statute for that of the agency whenever they face a pure question of statutory *construction*. *Id.* at 455.

191. Garrett, *supra* note 161, at 57.

192. Mayo Found. for Med. Educ. & Research v. United States, 131 S. Ct. 704, 713 (2011).

novo.[193] Moreover, "[w]here an administrative interpretation of a statute invokes the outer limits of Congress' power, we expect a clear indication that Congress intended that result. . . . Thus, 'where an otherwise acceptable construction of a statute would raise serious constitutional problems, the Court will construe the statute to avoid such problems unless such construction is plainly contrary to the intent of Congress.'"[194]

But the key question in many cases is the extent to which *Chevron* deference should be accorded to various "formats" of agency interpretations other than legislative rules, such as interpretive rules, adjudicatory opinions, manuals, briefs, policy statements, and the like.[195] In 1989, the Administrative Conference proposed that an agency intending to develop definitive interpretations should use notice-and-comment rulemaking, formal adjudication, or other procedures "authorized by Congress for, and otherwise appropriate to," the development of definitive interpretations. However, where the agency interprets its statute without using procedures authorized by Congress for the development of "definitive agency statutory interpretations," the agency should expect only that these interpretations will be entitled to "such special consideration as their nature and the circumstances of their adoption warrant."[196] In a series of Supreme Court decisions, the Court has basically adopted this view—though not without some remaining uncertainty.[197]

---

193. *See* Miller v. Johnson, 515 U.S. 900 (1995). *But see* Rust v. Sullivan, 500 U.S. 173 (1991) (applying *Chevron* in upholding regulation banning discussion of abortion in family planning centers); *see also* Reno v. Flores, 507 U.S. 292 (1993) (rejecting a facial challenge to INS regulations as violative of substantive and procedural due process). In this case, Justice Scalia, for the majority, said: "To prevail in such a facial challenge, respondents 'must establish that no set of circumstances exists under which the [regulation] would be valid.' [citing United States v. Salerno, 481 U.S. 739, 745 (1987)] That is true as to both the constitutional challenges, and the statutory challenge." *Id.* at 301 (citations omitted). This last statement seems inconsistent with *Chevron. See* Stuart Buck, Salerno *vs.* Chevron: *What to Do About Statutory Challenges*, 55 ADMIN. L. REV. 427, 429 (2003). *But see* Pub. Lands Council v. Babbitt, 529 U.S. 728 (2000) (reviewing a facial challenge to grazing regulations without mention of *Reno*, despite the court of appeals' reliance on it).
194. Solid Waste Agency of N. Cook Co. v. U.S. Army Corps of Eng'rs, 531 U.S. 159, 172–73 (2001) (citing Edward J. DeBartolo Corp. v. Fla. Gulf Coast Bldg. & Constr. Trades Council, 485 U.S. 568, 575 (1988)).
195. ACUS Recommendation 89-5, *supra* note 136. The recommendation is based on Robert A. Anthony, *Which Agency Interpretations Should Bind Citizens and Courts?*, 7 YALE J. REG. 1 (1990). For at least one area where courts seem to be ignoring an agency's guidelines, see Michael Higgins, *No Sudden Impact: Courts Rejecting Mental Disability Claims Despite EEOC Guidelines Intended to Protect Mentally Ill*, 83 A.B.A. J. 24 (Nov. 1997).
196. ACUS Recommendation 89-5, *supra* note 136.
197. In *Martin v. Occupational Safety & Health Review Comm'n*, 499 U.S. 144, 157 (1991) the Court first suggested that *Chevron* does not apply to interpretive rules. That same term, in *EEOC v. Arabian American Oil Co.*, 499 U.S. 244, 260, Justice Scalia, in a concurrence, maintained that *Chevron* should apply equally to legislative and interpretive rules. Justice Scalia lost that battle for the most part in *Christensen v. Harris County*, 529 U.S. 576 (2000) and *United States v. Mead Corp*, 533 U.S. 218 (2000), discussed *infra*, text at notes 217–41.

The *ABA Blackletter Statement* summarizes the application of *Chevron*'s principles as follows:[198]

The Scope of *Chevron*

1. *Chevron* principles apply to an agency's interpretation of a statute the agency administers, where
   (a) the interpretation is embodied in a rule that has the force of law;
   (b) the interpretation was developed in the course of formal adjudication, except where the adjudicating agency's lawmaking power is limited by virtue of a "split-enforcement" statutory scheme, in which lawmaking authority over the same subject has been vested in an enforcing agency;
   (c) the interpretation was developed in the course of informal agency action if the agency's conferred authority and other statutory circumstances demonstrate that "Congress would expect the agency to be able to speak with the force of law" in taking such action;[199]
   (d) the interstitial nature of the legal question, the related expertise of the agency, the importance of the question to administration of the statute, the complexity of that administration, and the careful consideration the agency has given the question over a long period of time indicate that *Chevron* deference is appropriate.

2. *Chevron* principles do not apply to agency interpretations
   (a) of statutes that apply to many agencies and are specially administered by none, such as the APA, FOIA, or the National Environmental Policy Act (although *Chevron* may apply to interpretations of statutes administered by two or a few agencies);
   (b) of criminal statutes where the agency's power with respect to the statute consists solely of the power to prosecute offenses in court;
   (c) that contradict a controlling judicial decision if the prior judicial decision holds that its construction follows from the unambiguous terms of the statute and thus leaves no room for agency discretion;[200]
   (d) that represent merely the agency's litigating posture developed after the agency's decision;[201] or

---

198. *Supra* note 13, at 39–40 (2002), as modified in 2012.
199. United States v. Mead Corp., 533 U.S. 218, 229 (2001). (Cited in Blackletter.)
200. *See infra* notes 247–51 and accompanying text.
201. *See* Natural Res. Def. Council v. Abraham, 355 F.3d 179, 201 (2d Cir. 2004) ("DOE's interpretation followed the petitioners' suits in both this court and the district court . . . and thus was arguably an interpretation advanced in contemplation of litigation; Catskill Mountains Chapter of Trout Unltd. v. City of New York, 273 F.3d 481, 491 (2d Cir. 2001) ("[A] position adopted in the course of litigation lacks the indicia of expertise, regularity, rigorous consideration, and public scrutiny that justify *Chevron* deference."); City of Kansas City, Mo. v. Dep't of Hous. & Urban Dev., 923 F.2d 188, 192 (D.C. Cir. 1991) ("The agency construction for which HUD seeks deference was never promulgated by the Secretary, or his designee, nor by administrative regulations, nor by decisions in agency adjudications; rather, agency counsel contends that the

(e) that are embodied in policy statements, manuals, enforcement guidelines, interpretive rules, and other such documents unless the agency's conferred authority and other statutory circumstances demonstrate that "Congress would expect the agency to be able to speak with the force of law" in taking such action.

3. Although in general courts have extended *Chevron* deference to agencies' interpretations of the boundaries of their own statutory jurisdiction, *Chevron* principles have uncertain application to an agency interpretation that significantly expands the agency's previously recognized jurisdiction.

C. *Chevron* or *Skidmore* Deference?

In situations in which *Chevron* principles do not apply, courts ordinarily will give some deference or weight to an agency's interpretation of a statute that it administers. In these circumstances, as the Supreme Court ruled in *Skidmore v. Swift & Co.*,[202] the agency's view can have "power to persuade," as distinguished from "power to control." In determining whether and to what extent an agency interpretation should benefit from *Skidmore* deference, courts are guided by such factors as the timing and consistency of the agency's position and the nature of the agency's expertise.

Taking the *Blackletter Statement* as our organizational guide, it can first be stated with some certainty that *Chevron* applies to interpretations made in notice-and-comment rulemaking (as in *Chevron* itself) as well as in formal adjudications (as long as the adjudicating agency is not purely an adjudicatory agency in a split-enforcement scheme, such as the Occupational Safety and Health Review Commission).[203] It is also quite clear that *Chevron* principles do not apply to agency interpretations of statutes that apply to many agencies and are specially administered by none, such as the APA, FOIA, or the National Environmental Policy Act,[204] although it may be appropriate when stat-

---

'permissible construction of the statute' for which it seeks approval as the agency's litigation posture in this case. For purposes of *Chevron,* this is patently insufficient."). But note also that in one case Justice Scalia was willing to grant *Chevron* deference to a statement made in an agency brief. *See Christensen, supra* note 197, at 591 (concurring opinion) ("But the Solicitor General of the United States, appearing as an *amicus* in this action, has filed a brief, cosigned by the Solicitor of Labor, which represents the position set forth in the opinion letter to be the position of the Secretary of Labor. That alone, even without existence of the opinion letter, would in my view entitle the position to *Chevron* deference.").

202. 323 U.S. 134 (1944).

203. *See* Martin v. Occupational Safety & Heath Review Comm'n, 499 U.S. 144 (1991) (stating that courts should defer to OSHA's interpretations, not OSHRC's); *see also* Collins v. Nat'l Transp. Safety Bd., 351 F.3d 1246, 1251–52 (D.C. Cir. 2003) (following *Martin,* deference should be given to Coast Guard, not NTSB). Formal adjudication can include adjudications beyond those conducted under the APA. *See, e.g.*, Negusie v. Holder, 129 S. Ct. 1159, 1164 (2009) (making clear that immigration decisions by the BIA can receive *Chevron* deference); Khalid v. Holder, 655 F.3d 363, 366 (5th Cir. 2011) (same).

204. *See* Ass'n of Am. Physicians & Surgeons v. Clinton, 997 F.2d 898 (D.C. Cir. 1993) (interpretation of Federal Advisory Committee Act); Prof'l Reactor Operator Soc'y v. NRC, 939 F.2d 1047 (D.C. Cir. 1991) (interpretation of APA); FLRA v. DOT, 884 F.2d 1446 (D.C. Cir. 1989) (interpretation of Privacy Act); Reporters Comm. for Freedom of the Press v. DOJ, 816 F.2d 730 (D.C. Cir.

utes are administered (especially jointly) by two or a few agencies;[205] or of criminal statutes where the agency's power with respect to the statute consists solely of the power to prosecute offenses in court.[206]

But until 2000 there was a lot of uncertainty regarding interpretations made in non-legislative rulemaking or informal adjudication. In that year, the Supreme Court addressed these issues in two major cases that have cleared up some points but left some remaining uncertainty.

The first major case was *Christensen v. Harris County*,[207] where the Court specifically refused to grant *Chevron* deference to a Department of Labor (DOL) opinion letter.[208] The opinion letter from the Wage and Hour Division of the DOL concerned the overtime and compensatory ("comp") time requirements of the Fair Labor Standards Act. Under the Act, workers working over 40 hours per week are entitled to time and a half. But under 1985 amendments, state and local governments may offer them comp time instead of cash payments. This meant that employees who left their jobs with a lot of accrued comp time could get large cash payouts. To guard against this, Harris County, Texas, wrote to DOL asking whether it could *force* employees to take unscheduled comp time once they hit a certain ceiling. DOL replied in a letter that its position was that this was allowed only if a public employer had a prior agreement to that effect with its employees. Harris County implemented the policy without such an agreement.

A group of deputy sheriffs sued the county, claiming its policy violated the Act as interpreted by DOL. The district court gave them a summary judgment, but the Fifth Circuit reversed on the grounds that the Act did not prohibit such a policy.

1987), *rev'd on other grounds*, 489 U.S. 749 (1989) (interpretation of FOIA). There is some dispute whether any (i.e., *Skidmore*) deference should be given to the agency interpretation of such statutes. *Compare* Thomas W. Merrill & Kristin E. Hickman, Chevron*'s Domain*, *supra* note 188, at 863 (2001) ("no"), *with* Cooley R. Howarth, Jr., United States v. Mead Corp.: *More Pieces for the* Chevron/Skidmore *Puzzle*, 54 ADMIN. L. REV. 699, 714–15 (2002) ("yes").

205. *See generally* Russell L. Weaver, *Deference to Regulatory Interpretations: Inter-Agency Conflicts*, 43 ALA. L. REV. 35 (1991). For a good discussion of this issue, *see* Collins v. Nat'l Transp. Safety Bd., *supra* note 203, at 1253 (holding that some level of deference (*Chevron* or *Skidmore*) is due to Coast Guard interpretation despite presence of other agencies' jurisdiction over the same sorts of activities). *See also* Individual Reference Servs. Grp. v. FTC, 145 F. Supp. 2d 6, 23–24 (D.D.C. 2001) (finding that where "the subject matter of the statute falls squarely within the agencies' areas of expertise, and the regulations were issued as a result of a statutorily-coordinated effort among the agencies, *Chevron* is the governing standard"). The court distinguished cases where one agency was claiming deference when several agencies administered the statute, e.g., *Salleh v. Christopher*, 85 F.3d 689, 691–92 (D.C. Cir. 1996) and *Wachtel v. OTS*, 982 F.2d 581, 585 (D.C. Cir. 1993). Courts may, of course, solicit the views of the other agencies in cases where one agency's interpretation is at issue.

206. *See* Crandon v. United States, 494 U.S. 152, 177 (1990) (Scalia, J., concurring); United States v. McGoff, 831 F.2d 1071 (D.C. Cir. 1987).

207. 529 U.S. 576 (2000).

208. The following discussion draws heavily on Daniel Cohen & Harold B. Walther, *Rulemaking* chapter, DEVELOPMENTS IN ADMINISTRATIVE LAW AND REGULATORY PRACTICE 1999-2000, at 143–47 (Jeffrey S. Lubbers ed., 2001).

Justice Thomas, writing for four Justices, held that DOL's interpretation was not entitled to *Chevron* deference:

> Here, however, we confront an interpretation contained in an opinion letter, not one arrived at after, for example, a formal adjudication or notice-and-comment rulemaking. Interpretations such as those in opinion letters—like interpretations contained in policy statements, agency manuals, and enforcement guidelines, all of which lack the force of law—do not warrant *Chevron*-style deference.[209]

Rather, it was "entitled to respect"[210] under the Court's 1944 decision in *Skidmore v. Swift & Co.*[211] Under *Skidmore*, the agency's position is entitled to deference, but only to the extent that it has the "power to persuade."[212] In *Christensen*, the majority found the agency's interpretation unpersuasive.

Justice Scalia concurred that the Labor Department's expansive comp-time interpretation should be rejected, but he disagreed with the failure to invoke *Chevron*. (In other words, he would have struck down the interpretation as unreasonable under step two.) According to Justice Scalia, *Chevron* has effectively replaced *Skidmore*, and even informal agency interpretations are entitled to *Chevron* deference if the agency has been given the power to administer the program in question and the interpretation "represents the authoritative view" of the agency.[213] He went on to say that the opinion letter itself may not have risen to the level of authoritativeness necessary, but that it attained that level because the position was accepted by an amicus brief of the Solicitor General of the United States that was co-signed by the Solicitor of Labor.[214]

Justice Breyer (for Ginsburg and Stevens) took a more equivocal position. He said he might well grant *Chevron* deference to this opinion letter and brief but accepted the majority's application of *Skidmore* in this case. Justice Breyer viewed the agency's decision as "eminently reasonable, hence persuasive, whether one views that decision through *Chevron*'s lens, through *Skidmore*'s, or through both."[215] In the end, though, the case seemed to stand for the proposition that interpretations of statutes made in nonlegislative rules normally get *Skidmore* deference, not *Chevron* deference.

Although the *Christensen* majority drew a clear distinction between the mere *opinion letter* at issue there and formal adjudication or notice-and-comment rulemaking, it left open the issue about whether a decision in an *informal adjudication* should also receive *Chevron* deference.[216] The Supreme Court has not decided this precise ques-

---

209. *Christensen, supra* note 197, at 587.
210. *Id.*
211. 323 U.S. 134 (1944).
212. *Christensen, supra* note 197, at 587 (quoting *Skidmore*).
213. *Id.* at 591 (Scalia, J., concurring).
214. *Id.*
215. *Id.* at 597 (Breyer, J., dissenting).
216. This issue became important in the notorious case of Elian Gonzalez. There, the Eleventh Circuit originally relied on *Chevron* to uphold the INS's determination that Elian lacked the capacity to file personally for asylum against his father's wishes. Gonzalez v. Reno, 212 F.3d 1338 (11th Cir. 2000). Then *Christensen* was decided. Elian's relatives argued strongly that

tion, but in *United States v. Mead Corp.*,[217] the Supreme Court extended the *Christensen* result to Customs Service letters and potentially other informal modes by which agencies announce statutory interpretations. Although the result of *Mead* may not have been a surprise after *Christensen*, *Mead*'s analysis went a step further by elaborating the circumstances under which courts will "tailor deference to variety"[218] when reviewing statutory interpretations, rather than affording *Chevron* deference.

The legal interpretation under review in *Mead* was made in a letter ruling issued by the Headquarters of the U.S. Customs Service. In the letter, the agency determined, contrary to its previous interpretation, that Mead Corporation's three-ring "daily planners" fell within a statutory category qualifying for an import tariff. The Supreme Court, over a dissent by Justice Scalia, agreed that the legal interpretation contained in the Customs Service letter ruling was "beyond the *Chevron* pale,"[219] and therefore was instead entitled only to the lesser *Skidmore* deference.[220]

More generally, *Mead* held that "administrative implementation of a particular statutory provision qualifies for *Chevron* deference when it appears that Congress delegated authority to the agency generally to make rules carrying the force of law, and that the agency interpretation claiming deference was promulgated in the existence of that authority."[221] The Court stated that implied delegation of authority "may be shown in a variety of ways, as by an agency's power to engage in adjudication or notice-and-comment rulemaking, or by some other indication of comparable congressional intent."[222]

Christensen should preclude *Chevron* deference for policy decisions made in the course of informal adjudication. The court granted a rehearing, but affirmed its decision to apply *Chevron* deference to what it termed an "informal adjudication." Gonzalez *ex rel.* Gonzalez v. Reno, 215 F.3d 1243, 1244 (11th Cir. 2000). The court said the agency had exercised delegated power, and the agency's decision was intended to have a binding legal effect unless reversed by the courts. *Id.* at 1245.

217. 533 U.S. 218 (2000).
218. *Id.* at 236.
219. *Id.* at 234.
220. Justice Scalia dissented in apocalyptic terms that the *Mead* decision "makes an avulsive change in judicial review of federal statutes," *id.* at 277 (Scalia J., dissenting) and that the "reasoning that produces the Court's judgment . . . makes [that] decision one of the most significant opinions ever rendered by the Court dealing with the judicial review of administrative action. Its consequences will be enormous, and almost uniformly bad," *id.* at 261. He continues to hold strong views on this matter. To listen to a podcast of a speech he gave on this matter on April 24, 2009, at Washington College of Law, American University, *see* http://www.wcl.american.edu/podcasts/podcast.cfm?uri=http://www.wcl.american.edu/podcast/audio/20090424_WCL_Chevron-Scalia.mp3&email.
221. *Id.* at 218 (syllabus). In *Gonzales v. Oregon*, 546 U.S. 243 (2006), the Court enforced this principle: "Since the Interpretive Rule was not promulgated pursuant to the Attorney General's authority, its interpretation . . . does not receive *Chevron* deference. Instead, it receives deference only in accordance with *Skidmore*."
222. *Id.* at 227; *see also* Edelman v. Lynchburg College, 535 U.S. 106 (2002) ("We agree with the Government as *amicus* that [*Chevron*] deference does not necessarily require an agency's exercise of express notice-and-comment rulemaking power. . . .") (citing *Mead*).

One commentator concluded:

> [T]he Court created effective safe harbors for the application of *Chevron* deference where an agency makes a legal interpretation in the context of notice-and-comment rulemaking or formal adjudication. The Court, however, left the determination of *Chevron*'s applicability to other agency decisionmaking formats to case-by-case analysis.[223]

This does not mean that any time an agency uses notice-and-comment procedures to issue an interpretation, it automatically obtains *Chevron* deference for it.[224] Nor did *Mead* specifically address whether *Chevron* applies to informal adjudication. While not ruling it out, the Court did not apply *Chevron* to the letter ruling in the case, which resembled the sort of action that might be made after an informal adjudication. Furthermore, the Court subsequently also added a few more ingredients to this stew in *Barnhart v. Walton*,[225] where the Court recognized that *Chevron* deference can apply even absent notice-and-comment rulemaking, noting that the Court will "normally accord particular deference to an agency interpretation of 'longstanding' duration." Justice Breyer focused on a series of factors, which have subsequently been termed the "*Barnhart* multi-factor analysis."[226] As characterized by the Second Circuit in a case applying them:

> Less formal interpretations may also be entitled to mandatory deference, depending upon to what extent the underlying statute suffers from exposed gaps in policies, especially if the statute itself is very complex, as well as on the agency's expertise in making such policy decisions, the importance of the agency's decisions to the administration of the statute, and the degree of consideration the agency has given the relevant issues over time.[227]

---

223. William S. Jordan et al., *Judicial Review* chapter, Developments in Administrative Law and Regulatory Practice 2000-2001, at 78 (Jeffrey S. Lubbers ed., 2002). *See also* Adrian Vermeule, *Introduction:* Mead *in the Trenches,* 71 Geo. Wash. L. Rev. 347, 350 (2003) (treating notice-and-comment procedures as affording the agency a "safe harbor" entitlement to *Chevron* deference). For a post-*Mead* case where the court granted *Skidmore* instead of *Chevron* deference to an interpretation rendered in an informal permitting proceeding, *see* Wilderness Society v. U.S. Fish & Wildlife Service, 353 F.3d 1051, 1067–69 (9th Cir. 2003) (en banc).
224. *See* text at notes 237–41 *infra*.
225. 525 U.S. 212 (2002).
226. *See* William S. Jordan III, *News from the Circuits*, 30 Admin. & Reg. L. News 22, 23 (Spring 2005). In his book, Justice Breyer explained that his view is that "*Chevron*'s rule is not absolute but simply a rule of thumb," and that he would ask whether a "reasonable member of Congress" "would likely have wanted judicial deference in this situation." Stephen Breyer, Active Liberty, *supra* note 170, at 103–08.
227. Kruse v. Wells Fargo Home Mtg., Inc., 383 F.3d 49, 59 (2d Cir. 2004) (granting *Chevron* deference to informal HUD policy statement); *see also* Mylan Labs., Inc. v. Thompson, 389 F.3d 1272, 1279–81 (D.C. Cir. 2004) (applying *Barnhart* factors to grant *Chevron* deference in context of informal adjudication).

It remains to be seen how *Mead*'s (and *Barnhart*'s) multifactored approach to discerning congressional intent for the purpose of determining whether *Chevron* applies to a particular agency interpretation will play out.[228] Professor Seidenfeld has opined that "*Mead* continues to confound lower courts, [which] hardly have settled on an approach for determining congressional intent to delegate interpretative authority that will fall with the scope of *Chevron*."[229] In some cases, the courts seem to demand "express delegation of congressional authority."[230] In other cases they do

---

228. For a set of articles commenting on *Mead*, see *Administrative Law Discussion Forum*, 54 ADMIN. L. REV. 1 (2002).

229. Mark Seidenfeld, *Judicial Review* chapter, DEVELOPMENTS IN ADMINISTRATIVE LAW AND REGULATORY PRACTICE 2002-2003, at 106 (Jeffrey S. Lubbers ed., 2004); *see also* Adrian Vermeule, *Introduction: Mead in the Trenches*, 71 GEO. WASH. L. REV. 347, 350 (2003) ("I suggest that the D.C. Circuit's day-to-day experience with *Mead* has been unfortunate, that its *Mead*-related work product is, in a nontrivial number of cases, flawed or incoherent. But I also suggest that these mistakes are traceable to the flaws, fallacies, and confusions of the *Mead* decision itself."); Lisa Schultz Bressman, *How* Mead *Has Muddled Judicial Review of Agency Action*, 58 VAND. L. REV. 1443 (2005) (documenting the muddle and arguing that both *Skidmore* and *Mead* should be abandoned in favor of application of *Chevron* as long as the agency issued an "authoritative" interpretation of the statute, but adding that such deference should also be restricted to procedures or interpretations that reflect transparency, rationality, and consistency). Justice Scalia cited the Bressman article approvingly as support for his view that the *Mead* decision is "inscrutable" and "incomprehensible." Coeur Alaska, Inc. v. Se. Alaska Cons. Council, 557 U.S. 261, 129 S. Ct. 2458, 2479 (2009) (Scalia J. concurring). The Ninth Circuit has declared with some exasperation that "[a]fter *Mead*, we are certain of only two things about the continuum of deference owed to agency decisions: *Chevron* provides an example of when *Chevron* deference applies, and *Mead* provides an example of when it does not." Wilderness Soc'y v. U.S. Fish and Wildlife Serv., 316 F.3d 913, 921 (9th Cir. 2003) (en banc).

230. *See, e.g.*, Am. Library Ass'n v. FCC, 406 F.3d 689, 699 (D.C. Cir. 2005) ("FCC's interpretation of its ancillary jurisdiction reaches well beyond the agency's delegated authority"); Pharm. Res. & Mfrs. of Am. v. Thompson, 362 F.3d 817, 822 (D.C. Cir. 2004) (finding that Congress had "expressly" delegated the power to interpret the Medicaid law, and therefore its interpretation of the relevant statutory provisions, "should have the force of law."); Motion Picture Ass'n of Am. v. FCC, 309 F.3d 796, 804 (D.C. Cir. 2002) (rejecting FCC rule mandating video description of television programs for the benefit of the visually impaired, on the grounds that Congress had delegated authority only to "promote the accessibility and universality of transmission, not to regulate program content"); *see also* Heimmerman v. First Union Mtg. Corp., 305 F.3d 1257, 1261 (11th Cir. 2002) (finding that because the power to issue interpretations is "expressly delegated" to HUD, the policy statement "carries the full force of law" and is entitled to *Chevron* deference), *accord* Kruse v. Wells Fargo Home Mortg., Inc., 383 F.3d 49 (2d Cir. 2004). *But see* Pub. Citizen, Inc. v. Dep't. of Health & Human Servs., 332 F.3d 654, 660 (D.C. Cir. 2003) (refusing to extend *Chevron* deference to agency manuals after failing to find *implicit* congressional authorization to issue binding requirements in such manuals in the particular agency program). The court in that case did allow *Skidmore* deference. *Id.* at 661–62.

not.[231] This issue obviously relates to the issues raised by Professor Thomas Merrill and Kathryn Tongue Watts,[232] who have argued that only those rulemaking grants that are "coupled with a statutory provision imposing sanctions on those who violate the rules" should be understood to authorize rules with the force of law and that "rulemaking grants not coupled with any provision for sanctions should be understood to authorize only interpretive and procedural rules."[233]

The Ninth Circuit recently meshed the *Chevron* and *Mead* cases by interposing *Mead* between steps one and two of *Chevron*:

> [P]rior to moving on to step two, we must determine whether the agency meets the requirements set forth in *Mead*: (1) that Congress clearly delegated authority to the agency to make rules carrying the force of law, and (2) that the agency interpretation was promulgated in the exercise of that authority. If both of these requirements from *Mead* are met, then we proceed to step two.[234]

In one case granting *Chevron* deference, the D.C. Circuit distinguished *Mead* on the grounds that, unlike the case at hand, "[t]he *Mead* Court observed that 49 different customs offices issued 10,000 to 15,000 customs classifications each year, that 'their treatment by the agency makes it clear that a letter's binding character as a ruling stops short of third parties' and that the agency 'in fact warned against assuming any right of detrimental reliance.'"[235]

Professor Merrill wrote after *Mead* that "[t]he area of uncertainty [as to whether *Chevron* applies] has been narrowed to things like interpretative regulations adopted after notice-and-comment procedures, and informal adjudications that are treated like precedents by the agency."[236] But he also opined, "I do not think the Court was say-

---

231. *See, e.g.,* Alfaro v. CIR, 349 F.3d 225, 228 (5th Cir. 2003) (no discussion); Hosp. Corp. of Am. & Subsidiaries v. CIR, 348 F.3d 136, 140–41 (6th Cir. 2003) (general rulemaking authority enough).

232. *See* discussion *supra*, Part II, ch. 2(A)(2).

233. Thomas W. Merrill & Kathryn Tongue Watts, *Agency Rules with the Force of Law: The Original Convention*, 116 Harv. L. Rev. 467, 469 (2002) (noting that "courts held that some agencies, such as the FTC, FDA, and NLRB, had legislative rulemaking powers that Congress almost certainly had not intended"). In this connection, *see* Elizabeth Garrett, *Legislating Chevron*, 101 Mich. L. Rev. 2637, 2640–41 (2003) (suggesting that Congress should create an action-forcing mechanism that would force it to determine "on an agency-by-agency basis whether to delegate the power to make policy through statutory interpretation with respect to all statutes that the agency administers, or with respect to some subset of decisions").

234. N. Cal. River Watch v. Wilcox, 633 F.3d 766, 772 (9th Cir. 2011). In this case the court allowed three agency regulations to "proceed" to step two but declined to allow an agency handbook to do so. In the end, it did not find the rules pertinent enough to the statutory question at issue and did not defer. It also found the three rules and the handbook to be unpersuasive under *Skidmore*. *Id.* at 780.

235. Pharm. Res. & Mfrs. of Am. v. Thompson, 362 F.3d 817, 822 n.5 (D.C. Cir. 2004) (citing *Mead*, 533 U.S. at 233).

236. Thomas W. Merrill, *The* Mead *Doctrine: Rules and Standards, Meta-Rules and Meta-Standards*, 54 Admin. L. Rev. 807, 821 (2002) (emphasis removed and emphasis added; citations omitted)).

ing, as some commentators and lower courts suggested before *Mead*, that if an agency adopts notice-and-comment or trial-type hearing procedures on its own authority, its interpretation is presumptively entitled to *Chevron* deference."[237] In other words, he did not think that an agency could "bootstrap" itself into obtaining *Chevron* deference for a non-legislative rule simply by using notice-and-comment procedures.[238] The Second Circuit cited this remark in holding a Department of Labor "interpretative" regulation to be deserving of only *Skidmore* deference, notwithstanding that it had been promulgated through notice-and-comment procedures.[239] However, the Supreme Court unanimously reversed the Second Circuit on this issue. Justice Breyer concluded that:

> Where an agency rule sets forth important individual rights and duties, where the agency focuses fully and directly upon the issue, where the agency uses full notice-and-comment procedures to promulgate a rule, where the resulting rule falls within the statutory grant of authority, and where the rule itself is reasonable, then a court ordinarily assumes that Congress intended it to defer to the agency's determination.[240]

So the agency's voluntary use of notice-and-comment procedures was not determinative, but it obviously played an important role in Justice Breyer's analysis. In a later case the Supreme Court applied *Chevron* after noting that the agency had issued a rule "pursuant to an explicit authorization to prescribe needful rules and regulations, and only after notice-and-comment procedures. The Court has recognized these to be good indicators of a rule meriting *Chevron* deference."[241]

Disputes have also arisen as to whether *Chevron* deference is warranted where the agency's statutory interpretation serves to expand the agency's jurisdiction. Some Justices have argued that it should be up to the courts, not the agencies, to decide the limits of the agencies' own power.[242] Others have argued that such a distinction is untenable because almost any issue of statutory interpretation can be phrased in terms

---

237. *Id.* at 814. This observation was cited approvingly in *Coke v. Long Island Care At Home, Ltd.*, 376 F.3d 118, 132 (2d Cir. 2004).

238. One commentator has referred to this as an "overpromulgated" rule. David R. Pekarek Krohn, Comment, *Cooper Technologies Co. v. Dudas: Laying the Foundation for Minimal Deference*, 104 Nw. U. L. Rev. 1213, 1233 (2010). He discusses the *Long Island Care* cases at 1237–39.

239. Coke v. Long Island Care at Home, Ltd., 376 F.3d 118, 132 & n.6 (2004). The court took pains to analyze two separate regulations, granting one of them *Chevron* deference and upholding it, and declining to grant *Chevron* deference to the other because the notice-and-comment procedure "was at best idiosyncratic and at worst insufficient."

240. Long Island Care at Home, Ltd. v. Coke, 551 U.S. 158, 173-74 (2007).

241. Mayo Found. for Med. Educ. & Research v. United States, 131 S. Ct. 704, 707 (2011).

242. *See* Miss. Power & Light Co. v. Mississippi *ex rel.* Moore, 487 U.S. 354, 386 (1988) (Brennan, J., dissenting) ("Agencies do not 'administer' statutes confining the scope of their jurisdiction, and such statutes are not 'entrusted' to agencies."); *see also* Ernest Gellhorn & Paul Verkuil, *Controlling* Chevron-*Based Delegations*, 20 CARDOZO L. REV. 989, 993 (1999), urging the Court to deny *Chevron* deference to "expansive agency readings of their jurisdictional claims"). In a

of agency jurisdiction.[243] The D.C. Circuit has ruled in favor of the latter position in *Oklahoma Natural Gas Co. v. FERC*.[244] The Supreme Court did not take advantage of an opportunity to comment on this issue in *Brown & Williamson*;[245] although the majority rejected the FDA's jurisdictional interpretation, the Court did not craft a different *Chevron* rule for that category of interpretations. There does, however, appear to be a trend in recent Supreme Court decisions to deny any deference to such agency determinations, sometimes without even mentioning *Chevron*.[246]

---

similar analysis in *American Bar Ass'n v. FTC*, 430 F.3d 457,467 (D.C. Cir. 2005), the court found the agency's attempt to include law firms within the statutory definition of "financial institution" was "turf expansion" and such a "poor fit" that the agency's claim failed at step one. It remonstrated:

> To find this interpretation deference-worthy, we would have to conclude that Congress not only had hidden a rather large elephant in a rather obscure mousehole, but had buried the ambiguity in which the pachyderm lurks beneath an incredibly deep mound of specificity, none of which bears the footprints of the beast or any indication that Congress even suspected its presence.

Id. at 469.

243. *Miss. Power & Light, supra* note 242, at 381 (Scalia, J., concurring) ("[T]here is no discernible line between an agency's exceeding its authority and an agency's exceeding authorized application of its authority."). *See also* Conn. Dep't of Pub. Util. Control v. FERC, 569 F.3d 477 (D.C. Cir. 2009) ("We afford *Chevron* deference to the Commission's assertion of jurisdiction."). But note Chief Justice Roberts's statement in a recent oral argument: "[this strikes] me as a purely legal, jurisdictional issue, are these wetlands or not? And I don't know why you give deference to the agency's determination on a legal jurisdictional issue like that." Transcript of oral argument in *Sackett v. EPA*, No. 10-1062 (Jan. 9, 2012) *available at* http://www.supremecourt.gov/oral_arguments/argument_transcripts/10-1062.pdf.
244. 28 F.3d 1281 (1994).
245. *Supra* note 160.
246. *See* New Process Steel, L.P. v. NLRB, 130 S. Ct. 2635 (2010) (rejecting, without mentioning *Chevron*, the agency's interpretation of quorum provision in its statute); *see also* Robin Kundis Craig, *Supreme Court News*, 35 ADMIN. & REG. L. NEWS 22 (Spring 2010) (discussing Union Pacific R.R. Co. v. Brotherhood of Locomotive Eng'rs & Trainmen Gen. Comm. of Adjustment, Central 23 Region, 130 S. Ct. 584 (2009), and Kucana v. Holder, 130 S. Ct. 827 (2010). Prof. Craig comments:

> As was true for *Union Pacific Railroad*, no discussion of deference to the agency appears in *Kucana*, even though the case clearly turned on an issue of statutory interpretation and even though the Attorney General was clearly acting on a particular interpretation of the Act—an interpretation that the Seventh Circuit, at least, found persuasive. *Union Pacific Railroad* and *Kucana* thus underscore a trend in the Roberts Court to limit (or eliminate) deference to administrative agencies in certain "core" contexts, such as when the extent of the agency's own authority is at issue—consider, for example, *Gonzales v. Oregon*, 546 U.S. 243, 255–69 (2006) (the Oregon assisted suicide case)—or when an agency interpretation raises constitutional concerns, as in *Rapanos v. United States*, 54[7] U.S. 715, 721–22 (2006) (considering the extent of federal authority to regulate the filling of wetlands).

Finally, with the advent of *Chevron,* cases have begun to occur where agency changes of interpretation have been litigated and the question becomes whether a *revised* interpretation deserves *Chevron* deference. Theoretically, of course, it should, where the statute is ambiguous and the revised interpretation is also a permissible or reasonable one. As the Supreme Court made clear in *National Cable & Telecommunications Ass'n v. Brand X Internet Services,*[247] "[I]f the agency adequately explains the reasons for a reversal of policy, 'change is not invalidating, since the whole point of *Chevron* is to leave the discretion provided by the ambiguities of a statute with the implementing agency.'" However, in an earlier case, the Court ruled in *Lechmere, Inc. v. NLRB*[248] that the agency's new interpretation should not be given deference if it contradicts an interpretation previously affirmed by the Supreme Court. In *Lechmere,* the Supreme Court had made its earlier decision in 1956 (that is, pre-*Chevron*), when the courts tended to review such questions of interpretations de novo. Thus, an argument could be made that the statute lost any ambiguity it might have had once the Supreme Court pronounced upon it.

If the earlier antecedent Supreme Court decision had come *after Chevron*, then *Brand X* makes clear that it would depend on whether the earlier decision was based on step one or step two of *Chevron.* If unambiguously step one, then presumably the matter is foreclosed, but if not, then the agency could revise its interpretation, because in that event the Court would have been exercising a more limited review, and the agency would have more leeway to arrive at a different but still reasonable interpretation.[249] Note that in the *Brand X* decision, the Court reversed a Ninth Circuit decision that had refused to give *Chevron* deference to an FCC classification of a cable operator's broadband Internet service as an "information service" because the Ninth Circuit felt that it was bound by one of its own earlier precedents. Justice Thomas held, "Before a judicial construction of a statute, whether contained in a precedent or not, may trump an agency's, the court must hold that the statute unambiguously requires the court's construction."[250] It is, of course, even more doubtful that the *Lechmere* prin-

---

247. 545 U.S. 967 (2005), *supra* note 177.
248. 502 U.S. 527 (1992). Three dissenting Justices would have applied *Chevron. See also* Neal v. United States, 516 U.S. 284, 285 (1996); Air Transport Ass'n of Am., Inc. v. Nat'l Mediation Bd., 663 F.3d 476, 479 (D.C. Cir. 2011) (upholding NMB election ballot-counting rule under step 2 of *Chevron*, but only after determining that the Supreme Court "came close to answering this question" in 1937).
249. *See* NLRB v. Viola Indus.-Elevator Div., Inc., 979 F.2d 1384 (10th Cir. 1992) (en banc) (upholding the Board's reinterpretation notwithstanding earlier Supreme Court affirmances of a previous Board position); *see also* Mesa Verde Constr. Co. v. N. Cal. Dist. Council of Laborers, 861 F.2d 1124 (9th Cir. 1988) (holding that when a prior panel of the court had applied an agency's interpretation of a statute after concluding it was reasonable under *Chevron* step two, a later panel of the court was free to accord deference to a new agency interpretation); *accord,* Tunik v. Merit Systems Prot. Bd., 407 F.3d 1326, 1338–39 (Fed. Cir. 2005); Garcia v. Dep't of Homeland Sec., 437 F.3d 1322, 1343–44 (Fed. Cir. 2006).
250. 545 U.S. at 985. Justice Scalia dissented vehemently. *Id.* at 1005–20. Justice Stevens joined the opinion that "correctly explains why a court of appeals' interpretation of an ambiguous provi-

ciple should still apply if the antecedent decision was by a different court of appeals rather than by the Supreme Court.[251]

In summary, it is certainly fair to say that the Supreme Court's *Chevron* decision has clearly had a significant impact on the way courts review agency statutory interpretations, if not the results.[252] In this regard, the comments by Professors Gellhorn and Levin in 1997 still seem apt:

> In practice, judges have proved so ingenious at finding "unambiguous" statutory mandates and "unreasonable" implementation of legislative commands that some writers suspect that the *Chevron* doctrine is a fraud: the courts invoke it when they wish to defer, and ignore it when they wish to go their own way. That assessment may be too cynical, but it seems fair to say the *Chevron* opinion, if read in isolation, would give an exaggerated picture of the deference that courts actually give to administrative constructions.[253]

---

sion in a regulatory statute does not foreclose a contrary reading by the agency. That explanation [however] would not necessarily be applicable to a decision by this Court that would presumably remove any pre-existing ambiguity." *Id.* at 1003. Subsequently, in a unanimous decision authored by Justice Stevens, the Court, without discussion of *Chevron* or *Brand X*, treated several questions of statutory interpretation as foreclosed by pre-*Chevron* decisions of the Supreme Court, *IBP, Inc. v. Alvarez*, 546 U.S. 21 (2005).

In *Brand X*, the Court's analysis essentially adopts (without attribution) the approach taken in Kenneth A. Bamberger, *Provisional Precedent: Protecting Flexibility in Administrative Policymaking*, 77 N.Y.U. L. Rev. 1272 (2002). For useful commentary on the *Brand X* case, see Randolph J. May, *Major Case for Agencies*, Nat'l L. J. (Aug. 8, 2005), *available at* http://www.pff.org/issues-pubs/other/opinion/05088may-agencies.html.

251. *See, e.g.*, Samuel Estreicher & Richard L. Revesz, *Nonacquiescence by Federal Administrative Agencies*, 98 Yale L.J. 679 (1979). *But see* Nat'l Mining Ass'n v. Fowler, 324 F.3d 752, 758 (D.C. Cir. 2003) (finding that agency's interpretation as to its jurisdiction was conclusively barred by an earlier negative decision by the same circuit in 1995).

252. There have been numerous empirical studies of the effects of *Chevron* vs. *Skidmore*. Professor Pierce has summarized them and found that reported rates of affirmance, across the different studies, when circuit courts invoked *Chevron* ranged from 64% to 81.3% and from 55.1% to 70% when they applied *Skidmore*. Richard J. Pierce, Jr., *What Do the Studies of Judicial Review of Agency Actions Mean?*, 63 Admin. L. Rev. 77, 84 (2011). Another study found an even narrower range between the two doctrines at the Supreme Court level. William N. Eskridge, Jr. & Lauren E. Baer, *The Continuum of Deference: Supreme Court Treatment of Agency Statutory Interpretations from* Chevron *to* Hamdan, 96 Geo. L.J. 1083, 1094, 1142 tbl.15 (2008) (analyzing 1,014 Supreme Court decisions between 1983 and 2005 "in which a federal agency interpretation was at issue" and finding an affirmance rate when *Chevron* was invoked at 76.2% and when *Skidmore* was invoked at 73.5%). Interestingly, the study found that in 53.6% of the cases the Court invoked no deference at all, yet the agency won 66% of the time. *Id.* at 1118.

253. Ernest Gellhorn & Ronald M. Levin, Administrative Process in a Nutshell 87 (4th ed. 1997); *see also* Linda R. Cohen & Matthew L. Spitzer, *Solving the Chevron Puzzle*, 57 Law & Contemp. Probs. 65 (1994) (presenting a positive political theory explication of the "puzzle" of why the Supreme Court adopted the *Chevron* test in the first place).

Moreover, there are many cases where courts engage in what has been called "*Chevron* avoidance":

> In many cases, the courts express their uncertainty about *Mead* by refraining from deciding clearly whether *Chevron* deference applies. Instead, they find an easier way out. Some refuse to choose between *Chevron* deference and *Skidmore* deference and simply determine that lower-level *Skidmore* deference supports the agency's interpretation. Others refuse to choose and simply determine that both *Chevron* deference and *Skidmore* deference support the agency's interpretation.[254]

e. When Chevron *does not apply, what does* Skidmore *deference mean?* Now that the Supreme Court (over Justice Scalia's protestations) has brought *Skidmore v. Swift & Co.*[255] back to the forefront as an alternative to *Chevron* deference, it is important to remember the key passage from that case:

> [T]he rulings, interpretations and opinions of the Administrator under this Act, while not controlling upon the courts by reason of their authority, do constitute a body of experience and informed judgment to which courts and litigants may properly resort for guidance. The weight of such a judgment in a particular case will depend upon the thoroughness evident in its consideration, the validity of its reasoning, its consistency with earlier and later pronouncements, and all those factors which give it power to persuade, if lacking power to control.[256]

As Professor Herz has summarized this paragraph, the agency interpretation in these situations "provides 'guidance' and has 'weight' but it does not 'control.'"[257] And as the *Blackletter Statement* concluded, in deciding "whether and to what extent an agency interpretation deserves *Skidmore* deference, courts are guided by such factors as the thoroughness evident in its consideration, the validity of its reasoning, and its consistency with earlier and later pronouncements."[258] But an empirical study that examined 450 court-of-appeals decisions citing either *Skidmore*, *Christensen*, or *Mead* for the five years after the *Mead* decision found that some courts used a "no

---

254. Lisa Schultz Bressman, *How* Mead *Has Muddled Judicial Review of Agency Action*, 58 VAND. L. REV. 1443, 1464–65 (2005). For an example, *see* Durr v. Shinseki, 638 F.3d 1342, 1348 (11th Cir. 2011) ("We need not decide whether the parts of the VA's personnel handbooks that we are considering are entitled to full *Chevron* deference or simply to *Skidmore* deference because the difference between those two measures of deference makes no difference to the outcome in this case.").
255. 323 U.S. 134 (1944).
256. *Id.* at 140.
257. Herz, *supra* note 145, at 127. *See generally id.*, ch. 5, at 125–46 (discussing "Judicial Review of Statutory Issues Outside of *Chevron*").
258. *See supra* note 13. This language regarding the factors is from *Mead*, 533 U.S. at 228 (quoting *Skidmore*).

deference" approach and applied their own judgment about the statutory interpretation, but most used a "sliding scale" approach that was based on factors such as the ones noted by Professor Herz.[259]

Since *Mead*, the Supreme Court has also often cited *Skidmore* in majority opinions, sometimes while upholding the agency's interpretation.[260] In one case, however, the Court said it did not have to choose between *Chevron* and *Skidmore*:

> Although we have devoted a fair amount of attention lately to the varying degrees of deference deserved by agency pronouncements of different sorts, see *United States v. Mead Corp.*, 533 U.S. 218 (2001); *Christensen v. Harris County*, 529 U.S. 576 (2000), the recent cases are not on point here. In *Edelman v. Lynchburg College*, 535 U.S. 106, 114 (2002), we found no need to choose between *Skidmore* and *Chevron*, or even to defer, because the EEOC was clearly right; today, we neither defer nor settle on any degree of deference because the Commission is clearly wrong.[261]

---

259. Kristin E. Hickman & Matthew D. Krueger, *In Search of the Modern* Skidmore *Standard*, 107 Colum. L. Rev. 1235 (2007). *See also* Matz v. Household Int'l Tax Reduction Investment Plan, 265 F.3d 572 (7th Cir. 2001) (upholding initially an IRS interpretation under *Chevron*, but on remand after *Mead*, changing its mind). *But see* Aeroquip-Vickers, Inc. v. CIR, 347 F.3d 173, 184 (6th Cir. 2003) (applying *Skidmore* to an IRS Revenue Ruling, but in a way that the dissenting judge charged "overstates the level of deference revenue rulings receive" under *Mead*). *See generally* Ellen Aprill, Linda Galler & Irving Salem, Mead *and Tax Law*, 29 Admin. & Reg. L. News 13 (Summer 2004).

260. For cases upholding the agency, *see* Federal Express Corp. v. Holowecki, 552 U.S. 389, 399 (2008) (upholding EEOC policy statements embodied in its compliance manual and internal directives, emphasizing the consistency of application); Raymond B. Yates, M.D., P.C. Profit Sharing Plan v. Hendon, 541 U.S. 1, 18 (2004); Alaska Dep't of Envt'l Conservation v. EPA, 540 U.S. 461, 487 (2004); Clackamas Gastroenterology Assocs. v. Wells, 538 U.S. 440, 449 (2003); Washington State Dep't of Social & Health Services v. Guardianship Estate of Keffeler, 537 U.S. 371, 383 n.6 (2003); and Meyer v. Holley, 537 U.S. 280, 287–88 (2003). Note that in *Meyer*, Justice Breyer cited both *Chevron* and *Skidmore* for the proposition that "the Court ordinarily defers to an administering agency's reasonable statutory interpretation." 537 U.S. at 281. For commentary on this, see William Funk, *Supreme Court News*, 28 Admin. & Reg. L. News, 16 (Spring 2003) ("Merging *Chevron* & *Skidmore*"). Other decisions have not upheld the agency's position. *See* Gonzales v. Oregon, 546 U.S. 243, 268 (2006); Gen. Dynamics Land Sys., Inc. v. Cline, 540 U.S. 581, 600 (2004); Nat'l R.R. Passenger Corp. v. Morgan, 536 U.S. 101, 111 n.6 (2002); *see also* Navarro v. Pfizer Corp., 261 F.3d 90, 99 (1st Cir. 2001) ("Under *Skidmore*, we are constrained to weigh the 'thoroughness evident in [the guidance's] consideration, the validity of its reasoning, its consistency with earlier and later pronouncements, and all those factors which give it power to persuade, if lacking power to control.' The EEOC's guidance does not fare well when measured against these benchmarks.").

261. Gen. Dynamics Land Sys., Inc. v. Cline, 540 U.S. at 600. For an inverse decision, *see* Tualatin Valley Builders Supply, Inc. v. United States, 522 F.3d 937, 942 (9th Cir. 2008) ("Even assuming that *Chevron* deference is not appropriate, under the less stringent *Skidmore* analysis, we hold that Revenue Procedure 2002–40 still should receive significant deference and that the Revenue Procedure is valid.").

But it is also important to recognize that "the distinction here is not simply one of degree or of 'weak' versus 'strong' deference. . . . Under *Skidmore*, the court independently interprets the statute; the agency's interpretation is one factor among many that will affect its conclusion. Under *Chevron*, the agency is the decision maker; under *Skidmore* the court is."[262]

f. Judicial deference to agency interpretations of their own regulations. Although *Chevron* remains the leading case in support of granting deference to agency interpretations of statutes, an earlier line of cases requires courts to accept reasonable agency interpretations of their own legislative regulations. The premise for this is that the agency is acting within its sphere of delegated authority and that agencies have special expertise in their own regulations.[263] The original case in this line is a pre-APA case, *Bowles v. Seminole Rock & Sand Co.*,[264] which is still being cited by the Supreme Court today:

> We must give substantial deference to an agency's interpretation of its own regulations. Our task is not to decide which among several competing interpretations best serves the regulatory purpose. Rather, the agency's interpretation must be given "'controlling weight unless it is plainly erroneous or inconsistent with the regulation'" (quoting *Bowles v. Seminole Rock & Sand Co.*).[265]

And in *Auer v. Robbins*,[266] the Supreme Court, citing *Seminole Rock*, unanimously deferred to a Labor Department interpretation of an existing regulation even though it was provided for the first time in a brief. This sort of deference, seemingly equal to *Chevron* deference, thus seems to be available to agencies when they interpret ambiguous regulations that they have previously issued. Indeed, the D.C. Circuit has stated:

> In the aftermath of *Chevron*, it may be that our deference to agency interpretations of ambiguous regulations is no different than that which we afford to interpretations of ambiguous statutes. It would seem that there are few, if any, cases in which the standard applicable under *Chevron* would yield a different

---

262. Herz, *supra* note 145, at 130–31. *See also id.*, 130–38 for a discussion of the "quality" and "quantity" of *Skidmore* deference.

263. *Id.*; *see also* Harold J. Krent, ch. 6.03, ABA GUIDE TO JUDICIAL REVIEW, *supra* note 13, at 152.

264. 325 U.S. 410 (1945).

265. Thomas Jefferson Univ. v. Shalala, 512 U.S. 504, 510–11 (1994) (footnotes and citations omitted); *see also* Long Island Care at Home, Ltd. v. Coke, 551 U.S. 158, 171 (2007). For a strong defense of *Seminole Rock*, see Scott H. Angstreich, *Shoring Up* Chevron: *A Defense of* Seminole Rock *Deference to Agency Regulatory Interpretations*, 34 U.C. DAVIS L. REV. 49 (2000). For strong criticism, see John F. Manning, *Constitutional Structure and Judicial Deference to Agency Interpretations of Agency Rules*, 96 COLUM. L. REV. 612 (1996).

266. 519 U.S. 452 (1997).

result than the "plainly erroneous or inconsistent" standard set forth in [*Seminole Rock*].[267]

The court acknowledged that the *Seminole Rock* type of deference has been criticized.

Of late, it has been argued that the Supreme Court should abandon deference to agency interpretations of ambiguous regulations, because it arguably creates perverse incentives for an agency to draft vague regulations that give inadequate guidance . . . . [T]here is, to be sure, an outer limit to that deference imposed by the Administrative Procedure Act. A substantive regulation must have sufficient content and definitiveness as to be a meaningful exercise in agency lawmaking. It is certainly not open to an agency to promulgate mush and then give it concrete form only through subsequent less formal "interpretations." That technique would circumvent section 553, the notice-and-comment procedures of the APA.[268]

The Supreme Court has recognized this problem by making clear that the government cannot claim "*Auer* deference" when it has issued a "parroting regulation" that "paraphrase[s] the statutory language."[269] It has however, continued to use *Auer* deference. *Chase Bank USA, N.A. v. McCoy*[270] arose out of a private dispute that concerned the proper interpretation of the Federal Reserve Board's Regulation Z governing credit card disclosures. The Board had filed an amicus brief suggesting its view that the credit card company was not required to provide notice to the cardholder of an interest rate rise under the version of the regulation applicable at the time of the dispute. The Court unanimously deferred to that view, saying, "Under [*Auer*], we defer to an agency's interpretation of its own regulation, advanced in a legal brief, unless that interpretation is plainly erroneous or inconsistent with the regulation."[271]

---

267. Paralyzed Veterans of Am. v. D.C. Arena L.P., 117 F.3d 579, 584 (D.C. Cir. 1997); *see also* Bigelow v. Dep't of Def., 217 F.3d 875, 878 (D.C. Cir. 2000) ("*Auer* does not require an agency to demonstrate affirmatively that its interpretation represents its fair and considered judgment."). However, see the strong dissent by Judge Tatel in *Bigelow*, 217 F.3d at 878.

268. *Paralyzed Veterans*, *supra* note 267, at 584 (citing Professor Manning's article, *supra* note 264). Since then, the chorus against *Seminole Rock* has gotten louder. *See* Robert A. Anthony, *The Supreme Court and the APA: Sometimes They Just Don't Get It*, 10 ADMIN. L. J. AM. U. 1 (1996); Jonathan T. Molot, *The Judicial Perspective in the Administrative State: Reconciling Modern Doctrines of Deference with the Judiciary's Structural Role*, 53 STAN. L. REV. 1, 107 (2000) ("An agency that creates law today knowing its own staff—rather than an independent judge—will interpret it tomorrow will be less likely to bind itself through precise drafting."). However, the Supreme Court has made clear that the government cannot claim "*Auer* deference" when it has issued a "parroting regulation" that "paraphrase[s] the statutory language."

269. Gonzales v. Oregon, 546 U.S. 243, 257 (2006); *see also* N. Cal. River Watch v. Wilcox, 633 F.3d 766, 780 (9th Cir. 2011) (declining to apply *Auer* deference because "[h]ere, the three rules cited by the United States essentially parrot the statutory language").

270. 131 S. Ct. 871 (2011).

271. *Id.* at 880 (quoting *Auer*). Interestingly, in the oral argument in this case, Justice Kagan began by saying, "I'm wondering whether [giving *Auer* deference to interpretations made in briefs] continues to remain good law after *Christensen* and *Mead*." 2010 WL 4974385 at *3–*4.

The Court shortly thereafter reaffirmed this approach in another private dispute involving an FCC regulation in *Talk America, Inc. v. Michigan Bell Telephone Co.*[272] Here, though, Justice Scalia broke ranks to suggest doubts about the *Auer* doctrine.[273] Doubts like this have led some commentators who are critical of *Seminole Rock* to suggest that the *Mead/Skidmore* standard should also be applied to court review of agency "interpretations of their own regulations that are contained in formats that are not legally binding."[274] Others have suggested that it would be a mistake to import the *Mead* complications into this area, and that if there is incongruity in reviewing informal agency interpretations of regulations under a more deferential standard than applies to informal agency interpretations of statutes, the cure is a consistent application of *Chevron* and *Seminole Rock.*[275]

The relationship between *Seminole Rock* and *Chevron* can be especially complicated when an agency seeks to rely on an existing rule as part of its statutory interpretation. In *Mission Group Kansas, Inc. v. Riley,*[276] the Tenth Circuit said, "Where an agency purports to act pursuant to an interpretation of its own regulations, the court should generally undertake a two-step [*Seminole Rock*, then *Chevron*] review of the government's action to determine whether it was statutorily authorized."[277] It went on to say that "*Seminole Rock* review only establishes that the agency's administrative action is a permissible construction of its own regulatory authority; it does not establish that that regulation, as interpreted, is statutorily authorized. . . . Thus, if the agency's

---

272. 131 S. Ct. 2254 (2011).
273. *Id.* at 2266 (Scalia, J. concurring):

> It is comforting to know that I would reach the Court's result even without *Auer.* For while I have in the past uncritically accepted that rule, I have become increasingly doubtful of its validity. On the surface, it seems to be a natural corollary—indeed, an *a fortiori* application—of the rule that we will defer to an agency's interpretation of the statute it is charged with implementing, see [*Chevron*]. But it is not. When Congress enacts an imprecise statute that it commits to the implementation of an executive agency, it has no control over that implementation (except, of course, through further, more precise, legislation). The legislative and executive functions are not combined. But when an agency promulgates an imprecise rule, it leaves *to itself* the implementation of that rule, and thus the initial determination of the rule's meaning. And though the adoption of a rule is an exercise of the executive rather than the legislative power, a properly adopted rule has fully the effect of law. It seems contrary to fundamental principles of separation of powers to permit the person who promulgates a law to interpret it as well. *Id.*

274. Robert A. Anthony & Michael Asimow, *The Court's Deferences—A Foolish Inconsistency*, 26 ADMIN. & REG. L. NEWS 10 (Fall 2000) (criticizing the *Auer-Seminole Rock* approach).
275. *See* Angstreich, *supra* note 265. This sentiment is also expressed by Professor Ronald Levin in an e-mail to the author (Sept. 30, 2005).
276. 146 F.3d 775 (10th Cir. 1998).
277. *Id.* at 780.

interpretation of its regulations survives *Seminole Rock* review, we then analyze the regulations as interpreted under the framework established by *Chevron*."[278]

In any event, to reap any of the benefits of deference to a reasonable interpretation, the agency must provide adequate notice of its interpretation.[279] And note that normally neither *Chevron* nor *Auer* deference is given when an agency is interpreting another agency's regulations.[280]

5. APA Section 706(2)(D): "without observance of procedure required by law"

This clause requires reviewing courts to invalidate agency rules for failure to adhere to legally required procedures. This provision must be considered, however, in conjunction with the last directive in section 706: "due account shall be taken of the rule of prejudicial error."[281] As the Supreme Court has put it, "In administrative law, as

---

278. *Id. See also* the Supreme Court's struggle with this in *Coeur Alaska, Inc. v. Southeast Alaska Conservation Council*, 557 U.S. 261 (2009) (finding relevant provisions of the Clean Water Act to be ambiguous, then finding that the agency's regulations did not resolve the issue, then deferring (under *Auer*) to an agency memorandum interpreting the regulations). Justice Scalia decried the complexity and would have deferred to the memorandum under *Chevron*. Occasionally an agency is rather bold about seeking deference in interpreting its own regulations. *See, e.g.*, DOL, Labor Certification Process and Enforcement for Temporary Employment in Occupations Other Than Agriculture or Registered Nursing in the United States (H-2B Workers), and Other Technical Changes, 73 Fed. Reg. 78,039, 78,041 (Dec. 19, 2008) (giving interpretation of a previously enacted regulation in the preamble, but not the text, of a new regulation and stating, "The Department states this as a definitive interpretation of its own regulations and expects that courts will defer to that interpretation.").

279. *See* Beaver Plant Operations, Inc. v. Herman, 223 F.3d 25, 30–32 (1st Cir. 2000) (finding the interpretation was inconsistent and therefore failed to provide adequate notice).

280. *See* Chao v. Cmty. Trust Co., 474 F.3d 75, 85 (3d Cir. 2007) ("When an agency seeks to piggyback upon another agency's regulation for its own enforcement purposes, such deference is inappropriate."); U.S. Dep't of the Air Force v. FLRA, 952 F.2d 446, 540 (D.C. Cir. 1991)("[W]e do not defer to the FLRA's interpretation of regulations promulgated by other agencies."). *See also* Amerada Hess Pipeline Corp. v. FERC, 117 F.3d 596, 600 (D.C. Cir. 1997) ("We generally do not accord deference to an agency's interpretation of regulations promulgated by another agency that retains authority to administer the regulations.") (citations omitted). But in this case the court *did* give deference because the promulgating agency's jurisdiction had been transferred to the agency doing the interpretation.

281. For another formulation of the "harmless error" rule, *see* the Clean Air Act, 42 U.S.C. § 7607(d)(8): "In reviewing alleged procedural errors, the court may invalidate the rule only if the errors were so serious and related to matters of such central relevance to the rule that there is a substantial likelihood that the rule would have been significantly changed if such errors had not been made." *Applied in* Husqvarna AB v. EPA, 254 F.3d 195, 203 (D.C. Cir. 2001). Failure to follow applicable notice-and-comment requirements will rarely if ever be considered harmless error. *See* Sugar Cane Growers Co-op. of Fla. v. Veneman, 289 F.3d 89, 96 (D.C. Cir. 2002) ("[A]n utter failure to comply with notice and comment cannot be considered harmless if there is any uncertainty at all as to the effect of that failure."); *see also* Riverbend Farms, Inc. v. Madigan, 958 F.2d 1479, 1487 (9th Cir. 1992):

in federal civil and criminal litigation, there is a harmless error rule."[282]

Clause (D) forms the basis for the third main prong of judicial review of rulemaking: review of the procedures used by the agency. Thus, when an agency violates a procedure mandated by the APA, an applicable statute, its own regulations, or a court,[283] and the violation is prejudicial to a participant in the process, the resulting rule must normally be remanded to the agency for a corrective proceeding.[284] The following are the main legal sources for procedural requirements, the violation of which may lead to court reversal of the agency rule.[285]

a. The APA—In the context of informal rulemaking, this refers to the provisions in section 553 requiring notice, an opportunity for comment, a statement of basis and purpose, a delayed effective date, and, under section 552, publication of the rule.[286] As discussed throughout this *Guide*, there have been numerous challenges to agency rules based on an agency having violated APA procedural requirements.

[We] must exercise great caution in applying the harmless error rule in the administrative rulemaking context. The reason is apparent: Harmless error is more readily abused there than in the civil or criminal trial context. An agency is not required to adopt a rule that conforms in any way to the comments presented to it. So long as it explains its reasons, it may adopt a rule that all commentators think is stupid or unnecessary. Thus, if the harmless error rule were to look solely to result, an agency could always claim that it would have adopted the same rule even if it had complied with the APA procedures. To avoid gutting the APA's procedural requirements, harmless error analysis in administrative rulemaking must therefore focus on the process as well as the result. We have held that the failure to provide notice and comment is harmless only where the agency's mistake "clearly had no bearing on the procedure used or the substance of decision reached."

(quoting Sagebrush Rebellion, Inc. v. Hodel, 790 F.2d 760, 764–65 (9th Cir. 1986)).

282. Nat'l Ass'n of Home Builders v. Defenders of Wildlife, 551 U.S. 644, 659–60 (2007) (quoting PDK Labs. Inc. v. U.S. Drug Enforcement Admin., 362 F.3d 786, 799 (D.C. Cir 2004); *see also* Columbia Venture LLC v. S.C. Wildlife Fed'n, 562 F.3d 290, 294–95 (4th Cir. 2009) (finding FEMA defective publication of required notices in the *Federal Register* to be non-prejudicial because the petitioner had been "deeply involved in the administrative process from the beginning, received actual knowledge of each development, had ample opportunity to be heard, and submitted voluminous data challenging the technical and scientific underpinnings of FEMA's conclusions").

283. However, the authority of a court to mandate procedures beyond those in the APA was sharply curtailed in *Vermont Yankee Nuclear Power Corp. v. NRDC, supra* note 32. *See* discussion *infra* subsec. (5)(d).

284. *See supra* note 2.

285. For a review of the evolution of procedural review of agency action in the lens of political and democratic theory, see Lisa Schultz Bressman, *Procedures as Politics in Administrative Law*, 107 COLUM. L. REV. 1749 (2007).

286. *See* discussion *supra*, Part II, ch. 1, on the APA procedures for rulemaking, as well as Part III, generally.

b. Other statutes—many regulatory enabling statutes contain additional procedures for informal rulemaking. These too must be followed and may constitute a basis for a court's vacating the rule. In addition, government-wide procedural statutes, such as the Government in the Sunshine Act, Federal Advisory Committee Act, Regulatory Flexibility Act, and Paperwork Reduction Act, as well as various executive orders, impose procedures on agencies that are applicable to rulemaking.[287] Some appropriations acts do as well.[288]

When the Regulatory Flexibility Act was amended in 1996, Congress reversed the Act's long-standing preclusion of judicial review of agency compliance with the Act[289] by providing that "a small entity that is adversely affected or aggrieved by agency action is entitled to judicial review of agency compliance with the requirements of [most sections of the Act]."[290] The first case reviewing agency action under the Act held that the scope of review of agency compliance was "whether the Secretary made a reasonable, good-faith effort to carry out the mandate of section 604 [containing the requirement for a final regulatory flexibility analysis]."[291]

On the other hand, the Unfunded Mandates Reform Act contains a provision for very limited judicial review, providing, among other things, that if an agency fails to prepare the statement required under the Act, a court may compel its preparation, but a failure to prepare an adequate statement is not to be used as a basis for staying or enjoining a rule.[292] Similarly, Executive Order 12,866 (like the other such orders affecting rulemaking) provides that it is intended to improve the internal management of the federal government and is not intended "to create any right or benefit, substantive or procedural, enforceable at law or equity by a party against the United States, its agencies or instrumentalities, its officers or employees or any other person."[293]

c. The agency's procedural regulations. Many agencies have procedural regula-

---

287. *See supra* Part II, ch. 3, and Part III, ch. 2, for a discussion of these generic requirements.

288. *See* Harbor Gateway Commercial Prop. Owners' Ass'n v. EPA, 167 F.3d 602 (D.C. Cir. 1999) (listing of hazardous waste site invalidated because it was not initiated in the manner required by appropriations act).

289. See the discussion of the amendments in Part II, ch. 3(C).

290. 5 U.S.C. § 611(a)(1).

291. Associated Fisheries of Me., Inc. v. Daley, 127 F.3d 104, 114 (1st Cir. 1997).

292. 2 U.S.C. § 1571. The information generated under the Act is, however, made part of the "rulemaking record for judicial review." *Id.* at (a)(4).

293. Exec. Order 12,866, § 10. The Administrative Conference endorsed this limitation. *See* ACUS Recommendation 88-9, *Presidential Review of Agency Rulemaking*, 54 Fed. Reg. 5207 (1989) ("The presidential review process should be designed to improve the internal management of the federal government and should not create any substantive or procedural rights enforceable by judicial review."). Others have argued for limited judicial review. *See, e.g.*, Peter Raven-Hansen, *Making Agencies Follow Orders: Judicial Review of Agency Violations of Executive Order 12,291*, 1983 DUKE L.J. 285.

tions governing rulemaking. It is a well-established principle that, if prejudicial, "an agency's failure to follow its own regulations is fatal to the deviant action."[294]

This principle is illustrated by *Rodway v. Department of Agriculture*.[295] In *Rodway*, the Department of Agriculture had promulgated a regulation making APA procedures applicable to otherwise-exempt rules relating to public property, loans, grants, benefits, or contracts. It later issued a food-stamp-related rule without using APA procedures. The reviewing court found that even though the regulation fell within an exemption from APA procedural requirements, it was invalid because the Department failed to follow its own procedural rules.[296]

The principle that an agency must follow its own regulations, whether mandated by law or not, may not apply, however, in cases where procedural regulations were not intended to benefit the aggrieved party or to vest rights in the public.[297]

d. Procedural requirements imposed by courts. In the 1970s, courts began to require use of procedures in addition to the APA's requirements, either to provide additional degrees of fairness to participants or to improve the record of the proceeding in aid of the courts' judicial review responsibilities. This development stemmed in part

---

294. Way of Life Television Network, Inc. v. FCC, 593 F.2d 1356, 1359 (D.C. Cir. 1979). This principle stems from two earlier Supreme Court cases, *Vitarelli v. Seaton*, 359 U.S. 535, 539 (1959), and *Service v. Dulles*, 354 U.S. 363 (1957).

295. 514 F.2d 809 (D.C. Cir. 1975).

296. *Id.* at 814.

297. *See* Am. Farm Lines v. Black Ball Freight Serv., 397 U.S. 532, 538–39 (1970) (agencies' procedural rules adopted for the orderly transaction of business before the agency are not enforceable against the agency, but a procedural rule that confers important procedural rights on regulated parties is binding where a failure to adhere to the procedural rule would result in substantial prejudice to the regulated party alleging a violation; PAM S.p.A. v. United States, 463 F.3d 1345, 1348 (Fed. Cir. 2006) ("[E]ven if a rule *does* confer important procedural benefits upon individuals, there may still be a reason—such as lack of substantial prejudice—to allow a court or administrative agency to relax or modify the rule"); Colo. Envtl. Coal. v. Wenker, 353 F.3d 1221 (10th Cir. 2004) (Department of the Interior procedure that specified the content of submissions to the agency prior to appointment of public advisory councils was a procedural rule for the orderly transaction of agency business, and did not confer important procedural benefits on the regulated entities). On the other hand, courts have enforced agency procedural requirements, even if found in internal manuals, where they are seemingly intended to protect regulated parties from abuses of discretion. *See* Campbell v. Attorney General, 256 Fed. App'x 504 (3d Cir. 2007) (provision of agency operations instructions was enforceable against the Board of Immigration Appeals where the instruction provided a procedural requirement relating to removal of former members of the military that had not been complied with); Nicholas v. INS, 590 F.2d 802 (9th Cir. 1979) (provision of INS's Instructions mandating deferral of deportation in certain cases was enforceable against the agency). These citations were extracted from a more comprehensive treatment of this issue in Geoffrey Forney, *The Administrative Appeals Office: Informal Adjudication, Administrative Appeals, and Judicial Review* (draft 2011, on file with author); *see also* Note, *Violations by Agencies of Their Own Regulations*, 87 HARV. L. REV. 529 (1974).

from the difficulty courts faced in understanding and digesting the large, technical records produced by many rulemaking proceedings. This difficulty led then-Chief Judge Bazelon of the D.C. Circuit to favor procedural review strongly over substantive review.[298]

However, the Supreme Court in 1978 decided *Vermont Yankee Nuclear Power Corp. v. Natural Resources Defense Council,*[299] which came down squarely against court-imposed procedures that go beyond the APA's rulemaking requirements. In reversing the D.C. Circuit's decision,[300] which had invalidated an NRC rule on the disposition of nuclear wastes for procedural insufficiencies—namely, the failure to allow intervenors the right to discovery or cross-examination—the Court characterized the lower court's approach as "Monday morning quarterbacking" and said that the APA's legislative history left little doubt "that Congress intended that the discretion of the *agencies* and not that of the courts be exercised in determining when extra procedural devices should be employed."[301]

The Supreme Court stated that if agencies were forced to operate under the "vague injunction" to adopt those procedures "perfectly tailored to reach what the court perceives to be the 'best' or 'correct' result, judicial review would be totally unpredictable," agencies would be encouraged or almost compelled to "adopt full adjudicatory procedures in every instance,"[302] and "all the inherent advantages of informal rulemaking would be totally lost."[303] Finally, the Supreme Court said that reviewing courts are to judge the adequacy of the record in informal rulemaking not by the type of procedural devices employed but rather by determining whether the agency has followed the procedural requirements of the APA and other relevant statutes.[304]

The reaction to *Vermont Yankee* among commentators was mixed, and opinion on the potential impact of the decision on judicial review of rulemaking varied widely.[305]

---

298. His approach was that courts should not "scrutinize the technical merits of each decision" but should "establish a decision-making process which assures a reasoned decision." Int'l Harvester v. Ruckelshaus, 478 F.2d 615, 652 (D.C. Cir. 1973) (Bazelon, J., concurring). Some of Judge Bazelon's colleagues on the court disagreed. *See, e.g.,* J. Skelly Wright, *The Courts and the Rulemaking Process: The Limits of Judicial Review,* 59 CORNELL L. REV. 375 (1974). For a thorough description of the debate on the D.C. Circuit at the time, see Reuel Schiller, *Rulemaking's Promise: Administrative Law and Legal Culture in the 1960s and 1970s,* 53 ADMIN. L. REV. 1139 (2001).

299. 435 U.S. 519 (1978); *see also* Gillian E. Metzger, *The Story of* Vermont Yankee, *in* ADMINISTRATIVE LAW STORIES 124 (Peter L. Strauss ed., 2006) (providing historical account of case).

300. Natural Res. Def. Council, Inc. v. NRC, 547 F.2d 633 (D.C. Cir. 1976) (Bazelon, J.).

301. *Vermont Yankee, supra* note 32, at 545–47 (emphasis in original).

302. *Id.* at 546.

303. *Id.* at 547.

304. *Id.*

305. *See, e.g.,* Kenneth Culp Davis, *Administrative Common Law and the* Vermont Yankee *Opinion,* 1980 UTAH L. REV. 3; Stephen Breyer, Vermont Yankee *and the Courts' Role in the Nuclear Energy Controversy,* 91 HARV. L. REV. 1833 (1978); Antonin Scalia, Vermont Yankee: *The APA, the D.C. Circuit, and the Supreme Court,* 1978 SUP. CT. REV. 345; Richard B. Stewart, Vermont

However, in years following, both the federal courts of appeals and the district courts have consistently followed *Vermont Yankee*'s proscription against judicial remands based on agency failure to follow procedures not mandated by the APA.[306]

It is important to note, however, that the *Vermont Yankee* decision has not been interpreted so broadly as to displace the case law that had already developed with regard to the adequacy of notice, the opportunity to comment, and, most significantly, the adequacy of the agency's statement of basis and purpose under section 553 of the APA. Indeed, in *Vermont Yankee*, the Supreme Court cited with approval an earlier D.C. Circuit decision for the proposition that "[public] comments must be significant enough to step over a threshold requirement of materiality before any lack of agency response or consideration becomes of concern."[307]

Also bearing on the reach of *Vermont Yankee* is the Supreme Court's 1982 *State Farm* opinion,[308] which reversed NHTSA's rescission of a rule requiring passive restraints in cars. There, the Court reaffirmed a reviewing court's obligation under *Citizens to Preserve Overton Park v. Volpe* to determine if an agency decision is "based on a consideration of the relevant factors and whether there has been a clear error of judgment."[309] The Court found the agency's rule rescission to be arbitrary and capricious because the rulemaking record failed to present evidence or a rationale for not considering an "air-bags-only" rule.[310] In so doing, the Court also disposed of petitioners' argument that *Vermont Yankee* foreclosed the placing of such an additional procedural burden on the agency, stating: "We do not require today any specific procedures which NHTSA must follow."[311]

Considering the needs of reviewing courts charged under *Overton Park* with conducting "a thorough, probing, in-depth review"[312] of agency action based on the administrative record, it is unlikely that *Vermont Yankee* will be read to overturn the pre–*Vermont Yankee* judicial decisions interpreting section 553's notice, comment, and statement of basis and purpose requirements. On the other hand, the Supreme

---

Yankee *and the Evolution of Administrative Procedure*, 91 HARV. L. REV. 1805 (1978); Clark Byse, Vermont Yankee *and the Evolution of Administrative Procedure: A Somewhat Different View*, 91 HARV. L. REV. 1823 (1978).

306. *See* Alfred S. Neely, Vermont Yankee Nuclear Power Corp. v. Natural Resources Defense Council, Inc.: *Response and Reaction in the Federal Judiciary*, 14 U. BALT. L. REV. 256 (1985) (providing a collection of court opinions).

307. 435 U.S. at 553 (citing Portland Cement Ass'n v. Ruckelshaus, 486 F.2d 375 (D.C. Cir. 1973)). *But see* Am. Radio Relay League, Inc. v. FCC, 524 F.3d 227, 245 (D.C. Cir. 2008) (Kavanaugh, J., concurring) (arguing that the requirement violates *Vermont Yankee's* strictures against mandated procedures not required by the APA).

308. *State Farm, supra* note 37; *see also* discussion *supra* subsec. (2).

309. *Id.* at 43 (citing *Overton Park, supra* note 16, at 416).

310. *Id.* at 50.

311. *Id.* at 50–51.

312. *Overton Park, supra* note 16.

Court decision has largely halted reviewing court imposition of procedures beyond those fairly read to be contained in the APA or other applicable laws.[313]

    (e) Need to decide substantive claims after vacating a rule on procedural grounds. The D.C. Circuit has admitted that its decisions are inconsistent on this point.[314] It requires a balance between letting the agency redo the rule with proper procedures and resolving substantive issues without undue additional delay.[315]

6. APA Section 706(2)(E): "unsupported by substantial evidence in a case subject to sections 556 and 557 of this title or otherwise reviewed on the record of an agency hearing provided by statute"

    The "substantial evidence" test is ordinarily applicable only to those adjudications or rulemakings (that is, formal rulemakings) conducted according to the trial-type procedures spelled out in sections 556 and 557 of the APA.[316] It typically has not been used in judicial review of informal rulemaking, which is subject to the arbitrary and capricious standard of review.

    However, in the late 1960s and 1970s, Congress began to insert a substantial evidence test into some specific informal rulemaking statutes. The combination of informal rulemaking procedures with procedural elements associated with the adjudicatory process, in statutes such as the Occupational Safety and Health Act of 1970 and the Magnuson-Moss FTC Improvement Act of 1975, caused such statutes to be referred to as "hybrid" rulemaking statutes.[317] Congress's use of the substantial evi-

---

313. *Vermont Yankee*, for example, has been cited by courts that have rejected the argument that notice-and-comment procedure is required for interpretive rules that have a "substantial impact" on the public. *See supra* Part II, ch. 1(D)(3)(a); *see also* KENNETH CULP DAVIS, ADMINISTRATIVE LAW TREATISE §§ 7:17–7:19 (2d ed. 1979).

314. Natural Res. Def. Council v. EPA, 643 F.3d 311, 321 (D.C. Cir. 2011) ("Our case law provides little direction on whether, having determined to vacate on procedural grounds, we should nonetheless address substantive claims."). The court cited *Sprint Corp. v. FCC*, 315 F.3d 369, 377 (D.C. Cir. 2003) (remanding without reaching substantive claims); *Syncor Int'l Corp.*, 127 F.3d at 96 (same); *Air Transp. Ass'n of Am. v. FAA*, 169 F.3d 1, 4–6, 8 (D.C. Cir. 1999) (reaching statutory claims but declining to evaluate arbitrary and capricious challenges); *Owner-Operator Indep. Drivers Ass'n v. Fed. Motor Carrier Safety Admin.*, 494 F.3d 188, 206 (D.C. Cir. 2007) (vacating a portion of a rule both because agency failed to provide an opportunity for comment and because agency failed to provide adequate explanation); and *Ala. Power Co. v. FERC*, 160 F.3d 7, 11 (D.C. Cir. 1998) (finding it appropriate to proceed to petitioner's argument that agency lacked authority to take challenged action after having found that agency failed to follow required procedure in taking that action).

315. *See id.* at 321–23. The court went on to not address the overall merits of a challenged guidance document once it found it should have been subject to notice and comment, but it did find one alternative addressed in the guidance document to be ultra vires.

316. *See supra* Part II, ch. 1(B) for discussion of formal rulemaking requirements.

317. *See* discussion *supra* Part I(C) & Part III, ch. 4(C)(2).

dence test for review of rulemaking reflected its view that the more stringent test afforded the courts more leeway to monitor agency actions in implementing the new regulatory programs.

The linking of the substantial evidence test with proceedings involving "legislative" or "policy" types of judgments by agencies involved in informal rulemaking was thought by some to be anomalous, because as Judge McGowan stated in *Industrial Union Department v. Hodgson*,[318] decisions in informal rulemaking are typically not based on factual findings but rather on a "prediction based on pure legislative judgment."[319] The court, nevertheless, sought to give meaning to the substantial evidence test in that case, which involved an OSHA regulation. The court concluded that in reviewing informal rulemaking decisions under the substantial evidence test, the court's "paramount objective is to see whether the agency, given an essentially legislative task to perform, has carried it out in a manner calculated to negate the dangers of arbitrariness and irrationality in the formulation of rules for general application in the future."[320] Another oft-cited formulation is that "[s]ubstantial evidence is 'such relevant evidence as a reasonable mind might accept as adequate to support a conclusion.'"[321]

While Congress's occasional application of the substantial evidence test to informal rulemaking may have been intended to increase the scope of judicial review, it is by no means clear that the use of the test has brought about any significant changes in review under those statutes. This is consistent with the view that, in court review of informal rulemaking, the substantial evidence and arbitrary and capricious tests have tended to converge.[322] The Supreme Court has cited approvingly then-Judge Scalia's view that there is little or no difference between the two standards when it comes to reviewing agency fact-finding.[323]

The Administrative Law Section of the American Bar Association, in its 1986 restatement of the scope of judicial review,[324] noted that there was no reason to preserve

---

318. 499 F.2d 467 (D.C. Cir. 1974).
319. *Id.* at 474.
320. *Id.* at 475 (citing Automotive Parts & Accessories Ass'n v. Boyd, 407 F.2d 330, 336 (1968)).
321. *See, e.g.*, Am. Iron & Steel Inst. v. OSHA, 182 F.3d 1261, 1267 (11th Cir. 1999) (quoting Am. Textile Mfrs. Inst. v. Donovan, 452 U.S. 490, 522 (1981)) (upholding an OSHA standard for respiratory protection under the substantial evidence test).
322. *See supra* subsec. (2); *see also* Matthew J. McGrath, Note, *Convergence of the Substantial Evidence and Arbitrary and Capricious Standards of Review During Informal Rulemaking*, 54 Geo. Wash. L. Rev. 541 (1986).
323. *See* Dickinson v. Zurko, 527 U.S. 150, 158 (1999) (Breyer, J.) (citing *Data Processing, supra* note 9, at 683–84 (Scalia, J.) (finding no difference between the APA's "arbitrary, capricious" standard and its "substantial evidence" standard as applied to court review of agency fact-finding)).
324. *See* Section on Administrative Law of the ABA, *A Restatement of Scope of Review Doctrine* (Feb. 8, 1986), *reprinted in* 38 Admin. L. Rev. 235 (1986). The Section's report on the Restatement by Professor Ronald M. Levin, Chair, Judicial Review Committee, is *reprinted in* 38 Admin L. Rev. at 239.

this distinction.[325] It went on to note in its resolution that the appropriate role for the courts in reviewing rules was to "determine whether the factual premise has substantial support in the administrative record viewed as a whole."[326] The Administrative Conference specifically urged Congress not to use the substantial evidence test for the review of agency rules and to delete the test where it exists in current rulemaking statutes.[327]

7. APA Section 706(2)(F): "unwarranted by the facts to the extent that the facts are subject to trial de novo by the reviewing court"

This clause covers the possibility that a reviewing court might determine the validity of agency action after holding a trial of its own on the factual issues involved in the proceeding. It applies in certain narrow categories of agency proceedings, such as civil rights cases under Title VII.[328] Otherwise, according to *Camp v. Pitts*,[329] de novo review is appropriate only where there are inadequate fact-finding procedures in an adjudicatory proceeding or where judicial proceedings are brought to enforce certain administrative actions.[330] Thus, this clause generally has no application to judicial review of informal rulemaking.

B. Record on Review[331]

Rule 17 of the Federal Rules of Appellate Procedure (F.R.A.P.) states that when review of a regulation is sought in a court of appeals, "The agency must file the record with the circuit clerk within 40 days after being served with a petition for review, unless the statute authorizing review provides otherwise. . . . The court may shorten or extend the time to file the record. The clerk must notify all parties of the date when the record is filed."[332] But nowhere in these rules is the composition of this record addressed. Various views on what the record in informal rulemaking proceedings should contain, and the recommendation of the Administrative Conference on the subject, have been discussed above.[333] While the Conference's recommendation would allow the agency

---

325. *Id.* at 272.
326. *Id.* at 236, 274–75.
327. ACUS Recommendation 93-4, *Improving the Environment for Agency Rulemaking*, 58 Fed. Reg. 4670 (1994).
328. *See* Chandler v. Roudebush, 425 U.S. 840, 862 (1976) (requiring district court to conduct de novo trial even after EEOC had concluded that federal employee's Title VII claim lacked merit).
329. 411 U.S. 138 (1973).
330. *See, e.g.*, McClory v. United States, 763 F.2d 309 (7th Cir. 1985).
331. See Part III, ch. 5 for a full discussion of the "rulemaking record."
332. Fed. R. App. P. 17(a). This deadline may be extended by the court for good cause. *See id.* at 26(b).
333. *See* ACUS Recommendation 74-4, *Pre-enforcement Judicial Review of Rules of General Applicability*, 39 Fed. Reg. 23,044; discussion, *supra* Part III, ch. 5(B)(3). *See generally supra* Part III, ch. 5.

to "proffer" documents in the record in addition to those it considered in the rulemaking, courts may be expected usually to require an agency to defend its rule in court on the record assembled during the course of the rulemaking proceeding. A contrary approach would seem to contravene the rule against post hoc rationalizations.[334]

As discussed above,[335] records in rulemaking proceedings are sometimes quite unwieldy, and courts may have little patience with unmanageable, unreadable records. Clearly, an agency can help its cause by preparing a well-managed, orderly record. Under F.R.A.P. Rule 17(b)(1)(A), agencies may file the actual physical record with the court of appeals. However, this is generally discouraged, and the procedure in (b)(1)(B) allows the filing of "a certified list adequately describing all documents, transcripts of testimony, exhibits, and other material constituting the record, or describing those parts designated by the parties." Under F.R.A.P. Rule 31(a), the petitioner must file its opening brief within 40 days of the filing of the record.[336]

The "appendix" is the term used for the separate volume or volumes containing those reproduced portions of the record submitted to the reviewing court.[337] It renders the record more manageable for the judges, though the "agency must retain any portion of the record not filed with the clerk . . . and, if the court or a party so requests, [it] must be sent to the court regardless of any prior stipulation."[338] For example, in *Natural Resources Defense Council, Inc. v. SEC*,[339] a record exceeding 10,000 pages was boiled down to a joint appendix of 877 pages. F.R.A.P. Rule 30 spells out the procedure for reaching an agreement on the preparation of a joint appendix. Such procedure generally involves either stipulations or cross-designations by both parties, and the appellant normally has to bear the costs of the appendix, though that is subject to a dispute resolution procedure.

C. Judicial Remedies[340]

As noted at the beginning of this chapter, section 706(2) of the APA directs reviewing courts to "hold unlawful and *set aside* agency action, findings, and conclusions found to [violate clauses A-F]" (emphasis added). In the rulemaking context, when a court that finds that an agency rule was unlawful or arbitrary and capricious, it will normally remand the rule to the agency.[341] This, of course, gives the agency

---

334. *See State Farm, supra* note 37, at 50, and discussion *supra* Part III, ch. 7(B)(1).
335. *See* discussion *supra* Part III, ch. 5(B)(3).
336. Fed. R. App. P. 31(a).
337. *Id.* at 30.
338. *Id.* at 17(b)(3).
339. 606 F.2d 1031, 1052 n.28 (D.C. Cir. 1979).
340. This section borrows heavily from Ronald Levin, ch. 10, ABA Guide to Judicial Review, *supra* note 13, at 205–09. *See also* Ronald M. Levin, *Vacation at Sea, supra* note 2.
341. *See* Fla. Power & Light Co. v. Lorion, 470 U.S. 729, 744 (1985) ("If the record before the agency does not support the agency action, if the agency has not considered all relevant factors, or if the reviewing court simply cannot evaluate the challenged agency action on the basis of the record

another chance to either revise the rule or provide additional justification for it. And often agencies are able to rescue some parts, or all, of their remanded rule.[342] Moreover, in some cases an agency may wish to voluntarily ask for a remand prior to the court's decision.[343]

But a threshold question is presented by the language in section 706(2) as to whether this compels a court to "vacate," or completely invalidate, an improperly issued rule or whether the court may simply remand the rule case back to the agency for additional proceedings without vacating it.[344] This practice has been termed "remand without vacation."

---

before it, the proper course, except in rare circumstances, is to remand to the agency for additional investigation or explanation.") For one of those "rare circumstances," *see* Earth Island Inst. v. Hogarth, 494 F.3d 757, 770 (9th Cir. 2007) ("We agree with the district court that the government's intransigence in following Congress's mandate renders this case one of the rare circumstances where generic remand is not appropriate.").

342. *See* William S. Jordan, *Ossification Revisited: Does Arbitrary and Capricious Review Significantly Interfere with Agency Ability to Achieve Regulatory Goals Through Informal Rulemaking?*, 94 Nw. U. L. Rev. 393, 418 (2000) (finding that of 61 remands of legislative rules by the D.C. Circuit between 1985 and 1995, in only 12 of them was the agency not able to "recover"); *see also* Daniel B. Rodriguez, *Gift Horses and Great Expectations: Remands Without Vacatur in Administrative Law*, 36 Ariz. St. L.J. 599, 601, 637 (2004) (arguing that remand without vacatur is a device used to "temper the draconian impact of hard look review," but as such may also "fuel the courts' aggressiveness"). For a public choice analysis that is largely critical of remand without vacation, see Boris Bershteyn, Note, *An Article I, Section 7 Perspective on Administrative Law Remedies*, 114 Yale L.J. 359 (2004).

343. *See* Toni M. Fine, *Agency Requests for "Voluntary" Remand: A Proposal for the Development of Judicial Standards*, 28 Ariz. St. L J. 1079 (1996).

344. *See* Honeywell Int'l., Inc. v. EPA, 393 F.3d 1315 (D.C. Cir. 2005) (withdrawing, after petition for rehearing, portion of previous per curiam opinion at 374 F.3d 1363, 1373–74, that stated that section 307(d)(9) of the Clean Air Act required the court to vacate EPA's erroneous action: "Even if § 307(d)(9) gives a court discretion to remand without vacating, we would vacate EPA's rule for the reasons given in Judge Randolph's concurring opinion, in which Judge Sentelle joined."). Judge Rogers objected: "Until the en banc court endorses the view expressed in Judge Randolph's concurring opinion regarding vacatur, binding precedent requires a remand when vacatur might be unnecessarily disruptive. . . ." *Id.* The two of them reprised their debate in *Natural Resources Defense Council v. EPA*, 489 F.3d 1250, 1261 (D.C. Cir. 2007). *Compare id.* at 1262 (Randolph, J., concurring) *with id.* at 1264–66 (Rogers, J., dissenting in part).

See also Milk Train, Inc. v. Veneman, 310 F.3d 747, 756–58 (D.C. Cir. 2002) (Sentelle, J. dissenting) (opposing remand without vacation); Checkosky v. SEC, 23 F.3d 452, 462–66, 490–93 (D.C. Cir. 1994) (providing an extended debate between Judge Silberman (favoring remand without vacation) and Judge Randolph (opposed)); Allied-Signal, Inc. v. Nuclear Regulatory Comm'n, 988 F.2d 146, 150 (D.C. Cir. 1993) ("An inadequately supported rule . . . need not necessarily be vacated."); Am. Mining Cong. v. U.S. Army Corps of Eng'rs, 962 F. Supp. 2, 4 (D.D.C. 1997) (holding that "the ordinary result" when a court finds an agency's rule unlawful is that the rule is "vacated," not just with respect to the plaintiffs who brought the action but with respect to all parties, citing numerous cases). For commentary on how the D.C. Circuit is

In August 1997, the ABA House of Delegates approved a resolution on this issue that suggested guidance to the courts:[345]

1. When a reviewing court holds that a rule or order issued by a federal administrative agency must be remanded to the agency for further consideration, the court may exercise discretion in determining whether or not to refrain from vacating the agency's action pending the remand proceedings. The Administrative Procedure Act should be construed, or if necessary amended, to permit the exercise of such discretion.

2. In exercising this discretion, a reviewing court should normally strike the balance in favor of vacating the agency's action, unless special circumstances exist. Such special circumstances may be most often found to exist where, in the context of the proceeding as a whole:

   (a) the agency's error did not preclude fair public consideration of a central issue in a rulemaking or a fair hearing on the necessary findings in an adjudication or other agency proceeding;

   (b) the court finds a substantial likelihood that the agency, after further consideration, will be able to remedy its error and reach a similar overall result on a valid basis; and

   (c) the challenging party's interest in obtaining relief from the agency's decision is clearly outweighed by the substantial and adverse impact that vacation of the agency's action would have on

   (i) persons other than the Government who over time have reasonably relied on the agency action being remanded, or

   (ii) persons other than the Government, during the interim period before agency action on remand to cure the error has become final, and such impact cannot be remedied after such interim period.

3. Where the court orders the remedy of remand without vacation, it should give serious consideration to specifying a time frame within which the agency is to comply with the terms of the remand order. The importance of setting a time frame is heightened if the burden of a remand on the challenging party noticeably increases with its duration.

4. Where the court orders the remedy of remand without vacation, it should also consider directing that, until agency action to cure the previous error has become final,

---

handling this issue, see Kristina Daugirdas, Note, *Evaluating Remand Without Vacatur: A New Judicial Remedy for Defective Agency Rulemakings*, 80 N.Y.U. L. REV. 278, 309–11 (2005) (suggesting that the courts bifurcate their hearings and decisions on the merits and the remedy). A good discussion by Judge Louis Pollak can also be found in *Comite De Apoyo A Los Trabajadores Agricolas v. Solis*, 2010 WL 3431761 *24–*25 (E.D. Pa. 2010) (vacating some parts of the rule remanded to agency but not other parts).

345. Recommendation No. 107B, Adopted by the ABA House of Delegates (Aug. 1997), *reprinted in* Levin, *Vacation at Sea, supra* note 2, at 387–88.

(a) any statutory or administrative deadline for compliance with the remanded action should be extended; and

(b) any proceedings brought to enforce compliance with the remanded action should be stayed, or pursued only with permission of the court.

5. In order to promote informed application of the above standards, courts should
encourage parties to address remedial issues, such as the possibility of remand without vacation, in their briefs and at oral argument. In a given case,
if further explanation is needed and undue delay will not result, the court
should also consider inviting supplemental briefs directed to this issue.

The legality of remand without vacation is still disputed, and several judges on
the D.C. Circuit have taken a strong position against it.[346] But the practice is still
widely accepted.[347] As Professor Levin concludes:

[A] court is relatively likely to resort to remand without vacation if it perceives that the agency has a good chance of curing its previous error with, at
most, minor changes in its rule or order. Conversely, a court normally will

---

346. *See supra* note 344. Former Chief Judge Wald has also opined that "there are inherent powers
in a reviewing court to postpone vacation until the agency has a chance to make things right."
Patricia M. Wald, *Judicial Review in Midpassage: The Uneasy Partnership Between Courts
and Agencies Plays On*, 32 Tulsa L.J. 221, 236 (1996). In many cases the remand order is silent
about vacatur. *See* William S. Jordan III, *Ossification Revised: Does Arbitrary & Capricious
Review Significantly Interfere with Agency Ability to Achieve Regulatory Goals Through
Informal Rulemaking?*, 94 Nw. U.L. Rev. 393, 410 & n.88 (2000) (finding that in 28 of the 68
rulemaking cases studied, the D.C. Circuit "did not explicitly state whether or not it was
vacating the rule at issue").

347. *See* Elec. Privacy Info. Ctr. v. U.S. Dep't of Homeland Sec., 653 F.3d 1, 8 (D.C. Cir. 2011) ("In
sum, the TSA has advanced no justification for having failed to conduct a notice-and-comment rulemaking. We therefore remand this matter to the agency for further proceedings.
Because vacating the present rule would severely disrupt an essential security operation,
however, and the rule is, as we explain below, otherwise lawful, we shall not vacate the rule,
but we do nonetheless expect the agency to act promptly on remand to cure the defect in its
promulgation."); Chamber of Commerce v. SEC, *supra* note 69, at 145 (remanding a rule,
without vacating it, to address the rule's deficiencies); La. Fed. Land Bank Ass'n, FLCA v.
Farm Credit Admin., 336 F.3d 1075, 1085 (D.C. Cir. 2003) (quotation marks omitted) (remanding—but not vacating—a rule because "it is not unlikely the FCA will be able to justify
a future decision to retain the Rule, inasmuch as its only error was its failure to explain what
seems to be a policy difference with the plaintiffs"); Ne. Md. Waste Disposal Auth. v. EPA,
supra note 71, at 949–50 (remanding without vacation); Cent. & S. W. Servs., Inc. v. EPA, 220
F.3d 683, 692 (5th Cir. 2000) (footnote omitted) ("EPA may well be able to justify its decision
to refuse to promulgate a national variance for the electric utilities and it would be disruptive
to vacate a rule that applies to other members of the regulated community. Accordingly, we
remand, without vacatur . . . ."). *But see* Massachusetts *ex rel.* Div. of Marine Fisheries v. Daley,
170 F.3d 23, 32 (1st Cir. 1999) (remanding and vacating fishing quota, while inviting petition
for rehearing on remedy and also noting that the agency retains power to issue emergency
regulations if necessary).

vacate an action if the agency's chances of being able to rehabilitate its prior action looks poor.[348]

In one case in which the D.C. Circuit found that the FCC had improperly failed to initiate a proceeding to repeal a rule, it went so far as to vacate the rule itself.[349]

A further question is raised in some circumstances: if a rule that replaced an earlier rule is vacated, does that create a regulatory void, or does the previous rule come back into force? In one case, the D.C. Circuit addressed this issue as follows:

> When an agency replaces an existing rule with a new rule, and we vacate all or part of the new rule, we must decide whether the prior rule continues in effect or whether our action leaves no rule in effect. In at least some cases, we have no power to reinstate the prior rule and must remand to the agency to determine the appropriate replacement. *See Burlington Northern, Inc. v. United States*, 459 U.S. 131 (1982) (Court of Appeals lacks power to reinstate old ICC rate after invalidating revised rate). On the other hand, we have sometimes assumed that a decision vacating a new rule will reinstate the old rule. *E.g.*, *Natural Resources Defense Council, Inc. v. Gorsuch*, 685 F.2d 718, 728 (D.C. Cir. 1982) (implicitly assuming that EPA will return to its previous regulation defining "source" under the Clean Air Act).
>
> We believe the better course is generally to vacate the new rule without reinstating the old rule. This avoids any problem of the court overstepping its authority and leaves it to the agency to craft the best replacement for its own rule. Failure to reinstate the old rule creates a temporary regulatory vacuum, but the court's power to delay the mandate in a case for a reasonable period, plus the agency's limited power to issue a replacement on an emergency basis

---

348. Levin, ABA GUIDE TO JUDICIAL REVIEW, *supra* note 340, at 208–09 (footnotes omitted). In extraordinary circumstances a court may issue a writ of mandamus to vacate agency rules. *See* Radio-Television News Directors Ass'n v. FCC, 229 F.3d 269 (D.C. Cir. 2000) (finding that mandamus would issue to require vacation of the FCC's personal attack and political editorial rules where the petition to vacate the rules had been pending for 20 years, the FCC had done nothing to cure the deficiencies in its justification for the rules, and the six reasons proffered in support of the rules were all wanting).

349. *See* Fox Television Stations, Inc. v. FCC, 280 F.3d 1027, 1052–53 (D.C. Cir. 2002) (holding that vacatur, rather than remand for reconsideration, was appropriate remedy for FCC's act of deciding not to repeal cable/broadcast cross-ownership rule, in violation of APA and Telecommunications Act, inasmuch as reasons set forth in FCC report for retaining rule were at best flimsy, its half-hearted attempt to defend its decision before court of appeals indicated that rule was hopeless cause, and vacatur would not be disruptive of FCC's regulatory program). In another unusual case, where the court remanded two provisions of a rule that had been largely implemented by the industry for additional notice and comment, the court stayed its vacation of those two provisions for 90 days to "afford the Commission an opportunity to reopen the record for comment on the costs of implementing the two conditions" and to file a status report with the court. Chamber of Commerce of U.S. v. SEC, 443 F.3d 980, 909 (D.C. Cir. 2006).

without notice and comment, should usually suffice to avoid untoward consequences.[350]

Of course, the court may find that only a portion of a rule is void and allow it to be severed from the valid portion.[351] And in some cases, if the agency action has not been stayed, vacation may not be feasible; as one court has put it, "the egg has been scrambled."[352]

Finally, an agency may not avoid notice and comment based on an argument that it is simply tweaking a remanded rule, where the earlier rule had been vacated.[353]

---

350. Small Refiner Lead Phase-Down Task Force v. EPA, 705 F.2d 506, 545–46 (D.C. Cir. 1983) (Wald, J.) (vacating an EPA lead-use standard for small refineries); *see also* Nuclear Info. & Res. Serv. v. United States, 918 F.2d 189, 196–97 (D.C. Cir. 1990) (Wald, J.) (vacating NRC regulations that streamlined nuclear power plant licensing procedures and recognizing that vacation of these subsections would "create a temporary regulatory vacuum"), *vacated on other grounds*, Nuclear Info. & Res. Serv. v. NRC, 969 F.2d 1169 (D.C. Cir. 1992). In one long-running rulemaking dispute the agency managed to persuade Congress to grant temporary relief from vacatur. *See* Owner-Operator Indep. Drivers Ass'n v. Fed. Motor Carrier Safety Admin., 494 F.3d 188, 197 (D.C. Cir. 2007) (recounting that "after our July 16, 2004 decision in *Public Citizen* vacated the 2003 Rule, FMCSA sought and received temporary relief from the vacatur in Congress. The Surface Transportation Extension Act of 2004, signed by the President on September 30, 2004, provided that the 2003 Rule 'shall be in effect until the earlier of—(1) the effective date of a new final rule addressing the issues raised by [*Public Citizen*]; or (2) September 30, 2005.' Pub. L. No. 108-310, § 7(f), 118 Stat. 1144, 1154 (2004).").
351. *See* Catholic Social Serv. v. Shalala, 12 F.3d 1123 (D.C. Cir. 1994) (holding a provision of Medicare rule that purported to apply retroactively was severable, rather than ultra vires or void ab initio).
352. Sugar Cane Growers Co-op. of Fla. v. Veneman, *supra* note 281, at 97 ("There remains the question of remedy. Normally when an agency so clearly violates the APA we would vacate its action—in this case its 'non-rule rule'—and simply remand for the agency to start again. Unfortunately, because we denied preliminary relief in this case, the 2001 program was launched and crops were plowed under. The egg has been scrambled and there is no apparent way to restore the status quo ante.").
353. AFL-CIO v. Chao, 496 F. Supp. 2d 76, 85 (D.D.C. 2007) ("Whatever discretion an agency may have to tweak rules that have been remanded disappears when the rule at issue has instead been vacated—that is, annulled, voided, rescinded, or deprived of force.").

Chapter 3

Judicial Review of Agency Failure to Act

A. General Principles

Judicial review in the rulemaking area traditionally has been associated with challenges to administrative agency actions, that is, challenges to rules promulgated by the agency. The Administrative Procedure Act's (APA's) judicial review provisions, however, are not so limited. Under section 706(1), a reviewing court may "compel agency action unlawfully withheld or unreasonably delayed." In addition, section 555(b) of the APA provides that "within a reasonable time, each agency shall proceed to conclude a matter presented to it."[1] Relying particularly on these provisions, courts of appeals have, on occasion, compelled agencies to initiate rulemaking proceedings[2] or to complete rulemaking "unreasonably delayed."[3]

The rationale for judicial review of agency failure to act has been described as follows:

> Statutes designed to protect regulatory beneficiaries would be undone if agency implementation and enforcement were inadequate or nonexistent. Responding to this possibility, courts have relaxed traditional principles of standing, ripeness and prosecutorial discretion in order to permit review of agency inaction or of action that is assertedly inadequate.[4]

---

1. 5 U.S.C. §§ 706(1), 555(b). Other provisions of the APA, notably 5 U.S.C. § 701(a)(2), have been cited as making review of agency inaction unreviewable. 5 U.S.C. § 701(a)(2) exempts from APA review provisions "agency action committed to agency discretion by law."
2. *See* Pub. Citizen Health Res. Grp. v. Auchter, 702 F.2d 1150 (D.C. Cir. 1983); discussed *infra* subsec. (B)(1).
3. Telecomms. Res. & Action Ctr. v. FCC, 750 F.2d 70 (D.C. Cir. 1984) [hereinafter *TRAC*]; discussed *infra* subsec. (B)(2). The courts have also reviewed agency actions terminating rulemaking proceedings without the issuance of a final rule. *See, e.g.*, Natural Res. Def. Counsel v. SEC, 606 F.2d 1031 (D.C. Cir. 1979); *see also* discussion *infra* subsec. (B)(3).
4. Richard B. Stewart & Cass R. Sunstein, *Public Programs and Private Rights*, 95 Harv. L. Rev. 1193, 1205 (1982) (addressing judicial recognition of "initiation rights," albeit with a deferential standard of review); *see also* Cass R. Sunstein, *Reviewing Agency Inaction After* Heckler v. Chaney, 52 U. Chi. L. Rev. 653, 680–82 (1985). The issues of ripeness and finality in the context of agency rulemaking inaction are discussed *supra* Part IV, ch. 1(E)(3)(d).

At the same time, courts have recognized that they are generally not equipped to make the comparative judgments necessary to determine priorities for allocating scarce agency resources in the face of the many competing demands for government regulation and other essential agency activity.[5] As a consequence, courts have traditionally applied a highly deferential standard of review in reviewing cases of agency inaction.[6]

The 1985 Supreme Court decision in *Heckler v. Chaney*[7] had a major influence on court review of agency inaction generally.[8] The Court held that the Food and Drug Administration's (FDA's) decision not to initiate an enforcement action was presumptively unreviewable,[9] relying particularly on the following four considerations:

1. In setting enforcement priorities, agencies must evaluate a wide range of factors, which are particularly within their expertise; these factors include resources, likely success of the action, how the requested action "fits the agency's overall policies," and whether the agency has "enough resources to undertake the action at all."[10]
2. Refusal to take enforcement action generally does not involve the "exercise of [an agency's] *coercive* power over an individual's liberty or property rights."[11]
3. Since the agency has not taken a specific action, there is no "focus for judicial review."[12]
4. Agency refusal to take enforcement action shares some of the characteristics of a prosecutor's decision not to indict, which has traditionally been held to be unreviewable.[13]

---

5. *See, e.g.*, Nat'l Cong. of Hispanic Am. Citizens v. Marshall, 626 F.2d 882 (D.C. Cir. 1979) (OSHA's refusal to issue field sanitation standard); WWHT, Inc. v. FCC, 656 F.2d 807 (D.C. Cir. 1981). *See generally* Neil R. Eisner, *Agency Delay in Informal Rulemaking*, 3 Admin. L.J. 7 (1989).

6. *Id.*; *see also* W. Fuels-Illinois, Inc. v. ICC, 878 F.2d 1025, 1027 (7th Cir. 1989) ("An agency decision not to institute rulemaking should be overturned only in the rarest and most compelling circumstances."). For an argument that courts should eschew any special prohibitions on judicial review of agency inaction, see Lisa Schultz Bressman, *Judicial Review of Agency Inaction: An Arbitrariness Approach*, 79 N.Y.U. L. Rev. 1657 (2004).

7. 470 U.S. 821 (1985).

8. For an illustrative modern case, *see* Riverkeeper, Inc. v. Collins, 359 F.3d 156 (2d Cir. 2004) (finding NRC's refusal to take actions to protect a nuclear plant from terrorist attack unreviewable under *Heckler v. Chaney*).

9. The Court distinguished *Citizens to Preserve Overton Park v. Volpe*, 401 U.S. 402 (1971), holding that *Overton Park*'s presumption of reviewability was inapplicable where an agency refuses to take enforcement action. Heckler v. Chaney, 470 U.S. at 831.

10. Heckler, 470 U.S. at 831–32.

11. *Id.* at 832.

12. *Id.* The Court said that because the agency "must have exercised its power in some manner," agency *action* can "at least" be reviewed to determine if the agency exceeded its statutory powers. *Id.*

13. *Id.* at 832.

The Supreme Court expressly noted in *Chaney* that it was not deciding the question of "agency discretion not to invoke rulemaking proceedings."[14]

Although several of the considerations relied on by the Court for not exercising review in the enforcement context would arguably justify a court's refusal in ordinary circumstances to review agency rulemaking inaction, courts of appeals have, since *Chaney*, considered claims of agency inaction in rulemaking on the merits, either distinguishing *Chaney* or not referring to the Supreme Court decision at all.[15] In 2007, the Supreme Court reaffirmed the reviewability of denials of petitions for rulemaking in the well-known global-warming case, *Massachusetts v. EPA*:[16]

> There are key differences between a denial of a petition for rulemaking and an agency's decision not to initiate an enforcement action. In contrast to nonenforcement decisions, agency refusals to initiate rulemaking are less frequent, more apt to involve legal as opposed to factual analysis, and subject to special formalities, including a public explanation.

However, where courts have found agency rulemaking inaction reviewable, they have continued to defer to agency decisions on the appropriate use of resources and determination of priorities. As the Court continued in *Massachusetts v. EPA*, "Refusals to promulgate rules are thus susceptible to judicial review, though such review is 'extremely limited' and 'highly deferential.'"[17]

On the other hand, the unanimous decision by the Supreme Court in *Norton v. Southern Utah Wilderness Alliance* has made some types of challenges to agency inaction highly problematic.[18] In that case, the environmental group sought declaratory and injunctive relief for the Bureau of Land Management's failure to act to protect Utah public lands from environmental damage caused by off-road vehicles, contending that they could sue under § 706(1).[19] The Tenth Circuit reversed the district court's dismissal of the claims, but the Supreme Court unanimously reversed. The Court held that a § 706(1) claim can "proceed only where a plaintiff asserts that an agency failed to take a *discrete* agency action that it is *required to take*,"[20] and this

---

14. *Id.* at 825 n.2. The Court also distinguished situations where the agency refused to institute proceedings "based solely on the belief that it lacks jurisdiction" or where the agency adopts a "general policy" that is "so extreme as to amount to an abdication of its statutory responsibilities." *Id.* at 833 n.4.

15. *See infra* subsec. (B) for a discussion of these cases; *see also* Ronald M. Levin, *Understanding Unreviewability in Administrative Law*, 74 Minn. L. Rev. 689, 762–73 (1990).

16. 549 U.S. 497, 527 (2007) (citation and internal quotation marks omitted).

17. *Id.* at 527–28.

18. 542 U.S. 55 (2004).

19. For a fuller discussion of this case, see Richard Murphy, *Judicial Review* chapter, Developments in Administrative Law and Regulatory Practice 2003-2004, at 84–88 (Jeffrey S. Lubbers ed., 2004).

20. 542 U.S. at 64 (emphasis in original).

limitation precludes a broad programmatic attack such as that rejected in *Lujan I*.[21] Moreover, the Court held that the required-action limitation rules out judicial direction of even discrete agency action that is not demanded by law.[22]

B. Types of Agency Inaction

Judicial review of agency inaction in the context of rulemaking has generally arisen in one of three situations: (1) agency failure to initiate rulemaking; (2) agency delay in an ongoing rulemaking proceeding; and (3) agency termination of a rulemaking without issuing a rule or issuing a very narrow rule.

1. Failure to Initiate a Rulemaking

In a notable pre-*Heckler v. Chaney* case, *Public Citizen Health Research Group v. Auchter*,[23] plaintiffs had filed a petition for rulemaking asking the Occupational Safety and Health Administration (OSHA) to issue a rule governing ethylene oxide. In 1983, the D.C. Circuit concluded that ethylene oxide was a carcinogen, that employees were exposed to "a significant risk of grave danger" from the toxic chemical, that OSHA delay in beginning a rulemaking proceeding amounted to "the least responsive course short of inaction," and that initiation of rulemaking would not disrupt other agency rulemakings of "higher or competing priority," and found that OSHA was not concluding its regulatory action for ethylene oxide "within a reasonable time"[24] as required by the APA.[25] Stressing the "documented risk to workers' lives and the children they may conceive,"[26] the court ordered OSHA to publish a proposal on ethylene oxide within 30 days and stated that it expected the rulemaking to be concluded within a year.[27]

---

21. Lujan v. Nat'l Wildlife Fed'n, 497 U.S. 871 (1990); *see* discussion *supra* Part IV, ch. 1(B)(3).
22. *Southern Utah*, 542 U.S. at 61–65. The Court cited § 706(1) but emphasized the word "unlawfully" and said, "but a delay cannot be unreasonable with respect to action that is not required." *Id.* at 64 n.1.
23. 702 F.2d 1150 (D.C. Cir. 1983).
24. *Id.* at 1157–58.
25. *Id.* The court relied on the provisions in the OSHA Act requiring the agency to "give due regard to the urgency of the need" in determining standards priorities. *Id.; see also* 29 U.S.C. §§ 655(b), 706(1).
26. 702 F.2d at 1150.
27. *Id.* at 1154, 1158–59. The court refused to dictate a date for the issuance of the final rule. The district court had earlier ordered OSHA to issue an emergency temporary standard, which can become effective without rulemaking procedures. Pub. Citizen Health Res. Grp. v. Auchter, 554 F. Supp. 242 (D.D.C. 1983). The court of appeals reversed the district court, emphasizing its reluctance to "*compel* the Assistant Secretary to grant extraordinary relief." 702 F.2d at 1157. A final ethylene oxide exposure limit was ultimately issued by OSHA and partially upheld by the D.C. Circuit. Pub. Citizen Health Res. Grp. v. Tyson, 796 F.2d 1479 (D.C. Cir. 1986). The short-term exposure limit was remanded to OSHA, and it took further litigation to force OSHA to issue

In a post-*Heckler v. Chaney* case, also filed by Public Citizen, the D.C. Circuit ordered OSHA to follow a detailed schedule for proposing and finalizing a permissible exposure limit to hexavalent chromium. The proceeding began in 1976 when the National Institute for Occupational Safety and Health petitioned for an emergency standard.[28] After no action was forthcoming, Public Citizen filed a petition for rulemaking in 1993. The petition was denied, and although the agency wrote a letter in 1994 anticipating issuance of a notice of proposed rulemaking in 1995, that did not happen. Public Citizen unsuccessfully petitioned the Third Circuit for an order requiring rulemaking in 1998.[29] But after continuing delays, the court granted this relief in 2002 and issued a specific schedule for completion of the rulemaking in 2003.[30]

American Horse Protection Association, Inc. v. Lyng[31] was one of the first post-*Chaney* cases involving agency refusal to initiate rulemaking. In that case, the plaintiff claimed that a U.S. Department of Agriculture (USDA) regulation against "soring"[32] had become outdated and should be revised in a new rulemaking.[33] The court addressed the reviewability of a refusal to institute rulemaking, saying that the issue has been a "source of some uncertainty" since *Chaney*.[34] Although conceding that *Chaney*'s reasoning applies "to some extent" to rulemaking, the court held it did not bar review in this case.[35] The court noted that the first two *Chaney* factors favoring nonreview—

---

it. *See* Pub. Citizen Health Res. Grp. v. Brock, 823 F.2d 626 (D.C. Cir. 1987). For an account of this litigation by Public Citizen's counsel, see David C. Vladeck, *Unreasonable Delay, Unreasonable Intervention: The Battle to Force Regulation of Ethylene Oxide, in* ADMINISTRATIVE LAW STORIES 190 (Peter L. Strauss ed., 2006).

In other OSHA cases, courts of appeals have indicated reluctance to compel emergency measures. *See, e.g., In re* Int'l Chem. Workers Union, 830 F.2d 369 (D.C. Cir. 1987); *see also* Int'l Union v. Chao, 361 F.3d 249, 256 (3d Cir. 2004) (upholding denial by OSHA of a petition for rulemaking despite 10-year delay in responding).

28. *See* Cindy Skrzycki, *OSHA Slow to Issue Standards, Critics Charge*, WASH. POST, Nov. 9, 2004, at E-1 (describing history).

29. *See* Oil, Chem. & Atomic Workers Union v. OSHA, 145 F.3d 120, 124 (3d Cir. 1998) (ruling that the facts did not yet "demonstrate [that OSHA's] inaction is . . . unduly transgressive of the agency's own tentative deadlines").

30. *See* Pub. Citizen Health Res. Grp. v. Chao, 314 F.3d 143 (3d Cir. 2002) (finding a nine-year delay in adopting a new standard was excessive and was not justified by scientific uncertainty or OSHA's competing policy priorities); Pub. Citizen Health Res. Grp. v. Chao, No. 02-1611, 2003 WL 22158985 (3d Cir. April 2, 2003) (unreported decision) (setting forth a detailed schedule for an expedited rulemaking process initiated for exposure to chromium). *See also* Emily Hammond Meazell, *Deference and Dialogue in Administrative Law*, 111 COLUM. L. REV. 1722, 1753–60 (2011) (discussing these cases as part of an examination of "serial litigation").

31. 812 F.2d 1 (D.C. Cir. 1987).

32. "Soring" is a practice of deliberately injuring show horses to improve their gait in public shows. *Id.* The Horse Protection Act, 15 U.S.C. §§ 1821–1824, prohibits soring, and the Department of Agriculture is authorized to issue regulations to implement these prohibitions. 15 U.S.C. § 1528.

33. The plaintiff relied on a study prepared by a school of veterinary medicine showing the harmful effects of various training devices on horses. 812 F.2d at 2–3.

34. *Id.* at 3.

35. *Id.* at 4.

agency expertise and nonexercise of "coercive" power—are "likely to be involved in an agency's refusal to institute a rulemaking."[36] However, the parallel to prosecutorial decisions not to indict, traditionally within exclusive executive prerogative, was not applicable to rulemaking.[37] In contrast to prosecutorial decisions, which are frequent and based "mainly on close consideration of the facts of the case at hand, rather than on legal analysis," refusals to institute rulemaking are "likely to be relatively infrequent" and to turn on issues of law.[38] The court also pointed out that an agency's denial of a petition for rulemaking provides "a focus for judicial review" because of the APA's requirement of a public explanation for the denial.[39]

The court went on to apply the "arbitrary or capricious" test to the agency's refusal to initiate new rulemaking but noted that such a "tag line" "encompasses a range of levels of deference to the agency" and reiterated the D.C. Circuit's oft-stated position that an agency's refusal to institute rulemaking "is at the high end of the [deference] range."[40] At the same time, the court held that refusal to initiate rulemaking "sets off a special alert" when a request for rulemaking is made on the basis of a "radical change in [the rule's] factual premises."[41] The court, stressing the cruel and inhumane nature of soring and the statute's goals, ultimately concluded that USDA had not presented a "reasoned explanation" of its failure to grant the rulemaking petition.[42] Nevertheless, the court did not order the agency to initiate rulemaking, an order appropriate "only in the rarest and most compelling of circumstances,"[43] but remanded to the agency for a "reasonable opportunity to explain its decision or to institute a new rulemaking."[44]

In *National Customs Brokers & Forwarders Ass'n v. Federal Maritime Commission*,[45] the D.C. Circuit applied the same deferential standard to a denial of request for rulemaking, this time in the context of economic regulation. Distinguishing such regulation from cases involving grave health and safety violations, the court deferred to the agency denial of the petition.[46] In various challenges to FAA's decision not to

---

36. *Id.*

37. *Id.*

38. *Id.*

39. *Id.*; *accord* Weight Watchers Int'l, Inc. v. FTC, 47 F.3d 990 (9th Cir. 1995).

40. 812 F.2d at 4–5.

41. *Id.* at 5. *Public Citizen Health Research Group v. Auchter*, 792 F.2d 1150 (D.C. Cir. 1983), was this type of case, because new scientific data developed after the original rule showed the carcinogenicity of the chemical.

42. *Id.* at 7.

43. *Id.* (citing WWHT, Inc. v. FCC, 656 F.2d 807, 818 (D.C. Cir. 1981)).

44. *Id.* The agency on remand again denied the petition for rulemaking. This action was successfully challenged in *American Horse Protection Ass'n v. Lyng*, 681 F. Supp. 949 (D.D.C. 1988), where the court did order the agency to initiate a rulemaking.

45. 883 F.2d 93 (D.C. Cir. 1989).

46. *Id.* at 103; *see also* W. Fuels-Illinois, Inc. v. ICC, 878 F.2d 1025, 1027, 1030 (7th Cir. 1989) (noting the "heavy burden" to show that rulemaking should be ordered, in a case involving rail regulation).

grant petitions for further rulemaking on its then-mandatory age-60 retirement rule for domestic commercial pilots, the D.C. Circuit held the FAA was not acting in an arbitrary or capricious manner because the FAA adequately justified its decision and reasoning supporting the age-60 requirement.[47] Contrariwise, in another case in which the D.C. Circuit found that the FCC had improperly failed to initiate a proceeding to repeal a rule, the court went so far as to vacate the rule itself.[48]

In *Massachusetts v. EPA*, the Supreme Court prominently quoted from both the *Horse Protection* and *Custom Brokers* cases.[49] However, in that case the Supreme Court did find the Agency's reasons for denying the petition to be arbitrary and capricious because it "offered no reasoned explanation for its refusal to decide whether greenhouse gases cause or contribute to climate change" and remanded to EPA with directions to "ground its reasons for action or inaction in the statute."[50]

When an agency does agree to accept a petition for rulemaking, may an intervener seek to challenge that agreement? In one case the D.C. Circuit said no and denied intervention.[51]

2. *Delay in a Rulemaking Proceeding*

A second area where agency inaction has led to requests for judicial review is where an agency is accused of "unreasonable delay." There is some overlap with cases involving an agency's failure to initiate a rulemaking,[52] but some cases involve situations where the agency had begun a proceeding, which then extended over a period of years.[53]

---

47. *See* Prof'l Pilots Fed'n v. FAA, 118 F.3d 758, 765–70 (D.C. Cir. 1997); *see also* Yetman v. Garvey, 261 F.3d 664, 679 (7th Cir. 2001) (affirming the FAA's denial of an age-60 rule exemption because the FAA provided enough evidence to support its denial even though the FAA has denied every exemption petition before it).

48. *See* Fox Television Stations, Inc. v. FCC, 280 F.3d 1027, 1052–53 (D.C. Cir. 2002).

49. *See* Massachusetts v. EPA, 549 U.S. 497, 527–28 (2007).

50. *Id.* at 534. Justice Scalia, for the four dissenters, accused the majority of misapplying its stated deferential standard: "No matter how important the underlying policy issues at stake, this Court has no business substituting its own desired outcome for the reasoned judgment of the responsible agency." *Id.* at 560 (Scalia, J., dissenting). For commentary, see Jeffrey A. Rosen, *A Chance for a Second Look: Judicial Review of Rulemaking Petition Denials*, 35 Admin. & Reg. L. News 7 (Fall 2009).

    Fifteen months later EPA finally responded with an Advance Notice of Proposed Rulemaking "solicit[ing] public comment on how to respond to the U.S. Supreme Court's decision," but the Bush Administration ended without further action, 73 Fed. Reg. 44,354 (July 30, 2008). The Obama Administration quickly issued a Proposed Endangerment and Cause or Contribute Findings for Greenhouse Gases Under Section 202(a) of the Clean Air Act, 74 Fed. Reg. 18,886 (Apr. 24, 2009), and finalized it on Dec. 15, 2009, 74 Fed. Reg. 66,496.

51. Alternative Res. & Dev. Found. v. Veneman, 262 F.3d 406 (D.C. Cir. 2001).

52. *See, e.g.*, Pub. Citizen Health Res. Grp. v. Auchter, 702 F.2d 1150, 1150 (D.C. Cir. 1983).

53. Of course, even "normal" rulemaking takes a long time. One study found that rules issued with NPRMs from 1983 to 1995 that resulted in a final rule or final action took an average of 452.6

Cases involving allegations of agency inaction inherently raise ripeness and finality issues[54] because the agency's failure to take final action is what the case is about. Despite this, courts have looked for ways to address the issue of agency delay. In *Public Citizen Health Research Group v. FDA*,[55] the D.C. Circuit, although unwilling to review the substantive merits of the case, which involved a challenge to the FDA's failure to require certain health warnings on aspirin bottles, remanded to the district court for a determination whether FDA had "unreasonably delayed" its resolution of the issue within the meaning of section 706(1) of the APA.[56] Noting that agency action must take into account statutory concerns for health and safety, the court of appeals said that "[i]f the [district] court finds unreasonable delay, it must fashion an appropriate remedy, which may include ordering rulemaking to begin immediately and proceed expeditiously, and ordering periodic reports to the court concerning the pace of rulemaking."[57]

In *In re International Chemical Workers Union*,[58] the D.C. Circuit set down four factors to be considered in assessing claims of agency delay in rulemaking:[59]

1. The court should ascertain the length of time that has elapsed since the agency came under a duty to act. Although there is no per se rule as to how long is too long, inordinate agency delay would frustrate congressional intent by forcing a breakdown of regulatory processes.

2. The reasonableness of the delay must be judged in the context of the statute that authorizes the agency's action.

3. The court must examine the consequences of the agency's delay. Delays that might be altogether reasonable in the sphere of economic regulation are less tolerable when human lives are at stake.

4. The court should give due consideration in the balance to any plea of administrative error, administrative convenience, practical difficulty in carrying out a legislative mandate, or need to prioritize in the face of limited resources.[60]

---

days. Rules labeled as "significant" took an average of 503.4 days (though the time period was different—from 1995 to 2008). *See* Letter from Professors Jacob Gersen and Anne Joseph O'Connell to OMB posted as a public comment on OMB recommendations for a new Executive Order on Regulatory Review (Feb. 27, 2009), *available at* http://www.reginfo.gov/public/jsp/EO/fedRegReview/Anne_Joseph_OConnell.pdf.

54. *See* discussion *supra* Part IV, ch. 1(E).

55. 740 F.2d 21 (D.C. Cir. 1984). This case is also discussed *supra* Part IV, ch. 1(E)(3)(d).

56. 740 F.2d at 34.

57. *Id.* at 35. The court stressed that agency inaction or delay may be "tantamount to denial" of a petition for rulemaking and asserted that "[i]n deciding whether the pace of decision is unreasonably delayed, the court should consider the nature and extent of the interests prejudiced by delay, the agency justification for the place of decision, and the context of the statutory scheme out of which the dispute arises." *Id.*

58. 958 F.2d 1144 (D.C. Cir. 1992).

59. The court had earlier provided guidelines for reviewing delay in agency proceedings. *See generally TRAC*, 750 F.2d 70, 77 (D.C. Cir. 1984).

60. 958 F.2d at 1149 (citations and internal quotation marks omitted).

In *Chemical Workers*, the court found that a six-year delay by OSHA in the issuance of a health standard on workers' exposure to cadmium was unreasonable, and it imposed a deadline for the issuance of such a rule.[61] In a case involving a 20-year delay by the FCC in acting on a petition to vacate the agency's "personal attack and editorial fairness" rules, the D.C. Circuit issued a writ of mandamus to vacate the rules after previously granting the agency several extensions.[62]

While these cases demonstrate that the courts of appeals are prepared to review agency inaction even after *Chaney*, the courts have generally strongly deferred to agencies' judgments on their priorities. An example is *Sierra Club v. Thomas*,[63] where the D.C. Circuit held that EPA's delay in concluding rulemaking was not unreasonable, stating: "Because 'a court is in general ill-suited to review the order in which an agency conducts its business,' we are properly hesitant to upset an agency's priorities by ordering it to expedite one specific action, and thus to give it precedence over others."[64] Similarly, the same court refused, in *United Steelworkers of America v. Rubber Manufacturing Ass'n*,[65] to order OSHA to expedite its rulemaking on benzene, saying that "judicial imposition of any overly hasty timetable at this stage would ill serve the public interest," because the rule and its rationale "must be constructed carefully and thoroughly if the agency's action is to pass judicial scrutiny."[66] In another case, the D.C. Circuit also refused to issue a writ of mandamus compelling rulemaking by the Mine Safety and Health Administration (MSHA) even though MSHA had not complied with statutory timelines for rulemaking; however, to ensure compli-

---

61. The court noted that "OSHA has cited to the resignation of a key staff member, the unanticipated delay in developing medical surveillance guidelines, and the need to respond to additional comments as contributing to the latest seven-month postponement." *Id.* at 1150. But it also concluded, "[F]or three years, OSHA has not met any timetable proposed to the court, and we have grave cause for concern that if we do not insist on a deadline now, some new impediment will be pleaded five months hence. OSHA's asserted justifications for the delay become less persuasive the longer the delay continues." *Id.*

62. *See* Radio-Television News Directors Ass'n v. FCC, 229 F.3d 269 (D.C. Cir. 2000) (granting writ of mandamus to require vacation of the FCC's personal attack and political editorial rules, where the petition to vacate the rules had been pending for 20 years, the FCC had done nothing to cure the deficiencies in its justification for the rules, and the six reasons proffered in support of the rules were all wanting).

63. 828 F.2d 783 (D.C. Cir. 1987).

64. *Id.* at 797 (quoting Envtl. Def. Fund v. Hardin, 428 F.2d 1093, 1099 (D.C. Cir. 1970)). In reaching this conclusion, the court relied on the facts that the statute gave no special priority to completion of this rulemaking, nor did the statute "instruct" EPA to regulate this subject matter; because EPA's entire docket consists of health regulatory issues, any acceleration in this proceeding would come at the expense of action elsewhere. *Id.* at 797–98. The court also noted that the agency had already proceeded through the comment period in the rulemaking, and because the proceeding involves "complex scientific technological and policy questions, [it] must be afforded the amount of time necessary to analyze such questions" so as not to risk judicial invalidation. *Id.* at 798.

65. 783 F.2d 1117 (D.C. Cir. 1986).

66. *Id.*

ance, the court retained jurisdiction and required MSHA to report regularly on its rulemaking status.[67] And in another mixed decision,[68] *In re Bluewater Network*, the court held that although Congress required the Coast Guard to initiate rulemaking for bodies of water explicitly named in the Oil Pollution Act, the Coast Guard was not required to begin rulemaking for other bodies of water. However, petitioners were entitled to a writ of mandamus when the Act required the Coast Guard to create some compliance standards by a certain date, the Coast Guard had not yet taken any action, and the date had since passed.[69] In *Bluewater*, the D.C. Circuit summarized its standards for analyzing unreasonable delay claims:

> (1) the time agencies take to make decisions must be governed by a "rule of reason"; (2) where Congress has provided a timetable or other indication of the speed with which it expects the agency to proceed in the enabling statute, that statutory scheme may supply content for this rule of reason; (3) delays that might be reasonable in the sphere of economic regulation are less tolerable when human health and welfare are at stake; (4) the court should consider the effect of expediting delayed action on agency activities of a higher or competing priority; (5) the court should also take into account the nature and extent of the interests prejudiced by delay; (6) the court need not "find any impropriety lurking behind agency lassitude in order to hold that agency action is unreasonably delayed."[70]

For a long-running dispute between the EPA and the Sierra Club in which the district court found EPA in repeated non-compliance with its duty to promulgate regulations governing the discharge of certain hazardous air pollutants, see *Sierra Club v. Johnson*.[71] EPA met an often-extended deadline by promulgating the mandated rules on the deadline date, but then stayed them two days before they were to become effective.[72] This order was deemed reviewable[73] and was vacated.[74]

---

67. *In re* United Mine Workers of Am. Int'l Union, 190 F.3d 545, 553–56 (D.C. Cir. 1999).
68. 234 F.3d 1305, 1315 (D.C. Cir. 2000).
69. *Id.* at 1315–16.
70. *Id.* at 1315 (citing *In re* United Mine Workers of Am. Int'l Union, 190 F.3d at 549 (quoting *TRAC*, 750 F.2d 70, 80 (1984))).
71. Sierra Club v. Johnson, 444 F. Supp. 2d 46 (D.D.C. 2006) (holding that "EPA did not demonstrate that it would be impossible to comply with plaintiff's proposed schedule for the enactment of remaining standards; however, it was appropriate for court to order a regulatory schedule that was slightly more relaxed than that proposed by plaintiff, but significantly more expedited than that sought by the agency"). For an overview of such cases, *see* Robert L. Glicksman, *The Value of Agency-Forcing Citizen Suits to Enforce Nondiscretionary Duties*, 10 WIDENER L. REV. 353 (2004).
72. *See* Sierra Club v. Jackson, Civ. A. No. 01-1537, 2011 WL 181097 (D.D.C. Jan. 20, 2011) (describing series of extensions and ordering promulgation by Feb. 21, 2011).
73. Sierra Club v. Johnson, 813 F. Supp. 2d 149 (D.D.C. 2011).
74. Sierra Club v. Johnson, — F. Supp. 2d ——, 2012 WL 34509 (D.D.C. Jan. 9, 2012).

In a case where an agency rule had been remanded for a better explanation but not vacated, and the agency had failed to respond in seven years, the court granted mandamus to a challenger seeking an explanation.[75] The court applied the *TRAC* factors but said that it also had the additional motivation to "prevent the frustration of orders previously issued."[76] The court explained that "the agency has effectively nullified our determination that its interim rules are invalid, because our remand without vacatur left those rules in place."[77]

3. Termination of Rulemaking

Termination of rulemaking without issuing a rule is also a type of agency inaction. In this situation, however, the agency has generally already expended resources and compiled a substantial record, making judicial review easier. In *Williams Natural Gas Co. v. FERC*,[78] the D.C. Circuit reviewed a FERC order terminating an ongoing rulemaking under the Natural Gas Policy Act of 1978.[79] The court, noting that the agency had issued a lengthy document expressing its tentative view that the regulation should be changed and received comments on the issue, concluded that there was a sufficient evidentiary basis for determining whether the agency decision was arbitrary or capricious.[80] Relying on *NRDC v. SEC*,[81] which "drew a clear distinction between an agency's refusal to undertake a rulemaking (reviewable, if at all, under an exceedingly narrow standard) and its decision to terminate a docket after a substantial record has been compiled," the court looked in detail at the agency's rationale in determining that FERC had not articulated a reasoned explanation for its decision. The court remanded to the agency for further consideration.[82]

---

75. *In re* Core Commc'ns, Inc., 531 F.3d 849 (D.C. Cir. 2008).
76. *Id.* at 856 (quoting Potomac Elec. Power Co. v. ICC, 702 F.2d 1026, 1032 (D.C. Cir. 1983)).
77. *Id.*
78. 872 F.2d 438 (D.C. Cir. 1989).
79. Pub. L. No. 95-621, 92 Stat. 3350 (codified in scattered sections of 15 U.S.C.).
80. 872 F.2d at 443.
81. 606 F.2d 1031, 1045–47 (D.C. Cir. 1979).
82. The court did not require the agency to issue a rule; it noted that the agency "retains wide discretion on remand." 872 F.2d at 450. In *Farmworker Justice Fund v. Brock*, the court reviewed OSHA's decision to terminate a 14-year-long rulemaking without issuing a rule. 811 F.2d 613 (D.C. Cir.), *vacated as moot*, 817 F.2d 890 (D.C. Cir. 1987). The court analyzed the *Chaney* case as not precluding judicial review where the "decision is based on factors that the court is competent to evaluate" or where the agency decision is contrary to law. *Id.* at 621–22. The court found that OSHA had based its decision not to issue a field sanitation standard for farmworkers on impermissible factors.

Inaction by the FCC was upheld in *N.Y. State Department of Law v. FCC*, 984 F.2d 1209 (D.C. Cir. 1993). In that case, the FCC entered a consent decree with affiliated companies accused of violations of the agency's rules prohibiting transactions between them. The D.C. Circuit held FCC's failure to reconsider its consent decree and instead take enforcement action was not subject to review. In so deciding, the court relied on its earlier decision in *Schering Corp. v. Heckler*, 779 F.2d 683 (D.C. Cir. 1985).

The same policy considerations would apply to court review where the agency, after rulemaking, issues a rule with exemptions for significant groups. Thus, in *United Steelworkers of America v. Auchter*,[83] the Third Circuit remanded OSHA's hazard communication rule for reconsideration of its decision not to apply the rule to non-manufacturing sectors of business.[84] The court rejected the agency's argument that its priority-setting authority barred review of its decision not to cover non-manufacturing industries, saying that because the rulemaking had been completed, the agency had failed to explain why coverage of non-manufacturing in the final rule "would have seriously impeded the rulemaking process."[85]

In a situation where the agency has failed to act in a timely fashion on the court's remand of a rule for reconsideration, the court had no difficulty in concluding that the agency's inaction was reviewable. Thus, in *Public Citizen Health Research Group v. Brock*,[86] involving the OSHA ethylene oxide proceeding after remand,[87] the D.C. Circuit scolded the agency for its failure to act on the remand order by promptly initiating rulemaking on the short-term exposure limit issue.[88] Although the court rejected a request to find the agency in contempt, finding that the agency schedule for completion of the rulemaking was reasonable, it warned that failure to meet that self-imposed schedule would constitute "unreasonable delay."[89]

C. Summary

In summary, despite the Supreme Court decision in *Heckler v. Chaney*,[90] the courts have reviewed agency failure to take rulemaking actions in a number of situations:

1. The court will ordinarily be most deferential where the question is whether the agency should initiate a rulemaking proceeding.[91] Where the court decides to

---

83. 763 F.2d 728 (3d Cir. 1985).
84. *Id.* at 739.
85. *Id.* at 738. *See also* United Steelworkers of Am. v. Marshall, 647 F.2d 1189, 1309–10 (D.C. Cir. 1980) (reviewing OSHA's exemption of construction industry from lead standard). The same principle was applied in *Colorado v. Department of the Interior*, 880 F.2d 481, 485 (D.C. Cir. 1989). There, the agency was challenged for not issuing "more comprehensive" regulations; the court held that the case was different from a petition to compel action where the agency had not yet acted, because "final agency action" was involved. *Id.*
86. 823 F.2d 626 (D.C. Cir. 1987).
87. *See* note 27, *supra*, for a discussion of this entire litigation. The court remanded the rule to OSHA for its consideration of a short-term exposure limit for the chemical. 823 F.2d at 629.
88. 823 F.2d at 628–29.
89. *Id.* at 629; *see also* United Steelworkers of Am. v. Pendergrass, 819 F.2d 1263 (3d Cir. 1987) (reviewing OSHA's failure to act on partial remand of hazard communication standard).
90. 470 U.S. 821 (1985).
91. *See supra* subsec. (B)(1).

compel action, it will typically require only that the agency issue a *proposed* rule.[92]

2. Where the agency commences rulemaking but delays its completion, courts will evaluate a host of factors in deciding whether to compel action.[93] These were summarized in the *TRAC* case.[94] Substantial deference will still be given to agency discretion in managing its priorities; however, circumstances may exist showing that the agency delay is "unreasonable." In some cases, the court will not decide on a deadline but will insist that the agency provide an appropriate timetable, which the court will monitor.[95]

3. A case in which the agency has completed rulemaking but decided not to issue a rule or issued a "less comprehensive" rule than is being sought represents the opposite end of the review spectrum. In that situation, because resource considerations are less important and there is a public record for court review, the court will review the agency failure to act in much the same way as it would agency action.[96]

4. Failure of an agency to act promptly on a remand from the court is likely to elicit a sharp rebuke and forceful response.[97]

Suits to compel agency rulemaking action often raise issues of timing (finality, ripeness, and failure to exhaust)[98] and also implicate the question of what is the appropriate "record" of agency actions before the court.[99]

---

92. *See supra* notes 23–27 and accompanying text for a discussion of *Public Citizen Health Research Group v. Auchter. See also supra* text accompanying notes 31 to 44 for a discussion of *American Horse Protection Ass'n v. Lyng.*

93. *See supra* subsec. B(2).

94. The *TRAC* case is discussed *supra*, subsec. B(2).

95. *See, e.g.*, Oil, Chem. & Atomic Workers Int'l Union v. Zegeer, 768 F.2d 1480 (D.C. Cir. 1985).

96. *See supra* subsec. B(3).

97. *See* Pub. Citizen Health Res. Grp. v. Brock, 823 F.2d 626 (D.C. Cir. 1987).

98. *See* discussion *supra* Part IV, ch. 1(E).

99. *See* discussion *supra* Part III, ch. 5; Part IV, ch. 2(B).

Appendix A

Selected Federal Statutes Affecting Rulemaking

1. **Unfunded Mandates Reform Act**
2. **Administrative Procedure Act**
3. **Negotiated Rulemaking Act**
4. **Regulatory Flexibility Act**
5. **Congressional Review of Agency Rulemaking**

1. Unfunded Mandates Reform Act
(Selected sections)
2 U. S. C. ____

§ 658. Definitions

For purposes of this part:

(1) Agency

The term "agency" has the same meaning as defined in section 551(1) of title 5, but does not include independent regulatory agencies.

(2) Amount

The term "amount," with respect to an authorization of appropriations for Federal financial assistance, means the amount of budget authority for any Federal grant assistance program or any Federal program providing loan guarantees or direct loans.

(3) Direct costs

The term "direct costs"—

(A)(i) in the case of a Federal intergovernmental mandate, means the aggregate estimated amounts that all State, local, and tribal governments would be required to spend or would be prohibited from raising in revenues in order to comply with the Federal intergovernmental mandate; or

(ii) in the case of a provision referred to in paragraph (5)(A)(ii), means the amount of Federal financial assistance eliminated or reduced;

(B) in the case of a Federal private sector mandate, means the aggregate estimated amounts that the private sector will be required to spend in order to comply with the Federal private sector mandate;

(C) shall be determined on the assumption that—

      (i) State, local, and tribal governments, and the private sector will take all reasonable steps necessary to mitigate the costs resulting from the Federal mandate, and will comply with applicable standards of practice and conduct established by recognized professional or trade associations; and

      (ii) reasonable steps to mitigate the costs shall not include increases in State, local, or tribal taxes or fees; and

   (D) shall not include —

      (i) estimated amounts that the State, local, and tribal governments (in the case of a Federal intergovernmental mandate) or the private sector (in the case of a Federal private sector mandate) would spend —

        (I) to comply with or carry out all applicable Federal, State, local, and tribal laws and regulations in effect at the time of the adoption of the Federal mandate for the same activity as is affected by that Federal mandate; or

        (II) to comply with or carry out State, local, and tribal governmental programs, or private-sector business or other activities in effect at the time of the adoption of the Federal mandate for the same activity as is affected by that mandate; or

      (ii) expenditures to the extent that such expenditures will be offset by any direct savings to the State, local, and tribal governments, or by the private sector, as a result of—

        (I) compliance with the Federal mandate; or

        (II) other changes in Federal law or regulation that are enacted or adopted in the same bill or joint resolution or proposed or final Federal regulation and that govern the same activity as is affected by the Federal mandate.

 (4) Direct savings

The term "direct savings," when used with respect to the result of compliance with the Federal mandate—

   (A) in the case of a Federal intergovernmental mandate, means the aggregate estimated reduction in costs to any State, local, or tribal government as a result of compliance with the Federal intergovernmental mandate; and

   (B) in the case of a Federal private sector mandate, means the aggregate estimated reduction in costs to the private sector as a result of compliance with the Federal private sector mandate.

 (5) Federal intergovernmental mandate

The term "Federal intergovernmental mandate" means—

   (A) any provision in legislation, statute, or regulation that—

      (i) would impose an enforceable duty upon State, local, or tribal governments, except—

        (I) a condition of Federal assistance; or

(II) a duty arising from participation in a voluntary Federal program, except as provided in subparagraph (B))*; or

(ii) would reduce or eliminate the amount of authorization of appropriations for—

(I) Federal financial assistance that would be provided to State, local, or tribal governments for the purpose of complying with any such previously imposed duty unless such duty is reduced or eliminated by a corresponding amount; or

(II) the control of borders by the Federal Government; or reimbursement to State, local, or tribal governments for the net cost associated with illegal, deportable, and excludable aliens, including court-mandated expenses related to emergency health care, education or criminal justice; when such a reduction or elimination would result in increased net costs to State, local, or tribal governments in providing education or emergency health care to, or incarceration of, illegal aliens; except that this subclause shall not be in effect with respect to a State, local, or tribal government, to the extent that such government has not fully cooperated in the efforts of the Federal Government to locate, apprehend, and deport illegal aliens;

(B) any provision in legislation, statute, or regulation that relates to a then-existing Federal program under which $500,000,000 or more is provided annually to State, local, and tribal governments under entitlement authority, if the provision—

(i) (I) would increase the stringency of conditions of assistance to State, local, or tribal governments under the program; or

(II) would place caps upon, or otherwise decrease, the Federal Government's responsibility to provide funding to State, local, or tribal governments under the program; and

(ii) the State, local, or tribal governments that participate in the Federal program lack authority under that program to amend their financial or programmatic responsibilities to continue providing required services that are affected by the legislation, statute, or regulation.

(6) Federal mandate
The term "Federal mandate" means a Federal intergovernmental mandate or a Federal private sector mandate, as defined in paragraphs (5) and (7).

(7) Federal private sector mandate
The term "Federal private sector mandate" means any provision in legislation, statute, or regulation that —

---

* The second closing parentheses is how it appears in the original statute and the U.S.C. The U.S.C. has a footnote recognizing this likely typo.

   (A) would impose an enforceable duty upon the private sector except—
      (i) a condition of Federal assistance; or
      (ii) a duty arising from participation in a voluntary Federal program; or
   (B) would reduce or eliminate the amount of authorization of appropriations for Federal financial assistance that will be provided to the private sector for the purposes of ensuring compliance with such duty.

(8) Local government

The term "local government" has the same meaning as defined in section 6501(6) of title 31.

(9) Private sector

The term "private sector" means all persons or entities in the United States, including individuals, partnerships, associations, corporations, and educational and nonprofit institutions, but shall not include State, local, or tribal governments.

(10) Regulation; rule

The term "regulation" or "rule" (except with respect to a rule of either House of the Congress) has the meaning of "rule" as defined in section 601(2) of title 5.

(11) Small government

The term "small government" means any small governmental jurisdictions defined in section 601(5) of title 5 and any tribal government.

(12) State

The term "State" has the same meaning as defined in section 6501(9) of title 31.

(13) Tribal government

The term "tribal government" means any Indian tribe, band, nation, or other organized group or community, including any Alaska Native village or regional or village corporation as defined in or established pursuant to the Alaska Native Claims Settlement Act (85 Stat. 688; 43 U.S.C. 1601 et seq.) which is recognized as eligible for the special programs and services provided by the United States to Indians because of their special status as Indians.'

§ 1501. Purposes

The purposes of this chapter are—

***

(7) to assist Federal agencies in their consideration of proposed regulations affecting State, local, and tribal governments, by —
   (A) requiring that Federal agencies develop a process to enable the elected and other officials of State, local, and tribal governments to provide input when Federal agencies are developing regulations; and
   (B) requiring that Federal agencies prepare and consider estimates of the budgetary impact of regulations containing Federal mandates upon State, local, and tribal governments and the private sector before adopting such

regulations, and ensuring that small governments are given special consideration in that process; and

(8) to begin consideration of the effect of previously imposed Federal mandates, including the impact on State, local, and tribal governments of Federal court interpretations of Federal statutes and regulations that impose Federal intergovernmental mandates.

§ 1502. Definitions

For purposes of this chapter—

(1) except as provided in section 1555 of this title, the terms defined under section 658 of this title shall have the meanings as so defined; and

(2) the term "Director" means the Director of the Congressional Budget Office.

§ 1503. Exclusions

This chapter shall not apply to any provision in a bill, joint resolution, amendment, motion, or conference report before Congress and any provision in a proposed or final Federal regulation that—

(1) enforces constitutional rights of individuals;

(2) establishes or enforces any statutory rights that prohibit discrimination on the basis of race, color, religion, sex, national origin, age, handicap, or disability;

(3) requires compliance with accounting and auditing procedures with respect to grants or other money or property provided by the Federal Government;

(4) provides for emergency assistance or relief at the request of any State, local, or tribal government or any official of a State, local, or tribal government;

(5) is necessary for the national security or the ratification or implementation of international treaty obligations;

(6) the President designates as emergency legislation and that the Congress so designates in statute; or

(7) relates to the old-age, survivors, and disability insurance program under title II of the Social Security Act [42 U.S.C. 401 et seq.] (including taxes imposed by sections 3101(a) and 3111(a) of title 26 (relating to old-age, survivors, and disability insurance)).

§ 1531. Regulatory process

Each agency shall, unless otherwise prohibited by law, assess the effects of Federal regulatory actions on State, local, and tribal governments, and the private sector (other than to the extent that such regulations incorporate requirements specifically set forth in law).

§ 1532. Statements to accompany significant regulatory actions

(a) In general

Unless otherwise prohibited by law, before promulgating any general notice of proposed rulemaking that is likely to result in promulgation of any rule that includes any Federal mandate that may result in the expenditure by State, local, and tribal governments, in the aggregate, or by the private sector, of $100,000,000 or more (adjusted annually for inflation) in any 1 year, and before promulgating any final rule for which a general notice of proposed rulemaking was published, the agency shall prepare a written statement containing—

(1) an identification of the provision of Federal law under which the rule is being promulgated;

(2) a qualitative and quantitative assessment of the anticipated costs and benefits of the Federal mandate, including the costs and benefits to State, local, and tribal governments or the private sector, as well as the effect of the Federal mandate on health, safety, and the natural environment and such an assessment shall include—

(A) an analysis of the extent to which such costs to State, local, and tribal governments may be paid with Federal financial assistance (or otherwise paid for by the Federal Government); and

(B) the extent to which there are available Federal resources to carry out the intergovernmental mandate;

(3) estimates by the agency, if and to the extent that the agency determines that accurate estimates are reasonably feasible, of—

(A) the future compliance costs of the Federal mandate; and

(B) any disproportionate budgetary effects of the Federal mandate upon any particular regions of the nation or particular State, local, or tribal governments, urban or rural or other types of communities, or particular segments of the private sector;

(4) estimates by the agency of the effect on the national economy, such as the effect on productivity, economic growth, full employment, creation of productive jobs, and international competitiveness of United States goods and services, if and to the extent that the agency in its sole discretion determines that accurate estimates are reasonably feasible and that such effect is relevant and material; and

(5) (A) a description of the extent of the agency's prior consultation with elected representatives (under section 1534 of this title) of the affected State, local, and tribal governments;

(B) a summary of the comments and concerns that were presented by State, local, or tribal governments either orally or in writing to the agency; and

(C) a summary of the agency's evaluation of those comments and concerns.

(b) Promulgation

In promulgating a general notice of proposed rulemaking or a final rule for which a statement under subsection (a) of this section is required, the agency shall include in the promulgation a summary of the information contained in the statement.

(c) Preparation in conjunction with other statement

Any agency may prepare any statement required under subsection (a) of this section in conjunction with or as a part of any other statement or analysis, provided that the statement or analysis satisfies the provisions of subsection (a) of this section.

§ 1533. Small government agency plan

(a) Effects on small governments

Before establishing any regulatory requirements that might significantly or uniquely affect small governments, agencies shall have developed a plan under which the agency shall—

(1) provide notice of the requirements to potentially affected small governments, if any;

(2) enable officials of affected small governments to provide meaningful and timely input in the development of regulatory proposals containing significant Federal intergovernmental mandates; and

(3) inform, educate, and advise small governments on compliance with the requirements.

(b) Authorization of appropriations

There are authorized to be appropriated to each agency to carry out the provisions of this section and for no other purpose, such sums as are necessary.

§ 1534. State, local, and tribal government input

(a) In general

Each agency shall, to the extent permitted in law, develop an effective process to permit elected officers of State, local, and tribal governments (or their designated employees with authority to act on their behalf) to provide meaningful and timely input in the development of regulatory proposals containing significant Federal intergovernmental mandates.

(b) Meetings between State, local, tribal and Federal officers

The Federal Advisory Committee Act (5 U.S.C. App.) shall not apply to actions in support of intergovernmental communications where—

(1) meetings are held exclusively between Federal officials and elected officers of State, local, and tribal governments (or their designated employees with authority to act on their behalf) acting in their official capacities; and

(2) such meetings are solely for the purposes of exchanging views, information, or advice relating to the management or implementation of Federal programs established pursuant to public law that explicitly or inherently share intergovernmental responsibilities or administration.

(c) Implementing guidelines

No later than 6 months after March 22, 1995, the President shall issue guidelines and instructions to Federal agencies for appropriate implementation of subsections (a) and (b) of this section consistent with applicable laws and regulations.

§ 1535. Least burdensome option or explanation required

(a) In general

Except as provided in subsection (b) of this section, before promulgating any rule for which a written statement is required under section 1532 of this title, the agency shall identify and consider a reasonable number of regulatory alternatives and from those alternatives select the least costly, most cost-effective or least burdensome alternative that achieves the objectives of the rule, for—

(1) State, local, and tribal governments, in the case of a rule containing a Federal intergovernmental mandate; and

(2) the private sector, in the case of a rule containing a Federal private sector mandate.

(b) Exception

The provisions of subsection (a) of this section shall apply unless—

(1) the head of the affected agency publishes with the final rule an explanation of why the least costly, most cost-effective or least burdensome method of achieving the objectives of the rule was not adopted; or

(2) the provisions are inconsistent with law.

(c) OMB certification

No later than 1 year after March 22, 1995, the Director of the Office of Management and Budget shall certify to Congress, with a written explanation, agency compliance with this section and include in that certification agencies and rulemakings that fail to adequately comply with this section.

§ 1536. Assistance to Congressional Budget Office

The Director of the Office of Management and Budget shall—

(1) collect from agencies the statements prepared under section 1532 of this title; and

(2) periodically forward copies of such statements to the Director of the Congressional Budget Office on a reasonably timely basis after promulgation of the general notice of proposed rulemaking or of the final rule for which the statement was prepared.

§ 1555. "Federal mandate" defined

Notwithstanding section 1502 of this title, for purposes of this subchapter the term "Federal mandate" means any provision in statute or regulation or any Federal court ruling that imposes an enforceable duty upon State, local, or tribal governments including a condition of Federal assistance or a duty arising from participation in a voluntary Federal program.

§ 1571. Judicial review

(a) Agency statements on significant regulatory actions

    (1) In general

        Compliance or noncompliance by any agency with the provisions of sections 1532 and 1533(a)(1) and (2) of this title shall be subject to judicial review only in accordance with this section.

    (2) Limited review of agency compliance or noncompliance

        (A) Agency compliance or noncompliance with the provisions of sections 1532 and 1533(a)(1) and (2) of this title shall be subject to judicial review only under section 706(1) of title 5, and only as provided under subparagraph (B).

        (B) If an agency fails to prepare the written statement (including the preparation of the estimates, analyses, statements, or descriptions) under section 1532 of this title or the written plan under section 1533(a)(1) and (2) of this title, a court may compel the agency to prepare such written statement.

    (3) Review of agency rules

        In any judicial review under any other Federal law of an agency rule for which a written statement or plan is required under sections 1532 and 1533(a)(1) and (2) of this title, the inadequacy or failure to prepare such statement (including the inadequacy or failure to prepare any estimate, analysis, statement or description) or written plan shall not be used as a basis for staying, enjoining, invalidating or otherwise affecting such agency rule.

    (4) Certain information as part of record

        Any information generated under sections 1532 and 1533(a)(1) and (2) of this title that is part of the rulemaking record for judicial review under the provisions of any other Federal law may be considered as part of the record for judicial review conducted under such other provisions of Federal law.

    (5) Application of other Federal law

        For any petition under paragraph (2) the provisions of such other Federal law shall control all other matters, such as exhaustion of administrative remedies, the time for and manner of seeking review and venue, except that if such other Federal law does not provide a limitation on the time for filing a petition for judicial review that is less than 180 days, such limitation shall be 180 days after a final rule is promulgated by the appropriate agency.

    (6) Effective date

        This subsection shall take effect on October 1, 1995, and shall apply only to any agency rule for which a general notice of proposed rulemaking is promulgated on or after such date.

(b) Judicial review and rule of construction

    Except as provided in subsection (a) of this section—

    (1) any estimate, analysis, statement, description or report prepared under this chapter, and any compliance or noncompliance with the provisions of this

chapter, and any determination concerning the applicability of the provisions of this chapter shall not be subject to judicial review; and

(2) no provision of this chapter shall be construed to create any right or benefit, substantive or procedural, enforceable by any person in any administrative or judicial action.

2. Administrative Procedure Act (Selected sections)
5 U.S.C. ____

§ 551. Definitions

For the purpose of this subchapter—

(1) "agency" means each authority of the Government of the United States, whether or not it is within or subject to review by another agency, but does not include—

(A) the Congress;

(B) the courts of the United States;

(C) the governments of the territories or possessions of the United States;

(D) the government of the District of Columbia;

or except as to the requirements of section 552 of this title—

(E) agencies composed of representatives of the parties or of representatives of organizations of the parties to the disputes determined by them;

(F) courts martial and military commissions;

(G) military authority exercised in the field in time of war or in occupied territory; or

(H) functions conferred by sections 1738, 1739, 1743, and 1744 of title 12; subchapter II of chapter 471 of title 49; or sections 1884, 1891–1902, and former section 1641(b)(2), of title 50, appendix;

(2) "person" includes an individual, partnership, corporation, association, or public or private organization other than an agency;

(3) "party" includes a person or agency named or admitted as a party, or properly seeking and entitled as of right to be admitted as a party, in an agency proceeding, and a person or agency admitted by an agency as a party for limited purposes;

(4) "rule" means the whole or a part of an agency statement of general or particular applicability and future effect designed to implement, interpret, or prescribe law or policy or describing the organization, procedure, or practice requirements of an agency and includes the approval or prescription for the future of rates, wages, corporate or financial structures or reorganizations thereof, prices, facilities, appliances, services or allowances therefor or of valuations, costs, or accounting, or practices bearing on any of the foregoing;

(5) "rule making" means agency process for formulating, amending, or repealing a rule;

(6) "order" means the whole or a part of a final disposition, whether affirmative, negative, injunctive, or declaratory in form, of an agency in a matter other than rule making but including licensing;

(7) "adjudication" means agency process for the formulation of an order;

(8) "license" includes the whole or a part of an agency permit, certificate, approval, registration, charter, membership, statutory exemption or other form of permission;

(9) "licensing" includes agency process respecting the grant, renewal, denial, revocation, suspension, annulment, withdrawal, limitation, amendment, modification, or conditioning of a license;

(10) "sanction" includes the whole or a part of an agency—

(A) prohibition, requirement, limitation, or other condition affecting the freedom of a person;

(B) withholding of relief;

(C) imposition of penalty or fine;

(D) destruction, taking, seizure, or withholding of property;

(E) assessment of damages, reimbursement, restitution, compensation, costs, charges, or fees;

(F) requirement, revocation, or suspension of a license; or

(G) taking other compulsory or restrictive action;

(11) "relief" includes the whole or a part of an agency—

(A) grant of money, assistance, license, authority, exemption, exception, privilege, or remedy;

(B) recognition of a claim, right, immunity, privilege, exemption, or exception; or

(C) taking of other action on the application or petition of, and beneficial to, a person;

(12) "agency proceeding" means an agency process as defined by paragraphs (5), (7), and (9) of this section;

(13) "agency action" includes the whole or a part of an agency rule, order, license, sanction, relief, or the equivalent or denial thereof, or failure to act; and

(14) "ex parte communication" means an oral or written communication not on the public record with respect to which reasonable prior notice to all parties is not given, but it shall not include requests for status reports on any matter or proceeding covered by this subchapter.

§ 552. Public information; agency rules, opinions, orders, records, and proceedings

(a) Each agency shall make available to the public information as follows:

(1) Each agency shall separately state and currently publish in the Federal Register for the guidance of the public—

(A) descriptions of its central and field organization and the established places at which, the employees (and in the case of a uniformed service, the members) from whom, and the methods whereby, the public may obtain information, make submittals or requests, or obtain decisions;

(B) statements of the general course and method by which its functions are channeled and determined, including the nature and requirements of all formal and informal procedures available;

(C) rules of procedure, descriptions of forms available or the places at which forms may be obtained, and instructions as to the scope and contents of all papers, reports, or examinations;

(D) substantive rules of general applicability adopted as authorized by law, and statements of general policy or interpretations of general applicability formulated and adopted by the agency; and

(E) each amendment, revision, or repeal of the foregoing.

Except to the extent that a person has actual and timely notice of the terms thereof, a person may not in any manner be required to resort to, or be adversely affected by, a matter required to be published in the Federal Register and not so published. For the purpose of this paragraph, matter reasonably available to the class of persons affected thereby is deemed published in the Federal Register when incorporated by reference therein with the approval of the Director of the Federal Register.

(2) Each agency, in accordance with published rules, shall make available for public inspection and copying—

(A) final opinions, including concurring and dissenting opinions, as well as orders, made in the adjudication of cases;

(B) those statements of policy and interpretations which have been adopted by the agency and are not published in the Federal Register;

(C) administrative staff manuals and instructions to staff that affect a member of the public;

(D) copies of all records, regardless of form or format, which have been released to any person under paragraph (3) and which, because of the nature of their subject matter, the agency determines have become or are likely to become the subject of subsequent requests for substantially the same records; and

(E) a general index of the records referred to under subparagraph (D);

unless the materials are promptly published and copies offered for sale. For records created on or after November 1, 1996, within one year after such date, each agency shall make such records available, including by computer telecommunications or, if computer telecommunications means have not been established by the agency, by other electronic means. To the extent required to prevent a clearly unwarranted invasion of personal privacy, an agency may delete identifying details when it makes available or publishes an opinion, statement of policy, interpretation, staff manual, instruction, or copies of records referred to in subparagraph (D). However, in each case the justification for the deletion shall be explained fully in writing, and the extent of such deletion shall be indicated on the portion of the record which is made available or published, unless including that indication would harm an interest protected by the exemption in subsection (b) under which the deletion is made. If technically feasible, the extent of the deletion shall be indicated at the place in the record where the deletion was made. Each agency shall also maintain and make available for public inspection and copying current indexes providing identifying information for the public as to any matter issued, adopted, or promulgated after July 4, 1967, and required by this paragraph to be made available or published. Each agency shall promptly publish, quarterly or more frequently, and distribute (by sale or otherwise) copies of each index or supplements thereto unless it determines by order published in the Federal Register that the publication would be unnecessary and impracticable, in which case the agency shall nonetheless provide copies of such index on request at a cost not to exceed the direct cost of duplication. Each agency shall make the index referred to in subparagraph (E) available by computer telecommunications by December 31, 1999. A final order, opinion, statement of policy, interpretation, or staff manual or instruction that affects a member of the public may be relied on, used, or cited as precedent by an agency against a party other than an agency only if—

    (i) it has been indexed and either made available or published as provided by this paragraph; or

    (ii) the party has actual and timely notice of the terms thereof.

******[Rest of § 552, the Freedom of Information Act, omitted]******
******[§ 552a, the Privacy Act, omitted]********************
******[§ 552b, the Government in the Sunshine Act, omitted]******

§ 553. Rule making

(a) This section applies, according to the provisions thereof, except to the extent that there is involved—

  (1) a military or foreign affairs function of the United States; or

  (2) a matter relating to agency management or personnel or to public property, loans, grants, benefits, or contracts.

(b) General notice of proposed rule making shall be published in the Federal Register, unless persons subject thereto are named and either personally served or otherwise have actual notice thereof in accordance with law. The notice shall include—

  (1) a statement of the time, place, and nature of public rule making proceedings;

  (2) reference to the legal authority under which the rule is proposed; and

  (3) either the terms or substance of the proposed rule or a description of the subjects and issues involved.

Except when notice or hearing is required by statute, this subsection does not apply—

(A) to interpretative rules, general statements of policy, or rules of agency organization, procedure, or practice; or

(B) when the agency for good cause finds (and incorporates the finding and a brief statement of reasons therefor in the rules issued) that notice and public procedure thereon are impracticable, unnecessary, or contrary to the public interest.

(c) After notice required by this section, the agency shall give interested persons an opportunity to participate in the rule making through submission of written data, views, or arguments with or without opportunity for oral presentation. After consideration of the relevant matter presented, the agency shall incorporate in the rules adopted a concise general statement of their basis and purpose. When rules are required by statute to be made on the record after opportunity for an agency hearing, sections 556 and 557 of this title apply instead of this subsection.

(d) The required publication or service of a substantive rule shall be made not less than 30 days before its effective date, except—

(1) a substantive rule which grants or recognizes an exemption or relieves a restriction;

(2) interpretative rules and statements of policy; or

(3) as otherwise provided by the agency for good cause found and published with the rule.

(e) Each agency shall give an interested person the right to petition for the issuance, amendment, or repeal of a rule.

§ 554. Adjudications

(a) This section applies, according to the provisions thereof, in every case of adjudication required by statute to be determined on the record after opportunity for an agency hearing, except to the extent that there is involved—

(1) a matter subject to a subsequent trial of the law and the facts de novo in a court;

(2) the selection or tenure of an employee, except a* administrative law judge appointed under section 3105 of this title;

(3) proceedings in which decisions rest solely on inspections, tests, or elections;

(4) the conduct of military or foreign affairs functions;

(5) cases in which an agency is acting as an agent for a court; or

(6) the certification of worker representatives.

(b) Persons entitled to notice of an agency hearing shall be timely informed of—

(1) the time, place, and nature of the hearing;

(2) the legal authority and jurisdiction under which the hearing is to be held; and

---

* Footnote "1" added to the U.S.C. to indicate that the incorrect use of "a" instead of "an" was so in original.

(3) the matters of fact and law asserted.

When private persons are the moving parties, other parties to the proceeding shall give prompt notice of issues controverted in fact or law; and in other instances agencies may by rule require responsive pleading. In fixing the time and place for hearings, due regard shall be had for the convenience and necessity of the parties or their representatives.

(c) The agency shall give all interested parties opportunity for—

(1) the submission and consideration of facts, arguments, offers of settlement, or proposals of adjustment when time, the nature of the proceeding, and the public interest permit; and

(2) to the extent that the parties are unable so to determine a controversy by consent, hearing and decision on notice and in accordance with sections 556 and 557 of this title.

(d) The employee who presides at the reception of evidence pursuant to section 556 of this title shall make the recommended decision or initial decision required by section 557 of this title, unless he becomes unavailable to the agency. Except to the extent required for the disposition of ex parte matters as authorized by law, such an employee may not—

(1) consult a person or party on a fact in issue, unless on notice and opportunity for all parties to participate; or

(2) be responsible to or subject to the supervision or direction of an employee or agent engaged in the performance of investigative or prosecuting functions for an agency.

An employee or agent engaged in the performance of investigative or prosecuting functions for an agency in a case may not, in that or a factually related case, participate or advise in the decision, recommended decision, or agency review pursuant to section 557 of this title, except as witness or counsel in public proceedings. This subsection does not apply—

(A) in determining applications for initial licenses;

(B) to proceedings involving the validity or application of rates, facilities, or practices of public utilities or carriers; or

(C) to the agency or a member or members of the body comprising the agency.

(e) The agency, with like effect as in the case of other orders, and in its sound discretion, may issue a declaratory order to terminate a controversy or remove uncertainty.

§ 555. Ancillary matters

(a) This section applies, according to the provisions thereof, except as otherwise provided by this subchapter.

(b) A person compelled to appear in person before an agency or representative thereof is entitled to be accompanied, represented, and advised by counsel or, if permitted by the agency, by other qualified representative. A party is entitled to appear in person or by or with counsel or other duly qualified representative in an agency proceeding. So far as the orderly conduct of public business permits, an interested person may appear before an agency or its responsible employees for the presentation, adjustment, or determination of an issue, request, or controversy in a proceeding, whether interlocutory, summary, or otherwise, or in connection with an agency function. With due regard for the convenience and necessity of the parties or their representatives and within a reasonable time, each agency shall proceed to conclude a matter presented to it. This subsection does not grant or deny a person who is not a lawyer the right to appear for or represent others before an agency or in an agency proceeding.

(c) Process, requirement of a report, inspection, or other investigative act or demand may not be issued, made, or enforced except as authorized by law. A person compelled to submit data or evidence is entitled to retain or, on payment of lawfully prescribed costs, procure a copy or transcript thereof, except that in a nonpublic investigatory proceeding the witness may for good cause be limited to inspection of the official transcript of his testimony.

(d) Agency subpoenas authorized by law shall be issued to a party on request and, when required by rules of procedure, on a statement or showing of general relevance and reasonable scope of the evidence sought. On contest, the court shall sustain the subpoena or similar process or demand to the extent that it is found to be in accordance with law. In a proceeding for enforcement, the court shall issue an order requiring the appearance of the witness or the production of the evidence or data within a reasonable time under penalty of punishment for contempt in case of contumacious failure to comply.

(e) Prompt notice shall be given of the denial in whole or in part of a written application, petition, or other request of an interested person made in connection with any agency proceeding. Except in affirming a prior denial or when the denial is self-explanatory, the notice shall be accompanied by a brief statement of the grounds for denial.

§ 556. Hearings; presiding employees; powers and duties; burden of proof; evidence; record as basis of decision

(a) This section applies, according to the provisions thereof, to hearings required by section 553 or 554 of this title to be conducted in accordance with this section.

(b) There shall preside at the taking of evidence—

    (1) the agency;

    (2) one or more members of the body which comprises the agency; or

    (3) one or more administrative law judges appointed under section 3105 of this title.

    This subchapter does not supersede the conduct of specified classes of proceedings, in whole or in part, by or before boards or other employees specially provided for by or designated under statute. The functions of presiding employees and of employees participating in decisions in accordance with section 557 of this title shall be conducted in an impartial manner. A presiding or participating employee may at any time disqualify himself. On the filing in good faith of a timely and sufficient affidavit of personal bias or other disqualification of a presiding or participating employee, the agency shall determine the matter as a part of the record and decision in the case.

(c) Subject to published rules of the agency and within its powers, employees presiding at hearings may—

(1) administer oaths and affirmations;

(2) issue subpenas authorized by law;

(3) rule on offers of proof and receive relevant evidence;

(4) take depositions or have depositions taken when the ends of justice would be served;

(5) regulate the course of the hearing;

(6) hold conferences for the settlement or simplification of the issues by consent of the parties or by the use of alternative means of dispute resolution as provided in subchapter IV of this chapter;

(7) inform the parties as to the availability of one or more alternative means of dispute resolution, and encourage use of such methods;

(8) require the attendance at any conference held pursuant to paragraph (6) of at least one representative of each party who has authority to negotiate concerning resolution of issues in controversy;

(9) dispose of procedural requests or similar matters;

(10) make or recommend decisions in accordance with section 557 of this title; and

(11) take other action authorized by agency rule consistent with this subchapter.

(d) Except as otherwise provided by statute, the proponent of a rule or order has the burden of proof. Any oral or documentary evidence may be received, but the agency as a matter of policy shall provide for the exclusion of irrelevant, immaterial, or unduly repetitious evidence. A sanction may not be imposed or rule or order issued except on consideration of the whole record or those parts thereof cited by a party and supported by and in accordance with the reliable, probative, and substantial evidence. The agency may, to the extent consistent with the interests of justice and the policy of the underlying statutes administered by the agency, consider a violation of section 557(d) of this title sufficient grounds for a decision adverse to a party who has knowingly committed such violation or knowingly caused such violation to occur. A party is entitled to present his case or defense by oral or documentary evidence, to submit rebuttal evidence, and to conduct such cross-examination as may be required for a full and true disclosure of the facts. In rule making or determining claims for money or benefits or applications for initial licenses an agency may, when a party will not be prejudiced thereby, adopt procedures for the submission of all or part of the evidence in written form.

(e) The transcript of testimony and exhibits, together with all papers and requests filed in the proceeding, constitutes the exclusive record for decision in accordance with section 557 of this title and, on payment of lawfully prescribed costs, shall be made available to the parties. When an agency decision rests on official notice of a material fact not appearing in the evidence in the record, a party is entitled, on timely request, to an opportunity to show the contrary.

§ 557. Initial decisions; conclusiveness; review by agency; submissions by parties; contents of decisions; record

(a) This section applies, according to the provisions thereof, when a hearing is required to be conducted in accordance with section 556 of this title.

(b) When the agency did not preside at the reception of the evidence, the presiding employee or, in cases not subject to section 554(d) of this title, an employee qualified to preside at hearings pursuant to section 556 of this title, shall initially decide the case unless the agency requires, either in specific cases or by general rule, the entire record to be certified to it for decision. When the presiding employee makes an initial decision, that decision then becomes the decision of the agency without further proceedings unless there is an appeal to, or review on motion of, the agency within time provided by rule. On appeal from or review of the initial decision, the agency has all the powers which it would have in making the initial decision except as it may limit the issues on notice or by rule. When the agency makes the decision without having presided at the reception of the evidence, the presiding employee or an employee qualified to preside at hearings pursuant to section 556 of this title shall first recommend a decision, except that in rule making or determining applications for initial licenses—

    (1) instead thereof the agency may issue a tentative decision or one of its responsible employees may recommend a decision; or

    (2) this procedure may be omitted in a case in which the agency finds on the record that due and timely execution of its functions imperatively and unavoidably so requires.

(c) Before a recommended, initial, or tentative decision, or a decision on agency review of the decision of subordinate employees, the parties are entitled to a reasonable opportunity to submit for the consideration of the employees participating in the decisions—

    (1) proposed findings and conclusions; or

    (2) exceptions to the decisions or recommended decisions of subordinate employees or to tentative agency decisions; and

    (3) supporting reasons for the exceptions or proposed findings or conclusions. The record shall show the ruling on each finding, conclusion, or exception presented. All decisions, including initial, recommended, and tentative decisions, are a part of the record and shall include a statement of—

    (A) findings and conclusions, and the reasons or basis therefor, on all the material issues of fact, law, or discretion presented on the record; and

    (B) the appropriate rule, order, sanction, relief, or denial thereof.

(d)(1) In any agency proceeding which is subject to subsection (a) of this section, except to the extent required for the disposition of ex parte matters as authorized by law—

    (A) no interested person outside the agency shall make or knowingly cause to be made to any member of the body comprising the agency, administrative law judge, or other employee who is or may reasonably be expected to be involved in the decisional process of the proceeding, an ex parte communication relevant to the merits of the proceeding;

    (B) no member of the body comprising the agency, administrative law judge, or other employee who is or may reasonably be expected to be involved in the decisional process of the proceeding, shall make or knowingly cause to be made to any interested person outside the agency an ex parte communication relevant to the merits of the proceeding;

    (C) a member of the body comprising the agency, administrative law judge, or other employee who is or may reasonably be expected to be involved in the decisional process of such proceeding who receives, or who makes or knowingly causes to be made, a communication prohibited by this subsection shall place on the public record of the proceeding:

    (i) all such written communications;

    (ii) memoranda stating the substance of all such oral communications; and

    (iii) all written responses, and memoranda stating the substance of all oral responses, to the materials described in clauses (i) and (ii) of this subparagraph;

    (D) upon receipt of a communication knowingly made or knowingly caused to be made by a party in violation of this subsection, the agency, administrative law judge, or other employee presiding at the hearing may, to the extent consistent with the interests of justice and the policy of the underlying statutes, require the party to show cause why his claim or interest in the proceeding should not be dismissed, denied, disregarded, or otherwise adversely affected on account of such violation; and

    (E) the prohibitions of this subsection shall apply beginning at such time as the agency may designate, but in no case shall they begin to apply later than the time at which a proceeding is noticed for hearing unless the person responsible for the communication has knowledge that it will be noticed, in which case the prohibitions shall apply beginning at the time of his acquisition of such knowledge.

(2) This subsection does not constitute authority to withhold information from Congress.

******************[§ 558 omitted]********************

§ 559. Effect on other laws; effect of subsequent statute

This subchapter, chapter 7, and sections 1305, 3105, 3344, 4301(2)(E), 5372, and 7521 of this title, and the provisions of section 5335(a)(B) of this title that relate to administrative law judges, do not limit or repeal additional requirements imposed by statute or otherwise recognized by law. Except as otherwise required by law, requirements or privileges relating to evidence or procedure apply equally to agencies and persons. Each agency is granted the authority necessary to comply with the requirements of this subchapter through the issuance of rules or otherwise. Subsequent statute may not be held to supersede or modify this subchapter, chapter 7, sections 1305, 3105, 3344, 4301(2)(E), 5372, or 7521 of this title, or the provisions of section 5335(a)(B) of this title that relate to administrative law judges, except to the extent that it does so expressly.

§ 701. Application; definitions

(a) This chapter applies, according to the provisions thereof, except to the extent that—

    (1) statutes preclude judicial review; or

    (2) agency action is committed to agency discretion by law.

(b) For the purpose of this chapter—

    (1) "agency" means each authority of the Government of the United States, whether or not it is within or subject to review by another agency, but does not include—

    (A) the Congress;

    (B) the courts of the United States;

    (C) the governments of the territories or possessions of the United States;

    (D) the government of the District of Columbia;

    (E) agencies composed of representatives of the parties or of representatives of organizations of the parties to the disputes determined by them;

    (F) courts martial and military commissions;

    (G) military authority exercised in the field in time of war or in occupied territory; or

    (H) functions conferred by sections 1738, 1739, 1743, and 1744 of title 12; subchapter II of chapter 471 of title 49; or sections 1884, 1891-1902, and former section 1641(b)(2), of title 50, appendix; and

    (2) "person," "rule," "order," "license," "sanction," "relief," and "agency action" have the meanings given them by section 551 of this title.

§ 702. Right of review

A person suffering legal wrong because of agency action, or adversely affected or aggrieved by agency action within the meaning of a relevant statute, is entitled to judicial review thereof. An action in a court of the United States seeking relief other than money damages and stating a claim that an agency or an officer or employee thereof acted or failed to act in an official capacity or under color of legal authority shall not be dismissed nor relief therein be denied on the ground that it is against the United States or that the United States is an indispensable party. The United States may be named as a defendant in any such action, and a judgment or decree may be entered against the United States: *Provided,* That any mandatory or injunctive decree shall specify the Federal officer or officers (by name or by title), and their successors in office, personally responsible for compliance. Nothing herein (1) affects other limitations on judicial review or the power or duty of the court to dismiss any action or deny relief on any other appropriate legal or equitable ground; or (2) confers authority to grant relief if any other statute that grants consent to suit expressly or impliedly forbids the relief which is sought.

§ 703. Form and venue of proceeding
The form of proceeding for judicial review is the special statutory review proceeding relevant to the subject matter in a court specified by statute or, in the absence or inadequacy thereof, any applicable form of legal action, including actions for declaratory judgments or writs of prohibitory or mandatory injunction or habeas corpus, in a court of competent jurisdiction. If no special statutory review proceeding is applicable, the action for judicial review may be brought against the United States, the agency by its official title, or the appropriate officer. Except to the extent that prior, adequate, and exclusive opportunity for judicial review is provided by law, agency action is subject to judicial review in civil or criminal proceedings for judicial enforcement.

§ 704. Actions reviewable
Agency action made reviewable by statute and final agency action for which there is no other adequate remedy in a court are subject to judicial review. A preliminary, procedural, or intermediate agency action or ruling not directly reviewable is subject to review on the review of the final agency action. Except as otherwise expressly required by statute, agency action otherwise final is final for the purposes of this section whether or not there has been presented or determined an application for a declaratory order, for any form of reconsideration, or, unless the agency otherwise requires by rule and provides that the action meanwhile is inoperative, for an appeal to superior agency authority.

§ 705. Relief pending review
When an agency finds that justice so requires, it may postpone the effective date of action taken by it, pending judicial review. On such conditions as may be required and to the extent necessary to prevent irreparable injury, the reviewing court, including the court to which a case may be taken on appeal from or on application for

certiorari or other writ to a reviewing court, may issue all necessary and appropriate process to postpone the effective date of an agency action or to preserve status or rights pending conclusion of the review proceedings.

§ 706. Scope of review

To the extent necessary to decision and when presented, the reviewing court shall decide all relevant questions of law, interpret constitutional and statutory provisions, and determine the meaning or applicability of the terms of an agency action. The reviewing court shall—

(1) compel agency action unlawfully withheld or unreasonably delayed; and
(2) hold unlawful and set aside agency action, findings, and conclusions found to be—

  (A) arbitrary, capricious, an abuse of discretion, or otherwise not in accordance with law;
  (B) contrary to constitutional right, power, privilege, or immunity;
  (C) in excess of statutory jurisdiction, authority, or limitations, or short of statutory right;
  (D) without observance of procedure required by law;
  (E) unsupported by substantial evidence in a case subject to sections 556 and 557 of this title or otherwise reviewed on the record of an agency hearing provided by statute; or
  (F) unwarranted by the facts to the extent that the facts are subject to trial de novo by the reviewing court.

  In making the foregoing determinations, the court shall review the whole record or those parts of it cited by a party, and due account shall be taken of the rule of prejudicial error.

3. Negotiated Rulemaking Act
5 U.S.C. _____

§ 561. Purpose

The purpose of this subchapter is to establish a framework for the conduct of negotiated rulemaking, consistent with section 553 of this title, to encourage agencies to use the process when it enhances the informal rulemaking process. Nothing in this subchapter should be construed as an attempt to limit innovation and experimentation with the negotiated rulemaking process or with other innovative rulemaking procedures otherwise authorized by law.

§ 562. Definitions

For the purposes of this subchapter, the term—

(1) "agency" has the same meaning as in section 551(1) of this title;
(2) "consensus" means unanimous concurrence among the interests represented on a negotiated rulemaking committee established under this subchapter, less such committee—

    (A) agrees to define such term to mean a general but not unanimous concurrence; or

    (B) agrees upon another specified definition;

  (3) "convener" means a person who impartially assists an agency in determining whether establishment of a negotiated rulemaking committee is feasible and appropriate in a particular rulemaking;

  (4) "facilitator" means a person who impartially aids in the discussions and negotiations among the members of a negotiated rulemaking committee to develop a proposed rule;

  (5) "interest" means, with respect to an issue or matter, multiple parties which have a similar point of view or which are likely to be affected in a similar manner;

  (6) "negotiated rulemaking" means rulemaking through the use of a negotiated rulemaking committee;

  (7) "negotiated rulemaking committee" or "committee" means an advisory committee established by an agency in accordance with this subchapter and the Federal Advisory Committee Act to consider and discuss issues for the purpose of reaching a consensus in the development of a proposed rule;

  (8) "party" has the same meaning as in section 551(3) of this title;

  (9) "person" has the same meaning as in section 551(2) of this title;

  (10) "rule" has the same meaning as in section 551(4) of this title; and

  (11) "rulemaking" means "rule making" as that term is defined in section 551(5) of this title.

§ 563. Determination of need for negotiated rulemaking committee

(a) DETERMINATION OF NEED BY THE AGENCY.—An agency may establish a negotiated rulemaking committee to negotiate and develop a proposed rule, if the head of the agency determines that the use of the negotiated rulemaking procedure is in the public interest. In making such a determination, the head of the agency shall consider whether—

  (1) there is a need for a rule;

  (2) there are a limited number of identifiable interests that will be significantly affected by the rule;

  (3) there is a reasonable likelihood that a committee can be convened with a balanced representation of persons who—

    (A) can adequately represent the interests identified under paragraph (2); and

    (B) are willing to negotiate in good faith to reach a consensus on the proposed rule;

  (4) there is a reasonable likelihood that a committee will reach a consensus on the proposed rule within a fixed period of time;

  (5) the negotiated rulemaking procedure will not unreasonably delay the notice of proposed rulemaking and the issuance of the final rule;

(6) the agency has adequate resources and is willing to commit such resources, including technical assistance, to the committee; and

(7) the agency, to the maximum extent possible consistent with the legal obligations of the agency, will use the consensus of the committee with respect to the proposed rule as the basis for the rule proposed by the agency for notice and comment.

(b) Use of Conveners.—

(1) Purposes of conveners.—An agency may use the services of a convener to assist the agency in—

(A) identifying persons who will be significantly affected by a proposed rule, including residents of rural areas; and

(B) conducting discussions with such persons to identify the issues of concern to such persons, and to ascertain whether the establishment of a negotiated rulemaking committee is feasible and appropriate in the particular rulemaking.

(2) Duties of conveners.—The convener shall report findings and may make recommendations to the agency. Upon request of the agency, the convener shall ascertain the names of persons who are willing and qualified to represent interests that will be significantly affected by the proposed rule, including residents of rural areas. The report and any recommendations of the convener shall be made available to the public upon request.

Note: Negotiated Rulemaking Committees—

Pub. L. 104-320, § 11(e), Oct. 19, 1996, 110 Stat. 3874, provided that:

"The Director of the Office of Management and Budget shall—

"(1) within 180 days of the date of establishment of this Act, take appropriate action to expedite the establishment of negotiated rulemaking committees and committees established to resolve disputes under the Administrative Dispute Resolution Act, including, with respect to negotiated rulemaking committees, eliminating any redundant administrative requirements related to filing a committee charter under section 9 of the Federal Advisory Committee Act (5 U.S.C. App.) and providing public notice of such committee under section 564 of title 5, United States Code; and

"(2) within one year of the date of the enactment of this Act, submit recommendations to Congress for any necessary legislative changes."

§ 564. Publication of notice; applications for membership on committees

(a) Publication of Notice.—If, after considering the report of a convener or conducting its own assessment, an agency decides to establish a negotiated rulemaking committee, the agency shall publish in the Federal Register and, as appropriate, in trade or other specialized publications, a notice which shall include—

(1) an announcement that the agency intends to establish a negotiated rulemaking committee to negotiate and develop a proposed rule;

(2) a description of the subject and scope of the rule to be developed, and the issues to be considered;

(3) a list of the interests which are likely to be significantly affected by the rule;

(4) a list of the persons proposed to represent such interests and the person or persons proposed to represent the agency;

(5) a proposed agenda and schedule for completing the work of the committee, including a target date for publication by the agency of a proposed rule for notice and comment;

(6) a description of administrative support for the committee to be provided by the agency, including technical assistance;

(7) a solicitation for comments on the proposal to establish the committee, and the proposed membership of the negotiated rulemaking committee; and

(8) an explanation of how a person may apply or nominate another person for membership on the committee, as provided under subsection (b).

(b) APPLICATIONS FOR MEMBERSHIP OR* COMMITTEE.—Persons who will be significantly affected by a proposed rule and who believe that their interests will not be adequately represented by any person specified in a notice under subsection (a)(4) may apply for, or nominate another person for, membership on the negotiated rulemaking committee to represent such interests with respect to the proposed rule. Each application or nomination shall include—

(1) the name of the applicant or nominee and a description of the interests such person shall represent;

(2) evidence that the applicant or nominee is authorized to represent parties related to the interests the person proposes to represent;

(3) a written commitment that the applicant or nominee shall actively participate in good faith in the development of the rule under consideration; and

(4) the reasons that the persons specified in the notice under subsection (a)(4) do not adequately represent the interests of the person submitting the application or nomination.

(c) PERIOD FOR SUBMISSION OF COMMENTS AND APPLICATIONS.—The agency shall provide for a period of at least 30 calendar days for the submission of comments and applications under this section.

§ 565. Establishment of committee

(a) ESTABLISHMENT.—

(1) DETERMINATION TO ESTABLISH COMMITTEE.—If after considering comments and applications submitted under section 564, the agency determines that a negotiated rulemaking committee can adequately represent the interests that will be

---

* So in original. Probably should be "on."

significantly affected by a proposed rule and that it is feasible and appropriate in the particular rulemaking, the agency may establish a negotiated rulemaking committee. In establishing and administering such a committee, the agency shall comply with the Federal Advisory Committee Act with respect to such committee, except as otherwise provided in this subchapter.

(2) DETERMINATION NOT TO ESTABLISH COMMITTEE.—If after considering such comments and applications, the agency decides not to establish a negotiated rulemaking committee, the agency shall promptly publish notice of such decision and the reasons therefor in the Federal Register and, as appropriate, in trade or other specialized publications, a copy of which shall be sent to any person who applied for, or nominated another person for membership on the negotiating** rulemaking committee to represent such interests with respect to the proposed rule.

(b) MEMBERSHIP.—The agency shall limit membership on a negotiated rulemaking committee to 25 members, unless the agency head determines that a greater number of members is necessary for the functioning of the committee or to achieve balanced membership. Each committee shall include at least one person representing the agency.

(c) ADMINISTRATIVE SUPPORT.—The agency shall provide appropriate administrative support to the negotiated rulemaking committee, including technical assistance.

§ 566. Conduct of committee activity

(a) DUTIES OF COMMITTEE.—Each negotiated rulemaking committee established under this subchapter shall consider the matter proposed by the agency for consideration and shall attempt to reach a consensus concerning a proposed rule with respect to such matter and any other matter the committee determines is relevant to the proposed rule.

(b) REPRESENTATIVES OF AGENCY ON COMMITTEE.—The person or persons representing the agency on a negotiated rulemaking committee shall participate in the deliberations and activities of the committee with the same rights and responsibilities as other members of the committee, and shall be authorized to fully represent the agency in the discussions and negotiations of the committee.

(c) SELECTING FACILITATOR.—Notwithstanding section 10(e) of the Federal Advisory Committee Act, an agency may nominate either a person from the Federal Government or a person from outside the Federal Government to serve as a facilitator for the negotiations of the committee, subject to the approval of the committee by consensus. If the committee does not approve the nominee of the agency for facilitator, the agency shall submit a substitute nomination. If a committee does not approve any nominee of the agency for facilitator, the committee shall select by consensus a

---

** Footnote "1" added to the U.S.C. to indicate that "negotiating" instead of "negotiated" was likely a typo in the original.

person to serve as facilitator. A person designated to represent the agency in substantive issues may not serve as facilitator or otherwise chair the committee.

(d) DUTIES OF FACILITATOR.—A facilitator approved or selected by a negotiated rulemaking committee shall—

    (1) chair the meetings of the committee in an impartial manner;

    (2) impartially assist the members of the committee in conducting discussions and negotiations; and

    (3) manage the keeping of minutes and records as required under section 10(b) and (c) of the Federal Advisory Committee Act, except that any personal notes and materials of the facilitator or of the members of a committee shall not be subject to section 552 of this title.

(e) COMMITTEE PROCEDURES.—A negotiated rulemaking committee established under this subchapter may adopt procedures for the operation of the committee. No provision of section 553 of this title shall apply to the procedures of a negotiated rulemaking committee.

(f) REPORT OF COMMITTEE.—If a committee reaches a consensus on a proposed rule, at the conclusion of negotiations the committee shall transmit to the agency that established the committee a report containing the proposed rule. If the committee does not reach a consensus on a proposed rule, the committee may transmit to the agency a report specifying any areas in which the committee reached a consensus. The committee may include in a report any other information, recommendations, or materials that the committee considers appropriate. Any committee member may include as an addendum to the report additional information, recommendations, or materials.

(g) RECORDS OF COMMITTEE.—In addition to the report required by subsection (f), a committee shall submit to the agency the records required under section 10(b) and (c) of the Federal Advisory Committee Act.

§ 567. Termination of committee

A negotiated rulemaking committee shall terminate upon promulgation of the final rule under consideration, unless the committee's charter contains an earlier termination date or the agency, after consulting the committee, or the committee itself specifies an earlier termination date.

§ 568. Services, facilities, and payment of committee member expenses

(a) SERVICES OF CONVENERS AND FACILITATORS.—

    (1) IN GENERAL.—An agency may employ or enter into contracts for the services of an individual or organization to serve as a convener or facilitator for a negotiated rulemaking committee under this subchapter, or may use the services of a Government employee to act as a convener or a facilitator for such a committee.

(2) DETERMINATION OF CONFLICTING INTERESTS.—An agency shall determine whether a person under consideration to serve as convener or facilitator of a committee under paragraph (1) has any financial or other interest that would preclude such person from serving in an impartial and independent manner.

(b) SERVICES AND FACILITIES OF OTHER ENTITIES.—For purposes of this subchapter, an agency may use the services and facilities of other Federal agencies and public and private agencies and instrumentalities with the consent of such agencies and instrumentalities, and with or without reimbursement to such agencies and instrumentalities, and may accept voluntary and uncompensated services without regard to the provisions of section 1342 of title 31. The Federal Mediation and Conciliation Service may provide services and facilities, with or without reimbursement, to assist agencies under this subchapter, including furnishing conveners, facilitators, and training in negotiated rulemaking.

(c) EXPENSES OF COMMITTEE MEMBERS.—Members of a negotiated rulemaking committee shall be responsible for their own expenses of participation in such committee, except that an agency may, in accordance with section 7(d) of the Federal Advisory Committee Act, pay for a member's reasonable travel and per diem expenses, expenses to obtain technical assistance, and a reasonable rate of compensation, if—

(1) such member certifies a lack of adequate financial resources to participate in the committee; and

(2) the agency determines that such member's participation in the committee is necessary to assure an adequate representation of the member's interest.

(d) STATUS OF MEMBER AS FEDERAL EMPLOYEE.—A member's receipt of funds under this section or section 569 shall not conclusively determine for purposes of sections 202 through 209 of title 18 whether that member is an employee of the United States Government.

§ 569. Encouraging negotiated rulemaking

(a) The President shall designate an agency or designate or establish an interagency committee to facilitate and encourage agency use of negotiated rulemaking. An agency that is considering, planning, or conducting a negotiated rulemaking may consult with such agency or committee for information and assistance.

(b) To carry out the purposes of this subchapter, an agency planning or conducting a negotiated rulemaking may accept, hold, administer, and utilize gifts, devises, and bequests of property, both real and personal if that agency's acceptance and use of such gifts, devises, or bequests do not create a conflict of interest. Gifts and bequests of money and proceeds from sales of other property received as gifts, devises, or bequests shall be deposited in the Treasury and shall be disbursed upon the order of the head of such agency. Property accepted pursuant to this section, and the proceeds thereof, shall be used as nearly as possible in accordance with the terms of the gifts, devises, or bequests.

§ 570. Judicial review

Any agency action relating to establishing, assisting, or terminating a negotiated rulemaking committee under this subchapter shall not be subject to judicial review. Nothing in this section shall bar judicial review of a rule if such judicial review is otherwise provided by law. A rule which is the product of negotiated rulemaking and is subject to judicial review shall not be accorded any greater deference by a court than a rule which is the product of other rulemaking procedures.

§ 570a. Authorization of appropriations

There are authorized to be appropriated such sums as may be necessary to carry out the purposes of this subchapter.

4. Regulatory Flexibility Act
5 U.S.C. _____

§ 601. Definitions

For purposes of this chapter—

(1) the term "agency" means an agency as defined in section 551(1) of this title;

(2) the term "rule" means any rule for which the agency publishes a general notice of proposed rulemaking pursuant to section 553(b) of this title, or any other law, including any rule of general applicability governing Federal grants to State and local governments for which the agency provides an opportunity for notice and public comment, except that the term "rule" does not include a rule of particular applicability relating to rates, wages, corporate or financial structures or reorganizations thereof, prices, facilities, appliances, services, or allowances therefor or to valuations, costs or accounting, or practices relating to such rates, wages, structures, prices, appliances, services, or allowances;

(3) the term "small business" has the same meaning as the term "small business concern" under section 3 of the Small Business Act, unless an agency, after consultation with the Office of Advocacy of the Small Business Administration and after opportunity for public comment, establishes one or more definitions of such term which are appropriate to the activities of the agency and publishes such definition(s) in the Federal Register;

(4) the term "small organization" means any not-for-profit enterprise which is independently owned and operated and is not dominant in its field, unless an agency establishes, after opportunity for public comment, one or more definitions of such term which are appropriate to the activities of the agency and publishes such definition(s) in the Federal Register;

(5) the term "small governmental jurisdiction" means governments of cities, counties, towns, townships, villages, school districts, or special districts, with a population of less than fifty thousand, unless an agency establishes, after opportunity for public comment, one or more definitions of such term which are appropriate to the activities of the agency and which are based on such factors

as location in rural or sparsely populated areas or limited revenues due to the population of such jurisdiction, and publishes such definition(s) in the Federal Register;

(6) the term "small entity" shall have the same meaning as the terms "small business," "small organization" and "small governmental jurisdiction" defined in paragraphs (3), (4) and (5) of this section; and

(7) the term "collection of information"—

    (A) means the obtaining, causing to be obtained, soliciting, or requiring the disclosure to third parties or the public, of facts or opinions by or for an agency, regardless of form or format, calling for either—

        (i) answers to identical questions posed to, or identical reporting or recordkeeping requirements imposed on, 10 or more persons, other than agencies, instrumentalities, or employees of the United States; or

        (ii) answers to questions posed to agencies, instrumentalities, or employees of the United States which are to be used for general statistical purposes; and

    (B) shall not include a collection of information described under section 3518(c)(1) of title 44, United States Code.

(8) RECORDKEEPING REQUIREMENT.—The term "recordkeeping requirement" means a requirement imposed by an agency on persons to maintain specified records.

§ 601 Note:

Regulatory Compliance Simplification

Definitions.

For purposes of this subtitle [Pub. L. No. 104-121, §§ 211 to 216, which enacted subtitle A of this note and amended section 648 of Title 15]—

"(1) the terms 'rule' and 'small entity' have the same meanings as in section 601 of title 5, United States Code [this section];

"(2) the term 'agency' has the same meaning as in section 551 of title 5, United States Code [section 551 of this title]; and

"(3) the term 'small entity compliance guide' means a document designated as such by an agency.

Compliance guides.

"(a) COMPLIANCE GUIDE.—For each rule or group of related rules for which an agency is required to prepare a final regulatory flexibility analysis under section 604 of title 5, United States Code [section 604 of this title], the agency shall publish one or more guides to assist small entities in complying with the rule, and shall designate such publications as 'small entity compliance guides'. The guides shall explain the actions a small entity is required to take to comply with a rule or group of rules. The agency shall, in its sole discretion, taking into account the subject matter of the rule and the language of relevant statutes, ensure that the guide is written using sufficiently plain language likely to be understood by affected small enti-

ties. Agencies may prepare separate guides covering groups or classes of similarly affected small entities, and may cooperate with associations of small entities
to develop and distribute such guides.

"(b) COMPREHENSIVE SOURCE OF INFORMATION.—Agencies shall cooperate to make available to small entities through comprehensive sources of information, the small
entity compliance guides and all other available information on statutory and regulatory requirements affecting small entities.

"(c) LIMITATION ON JUDICIAL REVIEW.—An agency's small entity compliance guide shall
not be subject to judicial review, except that in any civil or administrative action
against a small entity for a violation occurring after the effective date of this section [see section 216 of this note], the content of the small entity compliance
guide may be considered as evidence of the reasonableness or appropriateness of
any proposed fines, penalties or damages.

Informal small entity guidance.

"(a) GENERAL.—Whenever appropriate in the interest of administering statutes and
regulations within the jurisdiction of an agency which regulates small entities, it
shall be the practice of the agency to answer inquiries by small entities concerning information on, and advice about, compliance with such statutes and regulations, interpreting and applying the law to specific sets of facts supplied by the
small entity. In any civil or administrative action against a small entity, guidance
given by an agency applying the law to facts provided by the small entity may be
considered as evidence of the reasonableness or appropriateness of any proposed
fines, penalties or damages sought against such small entity.

"(b) PROGRAM.—Each agency regulating the activities of small entities shall establish a
program for responding to such inquiries no later than 1 year after enactment of
this section [Mar. 29, 1996], utilizing existing functions and personnel of the
agency to the extent practicable.

"(c) REPORTING.—Each agency regulating the activities of small business shall report to
the Committee on Small Business and Committee on Governmental Affairs of the
Senate and the Committee on Small Business and Committee on the Judiciary of
the House of Representatives no later than 2 years after the date of the enactment
of this section [Mar. 29, 1996] on the scope of the agency's program, the number
of small entities using the program, and the achievements of the program to assist
small entity compliance with agency regulations.

Services of small business development centers.

"(a) [Omitted. Amended section 648(c) of Title 15].

"(b) Nothing in this Act [Pub. L. No. 104-121, Mar. 29, 1996, 110 Stat. 847, for
distribution of which see Short Title note set out under this section and Tables] in
any way affects or limits the ability of other technical assistance or extension
programs to perform or continue to perform services related to compliance assistance.

Cooperation on guidance.

"Agencies may, to the extent resources are available and where appropriate, in cooperation with the States, develop guides that fully integrate requirements of both Federal and
State regulations where regulations within an agency's area of interest at the Federal and
State levels impact small entities. Where regulations vary among the States, separate
guides may be created for separate States in cooperation with State agencies.

§ 602. Regulatory agenda

(a) During the months of October and April of each year, each agency shall publish
in the Federal Register a regulatory flexibility agenda which shall contain—
   (1) a brief description of the subject area of any rule which the agency expects to
   propose or promulgate which is likely to have a significant economic impact
   on a substantial number of small entities;
   (2) a summary of the nature of any such rule under consideration for each subject
   area listed in the agenda pursuant to paragraph (1), the objectives and legal
   basis for the issuance of the rule, and an approximate schedule for completing
   action on any rule for which the agency has issued a general notice of proposed rulemaking,* and
   (3) the name and telephone number of an agency official knowledgeable concerning the items listed in paragraph (1).
(b) Each regulatory flexibility agenda shall be transmitted to the Chief Counsel for
Advocacy of the Small Business Administration for comment, if any.
(c) Each agency shall endeavor to provide notice of each regulatory flexibility agenda
to small entities or their representatives through direct notification or publication
of the agenda in publications likely to be obtained by such small entities and shall
invite comments upon each subject area on the agenda.
(d) Nothing in this section precludes an agency from considering or acting on any
matter not included in a regulatory flexibility agenda, or requires an agency to
consider or act on any matter listed in such agenda.

§ 603. Initial regulatory flexibility analysis

(a) Whenever an agency is required by section 553 of this title, or any other law, to
publish general notice of proposed rulemaking for any proposed rule, or publishes
a notice of proposed rulemaking for an interpretative rule involving the internal
revenue laws of the United States, the agency shall prepare and make available for
public comment an initial regulatory flexibility analysis. Such analysis shall describe the impact of the proposed rule on small entities. The initial regulatory flexibility analysis or a summary shall be published in the Federal Register at the time of
the publication of general notice of proposed rulemaking for the rule. The agency

---

* Footnote "1" added to the U.S.C. to indicate that use of a comma instead of a semi-colon is
probably a typo in the original.

shall transmit a copy of the initial regulatory flexibility analysis to the Chief Counsel for Advocacy of the Small Business Administration. In the case of an interpretative rule involving the internal revenue laws of the United States, this chapter applies to interpretative rules published in the Federal Register for codification in the Code of Federal Regulations, but only to the extent that such interpretative rules impose on small entities a collection of information requirement.

(b) Each initial regulatory flexibility analysis required under this section shall contain—

    (1) a description of the reasons why action by the agency is being considered;

    (2) a succinct statement of the objectives of, and legal basis for, the proposed rule;

    (3) a description of and, where feasible, an estimate of the number of small entities to which the proposed rule will apply;

    (4) a description of the projected reporting, recordkeeping and other compliance requirements of the proposed rule, including an estimate of the classes of small entities which will be subject to the requirement and the type of professional skills necessary for preparation of the report or record;

    (5) an identification, to the extent practicable, of all relevant Federal rules which may duplicate, overlap or conflict with the proposed rule.

(c) Each initial regulatory flexibility analysis shall also contain a description of any significant alternatives to the proposed rule which accomplish the stated objectives of applicable statutes and which minimize any significant economic impact of the proposed rule on small entities. Consistent with the stated objectives of applicable statutes, the analysis shall discuss significant alternatives such as—

    (1) the establishment of differing compliance or reporting requirements or timetables that take into account the resources available to small entities;

    (2) the clarification, consolidation, or simplification of compliance and reporting requirements under the rule for such small entities;

    (3) the use of performance rather than design standards; and

    (4) an exemption from coverage of the rule, or any part thereof, for such small entities.

(d)(1) For a covered agency, as defined in section 609(d)(2), each initial regulatory flexibility analysis shall include a description of—

    (A) any projected increase in the cost of credit for small entities;

    (B) any significant alternatives to the proposed rule which accomplish the stated objectives of applicable statutes and which minimize any increase in the cost of credit for small entities; and

    (C) advice and recommendations of representatives of small entities relating to issues described in subparagraphs (A) and (B) and subsection (b).

    (2) A covered agency, as defined in section 609(d)(2), shall, for purposes of complying with paragraph (1)(C)—

(A) identify representatives of small entities in consultation with the Chief Counsel for Advocacy of the Small Business Administration; and

(B) collect advice and recommendations from the representatives identified under subparagraph (A) relating to issues described in subparagraphs (A) and (B) of paragraph (1) and subsection (b).

§ 604. Final regulatory flexibility analysis

(a) When an agency promulgates a final rule under section 553 of this title, after being required by that section or any other law to publish a general notice of proposed rulemaking, or promulgates a final interpretative rule involving the internal revenue laws of the United States as described in section 603(a), the agency shall prepare a final regulatory flexibility analysis. Each final regulatory flexibility analysis shall contain—

(1) a statement of the need for, and objectives of, the rule;

(2) a statement of the significant issues raised by the public comments in response to the initial regulatory flexibility analysis, a statement of the assessment of the agency of such issues, and a statement of any changes made in the proposed rule as a result of such comments;

(3) the response of the agency to any comments filed by the Chief Counsel for Advocacy of the Small Business Administration in response to the proposed rule, and a detailed statement of any change made to the proposed rule in the final rule as a result of the comments;

(4) a description of and an estimate of the number of small entities to which the rule will apply or an explanation of why no such estimate is available;

(5) a description of the projected reporting, recordkeeping and other compliance requirements of the rule, including an estimate of the classes of small entities which will be subject to the requirement and the type of professional skills necessary for preparation of the report or record;

(6) a description of the steps the agency has taken to minimize the significant economic impact on small entities consistent with the stated objectives of applicable statutes, including a statement of the factual, policy, and legal reasons for selecting the alternative adopted in the final rule and why each one of the other significant alternatives to the rule considered by the agency which affect the impact on small entities was rejected.

(6) for a covered agency, as defined in section 609(d)(2), a description of the steps the agency has taken to minimize any additional cost of credit for small entities.[**]

[**] So in original. Two paragraphs (6) were enacted. [The Dodd–Frank Act, (Pub. L. No, 111-203, § 1100G(c)(2)) added this subsection (6); then the Small Business Jobs Act of 2012 (Pub. L. No. 111-240, § 1601(3)) amended subsection (a), adding a new subsection (3) and renumbering the old subsection (3), (4), and (5) as the new subsections (4), (5), and (6). However, it failed to renumber the new subsection added by the Dodd–Frank Act.]

(b) The agency shall make copies of the final regulatory flexibility analysis available to members of the public and shall publish in the Federal Register such analysis or a summary thereof.

§ 605. Avoidance of duplicative or unnecessary analyses

(a) Any Federal agency may perform the analyses required by sections 602, 603, and 604 of this title in conjunction with or as a part of any other agenda or analysis required by any other law if such other analysis satisfies the provisions of such sections.

(b) Sections 603 and 604 of this title shall not apply to any proposed or final rule if the head of the agency certifies that the rule will not, if promulgated, have a significant economic impact on a substantial number of small entities. If the head of the agency makes a certification under the preceding sentence, the agency shall publish such certification in the Federal Register at the time of publication of general notice of proposed rulemaking for the rule or at the time of publication of the final rule, along with a statement providing the factual basis for such certification. The agency shall provide such certification and statement to the Chief Counsel for Advocacy of the Small Business Administration.

(c) In order to avoid duplicative action, an agency may consider a series of closely related rules as one rule for the purposes of sections 602, 603, 604 and 610 of this title.

§ 606. Effect on other law

The requirements of sections 603 and 604 of this title do not alter in any manner standards otherwise applicable by law to agency action.

§ 607. Preparation of analyses

In complying with the provisions of sections 603 and 604 of this title, an agency may provide either a quantifiable or numerical description of the effects of a proposed rule or alternatives to the proposed rule, or more general descriptive statements if quantification is not practicable or reliable.

§ 608. Procedure for waiver or delay of completion

(a) An agency head may waive or delay the completion of some or all of the requirements of section 603 of this title by publishing in the Federal Register, not later than the date of publication of the final rule, a written finding, with reasons therefor, that the final rule is being promulgated in response to an emergency that makes compliance or timely compliance with the provisions of section 603 of this title impracticable.

(b) Except as provided in section 605(b), an agency head may not waive the requirements of section 604 of this title. An agency head may delay the completion of the requirements of section 604 of this title for a period of not more than one hundred and eighty days after the date of publication in the Federal Register of a final rule by publishing in the Federal Register, not later than such date of publication, a written finding, with reasons therefor, that the final rule is being promulgated in response to an emergency that makes timely compliance with the provisions of section 604 of this title impracticable. If the agency has not prepared a final regulatory analysis pursuant to section 604 of this title within one hundred and eighty days from the date of publication of the final rule, such rule shall lapse and have no effect. Such rule shall not be repromulgated until a final regulatory flexibility analysis has been completed by the agency.

§ 609. Procedures for gathering comments

(a) When any rule is promulgated which will have a significant economic impact on a substantial number of small entities, the head of the agency promulgating the rule or the official of the agency with statutory responsibility for the promulgation of the rule shall assure that small entities have been given an opportunity to participate in the rulemaking for the rule through the reasonable use of techniques such as—

    (1) the inclusion in an advanced notice of proposed rulemaking, if issued, of a statement that the proposed rule may have a significant economic effect on a substantial number of small entities;

    (2) the publication of general notice of proposed rulemaking in publications likely to be obtained by small entities;

    (3) the direct notification of interested small entities;

    (4) the conduct of open conferences or public hearings concerning the rule for small entities including soliciting and receiving comments over computer networks; and

    (5) the adoption or modification of agency procedural rules to reduce the cost or complexity of participation in the rulemaking by small entities.

(b) Prior to publication of an initial regulatory flexibility analysis which a covered agency is required to conduct by this chapter—

    (1) a covered agency shall notify the Chief Counsel for Advocacy of the Small Business Administration and provide the Chief Counsel with information on the potential impacts of the proposed rule on small entities and the type of small entities that might be affected;

    (2) not later than 15 days after the date of receipt of the materials described in paragraph (1), the Chief Counsel shall identify individuals representative of affected small entities for the purpose of obtaining advice and recommendations from those individuals about the potential impacts of the proposed rule;

    (3) the agency shall convene a review panel for such rule consisting wholly of full time Federal employees of the office within the agency responsible for carrying out the proposed rule, the Office of Information and Regulatory Affairs within the Office of Management and Budget, and the Chief Counsel;

(4) the panel shall review any material the agency has prepared in connection with this chapter, including any draft proposed rule, collect advice and recommendations of each individual small entity representative identified by the agency after consultation with the Chief Counsel, on issues related to subsections 603(b), paragraphs (3), (4) and (5) and 603(c);

(5) not later than 60 days after the date a covered agency convenes a review panel pursuant to paragraph (3), the review panel shall report on the comments of the small entity representatives and its findings as to issues related to subsections 603(b), paragraphs (3), (4) and (5) and 603(c), provided that such report shall be made public as part of the rulemaking record; and

(6) where appropriate, the agency shall modify the proposed rule, the initial regulatory flexibility analysis or the decision on whether an initial regulatory flexibility analysis is required.

(c) An agency may in its discretion apply subsection (b) to rules that the agency intends to certify under subsection 605(b), but the agency believes may have a greater than de minimis impact on a substantial number of small entities.

(d) For purposes of this section, the term "covered agency" means—

(1) the Environmental Protection Agency;

(2) the Consumer Financial Protection Bureau of the Federal Reserve System; and

(3) the Occupational Safety and Health Administration of the Department of Labor.

(e) The Chief Counsel for Advocacy, in consultation with the individuals identified in subsection (b)(2), and with the Administrator of the Office of Information and Regulatory Affairs within the Office of Management and Budget, may waive the requirements of subsections (b)(3), (b)(4), and (b)(5) by including in the rulemaking record a written finding, with reasons therefor, that those requirements would not advance the effective participation of small entities in the rulemaking process. For purposes of this subsection, the factors to be considered in making such a finding are as follows:

(1) In developing a proposed rule, the extent to which the covered agency consulted with individuals representative of affected small entities with respect to the potential impacts of the rule and took such concerns into consideration.

(2) Special circumstances requiring prompt issuance of the rule.

(3) Whether the requirements of subsection (b) would provide the individuals identified in subsection (b)(2) with a competitive advantage relative to other small entities.

§ 610. Periodic review of rules

(a) Within one hundred and eighty days after the effective date of this chapter, each agency shall publish in the Federal Register a plan for the periodic review of the rules issued by the agency which have or will have a significant economic impact upon a substantial number of small entities. Such plan may be amended by the agency at any time by publishing the revision in the Federal Register. The purpose of the review shall be to determine whether such rules should be continued without change, or should be amended or rescinded, consistent with the stated objectives of applicable statutes, to minimize any significant economic impact of the rules upon a substantial number of such small entities. The plan shall provide for the review of all such agency rules existing on the effective date of this chapter within ten years of that date and for the review of such rules adopted after the effective date of this chapter within ten years of the publication of such rules as the final rule. If the head of the agency determines that completion of the review of existing rules is not feasible by the established date, he shall so certify in a statement published in the Federal Register and may extend the completion date by one year at a time for a total of not more than five years.

(b) In reviewing rules to minimize any significant economic impact of the rule on a substantial number of small entities in a manner consistent with the stated objectives of applicable statutes, the agency shall consider the following factors—

    (1) the continued need for the rule;

    (2) the nature of complaints or comments received concerning the rule from the public;

    (3) the complexity of the rule;

    (4) the extent to which the rule overlaps, duplicates or conflicts with other Federal rules, and, to the extent feasible, with State and local governmental rules; and

    (5) the length of time since the rule has been evaluated or the degree to which technology, economic conditions, or other factors have changed in the area affected by the rule.

(c) Each year, each agency shall publish in the Federal Register a list of the rules which have a significant economic impact on a substantial number of small entities, which are to be reviewed pursuant to this section during the succeeding twelve months. The list shall include a brief description of each rule and the need for and legal basis of such rule and shall invite public comment upon the rule.

§ 611. Judicial review

(a) (1) For any rule subject to this chapter, a small entity that is adversely affected or aggrieved by final agency action is entitled to judicial review of agency compliance with the requirements of sections 601, 604, 605(b), 608(b), and 610 in accordance with chapter 7. Agency compliance with sections 607 and 609(a) shall be judicially reviewable in connection with judicial review of section 604.

    (2) Each court having jurisdiction to review such rule for compliance with section 553, or under any other provision of law, shall have jurisdiction to review any claims of noncompliance with sections 601, 604, 605(b), 608(b), and 610 in accordance with chapter 7. Agency compliance with sections 607 and 609(a) shall be judicially reviewable in connection with judicial review of section 604.

(3)(A) A small entity may seek such review during the period beginning on the date of final agency action and ending one year later, except that where a provision of law requires that an action challenging a final agency action be commenced before the expiration of one year, such lesser period shall apply to an action for judicial review under this section.

   (B) In the case where an agency delays the issuance of a final regulatory flexibility analysis pursuant to section 608(b) of this chapter, an action for judicial review under this section shall be filed not later than—

   (i) one year after the date the analysis is made available to the public, or

   (ii) where a provision of law requires that an action challenging a final agency regulation be commenced before the expiration of the 1-year period, the number of days specified in such provision of law that is after the date the analysis is made available to the public.

(4) In granting any relief in an action under this section, the court shall order the agency to take corrective action consistent with this chapter and chapter 7, including, but not limited to—

(A) remanding the rule to the agency, and

(B) deferring the enforcement of the rule against small entities unless the court finds that continued enforcement of the rule is in the public interest.

(5) Nothing in this subsection shall be construed to limit the authority of any court to stay the effective date of any rule or provision thereof under any other provision of law or to grant any other relief in addition to the requirements of this section.

(b) In an action for the judicial review of a rule, the regulatory flexibility analysis for such rule, including an analysis prepared or corrected pursuant to paragraph (a)(4), shall constitute part of the entire record of agency action in connection with such review.

(c) Compliance or noncompliance by an agency with the provisions of this chapter shall be subject to judicial review only in accordance with this section.

(d) Nothing in this section bars judicial review of any other impact statement or similar analysis required by any other law if judicial review of such statement or analysis is otherwise permitted by law.

§ 612. Reports and intervention rights

(a) The Chief Counsel for Advocacy of the Small Business Administration shall monitor agency compliance with this chapter and shall report at least annually thereon to the President and to the Committees on the Judiciary and Small Business of the Senate and House of Representatives.

(b) The Chief Counsel for Advocacy of the Small Business Administration is authorized to appear as amicus curiae in any action brought in a court of the United States to review a rule. In any such action, the Chief Counsel is authorized to present his or her views with respect to compliance with this chapter, the adequacy of the rulemaking record with respect to small entities and the effect of the rule on small entities.

(c) A court of the United States shall grant the application of the Chief Counsel for Advocacy of the Small Business Administration to appear in any such action for the purposes described in subsection (b).

5. Congressional Review of Agency Rulemaking
5 U.S.C. _____

§ 801. Congressional review

(a)(1)(A) Before a rule can take effect, the Federal agency promulgating such rule shall submit to each House of the Congress and to the Comptroller General a report containing—

    (i) a copy of the rule

    (ii) a concise general statement relating to the rule, including whether it is a major rule; and

    (iii) the proposed effective date of the rule.

(B) On the date of the submission of the report under subparagraph (A), the Federal agency promulgating the rule shall submit to the Comptroller General and make available to each House of Congress—

    (i) a complete copy of the cost-benefit analysis of the rule, if any;

    (ii) the agency's actions relevant to sections 603, 604, 605, 607, and 609;

    (iii) the agency's actions relevant to sections 202, 203, 204, and 205 of the Unfunded Mandates Reform Act of 1995; and

    (iv) any other relevant information or requirements under any other Act and any relevant Executive orders.

(C) Upon receipt of a report submitted under subparagraph (A), each House shall provide copies of the report to the chairman and ranking member of each standing committee with jurisdiction under the rules of the House of Representatives or the Senate to report a bill to amend the provision of law under which the rule is issued.

(2)(A)The Comptroller General shall provide a report on each major rule to the committees of jurisdiction in each House of the Congress by the end of 15 calendar days after the submission or publication date as provided in section 802(b)(2). The report of the Comptroller General shall include an assessment of the agency's compliance with procedural steps required by paragraph (1)(B).

(B) Federal agencies shall cooperate with the Comptroller General by providing information relevant to the Comptroller General's report under subparagraph (A).

(3) A major rule relating to a report submitted under paragraph (1) shall take effect on the latest of—

(A) the later of the date occurring 60 days after the date on which—

    (i) the Congress receives the report submitted under paragraph (1); or

    (ii) the rule is published in the Federal Register, if so published;

(B) if the Congress passes a joint resolution of disapproval described in section 802 relating to the rule, and the President signs a veto of such resolution, the earlier date—

    (i) on which either House of Congress votes and fails to override the veto of the President; or

    (ii) occurring 30 session days after the date on which the Congress received the veto and objections of the President; or

(C) the date the rule would have otherwise taken effect, if not for this section (unless a joint resolution of disapproval under section 802 is enacted).

(4) Except for a major rule, a rule shall take effect as otherwise provided by law after submission to Congress under paragraph (1).

(5) Notwithstanding paragraph (3), the effective date of a rule shall not be delayed by operation of this chapter beyond the date on which either House of Congress votes to reject a joint resolution of disapproval under section 802.

(b)(1) A rule shall not take effect (or continue), if the Congress enacts a joint resolution of disapproval, described under section 802, of the rule.

(2) A rule that does not take effect (or does not continue) under paragraph (1) may not be reissued in substantially the same form, and a new rule that is substantially the same as such a rule may not be issued, unless the reissued or new rule is specifically authorized by a law enacted after the date of the joint resolution disapproving the original rule.

(c)(1) Notwithstanding any other provision of this section (except subject to paragraph (3)), a rule that would not take effect by reason of subsection (a)(3) may take effect, if the President makes a determination under paragraph (2) and submits written notice of such determination to the Congress.

(2) Paragraph (1) applies to a determination made by the President by Executive order that the rule should take effect because such rule is—

(A) necessary because of an imminent threat to health or safety or other emergency;

(B) necessary for the enforcement of criminal laws;

(C) necessary for national security; or

(D) issued pursuant to any statute implementing an international trade agreement.

(3) An exercise by the President of the authority under this subsection shall have no effect on the procedures under section 802 or the effect of a joint resolution of disapproval under this section.

(d)(1) In addition to the opportunity for review otherwise provided under this chapter, in the case of any rule for which a report was submitted in accordance with subsection (a)(1)(A) during the period beginning on the date occurring—

(A) in the case of the Senate, 60 session days, or

(B) in the case of the House of Representatives, 60 legislative days, before the date the Congress adjourns a session of Congress through the date on which the same or succeeding Congress first convenes its next session, section 802 shall apply to such rule in the succeeding session of Congress.

(2)(A) In applying section 802 for purposes of such additional review, a rule described under paragraph (1) shall be treated as though—

    (i) such rule were published in the Federal Register (as a rule that shall take effect) on—

        (I) in the case of the Senate, the 15th session day, or

        (II) in the case of the House of Representatives, the 15th legislative day,

    after the succeeding session of Congress first convenes; and

    (ii) a report on such rule were submitted to Congress under subsection (a)(1) on such date.

(B) Nothing in this paragraph shall be construed to affect the requirement under subsection (a)(1) that a report shall be submitted to Congress before a rule can take effect.

(3) A rule described under paragraph (1) shall take effect as otherwise provided by law (including other subsections of this section).

(e)(1) For purposes of this subsection, section 802 shall also apply to any major rule promulgated between March 1, 1996, and the date of the enactment of this chapter.

(2) In applying section 802 for purposes of Congressional review, a rule described under paragraph (1) shall be treated as though—

(A) such rule were published in the Federal Register on the date of enactment of this chapter; and

(B) a report on such rule were submitted to Congress under subsection (a)(1) on such date.

(3) The effectiveness of a rule described under paragraph (1) shall be as otherwise provided by law, unless the rule is made of no force or effect under section 802.

(f) Any rule that takes effect and later is made of no force or effect by enactment of a joint resolution under section 802 shall be treated as though such rule had never taken effect.

(g) If the Congress does not enact a joint resolution of disapproval under section 802 respecting a rule, no court or agency may infer any intent of the Congress from any action or inaction of the Congress with regard to such rule, related statute, or joint resolution of disapproval.

§ 802. Congressional disapproval procedure

(a) For purposes of this section, the term "joint resolution" means only a joint resolution introduced in the period beginning on the date on which the report referred to in section 801(a)(1)(A) is received by Congress and ending 60 days thereafter (excluding days either House of Congress is adjourned for more than 3 days during a session of Congress), the matter after the resolving clause of which is as follows: "That Congress disapproves the rule submitted by the _____ relating to _____, and such rule shall have no force or effect." (The blank spaces being appropriately filled in).

(b) (1) A joint resolution described in subsection (a) shall be referred to the committees in each House of Congress with jurisdiction.

(2) For purposes of this section, the term "submission or publication date" means the later of the date on which—

(A) the Congress receives the report submitted under section 801(a)(1); or

(B) the rule is published in the Federal Register, if so published.

(c) In the Senate, if the committee to which is referred a joint resolution described in subsection (a) has not reported such joint resolution (or an identical joint resolution) at the end of 20 calendar days after the submission or publication date defined under subsection (b)(2), such committee may be discharged from further consideration of such joint resolution upon a petition supported in writing by 30 Members of the Senate, and such joint resolution shall be placed on the calendar.

(d) (1) In the Senate, when the committee to which a joint resolution is referred has reported, or when a committee is discharged (under subsection (c)) from further consideration of a joint resolution described in subsection (a), it is at any time thereafter in order (even though a previous motion to the same effect has been disagreed to) for a motion to proceed to the consideration of the joint resolution, and all points of order against the joint resolution (and against consideration of the joint resolution) are waived. The motion is not subject to amendment, or to a motion to postpone, or to a motion to proceed to the consideration of other business. A motion to reconsider the vote by which the motion is agreed to or disagreed to shall not be in order. If a motion to proceed to the consideration of the joint resolution is agreed to, the joint resolution shall remain the unfinished business of the Senate until disposed of.

(2) In the Senate, debate on the joint resolution, and on all debatable motions and appeals in connection therewith, shall be limited to not more than 10 hours, which shall be divided equally between those favoring and those opposing the joint resolution. A motion further to limit debate is in order and not debatable. An amendment to, or a motion to postpone, or a motion to proceed to the consideration of other business, or a motion to recommit the joint resolution is not in order.

(3) In the Senate, immediately following the conclusion of the debate on a joint resolution described in subsection (a), and a single quorum call at the conclusion of the debate if requested in accordance with the rules of the Senate, the vote on final passage of the joint resolution shall occur.

(4) Appeals from the decisions of the Chair relating to the application of the rules of the Senate to the procedure relating to a joint resolution described in subsection (a) shall be decided without debate.

(e) In the Senate the procedure specified in subsection (c) or (d) shall not apply to the consideration of a joint resolution respecting a rule—
  (1) after the expiration of the 60 session days beginning with the applicable submission or publication date, or
  (2) if the report under section 801(a)(1)(A) was submitted during the period referred to in section 801(d)(1), after the expiration of the 60 session days beginning on the 15th session day after the succeeding session of Congress first convenes.
(f) If, before the passage by one House of a joint resolution of that House described in subsection (a), that House receives from the other House a joint resolution described in subsection (a), then the following procedures shall apply:
  (1) The joint resolution of the other House shall not be referred to a committee.
  (2) With respect to a joint resolution described in subsection (a) of the House receiving the joint resolution—
    (A) the procedure in that House shall be the same as if no joint resolution had been received from the other House; but
    (B) the vote on final passage shall be on the joint resolution of the other House.
(g) This section is enacted by Congress—
  (1) as an exercise of the rulemaking power of the Senate and House of Representatives, respectively, and as such it is deemed a part of the rules of each House, respectively, but applicable only with respect to the procedure to be followed in that House in the case of a joint resolution described in subsection (a), and it supersedes other rules only to the extent that it is inconsistent with such rules; and
  (2) with full recognition of the constitutional right of either House to change the rules (so far as relating to the procedure of that House) at any time, in the same manner, and to the same extent as in the case of any other rule of that House.

§ 803. Special rule on statutory, regulatory, and judicial deadlines

(a) In the case of any deadline for, relating to, or involving any rule which does not take effect (or the effectiveness of which is terminated) because of enactment of a joint resolution under section 802, that deadline is extended until the date 1 year after the date of enactment of the joint resolution. Nothing in this subsection shall be construed to affect a deadline merely by reason of the postponement of a rule's effective date under section 801(a).
(b) The term "deadline" means any date certain for fulfilling any obligation or exercising any authority established by or under any Federal statute or regulation, or by or under any court order implementing any Federal statute or regulation.

§ 804. Definitions

For purposes of this chapter—

(1) The term "Federal agency" means any agency as that term is defined in section 551(1).
(2) The term "major rule" means any rule that the Administrator of the Office of Information and Regulatory Affairs of the Office of Management and Budget finds has resulted in or is likely to result in—
    (A) an annual effect on the economy of $100,000,000 or more;
    (B) a major increase in costs or prices for consumers, individual industries, Federal, State, or local government agencies, or geographic regions; or
    (C) significant adverse effects on competition, employment, investment, productivity, innovation, or on the ability of United States-based enterprises to compete with foreign-based enterprises in domestic and export markets.

    The term does not include any rule promulgated under the Telecommunications Act of 1996 and the amendments made by that Act.
(3) The term "rule" has the meaning given such term in section 551, except that such term does not include—
    (A) any rule of particular applicability, including a rule that approves or prescribes for the future rates, wages, prices, services, or allowances therefor, corporate or financial structures, reorganizations, mergers, or acquisitions thereof, or accounting practices or disclosures bearing on any of the foregoing;
    (B) any rule relating to agency management or personnel; or
    (C) any rule of agency organization, procedure, or practice that does not substantially affect the rights or obligations of non-agency parties.

§ 805. Judicial review

No determination, finding, action, or omission under this chapter shall be subject to judicial review.

§ 806. Applicability; severability

(a) This chapter shall apply notwithstanding any other provision of law.
(b) If any provision of this chapter or the application of any provision of this chapter to any person or circumstance, is held invalid, the application of such provision to other persons or circumstances, and the remainder of this chapter, shall not be affected thereby.

§ 807. Exemption for monetary policy

Nothing in this chapter shall apply to rules that concern monetary policy proposed or implemented by the Board of Governors of the Federal Reserve System or the Federal Open Market Committee.

§ 808. Effective date of certain rules

Notwithstanding section 801—

(1) any rule that establishes, modifies, opens, closes, or conducts a regulatory program for a commercial, recreational, or subsistence activity related to hunting, fishing, or camping, or

(2) any rule which an agency for good cause finds (and incorporates the finding and a brief statement of reasons therefor in the rule issued) that notice and public procedure thereon are impracticable, unnecessary, or contrary to the public interest,

shall take effect at such time as the Federal agency promulgating the rule determines.

Appendix B

Executive Order No. 12,866:
Regulatory Planning and Review
September 30, 1993
58 Fed. Reg. 51,735 (Oct. 4, 1993)

The American people deserve a regulatory system that works for them, not against them: a regulatory system that protects and improves their health, safety, environment, and well-being and improves the performance of the economy without imposing unacceptable or unreasonable costs on society; regulatory policies that recognize that the private sector and private markets are the best engine for economic growth; regulatory approaches that respect the role of State, local, and tribal governments; and regulations that are effective, consistent, sensible, and understandable. We do not have such a regulatory system today.

With this Executive order, the Federal Government begins a program to reform and make more efficient the regulatory process. The objectives of this Executive order are to enhance planning and coordination with respect to both new and existing regulations; to reaffirm the primacy of Federal agencies in the regulatory decision-making process; to restore the integrity and legitimacy of regulatory review and oversight; and to make the process more accessible and open to the public. In pursuing these objectives, the regulatory process shall be conducted so as to meet applicable statutory requirements and with due regard to the discretion that has been entrusted to the Federal agencies.

Accordingly, by the authority vested in me as President by the Constitution and the laws of the United States of America, it is hereby ordered as follows:

Section 1. *Statement of Regulatory Philosophy and Principles.*
(a) *The Regulatory Philosophy.* Federal agencies should promulgate only such regulations as are required by law, are necessary to interpret the law, or are made necessary by compelling public need, such as material failures of private markets to protect or improve the health and safety of the public, the environment, or the well-being of the American people. In deciding whether and how to regulate, agencies should assess all costs and benefits of available regulatory alternatives, including the alternative of not regulating. Costs and benefits shall be understood to include both quantifiable measures (to the fullest extent that these can be usefully estimated) and qualitative measures of costs and benefits that are difficult to quantify, but nevertheless essential to consider. Further, in choosing among alternative regulatory approaches, agencies should select those approaches that maximize net benefits (including potential economic, environmental, public health and

551

safety, and other advantages; distributive impacts; and equity), unless a statute requires another regulatory approach.

(b) *The Principles of Regulation.* To ensure that the agencies' regulatory programs are consistent with the philosophy set forth above, agencies should adhere to the following principles, to the extent permitted by law and where applicable:

  (1) Each agency shall identify the problem that it intends to address (including, where applicable, the failures of private markets or public institutions that warrant new agency action) as well as assess the significance of that problem.

  (2) Each agency shall examine whether existing regulations (or other law) have created, or contributed to, the problem that a new regulation is intended to correct and whether those regulations (or other law) should be modified to achieve the intended goal of regulation more effectively.

  (3) Each agency shall identify and assess available alternatives to direct regulation, including providing economic incentives to encourage the desired behavior, such as user fees or marketable permits, or providing information upon which choices can be made by the public.

  (4) In setting regulatory priorities, each agency shall consider, to the extent reasonable, the degree and nature of the risks posed by various substances or activities within its jurisdiction.

  (5) When an agency determines that a regulation is the best available method of achieving the regulatory objective, it shall design its regulations in the most cost-effective manner to achieve the regulatory objective. In doing so, each agency shall consider incentives for innovation, consistency, predictability, the costs of enforcement and compliance (to the government, regulated entities, and the public), flexibility, distributive impacts, and equity.

  (6) Each agency shall assess both the costs and the benefits of the intended regulation and, recognizing that some costs and benefits are difficult to quantify, propose or adopt a regulation only upon a reasoned determination that the benefits of the intended regulation justify its costs.

  (7) Each agency shall base its decisions on the best reasonably obtainable scientific, technical, economic, and other information concerning the need for, and consequences of, the intended regulation.

  (8) Each agency shall identify and assess alternative forms of regulation and shall, to the extent feasible, specify performance objectives, rather than specifying the behavior or manner of compliance that regulated entities must adopt.

  (9) Wherever feasible, agencies shall seek views of appropriate State, local, and tribal officials before imposing regulatory requirements that might significantly or uniquely affect those governmental entities. Each agency shall assess the effects of Federal regulations on State, local, and tribal governments, including specifically the availability of resources to carry out those mandates, and seek to minimize those burdens that uniquely or significantly affect such governmental entities, consistent with achieving regulatory objectives. In addi-

tion, as appropriate, agencies shall seek to harmonize Federal regulatory actions with related State, local, and tribal regulatory and other governmental functions.

(10) Each agency shall avoid regulations that are inconsistent, incompatible, or duplicative with its other regulations or those of other Federal agencies.

(11) Each agency shall tailor its regulations to impose the least burden on society, including individuals, businesses of differing sizes, and other entities (including small communities and governmental entities), consistent with obtaining the regulatory objectives, taking into account, among other things, and to the extent practicable, the costs of cumulative regulations.

(12) Each agency shall draft its regulations to be simple and easy to understand, with the goal of minimizing the potential for uncertainty and litigation arising from such uncertainty.

Section 2. *Organization.*

An efficient regulatory planning and review process is vital to ensure that the Federal Government's regulatory system best serves the American people.

(a) *The Agencies.* Because Federal agencies are the repositories of significant substantive expertise and experience, they are responsible for developing regulations and assuring that the regulations are consistent with applicable law, the President's priorities, and the principles set forth in this Executive order.

(b) *The Office of Management and Budget.* Coordinated review of agency rulemaking is necessary to ensure that regulations are consistent with applicable law, the President's priorities, and the principles set forth in this Executive order, and that decisions made by one agency do not conflict with the policies or actions taken or planned by another agency. The Office of Management and Budget (OMB) shall carry out that review function. Within OMB, the Office of Information and Regulatory Affairs (OIRA) is the repository of expertise concerning regulatory issues, including methodologies and procedures that affect more than one agency, this Executive order, and the President's regulatory policies. To the extent permitted by law, OMB shall provide guidance to agencies and assist the President, the Vice President, and other regulatory policy advisors to the President in regulatory planning and shall be the entity that reviews individual regulations, as provided by this Executive order.

(c) *The Vice President.* The Vice President is the principal advisor to the President on, and shall coordinate the development and presentation of recommendations concerning, regulatory policy, planning, and review, as set forth in this Executive order. In fulfilling their responsibilities under this Executive order, the President and the Vice President shall be assisted by the regulatory policy advisors within the Executive Office of the President and by such agency officials and personnel as the President and the Vice President may, from time to time, consult.

A Guide to Federal Agency Rulemaking

Section. 3. *Definitions.*

For purposes of this Executive order:

(a) "Advisors" refers to such regulatory policy advisors to the President as the President and Vice President may from time to time consult, including, among others: (1) the Director of OMB; (2) the Chair (or another member) of the Council of Economic Advisers; (3) the Assistant to the President for Economic Policy; (4) the Assistant to the President for Domestic Policy; (5) the Assistant to the President for National Security Affairs; (6) the Assistant to the President for Science and Technology; (7) the Assistant to the President for Intergovernmental Affairs; (8) the Assistant to the President and Staff Secretary; (9) the Assistant to the President and Chief of Staff to the Vice President; (10) the Assistant to the President and Counsel to the President; (11) the Deputy Assistant to the President and Director of the White House Office on Environmental Policy; and (12) the Administrator of OIRA, who also shall coordinate communications relating to this Executive order among the agencies, OMB, the other Advisors, and the Office of the Vice President.

(b) "Agency," unless otherwise indicated, means any authority of the United States that is an "agency" under 44 U.S.C. 3502(1), other than those considered to be independent regulatory agencies, as defined in 44 U.S.C. 3502(10).

(c) "Director" means the Director of OMB.

(d) "Regulation" or "rule" means an agency statement of general applicability and future effect, which the agency intends to have the force and effect of law, that is designed to implement, interpret, or prescribe law or policy or to describe the procedure or practice requirements of an agency. It does not, however, include:

    (1) Regulations or rules issued in accordance with the formal rulemaking provisions of 5 U.S.C. 556, 557;

    (2) Regulations or rules that pertain to a military or foreign affairs function of the United States, other than procurement regulations and regulations involving the import or export of non-defense articles and services;

    (3) Regulations or rules that are limited to agency organization, management, or personnel matters; or

    (4) Any other category of regulations exempted by the Administrator of OIRA.

(e) "Regulatory action" means any substantive action by an agency (normally published in the Federal Register) that promulgates or is expected to lead to the promulgation of a final rule or regulation, including notices of inquiry, advance notice of proposed rulemaking, and notices of proposed rulemaking.

(f) "Significant regulatory action" means any regulatory action that is likely to result in a rule that may:

    (1) Have an annual effect on the economy of $100 million or more or adversely affect in a material way the economy, a sector of the economy, productivity, competition, jobs, the environment, public health or safety, or State, local, or tribal governments or communities;

(2) Create a serious inconsistency or otherwise interfere with an action taken or planned by another agency;

(3) Materially alter the budgetary impact of entitlements, grants, user fees, or loan programs or the rights and obligations of recipients thereof; or

(4) Raise novel legal or policy issues arising out of legal mandates, the President's priorities, or the principles set forth in this Executive order.

Section. 4. *Planning Mechanism.*

In order to have an effective regulatory program, to provide for coordination of regulations, to maximize consultation and the resolution of potential conflicts at an early stage, to involve the public and its State, local, and tribal officials in regulatory planning, and to ensure that new or revised regulations promote the President's priorities and the principles set forth in this Executive order, these procedures shall be followed, to the extent permitted by law:

(a) Agencies' Policy Meeting. Early in each year's planning cycle, the Vice President shall convene a meeting of the Advisors and the heads of agencies to seek a common understanding of priorities and to coordinate regulatory efforts to be accomplished in the upcoming year.

(b) *Unified Regulatory Agenda.* For purposes of this subsection, the term "agency" or "agencies" shall also include those considered to be independent regulatory agencies, as defined in 44 U.S.C. 3502(10). Each agency shall prepare an agenda of all regulations under development or review, at a time and in a manner specified by the Administrator of OIRA. The description of each regulatory action shall contain, at a minimum, a regulation identifier number, a brief summary of the action, the legal authority for the action, any legal deadline for the action, and the name and telephone number of a knowledgeable agency official. Agencies may incorporate the information required under 5 U.S.C. 602 and 41 U.S.C. 402 into these agendas.

(c) *The Regulatory Plan.* For purposes of this subsection, the term "agency" or "agencies" shall also include those considered to be independent regulatory agencies, as defined in 44 U.S.C. 3502(10).

(1) As part of the Unified Regulatory Agenda, beginning in 1994, each agency shall prepare a Regulatory Plan (Plan) of the most important significant regulatory actions that the agency reasonably expects to issue in proposed or final form in that fiscal year or thereafter. The Plan shall be approved personally by the agency head and shall contain at a minimum:

(A) A statement of the agency's regulatory objectives and priorities and how they relate to the President's priorities;

(B) A summary of each planned significant regulatory action including, to the extent possible, alternatives to be considered and preliminary estimates of the anticipated costs and benefits;

(C) A summary of the legal basis for each such action, including whether any aspect of the action is required by statute or court order;

(D) A statement of the need for each such action and, if applicable, how the action will reduce risks to public health, safety, or the environment, as well as how the magnitude of the risk addressed by the action relates to other risks within the jurisdiction of the agency;

(E) The agency's schedule for action, including a statement of any applicable statutory or judicial deadlines; and

(F) The name, address, and telephone number of a person the public may contact for additional information about the planned regulatory action.

(2) Each agency shall forward its Plan to OIRA by June 1st of each year.

(3) Within 10 calendar days after OIRA has received an agency's Plan, shall circulate it to other affected agencies, the Advisors, and the Vice President.

(4) An agency head who believes that a planned regulatory action of another agency may conflict with its own policy or action taken or planned shall promptly notify, in writing, the Administrator of OIRA, who shall forward that communication to the issuing agency, the Advisors, and the Vice President.

(5) If the Administrator of OIRA believes that a planned regulatory action of an agency may be inconsistent with the President's priorities or the principles set forth in this Executive order or may be in conflict with any policy or action taken or planned by another agency, the Administrator of OIRA shall promptly notify, in writing, the affected agencies, the Advisors, and the Vice President.

(6) The Vice President, with the Advisors' assistance, may consult with the heads of agencies with respect to their Plans and, in appropriate instances, request further consideration or inter-agency coordination.

(7) The Plans developed by the issuing agency shall be published annually in the October publication of the Unified Regulatory Agenda. This publication shall be made available to the Congress; State, local, and tribal governments; and the public. Any views on any aspect of any agency Plan, including whether any planned regulatory action might conflict with any other planned or existing regulation, impose any unintended consequences on the public, or confer any unclaimed benefits on the public, should be directed to the issuing agency, with a copy to OIRA.

(d) *Regulatory Working Group.* Within 30 days of the date of this Executive order, the Administrator of OIRA shall convene a Regulatory Working Group ("Working Group"), which shall consist of representatives of the heads of each agency that the Administrator determines to have significant domestic regulatory responsibility, the Advisors, and the Vice President. The Administrator of OIRA shall chair the Working Group and shall periodically advise the Vice President on the activities of the Working Group. The Working Group shall serve as a forum to assist agencies in identifying and analyzing important regulatory issues (including, among others (1) the development of innovative regulatory techniques, (2) the methods, efficacy, and utility of comparative risk assessment in regulatory decision-making, and (3) the development of short forms and other streamlined regulatory approaches for small businesses and other entities). The Working Group shall meet at least quarterly and may meet as a whole or in subgroups of agencies with an interest in particular issues or subject areas. To inform its discussions, the Working Group may commission analytical studies and reports by OIRA, the Administrative Conference of the United States, or any other agency.

(e) *Conferences.* The Administrator of OIRA shall meet quarterly with representatives of State, local, and tribal governments to identify both existing and proposed regulations that may uniquely or significantly affect those governmental entities. The Administrator of OIRA shall also convene, from time to time, conferences with representatives of businesses, nongovernmental organizations, and the public to discuss regulatory issues of common concern.

Section. 5. *Existing Regulations.*

In order to reduce the regulatory burden on the American people, their families, their communities, their State, local, and tribal governments, and their industries; to determine whether regulations promulgated by the executive branch of the Federal Government have become unjustified or unnecessary as a result of changed circumstances; to confirm that regulations are both compatible with each other and not duplicative or inappropriately burdensome in the aggregate; to ensure that all regulations are consistent with the President's priorities and the principles set forth in this Executive order, within applicable law; and to otherwise improve the effectiveness of existing regulations:

(a) Within 90 days of the date of this Executive order, each agency shall submit to OIRA a program, consistent with its resources and regulatory priorities, under which the agency will periodically review its existing significant regulations to determine whether any such regulations should be modified or eliminated so as to make the agency's regulatory program more effective in achieving the regulatory objectives, less burdensome, or in greater alignment with the President's priorities and the principles set forth in this Executive order. Any significant regulations selected for review shall be included in the agency's annual Plan. The agency shall also identify any legislative mandates that require the agency to promulgate or continue to impose regulations that the agency believes are unnecessary or outdated by reason of changed circumstances.

(b) The Administrator of OIRA shall work with the Regulatory Working Group and other interested entities to pursue the objectives of this section. State, local, and tribal governments are specifically encouraged to assist in the identification of regulations that impose significant or unique burdens on those governmental entities and that appear to have outlived their justification or be otherwise inconsistent with the public interest.

(c) The Vice President, in consultation with the Advisors, may identify for review by the appropriate agency or agencies other existing regulations of an agency or groups of regulations of more than one agency that affect a particular group, industry, or sector of the economy, or may identify legislative mandates that may be appropriate for reconsideration by the Congress.

Section. 6. *Centralized Review of Regulations.*
The guidelines set forth below shall apply to all regulatory actions, for both new and existing regulations, by agencies other than those agencies specifically exempted by the Administrator of OIRA:
(a) *Agency Responsibilities.*
   (1) Each agency shall (consistent with its own rules, regulations, or procedures) provide the public with meaningful participation in the regulatory process. In particular, before issuing a notice of proposed rulemaking, each agency should, where appropriate, seek the involvement of those who are intended to benefit from and those expected to be burdened by any regulation (including, specifically, State, local, and tribal officials). In addition, each agency should afford the public a meaningful opportunity to comment on any proposed regulation, which in most cases should include a comment period of not less than 60 days. Each agency also is directed to explore and, where appropriate, use consensual mechanisms for developing regulations, including negotiated rulemaking.
   (2) Within 60 days of the date of this Executive order, each agency head shall designate a Regulatory Policy Officer who shall report to the agency head. The Regulatory Policy Officer shall be involved at each stage of the regulatory process to foster the development of effective, innovative, and least burdensome regulations and to further the principles set forth in this Executive order.
   (3) In addition to adhering to its own rules and procedures and to the requirements of the Administrative Procedure Act, the Regulatory Flexibility Act, the Paperwork Reduction Act, and other applicable law, each agency shall develop its regulatory actions in a timely fashion and adhere to the following procedures with respect to a regulatory action:
      (A) Each agency shall provide OIRA, at such times and in the manner specified by the Administrator of OIRA, with a list of its planned regulatory actions, indicating those which the agency believes are significant regulatory actions within the meaning of this Executive order. Absent a material change in the development of the planned regulatory action, those not designated as significant will not be subject to review under this section unless, within 10 working days of receipt of the list, the Administrator of OIRA notifies the agency that OIRA has determined that a planned regulation is a significant regulatory action within the meaning of this Executive order. The Administrator of OIRA may waive review of any planned regulatory action designated by the agency as significant, in which case the agency need not further comply with subsection (a)(3)(B) or subsection (a)(3)(C) of this section.
      (B) For each matter identified as, or determined by the Administrator of OIRA to be, a significant regulatory action, the issuing agency shall provide to OIRA:

(i) The text of the draft regulatory action, together with a reasonably detailed description of the need for the regulatory action and an explanation of how the regulatory action will meet that need; and

(ii) An assessment of the potential costs and benefits of the regulatory action, including an explanation of the manner in which the regulatory action is consistent with a statutory mandate and, to the extent permitted by law, promotes the President's priorities and avoids undue interference with State, local, and tribal governments in the exercise of their governmental functions.

(C) For those matters identified as, or determined by the Administrator of OIRA to be, a significant regulatory action within the scope of section 3(f)(1), the agency shall also provide to OIRA the following additional information developed as part of the agency's decision-making process (unless prohibited by law):

(i) An assessment, including the underlying analysis, of benefits anticipated from the regulatory action (such as, but not limited to, the promotion of the efficient functioning of the economy and private markets, the enhancement of health and safety, the protection of the natural environment, and the elimination or reduction of discrimination or bias) together with, to the extent feasible, a quantification of those benefits;

(ii) An assessment, including the underlying analysis, of costs anticipated from the regulatory action (such as, but not limited to, the direct cost both to the government in administering the regulation and to businesses and others in complying with the regulation, and any adverse effects on the efficient functioning of the economy, private markets (including productivity, employment, and competitiveness), health, safety, and the natural environment), together with, to the extent feasible, a quantification of those costs; and

(iii) An assessment, including the underlying analysis, of costs and benefits of potentially effective and reasonably feasible alternatives to the planned regulation, identified by the agencies or the public (including improving the current regulation and reasonably viable nonregulatory actions), and an explanation why the planned regulatory action is preferable to the identified potential alternatives.

(D) In emergency situations or when an agency is obligated by law to act more quickly than normal review procedures allow, the agency shall notify OIRA as soon as possible and, to the extent practicable, comply with subsections (a)(3)(B) and (C) of this section. For those regulatory actions that are governed by a statutory or court-imposed deadline, the agency shall, to the extent practicable, schedule rulemaking proceedings so as to permit sufficient time for OIRA to conduct its review, as set forth below in subsection (b)(2) through (4) of this section.

(E) After the regulatory action has been published in the Federal Register or otherwise issued to the public, the agency shall:

(i) Make available to the public the information set forth in subsections (a)(3)(B) and (C);

(ii) Identify for the public, in a complete, clear, and simple manner, the substantive changes between the draft submitted to OIRA for review and the action subsequently announced; and

(iii) Identify for the public those changes in the regulatory action that were made at the suggestion or recommendation of OIRA.

(F) All information provided to the public by the agency shall be in plain, understandable language.

(b) *OIRA Responsibilities.* The Administrator of OIRA shall provide meaningful guidance and oversight so that each agency's regulatory actions are consistent with applicable law, the President's priorities, and the principles set forth in this Executive order and do not conflict with the policies or actions of another agency. OIRA shall, to the extent permitted by law, adhere to the following guidelines:

(1) OIRA may review only actions identified by the agency or by OIRA as significant regulatory actions under subsection (a)(3)(A) of this section.

(2) OIRA shall waive review or notify the agency in writing of the results of its review within the following time periods:

(A) For any notices of inquiry, advance notices of proposed rulemaking, or other preliminary regulatory actions prior to a Notice of Proposed Rulemaking, within 10 working days after the date of submission of the draft action to OIRA;

(B) For all other regulatory actions, within 90 calendar days after the date of submission of the information set forth in subsections (a)(3)(B) and (C) of this section, unless OIRA has previously reviewed this information and, since that review, there has been no material change in the facts and circumstances upon which the regulatory action is based, in which case, OIRA shall complete its review within 45 days; and

(C) The review process may be extended (1) once by no more than 30 calendar days upon the written approval of the Director and (2) at the request of the agency head.

(3) For each regulatory action that the Administrator of OIRA returns to an agency for further consideration of some or all of its provisions, the Administrator of OIRA shall provide the issuing agency a written explanation for such return, setting forth the pertinent provision of this Executive order on which OIRA is relying. If the agency head disagrees with some or all of the bases for the return, the agency head shall so inform the Administrator of OIRA in writing.

(4) Except as otherwise provided by law or required by a Court, in order to ensure greater openness, accessibility, and accountability in the regulatory review process, OIRA shall be governed by the following disclosure requirements:

(A) Only the Administrator of OIRA (or a particular designee) shall receive oral communications initiated by persons not employed by the executive branch of the Federal Government regarding the substance of a regulatory action under OIRA review;

(B) All substantive communications between OIRA personnel and persons not employed by the executive branch of the Federal Government regarding a regulatory action under review shall be governed by the following guidelines:

(i) A representative from the issuing agency shall be invited to any meeting between OIRA personnel and such person(s);

(ii) OIRA shall forward to the issuing agency, within 10 working days of receipt of the communication(s), all written communications, regardless of format, between OIRA personnel and any person who is not employed by the executive branch of the Federal Government, and the dates and names of individuals involved in all substantive oral communications (including meetings to which an agency representative was invited, but did not attend, and telephone conversations between OIRA personnel and any such persons); and

(iii) OIRA shall publicly disclose relevant information about such communication(s), as set forth below in subsection (b)(4)(C) of this section.

(C) OIRA shall maintain a publicly available log that shall contain, at a minimum, the following information pertinent to regulatory actions under review:

(i) The status of all regulatory actions, including if (and if so, when and by whom) Vice Presidential and Presidential consideration was requested;

(ii) A notation of all written communications forwarded to an issuing agency under subsection (b)(4)(B)(ii) of this section; and

(iii) The dates and names of individuals involved in all substantive oral communications, including meetings and telephone conversations, between OIRA personnel and any person not employed by the executive branch of the Federal Government, and the subject matter discussed during such communications.

(D) After the regulatory action has been published in the Federal Register or otherwise issued to the public, or after the agency has announced its decision not to publish or issue the regulatory action, OIRA shall make available to the public all documents exchanged between OIRA and the agency during the review by OIRA under this section.

(5) All information provided to the public by OIRA shall be in plain, understandable language.

Section. 7. *Resolution of Conflicts.*

To the extent permitted by law, disagreements or conflicts between or among agency heads or between OMB and any agency that cannot be resolved by the Administrator of OIRA shall be resolved by the President, or by the Vice President acting at the request of the President, with the relevant agency head (and, as appropriate, other interested government officials). Vice Presidential and Presidential consideration of such disagreements may be initiated only by the Director, by the head of the issuing agency, or by the head of an agency that has a significant interest in the regulatory action at issue. Such review will not be undertaken at the request of other persons, entities, or their agents.

Resolution of such conflicts shall be informed by recommendations developed by the Vice President, after consultation with the Advisors (and other executive branch officials or personnel whose responsibilities to the President include the subject matter at issue). The development of these recommendations shall be concluded within 60 days after review has been requested.

During the Vice Presidential and Presidential review period, communications with any person not employed by the Federal Government relating to the substance of the regulatory action under review and directed to the Advisors or their staffs or to the staff of the Vice President shall be in writing and shall be forwarded by the recipient to the affected agency(ies) for inclusion in the public docket(s). When the communication is not in writing, such Advisors or staff members shall inform the outside party that the matter is under review and that any comments should be submitted in writing.

At the end of this review process, the President, or the Vice President acting at the request of the President, shall notify the affected agency and the Administrator of OIRA of the President's decision with respect to the matter.

Section. 8. *Publication.*

Except to the extent required by law, an agency shall not publish in the Federal Register or otherwise issue to the public any regulatory action that is subject to review under section 6 of this Executive order until (1) the Administrator of OIRA notifies the agency that OIRA has waived its review of the action or has completed its review without any requests for further consideration, or (2) the applicable time period in section 6(b)(2) expires without OIRA having notified the agency that it is returning the regulatory action for further consideration under section 6(b)(3), whichever occurs first. If the terms of the preceding sentence have not been satisfied and an agency wants to publish or otherwise issue a regulatory action, the head of that agency may request Presidential consideration through the Vice President, as provided under section 7 of this order. Upon receipt of this request, the Vice President shall notify OIRA and the Advisors. The guidelines and time period set forth in section 7 shall apply to the publication of regulatory actions for which Presidential consideration has been sought.

Section. 9. *Agency Authority.*
Nothing in this order shall be construed as displacing the agencies' authority or responsibilities, as authorized by law.

Section. 10. *Judicial Review.*
Nothing in this Executive order shall affect any otherwise available judicial review of agency action. This Executive order is intended only to improve the internal management of the Federal Government and does not create any right or benefit, substantive or procedural, enforceable at law or equity by a party against the United States, its agencies or instrumentalities, its officers or employees, or any other person.

Section. 11. *Revocations.*
Executive Orders Nos. 12291 and 12498; all amendments to those Executive orders; all guidelines issued under those orders; and any exemptions from those orders heretofore granted for any category of rule are revoked.

WILLIAM J. CLINTON
THE WHITE HOUSE
September 30, 1993

Appendix C

Executive Order No. 13,563:
Improving Regulation and Regulatory Review
January 18, 2011

By the authority vested in me as President by the Constitution and the laws of the United States of America, and in order to improve regulation and regulatory review, it is hereby ordered as follows:

Section 1. *General Principles of Regulation.*

(a) Our regulatory system must protect public health, welfare, safety, and our environment while promoting economic growth, innovation, competitiveness, and job creation. It must be based on the best available science. It must allow for public participation and an open exchange of ideas. It must promote predictability and reduce uncertainty. It must identify and use the best, most innovative, and least burdensome tools for achieving regulatory ends. It must take into account benefits and costs, both quantitative and qualitative. It must ensure that regulations are accessible, consistent, written in plain language, and easy to understand. It must measure, and seek to improve, the actual results of regulatory requirements.

(b) This order is supplemental to and reaffirms the principles, structures, and definitions governing contemporary regulatory review that were established in Executive Order 12866 of September 30, 1993. As stated in that Executive Order and to the extent permitted by law, each agency must, among other things: (1) propose or adopt a regulation only upon a reasoned determination that its benefits justify its costs (recognizing that some benefits and costs are difficult to quantify); (2) tailor its regulations to impose the least burden on society, consistent with obtaining regulatory objectives, taking into account, among other things, and to the extent practicable, the costs of cumulative regulations; (3) select, in choosing among alternative regulatory approaches, those approaches that maximize net benefits (including potential economic, environmental, public health and safety, and other advantages; distributive impacts; and equity); (4) to the extent feasible, specify performance objectives, rather than specifying the behavior or manner of compliance that regulated entities must adopt; and (5) identify and assess available alternatives to direct regulation, including providing economic incentives to encourage the desired behavior, such as user fees or marketable permits, or providing information upon which choices can be made by the public.

(c) In applying these principles, each agency is directed to use the best available techniques to quantify anticipated present and future benefits and costs as accurately as possible. Where appropriate and permitted by law, each agency may consider (and discuss qualitatively) values that are difficult or impossible to quantify, including equity, human dignity, fairness, and distributive impacts.

Sec. 2. *Public Participation.*
(a) Regulations shall be adopted through a process that involves public participation. To that end, regulations shall be based, to the extent feasible and consistent with law, on the open exchange of information and perspectives among State, local, and tribal officials, experts in relevant disciplines, affected stakeholders in the private sector, and the public as a whole.
(b) To promote that open exchange, each agency, consistent with Executive Order 12866 and other applicable legal requirements, shall endeavor to provide the public with an opportunity to participate in the regulatory process. To the extent feasible and permitted by law, each agency shall afford the public a meaningful opportunity to comment through the Internet on any proposed regulation, with a comment period that should generally be at least 60 days. To the extent feasible and permitted by law, each agency shall also provide, for both proposed and final rules, timely online access to the rulemaking docket on regulations.gov, including relevant scientific and technical findings, in an open format that can be easily searched and downloaded. For proposed rules, such access shall include, to the extent feasible and permitted by law, an opportunity for public comment on all pertinent parts of the rulemaking docket, including relevant scientific and technical findings.
(c) Before issuing a notice of proposed rulemaking, each agency, where feasible and appropriate, shall seek the views of those who are likely to be affected, including those who are likely to benefit from and those who are potentially subject to such rulemaking.

Sec. 3. *Integration and Innovation.* Some sectors and industries face a significant number of regulatory requirements, some of which may be redundant, inconsistent, or overlapping. Greater coordination across agencies could reduce these requirements, thus reducing costs and simplifying and harmonizing rules. In developing regulatory actions and identifying appropriate approaches, each agency shall attempt to promote such coordination, simplification, and harmonization. Each agency shall also seek to identify, as appropriate, means to achieve regulatory goals that are designed to promote innovation.

Sec. 4. *Flexible Approaches.* Where relevant, feasible, and consistent with regulatory objectives, and to the extent permitted by law, each agency shall identify and consider regulatory approaches that reduce burdens and maintain flexibility and freedom of choice for the public. These approaches include warnings, appropriate default rules, and disclosure requirements as well as provision of information to the public in a form that is clear and intelligible.

Sec. 5. *Science.* Consistent with the President's Memorandum for the Heads of Executive Departments and Agencies, "Scientific Integrity" (March 9, 2009), and its implementing guidance, each agency shall ensure the objectivity of any scientific and technological information and processes used to support the agency's regulatory actions.

Sec. 6. *Retrospective Analyses of Existing Rules.*
(a) To facilitate the periodic review of existing significant regulations, agencies shall consider how best to promote retrospective analysis of rules that may be outmoded, ineffective, insufficient, or excessively burdensome, and to modify, streamline, expand, or repeal them in accordance with what has been learned. Such retrospective analyses, including supporting data, should be released online whenever possible.
(b) Within 120 days of the date of this order, each agency shall develop and submit to the Office of Information and Regulatory Affairs a preliminary plan, consistent with law and its resources and regulatory priorities, under which the agency will periodically review its existing significant regulations to determine whether any such regulations should be modified, streamlined, expanded, or repealed so as to make the agency's regulatory program more effective or less burdensome in achieving the regulatory objectives.

Sec. 7. *General Provisions.*
(a) For purposes of this order, "agency" shall have the meaning set forth in section 3(b) of Executive Order 12866.
(b) Nothing in this order shall be construed to impair or otherwise affect:
  (i) authority granted by law to a department or agency, or the head thereof; or
  (ii) functions of the Director of the Office of Management and Budget relating to budgetary, administrative, or legislative proposals.
(c) This order shall be implemented consistent with applicable law and subject to the availability of appropriations.
(d) This order is not intended to, and does not, create any right or benefit, substantive or procedural, enforceable at law or in equity by any party against the United States, its departments, agencies, or entities, its officers, employees, or agents, or any other person.

BARACK OBAMA
THE WHITE HOUSE
January 18, 2011

Table of Cases

Index

A

Administrative Committee of the Federal Register, 346–48

Administrative Conference of the United States (ACUS), xii, xvii–xviii, 31–32, 54, 57, 86, 92–93, 101–03, 151, 178–79, 181, 192, 195, 204, 207, 211, 212, 267, 283–84, 292, 294, 299, 307, 310–11, 324–26, 335–37, 359–60 , 392, 395–96, 413–14, 484

Administrative Orders Review Act, 392, 395

Administrative Procedure Act (APA), 3–8, 113, 129, 279–81, 365, 369, 423–90

Attorney General's Manual on the APA, 44, 56, 64, 178, 253–54, 316

enactment of, 287–88

informal *vs.* formal rulemaking, xiii, 5, 34–35

Advance notice of proposed rulemaking, 188–90

Advisory committees, 148–50. *See also Federal Advisory Committee Act.*

APA judicial review provisions, 423–24. *See also Judicial review, scope of.*

APA rulemaking provisions, 43–111

distinction between informal and formal rulemaking, 44

formal rulemaking, 50–51

informal rulemaking, 52

publication requirements of Section 552, 110–11, 345–46

rule, defined, 43, 48

rulemaking, defined, 43, 48

rules and rulemaking, 43–50

adjudication, defined, 44, 49

rule, difficulty of determining, 44–50

rules of particular applicability, 48

rules exempt from Section 553 requirements, 52–110

agency management or personnel, 56

agency organization, procedure, or practice, 58–63

good cause, 93–109. *See also Good cause exemptions.*

interpretive rules and policy statements, 63–93

military or foreign affairs, 56–58

proprietary matters, 53–55

text, 514–26

APA Section 706(2)(A), 425–45. *See also Arbitrary and capricious test.*

APA Section 706(2)(C), 446–76. *See also Chevron doctrine.*

APA Section 706(2)(D), 476–82

need to decide substantive claims after vacating a rule, 482

procedures imposed by agency regulations, 478–79

procedures imposed by other statutes, 478

procedures imposed by the APA, 477

procedures imposed by the courts, 479–82

Arbitrary and capricious test, 425–45

hard-look doctrine, 7, 433–41

scope of review of agency policy changes, 441–45

Supreme Court application of arbitrary and capricious test, 429–33

Assessment of federal regulations and policies on families, 170–71

Attorney General's Manual on the APA, 44, 56, 64, 178, 253–54, 316

good cause, 93–109. *See also Good cause exemptions.*
interpretive rules and policy statements, 63–93. *See also Interpretive rules and policy statements.*
rules exempt from all of Section 553, 53–58
   agency management or personnel, 56
   military or foreign affairs, 56–58
   proprietary matters, 53–55
Rules of particular applicability, 111

S

Scope of judicial review. *See Judicial review, scope of.*
Small Business Administration, 136–39, 234
   Chief Counsel for Advocacy, 136–39, 233, 245–46
Small Business Jobs Act of 2010, 138
Small Business Paperwork Relief Act, 148
Small Business Regulatory Enforcement Fairness Act (SBREFA), 26, 133–34, 163–64, 203, 232, 278
Statement of basis and purpose, 38–39, 337–44
Statutory framework for rulemaking, 41–171
   APA rulemaking provisions, 43–111
   policy setting, rulemaking *vs.* adjudication, 113–28
   statutes affecting rulemaking, 129–71
Statutory hammer provision, 13–14
Statutory time limits. *See Time limits.*
Substantial evidence test, 482–84

T

Time limits, 319–20, 415–20
timing, judicial review, 397–422
Trade Agreements Act, 169–70, 327
Treasury and General Government Appropriations Act of 2001, 227

U

Unfunded Mandates Reform Act, 26, 155–57, 219, 234–36, 246
   Congressional Budget Office role, 155–56
   content of the analysis, 235
   coverage, 234–35
   limited judicial review, 157, 478
   purpose of, 155
   response to comments, 344
   review of the analyses, 236
   statement to accompany significant regulatory action, 156–57
   text, 505–14
Unified Agenda of Federal Regulatory and Deregulatory Actions, 23, 139, 222, 247
Updated Principles for Risk Analysis, 28

V

Vacatur, 486–90